To Rule Jerusalem is an historical and ethnographic account of the twentieth-century struggle for Jerusalem. The volume examines how Jerusalem is doubly divided, on the one hand between Israelis and Palestinians, both of whom ground their national identities in the city, as well as within each nation between those who put primacy in the democratic decisions of their nations and those who would yield to a higher divine law.

Professors Friedland and Hecht explore how Jerusalem has figured as a battleground in conflicts over the relation between Zionism and Judaism and between Palestinian nationalism and Islam. Based on hundreds of interviews with powerful players and ordinary citizens over the course of a decade, this book evokes the ways in which these conflicts are experienced and managed in the life of the city. *To Rule Jerusalem* is a compelling study of the intertwining of religion and politics, exploring the city simultaneously as an ordinary place and an extraordinary symbol.

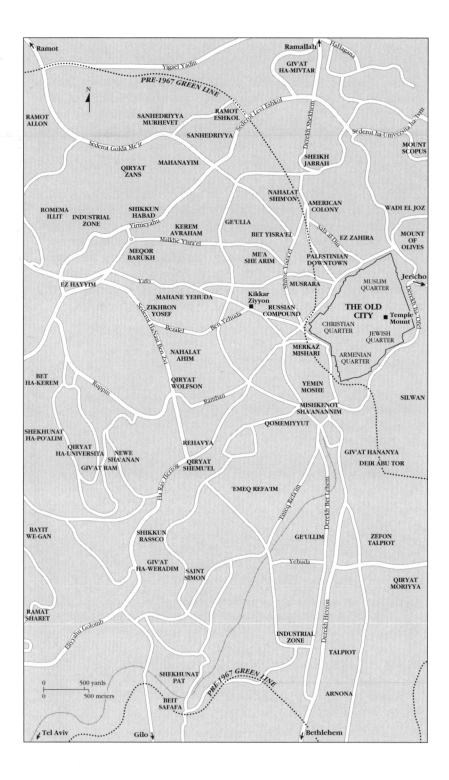

To Rule Jerusalem

Cambridge Cultural Social Studies

General Editors

Jeffrey C. Alexander, *Department of Sociology, University of California, Los Angeles*

Steven Seidman, *Department of Sociology, State University of New York, Albany*

Editorial Board

Jean Comaroff, *Department of Anthropology, University of Chicago*

Donna Haraway, *Department of the History of Consciousness, University of California, Santa Cruz*

Michele Lamont, *Department of Sociology, Princeton University*

Thomas Laqueur, *Department of History, University of California, Berkeley*

Cambridge Cultural Social Studies is a forum for the most original and thoughtful work in cultural social studies. This includes theoretical works focusing on conceptual strategies, empirical studies covering specific topics such as gender, sexuality, politics, economics, social movements, and crime, and studies that address broad themes such as the culture of modernity. Although the perspectives of the individual studies will vary, they will all share the same innovative reach and scholarly quality.

Other titles in the series

Ilana Friedrich Silber, *Virtuosity, Charisma, and Social Order*

Linda Nicholson and Steven Seidman (eds.), *Social Postmodernism*

William Bogard, *The Simulation of Surveillance*

Suzanne R. Kirschner, *The Religious and Romantic Origins of Psychoanalysis*

Paul Lichterman, *The Search for Political Community*

To Rule Jerusalem

ROGER FRIEDLAND
University of California,
Santa Barbara

RICHARD HECHT
University of California,
Santa Barbara

CAMBRIDGE
UNIVERSITY PRESS

Published by the Press Syndicate of the University of Cambridge
The Pitt Building, Trumpington Street, Cambridge CB2 1RP
40 West 20th Street, New York, NY 10011-4211, USA
10 Stamford Road, Oakleigh, Melbourne 3166, Australia

First published 1996

Printed in the United States of America

Library of Congress Cataloging-in-Publication Data
Friedland, Roger.
To rule Jerusalem / Roger Friedland, Richard Hecht.
p.   cm. – (Cambridge cultural social studies)
Includes index.
ISBN 0-521-44046-7 (hc)
1. Jerusalem – Ethnic relations. 2. Jerusalem – Social conditions.
3. Jerusalem – Politics and government. 4. Palestinian Arabs –
Jerusalem.   I. Hecht, Richard D.   II. Title.   III. Series.
DS109.94.F75   1996
305.8'009569442 – dc20   95–40499
                                                              CIP

A catalog record for this book is available from the British Library.

ISBN 0-521-44046-7 Hardback

For Debra – who will always take me to Jerusalem
Roger Friedland

For Joan – who cherishes Jerusalem and its people
with me
Richard Hecht

Contents

Part IV
Heart of Stone

Illustrations

Preface

Jerusalem is at war – with itself. In this city Judaism, Christianity, and Islam fought their defining battles. Here, in this century, two nations have declared themselves. Israelis and Palestinians both claim the city as their capital.

Rival prophets, warring nations. The war for Jerusalem has multiple fronts. At the edge, between forests to the west dropping precipitously to the Mediterranean Sea and deserts to the east stretching throughout the Arab world, lies a stone city creased by deep valleys. In reality, it is just a small, slightly dusty provincial town, cut of gray and pink stone, astride a small mountain range. But its air is seeded with pine pollen, the powder of bone, and memory. This last bends the light and makes the city a luminous medium of dream and nightmare.

The city is a central stake, a battleground, an ineffable symbol, not just to those who live within it, but to peoples and powers around the world. The conflicts that consume it reverberate in Washington, Rome, and Jeddah. And conversely even the smallest geopolitical shifts can shake its streets.

The contest between these larger nations and religions shows itself in Jerusalem, not just as ideology, but as life, in the daily struggles between the city's neighborhoods, which consider each other alien and dangerous zones. The city threatens always, everywhere, to crack into pieces or explode; yet it seems to grow inexorably, driven by the very forces that would tear it apart. And one must never forget that Jerusalem is also just a place whose residents must make do. There are understandings, interdependencies, codes of coexistence, as well as the bladed power of the state and the inertial force of life.

Others have told the history of its stones. We tell the city's contemporary story, the meanings its inhabitants imprint on its hard surfaces, how Jerusalemites experience and manage religious and national conflicts, of which the city is a chromosome. We explore the ways in which residents' ordinary lives shape and are shaped by this extraordinary city, and in so doing, we both map and chronicle the city's cultural wars.

To Rule Jerusalem presents the city's many voices. We have walked

Jerusalem's streets and alleyways, learning how its people live their lives, understand the lives of others, and defend themselves against rival claims. Our footsteps range across the entire ideological and social spectrum, from the clerics of the Muslim Brotherhood to the rabbis of Gush Emunim, from the Likud minister of foreign affairs who vowed Israel would never cede sovereignty over Judea and Samaria to the Palestinian construction worker building the settlements he hoped would one day disappear.

We have tried to convey the assumptions, the logic, the local justice, and indeed the common humanity of each of the city's communities. To convey the contours of each world, we have used its individuals' words. To represent a way of seeing, a cosmology, a point of view, what each individual says is legitimate data. But because we have also sought to find out what actually happened in particular places and times, we have also used many of these same individuals as informants. As representations of reality, an individual's words cannot necessarily be taken at face value. In Jerusalem, the real is always subject to contest. We have tried to check our informants' assertions against other sources. However, there inevitably will be accounts whose construction is strongly influenced by our informants' world views. In these cases, we have tried to offer alternative accounts of the same phenomenon or to indicate in the text what we believe actually happened. In such a complex and charged situation, we will have inevitably missed part of the story. All quotations not otherwise documented are from our interviews done between 1983 and 1993. A complete list of these is available from the authors upon request.

An urban and political sociologist and a historian of religions, we have been observing and interviewing Jerusalemites together since 1983, when we first began with more than a year of daily field work. Over the ensuing decade, we have returned repeatedly for shorter periods to the city, following the many figures we identified then as either influential leaders or emblematic articulators of the world views of a particular part of the metropolitan maze. Although the constellation of forces has shifted, although some may have become more visible and others less so, the stability of Jerusalem's political culture is attested to by the fact that most of these same individuals still represent, or count, within their respective worlds.

In the course of our research, we were stoned, shot at, physically assaulted, robbed, taken into custody in a "closed" military area, and verbally abused. But mainly we experienced some of the most profound hospitality two ethnographers could ever imagine. Jerusalemites' patience with our ignorance – and sometimes our insensitivity – astounded us. This was true even though Israelis sometimes resented our efforts to say anything about "their" country as American scholars; Orthodox Jews would often try to turn us toward repentance and occasionally refused to have anything to do with us as non-Orthodox Jews; Israelis would entreat us to settle in the land or implicitly denigrate us for our diaspora mentality as American Jews; Palestinians would mistrust our fundamental capacity to understand as Jews and had either great hopes that our country would someday compel Israel to recognize the Palestinian claim or bitterness that as Americans we were citizens of a blind neocolonial state. But through it all, people talked, offering up their lives for examination, for recognition, even for expiation.

And through it all we ate. In each home we entered, there were always coffee or juice, fresh-baked cookies and cakes, shortbread, strudel, baklava, and candies. The best cooks turned out to be the most bitter enemies, and most interviews could not have proceeded if we had not sampled the offerings that were so graciously provided us. Sometimes, after four or five interviews in a day, we could barely eat dinner.

Acknowledgments

We have received considerable assistance researching and writing this book. During our initial stay in Jerusalem, we were blessed with two research assistants who guided us to critical individuals and assisted in translations: Danny Felsenstein, then a graduate student in geography at the Hebrew University, and Muhammad Masslha, then a student in sociology at the Hebrew University. The first is a British-born Jew who supports the religious nationalist settlement movement, the second a Nazareth-born Palestinian Israeli who, early on, supported the Communist Party and a two-state solution. We have had research assistance as well from Gloria Blakemore, Sharon Chitin, Jared Epstein, Shoshanah Feher, Tarik Hamawi, Richard Hoch, Gerald Scher, and Sharon Shapira. Hundreds of students who have taken our course on Jerusalem at the University of California, Santa Barbara, have proved a receptive audience that helped us shape the ideas developed here.

In Jerusalem, we are grateful for the friendship and assistance provided to us by Chana and Naftali Arnon, Stan and Ruth Cohen, Jamil and Raeda Hamad, Yehuda and Levana Litani. The Reverend Colin and Carol Morton made the stones of St. Andrew's Scottish Hospice – our trusted redoubt – into a warm and welcoming refuge. We should like to thank the University of California, Santa Barbara, its Academic Senate Committee on Research, Interdisciplinary Humanities Center, and Office of Instructional Development, for providing us several times with monies to travel to Jerusalem.

We have benefited along the way from critical readings from a number of people. We want particularly to thank Chaia Beckerman, Director of Publications, at the Harry S. Truman Research Institute for the Advancement of Peace in Jerusalem, as well as Jeff Alexander, Robert Alford, Mitch Duneier, Sam Dunn, Richard Flacks, Helen Friedland, Mark Juergensmeyer, Harvey Molotch, Sandy Robertson, Mary Rakow, Gershon Shafir, Ehud Sprinzak, Susan Steiner, Lola Willoughby, and Ifrach Zilberman, all of whom carefully picked through these pages looking for false moves and undeveloped openings.

Finally our agent, Katherine Preminger, was a constant source of sweet cool water, carrying us onward, chiding us for our academic habits, insisting that we bring her "a book I can carry in my hands." This book landed in the Cultural Social Studies series at Cambridge University Press because Jeff Alexander understood and was willing to fight for its sociological significance. At Cambridge University Press, we have had the considerable benefit of criticism and editing, first from Emily Loose, who wanted to push Cambridge into more accessible texts, and then from Alex Holzman, our current editor, who has shaped our manuscript as though he were trimming his father's hair. We are truly grateful to both of these fine craftsmen for pushing us so hard and so gracefully.

Introduction

In Jerusalem, Israelis and Palestinians must confront each other, and the faithful must deal with those who do not believe. Its neighborhoods are divided among rival nations and religions. Although their residents may ride the same buses and walk the same streets, buy and sell from one another, draw their water and electricity from the same sources, they all strive to insulate themselves from those who live differently.[1] Each community is enclosed within its separate spaces, inhabited by those who order the world in the same way.

Contacts between communities must be carefully managed. The most uncomfortable encounters are often among kinsmen, within Jewish and Arab communities, not between them. Blood enemies evoke a mutual invisibility, fear, or hatred when one oversteps accepted boundaries. But fellow Jews and Arabs who violate the deeply felt commitments of their kinsmen are more likely to elicit disdain and anger.

On her way downtown, for example, a young Israeli woman takes a shortcut through an unfamiliar Jerusalem street. The *hamsin*, hot desert winds that will sweep the midday streets clean of people, are blowing from the east. She is wearing a t-shirt, blue denim skirt, and open leather sandals; her skin is the color of burnished leather; and one can just make out a flowered pattern on her brassiere.

Orthodox Jewish men in their late teens and early twenties stand around, cloaked in black. Their skins, alabaster from study, glisten with sweat. Side curls dangling, they hiss as the woman passes. One spits at her feet. Averting her eyes, she clutches her purse, hurrying to regain modern ground. The young men feel their neighborhood has been violated by a brazen woman whose nakedness bespeaks an empty freedom. Arriving home, the woman contemptuously recounts her treatment at the hands of the *schwartze*s, medieval fossils, the "blacks."

Jerusalem is a site of multiple sovereignties and sacralities. The routines of life easily get caught up in cultural battles over the identity of Israel and Palestine, Judaism and Islam. Personal choices express collective destinies, the taking of sides. Where to live, when to work and play, and with whom to be friends are choices freighted with deeper meanings.

Political debate among Israelis, Jerusalem, 1984.

Soccer is a Jerusalem passion, but the city failed to build a stadium during the first half-century of Israeli statehood. When the municipality finally set out to construct one in the suburbs, masses of devout Jewish men turned the streets into an angry, black-coated sea. They didn't want the stadium built near their neighborhoods. In fact, they didn't want it built at all. A football stadium, especially one where games would be played on the Jewish sabbath, would desecrate this holiest of places. They accused their municipal leaders of being "Hellenizers," a reference to Jews who thousands of years before had tried to make Jewish culture more cosmopolitan, more like the Greeks'. Then, too, there had been "games" in the city. Orthodox Jews performed a ritual exorcism of Mayor Teddy Kollek, intending to do him physical injury, even kill him. The decision to let the bulldozers loose almost brought down the national government, preventing Israel from responding to a diplomatic opening toward peace.

Similarly the decision to build a road, hire a worker, go to a movie, or live in a neighborhood can be absorbed into, or come to express, struggles between opposing social movements, between nations, between states far from Jerusalem. The right to rent an apartment, build a house, add a room, construct a synagogue or mosque, pray at a wall, or walk down a street can form the basis for communal warfare and government crisis.

In 1991, some Israelis bought title to some old stone houses in an Arab neighborhood inhabited by Palestinian tenants. They paid good money, signed contracts. It was all legal. Then, in the night, submachine guns slung over the men's shoulders, they moved into their new homes. Soldiers who accompanied them ate sandwiches left behind in haste by the Arab tenants as they fled. Other Palestinians, returning to homes in which they had lived for decades, found their furniture thrown out the window, their bedding stuffed into an outhouse.

"It's just like 1948," an old Palestinian man, his face field weathered, told us as he fingered amber beads, watching the news on Israeli televsion. Palestinians threatened to kill both their new Israeli neighbors and the Arab residents who had sold them the properties. "Apartheid!" a Palestinian cursed indignantly to us. "If a Jew can't live in Zion, that would be apartheid," a white-bearded rabbi replied. The Jews' move into the Arab neighborhood, which had to be defended around the clock by Israeli soldiers, was both authorized and financed by the Israeli government. It coincided with American pressure on the Jewish state to negotiate with the Palestinians and was accompanied by almost daily demonstrations and repeated protests by the American Department of State.

The routines of daily life in Jerusalem continually threaten to explode into partisan conflict, into demonstrations and rock throwing, into the deployment of troops and waves of terror. In other cities, citizens share a bedrock of belief; the metropolis is a more mundane and private landscape. Those who govern can manage the city through marginal adjustments in the distribution of office, honor, and wealth; through protection of life's routines from disruption.

But in Jerusalem, there is little common reality upon which citizens can stand and adjudicate their differences. Ordinary lives are suffused with extraordinary significance, radiating the power of collective purposes, irreconcilable and endlessly in conflict. The city is not just a profane backdrop to the daily round, a public instrument for the pursuit of private happiness. It is a symbol of each community's collective identity.

In other cities life can be lived as a relatively brief sequence of biographical moments, but in Jerusalem personal life derives its significance from shared understandings about the long sweep of history, from epic stories that revolve around this city and culminate here. Many see God's hand in that history, giving private life a cosmic, redemptive meaning. People who construe their days so differently cannot easily live as neighbors.

Separation in space is a way to manage conflicts between communities who cannot share historical time. Each community holds fast to the city, strives to multiply its numbers, to expand the space it controls. Each

Jewish graves on the Mount of Olives and Palestinian homes below Silwan, 1991.

battles with the weapons at hand. Simple acts of municipal construction incite group passions. The bulldozers threaten to disturb the past. It is not simply that in an ancient city digging anywhere is likely to unearth relics or graves. New construction threatens to disrupt the sedimented agreement about who can do what and where. Building reshapes the terrain of group conflict. The stones of the city mark too many miracles, too much ancestral blood, to be rationally rearranged. And so the cement mixers may be followed by demonstrations, litigation, fistfights, and riots. Jerusalem is a battleground with entrenched positions. It cannot be governed, but must be ruled.

A Nation in Mind

We can only make sense of Jerusalem's explosive energies if we understand the struggle is for identity, not just for stone. Even as Israelis and Palestinians strive to control the city, both are building new nations.

A century ago, the nations of Israel and Palestine did not exist. The Israelis and the Palestinians literally had to invent themselves, to imagine themselves as particular peoples armed with an essential, preeminent claim to this land. For both it was an arduous task. The Jews who would become Israelis needed to separate themselves from the nations among whom they had lived for generations. To build a national identity beyond ethnicity and religion, they felt compelled to assert their radical difference from those Jews who would not follow them to Palestine. The Palestinians, likewise, had to disengage themselves from the larger Arab nation that surrounded them and fought its enemies in their name.

A nation is a fantastic thing; making one involves an imaginary fusion of a people, a land, a history, and the authority of a single state. It requires the fashioning of a collectivity who believe there is an identity between them and the land, who understand themselves to have a history, a story tracking a distinctive path through time. This meaning of this location, this narrative binds a people to the state claiming sovereignty over the land in their name.

Communities of blood and belief must make claim to particular territories and histories as their own. Nation building is at once mundane, based in the material space and time of existence, and yet a magical transfiguration of people based on an imagined history and homeland that they envision together. Peoples who claim nationhood inhabit imaginary continents and literary fictions at the same time they live in and through real territories and histories shaped by the force of circumstance and state armies, schoolteachers and tax collectors. The national interest is the common reading of a map and a history. A nation must be manufactured in the imagination if it is to cohere through time on the land.

A people only makes history when they believe they have a history to make, when they understand themselves as distinct, with an essential nature, a character worth reproducing across the generations. The collective actions that mark off the land – settlement by pioneers and ancestors, the definition of boundaries and their determined defense – are seminal moments in the making of a people. Through the historical struggle to cohere in space, a people takes form, a truth exemplified by Israel and Palestine. Both measure their nation's character by how they take, hold, and husband the land. The bounding of the nation's body in space is essential to its bonding in time. Through that bounding a nation is born. The land becomes the body of the whole people. They defend it with their lives, for it embodies their collective life. In nationalist vision, Jewish settlement and Palestinian steadfastness, the first building the land and the other holding on to it, have always been imbued with a sacred aura.

Both the Israelis and the Palestinians were formed as new nations in this century. The Israelis, dependent upon immigration and new settlement, and the Palestinians, a population in place, faced different challenges in creating a nation and bounding the land as their own. Both initially faced serious doubt among their own people that a separate nation-state was necessary.

To form a nation, the Israelis were required to separate themselves, both physically and mentally, from a larger population of Jews who were indifferent, if not hostile, to the project of building a Jewish nation-state in the Middle East. The Zionists wanted to make an ancient memory that had become a messianic dream for religious Jews into a modern historical reality. An earlier Jewish nation, unified and fractured, vanquishing and then vanquished by its neighbors, incorporated and released by different empires, destroyed and rebuilt, had endured for a millennium. But it had been two thousand years since a Jewish state had existed in any form in *eretz-yisrael,* the land of Israel. Since Roman legions captured Jerusalem in 70 C.E., razed the city's Temple, and crushed the nationalists who wanted their freedom, Jews had been dispersed throughout the world.[2]

During the nineteenth century, the overwhelming majority of Jews believed they could find political freedom and personal security as citizens of the modern nation-states then being consolidated throughout Europe and the Americas. Wherever they were allowed, Jews became patriots of the new order, embracing the liberties of the marketplace, the classroom, and the ballot box. They would be good French citizens or Americans on the street, and good Jews at home.

Zionists, the nationalists who first began in the late nineteenth century to seek a Jewish nation-state, had to transform and transport themselves to a nation etched only in biblical imagination, not on the ground. The early Zionists were drawn from Russia and Poland, where liberties were few and fragile, where Jews faced official discrimination at every turn. Jews had lived in the land of Israel, particularly in Jerusalem, for centuries, but the land was overwhelmingly inhabited by Arabs.

For the Palestinians, building a nation was no less difficult. They had an important advantage: they were resident in the land the Romans renamed Palestine after crushing the Judeans. But Palestine had been a province in the Ottoman Empire for centuries. Over the course of the nineteenth century, the empire crumbled. At the close of World War I, when the European powers divided the Middle East among themselves, Palestine became a British mandate. Britain signed the Balfour Declaration promising the Jews a national home there, and as Jewish immigrants streamed into the land, local Arabs mobilized against what they understood to be European colonization. By what right did England in 1917, and later the United Nations in the aftermath of Nazi genocide in 1947, grant immigrant Jews the prerogative to fashion a state in their midst?

However, it was not evident in the region, even to the Palestinian Arabs themselves, that they should create an independent Palestinian state. After World War I, the Palestinians rose against the British and the Zionists in the context of a larger Arab mobilization against foreign domination, whether Turkish or West European. Arabic-speaking peoples declared themselves to be a single great nation that would beat back the colonial thrusts of the West and reclaim and replicate their glorious past, when the greatest mathematicians, doctors, poets, astronomers, and architects were Arab and the West lived in comparative squalor and ignorance. Palestine's Mediterranean shore was the Arab nation's most important western front.

Arab nationalists understood the divisions between Arab states as arbitrary colonial legacies traced on the maps by alien conquerors. Palestinians saw themselves as a vanguard of this larger Arab nation, *al-qawmiyya al-arabiyya*, in its struggle to throw off Western colonization. Indeed, Palestinian intellectuals, particularly the minority Christians, had been important in the first fashioning of Arab nationalism. Arab nationalists understood the expulsion of Jewish colonists as crucial to the liberation of the Arab homeland. The Palestine Liberation Organization was formed in 1964 under Egyptian tutelage as an instrument by which the Egyptians might bolster their claim to lead the Arab nation. Palestinians themselves counted on the armed might of the Arab world to free their land.

Colonial and ethnic rivalries quickly shredded the dream of a unitary Arab nation-state. Soon after the First World War, the one Arab nation was carved into a multitude of states. But the vision of unity endured, particularly as a mantle of legitimacy for expansion. As it took territory, each Arab state claimed it was reaching toward the larger nation. Neighboring Arab states naturally claimed Palestine as an extension of their own land. From the east, the Hashemite Kingdom of Transjordan considered these lands its territorial prerogative. To the north, the Syrians fervently believed Palestine should be a province in Greater Syria. Many Palestinians, including some of its preeminent warriors against Zionism, supported one or the other of their claims. That the Palestinians should or could fight on behalf of a separate state of their own was a premise that would have to be established.

The several Arab states won their independence. But after all the European soldiers had debarked, the Arab embassies had opened, and the oil fields had been nationalized, the Jews remained behind, their state in place, humiliating proof that the Arab nation was indeed more rhetoric than reality.

At the Center Stands a City

At the center of all great nations stands a city, a nucleus of power. From its ramparts, rulers ride out to pacify the periphery, commands are given and laws passed, revenues flow in and expenditures out. From this spot, elites attempt to orchestrate the life of their people, to bind them as a nation, and to protect those boundaries from others who would claim their loyalties. A nation's frontiers are at once physical and cultural.

This power center becomes the locus of a nation's identity, its most important signifier. Those who believe in the nation come here to hear its voice and to speak in its name, to see its face and be seen as one of its own. It is in the capital city where the mandate to rule is reaffirmed, where critical events in a people's history are compressed and ritually remembered, where its most important ancestors are often buried. The city, a physical concentration of buildings and bodies, becomes a symbol of the nation, the fixed point from which the global expanse and the chaos of time take on a particular perspective.

Israelis and Palestinians both see themselves through Jerusalem's eye. The city is the symbolic center of their two nations, the foundation stone of their claims to the land. Both stand on this city as their capital.

Israel was first forged into a unified nation from Jerusalem some three thousand years ago, when King David seized the crown and united the twelve tribes from this city, located on a stony spine in the no-man's-land between the fractious tribes. David renamed this conquered village Zion, a new capital of a new nation. For a thousand years, Jerusalem was the seat of Jewish sovereignty, the household site of kings, the location of its legislative councils and courts.

In exile, the Jewish nation came to be identified with the city that had been the site of its ancient capital. Jews, wherever they were, prayed for its restoration. The modern Jewish nationalists likewise called themselves Zionists. When the 1948 war ended, the new state of Israel had survived. But the frontiers marked by trenches and mine fields did not include Zion. Israel had lost control over King David's capital, had been expelled from the Old City by Jordanian Legionnaires.

Israel's Jewish citizens were concentrated along the Mediterranean coast. Nonetheless, David Ben-Gurion, the first prime minister, declared the modern Jewish part of Jerusalem outside the old walled city, dating back only to the nineteenth century, to be Israel's national capital. The Zionists built their capital outside the walls of Zion, in an even more modern suburb, their national future seemingly spread below them to the west along the sea. In the new Jerusalem they built a memorial to the Holocaust, the singular barbarity that to many provided the historical imperative for a new Jewish nation-state. And here they buried the heroes who had died to make it so.[3]

But Zion, the ancient capital, lay to the east in enemy Arab hands. The Zionists could only turn and look longingly at the monuments that provided the mythic template for their return. They could not go there until

1967, when Israel conquered the city from which its nationhood had originated. Israel declared the walled city to be an inseparable part of a unified Jerusalem. It had always been Israel's capital. It was as if it had been waiting for them. It was theirs now and they would never let go.

Jerusalem was also central for the Palestinian nation. Although the coast was peppered with nationalist leaders and intellectuals, only the old families of Jerusalem successfully vied for the right to speak in the name of the Arabs of Palestine. Divided between the more urban and urbane coast and the rural and traditional highlands, between Muslim and Christian, fragmented among jealous towns and villages, divided by intensely loyal networks of extended kin, penetrated and manipulated by agents of the surrounding Arab states, the Palestinians were forged into a nation from Jerusalem.

But the Palestinians never achieved a state of their own. Until the *intifada*, which exploded in 1987, their most determined effort was led by rival Jerusalem families a half century before. This rebellion, between 1936 and 1939, against British and Zionist colonization degenerated into a civil war between those who wanted independence and those who saw their future with the Jordanians, between those who refused to accommodate a Jewish state and those willing to make their peace with it. In 1948, those Palestinians who were still willing to fight for an independent state were beaten from the west by the Zionists, and from the east by the Transjordanians, who conquered the Old City and claimed all the lands the United Nations had allotted to the new Palestinian state for themselves. Although many Palestinians, particularly the large landed families, were happy to be part of the new Jordanian order, others rebelled. At the 1948 war's end, these Palestinians formed their first provisional government in Gaza, a sandy strip along the coast held by the Egyptians. They declared Jerusalem the capital of the new state they still hoped to form. In 1964, the Palestine Liberation Organization (PLO), a nationalist movement aiming to rid Palestine of Zionist occupation, was established in Jerusalem. But the city was then Jordanian territory and so the PLO did not claim it as their capital. In 1988, forty years after the Palestinians' first provisional government, the PLO finally declared an independent Palestinian state and reaffirmed their national claim to Jerusalem.

The Israeli–Palestinian struggle for Jerusalem draws its desperate energy from the fact that each nation grounds its existence, its right to sovereignty, in the city's history, in the memories imprinted in its landscape and the ancestors buried beneath it. For almost a century now, two peoples have fought each other to control this town, struggled to hang on when their prospects looked bleak. For the underdog, residence has always been a form of resistance. Each fights for the city as an essential part of the struggle to survive as a nation. The war for Jerusalem can never end because it is not just a war for the high ground of a stone city. It is a war to control a symbol.

Sacred and Sovereign

If Jerusalem were simply a piece of property on which to live and claim sovereignty, the conflict between Jewish and Palestinian nationalisms would be difficult enough. But this city is also a sacred center, the ground of faith. Over three millennia, the city has drawn pilgrims, a steady stream of new residents who waited and bore witness, warriors who fought for the faith. Many came because they believed God was near. Some believed their coming would bring him closer.

The site where God commanded Abraham to sacrifice Isaac stands within the city's walled core, the same place, it is believed, where King David's son, Solomon, built the Temple to the one God of Israel. In Jewish thought, this was the center of the world, the hinge between heaven and earth. Here human history began and here it would end. When the Temple stood, Jews believed that pilgrimage to and sacrifice in its sacred precincts kept both social order and cosmos in place.

For challenging this Temple's priesthood and its complicity with Rome, the Galilean wonder-worker Yehoshua bar-Yosef, whom the Christian world would later know as Jesus, son of God, was crucified a thousand years after Solomon built the first Temple. Jesus died the death of a political criminal, not a religious heretic. Yet if Christianity understood the loss of Jewish nationhood and the destruction of the Temple as proof that God had transferred his covenant to a new community, devout Jews still believed that the restoration of sovereignty and the reconstruction of the Temple would signal the coming of their messiah, finally a king in David's line.

Jerusalem was also the destination of the Prophet Muhammad's magical "night journey" before ascending to heaven in the seventh century. The Prophet, Muslims believe, tied his winged steed, al-Buraq, to the Western Wall of the Temple Mount, the same outer wall made of huge blocks of hewn stone where Jews still pray fervently for the Temple's rebuilding. Muhammad rose to heaven from an enormous rock in the midst of the platform that once housed Solomon's Temple, the same one where Isaac was bound for sacrifice.

Islam began as a religion of conquest, the veracity of its followers' faith proved by the military victories of those who wielded swords in the name of their Prophet. Shortly after Muhammad's death, Islam's second caliph (*khalifa*, from which the word derives, means "successor"), con-

Individual prayer at the Western Wall.

quered Jerusalem in 638 C.E. For those who followed the way of Allah, the city's conquest provided the foundational proof of Islam's primacy over Christianity and Judaism. Jerusalem's surrender treaty became the template by which those peoples in their midst who continued to follow the prophets – Abraham, Moses, Jesus – preceding Muhammad would be subordinated within the Islamic world. Purged from the Arabian peninsula containing Mecca and Medina, Jews and Christians were tolerated elsewhere as theologically subordinate peoples who were allowed religious freedom, but denied civil and political equality. Later in the seventh century, a Syrian caliph, Abd al-Malik (685–705), built the Dome of the Rock over the Prophet's stepping-stone to heaven. Inside the cool mosaic sphere, the calligraphy spells out, "Pray for your Prophet and Servant, Jesus the son of Miriam." A prior prophet yes; God, no.

Jerusalem, as both a sacred and a sovereign center, calls the relation between religion and state into question. Peoples of this region have not understood the nation-state as a compelling public power that relegates religion to a private confessional choice. Unlike Christianity, Judaism and Islam began as blueprints for all social life. Their models of righteousness were also models of rule, one hinging upon the other. Judaism and Islam each developed laws establishing their respective social orders, that linked ordinary existence to transcendental ideals: the Jewish *mitzvot*, or commandments, of the Torah, the Islamic *shari'a*, or law, based on interpretation of the Qur'an and the behavior, or *sunna*, of the Prophet and his companions.[4] Jewish kings and Islamic Caliphs grounded their authority as God's agents in this law and its enforcement.

Although the circumstances have differed, the Israeli and Palestinian nations have both been torn by tensions between religion and nationalism, between those who would ground their nation's destiny in divine dictates valid for all time and those who would trust to decisions made in history. At the same time that Israelis and Palestinians conduct a nationalist campaign against each other to control the city's streets, both groups fight among themselves over the meaning of their own nationhood, over the relation between Judaism and Zionism, between Islam and Palestinian nationalism. Because the city is simultaneously a central sacred site and a symbol of sovereignty, the contest within each nation is expressed here with particular ferocity.

To Rule Jerusalem

Although the peoples of Jerusalem live in the same city, they inhabit different worlds. The Israelis regard it as a liberated capital; the Palestin-

Sukkot at the Western Wall.

ians, as an occupied one. For both the city is the center of national desire. But many residents also understand it first and foremost as a holy city whose sanctity is to be protected against any who would defile her. Most believers, including the multitude of Christianities who squabble among themselves, want the city to be a plural, cosmopolitan center. However, there are Jews and Muslims who believe Jerusalem will ultimately be the exclusive patrimony of their own people. Many within each nation see the city as the frontier marking the limit of their people's legitimate claims to this land. Others look beyond, seeing the city as a gateway east or west to the rest they consider rightfully their own.

Jerusalem is simultaneously a material city shared by rival communities and a symbol whose meaning cannot be held in common. Each community jealously watches the others, waits for a chance to lean against history, to capture more of the city's space and time. Because Jerusalem is the center, it is a ritual theater for conflict. Each community conducts its own campaigns to control this place or that, defending or extending its claim to the center, the right to build Jerusalem according to its particular vision. By capturing this city, by reshaping its material organization, each hopes to refashion the identity of its respective nation. The struggle to control the profane choreography of daily life is part of a larger war to control Jerusalem as symbol. By capturing the center, each hopes to fashion its own nation and its relationship with the other opposing it.

The two nations who divide Jerusalem are themselves divided over the appropriate relation between religion and nationalism, democracy and the divine. *To Rule Jerusalem* explores Jerusalem's role as the most important battleground in the double struggle for Israeli and Palestinian nationhood, seeking to convey how the conflicts both between and within these nations are experienced and managed at the center they all claim as their own.

To Rule Jerusalem introduces these political contests not just as a clash of ideas, or a dissection of words and battle cries, but as the process through which these conflicts work in a Jerusalem that is both material metropolis and transcendent symbol. To do so, we focus on the ways in which national and religious conflicts are fought as a war for the city's space and time, a battle simultaneously to control the city's material organization and its cultural meaning. To understand the conflicts that organize Jerusalem, we address the dual reality of the city as a place to live one's daily life and as a symbol to which one accords ultimate meaning. People struggle to control both the real city and the ideal city. They cannot be kept apart. It is that meeting of earth and heaven we hope to convey here.

1

A Fearful Fusion

Zionists and Palestinian nationalists have both fought for Jerusalem as a symbol and sovereign site of their respective nations. Fashioning those nations has led them not just to bloody battles with each other, but into ferocious culture wars with their fellow Jews and Arabs who have understood their identities, and hence Jerusalem, in radically different ways. The struggles within the Israeli and Palestinian communities have often been just as intractable and uncompromising as those between them. Nation building has not been easy for either side.

The Israelis and the Palestinians confronted obstacles inside and out as they sought to forge their nations. Internally there were divisive conflicts between those who would follow the law of a sovereign people and those who would cleave to the law of God. Neither people could keep politicians and priests apart, nor could they establish a relationship between nationalism and religion that their citizens could abide.

From the outside, other countries refused to treat Israel or Palestine as they would nations like Brunei, Zimbabwe, or Albania. Both nations were picked out for exquisite scrutiny, either as a particular evil to be contained or as a supreme good for which one felt compelled to fight. In the 1948 war that gave it birth, Israel was unable to capture the Old City of Jerusalem enclosing the sites sacred to the world's three monotheisms. Particularly since 1967, when Israel recaptured this stone warren from the Jordanians, the conflict between Israelis and Palestinians has been subjected to global gaze and judgment. Neither has ever been allowed to understand itself as just another people.

Each nation had to face internal religious forces who refused to recognize a secular nation-state, who stood in the way of state making, who would not abide democracy. Both nations were vulnerable to challenge because two ancient religions – Judaism and Islam – were integral to their formation. Ever since the stone core of Jerusalem fell to the Israelis, these religious forces have become steadily stronger. The Israeli–Palestinian conflict may no longer be caught up in the drama of the superpowers, but both nations again confront the specter of militant religious nationalists willing to fight and die for an undivided city at the center of an undivided land ruled by believers in their one and only God.

The Meaning of Zion

From Zionism's earliest days, Jews could not agree about its meaning. And because they could not concur on the significance of the movement, they could not easily cooperate in the city from which it took its name. The Zionists not only confronted secular Jews who believed in the promises of modernity and chose to remain in exile, they were opposed by deeply religious Jews already in the land. The first rejected Zion; the second, the Zionists. The Balfour Declaration, Britain's 1917 pledge of support for Zionism, was opposed by prominent British Jews, including Herbert Samuel, the first Jew to sit in the British cabinet, who would later become Britain's first high commissioner for Palestine. Judaism was a religion, not a nation, they argued. These Jews feared Jewish nationalism would compromise their ascent in British society.[1]

Most of the religious Jews who got to Zion before the Zionists also saw a secular, democratic nation-state for Jews as anathema. They opposed it with all their might. They had to. The messiah's coming depended on it. Belief dictated that they wait for a messiah, a divinely chosen king, to restore sovereignty to Israel through Jerusalem. The devout Jews of Jerusalem, like most Orthodox Jews throughout the world, had a different understanding of what it meant to settle the land and restore Jewish sovereignty in Jerusalem. Coming here affirmed their belief that God would again send them a king, a scion in the line of David, who would enable them to possess the promised land one last time.

The territory of the new Jewish nation was spelled out in the Bible. The Torah, the five books God revealed to Moses at Mount Sinai, provided a legal, moral, and metaphysical foundation for a nation-state. Moses formed the nation in the desert as he led them to *eretz-yisrael*, the land of Israel, promised them by God. The Zionists, who largely did not believe, sought to settle just this divinely promised land. Although there were proposals to go elsewhere, including Mexico and Uganda, no other place would do.[2] It was here that the Jewish nation had been formed and taken root.

The Orthodox Jews understood the land of Israel as part of their covenant with God binding them to the laws revealed to Moses at Sinai. But the Torah also clearly stipulated that the Jews would possess the land only if they obeyed God's law. Law and land were contractually tied one to the other. Many Orthodox Jews believed they had lost the land two millennia earlier, had been forced into exile, because they had strayed from the law's requirements.

In exile, Judaism had become a personal faith and a moral code by which Jews regulated their communal affairs. But ever since the Romans had vanquished Jerusalem in 70 C.E., devout Jews had waited for God's kingdom to be rebuilt, a real kingdom, not a numinous dream. They understood Jewish history through a mythic pattern of exile and return. To return to the land of Israel, and most especially to Jerusalem, was an act of supreme faith that God had not forgotten his people and the promise he had made to Abraham so many millennia ago.

So when the overwhelmingly secular and predominantly socialist Zionists began to settle Palestine, they confronted a large, deeply religious Jewish community that had been present in Jerusalem for centuries. These devout Jews had come to Jerusalem to live, to study and pray, and to be buried in the city where they expected the messiah, a new king in David's line, first to appear. Many came because they believed he was near. They understood the messianic era would be marked by the ingathering of the exiles and by the restoration of Jewish sovereignty. By coming to Jerusalem, some believed they could help the messiah on his way.

By the middle of the nineteenth century, Karl Marx, whose theories the most radical Palestinians would later use to justify their drive to expel the Zionists, pointed out that these largely Orthodox Jews were already a majority of the city's population:

> Nothing equals the misery and the sufferings of the Jews at Jerusalem, inhabiting the most filthy quarter of the town, . . . the constant objects of Mussulman oppression and intolerance, insulted by the Greeks, persecuted by the Latins, and living only upon the scanty alms transmitted by their European brethren. The Jews . . . are only attracted to Jerusalem by desire of inhabiting the Valley of Jehosaphat, and to die in the very places where the redemptor is to be expected.[3]

These pious Jews confronted a wave of Zionist patriots who wanted to achieve many of the same goals for which they regularly prayed – gathering the exiled Jews in the land, reconstructing a Jewish polity. But instead of rejoicing, the Orthodox community was aghast.

In religious eyes, the return of Jewish sovereignty could be achieved only by the messiah, a divine agent. For human beings to achieve this was to force the hand of God. That its human agents did not cleave to the ways of their ancestors was incredible; that, once achieved, a state whose laws deviated from the Torah would be established was an abomination; and that the Zionists conducted their profane project in Hebrew, the sacred language, was too much to bear. Like many Orthodox Jews throughout the world, those of Jerusalem largely opposed Zionism as apostasy, false messianism, and a threat to Judaism itself. In 1881, Jerusalem's rabbis condemned the early Zionist settlers as "transgressors who pollute the land."[4] A Zionist state in Zion would profane its sacred center.[5]

Over the course of the twentieth century, the religious Jews who made up what the Zionists referred to as the old *yishuv*, or old settlement, were overwhelmed by secular immigrants of the new. Some among the deeply religious, the religious Zionists, ultimately came to understand Zionism as a strange and wonderful fulfillment of God's promise. But as it became clear that a Jewish state would be formed, most of Jerusalem's devout Jews viewed the prospect with great trepidation. Would they be able to protect their way of life under the sovereignty of a Jewish state? Upon what ultimate authority would the state base its laws?

In 1947, as the United Nations prepared to decide whether and how to divide Palestine, the Zionist movement engaged in frenzied activity to persuade the world's governments its cause was just. The Zionist leadership were convinced that vociferous objection by the pious Jews of Jerusalem would undermine their cause. To prevent their public opposition, David Ben-Gurion, the head of the Zionist movement who would shortly become Israel's first prime minister, promised that personal status – birth, death, marriage, divorce – would continue to be regulated according to religious law as interpreted by the Orthodox rabbinate. Although he and his wife, Paula, had been married in a civil ceremony in New York, Jews in the new state of Israel would be denied that right. The rabbinate also would be legally empowered to use religious law to determine who was a Jew and thus who had a claim to full membership in the nation.

In Jewish communities throughout the world, rabbis have been religious teachers, spiritual and moral leaders, selected for their knowledge of Jewish law and tradition. Under the Ottomans and the British, Jerusalem's chief rabbis had defended the Jewish community's interests in Palestine. The Zionists allowed this bureaucratic artifice imposed by outsiders, an adaptation to subjugation used to mediate between the Jewish community and non-Jewish kings and sultans, to be carried over into the sovereign Jewish state. As a result of Orthodoxy's legal monopoly, elementary ritual rights – to marry and to bury, for example – were denied to those non-Orthodox forms of Judaism – Reform and Conservative – that were flourishing in Western Europe and North America. Ironically the only group who would lack religious freedom in the Jewish state were the Jews themselves.

Ben-Gurion allowed both the anti-Zionist and pro-Zionist religious communities to maintain their own independent school systems and to finance them with public monies but forced the left-wing Zionist movement, Mapam, to fold its privately run city schools into a unitary secular state system. These religious Zionist schools provided the rabbis who staffed the new state rabbinate. Finally, Ben-Gurion permitted the rabbis to exempt a few hundred particularly gifted yeshivah students and all religious women from the Israeli army.

As the British prepared to depart Palestine on May 14, 1948, Ben-Gurion, a Jew from Plonsk, Poland, wove the foundational myth of the new Jewish nation-state. In proclaiming the state of Israel, he employed the Hebrew Bible, not as a religious or legal document, but as a history of nation building. The Hebrew prophets were construed not as the defenders of the particular powers of Jews, but as progenitors of the Enlightenment. "The State of Israel . . . will be based on the precepts of liberty, justice and peace taught by the Hebrew prophets," he wrote.[6] Ben-Gurion's Zionist movement sought to harness Judaism to the project of building a modern Jewish nation-state.

Although Ben-Gurion wanted to construct a secular Jewish state, synagogue and state had been fused in an uneasy weld. His fateful acts to secure Orthodox political support had crippled the state's institutional capacity to mold all its citizens in state schools, to register and regulate their passage through life, to mobilize them for military duty, and to shape the moral meaning of citizenship. Religious elites controlled a large, and because of their high birth rates, a growing component of mass education. Through the chief rabbinate, Ben-Gurion had perpetuated a mechanism by which caliphs and kings had earlier controlled the Jewish community. Unable to agree on the foundational principles of the state, Israel failed to write a constitution.

Each of Ben-Gurion's concessions became a beachead for different streams within the Orthodox community to expand their political influence, to secure more authority, to garner more funds. But more importantly, they created a base from which Jews would later undercut the legitimacy of their state. Israel failed to fix the relationship between nation and religion, between state and synagogue. The struggle between king and priesthood that had plagued the ancient Israelites debilitated the modern nation as well. Jewish law became an accepted basis from which to challenge, even disobey, state law. Disobedience and resistance came early from the Orthodox Jews who never accepted Zionism. It would come later, and more ominously, from those Orthodox Jews who understood the state as a divine instrument.

Zionists had believed that Jewish statehood would finally transform Jews into a people like any other, divided like the Irish, the Italians, and the Poles, between home and diaspora. But Zionism did not, as many of its early proponents believed it would, end anti-Semitism. The creation of Israel rendered Jewish life untenable in most of the Arab world, as the United Nations's partition resolution was followed by Arab pogroms and the burning of synagogues. In Russia and Poland, birthplace of many Jewish citizens of the new state, anti-Semitism was repeatedly used first to denigrate the enemies of the socialist state and later to deny Jews a secure place in the postsocialist order.

In the years immediately after World War II, when the specter of the Holocaust still stunned human imagination, socialists could support the fledgling state of Israel as part of what they understood to be the great progressive march of history. The Soviet Union was in fact one of the first nations to support Israel. The world construed the 1948 war as a heroic struggle of an infant nation to survive; in the 1949 May Day parade in Paris, the crowds cheered loudly for both the Algerians and the Israelis.[7]

Israel's capture of Jerusalem in 1967 changed all that. The Six-Day War was the first demonstration of Jewish power. But whereas the world could respect Jews who lived by the word, who could survive persecution, it was deeply uncomfortable when Jews showed themselves capable of military might, of shaping the existence of another people, of exercising sovereignty over the central symbols of Christianity and Islam. Nation after nation vilified Israel for incorporating Arab Jerusalem, for refusing to return the captured lands unconditionally, and even for purportedly starting the war.

Some nations broke their diplomatic ties with Israel. The Soviet Union withdrew its ambassador and year after year voted for Israel's ouster from the United Nations. Israel's contacts with other nations had to be conducted sub rosa, a clandestine diplomacy that could not be acknowledged by the offending nation. Israel, which had meant to be a model and a source of aid to the developing nations, was abruptly transformed into an outpost of Western imperialism. The low point was in 1975, two years after Israel barely escaped disaster in the Yom Kippur War started by several Arab nations, when the United Nations passed its resolution declaring Zionism to be a form of racism.

Internally, Israel was caught between secular Zionism and religious Judaism. In its foreign relations, the Jewish state was not treated as another fragment of sovereignty. Israel's existence did not prevent diaspora Jews from continuing subjection to the ugliest forms of discrimination and hatred.

Which Arab Nation?

The Palestinians faced a related dilemma. They, too, failed to fix the relation between Palestine and Islam, nation and faith. The early Zionist leaders, who were largely secular, had to protect their nationalist movement from religious Jews who opposed their state making. But Islam, the dominant Palestinian religion, was not an impediment to political mobilization of the Arabs; it was its source. Indeed, the men who vied for Palestinian allegiance all claimed to do so because of their Islamic ancestry and religious position. Palestinians were galvanized to action based on the defense of Jerusalem as a sacred Islamic center. Palestinian nationalism was joined to religion from the very beginning.

Like Judaism, Islam originated as a religion of rule. After centuries of statelessness, however, Judaism had lost much of its capacity to guide the construction of a real polity, relegating the restoration of a Jewish state to a messianic end game for which Jews must pray and wait patiently. Islam, in contrast, had never been shorn of sovereignty, first established in the seventh century, when Muhammad's armies swept victoriously out of the Arabian peninsula.

The Prophet's armies understood all the land they conquered to be part of the *umma*, or community, originally understood as an extension of the Prophet's household. Islam's initial territorial ambitions had no limit, and the Prophet's armies conquered much of the Near East and North Africa, whose peoples were compelled to accept the Prophet as the last word and to speak Arabic, the Prophet's tongue and the language of the Qur'an. Islam provided the law for these conquered lands and required the faithful to obey those who ruled in its name.

The Islamic God is sovereign; Islam, both religion and state. Although Islam understands religion and politics as separate spheres, the first eternal, the second subject to historical interpretation, both must be conducted according to the Islamic law, or *shari'a*. With the Prophet's death, authority flowed to the caliph, considered as a successor of the Prophet, his deputy on earth.[8] In theory, there could only be one caliph, one supreme sovereign, whose authority flowed from God. A singular caliphate endured well into the Middle Ages. Although the Islamic world was ultimately divided among rival caliphates, Islam justified no particular geographic division of sovereignty. The unitary caliph, who would rule the entire house of Islam, remained the ideal. Fragmentation into separate states, into little nations or *wattan*, went against the communitarian grain of Islamic thought. It would not be until the late eighteenth century that the Ottoman sultan, whose empire stretched over much of the Muslim world, would again claim to be caliph, the supreme religious head, for all Islam.[9]

Palestine's overwhelmingly Muslim population saw Palestine as part of the original community, and Jerusalem as a sacred step on the Prophet's itinerary to heaven. When the Zionists began to settle and the British later conquered Palestine in 1917, it had, except for a brief

Crusader interlude, been ruled by Muslims for more than a thousand years. The obligation to liberate lands lost to the infidel supplied the initial moral mandate for Palestinian resistance to both British and Zionist colonization. Many Palestinians saw the Zionists as new Crusaders, infidels with guns encroaching on sacred lands. The political pretensions of a theologically subordinate people had to be defeated. That Jews should have a state on Islamic ground, let alone in Jerusalem, known to Muslims as *al-Quds*, the holy, was unthinkable. The first forces to strike against the Zionists were Islamic militants.

While Islam spurred resistance to Zionism, it slowed the development of an independent Palestinian nationalism. Islam pointed beyond Palestine to a larger community of believers. Unlike Judaism, Islam did not justify a separate Palestinian nation-state. Indeed it provided a framework within which Palestinians could easily see themselves as part of something larger, whether it was the Islamic community or Arab nation. As a result of their Islamic commitments, large numbers of Palestinians were responsive to the claims of outsiders who sought to lead them, first from Istanbul, then Damascus, and finally Amman.

For more than four centuries before Zionist settlement, Palestine had been a small piece of an Islamic empire whose ruler claimed the title caliph. The Ottoman Empire faced the European powers as equals well into the eighteenth century.[10] Ottoman armies twice pushed all the way to Vienna, where, according to legend, besieged bakers fed Habsburg resistance by baking croissants so that the Islamic crescent could be eaten by all.

The Ottomans were expelled from Europe over the course of the nineteenth century. By the start of the twentieth, the empire had been cut into many European colonies and protectorates. Overwhelmed by the industrial nation-states battering the Ottoman Empire and the rise of Turkish nationalists seeking a secular state in which Arabic would no longer be the language of rule, new state makers emerged in the Arab heartland. These new leaders turned defiantly to Islam as the basis of a new national identity, and as a language of resistance to the Christian West.

At the same moment Jews were returning to the land and language of their ancestors, those who spoke the language of the Prophet were forging themselves into an Arab nation. The modern Arab nation was the original Arabic-speaking core of the house of Islam, the lands inhabited by those who spoke to each other in the same language as they spoke to God. For hundreds of years, Arab and Islam had been a natural identity, a community of belief, of law, of pilgrimage, of language. Modern Arab nationalists understood this Islamic heritage as the historical base of the Arab nation to which they now pledged their allegiance.

The first Arab nationalist leaders donned the mantle of the Prophet and dreamed of building a single state. Led by Sharif Hussein, who traced his clan all the way back to the Prophet's daughter and son-in-law, the Arab revolt, which began in 1916, helped break the Ottoman hold on the Middle East. Like the Prophet himself, Hussein was a member of the House of Hashem and called his family Hashemites. Hussein was part of a long line entitled to the name Sharif, guardians of Mecca and Medina, Islam's two holiest sites. Hussein's sons Faisal and Abdullah rode with T. E. Lawrence, intending to build a unitary Arab kingdom stretching from the sacred heartland of the Hejaz up the Arabian peninsula through Palestine, Syria, Lebanon, and Iraq.[11]

After World War I, imperial powers carved the Arab world into separate zones of influence, colonies, and protectorates. Regional loyalties to indigenous leaderships were strong. No unitary Arab nation-state was ever constructed. In the event, Hussein's son, Faisal, military leader of the Arab forces who had fought under British direction through Palestine and up into Syria, was crowned king of Syria. Although the Palestinians had not supported the Arab revolt, once the Ottomans had been shorn of their Arab holdings, the leading Palestinians were initially eager to be part of the larger Arab nation and did not seek a separate state. When Faisal was crowned the Syrian king, Palestinian political leaders clamored to be part of his regime until he was deposed by the French.[12] The Ottomans, after all, had for centuries treated Palestine as southern Syria, a territorial identity both familiar and acceptable to most of the Palestinians themselves.

Britain and France denied the Hashemites Lebanon, Syria, and Palestine. The British then engineered Faisal's ascent as king of an independent Iraq. In Jerusalem, Winston Churchill met with Faisal's brother, Abdullah, who had been en route to attack French-ruled Syria in 1921. When Churchill made him king of a nation that did not exist, Transjordan, on the eastern part of Britain's Palestinian mandate, substantial portions of the Palestinians now threw in their lot with yet another Hashemite king from Arabia.

Whereas most of Jerusalem's religious Jews had opposed Jewish nationalism, the city's religious Muslims were among the first ardent Palestinian nationalists. Just as in Syria and Iraq, important local families challenged the Hashemite claim to Arab leadership in Palestine, seeing them as alien interlopers. The Hashemites' greatest liability was their willingness to accommodate British-supported Zionism. The movement for a separate Palestinian nation-state was simultaneously a struggle against the Zionists, the British, and the new Hashemite leadership in Transjordan. It was launched by Palestine's highest Islamic cleric, the mufti, Muhammad Haj Amin al-Husayni, who used the Supreme Muslim Council in Jerusalem, a body established by the British to administer Islamic institutions, as his central power base. This Islamic hierarchy controlled landholdings throughout Palestine, appointed prayer leaders for the mosques, selected judges for independent courts who dispensed justice according to Islamic law, and hired teachers for the religious school system.

An ethnicity, yes, but Palestine had never existed as an independent nation. Loyalties were local, to extended kin in particular villages and regions, not to some historical nation as in Egypt. Palestinians in Transjordan were becoming loyal subjects of Abdullah, the Hashemite king. Haj Amin al-Husayni, Jerusalem's mufti, cast the struggle against the Zionists in Islamic terms, mobilizing vast pilgrimages to Jerusalem to unify the Palestinians, and opposition to Jewish demands for more ritual rights in Jerusalem to provoke violent confrontation with the Zionists. He chose the day in the Muslim calendar marking the Prophet's ascent to paradise from Jerusalem as "Palestine Day." Making the Palestinians into front-line defenders of the faith, he sought support for his nationalist leadership from Islamic movements and states around the world.

All Palestinians were thus torn between two Islamic power centers. The first was located in Amman, controlled by the Hashemite king, Abdullah and later Hussein, who were descendents of a family who once ruled Mecca. The second was centered in Jerusalem, controlled by Haj Amin al-Husayni, whose family traced its bloodline back to the Prophet's first followers. In the 1930s, sparked by guerrilla attacks by Islamic militants, a violent popular revolt exploded throughout Palestine, but particularly in the countryside, against the British and the Zionists. Many Palestinians, especially Christians concentrated in the cities, sought other means, such as a general strike, to convince the British to stem the flow of Jewish immigration and land sales. The conflict quickly degenerated into a bloody civil war between Palestinians supportive of Husayni and those more willing to cast their lot with Abdullah. Ultimately put down by British troops, the Palestinian revolt completely debilitated the Palestinian community a decade before the United Nations granted the Jews a right to found a state. As a result, when war came in 1948, King Abdullah of Transjordan easily conquered the lands the United Nations earmarked for a Palestinian state, including Jerusalem. When Israel took Jerusalem in 1967, the conflict between Jordanian Amman and Palestinian Jerusalem would begin in earnest once again.

Islam remained an essential component of Palestinian nationalism. The mufti's goal of an independent Palestinian nation was embraced by the Palestine Liberation Organization, founded in Jerusalem in 1964, and soon led by Yasser Arafat, a distant member of the mufti's family.[13]

Al-Fatah, his party and militia that dominate the PLO, retains a commitment to a polity that will be Islamic in orientation. Its fighters call themselves *fedayeen*, "those who sacrifice themselves," martyrs willing to die defending Muslim lands against the infidel.

After Israel's victory in the Six-Day War, Islamic institutions re-emerged as an important means by which Palestinians could organize themselves in the West Bank and Gaza, especially because Israel repeatedly repressed other forms of political organization. With mosques, schools and courts spanning every village and town, Islamic organization was a natural way for Palestinians to build a life free of Israeli control. Linked to Islamic movements throughout the Arab world, it became a platform for religious militants opposed to a secular Palestinian nationalism, particularly one that would accept partition, in much the same way that Israel's independent religious system produced religious nationalists willing to disobey their state to prevent what they understood as a perfidious territorial compromise.

The Islamic content of Palestinian nationalism has had calamitous consequences. In Islamic eyes, Jerusalem's seventh-century surrender had sealed Islam's supremacy as the last link in a chain of prophecy. For many, a Jewish state within the heart of the *umma* called into question the veracity of the Qur'an itself. How, then, could they agree to territorial compromise, to partition, particularly to any solution that compromised Islamic sovereignty over Jerusalem? As a result, it took Palestinians a very long time to accommodate themselves to the objective opportunities for state building in the region, to understand and to seize what was possible. It would not be until 1993, almost three decades after the PLO was founded, that Yasser Arafat would accept partition, decidedly less than the two-state solution the Palestinians had been offered and refused in 1948.

Unlike the Zionists, who are all Jews, the Palestinians include a significant minority Christian population, historically concentrated in and around Jerusalem. At the turn of the century, Christians made up about 15 percent of Palestine's Arab population; in Jerusalem, however, they were more than half of the city's Arab population.[14] Islam's Jewish problem was also a Christian problem. Christians had been repeatedly subject to persecution and political violence under Islamic rule. As the Ottoman Empire shattered, a politicized Islam was potentially prejudicial to their civil and political rights. The Islamic content of Palestinian nationalism thus made life difficult for the better-educated Palestinian Christians, who dominated commerce and the professions. Not surprisingly then, Palestinian Christians were more willing than their Muslim confreres to accommodate Zionism. Vulnerable to religious attack, large numbers of Palestinian Christians went into exile. Others, to prove their patriotism, were recruited disproportionately to the most radical Marxist–Leninist movements, which tolerate no public place for religion.

The Palestinians mobilized as part of a larger Arab nation. In consequence, it took them longer to develop an independent, local nationalism, to separate their struggle from that of others who claimed to be committed to the liberation of Palestine. The Arab nation was divided into a multiplicity of states run by autocrats, whether kings or presidents, backed by the machinery of a single party and a secret police. Each jealously guarded its own parochial interests. Efforts at larger Arab union failed. Border contests degenerated into war. Pan-Arabism was more myth than muscle.

Opposition to Israel was the singular glue uniting the Arab world, pan-Arabism's only important political reality. The Arab states demonstrated their commitment to the Arab cause by the resources they lavished on the Palestinians. And the Palestinians played their part by proclaiming themselves the avant-garde of the Arab nation or Islamic community, appealing to other Arab states for military protection and political sustenance. The Palestinian cause was an instrument of Arab foreign policy. Even the creation of the Palestine Liberation Organization in 1964 was an Egyptian strategy to undermine Jordanian influence. The PLO was founded over the opposition of Jordan's King Hussein. It was also opposed by the former mufti, Haj Amin al-Husayni, and a young engineering student, Yasser Arafat, head of al-Fatah, who would seize control over the organization five years later. In consequence, internal Palestinian political disagreements were embroiled in conflicts among the Arab states, making the formation of a national consensus much more difficult.

Throughout their history, the Palestinians have been torn between their own local nationalism and the larger Arab nation whose several states sought to control or exploit the Palestinian movement for their own political designs. The religious origins of Palestinian nationalism provided fertile ground for a militant Islam that refuses to recognize Palestine as a secular nation to emerge. The Palestinians themselves have been increasingly torn between a secular nationalism that has evolved toward coexistence with Israel and a militant Islam that refuses this accommodation.

The Palestinians were never treated by the world as just another nation seeking sovereignty, nor did they want to be. They variously cast their conflict as a critical anti-imperialist front, as an obligation of jihad, or holy war, as the ultimate testing ground for the Arab nation in its confrontation with the West. They made sure the liberation of Jerusalem became a rallying cry for Muslims throughout the world. But although the Palestinian cause is a badge of Arab honor, Palestinians, very much like Jews, continue to face hatred and discrimination within their Arab diaspora as dangerous outsiders, often highly educated professionals who play vital administrative and commercial roles in their host states, but are also caustic critics and living reminders that the Arab nation has never really paid its blood debt.

Dividing the City

The conflict over who rules Jerusalem has been raging for the entire twentieth century. During that time, Jerusalem has been enveloped within a large number of sovereign claims – a provincial town in the Ottoman Empire before World War I, the administrative center of a British protectorate during the interwar years, divided between a Jordanian Old City and the modern Israeli capital until 1967, and the unified capital of Israel after that. The reunification of Jerusalem under Israeli sovereignty in 1967 unleashed forces that have transformed both the Israeli and Palestinian nations, setting in motion the multiple battles for the metropolis that will concern us in this book. The people who lived these dramatic historical reversals experienced them in contradictory ways. These are their stories.

In November 1947, as the British prepared to withdraw from the territory mandated to them by the League of Nations at the close of the First World War, the United Nations (UN) passed a partition plan splitting Palestine into an Arab and a Jewish state. Jerusalem was set apart as an international entity. The United Nations' proposal to make Jerusalem a *corpus separatum*, or "separate body," was supported by the Vatican, which itself had hovered beyond reach of the state since Italian unification in the nineteenth century. Ever since the Crusaders had been pushed out of Jerusalem, the Catholics had had a tenuous position; the church hoped that history would now help its fortunes in the city of the Lord's crucifixion.

The Zionist movement took its biblical right to rule from the city, from Zion, where King David fashioned the first Jewish nation. A majority of Jerusalem's residents were Jews. But even as the entire Arab nation began to amass the men and material necessary to wipe out what they saw as a new Jewish colony, the Jewish Agency for Palestine, Israel's protogovernment, voted to accept the *corpus separatum* solution. The Zionist leadership feared that any insistence on sovereignty over Jerusalem would jeopardize the votes of the Catholic Latin American nations needed to pass the partition plan.[15] Even after the UN vote, with war against the entire Arab world imminent, in February 1948, three months before the British evacuated their last troops, the Jewish Agency still decided to place Israel's capital in a suburb of Tel Aviv, and Israel's war planning in anticipation of British withdrawal originally excluded Jerusalem. Why?

For one thing, America's support for partition was weak. Despite Harry Truman's personal commitment to Chaim Weizmann, Israel's first president, the American delegation at the United Nations had formally reversed its tentative support of partition and was garnering votes to make all Palestine a UN trusteeship. The Jewish Agency felt that going beyond the original partition plan and demanding Jerusalem would put American recognition of the new state at risk.[16]

Accepting Jerusalem's separate status was also integral to Israel's efforts to keep Transjordan out of the coming war. Contacts with King Abdullah continued right up to the outbreak of hostilities. Golda Meyerson, later Meir, the American who would become Israel's prime minister two decades later, was smuggled into Amman, where the king promised her he would deny other Arab armies access to Israel across the Jordan River if Israel would not oppose his incorporation of the West Bank of the Jordan River, which the partition plan intended as a separate Palestinian state. For Israel to claim sovereignty over Jerusalem would make the king's cooperation unthinkable. On May 14, 1948, the Israelis declared their statehood in Tel Aviv, not Jerusalem.

Over the opposition of the Arab League and against the advice of his own British commander, Sir John Bagot Glubb Pasha, King Abdullah committed his troops to capture Jerusalem. In 1925, Abdullah's father had been routed from Mecca and Medina by the ibn Sauds, a rival desert clan from central Arabia who led the puritanical Wahhabi sect.[17] Abdullah's brother had been pushed from Damascus by the French. To rule Jerusalem with its dome over the stone from which Muhammad leaped to paradise, the footprint still visible, was his family's last chance to retain a small piece of their heritage. On May 28, the Jewish Quarter of the Old City fell to Jordanian Legionnaires. The Jewish "New City" to the west was now besieged and under continuous bombardment. The Jews of Jerusalem faced the prospect of slowly starving to death.

The Zionist leadership determined that Jewish Jerusalem had to be saved and Jerusalem-born Yitzhak Rabin, commander of the Palmach's Harel Brigade and later Israel's prime minister, was charged with the defense of the city.[18] As Israel fought for its life, Ben-Gurion now proposed that Israel attack Jordan's Arab Legion and seize not only all of Jerusalem, but Bethlehem and Hebron as well. The Arabs, he hoped, would flee.[19] His cabinet rejected the proposal. Instead, Israel's forces eventually broke the siege of Jerusalem but at the war's end held only the western, predominantly Jewish city. Although half of Israel's casualties in the 1948 war fell in defending Jerusalem, the Jordanians still controlled the ancient stones of the Arab city to the east where King David had his capital, where King Solomon built the first Temple.[20]

Jerusalem's 1948 division had denied the Jews the symbol of their sovereignty; but for many Palestinians, the cleaving of the city by two occupying powers signified the denial of nationhood itself. Jerusalem had been the political center of those Palestinian forces seeking an independent state. From this city, the mufti, Haj Amin al-Husayni, had struggled to prevent Palestine's incorporation into Transjordan, to counter King Abdullah's treacherous willingness to divide it between a Jewish state and a new province of an expanded Jordanian regime. The mufti had been forced to flee Palestine at the beginning of the Palestinian revolt in 1936.

At the war's close, the mufti lived in exile in Cairo and King Abdullah controlled the city as his own. The war sent hundreds of thousands of Palestinians into exile. Arab Jerusalem lost half its population, including a large portion of its best businessmen and professionals, men and women from prominent families, and a goodly segment of its Arab Christians as well. Palestinians who had fled from Israeli-controlled territories closer to the coast took some of their places, but much of the nationalist leadership went into exile. Palestinian nationalists who remained were forced to swear allegiance to the Transjordanian regime.

King Abdullah encouraged those families from Hebron and Nablus supporting him to immigrate to the city to counter the dominant Palestinian families of Jerusalem. The Jordanians were determined to neutralize this Palestinian nationalist center and establish the centrality of Amman. Jerusalem's Supreme Muslim Council was disbanded and the Islamic *waqf*, the religious trust that had been a power base for the city's Palestinian nationalists, was brought under Jordanian control, its offices moved to Amman.

Jerusalem, however, remained a threat to the Jordanian claims. On Friday, July 20, 1951, King Abdullah was murdered by a Jerusalemite at the entrance to al-Aqsa mosque, where he had gone to pray. Abdullah's assassination had been planned by Abdullah Tal, a Palestinian supporter of the mufti in exile in Cairo; directed in Jerusalem by Musa al-Husayni, a member of the mufti's family; and executed by Mustafa Asha, a soldier in the mufti's army in the 1948 war. Testimony in the trial indicated the mufti himself had hatched the plot.[21]

At the king's side that day was his sixteen-year-old grandson, Hussein ibn Talal, who would succeed him as monarch two years later. King Hussein watched his grandfather die, narrowly escaping injury himself when a bullet ricocheted off a medal on his chest. As a result of this experience, Hussein feared the city and forbade the Palestinians of Jerusalem to carry weapons on pain of death. Not until 1963 did he begin to build an official residence there, significantly, far outside the city, at the same site where, according to Jewish tradition, King Saul, Israel's first warrior–king, had built his palace. Saul was displaced by King David. Hussein's official residence was never finished.

During two decades of Jordanian rule, Jerusalem's major business and government offices were forced to relocate in Amman. Requests for loans and grants for economic development were routinely turned down. Businesses in Amman got tax breaks; those in Jerusalem did not. Jordan reduced Jerusalem to a provincial town. Arabs who wanted to get serious business done had to move to Amman. Jerusalem was starved for capital investment, for infrastructure, for leadership, and in the nineteen years of Jordanian control, the Arab population of Jerusalem declined precipitously.[22]

The Six-Day War

Syrian sponsorship of repeated Palestinian paramilitary operations across Israel's northern border set in motion forces that led to the eruption of war in June of 1967. In April of that year the Israelis shot down six Syrian planes in an aerial ambush and flew over Damascus.[23] The Soviets and/or the Syrians informed Egypt that the Israelis were massing to attack Syria, with whom they had a mutual defense pact. In response, the Egyptians ordered the United Nations peacekeeping forces out of the Sinai and Nasser moved thousands of troops into the desert, closing the Suez Canal to all ships coming from or going to Israel. The world powers did nothing to counter this violation of international law. Israel's southern port of Eilat was shut off by a blockade at the entrance to the Gulf of Aqaba. Nasser announced his objective: "to destroy Israel." Millions marched in Cairo. "We will throw the Zionist vermin into the sea," the posters around the marketplace boasted. To many Israelis, it seemed the world would again watch while their enemies tried to destroy the Jews.

The tension mounted in Jewish Jerusalem. Rabbis sanctified the city's parks for possible use as cemeteries. Men and women rushed their work so as to leave no unfinished business. Buses stopped running as the drivers were called up to their units. Radio announcers read out the code words indicating this or that unit had been mobilized. Mail delivery stopped. Fewer and fewer men were seen on the streets.

On the basis of their cooperative sub rosa relations with the Hashemites and mutual hostility between the Egyptians and the Jordanians, the Israelis assumed Jordan would stay out of the war. Israeli plans for the eastern front were only defensive. Many Israeli soldiers stationed in Jerusalem were angry they were not posted in the Sinai or on the Syrian front. But suddenly, on May 30, King Hussein flew to Cairo in a dramatic volte-face to make peace with Abdel Nasser. Nasser, still bitter at Jordan's pursuit of its own territorial ambitions and its refusal to provide sufficient tactical support to the Egyptians during the 1948 war, had shortly before portrayed Hussein as a hireling of the British Empire. Their embrace at the Cairo airport meant Hussein would now put his forces under Egyptian command in the coming war.

At Nasser's insistence, Hussein returned to Amman with the first head of the PLO, Ahmad al-Shuqayri, who had vowed to drive the Jews into the sea. Hussein feverishly began to fortify positions, to bring more armaments into Jerusalem. The loudspeakers placed on top of the mosques called for Jewish blood – "Slaughter the Jews." The newspapers called for holy war. But the Palestinians of Jerusalem had been neither mobilized nor armed.

On Sunday, June 4, the Israeli cabinet met and decided to launch a preemptive strike the following sunrise. President Lyndon Johnson, who had sent repeated messages to Prime Minister Eshkol not to initiate hostilities, could restrain the Israelis no longer. At dawn the Israelis destroyed the entire Egyptian air force. But the Arab radio stations ebulliently reported that the Egyptian armies were advancing across the Sinai, that Tel Aviv was under bombardment from the sea. For a terrible day, because of enforced Israeli radio silence, that was all the Israelis knew.

On Monday, June 5, after the air attack on Egypt, Jordan declared war on Israel. Nonetheless, the Israelis still wanted to confine the war to the Egyptian front; the Jordanians had American-trained tank officers and superior armor and were reinforced by Iraqi brigades. Uzi Narkiss, Israel's commander of the central zone that included Jerusalem and a veteran of the failed 1948 attempt to take the Old City, had only reservists at his disposal. The Israelis therefore promised that if the Jordanians did not attack, neither would Israel, and sent King Hussein a message: "We are engaged in defensive fighting on the Egyptian sector, and we shall not engage ourselves in any action against Jordan unless Jordan attacks us. Should Jordan attack Israel, we shall go against her with all our might."[24]

But the Jordanians, who believed the radio reports from Cairo, rained artillery shells on Jewish Jerusalem, Tel Aviv, and Netanya. The Israeli cabinet once again voted to ask the Jordanians to keep out of the war, but Jordan continued to fire into Jerusalem. Shells fell on Hadassah hospital's outpatient ward, on Sha'are Zedek Hospital, the Jewish Agency (Zionism's administrative center), the new Hebrew University campus, and the main commercial streets. Machine guns fired into Jewish neighborhoods along the border, but from morning to afternoon that Monday, Israel did not counterattack. The Israelis desperately communicated to Hussein that the reports of Egyptian success were false and Jordan should stay out of the war. Hussein refused the Israeli overtures. Instead his troops advanced in the south of Jerusalem, attacking the undefended United Nations compound in an attempt to cut the city in two.

With Israeli troops stretched thin in the Sinai to the south and the Golan in the north, the Israeli cabinet decided to counterattack and assault Jordanian Jerusalem. After Israel's air force destroyed almost all Jordan's two dozen planes and stopped its tanks coming up from the Jordan valley, and after Israel's tanks and paratroopers had captured the northern approaches to Jerusalem, Jordanian defeat was inevitable. From that point on, with the predictable buildup of international pressures, Israel raced to make Jerusalem its own. By the end of the week, Jerusalem, as well as everything down to the Jordan River, lay in Israeli hands. Ben-Gurion's dream had finally been realized.

Erasing the Line

The white-haired remember Jerusalem whole, as it was before 1948; their children, only the division and the events of 1967, when the Israelis tore down the walls.[25] Many Arabs had never seen, let alone talked to, a Jew. The village Arabs around Jerusalem gaped at the modern Israeli city, the automobiles, the women in miniskirts. Groups of Palestinian men stood at the corner and stared, transfixed, at the stoplights. Each time the lights turned green and the cars proceeded on their way, some applauded.

For those who grew up with it, Jerusalem's partition had seemed immutable, a fact of nature like the winter rains. After Israel's victory, Nabil Tafakji, then a Palestinian teenager, fully expected the Israelis to keep the Jews and the Arab separate, to maintain the boundaries separating East and West Jerusalem. As a schoolchild, Nabil had gone with his friends to a place at the border where they could get a good view. "We went there," he told us, "to see the Jewish people. Sometimes we would throw stones at each other."

When the walls came down, Nabil was amazed. He was eager to see the territory he had only imagined. He had grown up hearing about the Rex Cinema, the movie house in the Jewish downtown where his uncle had once worked. To visit the "enemy," Nabil dressed for the occasion. Five days after the war ended,

I bought a jacket like the Jewish jacket . . . and I went to the Jewish side, the west side . . . I was afraid. I didn't know the language. I didn't know anything, so I was walking all the time until I reached the Rex Cinema. [Although it was partially burned down,] I was so happy that I told my mother "I saw that cinema that you told me about all the time." She said, "I don't believe it, you have been there?" . . . It's a beautiful city, and, it was really different, physically at least. There were traffic lights. The streets were big and beautiful. So it was like being in cinema or something in Europe.

Nabil Tafakji later became the director of the first Arab neighborhood self-government project started by Israel in A-Tur on the Mount of Olives.

As the walls came down, Arabs and Jews who had been forced to flee their homes in 1948 and earlier returned to see who lived there, and what had happened to the rooms, the walls, and the gardens they remembered. In some cases, they knocked at the door, introduced themselves as "previous owners," and asked to be allowed to come in for a few moments just to see.[26] On both sides of the city, there are those who inhabit homes left by the dispossessed from the other side who still live with a faint fear the former owners will one day return and claim what is theirs. Some talk of ghosts. The Jews who returned to the Jewish Quarter from which they had been forced also found their synagogues had been destroyed and defiled by the Jordanians. Not only had the Jordanians refused to allow Israelis access to the Western Wall as the 1949 armistice agreement stipulated, they had built a public latrine right up against it. Tens of thousands of Jewish gravestones on the Mount of Olives had been destroyed, others broken and defaced.

The Arabs who came to the Western city found their beautiful stone homes with tiled floors and pillared porches occupied by Jewish families. In one old Arab section, Malcha, Jews lived in an old mosque. The Arab graveyard was filled with broken and collapsed funeral stones. Many Arabs still held their titles and keys to these homes. They refused and even today refuse Israeli compensation for their lost properties. Not only were the Israelis only willing to compensate them at the market value of 1948, but to accept the money would be to admit defeat, to collaborate with occupation.

"We Opened Our Eyes and It Was a New World"

From 1948 to 1967 the no-man's-land marking the line of disengagement between Jordanian and Israeli forces cut Jerusalem in two. Barbed wire and mines lay at the base of the high walls of the Old City. New walls

Sylvia Farhi, homemaker and translator, 1984.

were built to protect Jews from Jordanian snipers who sometimes shot from the old. The deserted stores of the old commercial district in the now dangerous border zone on the Israeli side were repopulated with poor Jewish immigrants who had no place else to live.

Jerusalem, with a hundred thousand Jews, the second largest city in Israel after Tel Aviv, was chosen as Israel's capital only in 1949. Although it grew rapidly, the city remained a dead end, a vulnerable bulb of Jewish sovereignty surrounded by hostile Arabs. Guerrilla raids were frequent. Knesset members chose not to live in the city and commuted up from the coast for half the week. By Wednesday evening, few officials remained. Tourists would visit for the day and then return to their Tel Aviv hotels for the night. The cheapest rooms at the King David Hotel faced the Ottoman walls of the Old City.

With the border at their back, Jerusalem's Jews felt a proud solidarity in their new capital. Sylvia, a Jew from a small Welsh village, returned to Zion, where she had served as a British soldier during World War II. The daughter of a Russian Jewish watch repairman who had made his way to Wales, she was passionate about Zionism, and about Sam Farhi, who owned an import–export shop in downtown Jerusalem. "We had a country," she recounted over tea and biscuits in her tiny apartment, "and I was a Jew and where should I be?"

Ten days after arriving in the new state of Israel, she was working for the government of Israel. It was a good thing, too, for the Arabs had looted Sam Farhi's entire inventory during the war.

The Farhis lived in a rudimentary stucco structure for government employees in Katamon, then the last Jewish neighborhood before the Jordanian border at the southwest periphery of the city. Sylvia worked opposite the Old City walls, from which Jordanian snipers often fired into Jewish Jerusalem. More than once she spent hours on the office floor. Some days she couldn't get home. And at home, Palestinian guerrillas tried to infiltrate through the barbed wire fences along the no-man's-land to attack the enemy so close by. "At night there were the familiar sounds of shooting across the border," Sylvia said, her face soft and powdered. "It was very scary. My husband worked and didn't come home until the evenings and I used to wander around with an old lamp and . . . wonder what the next sound would be."

The 1967 war caught Sylvia Farhi's husband downtown. Disregarding instructions to go into the nearest shelter, he ran the whole way home. "He did not want to leave me home alone," Sylvia said. "He arrived absolutely soaking wet . . . We spent the time in the corridor . . . ." Their apartment wall faced directly on the Jordanian border, the direction from which the Jordanians launched their assault. Fearing the electricity would be cut off, Sylvia decided to cook everything in the freezer. "If we don't have anything else, for the first days of the war we'll certainly eat well, because I wasn't going to let food spoil . . . While the rockets were going off, I stood in the kitchen, put the pressure cooker on and cooked."

"When the ultimate came," she recalled, "and the Old City was captured, there was nothing more to wish for. This was just the beginning and the end, or let's say the end of the beginning. We opened our eyes and it was a new world. A new era started."

Like most Israelis, the Farhis never believed that one day they would walk in the Old City again. Before 1967 Jews on the Israeli side had climbed to high places and pointed longingly to the markers of an ancient Jewish nation. Some Jews crossed the Hinnom Valley on the Old City's western side and climbed up Mount Zion to an Israeli military enclave from which they could gaze down over the walls at the Jewish Quarter. The Farhis mounted the roof of Notre Dame de France, a huge pink-stone pseudo-Ottoman hotel for pilgrims owned by the French Catholic Assumptionist Fathers just outside the Jordanian city. The Notre Dame had been heavily damaged in the battle for the city in 1948. From here they could see the Damascus Gate and the Arab downtown.

The Farhis finally left their apartment, saw their neighbors, and heard the incredible broadcasts of the capture of all Jerusalem. The knowledge was overwhelming. "None of us could look at each other because we were all so emotional about it . . . The first time we went into town after the war, and we were in the bus and saw our flags waving on the Old City walls, and that was a sight never to be forgotten. I think there wasn't a dry eye in the bus. The Magen David [Star of David] fluttered on the edge of the wall near Mt. Zion."

Sylvia stood on a balcony on Ben-Yehuda Street, the city's most central commercial thoroughfare, and watched the Arabs who had come for the first time to the Jewish side of the city.

> They didn't know what to expect of us and we didn't know what to expect of them. And it was fascinating to watch how they looked at us. They saw Israelis and I think they realized that we were normal people . . . The looks on their faces were of bewilderment, of wonderment . . . Nobody bothered them. They were free to come. They weren't enemies. Nobody looked upon them as anything different from us. They were ordinary citizens. And we were prepared to accept them. I think they felt freer here . . . than we felt about going over there.

Although a number of Israeli soldiers were attacked in Arab Jerusalem, no Arabs who went to Jewish Jerusalem were molested.

Many Jews also expected Jerusalem to remain divided. When the Israelis began to build Ramot Eshkol, the first settlement over the 1949 cease-fire line along Israel's border with Jordan, called the Green Line, the Farhis were offered an apartment there. "I could kick myself now," she lamented.

> We were offered those beautiful apartments at very, very reasonable terms. We thought, "How could we, surely we'll have to give it back." We didn't dare think to undertake anything . . . So we didn't take advantage of the opportunity. We thought that everyone who went to settle over the Green Line, . . . they were real heroes . . . I didn't know then that it would develop into such fanaticism. I admired their courage and their nationalism.

"We Did Not Know What to Do"

Meanwhile, when the 1967 war began, hundreds of young Palestinian men worriedly gathered outside the office of Anwar al-Khatib, the Jordanian governor of Jerusalem, demanding weapons to defend themselves. Al-Khatib, a member of one of the prominent Hebron families the Jordanian monarch had brought in to rule Jerusalem, sent them to the police station. Now his own employees confronted Al-Khatib. A young worker in the Jordanian Passport Office, Ziad abu Zayyad, stood among them. "We did not know what to do," Ziad remembered. "So we asked the governor of Jerusalem . . . We asked, 'You are our boss, what are we supposed to do?' And he said, 'Well, I don't know.' "

As the firing intensified between Jordanian and Israeli positions, the employees were sent home. Ziad joined a large demonstration outside the police station. "They were shouting and asking for weapons and saying that they are not ready to die like sheeps [*sic*] because the Jordanian government did not give them weapons and they are not armed and the Israelis are armed. And if they come across the borders, they will kill us. We won't have anything to defend ourselves."

A jeep wheeled up, carrying a Jordanian general. After the men stopped shouting for arms, Ziad recounted, the general assured them: "Well, look, I have very good news for you. I don't want to tell you that we are already . . . approaching Tel Aviv, but I would ask you to keep it quiet and let the army do its job. So every one of you must go home immediately and don't disturb us."

Ziad, whose chiseled face wears a look of permanent concern, was doubtful. Taking a friend by his arm, he walked to a high place to survey the area. "It was very clear that he was telling lies, that he's not respecting even our boys because we knew that it's not that easy. We knew that Jordan was not ready to enter the war until the last moment. And even when they decided to enter the war, they did not give arms to the people."

Ziad walked home to Azariyah on the eastern side of the Mount of Olives. By Tuesday, the war's second day, the refugees had started to flow down the roads from Jerusalem, past his home, particularly from Abu Tor, right on the Israeli border. Fearful stories passed from mouth to mouth. "We saw women," he remembered,

> saying that the Israelis were crossing the border, and collecting every youth and every man which they see and take him prisoner. Some of the women even said that they saw them shooting youth and the men they catch. So there was a panic and there was a stream of people crossing Azariyah, and walking towards the east. Those . . . people . . . fled mainly because they were frightened of the stories and they did not realize the difference between the Israeli army in '67 and the Haganah and Stern and Lehi groups [separate 1948 Jewish militias], and they thought that if they stayed in their houses, they would be slain. They don't have any weapons and they cannot defend themselves.

Ziad stood in the middle of the road, pleading with the thousands of Palestinians streaming past him not to leave Jerusalem. "If you leave," he told them, "you will make it difficult for us. And if we all stay, the Israelis could not kill all of us. It was very hard, but at least four hundred people were convinced to come in and they were put inside the Greek

Orthodox convent which is by my house." Hundreds of Palestinians slept in the convent for two nights. "We stayed there simply because we thought the Israelis will not kill us if we were inside a church," he told us in a calm reedy voice. Nobody ventured outside into the river of fear. "Those people, they were inside the convent and they didn't know what was going on outside. Otherwise they would have left because all the time, the people [were] walking through the streets . . . and saying the Jews were killing everyone, the Israelis [were] killing everyone they catch."

Ziad and the refugees fearfully left the convent on Thursday and returned to their homes. The nights, confined to their homes by curfew, were particularly frightening. "The Israelis were shooting in the air . . . They were shooting all the night and there was curfew and when we were hearing the shooting all the night, we were all the time saying 'Ah, they are killing people, now our turn is coming, they will come to our house and we are just waiting for them to come to the house and shoot us.' "

Palestinians who had not fled across the Jordan River began gradually to return to their homes in and around Jerusalem. Each night Ziad followed their progress, sitting on his veranda counting the lit-up houses on the hill facing his house. "Every night we were discovering that the number of lights was more, and that all the time was giving us more confidence and more safety. It was very encouraging to see that one night, there were four, and the next night seven, then it was nine, and then fifteen, and then twenty and they were growing."

When the cease-fire came, the scope of the tragedy overwhelmed him. The Israelis had captured the entire West Bank and Ziad had never seen one of their soldiers. Ziad's father recognized somebody amid the first group of Israeli soldiers now moving into his neighborhood. "They both recognized each other as ex-workers in the Jerusalem municipality [under the British], and after gazing at each other for a while, each one asked the other about his name, and then I saw them hugging each other and kissing each other, and then the soldier came into my house, and my father introduced him to us."

Shimon Spiegel, an Israeli contractor, had not seen Ziad's father for nineteen years. Shimon assured Ziad that Jerusalem would soon be declared an open city, and to come immediately to the Jewish city and call him as soon as it was announced on the radio. When the walls came down, Ziad was among the first to go to the other Jerusalem, and Shimon gave him his first tour. In 1968, Ziad became the first Palestinian ever enrolled in a Hebrew language program for Jewish immigrants. Today, Ziad abu Zayyad is a balding nationalist laywer and journalist, a former reporter and editor of *Al-Fajr*, the Arab newspaper in Jerusalem most closely aligned with the PLO. He publishes a weekly newspaper on

Palestinian affairs in Hebrew called *Gesher*, "Bridge"; he is a close adviser to Faisal Husayni, head of the Palestinian team who negotiated with the Israelis after the Iraq war, and a confidant of Yasser Arafat.

"Mommy, Are We Going to Die?"

For Palestinians like Raymonda Tawil, a Christian from a wealthy Haifa family, Jerusalem had been an irreversible pathway between the Jewish and the Arab world. The sudden division of Jerusalem in 1948 cut off her brothers, studying in Arab Jerusalem, from their parents, who remained behind in Israel, the former becoming Israeli Arabs, the latter Jordanians. The Mandelbaum Gate was the only point at which diplomats and tourists were allowed to cross from one side of the city to the other. Tourists entering East Jerusalem had to present baptismal certificates or other proof they were not Jewish. The Israelis allowed Raymonda's parents to visit their sons once a year, at Christmas.

At twelve, Raymonda had been sent to a convent school in Haifa, its only Arab student. The others were mostly Jewish girls whose parents had saved them from Hitler by baptizing them and putting them in the care of the church. By school's end, she spoke fluent Hebrew and could sing Israeli songs and dance their dances. She also knew she did not belong in Israel.

The Palestinian elite had fled to Lebanon, to Jordan, to Paris, and her father feared she would marry below her station. At the age of seventeen, then, Raymonda took the seemingly irrevocable step of leaving Israel for Jordan. Passing through the Mandelbaum Gate in Jerusalem, she renounced her Israeli citizenship. Amman's restrictiveness was unbearable. "It was unbelievable, maybe like Saudi Arabia now," she said. Raymonda, who had read and loved the great Jewish poet Bialik in Israel, smuggled his poems into Jordan. Because the Jordanian police began random searches for "subversive books . . . with my own hands, I had to burn my precious Bialik."

Tawil, lipsticked and buoyant, was unable to go out in public unescorted, chastised for speaking to men at public parties, unable to prepare for a career. She longed for the freedom she had felt in Israel as a woman, and yet she remembered her humiliation there as an Arab. In Jordan, she married a wealthy bank manager from a well-known Jaffa Palestinian family. Her parents in Israel were unable to attend the Greek Orthodox wedding. At her request – a common practice of communication among friends and kin separated by the border – Jordan radio played, "Mommy, Don't Cry on My Wedding Day." Later, when her mother died, the Israelis did not allow Raymonda to attend her funeral.

The Jordanians were just as hostile to Palestinian nationalism as the Israelis. Palestinians who spoke of a Palestinian state were silenced, often disappearing in the night to be sent to concentration camps in the Jordanian desert. King Hussein broke up Palestinian demonstrations in the West Bank with Bedouin soldiers who fired indiscriminantly into the crowds, and Raymonda subsequently helped organize one of the first women's demonstrations against Jordanian repression.[27] A year after the Palestine Liberation Organization was founded in Jerusalem, Raymonda Tawil went to Jerusalem to attend its conferences.

In 1967 Tawil greeted the coming war with Israel with euphoric expectation. But as the Israeli tanks rolled into Nablus, Raymonda huddled in the shelter with her daughters, shells exploding outside. The machine guns made a horrible din. "My kids asked me, 'Mommy, are we going to die?' " When the war ended, Raymonda made her way to Jerusalem to contact foreign consuls and press for Red Cross aid for the Palestinian refugees in the West Bank. Israelis were celebrating everywhere – embraces, shouting, and ululation. For Raymonda, once again under Israeli control, this bitter defeat afforded her an opportunity to visit her parents' graves.

Raymonda, passionate and red-haired, was the first Palestinian woman to meet with the Israeli military governor, asking for aid to help refugees from Kalkilya who flooded the squalid Nablus camps set up by the United Nations after 1948 and left to fester by the Jordanians. Her house in Nablus quickly became a meeting place for journalists from around the world. By 1975 the *New York Times* was taking her stories on the Israeli occupation. The Israelis claimed she was a PLO agent, and in 1976 she became the first person to be placed under four-month house arrest "for poisoning the image of Israel abroad."[28] During this period, when she was not allowed to stand in her own garden, she wrote her widely read autobiography, *My Home, My Prison*.

Jerusalem residence was reserved for those Arabs who lived there at the time of conquest. But although Tawil could never live there, she, like many Palestinian political leaders, could work in Jerusalem. In 1978, she opened the Palestine Press Service, an information service used by writers like David Shipler and Thomas Friedman of the *New York Times* and William Quandt of the State Department. She was immediately arrested for forty-five days.

"Why are you so popular?" she recalled her interrogator's asking. "Why do all the people come to you?"

"Because," she snapped, "I serve the best coffee!"

The Israelis repeatedly closed Tawil's press service. Today, she lives in Paris and Washington. The daughter whose safety she used to fret about in local demonstrations against the Israelis married Yasser Arafat.

"When I Touched the Stones"

While most Israelis saw a perfect triumph in their victory, some saw the seeds of future tragedy. On June 7,1967, Israeli soldiers stormed the Old City, moving over the Temple Mount where al-Aqsa mosque now stands, and down into the narrow alleyway facing the Western Wall of the Second Temple.

Rabbi Shlomo Goren, then chief rabbi of the Israeli army, led a column of paratroopers into the Old City walls, a Torah under his arm, a *shofar* in his left hand. On the Temple Mount, Goren prostrated himself in the direction of the Holy of Holies and recited the ancient prayer of battle from Deuteronomy. "Hear, O Israel!" Goren intoned, "You are about to join battle with your enemy. Let not your courage falter. Do not be in fear, or in panic, or in dread of them. For it is the Lord your God who marches with you to do battle for you against your enemy, to bring you victory" (20:3–4). Goren kissed Motta Gur and then descended through the Mughrabian Gate down to the Western Wall, where he doned his *tallit* and began to blow the *shofar*, roaring, "Blessed be the Lord God, Comforter of Zion and Builder of Jerusalem, Amen!" The rabbi then recited the *Kaddish* and the *El Maleh Rachamim* for all those killed in the fighting to reach this most sacred of places. "*Leshanah hazot, be-sha'ah hazot, beyeurshalayim*," Goren repeated over and over again, "This year, at this hour, in Jerusalem."[29] Goren stood at attention, saluted the Wall, and sang "Ha-Tikvah," Israel's national anthem, joined by dozens of paratroopers, many of them crying.

When the radio announced that Jerusalem was in Israeli hands, soldiers cried and Jews poured out of their homes to wave to and embrace the soldiers who drove by on buses and trucks. The walls, the barbed wire, the mines – the physical barriers dividing the metropole – were destroyed. The Israelis rejoiced at the outer Western Wall of their ancient Temple, where Jews have prayed for millennia for its restoration, for a messianic ingathering in Zion. Shimon, a paratrooper, recalled, ". . . we got the Wall on the day the war finished. It was the climax of the war. When I touched the stones of the Wall, I knew it was all over, that moment, that very second, the war was over."[30]

Yisrael Harel grew up believing this moment would come. In 1947, at age nine, a child survivor of the Holocaust facing another war for survival, Harel arrived in Palestine with his parents. Twenty years later, he was among the paratroopers who fought for and captured the Old City and held the Temple Mount. The Israelis carefully refrained from shelling this sacred site, which it turned out the Jordanians had stockpiled with tons of ammunition and hand grenades. One explosion would have reduced the Temple Mount to a dusty crater.

A tough reporter, Harel watched machine gun fire mow down his friends, snipers pick off his officers, and enemy guns kill the sons of other survivors. "After the Six-Day War," he recalled, his slightly pudgy, but very strong hands, demonstrating the point, "everything was like a volcano . . . People went around like Messiah had come . . . When you went to Jerusalem, you did not touch the ground. Everybody felt it, including the secular Jews . . . I decided then that this is the time that I should be involved in settling the territories that were liberated." Harel had been raised in Bnai Akiva, the religious nationalist youth movement, had grown up with the expectation that one day biblical Israel would be delivered. Now was the time. One of the founders of the Land of Israel movement, Yisrael Harel later became the secretary-general of the settlement movement, and the editor of its magazine, *Nekudah*, or "Point."

But some Israelis saw shadows in this victory, the fetish power of the city, the dilemmas of occupation. Amos Oz, the Israeli novelist, had been born in Jerusalem in Mekor Baruch. The son of a comparative literature professor, he left Zion to become a real Zionist, working in the cotton fields of Kibbutz Hulda. Oz is deeply drawn, yet troubled, by Jerusalem's symbolic force. When we spoke, the German writer Günter Grass had just introduced him to Woody Allen at a writer's conference in New York. After an initial shyness and a few drinks, Amos began to press Allen to visit Jerusalem as his guest. "Not only didn't he want to go," he recounted, "but he told me that he didn't think that Jerusalem really existed." Perhaps coming to Jerusalem would change him, Oz mused. "Maybe I am glad that he doesn't come, because if he came he would no longer be Woody Allen."

On the eighth day, the day after the war ended, Amos Oz went to Jerusalem directly from the Sinai. Even then he could not share in Israel's victory as a liberation of the ancestral cities of the patriarchs. Amos went to visit the parents of one of the members of his kibbutz who had fallen in the battle for Jerusalem. The boy's mother was crying and his father was trying not to cry. "Look, after all, we've liberated Jerusalem," an older kibbutz member said. "He didn't die for nothing."

"The whole of the Western Wall isn't worth Micha's little finger as far as I'm concerned," the boy's mother replied.

Oz agreed with her, even then. "I do have a feeling for those stones – but they're only stones," he wrote. "And Micha was a person. A man. If dynamiting the Western Wall would bring Micha back to life, then I'd say 'Blow it up!' . . . Today, I'm completely opposed to all this myth of lands crying out and places calling for liberation. It's worth dying to liberate people. But to liberate places? It's not worth anyone's little finger."[31]

The City as Stage

The Six-Day War transformed not only the geography, but the cosmologies, of Jerusalem, not just its land, but its world views. As a result of the war, the Israelis and the Palestinians now confronted each other and the center each claimed as sovereign and sacred. Two nations now saw themselves through the eye of Jerusalem.

The very day fighting ended in Jerusalem, Moshe Dayan went to the Western Wall and declared: "This morning the Israeli Defense Forces liberated Jerusalem. We have reunited Jerusalem, the dismembered capital of Israel. We have returned to our most holy places; we have returned and we shall never leave them . . . We did not come to Jerusalem to conquer the Holy Places of others . . ."[32] As Dayan approached al-Aqsa mosque on the Temple Mount, the Muslim clergy waited tensely. Before entering, the minister of defense paused to take off his shoes, acknowledging their possession.

After almost two-thousand years, the Jews had come to assert sovereignty over their ancient capital, not to rebuild the Temple where high priests had once conducted ritual sacrifices. To Teddy Kollek, first elected Jewish Jerusalem's mayor two years before, it was an opportunity to govern the entire city of Jerusalem, something he would do for the next quarter century.

Jerusalem has been doubly rebuilt in that quarter century. The Israeli government mounted a massive construction campaign to ensure that Jerusalem could never be partitioned again. The Jewish quarter of the Old City, devastated in the 1948 war, in ruin and inhabitated by Arab squatters, was reconstructed and repopulated by Jews. The Muslim neighborhood abutting the Western Wall, in which Yasser Arafat had grown up, was razed and replaced by a plaza where thousands of Jews could congregate for religious observance and national holidays.

Israeli archaeologists launched excavations. Layer by layer, the successive waves of ancient Jewish habitation in the city were recovered, physically linking the modern national capital to its historical predecessors. By uniting the city, Israel had connected the present to the past. Now Jerusalem could truly become the nation's center.

Israel set out to claim all the city as its own. But by doing so, it freed Jerusalem from Jordanian subjugation, thereby allowing the Palestinians, too, to reclaim it as their own, to disengage their nationalist movement from the surrounding Arab nations who each claimed the Palestinian cause as their own. This would become one of the profound ironies of Israel's capture and unification of the city – Israeli control was the precondition of an independent Palestinian nationalism.

But at first the Six-Day War was only a catastrophe for the Arabs of

Jerusalem. It proved they could not rely on the protection of the Arab states. "[T]heir performance on the field belied the true intentions behind their bravado," noted Hanna Siniora, a Palestinian editor in Jerusalem. "They had not prepared adequately for war, and indeed did not really seek it. Their posturing was entirely for the sake of public image."[33]

In the wake of the 1967 disaster Palestinians determined that they would have to conduct their own armed struggle.[34] Palestinian guerrilla operations, which had scarcely begun before the war, intensified. The Palestinians increasingly asserted their specificity, separating themselves out from the larger Arab nation. They began to write their own histories and recite their own poetry. In 1968, the name of the PLO's covenant was changed, using the Arabic term *al-wattani*, making it a nationalist charter for the local Palestinian, as opposed to the larger Arab, nation. The movement's objective also shifted to the achievement of an independent democratic Palestinian state.[35]

The Israelis, through their victory in 1967, created a new political space in which these Jordanian Arabs could become Palestinians again. The Israeli occupation made the Zionists into intimate enemies and transformed the Palestinians into a nation that would match its wits, its history, its tradition against the Zionists. Israelis were no longer demonic colonizers, but real human beings whose occupation one hated, but whose model of nation building one used as a measuring stick to gauge the adequacy of one's own. The Palestinians studied Zionism's lessons. Under the influence of these Palestinians, the goals of the Palestinian nationalist movement began to be refashioned from Arab victory and return to the end of Israeli occupation and Palestinian statehood.

Under Israeli occupation, all the Arabs of the West Bank saw themselves as Palestinians. But unlike Palestinians elsewhere on the West Bank, the Palestinians of Jerusalem enjoyed the civil and political protections of Israeli law that applied to all Israeli Arabs. Jerusalem naturally became a privileged political platform from which Arabs could speak out against both Israel and the surrounding Arab world.

The unification of Jerusalem under Israeli sovereignty transformed both the Israelis and the Palestinians. It confirmed the power of one and the powerlessness of the other. Within both it unleashed religious forces who understood the Jewish liberation and the Arab subjugation as a play not of force, but of spirit; not as a glorious or tragic historical circumstance but as a divine dictate.

For the Orthodox Jews of Mea She'arim, the devout inhabitants of the old *yishuv*, Israel's victory made it possible to reach holy ground, the outer walls of the Temple Mount through which an ancient nation had once approached its God. As long as the most sacred sites of historic Israel had been beyond the confines of the Jewish state, Zionism's Orthodox opponents could deny its potential religious significance.[36] Zionist sovereignty in the ancient sacred center unleashed a ferocious struggle over what kind of city Jerusalem was to be and whether Judaism or Zionism would prevail here. By striving to control Zion, the Orthodox Jews of the old *yishuv* increasingly sought to reshape Zionism.

Many Zionist Jews believed Jerusalem had been delivered by God. Redemption had begun. These religious nationalists calculated time according to a new metric: 1967 became the year zero. Yoel Ben-Nun, one of their activists, wrote, "With the taking of the Temple Mount, we were suddenly thrust forward by a gigantic hand that propelled us out of the everyday and petty reality in which we had been submerged . . . It seemed that we could not possibly absorb all the divine and spiritual force that cascaded onto us from heaven."[37]

These religious Zionists saw the war as another step in the redemption of biblical lands to which they were through covenant bound by God. Jerusalem had been King David's capital, a site chosen to unify the warring tribes of Judah to the south and those of Israel to the north. Israel had been formed as a nation in these newly conquered highlands, not on the coastal plains that make up the body of the modern Jewish state. And so a new fusion of nationalism and religion was forged that compelled Jewish settlement of the conquered lands of Judea and Samaria as a preeminent religious obligation. Jerusalem became the center from which messianic suburbanites began to settle these biblical lands. They posited an alternative vision by which to believe in Israel. Rejecting the politics of state and citizen, they defined Israel as a nation of Jews chosen by God to inhabit this territory.

For the Arab world, the ability to defeat Israel has been the criterion against which the relative merits of different ideologies is measured. That the Jews had now taken al-Quds, "the Holy" [city], as Jerusalem is called by Palestinians and Muslims, sent shock waves through the Islamic world. For many, the loss of the sacred city was the proof text that secular pan-Arabism, the socialist statism of Egypt, Syria, and Iraq, had failed. The Israelis had won, many concluded, because they had never forgotten that they were Jews, children of Abraham.

After Israel's seizure of Jerusalem, more and more Palestinians also began to turn back to the sacred sources of strength, to the pillars of Islam and Allah.[38] The Jews had vanquished because they believed, and their victory proved the Arabs had lost their way. A politicized Islam that rejected any territorial compromise with the Zionists, that saw the reconstruction of the *umma* as the critical test for the Islamic world, began to make inroads everywhere. The Islamic movement was helped along by monies from the oil-rich Gulf States, who grounded their own legitimacy in Islam and who saw fundamentalism as a counterweight to the strident political radicalism of the Palestinians. Jerusalem ultimately became a bloody ritual battleground from which to engage the infidel and call the faithful to further resistance.

The unification of the sacred city under Israeli sovereignty reawakened ancient understandings of the nation as an instrument of divine will. The oneness of Adonai and Allah demanded an undivided city subject to the sovereignty of the believers, a land freed from the yoke of the unbeliever, the infidel. The energies released by reunification have made it extraordinarily difficult for either people to relate to the city and the lands around it as a territory to be shared or divided between two nation-states.

Jerusalem had become one city, unified by the force of arms. But now it would have to be governed. The force of symbols would make that an agonizing task.

Part I

The Two Zions: Jews Against Zionism in Jerusalem

2

Zion Against Zionism

It is ironic that Jerusalem lent its name to the Jewish nationalist movement, for Zionism was built largely outside Zion, in the countryside and along the coast. Theodor Herzl wanted to build the capital on Mount Carmel, not within Jerusalem. The city was filled, he wrote, with "musty deposits of two thousand years of inhumanity, intolerance and uncleanliness."[1] Poets and politicians – Bialik and Ben-Gurion, for example – avoided the city. Chaim Weizmann, Israel's first president, felt uncomfortable there and wanted to exclude the Old City in Britain's first partition plan. Jerusalem did not loom large in early Zionist imagery. In the early postcards celebrating Jewish settlement in Palestine, there are few images of Jerusalem.

The Zionists purchased little land in, or even around, the city. This was not because land was unavailable for purchase. Both the Greek Orthodox Patriarchate and the Catholic Church were acquiring property in Jerusalem. Prominent Arab families were also more than willing to sell to Jews, as their enemies repeatedly charged. When statehood came, Israel owned little in the city, not even a plot on which to build their new capital, which they constructed on expropriated Palestinian lands.[2]

To grasp Zionist discomfort with Jerusalem, it must be understood that the religious Jews of Zion opposed Zionism with all their might. The city's devout Jews fought to defend Judaism's sacred center against the secular nationalists whom they understood as a profaning presence. Although many religious Jews have accommodated, and even embraced, the Jewish state, the relationship between Judaism and Zionism is still an uneasy one. And it remains most difficult in Zion itself.

The Power of the Word

The dead do not sleep undisturbed in Jerusalem. The graves of Theodor Herzl, who created political Zionism, and Eliezer Ben-Yehuda, who modernized Hebrew, have been repeatedly desecrated. To compound the sacrilege, the spray paint sometimes traces out black swastikas on

the stone slabs. The tombs of the two men who created the idea of a
Jewish state and the words it would use are defiled not by Arabs, but by
Jews.

Rena Ben-Avi Raz's ancestors' graves had just been attacked. This
gracious grandmother, who carries her heritage on her tongue, is Eliezer
Ben-Yehuda's granddaughter. Ben-Yehuda migrated to Jerusalem from
Russia in 1881 to rebuild Israel through words, to refashion Hebrew, an
ancient language of liturgy and law, into a daily language for a new
Jewish nation.

Rena Raz's father, Itamar Ben-Avi, was Ben-Yehuda's first child.[3]
The boy's mother had promised her husband she would speak only
Hebrew to their children. For four years, their child remained mute, as
friends concluded the boy either was retarded or was being sacrificed for
the sake of his father's linguistic experiment. One day, Ben-Yehuda
returned to find his wife singing a Russian lullaby to their son. Enraged,
he lifted his clenched fist as if to strike her, bringing it down and shatter-
ing a small desk. Itamar leaped at his father, crying in Hebrew, "Abba!
Abba!" (Father! Father!). "Just as Isaac, the son of Abraham, before
you, was the first Hebrew child in ancient Jerusalem," Ben-Yehuda is
said to have exclaimed to his little son, "so you, too, are from now on
the first Hebrew child in modern Jerusalem."[4]

Itamar carried on his father's role as wordsmith and journalist. Rena
Ben-Avi Raz, Itamar's silver-haired daughter, lovingly recounted to us a
childhood that is both rich heritage and heavy burden. Sitting in front of
two enormous oil portraits of her parents, dressed in the finest Western
fashion, she is still proud of the thousands of Hebrew words her father
and grandfather constructed: "*chayyas*, pickpocket; *mivrak*, telegram;
hadish, modern." Wearing large winged glasses, she boasted how her
grandfather defended modern Hebrew against the importation of European words. " 'You can't say cafe,' he used to say, 'but *kahava*, from the
Arabic.'. . It's fantastic, unbelievable . . . hundreds and thousands of
words."

Languages not only represent reality in distinctive ways, they are tools
by which peoples identify and distinguish themselves from others. As
such, they are instruments of power. States have consolidated their rule
by forcing people to speak the same language, often crushing the regional dialects and minority languages as the English did in Wales, the
French in Provence. Languages become powerful by becoming the languages of power.

In the Turkish-controlled Jerusalem of Eliezer Ben-Yehuda's day, uni-
fying the Jews of Palestine through modernized Hebrew threatened both
the European powers and the Orthodox Jews of the old *yishuv*. As a
result of Europe's support when he confronted rebellion within his em-

Rena Raz, owner, Alba Pharmacy, 1984.

pire, the Ottoman sultan Abdul Majid was forced in 1840 to allow European states to establish consulates in Jerusalem. These consuls were granted legal jursidiction over foreign nationals in Palestine who sought exemption from Ottoman law. In their imperial scramble for influence, foreign states built institutions for pilgrims and residents – both Jews and Christians – to bolster their position in the city. Each state fostered communities who would seek its protection and speak its language – whether Russian, Spanish, German, French, English, or Dutch. A Hebrew-speaking community of Jews could dilute their influence.

But modern Hebrew was an even greater challenge to the city's existing Jewish community. Jerusalem had always attracted a small stream of Jews. Most Jews came on pilgrimage, whether to search for miraculous cures or to touch the rock remnants of their ancient nation. A few stayed on to study, to pray, to be buried close at hand for the messianic redemption of their nation. Jews came to the land because only here could one properly observe many of the Torah's commandments. They came to Jerusalem to be closest to God.

By the time Eliezer Ben-Yehuda arrived at the end of the nineteenth century, some seventeen thousand Jews, almost all deeply religious, made up the majority of the city's population. Jerusalem was the center of the old *yishuv*, the "old settlement," as the pre-Zionist Jews of Palestine were called by the new Zionist community.[5] The Jewish *yishuv* in Jerusalem was divided into two distinct ethnic communities. Worldly and olive-skinned, the Sephardim, from the Hebrew word *sepharad* for Spain, traced their origins to the Iberian peninsula. The Sephardim were the first large Jewish community in Jerusalem, seeking refuge here from the Dominican and Franciscan Inquisition in Spain and Portugal that culminated in the Jews' total expulsion at the close of the fifteenth century. Encouraged by the sultan, who could not believe his good fortune, the majority of the Sephardim entered the Ottoman Empire in North Africa and Southern Europe.[6] Sephardim first provided the Turkish armies with the capacity to produce firearms, enabling them to defeat the Persians and the Mamelukes at the beginning of the sixteenth century. Although most Sephardi Jews went to Istanbul and the Balkans, some went to Palestine, particularly to Jerusalem and Safed, a Galilean textile town and the center of Jewish mysticism.

The Ottoman Empire organized its relations with non-Islamic religious minorities through the *millet* system. Each *millet*, or community, was granted legal autonomy to regulate education, religion, and personal status – birth, marriage, divorce, and inheritance. The Sephardi Jews were the only Jewish community recognized as a *millet* by the Ottomans who enforced the rulings of its courts. Sephardi rabbis elected their own Hakham Bashi, or chief rabbi, who represented Palestinian Jewry to the Ottoman state. In Jerusalem, the Sephardim, the eminent among them donning the red Turkish fez, were the city's Jewish elite, merchants, owners of banks and real estate in downtown Jerusalem. Some had title to whole Arab villages. Sephardim built the railway from Jerusalem to Tel Aviv. When the Zionists later began purchasing lands in Palestine they often did so through Sephardi intermediaries.

With their skin chalk or rose pink, their forms cloaked in black cloth and sequestered in study, the *yishuv*'s second Jewish community, the Ashkenazim, arrived much later, in the nineteenth century, from Eastern Europe and the Russian lands. Because the Ottomans initially forbade the Ashkenazim, as Europeans, even to settle in Jerusalem, the greatest number also settled in Safed. It was only after Ottoman Palestine fell briefly to the Egyptian armies of Muhammad Ali, that the Ashkenazim were first given the official right to reside in Jerusalem in the 1830s.[7] This was shortly followed by a devastating earthquake that killed a third of Safed's Jews. The devastation was widely interpreted as divine wrath that Jews had neglected their messianic duty to rebuild Jerusalem. Thereafter Jerusalem reemerged as the preeminent Jewish center.

During the latter part of the nineteenth century, Ashkenazim poured into the city. The wealthier, more educated Sephardim, who spoke Arabic and Turkish as well as their own language, Ladino, a mixture of Latin, Hebrew, and Spanish, looked down on these Yiddish-speaking Jews as uncivilized and uncouth. Some Sephardim even refused to recognize them as real Jews. Ben-Yehuda's son, Itamar, was able to marry his wife, considered the most beautiful Sephardi woman of the city, only with great difficulty. However, by the end of the nineteenth century, the tables had turned and the Ashkenazim comprised a majority of the city's Jewish population.[8]

As the Jewish population of the walled city of Jerusalem grew in the nineteenth century, densities became unbearable. Jews pushed first into the Muslim area and then outside the walls of the Old City altogether. In 1860, Sir Moses Montefiore built the first Jewish residential quarters, Mishkenot Sha'ananim ("the dwellings of those who are at rest"), outside the city walls for families of rabbinical students.

Initially there was tremendous resistance to Montefiore's project and others like it. Living outside the Old City's protective walls exposed the new suburbanites to Arab bandits who looted their homes and attacked their families. Moreover, a number of Ashkenazi rabbis prohibited their followers to move there because, they argued, living outside the Old City's walls was moving outside Jerusalem's sacred space. Montefiore's Mishkenot only succeeded because it drew Sephardim, over whom the Ashkenazi leadership had no influence.

Small groups of Ashkenazi Jews likewise began to break out of the city, establishing small living complexes along Jaffa Road. In December 1873 Yosef Rivlin (1837–1896), who would distinguish himself as the city's most important Jewish builder, met with other Ashkenazi Jews to plan one of the largest new Jewish neighborhood projects. Their planning meeting ended during the week in which the Torah portion contained the narrative of how God blessed Isaac a hundredfold (*mea she'arim*). Since their building cooperative also called for a hundred subscribers, *Mea She'arim* was a propitious name for their new venture. Unable to purchase land near Jaffa Road, they secured a property to the north, called Kerem Kadkur by the Arabs, a rocky ridge unfit for agricultural use, with a malarial swamp at its base. A nearby heap of bones and ashes from the local soap industry would prove to be felicitous pollution, for their interpretation of this garbage mound allowed them to overcome the Ashkenazi rabbis' resistance to living outside the walls. Knowing that the walls of King Herod's Jerusalem in the first century B.C.E. had stretched farther to the north than the present walls, they contended that the hillocks of bone and ash were sacrificial refuse from the Temple, thus enabling them to advance their claim that the site was really within Herod's Jerusalem after all.

Many of those who supported Rivlin's project believed that building of Jerusalem was part of a redemptive process in which cosmic forces were at play. In the mystical literature, five spheres of holiness radiated outward from the innermost sphere centered on the Temple Mount.

Kerem Kadkur was propitiously located near one of the city's outer gates, a critical threshold through which the holiness of the city passed to the rest of the land. Jerusalem, it was interpreted, was being newly besieged by an invisible army of Amalekites, a nation whose forces had long ago attacked the Israelites as they passed from Egypt to the land of Canaan, attacking the rear of the Israelite column, killing women, children, the aged, and the sick. Wasn't the explosion of Christian activity outside the Old City's walls a manifestation of the unseen army of Amalek now massing around Jerusalem? By settling in their very midst, some of Joseph Rivlin's followers believed they were building a rampart to guard the city's innermost sanctity and doing battle with the evil forces congregating around its walls.[9] By the turn of the century there were as many Jews living outside the walls as inside.[10]

The Old Yishuv

Most Jews who immigrated to Jerusalem in the nineteenth century did not go to work, but to pray and to study. Judaism, at its root, is a religion built around the city, and the Jews who lived there strove to maintain Jerusalem's sanctity as an ancient center of sovereignty and sacrifice, to mark the memory of its greatness, and to affirm their faith it would be restored in some messianic future. Many believed that settling the city would speed the messiah on his way. The Jews who lived here were fulfilling a collective obligation and felt entitled to material support from Jewish communities outside Palestine.

Drawing upon ancient injunctions that Jews everywhere must support the Temple, a vast network funneled money from Jewish communities around the world to Jerusalem and the other three holy cities of Palestine: Hebron, Safed, and Tiberias. To raise monies for the Jews of Palestine, in 1759 Rabbi Moses Malki of Safed, for example, visited the prosperous Jewish community of Newport, Rhode Island, which built the Touro synagogue, America's first synagogue. This system of *hallukah*, or "portion," enabled thousands of Jews to live in Jerusalem with little or no productive employment.

Rabbi Shneur Zalman (1745–1813) of Lyadi in White Russia, the founder of the Habad *hasidim*, a more mystical form of Judaism, laid out the hierarchy of obligation: "Whoever cannot fulfill the commandment by actually living in *eretz-yisrael* should fulfill it by donating money to it, and whoever has no money should spend the effort in collecting money from others for *eretz-yisrael*."[11] Indeed Zalman argued that monies given for this purpose could never be returned. If a Jew took money to Jerusalem and found no Jews, he must give it to Arabs. If he could find no Arabs, he should throw the money on the ground in the expectation that somebody who needed it would find it.

The *hallukah* monies sent to Jerusalem kept the Jewish community alive.[12] The Sephardim, who controlled the flow of funds into the city, were unwilling to cede any of their authority to the Ashkenazim. As the Ashkenazi community grew in size, it made two strategic maneuvers. First, after 1840 its members chose not to become Turkish citizens, securing the protection of European consuls that exempted them from Ottoman courts and poll taxes, as well as the authority of the Sephardi communal institutions. A number of Ashkenazim were even appointed as European consular agents. Backed by the European states, the Ashkenazim were able to establish their own separate courts and other institutions.

Second, the Ashkenazim created their own networks to amass *hallukah* funds from abroad, usually from their home regions. The threat of Christian missionary activity sponsored by the same European states both propelled and helped them to raise funds abroad. At the same time the Europeans were establishing consuls, Western Christian communities, Catholic and Protestant alike, went on their own building spree in Jerusalem. For the first time since the Islamic leader Salah al-Din had retaken the city from the Crusaders in the twelfth century, the Christianities of the West were able to build new churches, convents, and hospitals.

French Catholics, German Lutherans, and British Anglicans all competed fiercely to harvest potential converts. Forbidden by the Ottomans to proselityze among the Muslims, the Christians used their new hospitals and schools to attract the many Jews who found themselves in abject poverty.[13] Free meals for one's children, adequate medical care, or a paying job was a powerful lure. The Jewish community threatened to excommunicate and to deny a proper burial to any Jew who used their services. And the Jews, both Ashkenazim and Sephardim, raised funds from wealthy Jews abroad to create their own community services to counter those of the Christians.

The Sephardim felt acutely threatened by the Ashkenazim's raising their own monies. There was only so much Jewish money and the Sephardim used the *hallukah* monies to pay taxes to the Ottomans, build community institutions, support gifted Torah scholars, and provide for the poor. The Ashkenazim did not have to pay Turkish taxes, which could be heavy, and, in contrast, used the funds to support everybody, with students receiving preferential treatment.

The Sephardim were more likely than the Ashkenazim to earn their living as artisans and merchants. For the Ashkenazim, not working was the ideal. Many sent their wives out to work rather than cut into their time for study and prayer. Because *hallukah* was rarely enough to live on and employment opportunities were limited, many Jews migrated away. European Jewish philanthropists like Baron Edmond de Rothschild and Sir Moses Montefiore felt an acute need to create a productive base for the Jewish community.[14] But the Orthodox Ashkenazim almost always greeted such efforts with hostility.[15] Jerusalem's Ashkenazi rabbis feared that if Jews in Jerusalem were expected to work for a living, it would divert energy from their mission: to build a community in Zion that walked in the ways of Torah. And they were anxious that economic independence would undercut their influence and might even reduce the flow of funds from abroad.

Religious Jewish leaders from the outside had little success encouraging Jerusalem's Jews to depend on their own labors for their livelihood. When the Kalischer *rebbe* arrived in Jerusalem, he preached to the Jews about the importance of engaging in agriculture rather than relying on *hallukah*. Jerusalem's rabbis answered that *hallukah* was a more steady source of income than farming. The *rebbe* then asked them, "What will you do if the *hallukah* money suddenly stops?"

"We are not worried about tomorrow," they replied.

"Then," exclaimed the *rebbe*, "you are like the wicked person who says, 'Why should I be concerned about the tomorrow of the world to come? I live only for today.' "[16]

When Moses Montefiore built the first Jewish residences outside the walled city, he also constructed a flour mill and a weaving plant. Although the housing was for the families of yeshivah students, he hoped to put Jews to work. Jewish suburbanization succeeded magnificently, but Montefiore's plans to introduce Jewish production did not. The historic windmill overlooking the Old City that attracts so many tourists today had to be shut down for lack of interest.[17] Other projects funded by Montefiore to establish workshops and agricultural settlements in and around Jerusalem also failed.

Ben-Yehuda, together with other Jewish moderns, was contemptuous of the *hallukah* system. Monies ultimately did not keep pace with the increasing number of Jews living in Jerusalem. Most families could not survive on *hallukah* funds alone. In the 1880s, the Russian czar, Alexander III, tried to push the Jews out of the Russian lands. His government sponsored pogroms and restricted Jewish residence, education, employment, and ownership. The repression created mass penury and millions of Jews fled Eastern Europe. A major source of funds for the old *yishuv* was all but closed off. The overwhelming majority made their way west to America, but significant numbers went to Palestine. Those who immigrated to Jerusalem were ashamed of the city's religious dole and promoted all manner of enterprises to make the Jewish community more self-sufficient.

Ben-Yehuda had arrived in Jerusalem determined to fit in. He let his beard grow, grew back his *payot*, convinced his cultured wife to cover her natural hair with a wig and run a kosher kitchen. He attended synagogue regularly. Ben-Yehuda believed if he dressed and behaved in a pious manner, his efforts to introduce modern culture would bear fruit. Instead he was soon ostracized by the city's Orthodox Jewish community.

Modern Hebrew threatened the Orthodox Jews of Jerusalem not only because it challenged their cultural distinctiveness as Yiddish-speaking Ashkenazim of Eastern Europe, but because it represented the linguistic medium of modernity and Jewish nationalism.[18] Ben-Yehuda promoted modern Hebrew in Jerusalem through new kinds of schools that taught history, science, and European languages, training their students for productive employment. They even accepted girls as students. Remaking Hebrew into the language of daily life linguistically unified sacred and profane discourse, which much of East European Orthodox Jewry separated by using Hebrew for prayer and study and Yiddish or other European languages for daily life.

Some of Jerusalem's rabbis even connived with the Turkish authorities to staunch the flow of Zionist immigrants whose children began to fill the secular schools. Young boys threw stones at Ben-Yehuda on his way to teach and his son was taunted and beaten up on the streets. Families who allowed their sons to attend his school and others like it were cut off from community financial support.

Because of the fierce opposition of the Ashkenazi religious establishment, the new schools recruited primarily among the city's Sephardim. Whereas Jerusalem's Ashkenazim drew a sharp line between sacred and profane, many seeing money-making as a diversion from their sacred mission, the Sephardim did not. Further, the Sephardim, drawing on a cosmopolitan cultural heritage of Arab Spain, were already more conversant than the Ashkenazim with the languages and learning of the wider world. The Sephardim expected individuals to make their own way and even their rabbis were glad to send their children to schools that would better enable them to make a living.[19] In consequence modern Hebrew today is based on Sephardi, as opposed to Ashkenazi, pronunciation.

Ben-Yehuda published a modern Hebrew newspaper, *Ha-Tzevi* – The Deer – which, until his first dictionary was published, helped diffuse the new Hebrew vocabulary. His articles attacked both the old *yishuv*'s school system and their dependence on foreign contributions. "Unfortunately, our community consists of 'Luftmenschen,' resting on no sound inner foundations, drawing its strength not from its own soil but sustained from abroad," he wrote.[20] Jerusalem's Ashkenazi rabbis banned the newspaper, most of whose readers were more secular Zionists outside the city.[21]

Jewish Ashkenazi religious leaders would ultimately even persuade the Turkish authorities to arrest Ben-Yehuda for sedition. And when his first wife, Devorah, died, the Ashkenazim refused to bury her, a fellow Ashkenazi, declaring her ritually unclean because of her contact with him. Only after the rival Sephardi community agreed to inter her did they relent and was she buried as an Ashkenazi. Shortly thereafter, three of Ben-Yehuda's children died. Some interpreted this as divine wrath on a heretic.[22]

Ben-Yehuda did more than restructure the syntax, vocabulary, and grammar of an ancient tongue. He challenged the dominant Orthodox community of late-nineteenth-century Jerusalem by seizing its linguistic patrimony and harnessing it to the needs of modernity. By creating new words for new realities, he challenged the Orthodox community in its own sacred language to name the new world around them. By naming that world in the language of their prayers, he provided a dangerous bridge between the walled city of Orthodox belief and the secular nationalists now landing on Palestine's shores.

In the end, modern Hebrew captured Jerusalem well before Zionism did. In 1904, Ben-Yehuda published the first part of his modern Hebrew dictionary. At the time, there were fewer than ten Hebrew-speaking families in all of Palestine.[23] Yet in 1917, the British declared that the three official languages of Mandatory Palestine would be English, Arabic, and Hebrew. Still, large segments of Jerusalem's Orthodox community never gave in; for many it is still blasphemous to use this sacred language to buy toilet paper and toothpaste. Ben-Yehuda's resting place remains to them a symbol of Zionist profanation of their city.

Today, the Jewish descendants of those members of the old *yishuv* who opposed Zionist pioneers like Ben-Yehuda call themselves *haredim*. Although they are predominantly Ashkenazim, they include a substantial Sephardi component, typically North African Jews who migrated to Jerusalem after Israel became a state. The Western press often mistakenly calls them "ultra-Orthodox." Literally, the term *haredim* means "those who tremble" or "those who are fearful."[24] Originally the term simply referred to those Jews who were rigorous in their religious practice. With the growth of Zionist settlement, it came to refer to the religious Jews of the old *yishuv* who opposed them. These Jews fear the punishment of God for violation of religious law, not only by themselves but by Jews around them. Judaism defines Jews not by belief but by descent from Jewish mothers. For the *haredim*, what the Jews do – any Jews – matters in the scheme of things. And naturally, it matters most in Jerusalem.

The *haredim*, in fact, may be no more religiously observant than the many Orthodox Jews who are Zionists. What distinguishes the *haredim* is that they deny – in varying degrees – the religious legitimacy of the Jewish state and secular, democratic nationalism as the foundations of that state. Today they either try to avoid contact with the Jewish state, push it to conform to religious law, or, when it violates that law, oppose it as though the heavens will not wait.

Zion Against Zionism

Wave after wave of Zionist immigrants began to break on the shores of Palestine. Most of the new immigrants who arrived in the first decades of the twentieth century settled in Jaffa, Tel Aviv, Haifa, and agricultural settlements in between, far from what they saw as Jerusalem's unproductive theocracy. Most of the religious Jews who settled in Jerusalem did so because they believed the messiah might be near. A scion in the line of King David would restore Jewish sovereignty in Jerusalem, gather the exiles, and rebuild the Temple the Romans had destroyed. The Zionist movement horrified them and their devout confreres around the world.

But Jerusalem did beckon to Jewish nationalists as well, particularly those who understood their Zionism as a natural expression of their Judaism. Zionist immigrants gradually established a vibrant community in Jerusalem. It was in Zion that Zionism faced its most profound challenge, a challenge that marked the very origins of Jewish nationalism.

Herzl had wanted to have the founding meeting of the Zionist Congress in 1897 in Munich. However, the city's Jewish leaders mobilized massive opposition and he was forced to relocate to Basel, Switzerland. "We shall keep our priests within the confines of their temples," Theodor Herzl had promised. Just before the rescheduled meeting began, Germany's Orthodox rabbis issued a statement: "The efforts of the so-called Zionists to found a Jewish national state in Palestine contradict the Messianic promises of Judaism . . ."[25] Although he was a secular Jew, Herzl nevertheless tried to assuage religious fears. The following year the Second Zionist Congress resolved that "Zionism will not undertake anything contrary to the commandments of the Jewish religion."[26]

As the Zionist movement grew, some Orthodox Jews came to approve it, seeing in Zionist settlement an ironic fulfillment of prophecy. The Zionists, they argued, misunderstood the forces moving them. Zionism was not a response to anti-Semitism, but to the spiritual crisis of diaspora Jews, who were rapidly assimilating. Besides, they argued, no believing Jew could turn his back on the fact that Zionism was a way to fulfill the commandment to settle in the land.

These observant Jews began to organize to make Zionism into an instrument of Torah, rather than its enemy. In 1902 they met in Vilna and founded the Mizrachi Party (*Mizrachi* is an acronym made from the words *mirkaz ha-ruhani*, "the spiritual center"). Their motto was "The Land of Israel for the People of Israel in accordance with the Torah of Israel." Their successors today make up the National Religious Party.

Some Orthodox Jews participated in the early Zionist movement because Herzl had pledged it would confine itself to settlement, leaving education to the traditional religious authorities. But it was soon clear Zionism was not simply a way to resettle an old land, but a movement to create a new Jew as well. That goal was manifest in the desire of the Zionist Congress to found a Hebrew University in Jerusalem where secular Jewish studies would be taught alongside the modern sciences. (Albert Einstein gave the university's first lecture, on the theory of relativity, in 1923, even before the buildings were completed.) The scientific study of Jewish history would show that Zionism was a natural culmination of changes in the Jews' material and intellectual conditions. Many Orthodox saw this project as a proof that Zionism intended a cultural revolution, not just settlement of the land. In 1911, when the Zionist Congress pushed ahead with its plan for a university in Jerusalem, many religious Jews felt they could no longer accommodate this new nationalism and left the Mizrachi Party en masse. The religious Zionists who remained launched their own modern religious school system in Palestine for their children, including a yeshivah to train rabbis for the new *yishuv*.

The Orthodox Jews who left the Zionist movement hated its secular nationalism and feared its spiritual deviation. In 1912, they formed Agudat Yisrael to fight Zionism throughout the world. When Britain in 1917 issued the Balfour Declaration supporting a Jewish homeland in Palestine, the Zionists took this as validation of their realpolitik. Returning to the land was a religious obligation, ingathering of the exiles traditionally understood as an indicator of messianic times. So while Agudat Yisrael and other Orthodox critics felt compelled to acknowledge the Balfour Declaration as a sign of the messianic advent, they argued that secular Zionism blocked the messiah's way.[27]

In the early years of the British Mandate, Agudat Yisrael was willing to sacrifice the establishment of a Jewish state if they could be sure that Jews could come and live in the land of Israel without harm. Settling the land was one thing; building a secular Jewish state quite another. Their leaders, Jacob Israel de Hahn and Rabbi Joseph Haim Sonnenfeld, conducted negotiations with Emir Abdullah of Transjordan, King Hussein's grandfather, in an attempt to secure guarantees of Jewish settlement, but without a national Jewish state. In 1924, de Hahn, an Orthodox Dutch Jew, was shot and killed in Jerusalem for his treachery to the Zionist cause. A note addressed to the "evil rabbinate," signed by a group calling itself the "Black Hand," was left on the body warning the *haredim* of a similar fate for any who "wished to murder us." The police never caught de Hahn's murderer, who, a Haganah member admitted forty years later, had been a Haganah agent.[28] Although Zionist writers have attempted to vilify de Hahn as a homosexual whose sexuality was exploited by his Arab friends, he is still mourned as a martyr in Jerusalem's *haredi* community.

History steadily pushed Agudat Yisrael toward cooperation with the Zionists. As a result of the great depression, *hallukah* funds from abroad slowed dramatically. Anti-Jewish violence in Europe became increasingly ferocious. Closer to home, the Palestinian townspeople and irregular forces who attacked the Jews in and around Jerusalem did not discriminate according to their nationalism. In the 1929 Arab riots, non-Zionist religious Jews in Hebron and elsewhere were hacked to pieces in their homes and synagogues.[29] By the mid-1930s, the Arabs had risen murderously yet again against the Jews, and the Nazis were ascendant. Finally, waves of Zionist immigration were swamping in demographic significance the Jews of the old *yishuv* centered in Jerusalem. And although they disagreed with its premises, large numbers of *haredim* were deeply moved by this massive Zionist ingathering of Jews.

In 1937, the Peel Commission envisioned the end of the British Mandate and raised the possibility a Jewish state would be established in Palestine. In an effort to unify religious support for the commission's findings, the pro-Zionist chief rabbi of Palestine initiated discussions with both the Mizrachi and Agudat Yisrael. The Mizrachi demanded only that the Jewish state's constitution reflect attachment to tradition and religious law. But when Agudat Yisrael held its world conference in Marienbad, it was almost torn into pieces. Whereas many leaders of the Agudat Yisrael outside Palestine were now willing to offer qualified support for such a state if they could be certain the *haredim* would be able to live separately in their own self-contained communities, Agudat Yisrael's leadership inside Palestine would not compromise. The Jerusalem branch rejected a Jewish state ruled by secular Zionists, dismissing it as "a hazard to the lofty role of the Jewish people as a holy nation."[30] Some even claimed that the barbarous acts against European Jewry that seemed to intensify daily were punishment for the deeds of the Zionists, that the Zionist sacrilege itself represented "tribulations" that indicated the messianic era was at hand.[31] The Jerusalem branch of Agudat Yisrael did not emerge victorious. In the end, Agudat Yisrael narrowly decided to endorse the British proposal for a small Jewish state.

After the Holocaust destroyed East European Jewry, the Jerusalem faction captured Agudat Yisrael's leadership. As the United Nations sent commission after commission to Palestine to implement the Peel

Commission's recommendations, the Zionists held two primary objectives: free immigration and a Jewish state. Agudat Yisrael supported free immigration, but was absolutely opposed to any Jewish state that did not operate according to the Torah.

The Orthodox feared the Jewish Sabbath would not be the recognized day of rest in a Jewish State. The holy day would be profaned by Jews. If government offices remained open on Saturdays, it would be impossible for religious workers to get government jobs. They pointed to the *kibbutzim*, where the day of rest moved through the week as work assignments rotated from person to person. Government offices and public institutions would have nonkosher kitchens where religious people couldn't eat. This was, they pointed out, exactly what had happened in the Labour Zionist "workers' kitchens." They also feared that secular Jews would close down their religious schools and impose their own educational system. Lastly, they believed that unless religious marriage laws were enacted by the state, an observant Jew would not take a chance on marrying the children of the secular Zionists. Each community would only marry, work, and eat with its own. Israel would be divided forever into two warring worlds.

In June 1947, representatives from Agudat Yisrael met with Ben-Gurion to present him with their demands. Ben-Gurion agreed that the state would enforce Orthodox religious marital laws; no civil marriages would be allowed. He saw several difficulties with the issue of the Shabbat, such as the operation of railways, the post office, and civil service, but he invited Agudat Yisrael to propose solutions that would allow the operation of these services without violating the Shabbat. Lastly, he declared that secular education would not be compulsory, allowing full autonomy of all religious educational systems, even that of the religious anti-Zionists. This letter, which Agudat Yisrael grudgingly accepted, is often referred to by the misnomer the "status quo agreement." It sealed Agudat Yisrael's passive support for the state. With the stroke of a pen, Agudat Yisrael moved from the anti-Zionist into the non-Zionist camp.

Many devout Jews in Jerusalem were enraged by Agudat Yisrael's progressive accommodation to Zionism. Already in 1935, large numbers had broken away from the Agudat Yisrael, forming themselves into the Edah Haredit, "the community of the those who fear God." Predominantly drawn from the courts of the more mystical *hasidim*, like the Satmar, these Jews refused to participate in Zionist state making in any way.

After the Arab uprising began in 1936, Agudat Yisrael cooperated in the establishment of a fund for Jewish defense. Several members of the Edah Haredit were even elected to Jerusalem's municipal council in 1939.

This motivated the formation of still another group, the Neture-Karta, to assert their radical opposition to the Jewish national movement.[32]

The Neture-Karta, "Guardians of the City," take their name from a passage in rabbinic literature. We are told that Judah the prince sent two sages to the land of Israel to organize Jewish life in accordance with his Mishnah. In one town, apparently so insignificant its name was not recorded, they asked the townspeople to show them their Neture-Karta, their "guardians of the city." The residents brought them their captain of the guard and the magistrate.

"These are the guardians of the city?" the sages responded. "They are 'the destroyers of the city [*haruve-karta*].'"

"Who are its guardians?" the people then asked.

The rabbis responded, "The teachers in Bible and Mishnah, who meditate upon, teach and preserve the Torah day and night." These are the real defenders of the city, they said; without them, a city would be defenseless, even if it has walls.[33] This group of *haredim* see themselves as the true guardians of modern Jerusalem.

"We Are at War"

To many Israelis, Moshe Hirsch, the self-appointed "foreign minister" of the Neture-Karta, is a perverse and ridiculous figure. The son of an observant Orthodox New York family, Hirsch immigrated to Jerusalem in 1955 to satisfy what he described as "an inner, soulish thirst to be in the Holy Land." Hirsch's powdery white face, a beard ruffle running ear to ear, is set against a wide black beaver hat, incredibly thick black-framed reading glasses, black coat, black knickers, and black socks.

When the Old City was recaptured in 1967, Hirsch refused to worship at the Western Wall because it was in "occupied" territory. Hirsch was unwilling to do anything that might be construed as legitimating Zionist property rights to the Holy of Holies. Only after receiving approval from King Hussein via the former Jordanian mayor of Jerusalem would he visit the revered ramparts of the ancient Temple.

On the first Friday night after the Six-Day War, Hirsch was walking in Mea She'arim with his father-in-law, Aharon Katzenelbogen, the successor to the founder of the Neture-Karta, Amram Blau. An army truck drove by.

"It's Shabbes [Ashkenazi pronunciation of Shabbat]," Hirsch and Katzenelbogen called out in reproof.

"You're shouting at me Shabbat! Who got you the Wailing Wall?" an Israeli soldier shouted back.

For Hirsch, this was not an accomplishment. As he saw it, the outer

Moshe Hirsch, foreign minister, Neture-Karta.

wall of the ancient Temple had been converted into a Zionist idol. It is the Wailing Wall, he said bitingly, that "brings people to the Golden Calf of Zionism."

Hirsch is not an Israeli citizen. He would prefer that Jerusalem be internationalized. He would even support the PLO's long proposed secular–democratic state if Jews could be assured of their religious freedom. In February 1988, the PLO were preparing for the departure of a "Ship of Return" from Athens, filled with Palestinians exiled from their homes over the decades. The ship would sail for the Israeli coast, its passengers willing to be seized, sent back, or even set adrift on lifeboats if the ship were sunk. Among the Palestinian passengers were three members of the Neture-Karta, with large stocks of their own kosher food. One of their rabbis, who had been born in Jerusalem, said he, too, was a "refugee from the Zionists. The Arabs are only fighting the Zionists about land. We are fighting about our faith. The Arabs can compromise. We can never compromise."[34]

In every confrontation with the Israeli police, Hirsch is there, arguing, granting interviews with the foreign press, refusing to move when the police try to clear the streets, arrested over and over and over again. He smiles beatifically as he is led away amid the truncheons.[35] When Hirsch's son was drafted into the Israeli army, his father used his status as an American citizen to get him released. "My son," he told us, "was taken and forced into an army . . . which is fighting people we have no enmity toward . . . One Jewish life is worth more than twenty Jewish states."

How many Neture-Karta are there in Jerusalem? "All those," he replied, "who want to link the past to the present and not break with it as Zionism is trying to do, transforming the Jewish people from a religious entity based on the teaching of God to an national entity, a godless national entity, they are Neture-Karta."[36]

Although religious Jews have always prayed for the end of exile and their return to Zion, most believed sovereignty could only be restored by divine intervention, not by ordinary human hands. "We are taught that God gave us the land," Hirsch told us, "and his messiah will return it." In his eyes, Zionism is a false messiah.

The Neture-Karta continue to hold firmly to the belief, codified in the Babylonian Talmud, that Israel and the nations must adhere to three divinely ordained oaths: Israel should not calculate the advent of the messianic era, Israel should not incite the nations, and the nations should not oppress Israel "too much."[37] "Zionism is . . . a movement which challenged a divine oath," he said. Jews are forbidden to "climb the wall," to take messianic tasks to hasten the messiah on his way.

"Zionism," he said, "began the strife which did not prevail before. The Arabs (were) the least anti-Semitic or anti-Jewish non-Jews throughout the world before Zionism . . . We are not at war with the Palestinians." Hirsch was certain Zionism would lead to punishment of the Jews. "Our flesh will become the prey of the deer of the forest and the wild animals," he said. Indeed he believed, as did the Satmar *rebbe*, that the Holocaust was God's punishment for Jews' turning from Torah and to Zionism.

To many, Moshe Hirsch is a political freak, an embarrassment. Yet, this outlying case provides information about the center. In fact, Moshe Hirsch speaks, in a Brooklyn accent, the original message of the Jews of the old *yishuv* who are still, in various ways, at war with the new. Hirsch still fights to defend the walls of Jerusalem's old *yishuv*, as if it were a new Jewish ghetto, against the Zionist state.

The Neture-Karta, like most other groups in the Edah Haredit, refuse any material support from the state, whether schools, national insurance, or welfare. Indeed, when Hirsch arrived in a taxi for our interview, he requested we pay his fare in American dollars, not wanting us to use Israeli shekels on his account. When the Edah Haredit accepted some state monies for its schools, the Neture-Karta paper carried an article condemning it. The Edah Haredit issued a *herem*, or ban of excommunication, against Rabbi Haim Katzenelbogen, the Neture-Karta leader. The order, plastered on Mea She'arim's walls, forbid wishing the rabbi "shalom," counting him for a prayer minyan, providing him with material means beyond those required for survival, or approaching any closer to him than four cubits. A Neture-Karta woman ripped down one of the posted orders. The man who had just put it up in turn tore off her black scarf, exposing her stubbled head. Fighting broke out and windows were smashed in the Neture-Karta yeshivah.

"We take an apartheid stand," Hirsch told us.

> We are at war with Zionism. It is an ideological war at this point. We must pick up sword and shield to combat Zionism which is converting more than a million children away from their roots. Strange, but very true. The state of Israel teaches the secular history of the Jews. But the history of the Jews is Tanakh [the Hebrew Bible]. The schools are secular, the teachers are secular and not God-believing. How can they teach our children? This is conversion and all of Jewry is commanded to take up sword and shield to protect a Jewish child from conversion.

When we ran into him on the street in the winter of 1989, he called us aside, pulling out a letter from his coat pocket bearing the PLO letterhead. Yasser Arafat, he whispered proudly, had appointed him "minister of Jewish religious affairs" in the new state of Palestine. That was too much, even for some of the members of his group. Reuven Katzenelbogen, one of Hirsch's rivals, told us, "I don't understand why he goes with Arafat. He thinks anything against Zionism is good – Hussein, Arafat, Reagan."

When Yasser Arafat returned to Gaza and Jericho in the summer of 1994, members of the Neture-Karta requested to be allowed to vote in the elections for the new Palestinian authority. Hirsch, the only Jew, as Arafat's "personal minister," to be included in the Palestinian government, would not, however, be able to attend the weekly cabinet meetings as they are held on Saturdays.[38]

Ben-Yehuda had harnessed sacred language to a secular purpose.

Haredim defaced Ben-Yehuda's grave in Hebrew. Traffic could travel both ways on that bridge of words. A century has passed since Ben-Yehuda first confronted the Orthodox world of Jerusalem, pitting the modern Hebrew of Zionism against the biblical language of Judaism. Religious Orthodoxy divided over Zionism. Some Orthodox groups accommodated Zionism, forming parties within the Zionist movement that tried to push the laws of the state to conform to religious law. Others remained bitterly opposed and either refused to have any dealings that would legitimate the state or became a force inside the Knesset, brokering for God.

The war between these two cities of Zion continues. It is, as we shall see, a struggle for territory, fought block by block, neighborhood by neighborhood. It is also a conflict over the categories of understanding, fought with words, over who has access to ultimate truths.

3

Black Zion

To an outsider Mea She'arim, the *haredi* center, appears dark and undifferentiated. "Black crow people," Yehuda Amichai, the Israeli poet, calls its residents, all clothed in black.[1] Given how threatened the *haredim* feel, one might imagine them solidary and united, densely packed into a few neighborhoods, all dedicated to preserving the traditions of their forefathers against Jewish modernity down at the corner. But, in fact, this community of those who have never fully made their peace with Zionism is still deeply divided between rabbis and *rebbes*, between Ashkenazim and Sephardim, between those who look to their religious leaders for privileges garnered from an alien Zionist state and those who demand their rights as its citizens. The community is rife with internal discord and mutual suspicion, a fertile ground for new political forces.

The Pious Ones

The most explosive cleavage within the *haredi* community, between *hasidim* and *mitnagdim*, first emerged among Eastern European Jewry in the eighteenth century. This division, between those who seek God's spirit and those who read his words, shattered the Jewish communities of Russia and the Polish lands. To understand it, we must return to the Sephardi Jews who trickled into Safed and Jerusalem in the fifteenth and sixteenth centuries.

The Spanish and Portuguese Jews who migrated to Palestine imported the intellectual wealth of the Iberian peninsula with them. Long before their exile, the Sephardim had developed a rich mystical tradition called the Kabbalah. In Safed, Sephardi thinkers grappled with the sudden failure of their assimilation, the destruction of their rich culture, and the emergence of the first truly racial form of anti-Semitism in which Spanish Inquisitors persecuted even Jewish converts to Christianity as "secret Jews" for their impurity of blood.

Many Sephardi Jews came to the land because they were sure the messianic era was imminent. In Safed, some among them even tried to reinstate the Sanhedrin, Israel's ancient high court, anticipating that God would rupture history and restore Jewish sovereignty. But Safed's mystics ultimately developed a doctrine that would later allow Jews everywhere to reinterpret their exile, to seek a gradual redemption, and to look for it within their own individual souls.

Safed's mystics read the Torah not simply as a literal codification of revealed law, but as the ineffable language of God. The nature of things could not be read off their surfaces, but was contained in hidden codes that those who knew could decipher. The world was awash with miraculous symbols, spirits, and souls. The dry rationalism of the Talmudists could generate reams of commentary, they argued; to know God a Jew would have to look elsewhere.

The greatest of the Safed Kabbalists was Rabbi Isaac Luria (1534–1572), a Jerusalem-born ascetic who worked wonders, who conversed with angels, as well as animals and trees. Luria fashioned a new myth of creation in which God's first act was to withdraw into himself, creating a vacuum devoid of divine matter. Into this void, God projected his divine light, which configured itself into a series of concentric circles, within which it crystallized into small vessels. God slowly withdrew the light, leaving only the minutest traces of the original formations. God then reintroduced the light. As the light coursed through the first tracings, they shattered, breaking into sparks, or *nitzutzot*, which adhered to the shards of the original vessels.

In Luria's account, the divine light of creation fragmented into chaos. Why had God done it? Luria had understood evil not in opposition to the divine, but as God's pure power of judgment, untempered by compassion. Luria's students reasoned that God had withdrawn his first light in order to project a light purified of this evil. But the vessels broke, commingling evil and good in the tumult of the world.

These obscure ideas converted Jewish exile into an arena of God's salvation. The divine was everywhere, not just in the land of Israel. Luria's students argued that the Jew's task was to redeem these divine sparks of compassion through piety and repentance, and thereby to restore the original structure of the universe. After Luria's death, his doctrine diffused throughout North Africa, the Middle East, and Europe via texts printed in Safed on Palestine's first printing press and transmitted by a global network of Sephardi merchants to which the city was connected.

Luria had made exile into a normal condition, indeed an intended act of God. The divine was omnipresent, even in evil. One could participate in redemption anywhere. By his or her own piety, each Jew could help to lift up the divine sparks trapped in matter, thereby repairing the cosmos and helping to bring on the messianic restoration of the Jewish nation.[2]

This mystical Sephardi tradition, nurtured in Safed in the sixteenth century, would bear fruit in Eastern Europe in the eighteenth. Hasidism first emerged in the Polish lands around the figure of a miracle worker, Yisrael Ben-Eliezer (1700–1760), known by his followers as the Ba'al Shem Tov, or "Master of the Good Name." In traditional Judaism, the name of God cannot be pronounced. Jews thus invented circumlocutions to speak about the divine. One of the most popular was simply *ha-shem*, "the name." A lore developed that a few select individuals knew how to pronounce God's unpronounceable name, and thereby had special powers to heal. Israel Ben-Eliezer's followers believed he was so endowed.

The Ba'al Shem Tov, or "the Besht" as he was known by his acronym, claimed to have telepathic and clairvoyant powers, to speak to animals, and to drive out evil spirits. He prepared amulets and charms for those who wanted to buy them. But more importantly, he fashioned a new form of popular piety, building on Kabbalistic ideas, known as Hasidism.

The Hasidic movement grew during the late eighteenth and early nineteenth centuries, when Jewish communal authority was being eroded by central rulers who wanted direct control over their citizens, unmediated by ethnic, communal, and ecclesiastic authorities. For millions of Jews in Eastern Europe, this meant forced assimilation, as they came under pressure to stop speaking Yiddish, were forbidden to wear traditional clothing and forced to cut their ritual earlocks (many hid them behind their ears or up in their hats), and brides were prevented from shaving their heads at marriage.

Hasidism also flourished in a setting where the rabbinical establishment, caught up and in many cases corrupted by the state's insatiable desire for revenue, had increasingly lost its legitimacy among the common people of Eastern Europe. In Poland, for example, Jews were subject to discriminatory taxes of all sorts. Some of these taxes exploited their ritual obligations, such as on candles used on Shabbat and on kosher meat that made it twice as costly as regular meat. Others were designed to undercut their ability to compete with Polish merchants. Jews paid a special tax, for example, to enter the capital city of Warsaw and to operate an inn.[3]

The right to collect these taxes was frequently leased out to Jews who derived considerable income from the privilege. Wealthy converted Jews, communal Jewish officials, and even rabbis became tax lessees. The rabbis had become a scholarly aristocracy, an insulated and self-satisfied stratum subservient to a wealthy Jewish elite. Under these circumstances, it was not surprising that the *hasidim*'s own unofficial small congregations, or *shtiblekh*, proliferated.

So threatened was the rabbinical establishment that in the early nineteenth century some rabbis supported the imposition of heavy state taxes on the *hasidim* for the right to hold their independent prayer meetings. Hasidism, which drew its original following from the poor and uneducated, nevertheless spread rapidly, drawing scholars skilled in Talmud to its ranks. Eventually half of the Jews of Poland and Russia were swept into the movement.

The *hasidim* (*hasid* means pious, *hasidim*, the pious ones)[4] elevated prayer over study, piety over scholarship, Yiddish over Hebrew, Kabbalah and the writings of their own spiritual leaders over Talmud. A *hasid* prepared carefully for prayer, purifying his mind, emptying his bowels to prevent "vapors" that would contaminate his thoughts, girding his loins with a special girdle to divide his heart from his genitals.[5] Swaying, gesticulating, shouting, and singing were ways for the *hasid* to achieve higher levels of concentration, to escape the body's constraints, so that his soul could soar to God.

In the beginning was the word. The Ba'al Shem Tov followed the Kabbalistic interpretation of creation as a materialization of divine speech. The observable world was a text, but its letters were only containers of divine light. Piety dictated focus on the light, not the letters. The logical wizardry of the Talmud, built around the tension between historical reality and Jewish law, was no substitute for meditation on the divine light that made that law possible.

The Besht claimed to make frequent visits, at times of his own choosing, to the messiah's dwelling place. The messiah apparently informed the Besht that he would come only after the Besht's teachings had been diffused throughout the world. Jews had for centuries, like Luria of Safed himself, held disappointed expectations of a messiah who would usher in an apocalyptic restoration of Israel to its land. The Besht recast the messianic process, pushing the messianic moment into a far-distant future.[6] In its stead, Hasidism opened up a personal spiritual territory that could be redeemed here and now. The *hasid* strove for personal communion with God, a communion open to all, not just to a scholarly or spiritual elite.

If God were everywhere, or more precisely if all life were contained in God, daily life itself could be a form of prayer, a way for each person to redeem those divine sparks – contained even in the soup he drank – available to him. One early *hasid* explained he had not gone to his *rebbe*[7]

> to learn interpretations of the Torah from him, but to note his way of tying his shoelaces and taking off his shoes . . . In his actions, in his speech, in his bearing, and in his fealty to the Lord, man must make the Torah manifest.

Each individual had his own divine sparks, and out in the mundane world there were sparks carrying his name. Each life could be a spiritual odyssey.

The most ordinary actions could be infused with redemptive meanings. Today, for example, the Satmar *hasidim* sew their shirt and coat buttonholes on the right with the buttons on the left so that the right side covers the left. For them the left represents a dark, malevolent "other side." When their shirts and coats are buttoned, right prevails over left, good over evil.

The *hasidim* use strange, intricate, and wondrous tales to instruct their followers. For them joy was to be the standard of prayer, experience more important than ideas, love than logic. Haunting and powerful melodies, wild dancing, somersaults, even drinking are used as adjuncts to prayer, ways to achieve the concentration, the joyful heart necessary to make their prayers acceptable to God. Against the dour behavioral conformism of the Judaism of the day, the *hasid* sought the ecstasy of a soul cleaving to God. Hasidism painted the black and white Ashkenazi world with luminous interior colors.

In Hasidism the guiding role of the one big messiah was taken over by the many little *zaddikim*, or "righteous ones," who were understood to act as intercessors with God, channels by which his blessings could reach humankind.[8] The *hasidim* used the Yiddish term *rebbe* to distinguish their spiritual leaders from the rabbis. Wherever the *zaddik* was located thus became a center of the cosmos. These men, it is still believed, have special powers to bless and to curse, to heal and strike down, to read the mind, to make barren or undo infertility, indeed to travel to the divine realm and intervene in the trajectory of the cosmos.

Jews went to the *rebbe* to be cured of diseases, to learn about their future, to seek repentance for past sins, to guarantee the success of their business ventures, and to be granted children. Hasids developed elaborate theories about the *zaddik*'s powers. The *zaddik* was no mere seer, but could anticipate and reverse decrees with which Gentile rulers were oppressing the Jews. A powerful *rebbe* might even alter divine will.[9] The Besht, for example, was said to have cancelled a divine decree that the Torah be taken from the Jews. More recently, the Stoliner *rebbe*'s followers claimed he delayed the start of World War II for two years.[10]

The *rebbe*'s tales, his clothing, his furniture, his behavior, his very being are all holy. One Friday night in Jerusalem, the time for the *rebbe* to tell his tales, we watched as the *rebbe* of the Hungarian Hasidic community of Toledot Aharon made the blessing over the wine and bread. As he finished, pandemonium broke out as men and young boys rushed from their places to get even a small bit of blessed bread. Course by course, the *rebbe*'s food was passed out to a jostling crowd hoping to partake of the blessings imparted to whatever their *rebbe* has eaten.

A Hasidic *rebbe* is revered a living saint armed with an inexhaustible reserve of spiritual power. Just like American children who trade bubble-gum cards of their favorite baseball players, the Hasidic children of Jerusalem buy small photographs of their *rebbe*s and recount their miraculous deeds. At major communal events, such as a ground break-ing for a yeshivah, posters of the bearded holy men are merchandised much like those of singers at a rock concert.

The *hasidim* consider their *rebbe* as the pathway by which their prayers might better reach God. Naturally, they seek the *rebbe*'s com-pany. He listens to their problems, instructs them in the mysteries of the universe, and advises them on the conduct of their most private lives. In exchange for the *zaddik*'s intercession, his followers accord him their absolute faith and provide for his worldy needs.[11]

Rabbi Talmi, a Gerrer *hasid*, is a good example. The Gerrer *rebbe,* Simcha Bunim Alter, lives in Jerusalem. He came here after the Holo-caust. Talmi is a personal secretary of the *rebbe*'s brother, Rabbi Pinchas Menachem Alter, who heads the Gerrer's big New York yeshivah – The Lips of Truth – and acts as the Gerrer's political leader. Together, the two brothers run Israel's largest Hasidic community.

"I would ask the Gerrer *rebbe*," Talmi told us, dressed in his finest black caftan, "Should I leave the United States for permanent? Should I do this deal for business? What name should I give my child? . . . Let's say that there is a *hasid* and his wife is going into the hospital to give birth . . . Immediately he picks up a phone and tells the *rebbe*."

Talmi is proud of his *rebbe*'s spiritual power. People, he boasts,

> run to the Gerrer *rebbe* . . . A man comes in brokenhearted with some kind of pain and the *rebbe* will laugh and hold his hand and say, "Don't worry." He listens and listens and then he laughs and laughs and then he takes out a fruit and gives it over to him and he went out as if a stone was taken from him. A cure is going to come; something good is going to happen to him. A *hasid* believes that the *rebbe* is a human being, but he has *koach ha-tefillah* ["the power of prayer"], which means that he can ask from *Ha-Kadosh boruch Hu* ["The Holy One, blessed be He"], O Lord, help this man.

Today the *hasidim* of Jerusalem are divided into the followers of differ-ent *rebbe*s, each with his own court, some centered in Jerusalem and many not. Although most individuals are born into their Hasidic group, only one thing is absolutely required for membership: a willingness to submit to the *rebbe*'s authority. Dissenting voices are not tolerated and those who disagree with the *rebbe* must leave.

As in any world divided into multiple royal dynasties, marriage is a critical political instrument. By exchanging sons and daughters between Hasidic courts, *rebbe*s forge new alliances and secure old allies. For example, the Viznitz *rebbe*, Rabbi Moshe Hager, became powerful by succesively marrying his three daughters to the Belzer *rebbe*, the Skver *rebbe*, and the eldest son and heir apparent of the Satmar *rebbe*. These dynastic marriages are unbelievably extravagant affairs. Thirty thousand guests attended when the Viznitz *rebbe* married his daughter to the Belzer *rebbe*.

Competition between different Hasidic courts can be ferocious. The Belz and Gerrer are Jerusalem's two largest Hasidic groups. Members of each can instantly recognize the other on the street, for each group's mark is inscribed upon its members' clothing, the movement of their eyes, even their gait. By the style of their hat, whether or not their eyes wander on the street, whether they let themselves pause for conversation on the corner, whether they are willing to stand next to a strange woman on the street, all persons can easily be positioned in cultural space. The Torah, for example, obliges observant Jewish men to let their *payot*, or sidelocks, grow long. The Gerrer *hasidim* leave their *payot* uncurled; the Belz curl their *payot* behind their ears.[12]

The Belz and Gerrer are bitter rivals. The Belz *hasidim* repeatedly claimed the Gerrer are not sufficiently zealous in their defense of Torah, that their membership in Agudat Yisrael is a shameless accommodation with Zionism. When both the Belz and the Gerrer chose the same non-*haredi* neighborhood, Mekor Baruch, in which to expand, the results were explosive.

In August 1982, after the Gerrer *rebbe*'s daughter's marriage, the spray paint on the Gerrer synagogue questioned the bride's virginity. A year later, in May 1983, two smoke grenades were thrown into the Belzer *rebbe*'s house in Mekor Baruch.[13] In retaliation, right before Passover, when a Jewish house must be completely cleaned of leavened items like bread and other products made from grains, a loaf of bread was sent anonymously to the Gerrer *rebbe*'s Passover residence. The package arrived after Passover had begun, violating the ritual purity of the *rebbe*'s house.

The right to rule a Hasidic community derives from the spiritual gifts with which one has been blessed, from claims about one's being. In many communities, the Hasidic courts are hereditary dynasties, in which the claim to lead is passed from father to son. Even so when a *rebbe* dies or becomes too infirm, succession can be a dangerous affair.

The Viznitz *rebbe*, who managed his foreign relations with such dexterity, watched helplessly as tensions within his own household blew his community apart. The *rebbe*'s eldest son, Yisrael, the natural choice to succeed his father, had amassed huge debts that made him vulnerable to challenge. When Yisrael's grandmother, who had been his stalwart, died at the age of one hundred, his mother seized upon his apparent financial impropriety in order to champion her youngest son as the rightful heir.

Hasid and son at the tomb of Rabbi Shimon bar Yohai.

In 1983, Yisrael's mother humiliated his wife and children, forcing them from the Passover meal in front of the entire community. Yisrael's followers claimed his debts were incurred to support charity. When a wealthy *hasid* offered to make good on them, the benefactor was physically attacked by a synagogue official. Yisrael was forced to flee with his family from Jerusalem to Tiberias. Forty families who supported him were also excommunicated. But even in Tiberias, the contender for the Viznitz throne was not safe. His home was broken into and his furniture burned. He was forced to flee once again to Monsey, New York, where he sought the protection of his father's brother.[14]

Because *hasidim* believe communion with God can be achieved anywhere, they have been ambivalent about territorial Jerusalem. The Ba'al Shem Tov himself began a journey to the Land of Israel but mysteriously changed his mind upon arriving in Istanbul and returned to Podolia. Likewise, in 1798 his great-grandson, Nachman of Bratslav, in great spiritual ferment, set out and actually arrived in Palestine but immediately returned home.[15] Many of today's Hasidic *rebbe*s have never been to Jerusalem and see no need to go, even though large numbers of their followers live there.

For example, in 1944, the Satmar *rebbe*, Rabbi Yoel Teitelbaum, was taken by the Nazis to Bergen-Belsen concentration camp. When the Zionists were able to negotiate freedom for a few thousand Hungarian Jews with Eichmann in his Blut gegen Ware ("blood for goods") program, they included this anti-Zionist in the convoy, saving his life. This didn't change the Satmar *rebbe*'s attitude toward Zionism. Shortly after arriving in Palestine in 1945, he turned around and emigrated to Williamsburg, New York, where he never stopped railing against the Jewish state as a satanic kingdom. Even the seemingly miraculous victories of the besieged state in 1948 and again in 1967 were created by Satan, the Satmar *rebbe* argued, "to dupe the children of Israel into supporting the Zionists and heretics who have come to uproot the entire Torah."[16] Satmar *hasidim* are forbidden by their *rebbe* from voting in the Knesset elections or even visiting the Western Wall.[17] When the Satmar *rebbe* finally visited Israel in 1959, a separate train was organized to take him to Jerusalem with special tickets with no Israeli markings.

Hasidism transformed the messianic hope of liberating the real Jerusalem into an effort to liberate the invisible city inside the *hasid*'s soul.[18] It sought redemption not from exile, but in exile. It is perhaps for this reason that the *hasidim* have been more hostile to Zionism than have other *haredi* groups who must come to terms with Zionism's material accomplishments. The *hasidim*, who are not very prominent in non-Zionist circles like Agudat Yisrael, dominate the anti-Zionist Edah Haredit, whose most important backer is the Satmar *rebbe*.

The Wrath of Reason

A rabbi's right to lead was based on his ability to interpret the vast body of Jewish law, to adapt its logic artfully to changing conditions, and to perceive its timeless order. A *rebbe* need have no such qualification. Whereas the rabbis had rigorously separated sacred from profane worlds, Torah study from ordinary work, the *hasidim* blurred the boundaries. The *hasidim* denigrated the value of a lifetime of study. The rabbinate seethed as young Jews flocked to the *zaddikim* during the nineteenth century, spurning the synagogue for joyful gatherings held in austere meeting rooms. The rabbis accused the *zaddikim* of being charlatans and heretics, of failing to pray appropriately and neglecting Torah study.[19] The *hasidim*, in turn, accused the rabbis of being "Jewish demons," more concerned with their own honor than the welfare of the Jews.

Opposition to the *hasidim* crystallized around the leadership of Elijah

Ben-Solomon Zalmon of Vilna (1720–1797), known to his followers as the Vilna Gaon. This towering intellectual was caught between what he saw as a corrupt rabbinate and a rapidly spreading heresy. Refusing any financial tie to the rabbinate, Elijah Ben-Solomon went directly to the Jews of Vilna for money. Like the *hasidim*, he too refused the title of rabbi, adopting the ancient title of Gaon.[20] So great was his stature that during his life, Vilna was called the Jerusalem of Lithuania.

The men who followed the Gaon's lead came to be known as *mitnagdim*, "those who are opposed."[21] In the late eighteenth century, the Vilna Gaon declared a *herem*, or ban, on the *hasidim*. Jews were forbidden to have business dealings with them, rent lodgings to them, allow their children to marry them, eat meat slaughtered by their butchers. *Hasidim* were even flogged and driven from their homes. In some places, the rabbinate concocted imaginary charges against the *hasidim* and had them arrested by the Russian police. In others, their sacred books were burned publicly in large bonfires.[22] Fearing for their safety, hundreds of *hasidim* made their way to Palestine, settling in Safed and Tiberias, both drawn by the former's mysticism and unable, as Ashkenazim, to reside in Jerusalem.

Considered one of the greatest Torah scholars of his day, the Vilna Gaon was not threatened by modern sciences, seeing in the latter an instrument to deepen one's understanding of the Torah. But the Vilna Gaon was no simple rationalist. He, too, had studied the Kabbalah. Unlike the Ba'al Shem Tov, the Gaon believed strongly that the messianic advent was near, very near. It profoundly troubled the Gaon and his followers that *hasidim* were streaming into the Holy Land.

The Gaon centered the geography of redemption on the real city of Jerusalem, not in the soul. Aliyah, going up to the land of Israel, and particularly return to and rebuilding of Jerusalem, were cardinal Gaon teachings. The Gaon himself set out for Jerusalem in 1782, returning, it was said, because of a dream in which a voice called out to him that his soul was a "spark from the soul of Moses," who likewise had been denied entry into the promised land. Nonetheless, the Gaon taught that now was the time to resettle the land of Israel. The Bible recounted that more than half a million Jews received the Ten Commandments at Mount Sinai. Only when an equal number of Jews lived in Jerusalem, the Gaon proclaimed, would the messiah finally come.[23] In 1771, some of the Gaon's followers formed Hazon Tzion, the Vision of Zion, dedicated to rebuilding Jerusalem. But the Turks had closed Jerusalem to Ashkenazim, and their followers were forced to settle in Safed. In 1812, in the midst of a cholera epidemic in Safed, a group of *mitnagids* bribed Turkish officials to allow them to move into abandoned buildings at the edge of the Muslim quarter. From there, dressed as Sephardim, they gradually made their way into the Jewish quarter. Thus began the Ashkenazi repopulation of Jerusalem. The Gaon was not ambiguous about when the messiah would arrive. He would arrive in 1840; the Gaon was sure. As a result of the Gaon's prophecy, thousands of his followers migrated to Jerusalem during the first half of the nineteenth century, forming the Ashkenazi core of the old *yishuv*. In Jerusalem today, the *mitnagdim* outnumber the *hasidim*, the tension between them still potent.

Agudat Yisrael: The Patron Kings

When the Ashkenazi Jews, who dominate the *haredi* community, migrated to Jerusalem during the nineteenth century, they replicated the social world of Eastern Europe, condensing their many religious centers into a few neighborhoods. Opponents and rivals, once separated by weeks of wagon travel, were suddenly side by side.

Today no single rabbi or *rebbe* dare speaks for all *mitnagid* or Hasidic Jews. The *haredi* community is fragmented among followers of rival *rebbe*s and rabbis, whose animosities are based on differences over Zionism, personal rivalries, competition for money and living space, and doctrinal differences, large and small. Although the *haredim* all share an antipathy to the secular Jewish world, the tensions between their separate communities are ferocious.

Each *haredi* community, whether *hasid* or *mitnagid,* is self-contained, providing its members with all their necessities, jealously guarding the resources it raises that enable it to insulate its members from the outside world. Each has its own newspaper, its own schools, its own cooperative, called a *kollel*, through which funds for housing and material support are allocated; its own residential neighborhoods; and sometimes even its own taxi or bus service. Within each, housing, jobs, places in the yeshivah, military deferments, and services of every kind are distributed at the personal discretion of the leader.

There is no overarching structure of governance to which all *haredim* will adhere. Certainly no *haredi* group fully recognizes the authority of the Israeli state. The *haredim* do not generally call the police when trouble arises, and they try not to use the Israeli civil courts to litigate their differences. Indeed, although the Israeli security forces have easily infiltrated the Palestinian communities, they have found it difficult to penetrate those of the *haredim*. Informants are rare and simulating the *haredi* life-style is difficult. As a result, the *haredim* host a significant number of smugglers and tax evaders. Some *haredi* communities have also operated largely unregulated banking operations in Jerusalem used by the PLO to launder money for their activists inside.[24]

But if the *haredim* will not recognize Israeli courts, where does a *haredi* go to get a divorce, to litigate about inheritance? The predominantly *mitnagid* followers of Agudat Yisrael, which sits in the government, nonetheless refuse to have anything to do with the official Israel rabbinical courts. Agudat Yisrael maintains its own. The followers of the Edah Haredit, backed primarily by the *hasidim*, whose members will not sit in the Knesset, in turn refuse to recognize the Agudat Yisrael courts. The Edah Haredit has its own legal system. And the Belz *hasidim*, who recognize neither of the non-Zionist courts, have formed their own.

These divisions have serious consequences. Each independent religious court, for example, supervises *kashrut*, the determination of whether food is properly prepared. Certificates are issued to slaughter houses, grocery stores, bakeries, retaurants, vintners, and all producers of food. Kosher certification, a major source of income, is also an instrument of control because it tightly regulates who will eat with whom. Each community's members will only accept certification by "their" court. An older religious Zionist woman, for example, who kept a strictly kosher home complained sadly to us that one morning her grandchildren, who were studying in an Agudat Yisrael yeshivah, refused to have breakfast at her table for fear the orange juice had not been properly tithed and would not thereby be considered kosher within their own community.

When people marry across these boundary lines, there are complex negotiations about whose court will supervise the preparation and serving of food. Guests sometimes arrive at weddings with large hatboxes containing their own dishes and utensils. If the groom's family is from a different community, it may even provide an entirely separate meal for its own guests.

Each segment of the *haredim* is a patronage machine. Because *hallukah* – donations from abroad – have not kept pace with *haredi* population growth, the *haredim* have not been able to resist the temptation of state monies. Agudat Yisrael, which evolved into a non-Zionist *haredi* political party, has been the uncontested broker through which the municipality and the national state funneled funds and services to the *haredim* who would take them.

Access to state funding gave Agudat Yisrael great leverage in the *haredi* world. It also made them vulnerable to political attack, as corrupt stooges of Zionism. In 1977, the *haredi* take from state monies suddenly rose beyond anything anyone in Mea She'arim had ever dreamed possible. Menachem Begin, the right-wing Revisionist, the man David Ben-Gurion had once reviled as an enemy of the Jewish state, had defeated the Labour Party. But Begin's Likud Party was still sixteen votes short of a parliamentary majority. The religious parties controlled seventeen. For Agudat Yisrael it was a chance to raid the government treasury.

Excepting Israel's very first government, when Ben-Gurion allied himself with Agudat Yisrael to avoid having to rely on the communists, Agudat Yisrael had never been part of the governing coalition. They were, after all, not Zionists. In 1977, Begin brought them in. In exchange for their support, Likud promised to widen the "status quo agreement" Ben-Gurion had signed before the state was created. Orthodoxy's hold on who was a Jew would be tightened, public activities on Shabbat circumscribed. But most importantly, Agudat Yisrael was able for the first time to garner truly massive state funding, which they funneled directly to their institutions in Jerusalem, enabling them to dole out more jobs, more military deferments, and more money in exchange for political loyalty.

Agudat Yisrael in Jerusalem is run as a fiefdom of the Porush family. The family patriarch, Menachem Porush, is a longtime member of Knesset; his son, Meir, sits on the Jerusalem city council. The family also owns the Central Hotel, an establishment catering to Jerusalem's most observant Jewish tourists. Menachem, in his seventies, heavy-set, with a distinguished gray beard, is the party's king.

Once an enemy of Zionism, Agudat Yisrael for four decades has led the struggle to make the laws of the Jewish state conform to those of the Jewish people. Although they sit in Knesset, members of the party make it a point not to be present at its inaugural session when Ha-Tikvah, the national anthem, is played. Even though they depend heavily on state monies, Agudat Yisrael's schools still do not celebrate Israel independence day.

There are no Israeli flags, no pictures of Israel's founding patriots on the walls of Agudat Yisrael's dingy headquarters in Jerusalem. They are lined with pictures of revered rabbis and sages. When we first sat in Menachem Porush's outer party office in 1983, it was filled with people waiting for an opportunity to present their petitions. Teachers and rabbis in their schools, fathers of yeshivah students hoping for military deferments, young families anxious to secure housing loans, supplicants of every kind try to tap into the money and influence that flow through this office.

Porush told us that the major issue in Jerusalem was whether, as he put it, "religious Jews" can "live in Jerusalem according to religious law . . . We feel," he told us, "Jerusalem is not Paris. Jerusalem is not Rome. Jerusalem is not London. Jerusalem is a holy city." Porush has kept a tight rein on Agudat Yisrael, refusing to step aside and let others have a turn in the Knesset. Over the objections of many in his party, he

Meir Porush, Agudat Yisrael member of Jerusalem city council.

was also successful in getting his son, Meir, then still in his twenties, to take the party's helm in the city council.

The Jews of the Other East

Agudat Yisrael had led the way to state power and to the rising volume of monies. But there were those *haredim* who wanted their own and others who despised what they saw as a corrupt, religious machine that Porush kept well oiled with public funds. Like most Western nations,

Israel has a proportional system of representation. A citizen votes for a list of candidates who speak on behalf of their parties, not for this or that district. Where a political party has to capture only a small percentage of the electorate to be heard, there are major incentives to break away and form new parties.

In this system of competing party machines, each dishing out jobs, favors, and services to its constituents, power has a personal basis. Cliques develop quickly and the stakes are too high to allow much constituent influence inside the party itself. Groups that cannot obtain representation in the parties that claim their allegiance reach for power by forming their own.

Rabbi Eliezer Shach, one of the most revered Lithuanian *mitnagid* rabbis in Israel, has led the way. Shach, who headed Agudat Yisrael's rabbinic court, was uncomfortable that there was any Hasidic influence within the party. In 1977, for example, Avraham Shapira, a Gerrer *hasid* Knesset member from Agudat Yisrael and then a wealthy manufacturer of carpets, captured the chairmanship of the Knesset Finance Committee. Shach made no secret of his disdain for the Gerrer *rebbe*, who sat on the rabbinic court with him as his co-chair. The conflict between them became so bad Agudat Yisrael's court literally fell apart in the mid-1980s as Rabbi Shach quit, leaving the party as well.[25] Shach was also enraged that Menachem Porush was taking the lion's share of monies for his own educational system, Kiryat Yeled.

Because of Shach's extraordinary influence, his leaving enabled other groups to break away from Agudat Yisrael. The first to bolt, with the blessing of Rabbi Shach, were the Jews of the "other" East, those of the Middle East and North Africa. When Israel became a state, the *haredi* community was, for all intents and purposes, Ashkenazi. The Sephardim of the old *yishuv*, although they did not respond with particular enthusiasm to Zionism, did not oppose it on theological grounds. Over time many were gradually caught up in, and almost all went along with, the Zionist project.

As Jews from Fez, Cairo, and Bagdhad, overwhelmingly devout, began to arrive in Israel after statehood, many uprooted from communities in which they had lived for hundreds of years, the Ashkenazi *mitnagdim* saw them as kin and allies, as reverent peoples to be protected from Zionist secularism.[26] A small number were inducted directly into *mitnagid* yeshivahs, where they dressed in East European clothes and spoke Yiddish. Later, parallel institutions, modeled on those of the Ashkenazim, were set up for them; there they were instructed by Ashkenazi teachers and rabbis.

Gradually a community of Sephardi Jews developed within the *haredi* world. These *edot ha-mizrach*, the olive-skinned "peoples of the east," were bitter their own distinctive rituals and liturgies were not respected, their songs not sung, their culture demeaned, and their institutions given short shrift in the allocation of resources. The Ashkenazi *haredim* regard them as social inferiors. Intermarriage is a sensitive index. Whereas secular Ashkenazim increasingly marry Jews of Moroccan or Iraqi origin (currently above 20 percent), among the "ultra-Orthodox," marriages with Jews from the Arab world are almost unheard of. "You'd have to be crazy," an Ashkenazi yeshivah student maintained.

The Oriental Jews concluded that ethnic dignity depended on power. In Jerusalem's 1983 elections, they formed their own party, the Sephardi Torah Guardians, or SHAS, as it is known by its acronym. Although the Oriental Jews call themselves Sephardim, the "true" Sephardim originating in Spain and Portugal don't regard them as such. These latter refer to themselves as the *samekh tet*, the Hebrew letters for *sephardi tehorah*, meaning pure Sephardi, to distinguish themselves from Oriental Jews who arrived in Palestine centuries later. If the classical Sephardim once disdained the Ashkenazi newcomers as uncouth and ill bred, both groups looked down upon the largely lower-class Jews from North Africa and the Middle East who poured into Palestine in the early 1950s, those of Morocco being the largest and most problematic group.

There had always been traffic between the Jews of Spain and North Africa, but they had never been a single people. When Spain and then Portugal exiled their entire Jewish communities in 1492 and 1495, Jews fled in waves across the channel to the Maghreb, the region to the "west" of Egypt. A great many exiles settled in Fez and Casablanca in Morocco, where they met Jews who were, by their standards, uncultured and desperately poor, some of whom had interrmarried with members of Berber tribes. The highly cultured exiles looked with disdain upon most of the indigenous Jews, whom they called Berberiscos. The skilled Jewish administrators and merchants from Spain and Portugal quickly dominated the community, many becoming brokers between the sultans in the Muslim interior and the Portuguese who held tenaciously to their outposts along the coast.

The Jews of the Maghreb, like other Jews living under Muslim rule, had their status delimited by the Pact of Umar, Jerusalem's seventh-century surrender treaty to Prophet Muhammad's invading armies led by the second caliph, Umar ibn al-Khattab. Wherever Muslims ruled, this pact became a prototype for Islamic treatment of non-Muslims. In exchange for protection of their rights to practice their religions, Jews and Christians were subjected to various kinds of taxes, as well as social, political, and legal restrictions. No synagogue, for example, could be higher than a mosque. Jews couldn't carry arms or ride horses. They were forbidden from testifying against a Muslim in court or from holding high office. The

Jews were considered a *dhimmi*, or protected, people, entitled to a legal status enjoyed by pre-Islamic monotheistic and prophetic traditions recognized by Muhammad: Christianity, Zoroastrianism, Judaism, and that of the Sabeans.

In some places, Umar's pact was loosely interpreted and Jews prospered. In others, life was harsh and Jews were particularly vulnerable. The Muslims of the Maghreb enforced the harshest subjugation of the Jews almost anywhere in the Arab world. If the Muslims wore white, a mark of purity, Jews were forced to wear black hats, black caps, and black slippers. In some towns, Jews were forbidden to wear shoes outside the *mellah*, or Jewish ghetto; in others, they were only allowed to wear sandals made of straw.[27] If Muslims could ride horses, Jews were confined to mules.

Before 1948, Zionists tried to persuade the Moroccan Jews to come to Palestine, but without success. The Zionists were seen as white moderns, socialists without faith, speaking about the incredible, while Jewish life in Morocco seemed to be improving steadily. In the 1950s, however, after Israel became a reality, almost a million Jews immigrated to Israel from Islamic lands. These Jews were both pushed by pogroms that swept through the Arab world in the wake of the 1948 war and pulled by the prospect of living in an existing Jewish state. Some walked thousands of miles across the deserts; others were airlifted in emergency convoys, like the Yemenite Jews, whose very existence was at stake. In the aftermath of the war, more Jews were forcibly exiled by Arab terror and the threat of it than Arabs who had been pushed out of their lands by the conquering Israelis.

Faced with a wave of immigration that would test any nation's capacities, especially an impoverished, infant state that had just won a war to secure its survival against tremendous odds, the Ashkenazi Zionist elite did not have time or temperament to assimilate these Jews in a delicate fashion. (They often called the Oriental Jews "primitives.") It did not help matters that many of the more prosperous, educated North African Jewish families, those who might have better brokered their people's entry into this new land, chose not to go to Israel, but left for Paris or New York.

The Israelis considered their job to make the new immigrants into Israelis as fast as possible and to use them to bolster the state's vulnerable defenses. Over the protests of the *haredim*, boys' earlocks were unceremoniously sheared as they passed through the transit camps. The Labour Zionists saw no great need to co-opt the Oriental Jewish leaders, and the old Sephardi elite did not want to be identified with these tattered masses landing on Israel's shore. North African Jews were not integrated into the *kibbutzim*, but used as unskilled labor to settle peripheral areas. Many a skilled artisan was forced to do unskilled manual labor in order to survive. Fathers held their shame, while their sons grew up with their rage.

In Jerusalem, many settled in bunker-like housing complexes and others squatted along the then dangerous border with Jordan.[28] The Marciano family, who had come from Morocco, moved in right after the war. Rafi Marciano, Musrara's first-born Jewish child, was born in 1950 into a family of eleven children who, together with three grandparents, lived in two rooms. Arab snipers fired randomly into the neighborhood. These Moroccan families often had little to eat, no heat, and insufficient clothing. To make extra money when he was young, Rafi Marciano scavenged among the houses in the mined no-man's-land for antiques and abandoned furniture to sell in the market. "We saw the border, the no-man's-land, as a fortune," he said. "We used the border as our work."

Today Musrara, which before 1948 had been a suburb built by affluent Palestinians, is a poor Moroccan neighborhood along the pre-1967 no-man's-land next to the Old City. When we attended a community play there, facetiously titled *Milk and Honey,* much of the community turned out. On stage a fair-haired, white-skinned Zionist emissary, a woman dressed in pith helmet and khaki shorts, conjured up the new Jewish society to the Jews in Morocco. Teenagers in the audience jeered and whistled at what they felt had been empty promises. Their parents were the poorest, the most likely to be illiterate, who now, if they were lucky, were supervisors of unskilled Palestinian workers who were doing the jobs they did before 1967.

Many Jerusalemites steer clear of the Moroccan neighborhoods, fearing violent gangs, drug dealers, pickpockets, prostitutes, and the unattended children who seem to roam there with no purpose except to make trouble. Despite years of community work, these neighborhoods remain central in the drug trade; heroin has replaced hashish as the primary narcotic on the local market. The Moroccan kids, who grow up tough, angry, and undisciplined, fill the Israeli prisons.

Jewish Saints

The Sephardim are different (and here we use the term – Sephardim – Oriental Jews use to describe themselves). You can hear it in their prayers, which are said in unison, melodically, unlike the discordant *mitnagid* liturgy. There was no European-style Enlightenment, no "rights of man," in the Arab world. Arab Jews are all deeply religious, but their Judaism is alien to the Ashkenazim, particularly the *mitnagdim* who dominate Agudat Yisrael.

Sephardi piety emphasizes good intentions, not behavioral conformity with the law. Pious Moroccan Jews pray fervently on Shabbat morning and then take their sons to football games in the afternoon. To many of them, the world is controlled by divine forces that can be placated, cajoled, bribed. Moroccan Jews still use talismans to ward off the evil eye. Old bread is never thrown away, but left on ledges and windowsills for the *shedim*, or spirits.

The religiosity of the North African Jews is simply an embarassment to many observant Ashkenazim. Ashkenazi tradition reveres the prophets; it does not worship them. The Moroccan Jews, in contrast, believe in saints. They obey their rabbi not simply because he understands the law, but, not unlike the Hasidic *rebbe*, because he is an intercessor to God with powers to cure and heal. In Musrara, we were told, the neighborhood rabbi had been angered by a young man who had repeatedly smoked on the Shabbat in his presence. This continued even after the rabbi asked him not to. The rabbi, it was said, caused the young man to go blind. Women who are not able to conceive go to neighborhood rabbis, who perform magical rituals designed to ensure their fertility.

Moroccan Jewish veneration of saints was adapted from Muslim custom.[29] Indeed, in some cases the two communities worshiped the same saints. Shimon Bar-Yochai is the most important Moroccan saint, a contemporary of the second Jewish revolt against Rome in 132–135 C.E. Bar-Yochai, the tradionally ascribed author of the *Zohar*, the most important Jewish mystical text of the Middle Ages, is understood to be buried in the Galilean mountain town of Meron. His memorial day falls on Lag ba'Omer, the thirty-third day of counting the *omer*, or wheat crop, between the holidays of Passover and Shavuot.

Each year hundreds of thousands of Sephardi Jews visit the grave of Bar-Yochai, camping out in tents for days at a time, drinking and feasting on meat ritually slaughtered on the spot. Sephardi Jews visit the tomb to ask Shimon Bar-Yochai to cure their infertility, to heal their illnesses. They go with their husbands and their wives to make love in their tents at night, for it is a propitious time to conceive. They go because they promised during battle that if they survived, they would make the pilgrimage. They go because Shimon Bar-Yochai has appeared to them in a dream. They go because they are his namesakes.

Carefully regulated by hundreds of police, we entered his tomb, hundreds of men, women, and children all pressed together. The room smells of sweat; bottles of arak, a potent alcoholic drink made of anise, pass mouth to mouth between strangers. It brings good fortune to share in this sacred spot. People pray in front of the tomb, tie pieces of cloth to its grating, and throw candles, rosewater, and even underwear on it. Up in the dry hills, hundreds of sheep are being slaughtered, the red blood running down the hill, soaking into the dust.

"Knives and Forks"

The Sephardi Jews who immigrated to Israel right after statehood were absorbed by organizations on the left and the right, religious and secular, largely controlled by Ashkenazim. The Sephardim were unable to reach beyond the lowest levels of the political hierarchy. And so it was the highly observant among them who became loyal clients in Agudat Yisrael's religious machine.

But beginning in the early 1970s, young North African Jews in Jerusalem – often unemployed, living in dilapidated state housing projects – launched a series of social movements that challenged, sometimes violently, their miserable condition. What galled them in particular was the juxtaposition of the state's apparent indifference to them to the loans and superior housing lavished on new immigrants from Russia, Poland, and Romania.[30] Ethnic hostility against the Ashkenazim of the ruling Labour Party steadily mounted.

By the early 1980s, the most devout Sephardi Jews who had been part of Agudat Yisrael had also had enough. Among North African Jews, the rabbis were always real, as well as ritual, leaders. In 1983, with the blessing of the former Sephardic chief rabbi, Ovadiah Yosef, and the renegade *mitnagid*, Eliezer Shach, they broke away to form the Sephardi Torah Guardians, or SHAS. Jerusalem's city politics would hatch a new national force.

Most of the rabbis who worked in synagogues and schools supported by Agudat Yisrael were then Ashkenazim; not a single member of Agudat Yisrael's Jerusalem secretariat was Sephardi. Ya'acov Cohen, who sold religious books, was a prime mover behind the party's birth in Jerusalem. Cohen explained to us that the party was born so that the Sephardim could get their fair share. "In order to eat, you need knives and forks," he said.

Getting resources for Sephardi institutions was a path to advancement, but it was also a means to promote Sephardi traditions and defend their dignity. The very first SHAS manifesto proclaimed:

> We came on Aliya along with our fathers, teachers and rabbis – behind us an ancient and prestigious past and it's as if all this had disappeared from us. When we look at our position today, we tremble at the sad and fearful spectacle that instead of sitting at the head along with our Ashkenazi brothers, they have pushed us . . . into a corner and have turned us into servants, reigning over us.

Shlomo Dayan, one of the new party's candidates, compared his people to Jacob, who had trusted Laban. The Sephardim, he said, had for too long put their faith in what he called the "people with beards."

Agudat Yisrael's bearded old Poles and Litvaks reacted indignantly, its rabbinical court forbidding the very formation of the new party. Sephardi teachers and rabbis employed by institutions funded by Agudat Yisrael were asked to sign political loyalty oaths. The Sephardi teachers refused. When the votes were tallied, the Sephardi Torah Guardians had scored a spectacular victory in 1983, capturing the same number of council seats as Agudat Yisrael. Agudat Yisrael's religious directorate tried to use the authority of its rabbinic court to stop them from going into coalition with Teddy Kollek. But the Sephardi Torah Guardians no longer recognized Agudat Yisrael's rabbinical court, having formed their own.

SHAS not only spoke for Sephardi *haredim*, it became the standard-bearer for Sephardim from all over the city. SHAS, which replaced Agudat Yisrael in Teddy Kollek's municipal coalition, proved to be just as intractable on religious issues and much more extreme in the handling of relations with the city's Palestinians than Agudat Yisrael had ever been. From their victory in Jerusalem, in elections the following year they catapulted to national power in the Knesset, a position they have subsequently consolidated.[31]

A Citizen in Torah

Among the devout, it wasn't just Sephardim who were dissatisfied with Agudat Yisrael. Many pious Ashkenazim had become equally outraged about the party's patronage machine. When we spoke to Meir Porush, Agudat's leader in the city council, during his 1989 campaign for council, he had been busy, he boasted, delivering twenty-nine thousand "favors" – personal interventions to secure services such as building permits, trash collection, installation of a street light, support for schooling – in his last five years as a member of Jerusalem's city council.

Again in 1989, the rebellious Rabbi Shach, now ninety-two years old, played patron to a new party. Rabbi Shach, a dove, was not happy about Agudat Yisrael's alliance with the territorial maximalist Likud. More-over, if the *mitnagid* rabbi disliked the *hasidim*, he positively hated the evangelizing Habad, which had waded into Israeli politics for the first time as supporters of Agudat Yisrael in the 1988 national elections. About Habad, Rabbi Shach can go apoplectic, calling the Habad *rebbe* "insane, an infidel, and a false messiah," whose followers are "eaters of *treyf* [nonkosher food]."[32] Their *rebbe*, Menachem Mendel Schneersohn, lived in Crown Heights, Brooklyn, and had never been to Jerusalem. It didn't help matters that the Habad Hasidim, the largest Hasidic community in the world, proclaimed that Schneersohn was the messiah.

When the Habad *rebbe* himself refused to deny interpretations that he was the messiah, Rabbi Shach demanded before the 1988 national elections that Habad be banished from Agudat Yisrael.[33] When the party refused, Shach struck again. To launch the new party, Degel ha-Torah, "The Flag of the Torah," he chose a group of *haredi* Jews who demanded that they receive their due because they were citizens, not because they were loyal clients of Agudat Yisrael. Large segments of the *haredim* had been moving, slowly but surely, toward a middle-class existence, toward acceptance of the state as an instrument to regulate public life according to Torah.

These middle-class *haredim* were led by Rabbi Avraham Ravitz, the son of one of Tel Aviv's eminent rabbis, who came to Jerusalem as a young boy to study in yeshivah. Ravitz fought in the right-wing Lehi underground in 1948. Once the battle for the state had been won, he threw himself against the forces of Jewish secularization, working with Sephardi immigrants who, he claimed, were being lured from their religious traditions. Later he helped build new yeshivahs for the city's burgeoning movement back to Judaism, teaching, for example, at Or Semeach, the "Happy Light" yeshivah for "born-again" Jews.

Ravitz lives in a modern apartment complex in one of the first middle-class *haredi* suburbs within the city, Beit Ve-Gan ("House and Garden"). Unlike their counterparts in Mea She'arim, the streets are clean with paved sidewalks and neat rows of apartments with small gardens front and back. Ravitz met us in his spacious living room. From one of Jerusalem's many high ridges, a large picture window looked out on the Knesset below.

Rabbi Ravitz was enraged that *haredi* Jews didn't receive the same level of services as the secular and that everything depended on one's political connections to Agudat Yisrael, who handed them out as political favors. "The truth is," he first told us in 1984, pointing his index finger at us, "that up 'til today, we don't get our rights. I'll take you to where my boys are learning and you won't believe it that such a place exists in Israel. We are not poor . . . [but] the teacher of my boys is not getting the same salary that a teacher who teaches the secular gets. Why? Because we don't get our rights in an established way."

In the run-up to the municipal elections of 1989, Ravitz angrily recalled a recent newspaper advertisement in Agudat Yisrael's newspaper, *Ha-Modiyah*. Mockingly, he recalled how neighbors on Tzefanniyah Street had taken out "a big ad of thank you to Meir Porush [who sits on the city council]. They thank him with such schmaltzy words, with titles and who knows what for being our hero, our big delegate. For what?

He, with his whole effort, made the city should bring garbage cans to Tzefanniyah Street."

"*I* want the garbage cans in their place," Ravitz continued, "because I'm a citizen and I don't want to give anybody a thank you."

In Jerusalem's city council and Israel's Knesset, Agudat Yisrael engages in continuous logrolling, trading monies for synagogues, schools, and housing for votes on other issues. Services for religious neighborhoods as a whole rarely become an issue. Indeed, Ravitz alleged, Menachem Porush had used his party's leverage to funnel public monies disproportionately into his private network of religious institutions.

Ravitz thought Agudat Yisrael's whole way of doing business undercut the legitimacy of religious Jewry. How, Ravitz asked us rhetorically, do secular voters see his community? "They are taking money and they are squeezing us," he imagined their answer. And everything, including issues Ravitz holds most dear, appeared to have a price. For example, when Jerusalem wanted to build an amphitheater in the Jewish Quarter of the Old City, Agudat Yisrael objected, arguing it would violate its sanctity. Ravitz recounted that the city then began to bargain with Agudat Yisrael with promises of more money for their synagogues. The horsetrading embarrassed him. When Porush speaks, he told us, "I am so ashamed that I want to bury myself."

Ravitz had tried in 1983 to form a break-away party, Tali, to challenge Agudat Yisrael in the city. When the new party failed to get even one seat, a relieved Menachem Porush dismissed Ravitz and his ilk as self-seeking upstarts, "fourth or fifth rank" people, he called them. But Ravitz kept on. In 1988, his Degel Ha-Torah Party won two Knesset seats, with considerable support from Jerusalem's *haredi* Jews. The next year, Degel Ha-Torah bid for city power. As soon as the returns came in giving the party three seats in Jerusalem's city council, Ravitz was on the phone to the mayor's office. "We are going to be your partners," he told a Kollek aide. "Tell Teddy I'm ready."

Ravitz is a kind of religious technocrat, a man who wants to plan the city's piety. Secular and religious Jews, he believes, provoke each other needlessly. The city should build all Jewish neighborhoods with synagogues, *mikvahs*, and religious schools so that religious families can live wherever they want.

Ravitz is a democrat. "We are not fighting the country should be religious," he claimed to us in 1989. But where democracy and Judaism collide, it is still democracy that must sometimes give way. That the rabbi wanted his rights did not mean he was any less demanding about Jerusalem's public life.

> Jerusalem . . . is not just a place to live . . . We religious people know what Jerusalem means. In the public we want Jerusalem to

look like a Jewish city. On Shabbat everything should be closed. The pornographic pictures [referring to bathing suit advertisements on bus shelters] should not be in the street . . . Jerusalem is different and you don't do things which profane it, even if it takes a little away from democracy.

That yeshivah boys throw stones at cars that come too close to their neighborhoods on Shabbat, Ravitz has no doubt, is wrong. "If I saw someone throwing stones, I would fight against him because it is against the *halakhah* [religious law]," he told us. One Shabbat in the early 1980s, an eminent Hebrew University professor, a Jerusalemite, made a wrong turn into a *haredi* neighborhood. When *haredi* youth stoned his car, one of the stones knocked him unconscious and for three months, he lay in a coma. The evening after he came to, Ravitz, together with other *haredi* leaders from the Edah Haredit, went to his hospital room to wish him a complete recovery. For Ravitz, their condolence call was an index of their responsibility, their morality. And, Ravitz wanted us to know, the *haredi* community found the boy who had thrown the near-fatal stone. He had been punished by the Edah Haredit's religious court.

"What was the punishment?" we inquired.

"I don't know," Ravitz replied; "perhaps they threw him out of the yeshivah. They sent him to Bene Berak [a *haredi* suburb of Tel Aviv]. I don't know, they are doing all kinds of things."

"They never turned him over to the Israeli police?" we asked.

"No, he was not given to the secular authorities. You know what they would do with this boy? . . . I am going to the jails a lot and lecturing there and jail is a very bad place for a young man. I think that they are very, very bad places. The police don't have any other choice, they have to put him in jail. We are against jails!"

Voting for Torah

The *haredim* have come out to vote in ever increasing numbers, winning a progressively larger share of Jerusalem's city council. The *haredim's* growing willingness to vote for representation in the Zionist state has many motives, some of them decidedly material. As a result of their population explosion and their ability to secure funds and deferments from the government, the number of full-time Torah students has sky-rocketed. Funds from abroad simply cannot keep pace. Nor is employment as schoolteachers, ritual slaughterers, scribes, supervisors of *kashrut* and ritual baths, shopkeepers catering to the religious – the traditional *haredi* sources of income – sufficient. *Haredi* women have been compelled to enter the work force in record numbers. For many

Heder students of the Stolin-Karliner *hasidim*, 1989.

haredi families poverty, real poverty, is already at the door. State funding has become vital to survival.

So, too, the electoral arena of the once-hated Israeli state has gradually become a vehicle to establish one's credentials within the *haredi*
community. Electoral politics has become a way to defend one's honor
and denigrate one's detractors. In 1989, even Neture-Karta rabbis, at
the anti-Zionist fringe, were privately phoning city officials in Kollek's
administration to lobby for one non-Zionist party or another as a coalition partner. Slowly, but surely, each part of the old *yishuv*, the first
Jewish pioneers in Zion who fought so strenuously against Zionism, is
being absorbed into electoral politics of the once profane state. Those
who understood Zionism as antithetical to Judaism increasingly seek to
use it to secure the moral authority and material success of their Judaism, and to make that Judaism the criterion against which the state's
action must be measured. Zionism's Jewish enemies now strive to set
themselves up as Zion's spiritual guardians.

4

Sabbath Wars

The United Nations chose May 15, 1948, as the day to partition Palestine into a Jewish and an Arab state. This choice presented a problem: May 15 was the Jewish Sabbath. And so Israel officially proclaimed its statehood on Friday afternoon, May 14.[1]

Time is at the heart of the struggle between Zionism and Judaism. The Bible narrates how God created the heavens and earth in six days, and on the seventh, he rested. Religious Jews understand the observance of Shabbat, from sunset Friday to sunset Saturday, both as a ritual reenactment of God's repose and as a reaffirmation of the covenant between God and Israel.

Identity is a matter of orientation, a common attention to particular places and times, to centers that bind a people to one another and identify them as so bound. These spaces, these times, become signs of the collectivity. Different use of time separates one people from another. For millennia, Shabbat observance has been fundamental to Jewish identity. To establish its distinctiveness, the early Christian community sacralized an alternative day. Still later, Muhammad called upon his followers to separate themselves with their own day of gathering.

For religious Jews, Jerusalem is the center of space, the Shabbat, the center of time. Those who hold this city sacred feel bound to protect the order of things; they cannot imagine that here, the most sacred of all places, the divisions of space and time would not be aligned one to the other. It should come as no surprise that in Jerusalem, the *haredim*, the religious remains of the old *yishuv*, fight with particular ferocity to defend this most sacred moment. They are fighting, after all, to protect the primordial signs by which Jews have always marked themselves off as a separate and holy people.

Medieval and early modern Jewish mystics imagined the Shabbat as a woman, and not just any woman, but a *kallah*, a "bride," or a *malkah*, a "queen." In the town of Safed, in the Galilee, dressed in royal white garments, Jews went to the town's boundaries to greet the Shabbat. The mystics envisioned the Shabbat as an elaborate marriage ritual between God and his *shekhinah*, or feminine presence, as symbolized by the

Shabbat bride. Separated by the profane time of the week, bride and groom now came together to take their marriage vows and consummate their union. This mystical symbolism still permeates Jerusalem's *haredi* communities. Men prepare themselves by immersion in the ritual baths. The *hasidim* don their finest clothing – freshly pressed white shirts, black or gold coats, topped with exquisite ermine or mink hats – as each prepares to meet the bride of God.

Shabbat is a creational time. Long ago the idea arose that on Shabbat new souls are created and introduced into the world, where they can enter the wombs of married women. This mystical gynecology has left a contemporary residue among many *haredim* who consider the Shabbat the most appropriate day for husband and wife to fulfill their obligation to be fruitful and multiply. By making their own sexual intercourse coincide with the day commemorating divine creation, they guarantee its success.

Observant Jews refrain from all forms of work on the Shabbat, replicating God's rest at the beginning of time. Work is not simply physical exertion but consists of specific prohibited activities drawn from the building of the Tent of Meeting as the Israelites wandered in the desert after their exodus from Egypt. Among other things, a Jew cannot sow, plow, or reap a field; bind sheaves; grind or sift grain; bake; spin wool; weave; light or extinguish a fire; or carry an object from one domain to another.[2]

Over the centuries, new forms of activity were interpreted within these categories. Moses did not prohibit the use of the automobile, but the rabbis interpreted the combustion starting a car's engine as the kindling of fire.[3] The turning of a light switch was understood similarly. Electric lights are either turned on before Shabbat and left burning or they are put on automatic timers. One of the last things an Orthodox woman might do before lighting the Shabbat candles is to tape the trigger in her refrigerator that automatically turns on the light inside when she opens the door. Otherwise, the refrigerator would be unusable.

City Tempo

Shabbat affects all of Jewish Jerusalem. Unlike Tel Aviv, a city built from scratch, where the *haredim* were never numerous enough to press their demands, everything in Jerusalem is closed for Shabbat's twenty-four hours: restaurants, markets, shops, and almost all drugstores. By Thursday afternoon, the pace quickens as people do their major shopping. By midday Friday, the bread bins in the markets have been picked clean. West Jerusalem's old central market, Mahaneh Yehudah, swarms with customers. Clerks leave offices early to do their own shopping. Never known for their queueing skills, lines of Israelis dissolve as each person presses on her or his own trajectory to the cash register or to the front door of ever more crowded public buses. Everybody desperately tries to finish business before the city closes down.

But by midafternoon Friday, Jerusalem is still. And by the time the city's air-raid sirens wail Shabbat's official beginning, few cars move anywhere in the commercial center. Without the traffic's din, one hears conversations, arguments, and solo musical passages as violins, pianos, and clarinets are played.

To secure their acquiescence in the Zionist project at its most fragile moment, David Ben-Gurion, as we have seen, came to an understanding with Agudat Yisrael in 1947 that declared Saturday would be Israel's official day of rest. Right after Israel became a state and Jerusalem an almost all-Jewish municipality, the religious Jews were able to close down most of the city's restaurants and all its theaters on Shabbat. The Orthodox used their electoral influence on the city council. They also used force. In 1949, for instance, when the city's cinema owners tried to squeeze in two shows on Saturday evening, one before Shabbat ended, mobs of Orthodox men broke into the theaters, physically attacking both the moviegoers and the policemen who tried to defend them.

The concentration of religious Jews of all types in the city was also a market businesses could not afford to alienate. Almost all restaurants were compelled to provide kosher food. An establishment serving on Shabbat would not be considered kosher, even by the state's own rabbis. Hotels placed their cash registers behind screens so their more observant guests would not be offended by the public exchange of money.

Saturday is Jerusalem's only night on the town. In the summer, darkness descends too slowly for the cafés and eateries. Each time Israel toyed with using daylight savings time, the *haredi* community opposed it. Darkness would come later and the shopkeepers would likely open their shutters before Shabbat was over in order to do a decent business on the one weekend night that Jerusalemites can go out to eat and to see movies.

The city's secular citizens gradually adapted. Special concerts and film screenings are scheduled right after work on Friday afternoons, before Shabbat comes in. On Saturdays, friends often walk long distances to visit each other so as not to disrupt the city's quiet. Few cars move along the city's residential streets. Groups, large and small, trek across the hillsides surrounding the city and ferret out the city's archaeological and historical secrets. Even nonkosher establishments like Fink's, Jerusalem's best bar, go along. Here you can get good whisky, good steaks, and pork cutlets (or "white meat" as the city's few butchers who sell it

Shimon Grama, rabbi and dean of Migdal Oz Seminary for
Teachers, with two of his daughters in Kiryat Tzanz, 1984.

euphemistically call it). But in deference to Shabbat, David Rothschild,
the moustached proprietor, closes down on Friday night and Saturday as
well. "I came to the conclusion that everybody has to have a day of
rest," he told us.

The Shabbes Queen

Shimon Grama will defend Shabbat with his life. Grama, who came
from New York's Borough Park more than two decades ago, lives in Beit
Mattisdorf, one of Jerusalem's more modern religious neighborhoods.
Sitting in a small spartan apartment he shares with his wife and their
eleven children, who ran noisily from room to room, he remembered, "I
came here as an American with my plaid jacket and my green pants, like
a good American yeshivah boy. And I had my straw hat in the summer. . . All the children would look at me."

Grama had been a youth leader in the largest American branch of
Agudat Yisrael. Orthodox outreach programs in the United States were
drawing in young Jews who had been through the sexual, chemical, and
political experimentation of the 1960s. Grama developed a street-wise
presentation of Orthodoxy that was legendary on the upstate New York
Jewish summer camp circuit.

In Jerusalem, Americans like Grama were the first to offer Judaism to the thousands of young people who gravitated here each year looking for moral anchorage. Today the city has a vast range of institutions serving this burgeoning community of "born-again" Jews. But it all started, he reminded us, "with five kids coming over for Shabbes." Originally the movement back to Jewish piety drew mostly immigrants from America and England, but it has increasingly attracted native-born Israelis, both poor young men from North African families and the more established native-born Ashkenazim.

When he arrived in Israel Grama was struck by the teenagers' singing "Jail House Rock" on the buses, mouthing words only a few actually understood. This hunger for American culture, he thought, was symptomatic of a nationalist movement that would invent Israel anew. "Anything American," he lamented, "*mamash* [really], you could make a mint on. Anything to get away from the past, from what you are." Unruffled by the constant shouts, giggles, and screams of his own enormous family, he continued, "There's no father, no mother. Everything had to come from nothing."

You can see the problem in the words of "Ha-Tikvah," Israel's national anthem, he insisted. The Israelis sing the words, *Leot am hofshi be'artzenu*, "to be a free people in our land."

> *Hofshi* means "free" and it was taken to be not only free from non-Jews, but free from everything. . . A non-religious Jew . . . wants to be free from the commandments . . . It was obvious when I came here that their objective was to be free of anything having to do with religion. Religion was archaic and they were thoroughly embarrassed by it. . . That's the reason why any [of our ambassadors] in the UN, whenever they got up to speak, they never mentioned God; while in America, there has never been a president who could not mention God. . . The first president that I really remember is John Kennedy. . . God was always on his lips. And it's obvious that every country must have some religion. That's the basis of countries and it should be the basis of this country.

The laws of the Torah constitute a seamless web, none of which can be compromised without eroding its entire basis. "The moment you begin to compromise on what is said in the Torah," Grama said, "you have lost it. Because Torah is from God and God is a noncompromising thing."

If the laws of the state contradict those of God, Shimon Grama says he will die rather than deviate from his obligations. "If the government says that you may not study Torah, you may not observe the Shabbat, or circumcise your children, as the Greeks did in their time, you must follow Torah. And even if it is punishable by death, that is how you show

your love for God, as your parents did and their parents before them."
In a Jewish country, Grama argued, "There can only be one law, the law
of the Jewish people. This is an ancient law. It did not start in 1948. It did
not come from the Romans and it did not come from the British. It is
thousands and thousands of years old."

Grama is Shabbat's ready defender. Jerusalem, of all places, he insisted vehemently, should stop working on Shabbat. He was not really
worried about who would prevail. "The problem of Shabbes has been
here for years," he confidently told us, using the Ashkenazi pronunciation. "But in each and every generation, a new guy gets up and tries to
stab Shabbes in the back, and he goes down like all the rest. Shabbes
never went down for anyone. Shabbes never got on its knees for anyone.
People who have tried with Shabbes never got anywhere. It just doesn't
work. What can I tell you, you're talking about a Queen."

Jerusalem Shabbat Circle

In 1949, David Ben-Gurion's government made Jerusalem the capital of
the infant state and began to strengthen the Zionist presence there.
Jerusalem had never been a Zionist stronghold and the *haredim* viewed
his secular nationalism with contempt. Ben-Gurion's government consciously restricted the *haredi* community's expansion in the capital.
Haredi neighborhoods were surrounded, by hostile Arabs on one side,
and by hostile Jews on the other. To the north and east they were
hemmed in by the armistice lines. To the south they were blocked by the
Zionists. Ben-Gurion reached an understanding with *haredi* leadership
that they would not jump westward over Jaffa Road, the major artery
linking the city to the coastal plain and Tel Aviv.

Between 1949 and 1967, the *haredi* population grew rapidly through a
high birth rate and immigration. Their population densities became unbearable, with whole families forced into one room, while their margin
for expansion was reduced even further by the government's policy of
settling newly arrived North African Jews in bunker-like housing blocks
along the border with Jordan. The municipal authorities were forced to
allow the *haredim* to add second stories to their buildings, but it was not
enough. Overcrowding became so severe, many were forced to migrate
to peripheral areas.[4]

The Six-Day War removed the barriers to *haredi* expansion. The
Knesset, Israel's parliament, expanded the borders of the now united
muncipality and began to "thicken" it, as the policy was called, with
Jews.[5] The Israeli government built model neighborhoods so that a big
chunk of the new Jewish population would be able to move into the

Interior court of a *haredi* housing complex in Mea She'arim, 1991.

newly liberated northern areas. However, the north was also the natural trajectory for *haredi* expansion. Conflict between the new, not particularly religious Jewish residents who were more than likely to profane the Shabbat and the rapidly expanding *haredi* community exploded a decade later in Ramot, a large northern suburb built within the new boundaries of the city.

In 1975, the Jerusalem city government planned a six lane motorway connecting Ramot with the city. Ramot, just like Gilo to the south, was planned as part of the government's efforts to surround the Arab neighborhoods of East Jerusalem with a line of Jewish settlement. Perched just below Nebi Samwil, where Muslims and Jews believe that the prophet Samuel is buried, Ramot has a panoramic view over the city below. The new suburb offered subsidized housing, space to build one's own villa with large backyards and ultramodern facilities. It was located on the old armistice line, and not far into newly conquered territory. Liberal Israelis could move into the new suburbs without compromising their consciences.

Beyond the government's desire to increase the number of Jews living in the newly expanded municipality of Jerusalem, key municipal planners like Meron Benvenisti, then deputy mayor, saw the road as a natural barrier, a way to set the limits for northward and eastward Jewish residential expansion. Benvenisti wanted to maintain the boundedness of the city, to keep Jerusalem free of urban sprawl. "Once it [Jerusalem]

"Build your own homes" on the western outskirts of Ramot, 1984.

will become a continuous housing estate all the way down to Tel Aviv,"
he told us, the feeling of going "up" to Jerusalem will be lost.[6]

But there was a problem. *Haredi* neighborhoods stood between
Ramot and the central city; the new road would have to cut right
through them. At a few points near its beginning, the road ran very close
to religious apartment buildings. Farther on, it ran along the bottom of
bluffs on top of which there were *haredi* neighborhoods. Because the
road would be a source of Shabbat traffic, Teddy Kollek, the city's
mayor, feared the *haredim* would protest. The city hired an Orthodox
architect to design an alternative route through the steep valleys, but the
grade turned out to be too dangerous.

In 1976, as the bulldozers began to shovel the red copper earth, *haredi*
residents demonstrated at construction sites and the municipality building. Surely, they argued, the secular residents would drive to their new
neighborhoods on Shabbat. The *haredim* claimed they had built their
neighborhoods up to the northern edge of the city precisely to prevent
secular desecration of the Shabbat. Over the years, small pockets of
haredi residents elsewhere in the city had gradually moved to join their
coreligionists in north Jerusalem. Ramot's largely secular residents
launched counterdemonstrations. If secular residents couldn't use the
road on Shabbat, they would be stranded up there on the mountain.

Efforts were made to strike deals between religious and secular neighborhoods. In one agreement some of the religious residents of Kiryat

Tzanz agreed to allow use of the road on Shabbat if it were limited to health emergencies and guests arriving from the outside. In return, the Ramot residents would oppose the construction of a sports stadium planned for north Jerusalem. Such agreements always broke down because the religious leaders could never get all the different religious communities to go along.[7]

On December 17, 1978, the road officially opened. The following Shabbat, *haredim* threw their first stones at motorists from the bluffs above. A week later, large numbers of black-coated *haredim* blocked the road with their bodies. The Israel Secular Association called for a mass pilgrimage to Ramot the following Shabbat to express solidarity with its besieged residents.[8] As the conflict escalated, driving to or from Ramot meant racing through a hail of stones thrown from above.[9] For seventy-seven straight weeks, the conflict continued. Claiming that public buses had transported secular demonstrators to Ramot, Mea She'arim residents in central Jerusalem flattened their tires and hurled garbage at their drivers when they stopped to repair them.[10] Residents willing to run the gauntlet drove by to cheering secular crowds.

Frustrated with the police's failure to keep the road open, the secular residents organized themselves into the Ramot Neighborhood Association and sent a convoy of forty cars with 250 men to confront a *haredi* demonstration blocking the road. At first, the *haredim* fled, but they quickly returned after the cars had left. Ramot's secular leader warned that if the police did not act, the next time members of the association would release guard dogs on the religious demonstrators.

In 1979, some sectors of the *haredi* community made another agreement, this time with the minister of interior, who planned to construct fifteen-foot-high barriers – at a cost of $10 million – to block any sight of cars traveling on the road. But this proposal was rejected by other *haredi* groups, notably the Neture-Karta, who continued to protest road traffic.[11] The minister, himself an Orthodox Jew, hammered out another pact, signed by the residents of Ezrat Torah, the *haredi* neighborhood closest to the road, and those of Ramot, to construct a bypass entirely out of view of the religious neighborhoods. Including a two-hundred-meter-long suspension bridge, the longest in Israel, the cost of construction was now estimated at $90 million dollars. Yosef Burg, the minister, said, "We've paid a lot more for peace [with Egypt] and if this brings peace, it's worth it." Again the Neture-Karta mobilized effectively against the plan.[12]

Finally, late in 1979, the residents of Ezrat Torah agreed to a city plan to construct a small bypass at the initial stretch of the Ramot Road slightly farther from *haredi* housing. But this didn't stop the demonstrations. Religious residents complained that people from Ramot drove right by their buildings on Shabbat afternoon, revving their engines and honking their horns. The *haredim* placed nails along the road. Time and again the police were called to remove *haredi* demonstrators blocking the road. Apparently angered that cars continued to drive on the main road, Moshe Hirsch, representing the Neture-Karta, warned, "Anyone driving along the road . . . will be doing so at the risk of his life."[13]

By 1980, three hundred police and reservists were required each Shabbat to keep the road open. In 1981, the police, under the command of Rachamim Comfort, took the unprecedented step of raiding the anti-Zionist Hungarian Hasidic yeshivah, Toledot Aharon, to arrest nine men charged with incitement to riot against the road. "The problem with Jerusalem," Comfort once quipped, "is that half the population thinks there's no such thing as a Jewish criminal and the other half doesn't believe there's a Jewish cop." Many *haredim* contend that once inside, the police rioted. "They make a real pogrom, like in the good old days," one rabbi told us. Neture-Karta supporters in London demonstrated at the Israeli Embassy, carrying banners comparing the Israeli police with the Nazis. In New York more than five thousand Hasidim demonstrated their support.

The following Shabbat, the March 15, 1981, fifteen thousand *haredim* from all over the country massed along the Ramot Road. This demonstration was not led by the marginal figures in the *haredi* world, but by the Edah Haredit, a confederation of the most important anti-Zionist communities. Most of the participants had never demonstrated against the road but had been radicalized by the police action against the Hasidic yeshivah Toledot Aharon.[14] And then, just as suddenly, the demonstrations ended. The minister of interior, Yosef Burg, flew to Williamsburg, New York, to convince the anti-Zionist Satmar *rebbe* to telephone the Edah Haredit in Jerusalem and personally ask them to call off further demonstrations. The Edah Haredit not only follows the *rebbe*'s spiritual leadership but are particularly dependent on his financial contributions. Mayor Kollek's office passed out flowers to the residents of Ramot, requesting they use the new bypass as a gesture of goodwill. For a while, most complied.[15] Major confrontations stopped, but occasional rock throwing continues to this day.

Power and Pollution

The *haredi* battle cry was that the Ramot road would violate the Shabbat. After the Six-Day War opened more territory, Kollek completely closed the *haredi* downtown to Shabbat traffic. Today, Jerusalem's police post barriers on most roads leading into the community. However, the desire to protect Shabbat in *haredi* neighborhoods is not an adequate explanation for the long, often violent campaign against Ramot Road. Before the road was opened, permits were issued to build new apartments for the religious near where the road would begin. The city demanded that both the *haredi* developer and the new religious residents sign statements acknowledging their acceptance of the proposed road. Moreoever, although the *haredim* had always blocked off any traffic moving down their own residential streets, they did not obstruct Bar-Ilan Avenue, a major cross-town avenue linking the secular neighborhoods around Mt. Scopus, which passes through a continuous *haredi* corridor. Why was the Ramot Road different?

Certainly part of the conflict between the Zionists and the *haredim* was a struggle over prime living space and who would control it. On every *haredi* street, long rows of diapers hang on the clotheslines. The average h*aredi* family has eight children, compared to two produced by the average secular Jew. Unlike those of other groups, *haredi* birth rates have not declined. Not only don't the *haredim* leave Jerusalem, they make up the bulk of its new immigrants. They are the fastest growing component of the city's population. As a result, they are under enormous residential pressure and their neighborhoods have higher densities than most other places in Jewish Jerusalem. In fact Mea She'arim, their residential center, has even more people living there now than it did in 1967, despite the expansion into many new neighborhoods.[16]

The *haredim* wanted to reserve the northern region for their own. "Many people," one *haredi* activist told us, "spent their life savings [on] where they wanted to live and to educate their children the way they wanted to have them educated. And the road infringed upon this way of life." By building a large secular neighborhood right in their path of expansion, the secular world once again appeared to have hemmed them in. Opposition was directed not to the existence of the Ramot Road, but to traffic driving along it on Shabbat. Blocking the road was an expression of their claim that the north belonged to them.[17]

As the protests against the Ramot Road ebbed, a new front opened up in the struggle for the north. In the late 1970s, in a small area near the top of Ramot called Ramot Polen, units in an ultramodern apartment complex were put up for sale. Although this gray and white honeycomb had received architectural awards, few Israelis were eager to reside in these austere, bizarre structures.

One of the cooperatives, called *kollel*s, which each major *haredi* group maintains to provide housing, services, and income for their yeshivah students and their families, decided to buy the whole thing. The *haredim* had their first foothold on the mountain. What the Ministry of Housing had originally intended as a small self-contained *haredi* neighborhood became a base for outward expansion. By 1988, the *haredim* made up 28 percent of the population of Ramot. Menachem Porush,

Ramot Polen, architected structure first controlled by the *haredim,* 1984.

Agudat Israel's most powerful member of Knesset, was predicting that it would not be long before the *haredi* residents would be a majority here.

Ramot's secular residents fought back by making the neighborhood as unappealing as possible. They constructed a mixed-sex swimming pool and kept it open seven days a week, surrounded their neighborhoods with recreational parks where their children could play tennis and ride horseback all week long, demanded meticulous adherence to the original zoning laws preventing construction of the new synagogues and ritual baths required by the expanding *haredim*, and promoted the construction of expensive single-family villas that would be beyond the means of almost all *haredi* families.

As the neighborhood became increasingly *haredi*, the city reluctantly decided to split it into two administrative districts, each with its own neighborhood council, to protect secular community services – like the swimming pool – from *haredi* interference. City officials felt helpless before the *haredi* onslaught. "What can you do?" asked Aharon Sarig, Jerusalem's city manager. "Nothing," he answered himself.

"Explain Me What Is Shabbes"

"Shabbes! Shabbes!" a *haredi* man, his young sons in tow, yelled at us, as we turned onto Ramot Road one Saturday afternoon. We randomly chose a white Subaru sedan to follow up the hill, beneath the bluffs from which the *haredim* still sometimes throw their stones. The car failed to turn off at the "alternative" route and continued up the main road. What, we wanted to know, did the secular residents of Ramot make of the regular Saturday siege on their neighborhood?

Isaac Mendelsohn immigrated to Israel from Mexico in 1968 just after the student demonstrations during the Olympic Games had been violently repressed by the state, leaving many dead. Mendelsohn, a leftist student of economics from a privileged family, no longer felt at home in Mexico. He found it difficult to identify as a Jew and as a member of the Mexican left at the same time. In Israel, he finally felt he belonged. "It's a strong fight to feel it," he admitted. "I have a deep feeling if this is my place, bad or good, I have to be here. And if I think that something has to change, so I have to try to change it."

When the first units were offered for sale in Ramot in 1977, the Mendelsohn family, attracted by location and price, bought an apartment. Mendelsohn returned to Mexico to finish a doctoral degree in psychology. When we spoke, he worked as a therapist and educational consultant for religious schools in Israel's Ministry of Education, although Mendelsohn is not himself religious. When he went to work at a school for underprivileged children, the headmaster requested he don a *kippah*, or skullcap. He refused. "I don't want to lie," he said, "not in front of the teachers, not in front of the children." Mendelsohn asked to be allowed to explain to the children why, contrary to Orthodox practice, his head remained uncovered. They granted his request.

Mendelsohn was studying in Mexico when the *haredi* tried to shut down Ramot Road. He was crazy to hold onto his flat, his friends told him. Why not sell and move in someplace else? But he refused even a generous offer, believing it would be possible to cooperate. "It's something that disturbs me very much, to live with a prejudice," he told us.

Problems with his religious neighbors began on moving day, which happened to be the holiday of Sukkot. It was the only time their carpenter was free to install their kitchen appliances and connect the water and heat. The carpenter, who lived in a religious neighborhood where residents had let the air out of his tires after he had driven his truck to work on Shabbat, was reluctant to drive up to Ramot himself. Mendelsohn picked him up in his own car.

Despite their best efforts, the work inside the apartment caused a lot of noise. The neighbors complained. Apologizing profusely, Mendelsohn pleaded for just another fifteen minutes. Otherwise, he told them, his wife and two children would be without a kitchen, let alone water or heat, for another week. His neighbors were not appeased. To make matters worse, the carpenter still was not able to finish the work.

Mendelsohn resolved to bring the carpenter back and complete the job the following week, coincidentally the holiday of Simchat Torah, celebrating God's gift of the Torah. He apologetically told his neighbors he would again have to work on the upcoming holiday. A neighbor confronted him, yelling that it was forbidden to work on the holiday. Again he pleaded for time, but to no avail. The outraged resident bellowed, "I am religious and I will break your head with a hammer." Mendelsohn dared him to try. Although he was furious, these were his neighbors and he posted a public apology for the inconvenience he had caused. His note was ripped down.

Mendelsohn often works inside his apartment on the Shabbat. Once, his downstairs neighbor sent one of his eight children upstairs "ordering" him to stop work. "He can order me all he wants, but he is no one to order," Mendelsohn firmly told the child.

The father burst out of his door. "You have to stop!" he yelled up the staircase.

"Why do I have to stop?" Mendelsohn yelled back.

"Because it's Shabbat."

"No, because it's Shabbat I *don't* have to stop!" he replied.

"Because my children are sleeping," his neighbor interjected.

"This is a different reason. If your children are sleeping and I make noise, this is right. I don't have any right to wake them up, but not because it is Shabbat! Because here in my house, I can do whatever I want!"

Mendelsohn was torn between his belief in cooperation and his growing anger at his neighbors. Sometimes, he tried to discuss their differences when he rode with them on the bus or when he picked up a *haredi* hitchhiker who couldn't find a bus for the long ride up the hill. "We don't know them enough. We have to if we want to live with them," he said.

But other times, his anger got the best of him. More than once he has pressed hard on the accelerator when he saw them crossing the street. They looked, he confessed, very "funny" when they ran.

And sometimes he played an aggressive game of words with them as he started his car or worked on Shabbat.

"Shabbes!" they predictably yell at him.

"Please again, what did you say, I didn't hear," he replies.

"Shabbes! Shabbes!" they yell even louder, more urgently.

"I don't know what it is, Shabbes, will you explain me?" he replies, feigning the rhythm and intonation of Yiddish. "What does it mean, Shabbes?"

And even louder comes the refrain, "Shabbes! Shabbes! Shabbes!"

"I'm not a Jew, what are you telling me, that it is Shabbes? So, it's

Shabbes for you; it's not Shabbes for me. What is Shabbes? I don't know
what is Shabbes. Explain me what is Shabbes?"

The *haredi* men who have gathered scurry away, leaving him alone.
Isaac Mendelsohn and his family have since moved out of Ramot.

Religiously Ramot

The religiously observant families of Ramot do not present themselves
as foot soldiers in a crusade to take over Jerusalem. Couples like
Chanoch and Chaya Slatin were just looking for a place to live and raise
their families. "Ramot is a good community for religious people,"
Chanoch Slatin told us, his daughter perched on his knee. "There are
very few places in Jerusalem . . . and many of these are too costly for
people like us who are studying and have wives and children." The
problem for the Slatin's secular neighbors is that the Slatins, a "modern"
Torah-observant family, want to live religiously as Jews both inside and
outside their homes.

The Slatins moved to Ramot Polen, the first *haredi* enclave within
Ramot, with the help of Chanoch's yeshivah, which assured them only
religious Jews would live there. If there were secular people, they would
be few in number and on the periphery of the community, they were
told. Some of their friends reassured them the nonreligious people
would probably move out as soon as the religious people moved in.

Originally, the Slatins weren't worried about getting along with the
more secular families surrounding their religious island. When they first
arrived, they invited their secular neighbors to their home. But goodwill
was not enough to overcome the frictions that quickly developed. One
secular mother took delight in baking cookies and cakes for the neighborhood children. Chanoch and Chaya explained to her that their children
could only eat kosher foods. "Since we did not know her and how she
kept her house," Chaya recalled explaining, her children "could not eat
the sweets she offered them." For the woman down the block it was just
a question of kids and cookies. When she refused to change, a mother's
kindness became a provocation.

As the Slatins interacted more with their nonreligious neighbors, tolerance turned to contempt. "I feel very sorry for them," Chanoch told us.
"They have no real community to be in and they always seem to be
chasing some false pleasure. That's why they want the swimming pool
here, for their pleasure, and they don't seem to have any idea of what
their pleasure will do for us."

Chanoch, wearing the black coat and pants with the white shirt, the
uniform of modern Orthodoxy, wasn't born into it. He grew up in a

nonobservant Reform home in the American Midwest. "I was happy without understanding," he recalled his youth, "and when I was in college, at one point I saw my whole life as a certain gift I had and I felt this need to express my gratitude. . . And I didn't have any pathways to do it, . . . but I knew that the Jewish people were very nitty gritty and down to earth. And I thought if there was a pathway . . . to some sort to divinity or some such like thing, I first must turn to Judaism, because I wanted, like, a nitty-gritty down-to-earth way of relating."

The number of commandments he observed increased one by one. By the last year of college, he was keeping all the *mitzvot*, or commandments. He approached a yeshivah in Cleveland to request permission to study. The director suggested he go to Jerusalem to Or Seme'ach, "the Happy Light Yeshivah," one of the many new schools designed for newly observant Jews like him. In Jerusalem, he was one among thousands of *hozre be-teshuvah*, "those who return in repentance."

Because of his high expectations of an instant Buddhist-like enlightenment, Jerusalem initially disappointed Chanoch. The city was arid, the Western Wall so small. "I had imagined . . . all I needed to do was to go to Israel and sit in yeshivah and that I would immediately reach tremendous spiritual heights." Chanoch perservered. He met and married Chaya, an American Jewish woman who had immigrated to Jerusalem to be a Jew, who was studying in a Torah institute for women, an Orthodox innovation to accommodate modernized Jewish women.

Why, we asked, are your neighbors so hostile and fearful toward you? Chaya and Chanoch ran through a series of explanations. The religious and nonreligious communities must be carefully segregated. Otherwise, Chanoch concluded, there will be friction.

"It's like the Quaker Village," his wife Chaya added.

> You ever been there? They have signs all over saying don't do this and respect us for being different. The thing is that everyone who goes there does have a respect for them. The problem with Israel, everybody is a Jew. In America, I always asked how the non-Jews would view me and I wouldn't talk too loudly on the streets and I wouldn't spit my *garinim* [sunflower] seeds on the ground, you know. And then you come here, one big Jewish family, right? The bus driver screams and everyone is kvetching at one another. There's too much familiarity here . . . and familiarity breeds contempt.

"There's a part of me," Chaya added, "that really feels for your taxi driver who can't take a bus to the beach on Shabbes, you know. It's his one day off. Why can't he take a bus? . . . The truth is that I'd like to see all Jews religious. I don't see the way to do it is through coercion, but through private example, and through people seeing that you live on a very high spiritual realm, almost like your spirituality would be contagious."

But Chanoch laid the blame on the secular Jews, particularly the media and the left. "The religious people look around," he argued,

> and they see that everything is against the religious people – the newspaper, the radio, the television. . . It is not our fault; it lies in the secular people. They are moving away from us and this is the root cause of the tension. I think that the leftists are most responsible; they are against Judea and Samaria, against the Likud, against everything. People from the secular society are living in a rat race and they never have time to ask themselves, "Why am I doing all of this, what am I running after?" . . . But then a tragedy comes along and they ask themselves, "Is this what is going to keep me going in this rat race? It's not enough!" Judaism assumes that there is more to a person than a cow that eats, sleeps, works, and drinks. There is something more!

But why is there so much tension *now*, we persisted?

"Why?" Chaya repeated our question. "I know why. . . They are afraid of the *hozre be-teshuvah* movement, the 'born-again' Jews. . . People are threatened . . . and they say, 'My God, this could happen to me. . . You mean, one day I might wake up with a hat on my head and *payot* [the side curls worn by observant men] and a beard. Oh no, save me from this."

A West Side Story

The *haredim* engage in classic block-busting behavior, strategically penetrating a secular neighborhood and then displacing its original residents. *Haredi* neighborhood expansion is not the result of uncoordinated individual decisions. Real estate acquisition and building are orchestrated through the *kollel*, which provides housing finance for the members of its particular community. The first move into a new neighborhood is usually the construction of a yeshivah, where single male students are housed and study. "It's not so easy to say 'no' to a sacred building," said Yisrael Kimchi, who throughout the 1980s was Jerusalem's chief planner and had to approve each *haredi* project.

The first real estate parcels are bought at prices well above the market. Other institutions and housing gradually grow up around the yeshivah. As the *haredim* expand into a new neighborhood, they exert subtle pressures on their neighbors not to drive on Shabbat. What begins as hostile glances at families driving to visit friends on the one weekly holiday often ends with slashed tires and broken windows. *Haredi* teenagers are usually the culprits. Once the *haredi* population reaches a certain size, the secular constituency for schools, day-care centers, and youth clubs declines, leading to closures and consolidations. Eventually, there is a mass exodus of non-*haredi* Jews and the remaining parcels are bought well below the market value. This has happened all around Mea She'arim, the *haredi* heartland, as the community has expanded inexorably.[18]

Menasseh Rejwan, for example, fought for more than two decades for the right to live where he wanted. A young Oriental Jew who had just finished his studies in physics at the Hebrew University, Rejwan lived in Mekor Baruch, a neighborhood built during the British Mandate and filled with large, well-crafted stone houses. Before 1948, the neighborhood was populated by East European Labour Party members and Holocaust survivors. The majority of his neighbors were now Oriental Jews who moved in after Israel became a state. Mekor Baruch stands directly in the path of Mea She'arim's expansion.

The *haredim* had pushed him out once before. This time, he told us, he intended to fight. Rejwan, clean shaven, head uncovered, once lived with his girlfriend, to whom he is now married, and his brother in Mea She'arim. One day, his girlfriend called him at work. Men from the neighborhood had yelled at her, "Whore!" "Shiksa!" (a derogatory Yiddish term for a young non-Jewish woman or a Jewish woman who is not observant). Rejwan and his girlfriend owned a dog. The *haredim*, who see dogs as filthy animals owned by non-Jews, warned them to get rid of it. Otherwise, they were told, their house would be burned to the ground.

A few days later, Rejwan received a telephone call. "Come and see what we have done to your house," the voice said. They rushed home to find their apartment and that of another neighbor in shambles. The furniture had been smashed with an axe. Everything in the refrigerator had been dumped on the floor. "We were heartbroken," he said.

A secular man who ran a shop on the ground floor of Rejwan's building was warned to cover his head. "I'm just working here," he responded. At midnight Rejwan heard the big plate glass window shatter on the pavement. Everything the intruders could reach they took and smashed on the sidewalk. The shopkeeper repaired the expensive window the next day. And the next night, they broke it again.

Desperate, the shopkeeper went to the local rabbis to plead for their intervention. "I am just working here. I have kids, too, and a house and family and I have to earn money for my family." The rabbis listened sympathetically and told him to cover his head. He agreed to wear a hat and the harassment ceased.

Rejwan was not so lucky. Not wanting to antagonize their *haredi* neighbors, he and his girlfriend were careful not to drive the car in the neighborhood on Shabbat. If they intended to drive on Shabbat, they would park their car outside the neighborhood and walk in and out.

Their car nonetheless became a repeated object of attack. One morn-

Menasseh Rejwan, resident, Mekor Baruch, 1983.

ing, they went out to find all four tires slashed. At great cost, Rejwan went out and purchased a new set. They too were slashed, with help from a few of his own neighbors. A note was left in their mailbox warning them to move out of the neighborhood. One Saturday night, his tires slashed for a third time, Rejwan put his car on blocks and took the tires yet again to his cousin's to repair them.

"When I returned to the car from my cousin," he recounted, "about two hundred young *haredim* came and they started to push the car and I scrambled inside and they pushed the car off the blocks. And they screamed at me, 'Get out of the neighborhood!' I got out of the car and they began to push me around, from one to another, and I began to scream at them asking them why they had done this."

Hearing the commotion, his girlfriend looked out to see him surrounded by a hostile mob. Terrified he would be injured or even killed, she called the police. It is a few minutes' walk to the main police headquarters, yet it took a half hour for a police car to arrive.

And when the police did arrive, Rejwan told us, "They . . . assume[d] that I was the problem. There were two policemen and they were very frightened. . . I told the duty officer what had happened and he said he was very sorry and that I should go to the newspapers, but there was nothing that he could do." "Go out from the neighborhood," Rejwan was told by the officer. "We are not going to give you any help. There is nothing that we can do about it."

Rejwan and company moved on. There is a huge Jewish star on the green metal gate leading to his home. "You can fight if you are not doing anything else," he said. "But if you want to live and do other things, you can't fight them."

But Menasseh Rejwan hadn't moved far enough. Now the *haredim* were moving into his new neighborhood, Mekor Baruch. The same thing was happening all over again. Although many of his Sephardi neighbors are deeply religious, unlike the Ashkenazi intruders, the Sephardim never attacked them for their lax observance. For the new Ashkenazi *haredi* residents, however, there could be no compromise. *Yeshivot* were popping up all over the neighborhood. Young Sephardi boys who played football after synagogue on Shabbat were being yelled at. The chorus of "Shabbes! Shabbes!" was getting more insistent. Women who walked alone on the street were called "prostitutes." The neighborhood was not officially closed on Shabbat, so the local *haredim* built makeshift barriers out of trashcans. Wires were stretched across the street between telephone poles. A tailor whose female asssistant was improperly dressed was beaten up by local yeshivah students, his assistant chased away, his shop set on fire. Residents were being offered 30 to 50 percent above market value for their apartments, often paid in U.S. dollars. Three neighborhood schools had been closed as the secular composition shrank.

Rejwan's neighbors tried to organize. Rejwan told the press. He appeared on television. And now he was watching the northern neighborhood of Ramot very closely. "[I]f . . . they go to Ramot and they . . . throw one rock there, all the secular people from Jerusalem must come and throw rocks back at them," he said.

> Just throw it at their houses. So that they will understand what it is
> to buy new windows and new doors. If we don't have our freedom
> to enjoy Shabbat as we want, they won't have their freedom to

enjoy Shabbat as they want. . . . I think that if they shout at you, we must shout back. If they throw a stone, we must throw a stone back at them. You have to fight back. I wouldn't want to do it, but I am prepared to do it if they push me. We have to show them that we are more powerful than them. . . . If they say that they cannot live with us, then we must say that we cannot live with them.

After the Belz Hasidim built a synagogue in the neighborhood, the number of *haredim* grew dramatically. Some of the younger secular residents began to take matters into their own hands. Windows were broken, apartments were broken into, and women were accosted and harassed, according to one *haredi* resident. Turf wars between secular and religious boys were becoming commonplace.

To the religious community, secular resistance seemed shockingly familiar. "The secular people said," we were told by a *haredi* resident, "God forbid that I should [even] say it: 'This place should be *Judenrein*.' "

The Walls of the New Ghetto

The conflict between secular and religious Jews over living space in Jerusalem is made acute by the tendency of the *haredim* to seek monopoly control over each area they enter. The *haredim* don't enter a new zone in twos or threes, but several dozen at a time. The followers of rival rabbis must be in walking distance of their respective centers to be able to congregate each Shabbat. More importantly the *haredim* understand Judaism not as a private confession, but as a system of laws regulating both private and communal life. Behavior in public places is of enormous importance. Public violations of Shabbat such as driving, watching television, dancing, smoking cigarettes profane the community. An observant Jew is obliged to make sure that his fellow Jews do not violate the Torah's commandments.

Living within a Jewish society makes the problem of communal control more complex than living in a non-Jewish world. For centuries, Orthodox Jews had to tolerate public violations of *halakhah*, their religious law, by outsiders. Their powerlessness as a small minority within non-Jewish societies made it impossible for them to claim anything but tenuous control over their living space. It was exclusion by the outside world, often into walled ghettos or homogenous villages, that enabled the community to discipline its own. These living spaces existed at the pleasure of popes and princes; Jews were powerless to control the flow of people across their boundaries.

Today in Jerusalem, *haredi* Jews are surrounded by Jewish neighborhoods under the authority of a Jewish state. Jewish police and Jewish soldiers ensure their safety. This has enabled them to demand and obtain greater communal control over their living space than at any time in history. Here in Jerusalem, fed by continuous streams of immigrants, natural population growth, and even conversions, the *haredi* Jewish community is rapidly expanding. The reason nobody leaves is that the *haredim* have enclosed themselves within impregnable symbolic walls, shutting out the larger Jewish world in every way possible.

Part of the exclusion of the outside, and thus a straining for homogeneity, is a desire for internal control. Homogeneity makes observance easy and deviance difficult. Living in a world composed exclusively of like-minded Jews, it is difficult to get away with much. The few *haredi* mothers with whom we were able to speak told us their biggest fear was that their children would play with other Jewish children who were not observant. "It is very important for children to live and play with their own kind," one *haredi* mother said. Children are warned not to speak to outsiders, and a secular Jew walking through the community is frequently treated with indifference. People do not give directions and often hurry past. Once we ventured into the *haredi* downtown with our heads uncovered. "The son of a bastard is your God," a *haredi* man grumbled after us, presumably referring to Jesus.

Sexual Pollution

To the *haredi* community, perhaps the most disturbing aspect of the Zionist city is the relationship between men and women. To the *haredim*, sexuality is a fearsome thing. Although they read in the biblical narrative that Abraham "knew" Sarah, on the eve of marriage, most young *haredi* men and women are ignorant of the mechanics of sexual intercourse. After the wedding ritual, it is expected a couple will consummate their union. A young man will perform *tashmish ha-mittah*, "the service of the bed," with a bride whom he barely knows, a woman with whom he has heretofore not even been allowed to be alone in a closed room.[19] In one Hasidic community, the young groom is taken aside before going home with his new wife. A man personally selected by the *rebbe* quickly instructs him. For a few the disclosures are simply too much. One young groom fainted. Another had a nervous breakdown.

Women, too, go into shock. For the young women the anticipation of the wedding is equally overwhelming and sudden onset of menstruation is not uncommon. One of the older, married women who counsel the brides explained that some young women do go into shock, but they come out of it very fast. And, this counselor believed, this shock was "not too high a price to pay for the way of life we lead. Better they should have one moment of shock and years of protection than they should wallow in impurity before marriage as the *chiloinim* [the secular people] and *goyim* do."[20]

In other cases, the community provides a two-page mimeographed checklist of dos and don'ts. This guide, used by Toledot Aharon, instructs the groom to close all blinds and curtains so that he will not "see" the nakedness of his wife. Genitals must be washed before and after intercourse. And in no case may a young man study religious law during the sexual act. Indeed, if there are religious books in the bedroom, they must be carefully covered with two cloths before the woman enters. Sexual intercourse must take place on a bed with mattress, sheet, and blanket. (A woman successfully secured a divorce because her husband liked to have sex in the bathtub.) To fulfill the commandment, the groom is told he must not ejaculate before entering his wife's vagina, and that in no case should sexual intercouse take longer than twelve minutes.[21]

This fear of sexuality is sustained by an elaborate mythology about semen and menstrual blood. In the *haredi* community, for example, a dead man's sons may not attend their father's burial. Sperm from noctural emissions, it is believed, generate spirits, or *dybbuk*s, who hover at the graveside awaiting the human heirs of the dead man. By occupying their bodies, these ghostly sons hope to gain access to the man's estate. One's sexuality, if not properly controlled, can wreak havoc.

A married couple's sexuality is tightly scheduled around a woman's menstrual cycle. Menstrual blood is considered a source of pollution, making the menstruating woman, or *niddah*, and many things she touches unclean for at least seven days. Menstrual blood was considered so powerful that the Talmud suggested women in menses were capable of warding off poisonous serpents.[22] Sixteenth-century mystical thinkers in Safed and elsewhere propounded the belief, widely diffused among Mediterranean Jewry, that a Jewish man who had intercourse with his menstruating wife would transmigrate in his next life into a Gentile woman who would copulate while menstrually unclean.[23] Many *haredim* understand a woman's body to be rendered impure by menstruation because she has missed an opportunity to conceive.[24]

The laws of *niddah*, which originally maintained the ritual purity of participants in the Temple cult, gradually developed into simple sexual taboos.[25] Jewish religious practice evolved such that men were prohibited from having sexual intercourse with their wives for fourteen days after the first menstrual blood appeared. Because masturbation is prohibited, for two weeks of every month *haredi* men and women are denied sexual outlet. The period of abstinence concludes with a woman's immersing herself in a *mikvah*, or ritual bath. Because this generally coincides with the time of ovulation, these proscriptions have contributed to high rates of *haredi* fertility.

In Israel, all Jewish couples – whether religious or not – must have their marriage ceremonies registered by the official rabbinate. The wedding date is carefully chosen according to the woman's menstrual cycle, determined in an interview by the rabbi's wife. A small pamphlet distributed to all engaged Jewish couples explains and defends the laws of *niddah*.[26] It is not just sexual intercourse that is forbidden during and after a woman's menstruation. The couple are forbidden to sleep in the same bed; the woman must not be naked in her husband's presence; they cannot eat from the same plate, nor sit close enough to each other that their bodies touch. Indeed, they are instructed not to sit on seats with springs, lest the motion of one be felt by the other. In the event of necessary travel, it is suggested a third person sit between them.

Certainly, the state rabbinate explains, these restrictions are God's law. But the Zionist rabbinate also seeks to make them materially rational as well. Enforced sexual abstinence, the pamphlet argues, maintains the unity of the Jewish family by making sexuality special. It preserves a husband's "health" and "vital energy." The manual explains that it allows women to be free of sexual duties during the low emotional period that coincides with the menstrual cycle's onset ("The woman thus experiences feelings of revulsion, as if she was being raped"). According to the rabbis, it preserves a man's potency, which declines with indiscriminate sex. And abstinence prevents contact with female menstrual blood, which, the rabbis claim, contains particles and bacteria from the womb's lining that cause disease. The state rabbinate thus seeks to show that there is no contradiction between the laws of Moses and those of what they construe as modern science.

Not only must a couple have sexual intercourse at the right time, they must do so in the right way. The *haredim* believe the thoughts of the parents at the time of coitus determine the quality of the offspring's soul. The Talmud thus warns a couple to refrain from intercourse when they are angry with each other, to keep their thoughts holy, and under no circumstances to think of another man or woman. Tradition has it that a woman returning from the *mikvah* should take care not to have any unpleasant encounters lest they affect the quality of her offspring. Otherwise, she is to return and undergo the ritual immersion once again. There are exceptions, of course. Seeing a scholar on the way home was no cause for alarm. So, too, it was thought that meeting a horse was not dangerous. A horse had a happy disposition and a son conceived while his mother thought about a horse would "rejoice in the study of Torah."[27] These rabbinic injunctions from antiquity are still alive. Thus the pamphlet distributed by Israel's rabbinate to couples before marriage argues that the "the brilliance of Jewish minds" and the "greatness of the Jewish soul" have been a result of these laws, whereas the rise of violent crime among the Jews is a consequence of their violation.

Mrs. Feinhandler, a heavyset Habad woman, went even further when the subject came up. This woman whirled between caring for her three children, serving us tea, cooking her family's supper, and sweeping the floor as she laid out her views on proper sexuality in no uncertain terms. If a Jewish woman does not maintain the *kashrut* [kosherness] of her home and the purity of the couple's sexuality, Mrs. Feindhandler told us, she jeopardizes the Jewishness of her family's souls.

"Why," we asked her, "was *kashrut* so important?"

She looked at us in disbelief, wagging her kerchief-wrapped head back and forth. "God has forbidden us to eat the blood," she patiently explained, "because the soul [of the animal] is in the blood. If you don't keep kosher, the blood will stop up your heart and mind. You can't be receptive to Jewish law. . . You can't be a proper vessel for a Jewish soul. . . You are what you eat."

Each Jew, she continued, spinning out the distinctive psychology of Habad Hasidism, has two souls: one animal and one divine. Both souls have a rationality. Both provide human beings with a purpose. But only by keeping the commandments of Torah can a Jew keep the animal soul at bay. Only thus can a Jew realize the *kedushah*, or divine component, of being.

"Do non-Jews have this divine soul?" we asked.

"No," she replied without hesitation, "they don't have it. They have a soul that comes from a different place."

The sexual reproduction of Jewish bodies and souls is of a piece. If a Jewish woman has intercourse at the improper time, if she does not purify herself monthly in the waters of the *mikvah*, she degrades the souls of her family – husband, wife, and the children they might bear.

"If a wife does not use the *mikvah*," Mrs. Feinhandler said, "she runs a very real possibility of having a retarded child or a child with birth defects. Religious law is given so that we become complete people and retarded children are in a way incomplete because their parents, especially the wife, have not followed the religious laws of the *mikvah* and family purity."

"But," we responded, "you can't really believe that God would punish the offspring of parents by such horrible things as retardation and birth defects?"

"Yes," she said, "that's what I meant about the *kedushah* of the Jew. If the Jew rejects this *kedushah*, very strong things can happen. That's what it means to be a religious Jew."

Naturally, the *haredim* of Jerusalem find the women of the modern city disconcerting. Women soldiers dressed in skin-tight pants or in summer shorts and short-sleeved blouses know to stay well away from the streets of Mea She'arim. The untutored visitor is warned by large signs demanding the daughters of Israel be modestly dressed. Those who do not know or will not heed are frequently greeted by hisses, spittle, and verbal insults. Even acid has been thrown at the unwary.

But it is more than immodesty that troubles the *haredim*. The public status of Jewish women is just as problematic. In Orthodox Judaism, as in Catholicism, males exercise a ritual monopoly. Women are considered private persons, exempt from the obligations of public prayer. Men are required to hear the weekly reading of the Torah portion, which derives from its original function to teach the law to the public. Women are not. Women cannot be counted as legitimate members of a minyan, the ten Jewish males necessary for public prayer to take place.[28] Indeed, they are prohibited from reading from the Torah portion, a public honor. The Jewish body politic has been an all-male body for three thousand years. To depend on female voices would cast doubt on the capacity of its male members.

In 1989, when Jewish women, wrapped in prayer shawls, began to read from the Torah – both traditional male prerogatives – at the Western Wall, they were kicked, spat upon, cursed, and assaulted by *haredi* men and women who found their ritual incursion to be blasphemous, a perversion of the order of things. Police had to use tear gas to break up the melee. Since then police have repeatedly removed women praying or singing at the Wall. The Ministry of Religious Affairs claimed female song in the presence of praying men was a violation of Jewish law. It took five years for the Israeli courts to act. In January of 1994, the Supreme Court ruled that although the women's request was not against *halakhah*, or religious law, women would be forbidden from holding any kind of prayer service until the Israeli government made its own determination.

In the *haredi* world, public contact with women is prohibited. Because it is impossible to know when any particular woman is menstruating, many *haredim* try to avoid contact with all women. Men and women do not walk side by side, let alone touch, in public. A woman, even a married woman, is forbidden from conversing alone with another man. Our interviews with *haredi* women were always conducted in the presence of their husbands. Woman is temptation and lure. Men are taught in the proverbial wisdom of the Talmud that it is better "to walk behind the back of a lion than that of a woman."

Seeing a woman or hearing her voice in a synagogue, it is believed, gives rise to evil impulses. Hence, Orthodox synagogues position women behind and often above the main hall where the men pray. There is also a partition making it difficult to see women, even if one were tempted to look around. Woman's place within Orthodox synagogues varies. In Orthodox synagogues that serve the Zionist community, women are separated – in upstairs balconies or in their own section behind or to the side of the men – but clearly in view. In the anti-Zionist community, women's galleries are more often airless cages without any prayer books. In Toledot Aharon, the community charged with incitement in the Ramot Road protests, the women's gallery above the synagogue floor is completely shut off by a screen containing small nickel-sized peep holes through which they can barely make out the service below. The more anti-Zionist the community, the more women are made invisible within the synagogue, and the more dangerous contact with them is understood to be. Like secular Zionism, public woman is out of place, a modernist erasure of boundaries, a siren leading Jews from their path to redemption.

When we broached these issues with an educated Orthodox woman, she leaped to defend her community. Extreme modesty in dress and separation in ritual life did not indicate devaluation, but esteem, she argued. "People could take the idea of covering up something . . . you are ashamed of. . . On the other hand, you could take the idea of covering something up that you value." Wasn't it the case, she queried, citing a rabbinic parable, that one put cheap jewelry out for everyone to see and touch, while the more expensive was kept behind glass, and the most precious stones of all were stored away in a locked safe?

Before marriage, older boys with hormones coursing through their bodies are rigidly controlled. Many *haredi* boys are taught never to touch one's penis or even move one's hands to the lower body, for it will lead inevitably to "hardening" themselves, followed by masturbation.[29] Young boys who admit to masturbation are sometimes told they will be struck down with horrible illnesses, or that the *rebbe* will delay the year they are allowed to marry. Not surprisingly, young women are often feared as a source of temptation, of pollution. In disgust, *haredi* boys have smashed windows where bathing suit ads are displayed. They have burned down city bus stop shelters, constructed to protect the traveler from Jerusalem's weather, which carry offending ads.

Some of the communities organize their young men to protect their boundaries. Toledot Aharon's "Soldiers in the Modesty Patrol," for example, are renowned as sex police.[30] When the secular world brings its sexuality too close, the results can be explosive. In the early 1980s, for example, two teenagers had parked their car at the periphery of Mea She'arim to do some serious necking. A group of young *haredi* men discovered them and hauled the young man out of the car and beat him mercilessly, breaking his arm and wrist. They also beat him with a stick, hitting him so hard in the groin that one of his testicles was crushed. They also hit the girl, breaking her nose. "Whore, whore, whore!" they screamed at her as the blood ran down her face.

Purity and Danger

The *haredim* see the Zionists as a dangerous source of pollution. Cleanliness is not purity and the Zionist world offers a cornucopia of pollutants. The Zionists' food may be ritually unclean, their bodies may be uncovered, and their heterosexuality too public.

Even their money may pollute. Israeli shekel notes use the holy language and in some cases include whole sacred texts. In 1983 the *haredim* objected to a new note containing the portrait of Maimonides against a background composed of his Mishneh Torah. Most *haredim* refused to touch this profane use of a sacred Hebrew religious text. Besides, the idea that this text could be taken in one's wallet into a place like a toilet was repulsive.

The *haredim* have done their best to shut out Israeli institutions. They have their own schools, their own sources of housing, hospitals, places of employment, and newspapers. They even have their own transit systems, which separate men and women. In this alternative network, men do not have to look upon women who are scantily clad. They do not have to sit next to women who are menstruating. Because of the *haredim*'s total dependence upon the services of their own community, deviance is materially dangerous.

Looking out across the rooftops of the *haredi* neighborhoods, one sees no television aerials. It is forbidden to receive the messages of the Zionist state. Television camera operators, even foreign ones, are frequently chased from the community. Some understand the ownership of even a radio as a mark of impiety. They do not read secular Israeli newspapers. Without access to mass media, word of mouth and wall posters are a very important form of communication, particularly between different groups.

There are few public telephones in Mea She'arim. Public telephones would make it too easy for young men and women to communicate unobserved. Skirmishes have taken place over the placement of phone booths, with *haredi* youth ripping out unwanted phone receivers. In one case, we observed three young boys from *heder*, or elementary school, use a four by four post to batter a new public phone at the border of their neighborhood. Adults walked by without intervening.

Many of the *haredi* communities have their own "police" who have been known to dispense a rough justice to those who violate the rules. Every pair of eyes on the street is a potential source of information. But still the larger city outside provides for illicit sexual encounters. There are, for example, a group of prostitutes who specialize in servicing the sexual needs of *haredi* men. *Haredi* "police" patrol zones near the community where these prostitutes are known to solicit, as well as try to intercept young *haredi* men who arrange liaisons in public parks outside their own community.

The *haredim* strain to control their own, to expand the territorial boundaries of their community within the city. The conflict is intractable because the *haredim* seek to regulate the public, as well as the private, behavior of their Jewish neighbors. The *haredim* do not present themselves just as families who wish to have their private lives respected. They demand that Jews in Jerusalem – all Jews – obey particular standards of public behavior. Locked in moral battle with the Zionists around them, they increasingly threaten to make Zion unlivable for the Zionists.

5

To Control the Center

Mayor Teddy Kollek entered the Persian synagogue in the Bukharian quarter with the best intentions. Attending services in a *haredi* neighborhood on the last Shabbat before the municipal elections wouldn't give him any votes. Many people in these neighborhoods didn't vote. And if they did, they wouldn't vote for him. This act of respect by a mayor who believes in mutual tolerance would soon become a grim reminder of the city's fault lines.

Haredi children who saw the mayor enter the synagogue told their parents. When he emerged, hundreds of young men from different anti-Zionist communities were waiting for him. What began as shouting of insults ended in mob violence. Kollek, a barrel-chested senior citizen, landed a few punches of his own. He was thrown repeatedly to the ground, kicked, spat upon, and beaten, along with others who accompanied him. For the rest of the the 1983 electoral campaign, he walked with difficulty, using a gold-tipped cane to support himself.

Moshe Hirsch, the anti-Zionist Neture-Karta activist, returned home to find police waiting to take him away. "I don't mind," he told us, "I like to help out a fellow Jew." *Haredim* had violated Shabbat's sacred time to mug the mayor. The Edah Haredit, the umbrella organization of anti-Zionist Jews, was unrepentant about the behavior of Jews who looked to them for leadership. "I am not upset about what happened," its secretary remarked. "He is considered by us as a religion hater and a hater of Judaism. We have many unclosed accounts with him. In my opinion, he deserves more punishment than he got. Those who attacked him weren't behaving correctly because it is for heaven to judge, not man."

Many *haredim* were displeased with their fellow Jews' behavior, no matter how much they disagreed with the mayor. Some saw the beating as a desecration of Shabbat pure and simple. Others said it reflected badly on the community. Unable to drive on Shabbat, one rabbi walked miles across town to Hadassah Hospital, where the mayor was recuperating, to express his concern. A few yeshivah students announced to their teachers they would even vote for Kollek to express their outrage. Some thought the attackers should be punished and posters appeared offering a reward for information, with the promise it would *not* reach the police. The *haredi* community would handle its own.

But even *haredim* who condemned the excesses could understand the anger and even the violence heaped upon the mayor. "From a logical point of view, it makes no sense," a *haredi*, an Agudat Yisrael supporter, told us. "And from a humane point of view, it makes no sense. But from a Torah point of view, it makes sense – he was dealt the law of the unbeliever."

The mayor was troubled by the attack. "There's a reluctance to move against the *haredim* because they all look like our grandfathers," he said. "The government has always regarded them as quaint, but when stones are thrown and people are hit and the mayor is beaten up, things are getting out of hand."[1]

Culture Wars

For the *haredim* the conflict over the northern suburb of Ramot is more than a desire to live with one's own kind, more than a battle for living space. It is part of a war over who will control Jerusalem. The *haredim* seek to make Jerusalem their kind of Jewish city, to build its sanctity and monopolize its meaning.

What once seemed a doomed, backward-looking community resisting Zionist efforts to bring the Jewish people into the modern world is today a formidable opponent. Like all important wars, the conflict between the *haredim* and the Zionist mainstream is not simply over material resources and power, which can be redistributed, but over meanings, which cannot be compromised.

Some city officials hold a portentous interpretation of *haredi* settlement. It is, they warn, designed to choke off Jerusalem from the outside world. Just as the *haredim* had built housing on both sides of the road to Ramot, raining rocks down upon cars which dared travel there, these city planners fear similar concentrations on both sides of the main road to Jerusalem from Tel Aviv will someday lead to a confrontation over access to the city itself.

The *haredim* have already made sure that Jerusalem's Shabbat will not be publicly profaned from the outside. As a result of political pressure at the national level in the 1950s, public buses can neither leave nor enter Jerusalem during Shabbat. To make the last bus into Jerusalem, soldiers stationed on the Golan Heights, for example, must leave early on Friday afternoon. Because of the truncated bus schedules, Jerusalem's central station is jammed with people trying, sometimes desperately, to get out of the city before the last bus early Friday afternoon. Buses entering Jerusalem from far away often have to wait outside the city's borders until the requisite three stars appear in the sky, marking Shabbat's end. Originally these restrictions on public transport affected the large bulk of the population. Over the decades, they have become increasingly discriminatory against the less affluent who cannot afford a private automobile and soldiers who must hitchhike back to their military posts after Shabbat leave.

The *haredim* are fighting simultaneously to control the symbolic and the material city, for cultural as much as for political power. Each is an instrument to obtain the other. For by excluding those cultural practices that would profane Jerusalem, they both build the city's sanctity and make its life unpalatable to secular Jews, thereby causing them to emigrate and increasing their own numerical weight. The *haredim* have had to confront a multitude of plagues.

Swimming Pools. The construction of each swimming pool, particularly open air ones for mixed bathing, has been accompanied by acrid conflict. Jerusalem summers are hot and dry. Visitors to any office are offered a glass of juice or water. People stay inside to escape the midday sun. By late summer, dry, hot *hamsin* winds blow in from the Arabian peninsula. For many Jerusalemites, a swim offers a brief relief and the few public pools are filled to capacity.

Ramot's *haredim* claimed the pool to be constructed there would cause divorces. In 1983, Agudat Yisrael actually demanded that Menachem Begin's government agree to stop the pool as a condition for entering the coalition. The city had no intention of complying, but they agreed to cover it. "You can buy binoculars and look from Mt. Zion to the Dead Sea also," said Yisrael Kimchi, the city's top planner. "It doesn't mean that we have to abolish the Dead Sea because people are bathing there."

When the Ramot pool was finally opened in 1985, visitors had to wade through one of two opposing waves of demonstrators. Agudat Yisrael bussed in thousands of Orthodox opponents. The secular residents saw the pool as their civic right. "Live and let live," a secular placard read. "Religion, yes; Khomeini, no." To its Orthodox opponents, the pool was another source of pollution in the holy city. Rafi Davara, Mayor Kollek's adviser, had pushed the construction crews to work twenty-four hours a day. He was so excited, both he and the head of the Ramot council jumped into the pool with their clothing on.

Archaeology. Digging for relics in the city's dirt also raises *haredi* ire. In Jerusalem, archaeology is a nationalist passion. Unearthing the Jewish past, each relic supports contemporary possesssion. The *haredim*, in contrast, regard each excavation as a potential sacrilege. In 1983, when Eliezer Ben-Yehuda's family's graves were desecrated, the memorial stones overturned and broken, it was in protest over the excavation of King David's original settlement in Jerusalem. In 1986 *haredi* activists struck again in Jerusalem's Mt. Herzl Cemetery. Swastikas and slogans were spray-painted on the graves of Theodor Herzl, Ze'ev Jabotinsky, Levi Eshkol, Zalman Shazar, and Golda Meir. "Government sponsored archaeologists should dig here rather than at sites in Jerusalem and the Negev," one read. This implied it was better to disturb the graves of these "non-Jews" than the ancient bones of the pious.

Police have to protect archaeologists' excavations from violent *haredi* protests. The *haredim* claimed the King David excavation would desecrate Jewish graves, disturb Jewish bones that had to be kept whole and ready for resurrection. This was so even though the dig was at the Canaanite level, below the Israelite strata, before properly Jewish habitation. Given the age and length of Jewish settlement here, there are probably few places where Jewish bones are not buried. Some contend one can find Jewish skeletal remains in the basements of Mea Sh'arim itself.

The *haredim* threatened the archaeologist Yigal Shilo, as well as government officials, with death for desecrating what they claimed was a medieval Jewish cemetery. At one demonstration of six thousand *haredim*, a rabbi read a centuries-old prayer through a loudspeaker asking God's forgiveness for this violation by the *goyim*, praying as well that their hands be chopped off. In the ensuing riots in Mea She'arim, municipal garbage bins were set on fire and rocks and cinderblocks were dropped from the roofs onto the police below.

In 1983, Agudat Yisrael, as part of its coalition agreement with Likud, introduced a bill that would require any archaeological dig that discovered human bones to stop while the remains were reviewed by the Chief Rabbinate to determine whether it were a Jewish cemetery. Yigael Yadin, the famous archaeologist, argued that, if the proposed law passed, Israel's renowned archaeologists would have to dig "like thieves in the night" to evade the religious inspectorate.[2] Israel's archaeologists vowed to go to jail rather than comply and the bill was defeated. When Shilo died of stomach cancer, announcements on the walls of Mea She'arim celebrated his demise, saying he got what he deserved and hadn't really suffered enough.

Jerusalem is the central staging ground for *haredi* protests against desecrations of Jewish gravesites around the country. The *haredim* alleged in 1984 that Israel's Bank Leumi was financing a new hotel complex in Tiberius that had unearthed a Hellenistic Jewish site, which the *haredim* claimed, contained Jewish graves. A massive *haredi* demonstration was held in Shabbat Square, Kikkan Shabbat, in Jerusalem's religious downtown against the government-directed archaeological excavation of the site and the conduct of disfiguring autopsies on the Jewish dead, as well as cinema openings in a suburb of Tel Aviv and the relatively liberal government abortion laws.

A branch of Bank Leumi faced Kikkar Shabbat. The *haredi* community had already been asked by their leaders to sever their relations with the bank. *Haredi* clients withdrew their savings and sold their shares. A week after the demonstration, minutes before the beginning of Shabbat, the bank was firebombed, destroying much of its interior. No one was ever charged.

In 1991, we happened upon three Israeli soldiers guarding archaeologists excavating Byzantine ruins near the Old City, as several *haredim* wandered from trench to trench, scanning for the first bone. What did they think of these *haredim*, we inquired? "I think you should put them in there," one young soldier replied, pointing to the trenches dug by the archaeologists. "Then it would be a Jewish cemetery."

Nonkosher Food. What Jews in Jerusalem put into their mouths is also a source of conflict. The *haredim* want to control what Jews can eat in the city. They have demanded, for example, that the city's major hotels use their rabbis, as opposed to the religious Zionist rabbis, for kosher certification. The hotels comply because the *haredim* are a growing segment of the market and because religious Zionist Jews will accept the *haredi* certificates, whereas the reverse is not true. Once the hotels agreed, the *haredim* went to the bakers and greengrocers who supply them with the same demand. Not only does the dispensation of *kashrut* certification pay the *haredim* large material dividends, it multiplies their points of leverage in the cultural politics of the city.

The ice cream at Sefer ve-Sefel, a downtown ice cream parlor–bookstore, is both creamy and kosher. In 1982, the press interviewed its owner, an observant Conservative Jew, about the reading habits of his clientele. The Israelis liked history, the Americans fiction, and the Orthodox pornography, he quipped mischievously. In fact, the store carried sexual education manuals read by *haredi* women who lived nearby. The rabbinate immediately threatened to revoke the store's license as a kosher establishment, meaning no religious Jew would eat there, unless the "pornographic" books were withdrawn from the shelves. Only after the store owner convinced the rabbi it was better for observant women to get their information from books than from male gynecologists, and the store owner agreed to sign a statement the bookstore would not carry "pornography," was the certificate granted.

In 1991, the *haredim* pushed through a bill in the Knesset making it illegal to sell pork products in Jerusalem. Although most of the city's butchers do not sell pork, a few do sell the particularly good bacon and chops produced by Israel's farmers. Customers ask for it under the innocuous name of *basar levan*, or "white meat." In protest, a number of Jerusalem's butchers handed out free ham sandwiches to any and all downtown. There were not many takers.

Christian Institutions. For most secular Jews, Jerusalem's Christian life is an accepted part of a cosmopolitan city. Jews enjoy the ritual drama of Christmas Mass, the pageantry of Easter, and the multitude of concerts held in churches and monasteries across the metropole. But the *haredim* and large numbers of other Orthodox Jews are deeply suspicious that the Christians' ultimate objective is the conversion of Jews. That fear is not without foundation in Jerusalem's history, as in the nineteenth century, when it was explicitly hoped that the services provided by Christian hospitals and workshops would draw Jews away from Judaism.

The *haredi* community's vociferous opposition to Mormon efforts to enlarge their presence in the city are illustrative. When the Mormon Tabernacle Choir performed Handel's *Messiah* to enthusiastic Jewish crowds, *haredim* disrupted the performance. Still, Brigham Young University's plans to build a center in Jerusalem began auspiciously enough. Mormon students had studied here since 1968. In 1973, the Church of Jesus Christ of Latter-Day Saints first broached the idea of constructing a visitors' center. Four years later they began looking for a location. Finally in 1981, the municipality of Jerusalem offered a long-term lease on a parcel of land between Mount Scopus and the Mount of Olives. By 1984, the proposed Mormon center had been approved by Teddy Kollek and both the Education and Foreign Ministries.

Then suddenly in 1985, the project was engulfed in controversy. Tens of thousands of *haredim* massed in front of the building site. Large demonstrations in front of the city hall harangued the city council and forced traffic to a halt in the city center. David Galbraith, director of the Mormon Study Center, received telephone death threats. The police logged menacing calls threatening to blow up the center. These threats were not empty. In 1982, the city's Baptist church had been burned to the ground. In 1987, St. Paul's Church, near Mea She'arim, would twice be attacked by arsonists, destroying the oak choir gallery.

Mission is at Mormonism's doctrinal center. Because the Mormons believe even one's ancestors can be posthumously baptised into the church, they maintain unparalleled genealogical records. However, Mormon doctrine holds that conversion in Jerusalem itself is forbidden until the messiah returns, at which point it will not be necessary. "Jerusalem,"

Brigham Young said, "is not to be redeemed by our going there and preaching to the inhabitants. It will be redeemed by the high hand of the Almighty."[3] Although Mormon apostles have gone to Jerusalem to offer prayers on the Mount of Olives, they have never been sent there to proseltyze.

Given the centrality of mission to Mormonism and the existence of some dissenting voices within the Mormon Church, the *haredim* believed the Mormons would seek to do the same in Jerusalem. Indeed, the *haredim* even obtained a document from an informant in the church's Salt Lake City headquarters stating that the "center in Jerusalem could serve as a great missionary tool." Calling it a "study center," the memo argued, might mask its missionary intent. Church officials claimed the leaked memo was not the official position of the church.

Although Dr. Jeffrey Holland, president of Brigham Young University, stated that it was not church policy to proseltyze in Jerusalem and that his church does not proselytize without local government permission, Jerusalem's Orthodox were unconvinced. "Conversion is murder!" read the banners outside President Holland's hotel in Jerusalem. That Christians converted Jews in the diaspora was bad enough, but that they might be allowed to do so in the holy city of Jerusalem was unconscionable. The Orthodox religious parties even tried to make the closure of the Mormon center a prerequisite for their participation in the next coalition government. The domed Mormon center, overlooking the esplanade of the Temple Mount, was eventually built, one of the most elegant structures in the city.

The Fourth Religion

And finally, there is English football, or soccer, which after Judaism, Christianity, and Islam is Jerusalem's fourth religion. Games are played on Saturdays to fanatically devoted crowds who not infrequently throw bottles or rolls of toilet paper on the field during play.

Football games were played at the small and relatively unsafe stadium at the YMCA. Jews and Arabs without money for a ticket shinnied up telephone poles and light standards covered with axle grease and over barbed wire enclosures to get into the games. Betar, one of the city's two teams and often the national champion, was headquartered and trained in Tel Aviv. Mayor Kollek had long promised to build a large modern stadium for his city. He raised half the money for its construction and chose a site on confiscated Arab lands in Shuafat in north Jerusalem. The *haredim* were promised that the road to it would not go through their neighborhoods.

Nonetheless, the proposal mobilized intense *haredi* opposition. The *haredim* have always opposed Shabbat football in Jerusalem. In the pre-state days, Amram Blau, the leader of Neture-Karta, used to dash onto the field and steal the ball. To the *haredim*, the construction of a sports stadium spoke of the Romans and their cultural allies among the Jews who had defiled the city with a stadium where uncircumcised athletes had competed in sight of the sacred Temple. King Herod himself had sponsored an Olympic Games. The *haredim* conducted the ancient ritual of *pulsa de-nura*, "the tongues of fire," designed to debilitate or even kill its intended victim. The *haredim* believed it could work. Twenty years earlier hadn't two officials died shortly after this ritual was conducted against them in response to their disobedience of the *haredi* court? Some *haredim* argued Kollek had a worsening case of palsy as a result of their ritual.

In 1979, with stadium construction imminent, the Agudat Yisrael demanded that Menachem Begin, their Likud coalition partner in the national government, stop the stadium. Anxious to maintain their support, Begin complied. Kollek had to find another site.[4] After five years of juggling the municipal maps, the city decided upon a new site in Manahat on the city's western rim.

Still the religious parties opposed it. It would be too close, they said, to Bayit Ve-Gan, a middle-class Orthodox suburb.[5] Menachem Porush, the rotund, white-bearded head of the Agudat Yisrael, complained to us: "If you are living in Bayit Ve-Gan you don't need to have a ticket to see the game. Standing there you will be able to be there at the game. The new site is just as objectionable as the old site. We don't want the stadium near the Tomb of Rachel. . . I don't understand why he [Kollek] wants to build it right here in our very midst."

For the Sephardim, football is everything. Their heroes are young men from the neighborhoods who have made it on the playing field. Even so the reaction of the Sephardi Torah Guardians (known by its acronym, SHAS), an Orthodox religious party supported by Oriental Jews, was only slightly different. The Sephardim do not sharply separate the sacred and the profane, Ya'acov Cohen, a SHAS activist, told us. "Man is a combination of body and soul. . . You can't separate them. If you do, you've killed him."

This didn't mean the Orthodox Sephardi leader was willing to condone football games on Shabbat. "Football is the opposite of this," he told us, "a sport where the brain follows the foot and not vice versa. We try to wean people away from football and towards Shabbat." Cohen was willing to support the new stadium, but only if football games were played on Saturday night, after Shabbat ends.

Even when the proposed stadium had passed all the planning hurdles, the bulldozers still could not move. There was one last signature from the minister of interior. But the minister of the interior was Yitzhak Peretz, a member of the Oriental religious party, SHAS. Peretz was not about to be less militant pursuing religious objectives in Jerusalem than Agudat Yisrael, his Ashkenazi rivals. Peretz refused to sign off on the stadium.

In 1987 – before the Palestinian uprising – the Labour Party wanted to dissolve the "unity" government with Likud in order to take up peace negotiations with the Arabs. But the religious parties held them hostage on this football stadium in Jerusalem. Because Likud was willing to meet the religious demands, the Labour Party couldn't bring down the government and present their strategy for peace to the Israeli voters.

Municipal officials became increasingly enraged. "We are trying to allow them to do what they want to do . . . but they are parasites who do nothing, I am sorry to say. . . They sit in the *yeshivot* [plural of *yeshivah*] and do nothing," Aharon Sarig, Jerusalem's deputy general, the city's highest staff member, told us. In desperation Teddy Kollek opened a mobile "office" in front of Prime Minister Shamir's office, complete with portable telephone, secretary, and beach umbrella, to embarrass the prime minister into signing the final go-ahead. Shamir, now acting minister of interior and fearful of losing the support of the religious parties in the upcoming 1988 election, dragged his feet. He would only sign if Kollek assured him soccer games would not be played on Shabbat. Kollek refused. It took the High Court of Justice to force the government's hand and today Teddy's Stadium, as it is officially known, hosts games to capacity crowds.

"I'm Mad and I'm Not Going to Take It Anymore"

Faced with greater militancy by the rapidly growing *haredi* community, many Jerusalemites have migrated to Tel Aviv, where cafés, restaurants, discos, ice cream parlors, galleries, and cinemas teem with clients into the wee hours of Friday night. Friday afternoon, the road down the mountain to Tel Aviv is packed with cars leaving for the coastal nightlife. And each year thousands of Jews – mostly young, secular, professional – leave Jerusalem permanently. While they are pulled by the better jobs and cheaper housing that can be found elsewhere, some are also pushed by the growing power of the *haredim*.[6]

Those who have left complain that Jerusalem is a "dead" city; they speak of the loneliness, of the growing sense of religious siege. "I once had good friends in Ramot Eshkol [a northern neighborhood near Mt. Scopus]," one ex-Jerusalemite recounted. "But slowly the connection lessened as a visit on Shabbat to them was bound up with barriers, stones and encircling half the city to get there." As their share of the city grows, the *haredim* have become more strident. More secular Jews leave. The pattern is self-reinforcing.

There is a mutual antipathy between the *haredim* and the more secular Zionists. The names by which the two communities call each other reveal it nicely. The *haredim* refer to the secular community as *hillunim*, which doesn't translate as "secular," but as "those who actively profane the name of God." The secular Zionists have gladly adopted the term as their own. Sometimes the *haredim* disparagingly call them *freirim*, "the free ones."

The Zionist community has its own arsenal of denigration. The most common terms throw the "foreignness" of the Orthodox East European Jews back at them. Many secular Israel's complained to us that the "schwartzehs" had moved too close to their neighborhoods. *Schwartzeh* is Yiddish for black. They were not referring to black Jews from Ethiopia then being relocated in their new homes, but the *haredim* with their distinctive black clothing. Other examples are *voos-voosnik*, from "voos, voos," Yiddish for "What is this?" or *dossim*, the East European and hence non-Israeli pronounciation of the Hebrew term *dati'im*, or "religious." "I have a fantasy," a secular Israeli told us. "The messiah would come and these people will follow him to Sinai. Then we could solve our other problems." "I'm not biased," another Israeli said, "I hate them all."

As the *haredim* have grown in size, invading more and more Zionist neighborhoods, politicizing the cultural life of the city, secular residents have begun to fight back. In some cases, the symbolic counterviolence against the *haredim* has been ugly. "Run down the religious!" "Burn the *yeshivot!*" have been spray-painted on *haredi* schools and school buses.

This parallels the linguistic violence of the religious extremists. In Petach Tiqvah, after the movie house opened, the spray paint on City Hall read: "Dov Tavori [the mayor] should be killed." In Mea She'arim, we found graffiti equating Zionism with Nazism, posters comparing the police chief to Adolph Hitler. At the end of a narrow street, there were hastily scrawled denunciations: "Death to the archaeologists!" "Death to Kollek!" and "Death to Comfort!" (referring to the city's former chief of police).

After Kollek was attacked on his Shabbat visit to the Persian synagogue, Yosef Goell, then the managing editor of *The Jerusalem Post*, penned an opinion piece that could only be interpreted as a call to secular vigilantism. "I believe," he wrote,

> that the situation has escalated sufficiently to justify a call for action
> by citizens in their own defense. If the police will not act because of

political constraints, then the threatened victims must act. . . In post-Holocaust Israel, calling an Israeli a Nazi . . . is legitimate cause for mayhem. . . Drunken foreign sailors in Haifa bars who descend to the Nazi bit usually get bashed in the face and are jailed for their troubles. The same treatment should be meted out on *haredi* Khomeinis who, in altercations with the police, resort to call them Nazis. Under such provocation, any policeman worth his salt should feel free to let loose with his baton. . . The right to freedom of travel on Shabbat over the Ramot Road should be defended not there but in counter-measures in the heart of Mea She'arim."[7]

The biggest break came in May 1987, when Lia van Leer, the founder of Jerusalem's Cinematheque, decided to roll the reels in her movie house on Friday nights. Jewish movie houses in Jerusalem had been prevented from selling tickets or showing films on Shabbat ever since Israel achieved statehood. "Somebody has to start standing up to those people," she said.[8] Other cinemas and restaurants soon followed suit. The movies they chose, like *Body Heat* and *Midsummer Night's Sex Comedy,* couldn't have been better calculated to offend, to suggest that Babylon had come to the Holy Land.

The fragile consensus, which had maintained an uneasy peace between Jerusalem's secular and militantly Orthodox Jewish residents, had cracked. Mea She'arim exploded. The Israeli court ruled that municipalities had no authority to infringe upon such matters of conscience. The religious parties threatened to leave both municipal and national coalitions unless legislation was passed enabling the cities to ban legally such public Shabbat violations.

Led by the country's chief rabbis, thousands held a pray-in at the Western Wall. There were three stages in the religious struggle for Jerusalem, claimed Agudat Yisrael's most prominent Knesset member, Rabbi Menachem Porush: persuasion, prayer, and war. And war they did. After weeks of shoving and verbal Friday night confrontations on the movie lines, they massed to march on the secular downtown. Fearing a full-scale riot if the secular and religious Jews came into direct confrontation, Jerusalem's police trained their water cannons on the *haredim*, charged into their ranks with horses, beat them with truncheons. The *haredim* spat on the police and taunted them, "Nazi! Nazi! Nazi!" When the *intifada* exploded, the *haredi* street wars against cinema screenings evaporated. Nevertheless, posters appeared in Mea She'arim claiming that the Arab unrest was God's punishment for desecrating Jerusalem's Shabbat.

Rabbi Menachem Porush told us the relationship between the *haredim* and the more secular Zionist community in Jerusalem was the worst he could remember. "All communication seems to have broken down between us," he said. The militance of his own party members had threatened the frontiers of the permissible. Secular Jews had begun to fight back.

In the 1989 municipal election, for the first time, growing *haredi* boldness finally mobilized a fierce anti-*haredi* electoral opposition. Although Kollek had supported secular efforts to open cinemas and restaurants on Shabbat, to build a football stadium, to construct mixed-sex swimming pools, many secular Jewish Jerusalemites felt it was not enough. The *haredim* were growing rapidly, taking over the north of Jerusalem, and now jumping southward over Jaffa Street into long-middle-class secular Zionist neighborhoods. The *haredim* would eventually convert their reproductive powers into cultural control.

In 1989 municipal elections, for the first time, the left-leaning civil rights parties – Ratz and Shinnui – ran on a platform opposing *haredi* coercion and promoting civil equality of the Palestinians. With their slogan "A free Jerusalem," they embraced the *haredi* charge that Zionist "freedom" meant freedom from religious law as something of which to be proud. Two weeks before the election, the party distributed a map that shocked the city.[9] The map showed all of the Jewish neighborhoods of Jerusalem with black dots of various sizes and densities indicating the extent to which the *haredim* had "spread" in Jerusalem. Many secular Israeli Jerusalemites, however, were outraged at what they perceived as an anti-Semitic campaign. How, they demanded, would Jews respond in a Christian country if the dots represented them rather than the *haredim*? Or, how would these same Israeli civil rights activists respond if the dots had marked Palestinian residences?

When asked about the map, one of Agudat Yisrael's campaign organizers grinned from ear to ear. "It's much worse than they think," he told us. If anything, the map had underestimated *haredi* strength, he boasted. "We've got people where they don't show any dots." The *haredim* had their own wordplay on Ratz–Shinnui, which, when read backward, spelled *sheretz*, the Hebrew term for flying insects that are ritually unclean to eat.

Although Teddy Kollek was overwhelmingly reelected mayor, his party lost its majority on the council in 1989, plummeting from seventeen to eleven seats. Anti-*haredi* sentiment had cut deeply into his support. Although Ratz–Shinnui's attempts to create a joint Israeli–Palestinian list and to bring out Palestinian voters failed miserably, their ability to harness anti-*haredi* rage succeeded magnificently. So many Jerusalemites voted for Ratz, they ended with four seats on the city council, the same number as Likud.[10] But the Orthodox religious parties were unfazed. The secular parties were fighting over a shrinking portion of the political pie, while theirs was steadily rising. Meir Porush, local head of Agudat

Agudat Yisrael campaign workers talking on mobile phones during the 1989 municipal election.

Yisrael, crowed, "This is going to be a religious city. It may take five years or ten years, but Jerusalem will be a kosher city."[11]

The Politics of Protest

The *haredim* fight for the sanctity of the city, but they do so under material conditions that shape the struggle in particular ways. Three dynamics organize the pattern of their protest.

First, to obtain *hallukah* funds, the donations from abroad, the *haredi* communities of Jerusalem have to justify themselves in the eyes of the diaspora that gives them these monies. The *haredi* community evolved from the fragmented world of East European Jewry, each segment of which derived its material support from donations from abroad, monies sent to Jerusalem to support their performance of commandments to live, study, and pray in the Land of Israel. Although *hallukah* has been modernized, the system remains essentially intact.

One of the most effective ways to appeal for funds is to appear as particularly reverent defenders of Jerusalem. *Haredi* activists regularly appear at photo labs first thing Sunday morning after their weekly Shabbat protests to get photos for fund-raising abroad. Pictures of police wading into crowds of rabbis and yeshivah students with horses and truncheons are quite effective in demonstrating the front lines of the war to protect Jewish tradition in Jerusalem.[12] Some photographers earn a lot of money specializing in Shabbat conflicts.

The *haredim* now compete for new, lucrative sources of foreign monies. In the United States and Canada there have been some enormously successful Orthodox-owned business enterprises, like the development corporation owned by the Reichman family, whose wealth was once measured in the billions. In one year in 1988, they reportedly sent $100 million to Jerusalem for *haredi* yeshivahs and their students.[13] 47th Street Photo, the mail-order house, is another very successful *haredi* enterprise, owned and staffed by *hasidim*. When the Satmar rebbe visited Jerusalem in 1983 to put down a revolt against his leadership, he had with him a suitcase filled with *hallukah* funds to bolster his most loyal faction. Some claimed those monies were derived in part from the profits of these Hasidic enterprises. Demonstrations against Shabbat violations or archaeological disturbances of ancient Jewish graves are not infrequently timed to coincide with the cycle of high holidays, a traditional time for solicitation.

The second dynamic derives from competition among the fragmented courts and *yeshivot* of the community. "They are like the PLO," quipped Jerusalem's city manager, referring to its many factions. Each competes to be the most pious, the most reverent, the most abiding of the dictates of the Torah. The smallest, poorest groups often have just one resource upon which to build – their piety, which they manifest through public displays of outrage at the violation of their holy city. By politicizing an issue, they can often force other groups to follow suit and thereby set the agenda for the entire community.

There are always incentives for moral entrepreneurship. The major religious players in the city each attempt to defend their claim to purity. The National Religious Party – religious Zionists – and parties like Agudat Yisrael and SHAS – religious non-Zionists – all participate in electoral politics and derive monies and authority from the state. The Edah Haredit, the main religious anti-Zionist communal organization, and radical anti-Zionist communities like the Neture-Karta refuse any formal connection with the state.

Those who truck with the Zionists are always defending themselves against charges by those who don't that they are lax in their defense of Torah. A moral pecking order is constantly in play. The Edah Haredit and the Neture-Karta politicize an issue, generating a confrontation with the state. Yehudah Meshi-Zahav, considered the Edah Haredit's operations officer, claims to have organized the initial confrontations over the Ramot Road, as well as the interchange at French Hill, at the direction of the Edah Haredit.[14] The demonstrations, even though they may be violent, are not forcefully controlled because religious Zionist parties, like the National Religious Party and SHAS, hold the Ministry of Interior, which in turn controls the police throughout the country. These religious parties are unwilling to appear as approving ordinances that violate Torah or as repressing those who defend it.

As a result, the police often respond slowly and ineffectually to *haredi* lawbreaking. Under political pressure, even those caught with stones in their hands are often released in time for Shabbat. Jerusalem's district commander, Haim Albaldes, for example, actually attends family celebrations of the Edah Haredit's Jerusalem point man. This attitude both emboldens the *haredi* activists and forces their secular opponents to try to take matters into their own hands. The non-Zionist parties often get morally outflanked by the anti-Zionists, as happened to Agudat Yisrael in the siting of the football stadium for Jerusalem, to which they had given their de facto assent. Once the Edah Haredit and the Neture-Karta politicized the issue, "we put them in a cage," a member told us, and Agudat Yisrael was forced into public opposition. As the confrontations escalate, the inevitable conflicts galvanize the remaining anti-Zionists outside the goverment and the non-Zionist parties within it as well.

Organizing conflict in Jerusalem is not just a way for the *haredim* to gain influence in their own world. Conflicts over land use in Jerusalem are a way to reach for political power and public funds within both the national and the local government. *Haredi* demands for housing in the city cannot be separated from their efforts at increasing their political power.

Land-use conflicts in Jerusalem are an effective instrument by which to reach for money from the national government. In the fragmented structure of Israeli politics, where coalition building requires adroit combinations and trade-offs between small parties, the religious parties exercise an influence far beyond their numbers. The Orthodox communities associated with the Ashkenazi-dominated Agudat Yisrael and its Oriental counterpart, SHAS, use disruption and social protest over issues like Shabbat violations, autopsy, and archaeological digs as a way to threaten to bring down the government and thereby to maintain high levels of funding.[15] With electoral support at the national level finely balanced between Likud and Labour and both parties steadily losing supporters to smaller parties on their right and left, respectively, the small religious parties have been able to obtain large payoffs for their support, even when other public institutions were operating on skeletal budgets and cuts were being made in the training time and materiel used to keep Israel's army battle-ready. Vast sums are at stake. (The 1991 government budget, for example, contained over $200 million in funds earmarked as "special allocations" for particular *haredi* institutions.[16]) In some cases, state monies flow even to fictitious religious institutions that exist on paper alone. Naturally the funds won by non-Zionist Orthodox parties in these political negotiations allow them to build and expand in Jerusalem.

The municipal and national governments have attempted to reserve some new neighorhoods exclusively for Jerusalem's *haredim*. In 1987, Betar, a new settlement southwest of Jerusalem, was designated a completely *haredi* neighborhood. Here the Orthodox would be able to live exactly as they wished, undisturbed by secular Israelis. Agudat Yisrael, the major non-Zionist party, rejected the offer because Betar was outside the city's boundaries and going there would siphon off *haredi* voters from the city. Housing, per se, was not the issue. Although Agudat's leaders drew upon the sanctity of the city to explain the unsuitability of the site, their interests were clearly political.

Because their primary occupations are study and prayer, supported by private funds from abroad and public funds from Israel, *haredi* growth in Jerusalem does not depend on their ability to find employment. The explosion of Israeli government support to non-Zionist *haredi* groups since Likud came to power in 1977 has enabled them to expand dramatically in Jerusalem, a relatively poor city whose more Zionist youth must migrate to Tel Aviv to find jobs. By 1985, the *haredim* already constituted 27 percent of the city's Jewish population and were still growing. Faced with a Palestinian population with high birth rates, the government's primary objective has been to maintain a substantial Jewish majority in the city. Jews, even *haredim* hostile or indifferent to Zionism, need not fear housing will be denied them.

In a city where a majority of the city's Jewish population now considers itself Orthodox and thus, even though they are Zionists, share elements of the *haredi* world view, where large numbers of previously secular Jews are returning to Orthodoxy, where biblical sources are increasingly used to justify Israel's claim to territory, the *haredim* are

Dedication of Kiryat Belz in Jerusalem, the largest synagogue in the world.

hopeful about their political future. "When I look at my great-grand child," Menachem Porush, the head of Agudat Yisrael, said, "I say to myself: In 20 years, he will live in a real holy land, with a real holy people. . . Remember, the past is ours; the future is ours. We just have to bridge the present."[17]

Menachem Porush is probably right. The *haredim* migrate to Jerusalem in large numbers and have more babies than anyone else. Their children already make up almost half of all primary students in the city.

Indeed, if the students enrolled in the religious Zionist schools are included, an overwhelming majority of the future generation of Jewish Jerusalemites will be Orthodox Jews of one sort or another.[18] For the first time in 1993, the *haredim* constituted a majority of first grade pupils within Jewish Jerusalem. The *haredim* believe it is just a matter of time before they can impose their political agenda.

Time and Identity

And so the battle for Jerusalem's roads, restaurants, and cinemas is more than an effort to defend Shabbat from violation. It is a struggle to make the Jewish state observe religious time in its national capital. By organizing the city's time, the *haredim* seek to capture its space. By constantly fighting the Zionists, the *haredim* raise the psychological barriers that make them "other," reinforcing cohesion within the *haredi* community. But no matter how anti-Zionist any particular *haredi* community, each is willing to use the state's authority to enforce the dictates of Torah on their fellow Jews.

In all modern societies, the authority to organize time has been concentrated in the state. In Christian nation-states, the church's ability to maintain holidays and saints' feast days declined and national holidays became progressively more important over the centuries. The municipal clock tower and the factory whistle supplanted the centrality of the cathedral's bells.[19]

The capacity to regulate time is a power to assert the categories of social life that matter most. The Orthodox rabbinate – whether inside or outside the state – is attempting to expand their control over the rhythms of daily life and the course of each individual's biography within it – work and rest, birth, marriage, divorce, and death. Whoever controls the organization of time controls the basis upon which society defines its identity. And by controlling time in Jerusalem, they hope to capture its space, and thereby assert the primacy of its sanctity, as opposed to its sovereignty. The battles to defend Shabbat in Jerusalem are fought to shape the moral basis of public authority.

But they are also fought to defend the identity of the Orthodox Jew. The laws of Torah not only regulate what is right or wrong: they define the categories in which the world is understood. They organize time, space, species, generations, social strata, and the sexes. Their system of classification, their categories of reality, are as certain to the believer as gravity is to the post-Newtonian. To have power, categories must organize human activity, especially in the believers' most sacred city. Otherwise, they lose their meaningfulness.

When a people establishes the order of the world, they simultaneously determine their position within it and fashion the meaning of their own existence. The defense of a collective identity thus becomes bound up with the reproduction of the categories with which the universe is understood. The object of the elaborate systems of classification that regulate Jewish behavior – by which the clean is divided from the unclean, the holy from the profane, man from woman, Jew from non-Jew – is to maintain the status of the Jews as an *am kadosh*. These words are most often translated as "a holy people." But the term *kadosh*, or "holy," literally means to be separate.

To be an *am kadosh* means to be a separate people, a separateness announced by the distinctiveness of the patterns by which it defines and organizes the world. Yet it has a deeper meaning as a people who maintain the "natural" divisions within creation itself, divisions imposed by God at the very beginning of time. The Book of Genesis tells us that God created the world not through combination, but through distinction or separation. In the traditional reading, the most fundamental aspect of creation was that God distinguished the order of the cosmos, simultaneously bringing it into material existence. The real meaning, then, of *am kadosh* is not only a separate people who understand their unique place in the world through their specific categories of reality, but a people whose chief task, the very meaning of their being in the world, is to maintain the cosmic order, maintain the distinctions placed there at the beginning of time. An *am kadosh* is a people who repeat that divine action. Through daily life, a system of distinctions is brought to life, given material reality, and through this work, observant Jews both define themselves and make themselves holy.

Part II

Zion Divine: Jerusalem as the Messianic Central City

6

A Few Footsteps for the Messiah

In 1967, Israel won a war and power over new places. The Jewish state
finally controlled Jerusalem, indeed all the lands the United Nations had
laid out in 1947 as a Palestinian state. These captured spaces provided
strategic depth and bargaining chips for the negotiations Israel believed
would soon follow. But the soils of war were also symbols with a power
all their own.

Conquest can transform the conqueror. In this case, Israel's victory
and the failure of the vanquished to sue for peace set in motion social
forces that transformed Israel's political culture, its understanding of
itself and its place in the family of nations. Those, religious and secular,
who believed in the Jews' singularity – that Israel could not and should
not be like other nations – came forward to take the land.

Zionism had been a largely secular affair, grounded in a belief that
statehood would birth a new people, an exemplary, but normal nation,
who would take its appointed place in the region and the world.[1] Judaism was a cultural fact, not the metaphysical basis of statehood. But two
decades after Israel declared a state in a Tel Aviv movie theater, Israel's
1967 victory ignited the fires of messianism. A marginal group of rabbis
whom David Ben-Gurion had brought inside the state were able to
reactivate the messianic meanings of the land and its settlement that had
so moved the Jews of the old *yishuv*. These men and women did more
than build houses and roads. Fired by God's historical instruction, the
religious nationalists captured the commanding heights of a once-
secular, but territorially maximalist Revisionist Zionism. As they built
the newly conquered lands, they reconstructed the relation between
Zionism and Judaism.

Bringing Jerusalem's foundational stones into the territorial body was
an electrifying moment, a defining cusp in Israeli history. As ancient
Israel's sacred and sovereign center, the city was axial to all Zionist
maps. But Jerusalem's power pointed beyond the city's limits. The city
signified a larger territorial claim on both registers. For the lands beyond
its new perimeter were not just any lands. Jordan's defeat had put ancient Israel – Judea to the south of Jerusalem and Samaria to the north –

under Israeli control. The Arab towns and villages dotting the West Bank of the River Jordan stood on sites dating back to biblical times. These mountains, not the lowland marshes and plains along the Mediterranean coast where most Jews now lived, were the core of the "promised land."[2]

It is not possible to understand the moral and material logic of Jewish settlement in Jerusalem apart from that which governs the the territories around it that were taken in the Six-Day War. Jerusalem is the magnetic metropole for the larger Palestinian and Israeli population of the West Bank, drawing Israeli and Palestinian workers who live in "occupied" territory outside its borders. It is not just Palestinians who make no distinction between Israeli suburbs on annexed territory inside and outside Jerusalem's municipal limits. In Jerusalem the Israelites had once been able to approach God. The city's liberation was read by many Jews as a divine writ to take all the covenanted lands. If it was right to take the lands on which the Temple once stood, why should Jews likewise not absorb the Hebronite burial ground of Abraham, their founding father? What, after all, was the essential difference? The same redemptive visions and messianic impulses that have always drawn Jews to Jerusalem also pointed to the city's suburbs. Soon after Israel moved into the Arab side of the city, Jews pushed beyond to claim the rest of the promised land.

To treat Jerusalem's suburbs as though they were a different order of place would fortify Israel's municipal boundaries as the definition of where Israel ends and Palestine begins, one that the Israelis themselves increasingly understand to be problematic in the event of any territorial partition. As we shall see, a quarter of a century later, when a peace treaty with the PLO put the Jews' right to settle those larger lands in jeopardy, it was to Jerusalem that the struggle between rival national claims would return.

A Normal Nation

The 1967 war unleashed forces that challenged Zionism's central premises. Jewish nationalism was a response to the failure of many European nations to treat Jews as equal citizens, as essential members. Zionism emerged most forcefully where emancipation, the formation of a social body composed of equal citizens, failed. The early Zionist leaders came not from America, England, or even France, where the Dreyfus trial unleashed a virulent wave of anti-Semitism, but from Russia, Poland, Germany, and the remains of the Austro-Hungarian Empire. The Zionists derived not from those places where democracy had been tested and survived, but from those where the experiment was barely tried or did not flourish.

The Russian empire and its "pale of settlement," the area to which tsars had confined the Jews, which would later become Hitler's *lebensraum* – living space for the Reich's expansion – was the Zionist heartland. In tsarist Russia, Jews suffered violent pogroms in the early 1880s, the worst attacks on Jews anywhere in the nineteenth century. This reversal, coming on the heels of liberalization, convinced many who hoped to assimilate or become a distinct but landless cultural nation, that Zionism was the only way out. A decade later, Russian secret police first forged the "Protocols of the Elders of Zion," a tract claiming the Jews sought world hegemony through such devious means as democracy, liberalism, trade unionism, and modernism.[3]

The early Zionist thinkers fought the new anti-Semitism, while accepting its basic premises. Jews were, they agreed, an abnormal people, without a land and thus without authenticity. In his pamphlet *Autoemancipation* (1882), Leo Pinsker, a Russian Jew, argued that the Christian world feared the Jews because they appeared to them as ghosts, spirits without bodies. To join spirit and body, Jews required their own land, their own sovereignty, their own nation.

Theodor Herzl, a Viennese Jewish reporter, was originally assigned by the *Neue Freie Presse* to its Paris bureau to write on French culture. He was drawn to the Dreyfus trial of 1893–94, where enemies of the new French republic ruined the career of the first Jew ever to be included in the French army general staff. For Herzl, the hateful prosecution and the way the trial enflamed the French masses against the Jews were portents, which motivated him to write *Die Judenstaat*, "The Jewish State." "I see dark clouds gathering over Europe which will sweep away the Jews in a catastrophe," he wrote half a century before the Holocaust. Herzl accepted Europe's rejection. Referring to the popular Berlin rallying cry "Juden raus!" "Jews out!" he wrote, "I shall now put the question in the briefest possible form: shouldn't we get out at once, and if so, whither?"

Herzl also thought the anti-Semites' plaint that the Jews wielded great power in the councils of Europe was correct. But he believed he could use that power to create a new Jewish state. Such a state was necessary, the Viennese reporter contended, to build a new society that would normalize the Jewish people, make them like other nations. Only in their own state would Jews be required to take up all occupations, to be police as well as composers, farmers as well as grain merchants.

The Zionist pioneers also shared this belief in the abnormality of exile where Jews used their heads more than their hands, influence rather than power, accumulated money rather than might. It seemed to them that everywhere Jews were casting off or covering up their Jewishness in exchange for social mobility and fragile political rights. The revered early Zionist settler A. D. Gordon, a Russian who immigrated to Palestine in 1904, called the diaspora Jews a "parasitical people," manipulators of symbols – words and money – dependent on others. Only through manual labor's muscle and sweat, he argued, would Jews be able to reclaim the land and establish an essential bond with it. And only thus would they reconstitute themselves as a normal, self-reliant nation.

In the eyes of the Labour Zionist "pioneers," the Jews of the cities of Europe and Russia lived the archetype of *galut*, or exilic, existence, which had to be negated.[4] It was in the cities that Jews were exploited, that they assimilated, that they came into conflict with the non-Jewish world and confronted their own powerlessness. Cut off from nature in Europe's cities, the Jews who went to Palestine would reconnect with their own nature by forming a new relationship with its land. Living in the land, a Jew redeemed both his or her own physical body and the collective political body. The Zionist harvesting oranges or cotton on the kibbutz often looked down on the urban merchant in Tel Aviv or Haifa. Settlement was not just a clearing of a platform for sovereignty. Working the dirt was a way to wash off the diaspora and to form a new Jew.

But it did not work out the way the Zionists expected. The world did not treat Israel as just another nation. The formation of a Jewish state did not eliminate anti-Semitism, as many Zionists had hoped it would. Particularly after Israel took Jerusalem in 1967, the Jewish state became a pariah in much of the world. The failure of normalization led many Israelis to reject the possibility altogether, to withdraw from the universal and to celebrate their specialness.

The Zionists built their nationhood in radical opposition to diaspora Jewish life. They saw themselves as proud Hebrews, nationals in the land, not as diaspora Jews, defined by race or religious beliefs, outside it. They repudiated the past, inventing themselves anew, with a new culture, new names written in a newly modernized language. But after 1967 many were now forced to interpret Israel's growing isolation as just another form of anti-Semitism. With one important exception, the world's nations had done nothing to prevent Arab aggression against Israel. In the final analysis, Israel was alone. Only Jews could be counted on to rally to her cause.

Through the world's eyes, Israelis increasingly saw themselves as fellow Jews, as opposed to nationally distinctive Israelis.[5] And many turned to Judaism, to religion, to explain the failure of normalization, to sources that stressed the singularity of the Jews, a nation alone, burdened and blessed with a messianic role in history. In the aftermath of the Six-Day War, the fusion of Judaism and Zionism flourished, a resonant creed penetrating deep into Israel's political culture. The nation's central definition began to shift from citizens of a democratic, secular state to a particular people divinely wedded to a piece of territory. Ideas that had begun at the margins of Israeli life, notions of the old *yishuv* swamped by those of the new, now made their way into its mainstream. Israel is now in the throes of a cultural war over which definition shall prevail.

Divine Promise

At the Six-Day War's end, the historic land of Israel was there for the taking. Those who now insisted most forcefully that it was right to do so were not secular Zionists; they were observant Jews whose reading of the texts told them Jews could never be a nation like the others. There was a job for which they alone were equipped – preparing the way for the messiah. To accomplish it, they had to take the land God had promised their ancestors.

To the Zionist mainstream, the fusion of Judaism and Zionism on which these new Jewish pioneers based their right to reclaim the promised land looked like something alien, un-Israeli, a madness even. In fact, it had always been there, buried in Zionist prehistory. Ever since the Romans had crushed the Jewish revolt for sovereignty in 70 C.E., culminating in the destruction of the Temple in Jerusalem, the messianic advent has been understood as a condition of possibility for the formation of a new Jewish nation. There has always been a messianic connection between Jews and Jerusalem. In their centuries-long exile, Jews prayed daily that a scion of David would emerge who would take them back to the Land of Israel, reestablish Jewish law, and rebuild Solomon's Temple. Jews who believed prayed fervently, but in the main waited passively, for a miracle man who would take them out of history and lead them back to Zion. A Jew's role was to struggle personally for redemption, to be ready when that time out of time finally arrived.

Sometime between the third and the sixth century C.E., the rabbis composed an oral tradition, later codified in the Talmud, which sought to neutralize the messianism that had contributed to three disastrous revolts against Rome. They argued that God had made three oaths with Israel: Jews should not rebel against the nations, the nations should not oppress Israel too harshly, and Israel should neither calculate the messianic advent nor attempt to hasten it.[6] Jews were to be forever ready to pack their bags, but do nothing in order to know when the train might leave. The rabbis knew their history: messianic impulses could have catastrophic consequences for the Jews.

But some Jews refused to wait. Periodically, men emerged who claimed to be the messiah. Sometimes few followed; sometimes almost the entire Jewish world seemed to believe. But each one failed.

The High Priest of Religious Nationalism

As increasing numbers of secular, socialist Eastern European Zionists found their way to Palestine, much of the preexisting religious Jewish community in Palestine reacted with distaste, if not horror. But for a few, the tradition of messianic activism provided a bridge enabling them to see these nonobservant Jews as the harbingers of something positively divine.

The most important bridgebuilder was Avraham Yitzhak ha-Cohen Kook (1865–1935).[7] Arriving in Jaffa to assume the post of rabbi in 1904, Kook grappled with secular Zionism's evident dynamism. He, too, believed fervently in the ingathering of the exiles. Yet when Kook looked at the land in Palestine, it was being settled and worked by young men and women wearing shorts and open shirts, working together in the fields, even sleeping together at night. The pioneers neither prayed nor kept kosher, nor did they honor the Sabbath. How could such unbelievers do God's work?

To make sense of it, Kook revolutionized the relation between Judaism and Zionism. Kook drew on the writings of Moses Ben-Maimon – a twelfth-century rabbi from Cordoba, Spain, known in Christian sources as Maimonides; among the Jews by his acronym, the Rambam. The Rambam made ordinary human history into a medium by which Jews could bring on the messianic age. In the final book of his monumental digest of Jewish law *Mishneh Torah*, he reinterpreted rabbinic tradition that had discussed not one, but two messiahs.[8] The first messiah, son of Joseph, would be a real historical man who would not have to create signs and wonders, nor revive the dead. This "king messiah" would work in human history, gathering the Jews in Israel, restoring Jewish sovereignty in Jerusalem, and rebuilding the Temple.[9] The human messiah would prepare the ground for a second divinely sent messiah, messiah son of David, who would end history. The Rambam made the historical achievement of sovereignty in Zion into a human-made mark of the messianic age.

Drawing on mystical tradition, Kook argued that for Jews even the profane necessarily contained sacred elements. Kook seized the very same passage that some *haredim* used to attack the Zionists: "In the footsteps of the Messiah, insolence [*hutzpah*] will increase."[10] Traditionally used to denounce false messiahs, the passage, Kook argued, contained the key to decode the messianic meaning of an apparently godless Zionism. As unbelievable as it seemed, Kook argued the Zionists were, collectively, none other than the first messiah, the messiah son of Joseph. Zionists were profane but necessary precursors to the second holy phase of redemption. "The holy," he wrote, "can only be built on the basis of the profane. The profane is the matter of the holy and the holy gives it form."[11]

Zionism was the *hutzpah* preceding the messiah. The more secular, the more insolent Zionism was, the more it accomplished its purpose, as necessary to redemption as yeast was to winemaking.[12] Zionism was essential, Kook argued, to reinvigorate the Jewish life force that had declined in exile. But, like yeast, Zionism was ultimately contradictory to its messianic end point. In the messianic era, Kook argued, secular Zionists would fall to the bottom of the wine cask, inert and lifeless, having served their necessary function. Until then, Zionism would be hideous but had to be tolerated because it created the material base for the messianic world.

The *haredim* of Jerusalem, who were also waiting for the messiah, rejected Kook's interpretation. Most *haredim* still believed redemption would break with human time, not evolve out of it. The footsteps of the godless Zionists, they contended, could not prepare the path for redemption, only set it back.

Rabbi Kook chastised Jerusalem's *haredim* for opposing Zionism. "The spirit of God and the spirit of Israel are identical," he told them. A religious Jew's task was to reveal the holiness lying hidden in nationalism. Just like a Marxist who contends that workers have false consciousness and cannot understand their true historical mission, Kook believed the secular settlers would ultimately realize their acts were "rooted in the life of God."[13] Religious thinkers like Kook built an intellectual bridge that would allow observant Jews to participate in Zionism as a religious duty. The *haredim* were wrong – Zionism was not an obstacle to redemption; it was its instrument. By building the new Jewish state, one could hasten the messiah's coming.

While the *haredim* chose to remain outside the new Jewish state, Rabbi Avraham Yitzhak Kook, the first Ashkenazi chief rabbi of British Palestine, provided theological leadership to the religious nationalists who came inside. In 1922, Rabbi Kook founded a yeshivah in Jerusalem, Merkaz ha-Rav, hoping to provide new generations with a new synthesis of Judaism and Zionism. The *haredim* looked down on this small religious college, but in the years of struggle for statehood, it attracted religious Zionists, including members of all the Jewish undergrounds, eager to ground modern Israel in ancient Judaism.

When Rabbi Kook died in 1935, he could not have imagined his son's harvest. On November 29, 1947, Zvi Yehuda ha-Cohen Kook, Rav Kook's only son, wept bitterly when he heard the United Nations had voted to create a Jewish state.[14] It was, he believed, a dreadful fulfillment of biblical prophecy (in Joel 4:2) that the land would be divided, that the heart of ancient Israel – Shechem (Nablus), Hebron, and Jerusalem – would be torn from the body of Israel. It took two days before Kook's son could bring himself to rejoice at the coming statehood. However incomplete, he concluded, it was surely a step on the way to redemption and thus came from God.

Initially working in relative obscurity, the younger Kook both edited and drew out the practical implications of his father's abstract ideas, developed before Jewish sovereignty had become a reality. The younger Kook believed, unlike his father, not only that was redemption well under way, but that it would precede repentance.[15] Kook transformed the state's tax collectors and soldiers into agents of the "Kingdom of Israel." The Jews, he argued, were commanded to reconquer all of the lands God had promised them. "We are commanded both to possess and to settle," he wrote. "The meaning of possession is conquest. . . Torah, war and settlement – they are three things in one."[16] The *haredim,* by neglecting these duties, were little better than heretics.[17] Until the state achieved sovereignty over the entire promised area, redemption was impossible.

In 1952, Kook was chosen head of his father's yeshivah and quickly became the spiritual mentor of a group made up of some of the most dedicated youth of the religious Zionist movement, the B'nai Akiva.[18] In 1967, on the eve of Israeli independence day, these young men gathered to hear Rabbi Kook speak. This was three weeks before war began, before Nasser ejected the United Nations force from the Sinai, before Israel had mobilized for battle. Kook spoke to them of how God works through history, through visible physical realities. And then he asked them:

> And where is our Hebron; have we forgotten it? And where is our Shechem [Hebrew name for Nablus]; have we forgotten it? And where is our Jericho; have we forgotten it? And where is our *Ever ha-Yarden* [Transjordan]; have we forgotten it? . . . Can we give up even a millimeter of them? God forbid!

"It was as if his body were a map of Israel," Hanan Porat, one his students who would later become a member of Knesset, recalled feeling.[19] The day after Kook spoke, events began to march toward war.

Jerusalem fell to the Israelis on exactly the same day, May 14, that Zvi Yehuda's father, Avraham Kook, first arrived in Jaffa with his family in 1904. Kook's students were among the first soldiers to arrive at the

Rabbi Eliezer Waldman, head rabbi, Nir Kiryat Arba, 1991.

Western Wall. Motta Gur, the commander, granted their request that a military jeep be sent to carry their teacher, Rabbi Zvi Yehuda Kook, to the wall. Hanan Porat, a paratrooper, was there to meet his teacher and hear him declare,

> We hereby inform the people of Israel and the entire world that under heavenly command we have just returned home in the elevations of holiness and our holy city. We shall never move out of here.[20]

Liberation of these lands gave them positive proof redemption was on the way. The kingdom of Israel was in the process of being rebuilt. Rabbi Kook's students were determined to do their duty. When the war ended, they were first over the line to settle what others would only occupy.

"Such a Power in the Land"

Rabbi Eliezer Waldman had listened to his teacher with rapt attention on that evening just before independence day. Kook reminded them that all the lands of ancient Israel, even though they lay in Jordanian hands, were really theirs. "We have not accepted it," Waldman recalled the rabbi's words. "We have no choice at present, but we've not forgotten."

For Waldman, as for many of Kook's students, the time leading to war glowed with an imminent greatness. He was certain the ancient heartland would at last be liberated.[21] When that greatness was realized, Rabbi Waldman was convinced his teacher had been blessed with the power of prophecy. After the war, in September 1967, Kook declared to them that "any transfer of our land to non-Jews" would be "a sin and a crime," "null and void."[22]

Waldman was among the first to respond, to reclaim these holy lands for the Jewish people. Rabbi Waldman now lives in Kiryat Arba, a Jewish settlement of nearly twelve thousand encircled by barbed wire overlooking Hebron, the city where Abraham, the founding patriarch and the first Jew, settled and buried his family. In 1968, Waldman, together with two other rabbis – Moshe Levinger and Haim Druckman – led ten families to Hebron. The families checked into the Park Hotel, presenting themselves to the hotel clerk as Swiss tourists. As far as the Israeli military was informed, they had come to celebrate the Passover seder in Hebron. To Moshe Dayan's great irritation, at the festival's end, they announced their determination to stay.

Waldman heads the yeshivah called Nir Kiryat Arba, after the furrow Abraham plowed to mark his land in the Village of the Four, one of Hebron's biblical names. A chill wind whipped across the ridge. In the yeshivah's warmth small groups of students from all over the world studied intently together. Some stood, hunched over desks, pondering a textual interpretation. Amid stacks of books of religious law and commentary, volumes by and pictures of the Rav Kook and his son were everywhere.

Rabbi Waldman, his dark moustached mouth waiting in a white field of beard, bristled. We had referred to the lands where ancient Israel once stood as the West Bank. "No one ever called the country of Jordan the East Bank," he reprimanded us. "In the same manner, you cannot call this the West Bank if you want to relate to the essence of this area."

Naming is rarely innocent; choice of place names carries meanings, forwards claims. To those who would trade land for peace, this is the "West Bank." The military authorities who administer these lands, for whom they are mainly a troublesome job, call them "the territories." To the religious nationalist settlers they are Judea and Samaria (Yehudah and Shomron in Hebrew), the historical core of the ancient Jewish nation. "Our rights [to *eretz-yisrael*] do not stem from Tel Aviv or Haifa," Waldman continued. "They stem from Judea and Samaria, and this is truly the heart of our land."

A portrait gallery hangs in the rabbi's austere office. Waldman works surrounded by the faces of his students who died defending Israel and its right to settle these lands. His yeshivah students, unlike many in Mea She'arim, understand their military service as a religious obligation. Some fell in the war in Lebanon; others were murdered by Palestinian terrorists in the city of Hebron below. In Waldman's view, they sacrificed for the same cause, the same reason.

Waldman is a child of Palestine, born here, where his parents fled to escape the Nazis. For them it was a transit point on the way to America, where they raised their son. For him, it was destiny. He returned through the religious Zionist youth movement B'nai Akiva.

A triptych faces his desk. Following rabbinic tradition, it declares, "The three things which Israel purchased but the nations of the world will accuse Israel of stealing." The three panels portray Hebron's Cave of Machpellah, which Abraham bought from Ephron the Hittite to bury his family; the Temple Mount, which David purchased from the Jebusites; and the grave of Joseph, which the Israelites acquired after returning from Egypt. For Waldman, these ancient property titles still bind.

Israel's security, Waldman believes, is tied to the ferocity with which it clings to its land, not as a military buffer but as the source of its identity and its right to exist as a nation at all. God has given these lands an essence of holiness, this father of six patiently explained. "It has to be activated. It is there even if it is not activated, just as a human being is a human being even if he acts like an animal."

As Jews returned to their ancestral lands after the war, Waldman contended, the latent holiness of the Jewish people surged forward. Cause and effect. Everyone saw that after the war, more and more Israelis began returning to the faith of their fathers, but Rabbi Waldman understood why. "Touching the land . . . brought about an arousing of spiritual feelings, . . . everyone according to his ideology and belief . . . because there is such a power in the land." There is an inexorable, if mystical logic to it. Taking possession of the land unleashed the Jewish soul hidden inside Zionism's secular form.

An Egyptian reporter once visited the rabbi in Kiryat Arba. "If you say that you need these areas for security reasons," he remembered her telling him, "that I am willing to accept. But if you say that it is yours, we will never accept that."

"If I would say that I need these areas for security reasons," Waldman replied,

> and *not* because it is mine, . . . this is imperialism. This is what Hitler, God forbid that you should think this, did. What right do I have to take someone else's land for security reasons? On the contrary, the only thing that should be said is that it is *ours*! The security of a nation is dependent on its land. . . A nation cannot be a nation without its land.

Rabbi Waldman did not want to "normalize" the Jews. For a chosen people, it was impossible in any case. In order to hold the land, Israelis needed to understand their specialness, the mission for which they, and they alone, were selected. Rav Kook had argued most states were just bureaucratic shells. True, a few serve their citizens' interests. But Israel, Israel must serve God. "The state of Israel is the foundation of the throne of God in the world," Waldman said, "its only desire that it unify God and His name."

For Israel to be a state like others would contradict the chosenness of Abraham and his descendants. Hadn't God promised to bless the nations through these children? Hadn't the prophets foretold Israel would be a light unto the nations? "We're not missionaries," he said, "mainly because it won't help. . . We believe that certainly all of them in the end will come . . . to the godly mount and want to study our ways."

But for Israel to perform its chosen role, to bring on the messianic age, it would have to recapture, reclaim, and hold on to its promised land. "We believe," he told us earnestly, "that nothing bad or evil can come to our neighbors by us being an independent people in *eretz-yisrael*."

And that meant *all* the land. Although the rabbi had no intention of aggressive military action, he reminded us that "there are many parts of *eretz-yisrael* which are not in our hands today." Indeed, the promised land, as laid out by Moses, stretches from Iraq to the Mediterranean. Someday, he implied, when the Lord's work was finally done, Transjordan would fall, too. If any of this land, the rabbi wanted us to know, "comes into our hands . . . only through defending ourselves, we certainly see it as an act of God and we certainly have no right to give it back. So we believe that by standing upon this it will bring in the end a blessing to the other nations."

Throughout history, Jews passively awaited a messianic figure who would take them out of exile, who would end history. But the messiah tarried. And people tired of waiting. Jewish messianism led periodically to more active attempts to bring history to a close, to create the perfect world the prophets had envisioned. An elect emerged to read history for signs the time was ripe and by their actions they could speed the messiah on his way.

These apocalyptic communities claimed to see the finger of God in history. In their hands, the texts of the Hebrew Bible took on new meanings others had failed to see. History, heretofore horrible and capricious, revealed its secret pattern, a trajectory leading to a new heaven, a new earth. If the traditional rabbis cut themselves off from history to devote themselves to Torah, the new leaders seized upon the patterns of history to unlock the Torah's secrets. Rabbi Kook's students, many of whom went on to staff the state's official rabbinate, including its highest offices, were trained to understand the Jewish state as an instrument of God, both the means and the end of history.

Waldman, too, believes he can see clearly. For Eliezer Waldman, rabbi and reserve tank commander, history is not random. His teachers had already perceived its pattern. All of human history leads inexorably to the ingathering of the Jews, a national restoration that will prepare the ground for the messiah who will end history. The patterns of pain in Jewish history are a divine text written to push his people in the right direction.

Many Jews refused to believe in God after Auschwitz. But Waldman believes God even delivered the Holocaust, this most monstrous of events. Unlike many of Jerusalem's *haredim*, who see it as God's punishment for Jewish assimilation and their flirtation with secular Zionism, Waldman interprets it as a desperate divine effort to push the Jews to Zion. That six million perished was not revenge for the dereliction of Torah, but a final lesson that Jews could no longer live outside the land of Israel.

"What God wanted," he told us, watching for our reactions through his wire-framed glasses,

> was to make it clear that the direction of the Jewish people now is to come out of *galut* [exile]. The time has come for redemption. The time has come that the Jews should be independent. . . This time . . . came a hundred years ago, the beginning of the process. Jews did not understand, [they] wanted to remain in the *galut*. God wanted . . . to show the Jews there's no possible future of life in the *galut*. They didn't understand it by little pogroms. . . There were pogroms through all the years, but God never brought about the arising of a movement for independence, of coming back to *eretz-yisrael*. This is what God brought about in our generation.

The consequences of the Holocaust seem to confirm his explanation of its causes. Not only were the Jews of Palestine spared the death machine, but in its aftermath, hundreds of thousands of survivors made their way here and the Zionist movement gathered sufficient strength to create Israel. Israel's victory in the 1948 war was a "miraculous act of God." How else to explain the survival of its small army against the enormous force of its enemies? The center of the world's Jewish life shifted to Jerusalem.

Before the 1967 war, Israel had not intended to capture Jerusalem, let alone all of Judea and Samaria. That "sovereignty came by accident," Waldman told us, was proof the city was delivered by God.

> Certainly we had no plans and we didn't dream of getting to Yerushalyim. . . God brought us back. If we would have planned it,

it wouldn't have . . . such a deep Godly dimension or inspiration. . . Certainly something not planned by us . . . shows to us that this is God's will. God expects us to take advantage of this occurrence, meaning to fulfill our obligations with regard to *eretz-yisrael*. Just as if God was saying, "Well, I've done my part, now you do your part," meaning the settling of the land. . .

The swiftness of Israel's victory, the coming in contact with the Western Wall, and the relatively few Israeli casualties – all these were further proofs that God was the architect of this history.

To Waldman's horror, the Jews did not immediately accept God's gift. Waldman, like Zvi Yehudah Kook's other students, had assumed the government intended to populate immediately the newly conquered lands.[23] But Judea and Samaria remained unsettled, held at arm's length as occupied territory. As a result, Waldman believes, God delivered another "shock," the Yom Kippur War, six years later. For more than a week, the state's survival was in doubt. To repulse the Egyptians and the Syrians, Israel sustained huge losses, more than three thousand killed in one month, proportionally the same as all the Americans killed in the Second World War. God's chosen people had not understood the choice they were intended to make, and so God had inflicted "pains" to push them toward their land.

"We can cause the redemption to go at a quicker pace with less problems and less sacrifices and less pains," the salt and pepper bearded rabbi explained, ever so sadly. "We can also cause it to be more painful by our actions, by our disbelief, by our not understanding God's will. . . God opens the doors of redemption and you don't come in. This is just as if saying to God, 'Well, it doesn't matter to me. It's not important to me.' And that is even a worse crime than the usual crimes of not heeding God's will."

Even when, in the late 1980s, the United States started to press Israel to consider territorial partition as the price for peace, Waldman was not unduly concerned. In 1991, the rabbi told us that a few years before, when Secretary of State Baker announced Israelis would have to give up the "dream" of a greater Israel for peace, Waldman had written him a letter. "You know," he recounted, "we were used to the American administration telling us what to do and what not to do. Now they . . . were also going to tell us what to dream. . . Only Americans are allowed to dream, and dream of a great America." This Israeli "dream," Waldman wrote to Baker, is a few thousand years old. There is a verse in Psalms, Waldman reminded us, that says, When God will return us to Zion, we will be like dreamers. "It's a dream. It's a prayer. It's a hope that kept the Jews alive for thousands of years, for two thousand years of *galut* [exile]." The dream that returned the Jews to Israel, Rabbi Waldman said, would outlast Mr. Baker, "the leader of a great nation that is only two hundred years old."

The growing American pressure on Israel did not fluster Waldman. And, anyway, just like the Muslim Brotherhood clerics with whom we spoke, the rabbi was confident God would punish the United States for its attempted obstruction of the redemptive process. America mistakenly believed it had won the cold war. But look at the Talmud, the rabbi said. Didn't the sages prophesy that any nation that hurt the Jews at the time of redemption would "fall apart"? Examine the history of each nation that got in the way of building the Jewish state.

> The first empire . . . that tried to prevent this Godly process of redemption was Turkey. . . That was the end of that empire. The second empire here [that] tried to prevent this was England, who was a superpower, and they also went down to the correct proportions. . . And of course Russia. All the years, they were the ones who armed our enemies and incited them to fight us. They are now falling apart.

The United States, Rabbi Waldman was confident, would be next. The public address system played an electronic version of "Look Away, Dixieland," announcing the next round of classes. Waldman had to leave.

Zionist Perfidy

When Israeli soldiers swept down to the Jordan River in 1967, others understood what needed to be done and did not need a divine mandate to do it. It did not surprise them that Israel failed to claim these lands as its own. They were already prepared for perfidy. The Likud, the opposition to the Labour Zionists, originated in Revisionist Zionism, founded by Vladimir (Ze'ev) Jabotinsky, the son of a wealthy Russian Jewish merchant. A charismatic speaker and prolific writer in more than a dozen European languages, Jabotinsky mobilized thousands by his celebration of the innate racial power of the Jews. On more than one occasion, David Ben-Gurion referred to Jabotinsky, who placed great emphasis on nationalist ritual and paramilitary discipline, as "Vladimir Hitler."[24]

Britain, which had been granted mandatory authority in Palestine by the League of Nations, in 1917 made its historic Balfour Declaration supporting the establishment of a "national home" for the Jewish people there. Four years later, with the approval of the League of Nations, the British split off the territories east of the Jordan River, creating Transjordan, an independent state under King Abdullah, a prince of the Hashemites.

Britain's first partition of Palestine and the exclusion of Jewish settlement from the eastern part enraged the Zionist movement. In fact, both the Labour Zionists and the Revisionists initially wanted the "Jewish commonwealth" to include both banks of the Jordan.[25] Both tried to reverse the decision, Labour through diplomatic maneuvering and the lure of Jewish labor and capital for development, the Revisionists through force. Jabotinsky wanted to establish a Jewish state on both sides of the Jordan River through mass colonization defended by a new Jewish army drawn from around the world.[26]

After the Palestinians rose in revolt in the mid-1930s against ever-increasing Jewish immigration and land acquisition, the British proposed a second partition of Palestine, allocating a small piece of what remained to the Jews. It would not be until after World War II and the Holocaust that the Labour Zionist movement would enthusiastically and publicly endorse this partition. The Revisionists, however, never resigned themselves to this second dismemberment. Ben-Gurion's willingness to accept territorial partition, even though he himself saw it as a tactical maneuver to create a base from which to reach later for more territory, was understood as a perfidious betrayal, a failure of will, an indication Jews were not yet morally prepared for power.

The Revisionist movement broke with the Labour-dominated Zionist leadership in the early 1930s, creating a "New Zionist Organization." Jabotinsky instructed his followers who wanted to immigrate to Palestine to shun the Labour-led *kibbutzim* and the socialist labor exchange.[27] In the new Jewish nation, he argued, class struggle would be suicidal. Anyway, it was right that the new Jewish middle class in Palestine should lead. "If there is a class in whose hands the future lies," he wrote, "it is we, the bourgeoisie, the enemies of a supreme police state, the ideologists of individualism. . . We don't have to be ashamed, my bourgeois comrades."[28]

While the Labour Zionist farmers plowed their fields, the Revisionist youth groups strutted in the cities of Jerusalem and Tel Aviv. Unlike his political enemies, Jabotinsky believed the Jewish race would be reborn in Palestine's cities, not its countryside. Jerusalem was Zionism's symbolic center and namesake. Revisionists could not stomach Labour Zionism's ongoing willingness to bargain it away for the sake of Jewish sovereignty.

In the prestate days, the Zionists, not unlike their Palestinian opponents today, were divided into clandestine rival armies, each of which had a different territorial vision of the state and its own terms of engagement with the enemy. The Haganah, the embryonic Israeli Defense Forces, was based in the Zionist Labour movement. The Palmach, a crack strike force, recruited left-wing soldiers from the *kibbutzim* and among East European immigrants to Palestine. The territorially maximalist Lehi and Irgun, though led by East Europeans, drew from the Jews of North Africa and the Middle East who lived in the cities. Thus Israel's armed forces were politically divided into socialist armies drawn disproportionately from the countryside and conservative armies recruited predominantly from the cities, something neither Marx nor Lenin would have understood.[29]

When Ben-Gurion declared Israel a state, the Irgun agreed to integrate its soldiers into the army of the new state. But Menachem Begin still bitterly opposed confining that state to the United Nation's boundaries, and especially Ben-Gurion's acceptance of the internationalization of Jerusalem. Many in the Irgun and Lehi wanted to continue fighting on their own outside the new boundaries, particularly in Jerusalem. Their agents abroad continued to raise money and find arms.

In the midst of the 1948 war, during the truce overseen by the United Nations, both Israel and the Arabs feverishly acquired arms. At the behest of the French government, the Irgun had obtained thousands of rifles and machine guns with enough ammunition to supply an entire brigade. Near Marseilles, they loaded their precious cargo into a converted World War II landing craft called the *Altalena,* bound for Kfar Vitkin on the coast north of Tel Aviv. *Altalena,* an Italian word for a "seesaw" or "swing," was also Ze'ev Jabotinsky's pen name. There were over nine hundred Jews on board, many of whom stood with the Revisionists.

Begin was willing to turn over the bulk of the weapons and ammunition to the armies of Ben-Gurion's provisional government, but he demanded that 20 percent be given to his forces in Jerusalem, and that the Irgun be responsible for their unloading and storage. Despite the acute need for arms, Ben-Gurion refused Begin's deal. Ben-Gurion wanted to assert his authority as commander in chief of a new unified army, and he also feared that Begin and his troops intended to launch a coup against the new government. According to some sources, Begin's chief of operations officer was preparing a plot to overthrow Ben-Gurion and murder him, if need be.[30] Ben-Gurion ordered the arms confiscated.

Irgun soldiers deserted their new army units and streamed toward the *Altalena.* The rival armies began to shoot at each other. The ship steamed onward to Tel Aviv, a city where the Irgun enjoyed considerably more popular support, and for a time, it appeared the Irgun had actually captured Israel's largest city. That members of Irgun, newly integrated into the Israeli army, deserted their posts in the midst of the war to unload "their" arms alarmed Ben-Gurion. Declaring the Irgun's resistance an attempt "to kill the state," Ben-Gurion ordered Yigal Allon, the commander of the Palmach, to take Tel Aviv and prevent the Irgun from unloading its arms on the beach.

The two sides began to fire at each other across the Tel Aviv waterfront. Fearing the outbreak of civil war, Ben-Gurion ordered his forces to sink the *Altalena,* with its precious arms, and to capture Begin. In the firing, the boat and all its cargo were lost. The artillery piece used to bombard the *Altalena* came to be known as "a holy gun."

To Ben-Gurion, any independent army threatened the existence of the state. To Begin, the requirements of achieving a state had compromised the territorial premises of the nation. The struggle between these principles would structure Israeli politics for decades to come.

Begin was hardly alone in his desire to fight for Jerusalem, even against the orders of the leader of the fledgling Jewish state. Yisrael Eldad, a soldier in the Lehi, was one of many. When we asked Eldad where he was born, he answered by quoting S. Y. Agnon, who, when asked the same question by Swedish television after receiving the Nobel Prize for literature in 1966, responded, "I am from Jerusalem, but because Titus burned the Temple, I was born in Galicia." Eldad, too, was born in Galicia, in 1910. "I belonged to Jerusalem before I was here."

Eldad had met Menachem Begin, the young head of the Revisionist youth movement Betar, after Eldad had just begun teaching at the University of Vilna. Eldad had written his doctoral thesis on Schopenhauer, the German philsopher who believed men of genius could intuit the movement of history and thereby shape it. Begin recruited Eldad into Betar's high command.

While the *Altalena* was still burning, Eldad made his way to Begin's command ship in Jaffa harbor with a dramatic proposal: take the four thousand soldiers of the Irgun and Lehi out of the army of the new state and march on Jerusalem. Eldad suggested to Begin that their forces "go to Jerusalem, to take over Jerusalem, to proclaim an independent Jewish state in Jerusalem. Like most of the old history, Judea and Israel, Ben-Gurion will have Israel and we will have Judea." Begin refused, arguing this would lead to a full-scale civil war. To get to Jerusalem, their soldiers would have had to march directly through the lines of Palmach's Har-El Brigade, commanded by Yitzhak Rabin.

At the time, Eldad was not convinced. "Begin, Menachem," he remembered replying, "You are against civil war? You are very ardent about the French Revolution. The French Revolution is an ideal for you. In the French Revolution, I think that two or three people got killed. . . If it is necessary, make a civil war."

"Today," Eldad conceded, "I know that he was right, not me." A civil war during the struggle against the Arab armies would have denied the Jews the possibility of any state. Eldad sees Begin's decision as comparable to that of Lenin, who chose to finish the war with Germany – thereby losing considerable territory – before he launched the Russian Revolution.

How, we asked, could the Jewish Agency for Palestine agree in 1937, and again in 1947, to partition plans that excluded Jerusalem, a city in which Jews were actually the majority? Eldad believes the Labour Zionist movement was afraid of Jerusalem, of truly claiming it as its capital. The Zionists, he told us, did not understand the strategic implications of Jewish history. Their orientation toward the land was too pragmatic: settlement was determined by where land could be purchased and defended. Because the Zionists built along the coast, reclaiming marshlands in the north and desert in the south, the central mountain range, running from Nazareth in the north to Hebron in the south, the core of ancient Israel, was largely unsettled. "It was one of the mistakes of the Zionists," Eldad said. "Why didn't they start with the mountains? Joshua started with the mountains and the Philistines were down [on the coastal plane], and therefore, he threw them out."

And then there was the Zionist concern for what other nations might think. The Zionists knew their claims to Jerusalem would conflict with those of the Christian, and particularly the Catholic, world. "Tel Aviv, nobody cares," Eldad recounted how he imagines they thought. "Another city more. *Kibbutzim*, everybody likes *kibbutzim*, why not? Even Churchill, the conservative, the imperialist, he likes communism in the Jewish *kibbutzim*. He would not like *kibbutzim* in England. Beautiful, such an experience!" But the Christian nations of the West would not support Jewish sovereignty over Jerusalem. "There's a Jewish saying, Messiah, Messiah, we've waited two thousand years, maybe one hundred years more. We have to leave something for the Messiah to do. We will leave Jerusalem."

Finally, Zionism was afraid of Judaism. Including Jerusalem would bring the largely secular nationalist movement into conflict with the Orthodox Jews concentrated there. For the Jews of the old *yishuv*,

> Messiahs have to come from the heaven. But Doctor Herzl is the Messiah? Dr. Messiah? Messiah with an academic degree? Nordau! Max Nordau, this is the messiah? His wife was a *goyah*, a *shiksah*. [Nordau – a fellow Hungarian who, like Herzl, came to Zionism through journalism – had married a non-Jewish Danish opera singer.] This is the messiah? Look at their Shabbat. They eat *tref* [nonkosher food]!
>
> We have to understand them psychologically. . . I understand them very well. All two thousand years we are waiting for the messiah. And the messiah will be an Orthodox Jew, of course. . . Zionists

are messiahs? Impossible. This was Jerusalem, a very, very hard city. . . What do we need it? Let it out, we will build the country. Maybe there will come a day that it will be ours.

To men like Yisrael Eldad, Zionism's failure to demand and take Jerusalem in 1948 – its inability to understand Israel's ancient history, its sensitivity to the opinions of non-Jews, its inability to come to grips with Judaism – is as relevant today as it was then.

7

Staking the Claim in Judea and Samaria

Israelis entered the 1967 war feeling alone, inhabitants of a vulnerable sliver of territory. Yet in the wake of its tremendous victory, the Labour government's first impulse those first months was to exchange much of the land that had been won for a separate peace, not with the Palestinians, but with King Hussein's Jordan. Prime Minister Eshkol pressed for a formal peace treaty with all the Arab states. While the government was already planning strategic settlement on the Jordan River and around Jerusalem, Abba Eban, Israel's foreign affairs minister, was telling Arab leaders that "everything" was negotiable. Three months after the war, the Arab world's answer at Khartoum was an unequivocal no: no to negotiations, no to peace, no to recognition.

In the face of this implacable Arab hostility, most Israelis felt it was their right to take what history had given them by no fault of their own. "The feeling in Israel," Mordechai Gur told us, "was 'OK, so maybe that's how history decides it should be.' " The Labour government was nonetheless internally divided, as it has always been, over the negotiability of the territories. Whereas many Labour leaders saw much of the land as bargaining chips to be exchanged for demilitarization and Arab concessions on Jerusalem, others argued there was no going back. They had fought for keeps.

Zionists had always sanctified the land, had cultivated a profound sense of *moledet*, or birthplace. Boy Scout troops criss-crossed the countryside; schoolchildren learned to identify each species of bird and flower; young men and women trekked through the deserts with little water. To know the land, to restore its fecundity, became a claim to possession. In the mythology of *moledet*, a belief inherited from European travelers and researchers who visited Palestine in the late nineteenth and early twentieth centuries, Arabs were portrayed as poor husbands to the land, allowing its deforestation and erosion. Only the Zionists could make it bloom again. Israelis quoted approvingly a British officer's remark, "The Bedouin is not the son of the desert; he is its father."

Many on both the left and the right believed Israel's territorial gains were irreversible. A besieged Israeli army had, incredibly, righted a historic wrong, reversing the partition of the land forced upon the new nation two decades before. Only now did Israel control the part of Palestine that "really" belonged to her. A number of Labour Zionists, including some leaders of the kibbutz and *moshav* cooperative agrarian movements and those loyal to David Ben-Gurion, now joined together with men and women they had always despised, the Revisionists, who, before there was a state, had been willing to fight recklessly against the Arabs, the British, and even against their fellow Zionists to hold on to all of Palestine.

In September 1967, men and women who were not identified with the right, like Isser Harel, the founding director of Mossad, Israel's secret service; Rachel Ben-Zvi, the wife of Israel's second president, the famed poet Nathan Alterman; and Uzi Feinerman, the secretary-general of the *moshav* movement, threw in their lot with Revisionists like Israel Eldad, once a commander in Lehi; Eri Jabotinsky, the son of Revisionist Zionism's founder; and the poet laureate of the right, Uri Zvi Greenberg, to form the Land of Israel Movement. The movement had one objective: goading the government into settling the land with Jews. Settling the land was a way to manifest and build the material and moral power necessary for survival, to secure strategic depth as well as a platform for spiritual renewal of the pioneer tradition. Their manifesto read: "We are obliged to be faithful to the completion of our land, . . . and no government has the right to compromise on this completion."[1] The young religious nationalist followers of Rabbi Kook went along, with Rabbi Kook issuing a proclamation declaring it "a sin and a crime" to "transfer our land to the *goyim*."[2]

The Labour Zionists, who had governed the country since 1948, would soon disappoint them. Labour has always held to one version or another of the "Jordanian option." Israel, along with Britain, was one of the few nations that recognized Jordan's 1948 incorporation of the lands originally promised to the Palestinians at the United Nations. Every single Arab state repudiated Jordan's land grab. Now Jordan had lost it all.

After the Six-Day War, Israel secretly proposed a peace plan to the defeated King Hussein. Yigal Allon's plan would return most of the densely populated highlands Israel had just conquered to Jordanian sovereignty. The Jordanians would regain Nablus and Ramallah to the north of Jerusalem, and Bethlehem and Hebron to the south. They would also secure the Gaza Strip, giving Jordan access to the Mediterranean coast. Jerusalem would remain in Israeli hands.

The Allon plan was a territorial jigsaw. Jerusalem would become the center of a new Israeli zone extending down to the Jordan River, then spreading out north and south along it. This desert zone along the western side of the Jordan River would provide Israel with a defensive buffer from which it could deploy against advancing Arab armies. The Israeli corridor connecting Jerusalem to this buffer zone would cut the main Arab landmass in two. The two Jordanian pieces would be connected to each other by an Israeli-controlled road and to Jordan proper by another corridor running down the mountains through Jericho. Jordan would control the heavily populated mountain ridges surrounded on all sides by Jewish soldiers. (The territorial outline of the plan has remained, down to the present, the Labour Party's blueprint for territorial partition.)

Although King Hussein was delighted the Israelis allowed him to remain custodian of the entire Islamic complex controlled from the "noble sanctuary" in the Old City, he refused Israel's territorial requirements for peace. Not only would Hussein be denied Jerusalem, Allon's proposed patchwork quilt ceded one half of the West Bank to Israel. "We prefer secure borders that are not agreed to, to agreed borders which are not secure," Allon responded. After the king crushed the PLO in 1970 and expelled it from Jordan, Allon met the monarch once again. This time he offered him an additional prize: a corridor of Jordanian territory that went all the way to the Mediterranean. Again, the king refused.

Moshe Dayan, minister of defense in 1967, believed Israel should act on the assumption that its occupation would be permanent. Burying Israel's war dead on the Mount of Olives right after the war, he said, "We have returned to the mountain, to the cradle of our people, to the inheritance of the Patriarchs, the land of the Judges and the fortress of the Kingdom of the House of David."[3] Jordan's king had not come forward; peace seemed remote. Although Dayan's concern for the Jewish–Arab demographic balance prevented him from urging outright annexation, he encouraged Jewish settlement throughout the conquered territory, *especially* in areas adjacent to Palestinian cities. Israel, he advised, should "create facts," including four new Jewish cities along the north–south mountain ridge on which Jerusalem sat, each composed of tens of thousands of civilians as well as a military base.

Dayan was willing to grant functional autonomy – control over basic services – to the local Palestinians, but he believed sovereignty would never have to be negotiated. To remain a Jewish democracy, Israel could not officially annex the lands, but it should keep them forever. Moshe Dayan's vision of de facto incorporation without formal annexation provided the template for Israel's evolving relationship with these new lands.

Jerusalem was never up for discussion with the Arabs, not in the Allon plan, not anywhere. Right after the 1967 war, the Israeli government redrew the city's borders to include a maximum amount of land with a minimum number of Arabs. The capital of the Jewish state would have to have a strong Jewish majority. Within the new municipality, Palestinian properties were expropriated to build new suburbs. The Arab owners were largely unwilling to contest the expropriations in Israeli court. East Jerusalem was occupied; to argue before the Israeli bar would grant legitimacy to that occupation. And they refused compensation. To accept the money would be a disgrace; for those who wavered, Jordanian radio announced death sentences imposed in absentia against those Arabs who had had the audacity to sell their patrimony to the Jews.

In 1969, William Rogers, the U.S. secretary of state, proposed a peace plan that called for joint Jordanian–Israeli governance of a unified Jerusalem. The Israelis responded by siezing thousands of acres of Arab-owned land in Jerusalem and bringing in bulldozers to build more Jewish housing. (Rabbi Zvi Yehuda Kook opposed the Labour government's decision to build on lands confiscated from Arab villagers. In Kook's view, Jewish national rights, absolute and sacred as they were, did not abrogate the individual rights of the Arabs.) In 1970, the Israeli government decided to "thicken" the metropolitan area of Jerusalem, to consolidate a Jewish presence not only in each corner of the enlarged and united city of Jerusalem, but all around it as well. Israel built vast new Jewish suburbs, Ramot to the north, Gilo to the south, and East Talpiot to the east. Although Jews had owned some of the lands for these projects before 1948, most was expropriated from private Arab owners or declared state lands.[4] Ringing the Arab part of the city with Jewish housing projects would, the government believed, make it impossible for it ever to revert to Arab sovereignty.[5]

However, outside Jerusalem, Israel was not quick to settle the territories it had just won. The first Jewish settlers across the "Green Line," the old armistice line with Jordan, moved outward from Jerusalem. They returned first to places from which Jews had been driven by Arab forces before statehood. By the end of 1967, Jews returned to Kfar Etzion, just south of Jerusalem, which had been overrun during the 1948 war. The returnees included followers of Rabbi Kook and children of the original settlers, some of whose parents had been massacred by Arabs in 1948, a first wave of soldiers doing the killing, while a second wave of Palestinian villagers gouged out eyes from the corpses and placed castrated genitals in the mouths of dead men. In 1968, with the support of the Land of Israel movement, Rabbis Waldman and Levinger led Jewish families back to Hebron, the first Jewish presence there since the Arab pogrom of 1929.

For the first decade, government settlement initiatives were largely confined to the boundaries of the Allon plan – around Jerusalem and along the Jordan valley. A new north–south road, the Allon Road, was built along the western edge of the arid Jordan valley to define the security corridor. The Labour government's slow and territorially restrictive moves made it clear to members of the Land of Israel movement that their political future lay with Menachem Begin and the parties of the right. The movement was soon absorbed into Begin's Likud Party.

However, if it hadn't been for the trauma of the Yom Kippur War in 1973, in which Israel was attacked on the holiest day in the Jewish calendar, the Labour government might have slowly incorporated the new lands. Israel had earlier rebuffed Egyptian and American efforts to trade the Sinai for bilateral peace. President Anwar Sadat, speaking to the Egyptian parliament, claimed he was willing to lose a million men to regain the Sinai. Hirsh Goodman, who was then *The Jerusalem Post*'s defense correspondent and who would fight in the war, wrote:

> I remember well that day in the Knesset, Golda [Meir] on the podium, the plenum and press gallery filled to capacity. I remember the arrogance of her reply to Sadat's threat. In a speech devoid of emotion, her voice husky with cigarette smoke, she unabashedly mocked Sadat, making light of both his overtures for peace and his threat of war. I remember well the dismissive wave of her hand as she called Sadat's threat to sacrifice a million men a hoax and her expression as she called him a clown.[6]

Israel lost over twenty-five hundred soldiers; a quarter of its air force was destroyed. An emergency American airlift was required to keep its army supplied. It did not matter that Ariel Sharon had punched across the Suez Canal into Egypt and that Egypt's Third Army was encircled. The war shattered Israel's sense of invincibility.

The Palestinians Israel had absorbed six years earlier were jubilant; the PLO, on the rise. Yet there were sounds of Palestinian pragmatism, voices for coexistence. In this context, the overwhelming majority of Israelis were now willing to exchange territory, large chunks of it, for peace. There were arguments pro and con about the strategic value of the lands taken in 1967. Those in the Land of Israel movement argued that they had proved decisive during the war. In contrast, many in the Labour Party argued that when war came in 1973, the few Jewish settlements had been ineffective as defensive outposts, their evacuation – particularly in the Golan – consuming precious time and personnel. The Labour Party platform moved increasingly toward negotiated withdrawal.[7]

The change in Labour Party orientation and the loss of faith in its capacity to govern created the conditions for the practical messianists, those who had been trained by Rabbi Kook, to make their move. They understood what the Lord was saying. Moreover, Labour Zionists who controlled the state had always deprecated the religious Zionists as an insignificant appendage of the main movement, devoted to Torah at the expense of their conquest of the land. This was their chance to replicate the daring of the original pioneers, this time in the vanguard, against their own state if necessary.

Young men trained in religious nationalist *yeshivot* now formed an extraparliamentary movement to challenge the Labour government's apparent unwillingness to intensify Jewish settlement. With the backing of Rabbi Shlomo Goren, now the Ashkenazi chief rabbi, they founded Gush Emunim, the "Bloc of the Faithful," in Kfar Etzion in March 1974. The young settlers demanded that the National Religious Party, the only religious Zionist party and the party to which they had always been loyal, refuse to remain in any coalition government that would not annex the territories. When the party leadership, then part of the Labour government coalition, rejected their demand, they bolted, determined to settle the land and to support only those parties who believed as they did.

The settlement movement they founded was determined to break out, to make it impossible ever to divide Judea and Samaria between an Arab and a Jewish state. An enlarged Jerusalem and a security zone along the Jordan were not enough. The movement was ready to leap into every area of Judea, Samaria, and Gaza. They organized mass processions through Judea and Samaria, usually during the pilgrimage festivals of Passover and Sukkot, symbolically laying claim to the soil. By 1976, tens of thousands of Israelis – including the rising elites of Menachem Begin's Likud Party – were marching through the rocky hills, wending their way through hostile but impassive Palestinian towns and villages.

These mass demonstrations occurred simultaneously with legal and illegal attempts to found new settlements. In the last years of Yitzhak Rabin's Labour government (1974–1977), it was not difficult for Jewish settlers to exploit partisan and personal rivalries, as well as the sympathies of those across the political spectrum who saw these new settlers as successors to the old. While the Labour government still held out the possibility of partition, this movement kept expanding the boundaries of acceptable Jewish settlement. Gush Emunim induced the government to establish military work camps, which became nuclei for civilian settlements. Their members made repeated illegal attempts to settle at Ofrah, Jericho, Nablus, Ma'aleh Adumim, and elsewhere. And their efforts bore fruit. Temporary, unofficial, illegal – but Jews were being allowed to build outside the boundaries of the Allon plan. Allon railed that they were a "political movement of false Messiahs and nationalistic demagogues."[8]

The Labour government increasingly allowed settlement anywhere in the territories as long as it was well away from major Arab population centers. But the Gush Emunim would not be confined. In 1974, they had begun a campaign to create a settlement, called Elon Moreh, the biblical name for Nablus, on a hill overlooking the Arab city. Nablus was a traditional center of Palestinian nationalism, a politically mobilized Palestinian city at the heart of the most densely populated region in Samaria. If Gush Emunim could establish the right of Jews to live here, they would undercut what remained of the Allon plan.

Seven times the settlers camped and constructed makeshift dwellings. Each time the army, under the direction of Prime Minister Rabin, forcibly removed them. Rabbi Zvi Yehuda Kook himself participated in the first attempt to settle Elon Moreh. When the soldiers came to take him away, he opened his black coat and said: "If you wish, take a machine gun and kill me . . . Just as it's impossible to force me to eat pork and desecrate the Sabbath, you won't force me to move from here." In the end, the rabbi was alone at the site, until finally, he left too.[9] Ariel Sharon, then a Knesset member, later Begin's minister of defense, protested that the orders were immoral and "orders like that we have to refuse to obey."[10]

The battle to settle near Nablus shifted to Sebastia, an old rail station. Thousands of Israelis responded to Gush Emunim advertisements: "Join the great procession: The People of Israel are coming home again." The Israelis were evicted once more. On November 10, 1975, the United Nations passed its infamous resolution equating Zionism with racism. There were thunderous calls by the World Zionist Organization and others to respond by establishing new Jewish settlements. Gush Emunim immediately resolved to try again to settle Sebastia. Two thousand Jews squatted around the abandoned railroad depot; some chained themselves to the site. For a week they held the army at bay. At week's end, even a school and a nursery had been constructed.

The minister of defense, Shimon Peres, ever rivalrous with Yitzhak Rabin, his prime minister, not only did not immediately remove the settlers, he allowed them to take provisions through Israeli army lines. Members of the National Religious Party (NRP), who were in the Labour coalition, threatened to bring down the government if the Jews were not allowed to remain. In Jerusalem, an international conference had been hurriedly called to express its solidarity with Israel after the UN vote. At the request of Gush Emunim, the delegates affirmed "the historical right of the Jewish people to the Land of Israel."

It was in this context, in December 1975, that Rabin allowed these determined Jewish settlers to move into an army post in nearby Kadoum. Rabin intended the settlement to be temporary and to relocate them later *within* the confines of the Allon plan, not in the heart of Samaria. The settlers, however, refused to move. After all, they had the backing of

Shimon Peres, Moshe Dayan, and the National Religious Party members; several government ministries were providing material support. In March 1976, the settlers were allowed to remain in Kadoum, which they Hebraicized to Kedumim. The activists described this as the "Hanukkah miracle of our own day."[11] The capacity of the government to control the settlement process was breaking down.

In May 1977 Menachem Begin was elected prime minister. Even though the election had not been fought on the territorial question, Gush Emunim's expectations rose. The National Religious Party was now allied to Herut, the core of the Likud coalition, a party opposed to any kind of territorial compromise, a party whose members had wanted a Jewish state on both sides of the River Jordan. Begin had marched with Gush Emunim through the olive groves and stony pasture lands of Judea and Samaria, had referred to the Gush Emunim's members as his "darling children."[12] Soon after the election, the prime minister attended the synagogue dedication in Kedumim. From the pulpit, he proclaimed, "We will establish scores of Elon Morehs."

The Begin regime appointed Ariel Sharon to replace Yigal Allon as head of the Inter-Ministerial Settlement Committee. It was Sharon, one Israeli contended, who, in 1964, had authorized a study of the feasibility of putting all the Arabs in Samaria on trucks and transporting them to another Arab country.[13] Sharon immediately drew up a plan for two million Jewish settlers on the West Bank by the end of the century. All the unofficial settlements started by the Gush Emunim in the last years of the Labour government were legalized.

In this politically friendly environment, the Gush Emunim decided to establish its own institutionalized settlement body, just like those formed by other political streams in Israel's history. Headquartered in Jerusalem, Amana, or Covenant, gradually took the place of Gush Emunim itself. Amana presented the new Begin government with a plan to settle Jews throughout the territories.[14]

The movement, downplaying the restoration of biblical sites, now called for the construction of whole cities. A road network would be built linking the new Jewish towns and villages to the main body of Israeli territory to the west. The plan, if implemented, would make it impossible to find a continuous north–south corridor of Palestinian territory to give back to anybody. The Likud government immediately provided a half dozen new sites – all military camps – that would be gradually converted to civilian settlements. The campaign to make partition impossible had begun.

And then in 1978, the prime minister appeared to betray the Jewish settlement movement. All new settlement activity was frozen during Israel's Camp David negotiations with Egypt. In exchange for peace,

Begin agreed to return the Sinai desert. Not only was Israel willing to relinquish a desert that provided critical strategic depth to the south, but even part of the promised land, the Rafiah salient where Jews had returned to live again in Yamit.

To the stupefaction of the Jewish settlers, Begin even promised "full autonomy" to the Palestinians. The 1978 accord stated, "The Israeli military government and its civilian administration will be withdrawn as soon as a self-governing authority has been freely elected by the inhabitants of these areas."[15] Begin appeared willing to give up the heart of the land of Israel! "All of Zionism is about to be wiped out," wrote one of Gush Emunim's rabbis. And to Gush Emunim's bitter disappointment, the Israeli public did not respond to their calls for mass resistance to the required evacuation of Yamit in the Sinai.

Gush Emunim again intensified its confrontational tactics, attempting to squat illegally in Nablus, Mesha, Givon, Jericho, and Hebron. Adding to their sense of betrayal, the National Religious Party, the only religious Zionist party, agreed to support the Camp David Accords. In 1979, with the support of Rabbi Zvi Yehuda Kook, Rabbi Waldman and Hanan Porat spearheaded the formation of a new political party – Tehiyah, or "Renaissance," dedicated to the inviolability of the land.[16] Waldman told us he had entered politics reluctantly. He would rather study Torah and settle the land, he said. But just as his yeshivah boys had borne arms, it was time to "purify" the "political field."

Gush Emunim's fears were only partially founded. Unlike President Jimmy Carter and Egyptian president Anwar Sadat, Prime Minister Begin saw "autonomy" as an alternative to Palestinian statehood. Moreover, Begin, like Moshe Dayan, whose concept it was, did not understand "autonomy" to preclude Jewish settlement. Quite the contrary. Begin had negotiated Israeli withdrawal from the Sinai on the assumption that Israel would later be free to continue settlement in Judea and Samaria. Indeed, the government wanted to build as widely and as quickly as possible before "autonomy" became a reality.

Within a week of signing the peace treaty with Egypt in 1979, Begin established three regional councils in the West Bank that would enable Jews living there to make long-term plans for a permanent presence under Israeli law. Gush Emunim activists consequently formed an umbrella organization to represent the interests of all Jewish settlers, most of whom are not actively messianic, but religious nationalists doing what they see as their patriotic duty or ordinary Israelis drawn by subsidized housing. This body is called Moetzet Yesha, or the Council of Settlements in Yehudah, Shomron, and Aza (*Yesha* is an acronym for the Hebrew names for Judea, Samaria, and Gaza). The government now recognized Amana as an official settlement movement, entitling it to the same financial and technical support provided to the *kibbutzim* and *moshavim*. Institutionalized in this way, with its activists serving as officials in the many municipal and regional governments, Gush Emunim, as an organized social movement, had ceased to exist. Its activists nonetheless dominate Amana and Yesha, which have been able to claim that their settlements are eligibile for subsidies as development towns, as well as pioneering and confrontation settlements.[17] As a result, their villages and towns have received massive amounts of state monies compared to the funds received by localities within Israel, even desperately poor development towns inhabited by North African and Russian Jews in sparsely populated areas.[18]

Lands Away

Under the auspices of Begin's regime (1977–1984), Jewish settlement exploded throughout the territories. During the previous decade, the Labour government had only expropriated lands that had belonged to the Jordanian government or had been abandoned by Palestinian refugees. A small amount of private land had been requisitioned for military uses, which included the building of a few civilian settlements, that the Israeli High Court ruled were integral to regional defense and thus justifiable by international law.

Elias David Khoury, an Arab Israeli lawyer from Jerusalem who learned his trade at the Hebrew University law school, tried to challenge these Israeli expropriations in court. It was a daunting task. When the Israeli High Court ruled that taking private lands for civilian settlements was legal because it served Israeli security needs, it seemed to him there was no basis for challenging any land seizures. "So then all the West Bank should be needed for such settlement," Khoury told us. "Any settlement you put there, it will serve . . . interior Israeli security. And if you create such a settlement, you create the necessity to protect such a thing and therefore this land. It's like a chain, one link to another."

At Elon Moreh, the Gush Emunim's first big push into Samaria outside the Allon plan, Khoury managed to prove the military had responded to Gush Emunim's political initiative rather than to considerations of military strategy. In 1979, the High Court ruled that *this* Israeli settlement on private Palestinian land had to be dismantled because it did not serve security interests. It was the last major case Khoury won.

In response to the High Court's ruling, the Likud government devised an alternative strategy to seize vast amounts of privately owned lands for Jewish settlement. The government now took the position that Israel could claim all lands for which Palestinians lacked valid Jordanian registration. Under British and Jordanian occupation, land registration had been well advanced in the desert valleys. But in 1968, Israel stopped the land registration process. And among the scattered highland villages, there were thousands of family plots without proper title. In 1980, the Israelis began to apply Ottoman law from the midnineteenth century, which held that all uncultivated land without registration was *mawat*, or "dead" land, and thus could be claimed by the state.[19]

The Israelis did not carry out a survey that might have enabled Palestinians to register their land. On the contrary, Palestinian peasants had a very short time to prove that they had valid title; otherwise, they would lose the land. The military committees who administered the process often did not speak Arabic. Many Palestinians had worked unparceled, unregistered land without formal title for decades. Others, unable to make a living off their land, had become wage workers so that their land had not been cultivated for some time.

Issam al-Anani neither speaks nor reads Hebrew. Al-Anani will only practice law in the West Bank. Like other Palestinian lawyers in Jerusalem, he won't defend clients in Jerusalem courts because they are run according to Israeli law. A dapper man who is tightly connected to King Hussein, he helped keep his friend Anwar Nusseibeh's East Jerusalem Electricity Company from being taken over by the Israelis. He has spent much of his adult legal life defending Palestinians against expropriation, trying to keep them out and get them out of jail, to allow them to open new businesses and plant crops.

How did it feel to defend his clients in these military courts? we asked him. "Show of justice, perfect," he replied. "They give you the right to talk, to give documents, to ask the witnesses, to make cross examinations, as you like. But the results are always against us. And we always try to go again because we have no other choice."

According to the law, lands planted for seven continuous years belong to the planter. When Palestinians tried to plant trees or vines to maintain their right to possession, the Israelis often stopped them. In some cases, Israeli settlers or troops would uproot trees staking an Arab claim to lands they believed should properly be categorized as "state" lands. It was partly for this reason that the Jewish National Fund (JNF) planted millions of trees all around Jerusalem. "Trees represent people who aren't here yet," a JNF official told us.[20]

It is no different in Jerusalem. When in the late 1980s, for example, a new neighborhood, Har-Homah, was being planned for a forested area between two Arab villages in Jerusalem, the left-wing Ratz city council members objected. Besides, they said, these forty-five hundred housing units would be constructed right in the middle of a "green area." Teddy Kollek reportedly replied, "Green? This is green for Arabs." When

Jewish suburbs north of Jerusalem.

Arnon Yekutieli, a Ratz member, inquired what he meant, Kollek replied that some places had been forested so that Arabs wouldn't build
there. "We just needed time until we get there," the mayor reportedly
replied. "That's green for Arabs."[21]

Tens of thousands of Palestinian landowners were vulnerable to expropriation. When the Israelis took control of the West Bank, Jordan
claimed 527,000 dunam as state land. By 1988, the Israelis had claimed
2.15 million dunam, close to 40 percent of the total landmass, as state
land.[22] In addition, some lands owned by the Palestinians were declared
military areas; others, nature preserves; still others were subject to construction bans of various sorts.

Under pressure from Jewish settlers, Likud, for the first time, allowed
private individuals to purchase West Bank lands from Arabs. This contradicted the historic Zionist pattern of collective, national ownership. By
turning the buying of Arab lands over to private individuals and firms, the
Israeli state was able to distance itself from some of the controversial
process of Jewish residential penetration, and at the same time to institute
mechanisms of legitimate, noncoercive land acquisition that would endure after the Likud was no longer in power. A shadow world of clandestine land purchase, sometimes coerced, sometimes fictitious, and sometimes real, quickly emerged. There were few Jewish settlements that were
not approached by Palestinians, sometimes in the dead of night, about the

sale of land. In just the first five years of Begin's government, Israelis were able to buy 200,000 dunam on the private market from Palestinians.[23] If the dreams of the Gush Emunim were realized, there would be millions to be made from real estate in the territories. Private developers and speculators moved in to complement the work of Amana.

The Labour government had been loath to integrate the West Bank's north–south road network into the Israeli system. Likud cut new roads, designed to bypass built-up Arab areas, from Jewish settlements to the Jerusalem and Tel Aviv metropolitan areas. Enormous setbacks were established to prevent Palestinians from building on their own land along the main roads out of the city. Not only could Jewish commuters move more quickly and safely into Israel's cities, troops could move quickly out to control the Palestinian population.

With heavy government subsidies, a family could buy an affordable detached house and at the same time participate in the foundational pioneer tradition. Although veterans of the early *kibbutzim* sneered at the comparison, commuting became patriotic. The new roads placed the Palestinians out of sight, much like the early Zionist art, which lovingly chronicled the landscape of the new–old land, while erasing its resident population.[24] Many government maps of planned Jewish settlement were devoid of indicators of Arab habitation.

Israel placed new settlements so as to fragment the field for Palestinian settlement and block the expansion of Palestinian cities.[25] New regional councils – Shomron, Binyamin, Midbar Yehudah – provided the Jewish settlers with the same municipal services their fellow citizens received on the other side of an invisible former border. The West Bank's scarce water resources were diverted to service the Jewish settlements. Jewish residents of the West Bank remained full citizens of Israel proper, subject to its laws and courts; the Palestinians were ruled by military occupation. A dual legal system was put in place, with one law for Arabs and another for Jews.

Under the Likud regimes, new public construction monies poured into the West Bank. If the major construction companies, which had grown up symbiotically with the Labour Party and depended heavily on public contracts, wanted to survive, they had to follow the demand out into the territories. The speed of construction was incredible – power grids, schools, sewers, housing. Most Jerusalemites rarely had occasion to travel north or south from Jerusalem. Despite two decades of occupation, most still oriented themselves to the west, toward Tel Aviv and the Mediterranean. Every week, somebody would announce incredulously, "Have you been up there? A small city has been built!"

In the second decade of Israeli rule, Jewish population grew dramatically in the West Bank. In 1977, when Begin came to power, there were only five thousand settlers in thirty-four locations. By the end of the next decade, there were sixty-seven thousand Jews spread out over 140 separate settlements, dotting the entire area to be exchanged under the Allon plan.[26] The World Zionist Organization's master plan called for over ten times that number of Jewish settlers by the year 2010.

With Likud's electoral victory in 1988, the construction of new settlements began again. The Palestinian uprising changed nothing. In July 1988, Rabbi Moshe Levinger, the Gush Emunim stalwart, reminded the movement faithful that Likud's massive settlement drive took place *after* they had successfully forced the government to create a dozen new settlements in the first six months of Begin's rule. "If we do our part," he told them, "it can be expected that the state will follow in our footsteps as it did in the past."[27]

In 1989, the Soviet Union, desperately in need of American aid, investment, and markets, decided to let its Jews emigrate. It was impossible for the Russian regime to legitimate this legal exodus under anything other than a logic of repatriation. And as the Soviet Union began to disintegrate, the Jewish exodus received a nasty, if predictable, shove from a wave of anti-Semitism. Most of the Jews wanted to immigrate to the United States, but by closing their doors to new Russian Jewish emigrés, the Americans cooperated in funneling them to Israel. The Americans and the Soviets successfully pressed Israel to make assurances the new immigrants would not be settled in occupied territories. Even though Ariel Sharon was Israel's minister of housing in Shamir's Likud government, with the exception of Jerusalem, the Russian Jews who flooded Israel were not directed to settlements over the "Green Line," the armistice line separating Israeli and Jordanian forces from 1948 to 1967. But there simply wasn't enough affordable housing within Israel proper to accommodate them. Rents and housing prices skyrocketed. Although the new immigrants had access to rental and mortgage subsidies, there were Israeli families who lived with friends, in tent camps, and even on the streets because they could not find an affordable roof. In spite of the *intifada*, the housing pressures pushed more and more ordinary Israelis to reconsider the cheaper, subsidized housing waiting for them out there in the West Bank.

Even after Egypt, Syria, Jordan, Lebanon, and Israel had all agreed to the peace conference convened in Madrid in October 1991, and Saudi Arabia and Kuwait were willing to suspend the Arab boycott if Israel stopped its settlement of the occupied territories, the Shamir government's response to America's call for reciprocal confidence-building measures was to dig feverishly. The pace of new housing starts in the occupied territories accelerated to record levels.[28]

Five Minutes to Midnight

After the Begin regime came to power, Ra'anan Weitz, longtime head of the Jewish Agency's Settlement Department, the man who had orchestrated Israel's settlement policies, was pushed out of any ministerial responsibility. In 1978, a year into Begin's reign, Weitz was architect of a settlement plan anticipating the eventual creation of a Palestinian state. The plan engendered a firestorm of controversy, including calls for his expulsion from the agency. A Palestinian state was unthinkable to most Israelis.

In the same year, the movement Shalom Achshav, or Peace Now, was founded. Its demonstrations against expansive Jewish settlement were small, drawing heavily upon university students and left intellectuals. This movement said loudly what many Israelis already knew, that the conquered lands presented Israel with a choice between being a Jewish and being a democratic state. Keeping the territories, they warned, would lead Israel back to a nondemocratic dualist structure not unlike those that Jews endured in pre-Enlightenment Europe. If Israel held on long enough, it would slide, de facto, into apartheid. But even at the height of the movement's powers, when it brought hundreds of thousands of Jews out against the war in Lebanon, Peace Now was never able to convert its members' desires for peace into concerted opposition against settlement. With structures and subsidies in place, the logic of suburbanization did its work. Jerusalem has become the hub of West Bank Jewish settlement. Despite the demonstrations, the angry confrontations, the bulldozers continue to move, the planning permissions never stop.

Meron Benvenisti, Kollek's former deputy mayor, compared the Israeli left, and particularly the peace movement, to the Social Democrats in Weimar Germany, who were incapable of positing new mechanisms of mobilization, of change, as the nation slid into fascism around them. Pointing to his lips, jutting out his chin, he said:

> They are still with the milk of their mothers just here . . . If [the Israeli left] is committed, it is committed to their own conscience. "We don't care about the Arabs; we just care for the nature of the Jewish state." That is a typical Peace Now slogan . . . I call them a big laundry for their own conscience. Going between eleven and one on Shabbat, after their brunch and before their nap, to go to demonstrate on the West Bank. They feel for the whole month that they took the old lady across the street.

He stopped abruptly. "You make me angry, you provoke me, with your questions."

Benvenisti angrily chronicled the Jewish penetration. As creator and director of the West Bank Data Project, he wielded his skills as mapmaker and planner against it. Built like a linebacker on an American football team, and like many Israelis his age, he has fought in four wars. But unlike most, he has had intimate contacts with Palestinians.

And he knows their land. As a child, he traveled with his father, one of Israel's founding cartographers. The elder Benvenisti mapped the topography of his new land, devising Hebrew names for the villages and towns the Jews were constructing everywhere they could purchase land. Young Benvenisti not only learned the new names, he also learned the Arab place names they replaced. Meron Benvenisti watched as the dots diffused across the government maps; he counted the millions of dollars diverted to new settlements, when development towns in the Negev and the Galilee were faltering; he monitored the cycle of repression and resistance that accompanied occupation. He became impatient, even desperate.

"What," we inquired, "is the difference between Likud and Labour regarding the territories?"

"Like a loved wife and a kept woman, pure and simple," he snapped at us.

> The Labour government is a Protestant husband. They always felt ashamed of their mistress . . . That's typical Alignment [Labour], Peace-Now, bourgeois, boy scout psychology. "We want to keep both our values intact. Yes, we are for territorial compromise. We are ready. What can we do if the other side is not ready? So we tell them, we put settlements there because we want to explain to you the price." So there's a liberal approach in building more settlements so that the Arabs will be more frightened to come talk to us.

There was, he said, an essential continuity between Israeli state-building before 1967 and its "occupation" after, between the state's relationship to the land to the west and the east of the "Green Line."

Most Palestinians shared Benvenisti's vision. "The Labour are very dangerous for us," Akram Haniyeh, a newspaper editor, told us. "The Likud is going to kill us by a gun, you know, but the Labour, they will put a silencer on the gun so we will be killed without giving us the right to scream or without giving the world the right to know."

Labour Zionists once celebrated the building of socialism. But after statehood, their successors increasingly honored just the building itself. The hardscape rising over the land was both a territorial claim and an assertion of presence. As a result, Benvenisti told us, the Labour Party was not morally equipped to resist pressures by a new generation of pioneers to do what had become the state's central legitimation – to build. The Labour government's ad hoc concessions to settlement pressures, the elasticity of the Allon plan, its justification of ever more settlement on military criteria, its desire to establish Jewish hegemony in the Jerusalem metropolitan area – all these had contributed to the waves of settlement that came later. Officially Labour treated its territorial occupation as though it were temporary. But by its actions, it created the framework for permanence.

In his technical reports, his news conferences, his lectures, and his testimony before the U.S. Congress, Benvenisti hammered at the same theme: the occupied lands were being knit to the motherland by a thousand threads – by tarmac and concrete; by flows of commuters, workers, and consumer goods; by water lines, sewer pipes, and electric grids; by the application of Israeli laws to the Jewish settlements. The separation between Israel and the "territories" had become a fiction, a cartographic fetish.

By the early 1980s, Benvenisti was arguing that the forces of incorporation had a momentum all their own. The hour, he warned, was close to midnight. These claims of "irreversibility" provoked anger and anguish almost everywhere. In Amman and Tel Aviv, both King Hussein and the Israeli left rejected his conclusion that the forces connecting the new lands to the old had reached the point of no return. Israeli critics claimed he was under the "spell of those little black dots on the settlement map."[29] If France, with one million of its citizens ensconced in Algeria – one eighth of the total population – could be forced to grant its former colony independence after 120 years of occupation, so could Israel. The Palestinians, the world, and ultimately even the Israeli public would make the price of occupation too high. Abba Eban, one of the staunchest defenders of the possibility of partition, a Labour leader who even initially refused to visit the West Bank, wrote of the Benvenisti thesis, "I find it rather hard to speak calmly about that thesis. Its consequence is to enfeeble our front, to create defeatism – after all, if it is really all over, why fight?"

But in Washington, some State Department officials concluded Benvenisti was right: all that could be done was to force Israel to improve the "quality of life" of the West Bank's Arab residents. Only Benvenisti's enemies, Israelis who wanted to believe these lands would always be theirs, celebrated his conclusions. His apparent contribution to their cause angered the Israeli left. Amos Oz, the novelist, dismissed Benvenisti. "He wants to be a prophet; or maybe a messiah," he sighed to us. "Jerusalem is filled with angry prophets."

8

Building the Capital

Jerusalem is a wise old town. Things will come and things will go, and it always has its very calm hysteria.

– Elinoar Barzaki, Jerusalem's chief engineer[1]

As Israeli troops stormed onto the Temple Mount in 1967, a Jewish state controlled this ancient site of sacrifice to the one God and symbol of sovereignty of the one people for the first time in two thousand years. One soldier thought it natural to raise the Israeli flag from the dull black dome of al-Aqsa mosque, once a stable for the Knights Templar. Moshe Dayan, the minister of defense, ordered it taken down. The Muslims would keep the platform they called the *haram as-sharif*, and the Jews would again pray below the complex at its outer "Western Wall." When Israelis first touched this wall, many wept uncontrollably. Israel's prime minister, Levi Eshkol, pressed his body, arms outstretched, against the wall as if to embrace it for the nation, sovereign flesh against sacred stone. The Western Wall became a site where soldiers were initiated into elite military units, where Israel commemorated the sacrifice of its soldiers.

The Israelis believed that by dividing the holy places between Muslims and Jews, they could unite this city of Arabs and Israelis. Moshe Dayan removed the barbed wire, the mine fields, and the walls dividing Jerusalem, and a remarkable young mayor, Teddy Kollek, elected two years before, began to govern the city in a way he hoped would serve Arab and Jew alike.

The Redemption of Zion

History had prepared Kollek for the job. Teddy, as he is known by every Israeli, grew up in Vienna, a city torn between modernity and its victims, a city inhabited by cultured Jews and rabid anti-Semites. One man from Vienna first coined the term *Zionism* and another invented the gas

Teddy Kollek, former mayor of Jerusalem, 1989.

chamber. The connections between the two phenomena made Teddy Kollek; Vienna is stitched into his political genes.

In 1935, Kollek, named Teddy in honor of Theodor Herzl, left for Palestine on a boat called *Gerusaleme*. In 1939, he returned to Vienna with British entry permits to negotiate Jewish exit visas with a young Nazi who had been given authority over the "Jewish problem"; twenty-two years later, Adolph Eichmann would stand trial in Zion for crimes against humanity. Kollek, then the director of Prime Minister Ben-

Palestinian bearing pita in the Muslim Quarter of the Old City, 1993.

Gurion's office, technically prepared the trial.[1] Four years later, in 1965, Jerusalem would be his, elected mayor over and over again, until he was finally defeated in 1993. For more than a quarter century, he tried to make the ideal of a cultured, multiethnic Vienna real in Jerusalem. Even as Kollek sought to make Jerusalem a cosmopolitan jewel, he feared the religious and national hatreds that had destroyed the city of his youth.[2]

After 1967, the Israelis poured money into the city, not only on the Jewish side, where neighborhood after neighborhood sprung up in the rocky hills, but on the Palestinian side. The Old City's alleyways were repaved, its plumbing and decrepit sewage system that ran towards the Western Wall were replaced, its fabled gates refurbished. Kollek's administration built sewers, laid pipes, renovated schools, and graded roads in East Jerusalem, reversing almost twenty years of Jordanian neglect. For two decades, the Israelis, and Teddy Kollek in particular, believed they could run Jerusalem as a pluralistic city in which all residents would benefit while they waited for the Jordanians to return to the negotiating table.

Before the city was cut in two in 1948, Jerusalem had had a downtown in which Jews and Arabs mixed uneasily. During two decades of division, the two downtowns moved steadily away from the dangerous walled center of the city. In the first flush of unification, Kollek wanted to recreate a common downtown, to show that Jews and Arabs could shop and work together. Plans to rejoin the two downtown centers went nowhere. He left the two sides each to go their own way.

Kollek not only tried to promote the individual prosperity of the Palestinians, he protected their pride. Kollek braved tremendous outrage when he allowed the city's Palestinians to build a memorial to their soldiers who fell fighting his friends and countrymen in the 1967 war. Later, he allowed them to build a memorial to the Palestinians who fell at Sabra and Shatilla, in a Christian Phalangist massacre for which the world and the Palestinians held the Israelis, at least indirectly, responsible. Kollek was even willing to state for the record that someday an Arab flag might fly above the *haram as-sharif*.[3]

As mayor, Kollek railed against the Jewish settlements built in a ring around his city. After Palestinians withdrew en masse from government schools, Kollek successfully pressed for the Palestinians of Jerusalem to be allowed to follow the Jordanian curriculum in state-funded Israeli schools provided it was stripped of its anti-Israeli and anti-Semitic content. He opposed those Jews who demand what they consider their right to pray on the Temple Mount. Kollek pressed to exempt Jerusalem from the West Bank procedure, started by the British, of dynamiting the family houses of those Palestinians suspected of terrorism.[4]

This is remarkable, for Jerusalem is a right-wing city, repeatedly and disproportionately casting its vote with Likud in the national elections. The city has been a bastion of support for right-wing parties racing to settle the territories, parties that would minimize the political rights and the economic benefits received by the Palestinians under Israeli governance. Even while they endorsed the uncompromising aims of more right-wing parties at the national level, the people of the city voted time after time for moderation at home. Jerusalem is the center of the storm and Teddy Kollek devoted his life trying to prevent the walls from closing in. He did it in part by attempting to disengage the politics of his city from those of the nation. By insisting that Jerusalem is different from any other place in Israel, Kollek demanded Jews treat Zion with special care.

Kollek made his reputation as a master builder, a fund-raiser, a gruff man with a gentle touch, a *bitzuist*, "doer of deeds," who busted through bureaucratic obstacles or went around them altogether, a patronage politician who remembered the particular problems of poor people, a peacemaker. His telephone number was listed in the phonebook; ordinary citizens called him at home. He arrived at work before seven and often left close to midnight. Kollek could fall asleep at public functions and nobody minded. He delivered short speeches using simple and sometimes ungrammatical Hebrew. "Do me a favor and start at the end" became the mayor's standard interruption of a committee chairman's lengthy peroration.

"He's a miracle," Ari Shachar, the head of Hebrew University's Department of Geography and one of the city's top planners, told us in 1989.

> If there was anything that God sent to this town, to this country, it was Teddy Kollek in Jerusalem . . . He's a simplistic person, not too intelligent, not too cultured. Nevertheless, he has this sort of deep understanding of human beings . . . Without Teddy I don't know what would have happened in Jerusalem. It deeply concerns me what will happen in Jerusalem when he will retire.

To keep national politics out of Jerusalem is impossible. Israel is a centralized state; the most important initiatives to build in Jerusalem come from the central government. The city can react, modify, but rarely resist for long. Whenever Kollek decided to build a public building, a housing project, a stadium, he first had to obtain clearance from the national government. Jerusalem's police followed orders from the Ministry of the Interior, a ministry controlled by a small religious party. Most of the city's tax revenues were collected by the central government. Which party held national power had a major impact on Kollek's policy options.

So, too, Israel is a country where every job, every building, every project has a party label. Israel's government is bloated with political appointments. Local politics are harbingers of new political forces that burst onto the national scene. The major political blocs – Likud and Labour – each rely upon the party machines in the large cities, including Jerusalem. Kollek, too, depended on the Labour Party to get out the vote, particularly among his lower-income constituents.

Kollek, however, was able to create space to maneuver. Like his mentor David Ben-Gurion, Kollek broke from the Labour Party and began to run as an independent in 1978. He won. Until his defeat in 1993, the Labour Party was forced to follow their charismatic mayor. He was a consummate fund-raiser, alternatively charming and bullying the rich and the glamorous to give to and perform in his city. Not a few philanthropists proudly handed the mayor a very large check only to hear him tell them that it was not enough. Hundreds of millions of dollars coursed through Kollek's independent agency, the Jerusalem Foundation, which evolved out of his first campaign fund.[5] The foundation financed over a thousand projects ranging from parks, theaters, and archaeological restorations to community centers and synagogues.[6] Such resources gave him a margin of autonomy from the government, a lever to prod the ministries. Indeed, some argued he had created a private government accountable to neither city nor national government.

Representing the Unrepresentable

Most Palestinian residents of Jerusalem refuse to do anything that would legitimate Israel's claim to sovereignty in what they understand as their nation's capital. Almost all Palestinians with Jordanian passports who reside in Jerusalem rejected Israel's postwar offer to become citizens. Local Palestinian lawyers decline to try cases in Jerusalem courts, where Israeli law applies, and largely confine their work to the officially "occupied" West Bank. Jerusalem's Palestinians rely upon Israeli Arabs to defend them.

But if most of its Palestinian residents refuse to work with or for the Israeli municipality, they accept having the city work for them. As official residents, they are glad of the new roads and sewers the Israelis build in their neighborhoods, of the kindergartens, for the health care and social insurance. The mother of Abu Mussa, the Palestinian radical, lives in East Jerusalem and draws a National Insurance pension.[7] Many of Jerusalem's Arabs join the Zionist labor union, the Histadrut, vote in union elections, and take full advantage of the health benefits available in Jerusalem's hospitals.

Because the mayor preserved the Jordanian curriculum in East Jerusalem's public schools, unlike other Israeli Arabs – whom the West Bank Palestinians regard suspiciously – the Palestinian youth of Jerusalem attend West Bank Palestinian universities. Rashidiyah, an Arab boy's high school in Jerusalem, is an Israeli-run school following the Jordanian curriculum. By both Israeli and Jordanian design, the history of the Palestinian nation is not taught. The Israelis forbid Palestinian teachers in Jerusalem to discuss politics with their students. The students learn their history and its heroes, their politics, and their poetry at home, in youth clubs, and on the street. "I know it from my father. He can tell us. And my grandfather, he told my father," one said. They rattle off their favorite poets. They learn their own history lessons: "Israel . . . must take a good lesson from history about how many empires have collapsed," one dark-eyed student told us.

Kollek jumped to defend the individual rights and liberties of Palestinians, as well as the religious sensibilities and ritual rights of Muslims and Christians. But he would not and could not represent the unrepresentable: the national rights of the Palestinians. Even though they refused to become Israeli citizens, Palestinians were granted the right to vote and run for office in the now-united Israeli city. Most Palestinians nonetheless refused to exercise their franchise in Jerusalem at all.

Jerusalem's contending political parties have been finely balanced; a unified Arab party speaking for almost a third of the city's voters would wield considerable influence. At various times, Kollek barely managed a majority and was forced into coalition with non-Zionist religious parties with whom he violently disagreed. A Palestinian bloc would have provided an almost irresistible alternative.

If the Palestinians didn't want to vote for Zionist parties, why not form their own Palestinian party to run for city council? In the decade we covered the city, only a few prominent Palestinians considered this a thinkable, let alone desirable Palestinian strategy. We heard it first around the time of the 1983 election from Elias Khoury, the Jerusalem-based Israeli Arab lawyer who had fought so ferociously against expropriation of Palestinian lands. Staying out of the city's politics, Khoury said, only served the Zionists. The Jews were staking claims to larger portions of the city and the Arabs could neither resist effectively nor build on their own. It was stupid, he said, for the PLO and Jordan to object. Didn't they allow Palestinians in Jerusalem to be represented in Israeli courts by Israeli Arabs? Why not let Israeli Arabs in the capital run for office? "If the Arab voters all will vote for one person to be a mayor and the Jewish voters will be divided," Khoury told us, "I believe the mayor can be also an Arab."

Several years later, before the 1989 municipal contest, Hanna Siniora, the *al-Fajr* editor, publicly supported the idea. His opponents argued that to run for the council would legitimate Israeli sovereignty, would validate the authority of the municipal council on which the Palestinians would sit. Israelis on Jerusalem's council city claimed just this.[8] After his car was twice firebombed, Siniora withdrew the proposal. Asked about the idea, Faisal Husayni, Fatah's top man in the city, said,

> When I speak about a Palestinian state, I can't get the capital of the state out of it. A Palestinian state means the capital in Jerusalem, in this case one-half of Jerusalem, East Jerusalem. So I wouldn't allow anything to cut East Jerusalem from the . . . remains of Palestine, and to tell me, "Make your own state without this capital." No Palestinian state without Jerusalem . . . To ask me to have six people to be in that municipality, it means that I am part of Jerusalem, the capital of Israel, not the capital of Palestine. So maybe we are losing a lot of services here. But to lose services is better than to lose the capital.

Kollek initially tried to recruit Palestinians to stand for office on his own list. He wanted his party to speak for all Jerusalem's citizens. Most Palestinians he approached refused, and when they did not, they retreated in the face of threats of violence from their more militant nationalist neighbors. The only Arabs Kollek could have found to run on his list would have been "simple people from the village edges of Jerusalem," the mayor told us. To the Arabs, he said, "they would be regarded as some kind of fig leaf . . . They might make a good impression when they are being filmed on television abroad, but it wouldn't mean anything here . . . and after all, life here is the important thing and not the impression abroad."

The PLO always organized campaigns to prevent Palestinians in Jerusalem from voting in the municipal elections. At the time of the 1983 municipal election, the PLO was in disarray, militarily shattered and split into warring factions. There was no official campaign to deter Arabs in Jerusalem from going out to vote. "We are getting used to living together," Kollek then remarked. "This doesn't mean . . . that the Arabs of Jerusalem are turning into Zionists or beginning to love us. But they're beginning to get used to living here."

Afraid to unleash Palestinian political activism of any kind, serious campaigning in East Jerusalem was kept to a minimum. Nonetheless, in a close election, the temptation of all those Arab votes was too great. For Likud and the religious right, with their insistence on permanent territorial control of Judea and Samaria, gaining Arab votes was difficult. But for Kollek, with his record of building infrastructure in the Arab areas, his administration of welfare and education for large segments of the Arab population, his provision of numerous jobs to Arabs, and his record of support for territorial compromise, it was much easier. Kollek's posters, printed in Hebrew and Arabic, were plastered all over the Arab side of the city. Some Palestinian teenagers and even some adults wore T-shirts with his picture on them.

The act of voting was conspicuous. Polls were located in each Palestinian neighborhood. All Jerusalemites' identity cards are stamped after voting. It was not easy for a Palestinian to evade hints by Israeli employers or city workers who provide services that one ought to vote. The right-wing opposition accused Kollek of padding his work force with low-level Arab workers whose families would exercise their franchise in support of their employer. According to news accounts, Kollek's campaign workers used the recent census to pinpoint households receiving welfare payments, conveying the message that voting for the regime providing those benefits would be in their best interests. The Israeli parties hired workers to bring out the Arab vote, often the same contractors who took Arab workers to Israeli construction sites. And there were those who were waiting for a permit to build, to start a business, to reunite their families, to allow their children to visit during the summer, or to place a student in school. Evidence of voting might speed the processing of their case. The bureaucracies were not blind.

More than patronage politics got Arabs to the polls. Even though they knew he represented the liberal face of Zionist occupation, Teddy Kollek made a difference in their lives. The Palestinians of the villages who couldn't afford not to send their children to the municipal schools, who were most dependent on Israeli labor unions to improve their working conditions and on the Israeli social insurance for material support in the event they could not work, were more likely to vote than the more urban and urbane Palestinians who had other means at their disposal and could fall back on family networks in the event of disaster.[9]

At headquarters on election night in 1983, Kollek's small army of Israeli volunteers were jubilant. Jerusalem had given the mayor his largest mandate ever. Not only was Kollek chosen mayor once again, but for the first time, his party had a clear majority in the city council. More Palestinians – thirteen thousand – had come out to vote, largely for him, than ever before. Kollek owed his majority on the city council to his Arab constituents. "The election proves," he told Israeli reporters, "that there is *one* Jerusalem." As he faced the world press late that night, still supporting himself with a cane against the injuries sustained at the hands of his *haredi* opponents, he was proud. Through substantial support from one group of enemies of Zionism, he could rule Jerusalem without having to depend on the support of another. This was a highwater mark for Kollek's vision of unified Jerusalem, one city under liberal Zionist rule. It was, in fact, the beginning of a long slide in his political fortunes. Kollek's vision would come under attack from both inside and out.

Points of Contact

Because the Palestinians of Jerusalem won't represent themselves, the Israelis have had to construct their own channels of communication and control. The mechanisms combine the colonial bureau of "native affairs" and the premodern *mukhtar*, local notables dating from the Ottoman Empire.

An Arab Jew whose parents came to Palestine from Iraq in 1933, Morris Zilka had just finished a long stint as Kollek's adviser on Arab affairs when we met him in 1984. This tough-minded Zionist was the point man to whom the city's Arab residents turned when they wanted something from the city. He had his own budget, his own bureaucrats, and his own network of connections to the bureaus that impinge on the lives of the Arabs. He worked hard at a job he believed should be eliminated. Jerusalem was the only Israeli city with a special liaison to the Palestinian community; Zilka thought Jerusalem should relate to its Arab residents in the same way as any other Israeli city with a large Arab population – like Haifa or Jaffa.

"Because the mayor has no Arabs in the city [council], he needs someone to protect their rights," Morris Zilka told us. The job fell to Zilka. "You know," he said, "[for] every single thing on earth they come to us, to our office. Even when they have problems among themselves, they come to us to fight." Zilka spent a lot of his time acting as an intercessor for individuals, families, and neighborhoods who wanted something done or undone by the city's bureaucracies. Many of Jerusalem's Arabs turned to Zilka to help get their relatives through the Israeli checkpoint at the Jordan River bridges, to contest their tax assessments, or to keep a brother out of an Israeli jail.

"I protect them deeply, protect their rights as citizens," he said. "Otherwise I wouldn't survive . . . Otherwise, I would hate myself, because I think that they need this help, have no one to help them, because they are in the shadow . . . even though I know sometimes it's not probably the best thing to do because I'm still a Jew and my concern is the Jewish people."

Teddy Kollek and his Arab affairs adviser related to the Arabs of Jerusalem through *mukhtars* who represent the most important families, neighborhoods, and villages incorporated in 1967 to an enlarged Israeli capital. For example, the residents of A-Tur, a small suburban village on the lip of the Mount of Olives, still do not identify themselves as *Qudsi*, after al-Quds, or "Jerusalemites," but as *Aturi*. Go into any office in the Jerusalem municipality where building permits are issued, to the prison gate where relatives are waiting to visit a son or grandchild, and you will see the Palestinian *mukhtars* trying to intercede, to cajole, to argue for their constituents. The *mukhtars* register births and the transfer of land ownership. Traditionally it was to the *mukhtars* that the Israeli police would go when a neighborhood caused trouble, harboring somebody who had crossed the ever-changing line of acceptable political expression.

Israeli political elites saw Arab Jerusalem as fragmented among many personalities and clans, a city in which the Palestinians lacked a recognized political leadership. This made Zilka's job both harder and easier. Harder, because it took so much time to deal, as he put it, with "the small pieces." And easier because contacts with the city's Arabs tended to be personal, fragmented, invisible, between patrons and very local clients still pulled by primitive rivalries stretching back over the centuries. It was easier to maneuver, but harder to coordinate.

From where Morris Zilka sat, it seemed the Palestinians of Jerusalem led a blessed life. "Life in Jerusalem is the best life on earth for Palestinians," he said. Compared to the diaspora Palestinian communities, the Palestinians of Jerusalem have it sweet indeed, he argued. Kuwait, Saudi Arabia, and Lebanon had all enacted discriminatory laws against Palestinians. In Syria, Palestinian political prisoners disappeared with no account, no television cameras, no international investigation. Certainly it was better than the militarily administered West Bank, where, he reminded us, they "can hold a person for questioning for a year. In Jerusalem, you can't. It's exactly like my right I have by law. And social security, free education. You're free."

"They eat the cake from both sides," he told us in 1984. "That is why, in this city, we've had no problem whatsoever for seventeen years . . . So they strike, so a few kids throw stones. This is not a serious thing . . . They are only kids. Capture those kids."

A Separate City

Kollek tried to separate his city from the politics of the West Bank, both from the claims of Israeli settlers who want these lands to be part of Israel and from those of the Palestinians who see them as their last hope for a state of their own. To do so, Kollek had to manufacture a myth that the new lines the Israelis drew in the dirt after 1967 for the enlarged municipality of Jerusalem delineated an entity somehow different from the other conquered lands.

The city of Jerusalem includes a huge chunk of land that used to be part of Jordan. In fact, most of the lands that make up postwar Jerusalem are on the Jordanian side of the "Green Line" and thus constitute "occupied" territory according to international law.[10] Although many Israelis will not buy real estate on the other side of the old armistice line, for most the old Green Line in Jerusalem has ceased to be any kind of constraint. More Israelis live on "occupied" lands in the city than in the rest of the West Bank and Gaza together.[11] Consider the amazement, then, of one Israeli woman living in a new neighborhood in the old Jordanian sector of the city when she volunteered her home for an Israeli–Palestinian women's peace group. It hadn't occurred to her that even moderate Palestinians would be uncomfortable meeting in a Jewish neighborhood they considered just like any settlement on the West Bank.

Jerusalem's municipal boundaries stake out a national claim that the world refuses to acknowledge. Since 1953, when Israel moved its Foreign Ministry to Jerusalem, the world's nations have played diplomatic cat and mouse with the city. On the eve of the Six-Day War, twenty-three embassies were located in Israeli Jerusalem. Within weeks after the war, almost every embassy had left for Tel Aviv. Some, such as the Soviet Union, left altogether.

Slowly and quietly, the embassies began to return to Jerusalem during the 1970s. And then in 1980, Begin's government passed the Jerusalem Law declaring united Jerusalem the eternal capital of Israel. The law's passage infuriated Kollek. "It was meant for popularity, not for any substance," he told us. Jerusalem *was* already Israel's capital; although the rest of the city had never been formally annexed, Israeli law applied to the entire city. As a result of the Jerusalem law, the embassies that had relocated in Jerusalem packed up again and moved down to the Mediterranean coast. (Jerusalem's famed tulip gardens date from this period. Dutch citizens sent the city over 100,000 tulip bulbs to protest their government's departure.) Foreign investors shied away. "It was a terrible setback," Kollek said.

While Teddy Kollek refused to attend national celebrations of countries, like the United States, whose embassies or consulates held separate affairs for each side of the city, he was committed to Jerusalem – all of it – as a Jewish city, as Zion. But, not one dunam more. When, for example, the Labour government authorized Ma'ale Adumim, which would become a huge suburb just over the new municipal boundaries at the eastern edge of the city, Kollek was incensed. He was not convinced by Moshe Dayan's argument that it would serve as a fortification to block future Arab tank advances from the Judean desert below.[12] What Kollek understood was that most of its residents would be Jerusalemites drawn to the greatest real estate deal in town and that they would use Jerusalem's services while paying no taxes to finance them. Kollek saw it as an inefficient use of public monies, all the more galling because Jerusalem received short shrift in the allocation of the national budget. However, when it came time to inaugurate the massive complex, Kollek was there to give his blessing. Although it compromised his plans to strengthen Jewish presence in Jerusalem, Kollek was powerless to shape the government's settlement policy, not only in the suburbs, but in the city itself.

The outward thrust from Jerusalem became exponentially more expansive once Likud came to power in 1977. Kollek's vision of Jerusalem entailed the prospect of territorial compromise, whereas Likud saw Jerusalem as the territorial center of a network of Jewish settlement through Judea and Samaria. Kollek's political opponents in the city all supported the profusion of satellite towns and settlements around Jerusalem. In most American cities, except the most beautiful or exclusive, it would be bizarre for a mayoral candidate to campaign on a platform encouraging growth *outside* his city. Yet here in Jerusalem, that has always been Likud's municipal platform. With dense Jewish settlement ringing the city, it would be impossible ever to use the municipality to define Israel's negotiated borders.

Kollek opposed these policies. Likud, Kollek railed to us in 1984, was draining Jerusalem of Jews, who were resettling in the West Bank suburbs around his city. He had settled seventy thousand Jews beyond the Green Line in "comparative quiet," he boasted. There was still room, he claimed, for tens of thousands of more Jews inside the city. Not only did Likud's settlement policy promote "urban sprawl," he prophesied, these government policies were laying the ground for a non-Zionist majority in the city made up of *haredi* Jews on the one side and Palestinians on the other. "It's just abysmal stupidity," he said. "We will end up with a Jerusalem metropolitan area stretching from Ramallah to Bethlehem with an Arab majority, instead of a smaller, stronger Jerusalem with a Jewish majority."

Hometown Advantage

After the Six-Day War, the Israelis redrew the municipal boundaries so as to maximize the areal size of "united" Jerusalem, while minimizing the number of its Arab residents.[13] The government showered the city with money to expand the Jewish presence there. Officials wanted to shake off the city's image as a sleepy dead end, a poor cousin to Tel Aviv down the hill. Some of its huge hotel towers, like the Plaza, which planners now concede are aesthetic and functional mistakes, date from this period. Fueled by the growth of its public sector, which employs half of its Jewish residents, Jerusalem outgrew both Tel Aviv and Haifa. In 1967, Tel Aviv was the largest city in Israel. By 1987, more *Jews* lived in Jerusalem than the total population of Tel Aviv. Jerusalem had become Israel's premier city.[14]

The Arab population of East Jerusalem, which had stagnated under Jordanian rule, doubled during these first two decades of Israeli administration.[15] Whereas the city's Jewish population is fed by continuous streams of immigrants, Arab population growth has depended almost exclusively on natural increase. The Israeli government makes it very difficult for Palestinians who live on what most Israelis consider to be "occupied" territories, even if they own property in Jerusalem proper, to migrate into the city. According to Israeli law, a Palestinian from the West Bank is not allowed even to stay overnight in Jerusalem without formal permission. Despite this prohibition, the economic lure of Jerusalem – both jobs and the health, insurance, and educational benefits that come with residence – has been such that thousands of West Bank Palestinians maintain an illegal residence in Jerusalem.[16] Only a handful of Palestinian immigrants from the West Bank and Gaza are allowed to settle officially in the city each year, some handpicked by the mayor after they have been cleared by the security forces.[17] Arab Jerusalemites who leave to work elsewhere in the world often lose their right to return as official residents of the city, and even Palestinians from the outside who are married to Jerusalemites have difficulty taking up residence in the city.[18]

After Likud came to power in 1977, Israel made it almost impossible for Palestinians to obtain residence permits for their family members located elsewhere. For example, as head of the East Jerusalem Chamber of Commerce, Faiq Barakat was as well connected as an Arab could be in Jerusalem. He was on the best of terms with Teddy Kollek. "We don't deny that he is a good man," Barakat told us. But such a posture didn't do him any good. Barakat, whose family has the best antiquities shops in Jerusalem, wished to bring in a sister in Amman whose husband had just died. "It is my obligation to protect her," he complained to us. "What should she do, become a prostitute on the street?"

In contrast, each year thousands of Israeli Jews migrate to Jerusalem from elsewhere in Israel and thousands leave. Indeed, more leave than come. If it hadn't been for Zionist immigrants from abroad, for whom Jerusalem was destiny, Jewish predominance in the city might have slipped dramatically in the first quarter century of Israeli rule in the unified city. (Between 1967 and 1993, Jews remained more or less stable at 72 to 73 percent of the city's population.)[19] But if Palestinians can't easily take up residence in the city, the Palestinian residents of the city and their children still cling to it as if their very lives were at stake. If immigration to the city is impossible, for most emigration is unthinkable, a constrained last choice.

Yisrael Kimchi is a soldier in the struggle for Jerusalem. Born and bred there, he commanded the first group of Israeli soldiers who counterattacked against the Jordanians in 1967 as they tried to slice into Jewish Jerusalem from the United Nations compound. "We started the battle for Jerusalem," he told us proudly. As the city's mapmaker and chief planner, he was still fighting. Instead of rifles and tanks, he deployed pencils and plans followed by bulldozers. The Israelis intend to hold this position and he was their urban commander.

Kimchi knows every alley, street, and gate, both those that exist and those that are no longer. Until Kollek was ousted from power in 1993, he was involved in every planning choice in the city since the Master Plan of

Yisrael Kimchi, former head of Policy Planning Section, Municipality of Jerusalem, Senior Researcher, Jerusalem Institute for Israel Studies, 1984.

1968, when the Israelis' strategy of residential invasion of the eastern portion of the new city and encirclement of its Arab center was first outlined. On this, he said, Teddy Kollek and the national government did not disagree. Conflict only took place over what was to happen *outside* the new city boundaries. Kimchi had wanted to surround the new Jerusalem with small villages, he told us, "to keep as much as possible the nature of the biblical area around Jerusalem." But the national government's Housing Ministry listened neither to him nor to Kollek.

Kimchi was the municipality's strategist in the competition between Israelis and Palestinians to control Jerusalem's space. "It is basically a race," Kimchi said. The way he saw it, the Palestinians held their own. True, Israel committed its treasury to residential expansion. But the PLO and Jordan also donated tens of millions for Palestinians who wanted to build a home around, or especially in, Jerusalem. To get the subsidy of seven thousand dinars, about twenty-seven thousand dollars, in the mid-1980s, a Palestinian needed the signature of men like the late Anwar Nusseibeh, the director of the East Jerusalem Electricity Company, or Faiq Barakat, the head of East Jerusalem's Chamber of Commerce. But he or she also needed a municipal building permit, which required application to the municipality of Jerusalem. To get the permit, the proposed structure had to be inspected. The PLO, Kimchi mused, reinforced the city's tough building codes.

The Palestinians have had one advantage. Israelis have always built dense, self-contained neighborhoods, residential compounds on high places, so that in the event of war, they can be defended. Facing something less than war, their perimeters can be controlled. So, too, Jerusalem's suburbs have been built for lower-income families. To capture that market, the Israelis have had to build low-cost, high-density settlements.

The Arabs have rushed to build in, and especially around, Jerusalem, constructing houses for extended families on large parcels of land. The Israelis have built new roads between the dense suburban settlements spreading out into the hills around Jerusalem, while the Palestinians have spun residential ribbons along those same roads with the monies they earned building the Jewish settlements. Mattitiyahu Drobles, the co-chair of the World Zionist Organization's Settlement Department who spearheaded Jewish settlement throughout Judea and Samaria right after Likud came to power, called this Arab urban sprawl around Jerusalem "a cancer." One of Jerusalem's planners told us that he wanted to vomit when he had heard Drobles's statement.

In this Go game between Arab and Jew, if the market were left to itself, because of the high value they put on land, per se, the Arabs would end up controlling much more land than they own today. Kimchi made sure that inside the city, it was not just the market that was at work. For example, a single road stretches through the northern panhandle of Jerusalem toward Ramallah. After the Arabs began building along the road between the two Jewish suburbs the city had placed there, Israeli planners became alarmed the two Jewish neighborhoods would be cut off from each other. Kimchi got the national government to declare most of the land between them as "state" land, meaning that the Arabs could no longer build on it.

Although Kimchi is committed to Jerusalem as a Jewish city, he also considers himself a fair-minded planner who wanted to service the needs of all the citizens of the city. "It is absolutely not true," Kimchi told us, "that non-Jewish people have difficulty getting permits." Two out of three requests to build are made by non-Jews, he claimed. Indeed, he maintained, getting a permit was easier for an Arab than for a Jew. And, he claimed, the city has had an easier time displacing Jews from their homes to make improvements in this ancient hodge-podge city than it has Arabs.

Although Israel expropriated large amounts of Palestinian land in Jerusalem after 1967 – more than a third of the annexed area – it did not displace many Arabs, with the exception of the massive clearance of Palestinians from the Jewish quarter right after the war.[20] The government has, in contrast, repeatedly removed Israelis. For example, after the 1948 war divided the city, thousands of North African Jews squatted in the old stone neighborhoods along the dangerous no-man's-land. Gradually their tenure was regularized. After the city was united, Israel forced out these Jews all along the border area to make way for fashionable residential reconstruction of now-valuable downtown real estate. Once new alternative housing estates were ready, Kimchi told us, "We kicked the Jews out from there . . . We were ready to do the same for the Arabs, but nobody dared do it because of the political implications." Just look at the string of Arab garages, grease-stained pavements, and side lots piled with rusted metal and old car parts right down the hill from the Old City, he said. Kimchi had wanted to excise this "ugly spot" but was prevented from doing it, he claimed, because it was Arab property and too politically sensitive.

The government of Israel never formulated comprehensive plans for the Arab side of the city. We had heard many reasons from politicians and bureaucrats: complex land title battles, the political difficulties of expropriating Arab-owned lands for public infrastructure, the existence of squatting and illegal construction. Kimchi dismissed all that. "I believe," he said, "that plans . . . bind the hands of the politicians . . . If there is no plan, [the politicians] are the ones that make the decisions." Arab Jerusalem was too important to be left to professional planners. Without a plan, the politicians could keep their options open; they could use approval to build as a carrot to win allies. A blueprint would establish general rights; it would only box them in.

As a result the Palestinians have built helter-skelter through the city without sewers, schools, or adequate roads. Jews would sometimes construct illegal additions, Arabs built whole structures, hundreds of them. Initially, the city did nothing except demand they pay taxes. In 1982, the city began to demolish illegal structures, assuming they hadn't been completed. Still the Arabs would build in the night or on the Shabbat to evade the building inspectors. They even built a small mosque on the Mount of Olives. Right-wing city council members complained the mayor looked the other way. If it continued, Kimchi complained, the shortage of public services on the Arab side of the city would reach crisis proportions. There wouldn't even be land to give them for the public infrastructure they had the right to demand. In 1984, the city was finally given permission to tear down any and all illegal structures built by the Arabs. In consultation with the *mukhtars*, Kimchi was laying out plans for the Arab side of the city. By the year 2000, there will be 700,000 people in the city, he told us. "Its exactly the same for us [the municipality] whether they are Arabs or Jews," he said. By 1992 the national government still had not authorized a master plan for the Arab side of the city.[21] Mayor Kollek, in protest, began to refuse to sign destruction orders for illegally built Arab houses.

The Palestinians, however, have never understood the municipality as even a potentially fair-minded government. Hassan Abu-Assali did what he could so Palestinians might remain in the city. A municipal employee in Jordanian Jerusalem, Assali worked as the chief Arab technician in the Israeli city's planning department. He dealt with the city's Arab neighborhoods, approving and disapproving Arab building permits, acting as an advocate for his fellow Palestinians, trying to pry loose space and permission for them to build and expand within the city. It was a tough and controversial job.

An educated professional and a devout Muslim who made the pilgrimage to Mecca, he had no illusions about Teddy Kollek when we interviewed him in 1984. Behind the bureaucratic rules, Assali discerned a political objective: to prevent too rapid Palestinian growth, to conserve the lion's share of public resources for the Jews. The Israelis had improved conditions on the Arab side of the city, he was the first to admit, but there was no intention of equalizing living conditions for Arabs and Jews. Just look at the wide, clean, smooth asphalt roads with street lights overhead on the Jewish side of the city, he said. "From '67 'til now, they've built one street in the Arab areas like that." His own village in the south of Jerusalem still had no sewer system and the school classrooms were spread throughout the village in rented rooms because of lack of space in the main schoolhouse.

Illegal Arab construction originated, Assali contended, in the roadblocks the Israelis put in the way of Palestinian building. Large amounts of Palestinian land – one third of East Jerusalem – were seized by the Israelis after 1967 without prior notification or consultation with the Arabs of Jerusalem, he said. Most of the Jewish Quarter had been owned by Arabs. Israel's massive seizure of Palestinian lands stopped natural expansion of the built-up area of Arab Jerusalem.[22] Although most of the land the Israelis took had not been developed, it was almost all privately owned by thousands of local people. Assali himself, he claimed, had seven dunams seized. Some families lost everything they had. For some, it was too painful to see the properties their families had lost. However, we met many Palestinians who would point to this housing project or that road as their family's land. The compensation offered, such as it was, was refused. Teddy Kollek, the Arab planner reminded us, never opposed these seizures.

For those Arabs who still own their own lands, there are other difficulties. The city, Assali asserted, repeatedly denies Arab building permits. We met dozens of Palestinians who claimed they had been waiting for years, some more than a decade, to get a building permit. As a member of a proposed housing project, Bernard Sabella had been waiting for thirteen years. "I am living in this city for the past forty-five years," he told us angrily in 1993. "And I cannot have a housing unit. Why? Isn't this my right?" Since 1967, he contended, the Israeli government had built as many as a hundred thousand housing units for Jewish families in Jerusalem, while providing a few thousand for Arabs, even though the Arab population had doubled during that time.[23]

When we asked Sabella, a Palestinian Christian, about Israeli allegations of high levels of Arab building without permits, his voice strained to contain his rage. "What are you telling me about massive illegal Arab housing!" he ranted. "Put all of these Arab houses together and they don't come to one quarter of Pisgat Ze'ev [a Jewish post-1967 suburb within Jerusalem that is rapidly expanding during the 1990s]." Or take Ali Ghuzlan, a prominent Palestinian attorney who had three hundred dunam confiscated in Jerusalem. "Nine years to get a permit to build a house and I am a lawyer," he told us. In the midst of constructing his two story house, the authorities came to him, he said, and retracted the permit to build the second floor.

In fact, since 1967, only about 12 percent of all new construction in the city has been for Palestinians although their proportion of the city's population is more than twice that (28 percent in 1993). Israel had built ten new neighorhoods for Jews, but none for Arabs. Building permits have been strictly rationed to prevent an increase in their proportion of the city's population.[24] Israel's obstruction of Palestinian building has been completely legal. Because all construction must be consistent with the Master Plan and the municipality has been slow to develop and approve formal plans for most Arab neighborhoods, much building has not been able to proceed. Many Palestinian proposals for housing projects, for example, have been turned down on this basis. Many Palestinians don't even bother to apply. The vacant lands ringing the Old City, planned as a "green belt" since the British Mandate, thus are not open to construction. And in other places, unlike in typical Jewish neighborhoods, Arab-owned areas have been zoned such that very large lots are required, putting them within reach of only the wealthiest of families.

On the Arab side of the city, demand has always far outstripped supply. Arab families are desperate to find a home of their own, in part to avoid the rapacious rents Arab landlords can charge in a very tight market. "People die for a house of their own where they would not be subject to the cruelty of owners of building . . . I'm dying to have a house of my own," Sam'an Khoury, an editor at *Al-Fajr*, told us.

Kollek, who argues that these biases derived from the Palestinians' failure to participate in municipal governance, began in 1984 to push in earnest to build more Arab housing in Jerusalem. Kollek initially proposed building seventeen thousand units. Over and over again, city planning initiatives for Arab housing died mysteriously in ministerial committees. In the late 1980s, Kollek released lands in the northern part of the city that would allow twelve thousand Arab units, but the Likud-controlled government ministries refused to grant approval, nor to issue licenses for construction.[25] It was not until 1992 that the first outline plan for major Arab housing construction in northern Jerusalem was approved. By this time, political pressures from the Likud-dominated ministries had cut the number of housing units to just seventy-five hundred units and significantly reduced the area covered by the plan.[26]

Those Palestinians without land cannot easily buy it and those with land cannot easily build on it. As a result many of Jerusalem's Arab sons and daughters are forced each year to take up residence outside the city's borders, where it is easier and cheaper to buy land, where building permits are easier to obtain. Abu-Assali tries his best. But each year, there are Palestinian families who refuse to wait another year for a man like Abu-Assali to plead their case, for the bureaucracy to bend; who tire of living in cramped quarters with their relatives; who are willing to take the risk that the Israelis will tear down their structures built in the night, on the weekend, in the back, out of sight.

9

Suburbs of the Messiah

The Gush Emunim, or "Bloc of the Faithful," dedicated to populating the land of Israel, moved outward from Jerusalem and Tel Aviv. The success of this settlement movement lay in its ability to recast Israel's foundational myths religiously. Gush Emunim claimed to reincarnate the hero of Israeli history – the pioneer – and to be the vital, expansive successor to the kibbutz settlements they founded. For decades, the religious Zionists, who had a kibbutz movement of their own, had been looked down on by the Labour Zionists as not measuring up to the ideal of the new Israeli, somehow tainted by their continued attachment to Torah, holding to traditions of exile.[1] As the religious nationalist movement grew and held tenaciously to one place after another, the settlers' claim that they were the true embodiment of the Zionist settlement did not go unheeded.

The Ancien Regime

The pious Jewish families who have braved Palestinian violence and the hostility of their own government to live in Jerusalem's remote suburbs see themselves as the natural heirs of the pioneers who endured considerable hardship and broke British law in the prestate years to carve out a place Jews could call their own. Religious nationalist Jews led the drive to resettle Judea and Samaria; secular Jews who shared their territorial objectives followed their lead.

Eliakim Ha-Etzni was a party leader and polemicist for Tehiyah, the political party established in 1979 with the support of Rabbi Zvi Yehuda Kook, in response to Begin's signing of the Camp David Accords granting Palestinian autonomy in Judea and Samaria. Tehiyah was intended to unite all those, religious and secular, who were most zealous about the land.

Ha-Etzni was a secular Tel Aviv lawyer when he helped organize the first push into Hebron with Rabbi Moshe and Miriam Levinger. He himself went to live in Kiryat Arba, at Hebron's edge, in 1972. Like many others in this suburb, he commutes to Jerusalem to work. On the same day that Palestinian Black September terrorists murdered eleven Israeli Olympic athletes in Munich, Ha-Etzni, who was seriously wounded in the 1948 war for independence, moved his wife and four children to Kiryat Arba in response.

Ha-Etzni believes only power can protect, can guarantee Jewish survival. This fact is grounded in his life. Born in Kiel, Germany, he barely escaped Hitler's Reich in 1938 with his parents, who made their way to Palestine.

A German television crew entered the Jerusalem café where we were speaking with this wiry lawyer in 1983. Newspapers were reporting that Jewish gunmen had opened fire on Palestinians in Hebron. "Why has Israel not captured the Jewish terrorists?" the German reporter asked him. "Why are these criminals not tracked down, arrested, and punished?"

"Nasty questions, Nazi questions!" the lawyer muttered to us in Hebrew.

"Tell me," he replied to the reporter in an acid German, "why does the German government allow its Nazi war criminals to remain free?"

As Ha-Etzni sees it, Jews are forever subject to selective moral assault. Herzl had been wrong: the Jewish state did not end scapegoating of Jews. Hostility had deeper sources. Stretching his syllables, Ha-Etzni said, "It is Juuu-daaa-iiism which is not wanted. There is something in the 'ism' of the Jews which repels them. And if there is a Jewish state, then the state is the cause of it."

Ha-Etzni does not see the conquest of Judea and Samaria as gaining a buffer zone, to be negotiated away in exchange for peace. Rather, the lands are a "trial" of the young nation's mettle. Israel's ability to settle and hold these new lands would be proof of its strength, its durability.

Ha-Etzni, like many secular nationalists who believed Judea and Samaria had been liberated and were ready for Jewish settlement, searched in vain among the old Zionist pioneers for those who would go with him. Many of Israel's political leaders – like Golda Meir, Moshe Dayan, Levi Eshkol – had been drawn from the *kibbutzim*. So were a disproportionate number of soldiers selected for elite military units.

The children and grandchildren of the founders, Ha-Etzni recounted, comfortable in the *kibbutzim*, did not rise to the new territorial challenge. Once lonely outposts eking out an existence in a hostile sea of Arab villages, many were now wealthy, with automobiles, swimming pools, spacious houses, paid vacations to Europe and America. The *kibbutzim* had become self-interested secularist islands, he charged. They failed to absorb the new immigrants from Morocco and Iraq. Their sons and daughters looked down their noses at the religious youth movements whose momentum grew as their own declined. They were unable to keep even their own youth. "They don't have the power," he claimed, "to fill up their *kibbutzim*."

Israel had become all too normal, a society whose members were devoted, within the tight limits of full-scale military mobilization, to personal pleasures and interests. The spirit of self-sacrifice that had brought the state into being had naturally slackened. Tel Aviv, Ha-Etzni contended, had become Babylon, its youth like their distant cousins in New York and Buenos Aires, "without any ideals, without any moral and spiritual content, which may be OK in Norwegia [Norway]. It is not OK! They're not happy. But Norwegia will continue to exist," he concluded. Israel, however, would not.

Ha-Etzni understands holding the land as a way to project and rebuild the power of the social body. But, like many other secular nationalists who wanted to keep what they believed was theirs, Ha-Etzni was forced to turn to the young religious nationalists who were forging a movement to resettle and hold these lands. In this ascendent social movement Ha-Etzni saw a way to build a moral fortress, to reconstruct the ramparts of idealism against Western decadence and superficial liberalism.

Israel, surrounded by implacable enemies, could not be like other nations. "I don't want to be normal!" this spectacled man you would expect to see in a college library, almost shouted at us. "No! Vehemently, I don't want to be normal." Ha-Etzni believes a terrible mistake was made in trying to make Israel over in the image of other secular Western democracies. Although not religious in a traditional sense, he believes the state must have a religious foundation. Only Judaism will ensure the moral code necessary for power. "The religion is nationalistic and the nationalism is religious," he said. "I think that even if the Russians would be ready to tolerate religions, they still would have problems with the Jewish religion. Why? Because the Jewish prayer book is a Zionist pamphlet."

Ha-Etzni thinks it is stupid to divide his people, as the *haredim* do, into those who are religious and those who are not on the basis of their observance of the minutiae of *halakhah*. Mocking the rabbis of Mea She'arim who worry whether an individual has skin blisters that are "white as snow," the Torah's criterion for expulsion as a leper, he wryly told us, "We do not know how *ha-kodesh boruch hu* [the Holy One, blessed be He] weighs the *mitzvah*s, whether this *mitzvah* [a commandment of the Torah] or that *mitzvah* is in his eyes so many kilowatts or so many ohm."

But he did know that one commandment trumped all the rest. Settlement of the land of Israel, Ha-Etzni believes, existence on this land alone, is sufficient to define a Jew as religious. Although Ha-Etzni provides legal armature for Jewish settlement, he has also provided counsel to myriad Palestinian clients who have, for one reason or another, fallen afoul of Israeli military administration in the West Bank. But there is a limit: he has refused to involve himself in land cases. "I don't want to enrich myself on the thing which for me is a matter of utmost holiness," he said. The land is beyond the law.

Was there a place in the new Israel, we asked, for the secular? He recalled Ben-Gurion's answer when he was asked the same kind of question about religious Jewry. Let them bring three million and the state will be theirs, Ben-Gurion replied. Ha-Etzni respects the long rows of diapers hanging from *haredi* balconies. Unlike secular Israelis, who raise dogs, religious Jews, he reminded us, have many children. (Orthodox Jews view dogs as unclean animals.) Survival is the test, numbers the only morality.

As young men, wearing leather sandals, semiautomatic weapons strung over their shoulders, their heads capped with colorful knitted *kippot* (the yarmulka that is the badge of the new religious nationalists), scrambled over the rocky hills of Judea and Samaria, secular left intellectuals looked on in horror. One of the most eloquent spokesmen for the old order is Amos Oz, a Jerusalemite who now lives and works in Kibbutz Huldah.

Oz's prodigious output of novels, short stories, and essays has increasingly focused on the moral erosion of Labour Zionism. Oz's essays in the *New York Times* cry out to American Jewry that his Zionism, secular and socialist, is the true one, and the new religious Zionism, an antediluvian heresy.

Ha-Etzni regards Oz as emblematic of a creed that had to fail. "Mr. Amos Oz, the blue-blooded, the blue-eyed aristocrat of Labour," Ha-Etzni drummed, "can only ask, 'Who are you? You have no culture, you have no writers, no nothing. You are parvenus.'. . It is exactly like the French nobility during the French revolution, like the *ancien regime*."

Labour's intellectuals saw no culture amidst the new religious nationalists, only obscure interpretations of dead rabbis. But to Ha-Etzni such culture was not powerful. And to Ha-Etzni, power is everything. "I saw what was deemed relevant," he said.

> It failed in the trial of life. You have two trees, one looks very beautiful from the outside and the other looks quite poor. But you look at the fruit. The beautiful tree brings no fruit, is barren, and the other one brings a wonderful fruit. So I begin to wonder, which tree is better, my dear friend. This is what happened to me in 1967. I was desperately looking for people without a knitted *kippah* to carry

on the battle of the people of Israel, which I saw the old regime was
not able to carry on.

Cosmology and Strategy

It was not just right-wing Revisionists who fell under the spell of the
religious nationalists. There were Labour Zionists, too, who were drawn
to their mission. In a April 1976 meeting at Ein Vered, some oldtime
kibbutz leaders endorsed the Gush Emunim settlement idea. Moshe
Tabenkin, the kibbutznik son of the great Labour Zionist Yitzhak
Tabenkin, rose and said, "I am afraid that too many successive years in
power have caused the Labour government to forget its real content and
purpose – the settlement of *eretz-yisrael*."[2]

The Gush Emunim and the largely Labour Zionist *kibbutzim* diverge
dramatically in their cosmology. The differences have consequences for
the pattern, form, and strategy of settlement. These differences help
explain why Gush Emunim was so effective in moving from a marginal
social movement of a few hundred people to an institutionalized structure that, until Labour's victory in 1992, had vast resources at its control,
access to the highest centers of power, and an ability, still perhaps, to
wreck any peace negotiations between Israel and the Palestinians.

For the first Zionist settlers in Palestine, the primary objective was to
create a national state, to bring together the Jewish people in at least
part, even the most peripheral part, of ancient Israel. Territory was a
means to state power, not the other way around. Which territory within
Palestine should be settled was largely a matter of realpolitik, of opportunities for purchase and possibilities of defense. Although each settlement was a claim to land for the eventual national state, settlement was
evaluated on the basis of its contribution to economic autonomy and
physical defense. The *kibbutzim* were distinguished by their well-
cultivated fields and orchards and their high watchtowers from which
guards could monitor hostile Arab activity around them. Each settlement was a self-contained, productive fighting unit.

For the Labour political establishment that created the state of Israel,
territory, even if it was biblical land, was evaluated in terms of its contribution to the military and economic capacities of the Jewish state. In
contrast, the Gush Emunim have often used biblical geography to
choose settlement sites. The identification and building of the sacrality
of each site have been a key ideological weapon by which they have
gained access and legitimated their presence. Gush Emunim's first surprise strike into occupied territory was typically to a spot to which a
ritual connection was made and worship organized. When the military

pushed them out, the compromise was that a yeshivah be established and the original community be allowed to remain, albeit often at another proximate site, usually a military zone. Eventually a permanent settlement was created.[3]

Many of these sites did not, in the main, make any strategic sense. The first Jewish settlement in the heart of Hebron, for example, is surrounded by tens of thousands of hostile Muslims who could easily overrun these few Jewish apartments in the event of war. It was, in fact, their military vulnerability that had motivated the government's opposition. Although Hebron's Jewish residents are heavily armed, they have not been able to defend their members from repeated violent attacks and large numbers of Israeli soldiers have had to be brought in to protect them.

Gush Emunim's failure to consider the strategic value of its settlements was evident in its first major penetration into Samaria, the whole region to the north of Jerusalem. In 1973, led by two yeshivah students from Kiryat Arba, a group began a long bitter struggle to settle Elon Moreh, near Nablus, the largest Palestinian city, where Abraham had built an altar to the Lord after he had promised the land of Canaan to Abraham's offspring.

The Israeli High Court had previously ruled that taking private lands for civilian settlements, such as those along the new confrontation line with Jordan, was legal because it served Israeli security needs. The land that the Jewish settlers of Elon Moreh had seized had also been expropriated earlier by the Israeli military for "reasons of national security."

But did this Jewish community contribute anything to security? Encouraged by large Israeli protests against it, the Palestinian landowners filed suit in 1979. They came up against Menachem Begin's Likud government, elected two years earlier, which supported Jewish settlement throughout Judea and Samaria. Rafael Eitan, Begin's chief of staff, testified the settlement was of military value. In the event of war, the settlers could be of use, he said. But Elias David Khoury, the Arab Israeli lawyer from Jerusalem who represented the Palestinians, was not allowed to cross-examine Eitan. "How can the High Court of Justice decide," Khoury remembered asking in court, "if Mr. Eitan is a liar or is a truth-speaker if you will not permit me to cross examine him for his testimony?"

But there were others, high in the Israeli military, who not only saw no strategic value in the Jewish settlement but argued it was a drain on Israel's fighting capacity. Begin's own minister of defense, Ezer Weizman, against Begin's orders, entered an affadavit that the settlement had no security rationale. Chaim Bar-Lev, a former chief of staff, stated for the record:

I absolutely reject the notion that there is any security value in the fact that a few dozen Jewish families live in some settlement outpost in a broad area entirely populated by Arab villagers. They are a target for attack. Any attempt to attribute motives of security to these settlers is misleading and distorted. These settlements are detrimental to security.[4]

The High Court ruled with the Palestinian landowners and *this* Israeli settlement on private Palestinian land had to be dismantled.

Many of the settlements founded by Gush Emunim are not militarily defensible. Their male residents, who work elsewhere, are absent most of the day. Most are quite small, a dozen or so families, and must recruit reserve soldiers from outside to protect them. During the latter half of the 1980s and the early 1990s, the security implications of diffused Jewish settlement throughout the West Bank and Gaza became clear. Violent Palestinian attacks on Israeli settlers and soldiers became increasingly frequent well before the *intifada* exploded in 1987. As a result, elite troops, demobilized from the war in Lebanon, had to be deployed to protect the Jewish settlers. During the *intifada*, some argued that the settlers' indiscriminate responses contributed to, rather than controlled, Palestinian violence. This was also a period of sustained Israeli mobilization made necessary by the growing Syrian and Iraqi military threats. As a result of these internal and external challenges, Israeli forces were stretched thin and Israelis were called upon to serve longer and longer stretches of reserve duty.

Many military analysts argue that the settlements have been a serious drain on Israel's defensive capabilities, precisely because each is treated as an integral part of the territorial defense system designed to delay the advance of the enemy in the event of war. Not only are these military resources denied to external territorial defense units, but in the event of a full-scale war, they claim these isolated settlements will tie down large numbers of soldiers to rescue or defend the Jews living there.

The original Zionist movement was dominated by socialists who built up their army and infrastructure in the countryside of Palestine. Working the land was a way to normalize the Jews, "unnaturally" confined to cities, often forbidden to own or farm land. The early Zionists were ideologically opposed to the cities, seeing them as sources of decadence, alienation, and capitalism. Each settlement they created was to be a country island of socialist living. Unlike in Russia, from which many of them had fled, socialism came to Israel from the fields of Palestine, not its factories.

Gush Emunim, in contrast, rejected socialism. Its community villages aim at a communitarian life-style without the leveling and compelled economic cooperation typical in the *kibbutzim*. Unlike in the *kibbutzim*, individuals privately buy and sell their homes. The ability to choose one's own job and living conditions is suited to idealistic, upwardly mobile, highly educated individuals who would be attracted to suburbs anywhere and whose occupational prospects remain brightest in the city. Gush Emunim was thus able to build a new pioneering tradition on a middle-class base.

Although members of the Gush Emunim were themselves highly observant Jews, their theological differences with the *haredim* enabled them to co-opt and cooperate with secular nationalists who love the land just as much as they do. For Orthodox Jews, the commandments are all equally binding. Not so for these religious Zionist pioneers: for them, settlement and possession of the land are supreme. By elevating this *mitzvah* above all others, they can both bridge to Israel's secular pioneering tradition and avoid confrontation with Israel's secular majority, who are unwilling to abide governmental enforcement of religious law but can be persuaded to support Jewish settlement. The settlers need not demand that those secular Israelis who wish to join them adhere to the Torah's other dictates. Their mix of modernity and religious observance makes it possible for women to play a prominent role in the movement, indeed to be among some of its most important public faces.

Because possession of the land, in itself, is the highest value, the settlements are not established with an eye to self-sufficiency. They are not engaged in any form of collective or cooperative production. Often they engage in no production at all. Unlike the kibbutzim which provided work for Jews, these Jewish outposts have typically provided work for Arabs, who actually build the Jewish houses and roads, tend the gardens, and collect the garbage. Because the settlements do not organize production themselves, settlers must rely upon private investors to locate their plants and offices within their boundaries. In this they have been only marginally successful. As a result, settlement has been concentrated within commuting distance of Israel's major cites, and the overwhelming majority of Jewish settlers live in suburbs of Jerusalem or Tel Aviv.[5] Because most settlements are not engaged in substantial productive activity, they are not an engine of self-sustaining economic growth, but a very expensive way to provide housing for Israel's metropolitan labor markets inside the "Green Line." Many of the more remote settlements have been able to survive only because of the provision of government jobs operating the settlements themselves and are thus a fiscal drain on the state.

Unlike early Zionist settlements, which were predominantly rural, Jewish settlements in the West Bank are primarily dormitory suburbs for workers who commute to Jerusalem and Tel Aviv. As followers of Rabbi Kook, Gush Emunim activists believe that one builds the sacred through the medium of the profane, that settling the land itself makes a Jew holy and extends the state's sacrality. This vision has enabled the movement to exploit the natural logic of suburbanization, not cynically, but as a practical messianic tactic perfectly consistent with their world view.

The profitability of building vacant land at the city's rim, the city dwellers' search for better, more spacious housing at lower cost – these drive suburban sprawl in any market society. In Jerusalem, Gush Emunim was able to exploit the logic of suburbanization to the hilt. In addition, government-subsidized cheap loans and mortgages, lower taxes, and government jobs were offered to those who would settle in its suburbs. The developers saw handsome profits to be made from the enormous differentials in land values between the two sides of the old armistice line. The natural push for more space at lower cost and the governmental pull of subsidized housing have assembled an enormous suburban constituency of homeowners – middle-class professionals drawn to modern amenities, Oriental Jews who can afford nothing else, secular Zionists of the right and left who see a chance to live a better life and participate in something meaningful, and even some *haredi* families who want to escape an expensive and still too secular city.[6]

With the construction of each new settlement, the members of the movement have been provided with salaried positions and with the resources – contracts, jobs, services – with which to institutionalize themselves as a self-sustaining network of municipal organizations. Although those who have been actively involved in the Gush Emunim constitute perhaps only 20 percent of all Jewish settlers, their members dominate the local and regional councils that govern the Jewish settlements in the West Bank.[7]

As of 1994, approximately one hundred and thirty thousand Jews lived in the West Bank and Gaza, exclusive of Jerusalem. They have been drawn by a mixture of messianic, materialist and nationalist motives. Neither their number nor their diffusion throughout Judea and Samaria has ever impressed Ra'anan Weitz, the Labour Zionist architect of Israel's settlement policies. Weitz dismisses them contemptuously as "fake settlements." "Just giving people houses so as to stake a claim isn't settling land," he said.[8] "I can't imagine these 'settlers' fighting for their villas . . . Their interest remains . . . financial . . . Building these colonies is merely an episode, a false turn and tragic mistake . . . And one day it will all vanish . . . These Likud projects are totally unplanned, unviable, and not only don't enhance our self-determination, they're done at the expense of the self-determination of others." They were, he said, a return to "the rotten past."

Weitz wanted to discredit the settlement movement, to denigrate it as "merely" materialistic, to lay bare its profane core so that the messianism of its most committed members could be exposed as window dressing, a veneer over something base. But that is the way movements wishing to transform the meaning of the world often operate. To succeed they must reshape the material world so that their vision "works," so to speak, so people can do well while doing good, so that meanings matter. Social movements that seek to remake the world must work through people's daily lives. The road to institutionalization is to a place whose upkeep does not depend on good intentions alone; where many people will behave appropriately not because they believe, but because it is in their interest to do so, and where many others will come to believe truly because those beliefs account for their behavior, protect their interests, and enable them to identify with their ideologically committed neighbors. Indeed, the evidence indicates that Jews attracted to affordable suburban homes quickly moved toward the religious and right-wing maximalist parties after taking up residence in the settlements.[9] For a social movement to succeed, it must make extraordinary behavior ordinary. Success requires just such a weld of ideals and interests.

Looking for a Lawn

In any American city, the farther one drives from the center, the larger the lot size, the higher the income, the whiter the neighborhood. From Jerusalem, a different gradient operates. The farther one drives from downtown Jerusalem, the more ideological commitment and fervor one finds. Closer to the city's rim, the messianic and the monetary begin to blend one into the other.

The day after Tami and Morris Rubin were married, they laid the foundation for their seven-bedroom home in Efrat, twelve miles south of Jerusalem, near Bethlehem. At Jerusalem's edge, you can see Bethlehem clearly. Efrat is part of the Etzion bloc, an area every Labour government has insisted will be retained in the event of any territorial redivision. Although it is beyond the "Green Line," living here need not imply a commitment to territorial maximalism.

Begun in 1983, Efrat is intended to be a small town, stretching over seven hills with five thousand families. Two hundred families came during that first year; the Rubins were among the very first. It then cost a minimum of $100,000 to buy a house in this upper-middle-class dormitory suburb for Jerusalem. Because there are virtually no long-term mortgages offered by Israeli banks, young couples must come up with almost the entire purchase price.

The glossy brochures depicting five types of available houses appeal to solid middle-class immigrants from South Africa, South America, Eu-

rope, and America. The houses are handsome, stand-alone, stone structures with red tile roofs and large backyards. Half of the community's
residents come from English-speaking countries.

Rabbi Shlomo Riskin, who also writes a regular column in *The Jerusalem Post*, is their rabbi. "I am not a settler; I am a citizen. I am not an
occupier; I am a resident," he said.[10] Riskin used to be the rabbi at the
Lincoln Square Synagogue in New York, a place that drew young, newly
Orthodox Jewish singles. Then he called himself Steven Riskin, fondly
referred to as "Stevie Wonder." Riskin bridged the gap between modernity and Orthodoxy. On some Saturday mornings, you couldn't find an
empty seat. In his synagogue in the round, men and women both faced
the Ark containing the Torah, and each other, separated only by a clear
Plexiglas screen, or *mehitzah*. Because the female lawyers, doctors, and
therapists at Lincoln Square are fully present, in sight of the Ark, Lincoln Square was often called "Wink and Stare." In 1984, the rabbi, who
had adopted his Hebrew name, Shlomo, announced to his congregation
that he would move to Efrat; he hoped they would follow him. Two of its
seven hills, he told them, were reserved for them. By 1994, two hundred
of Efrat's nine hundred families were former congregants at Lincoln
Square Synagogue.[11]

Tami Rubin, the daughter of a Conservative American rabbi, moved
out of Jerusalem to live in Efrat. When we spoke in 1983, she was in her
midtwenties, the community's youngest mother, and found Jerusalem's
apartments noisy and crowded. The endless and often acrimonious discussions among the apartment's residents about how much to heat the
apartment building irritated her. "It was degrading," she complained,
"knowing what everybody was doing." Morris, her fiancé, had a solution. Although the couple were both trained as lawyers, Morris seized
on the Likud government's rush to settle and decided to become a
developer. When we met he was building twenty homes on the hills of
Efrat, using Palestinian laborers. Each time they finished a house, Morris bought a sheep for the Arab workers to roast, in keeping with Palestinian custom.

Morris had also grown up with a large lawn and shade trees, something unattainable at any price in Jerusalem. Tami, the kind of fast-
talking woman who might have become a silk bowtied corporate lawyer
had she remained in Chicago, repeatedly spoke for her quiet husband.
"Morris wanted his children to grow up in that kind of atmosphere . . .
where he didn't have to worry about crossing the streets, a small-town
atmosphere. It's a matter of quality of life."

Tami Rubin's American liberalism affects her views here on Jerusalem's suburban frontier. Whereas a number of settlements are restricted
to religious Jews, nonreligious Jews are welcome in Efrat. Tami's neigh-

bor, for example, moved to Efrat solely in search of a backyard. Although deeply religious, Tami was willing to live next to those who don't believe. And although a fervent religious nationalist, she hoped to live peacefully among the Arabs whose towns and villages surround her suburb. "There's no reason why they can't live here also," she said. "My argument is with those Arabs who don't want us to be here. And they, I wouldn't mind being removed from the immediate vicinity and sent to other Arab countries."

Tami trusted the Arabs who worked on her husband's construction sites and who moved freely in and out of her house. She had to. When the Rubins moved to Efrat, she had been afraid. There were only twenty-eight families then. There was no fence at the perimeter. "There were no people, no lights," she recalled. "And no sidewalks. There was nothing here, just our house and a lot of rubble. And the first few weeks, when there was nobody here at all, and you could scream, no one would hear you. No one would hear a gun shot."

Now that hundreds of Jews live around her, the fear has subsided. But it was still there. From the lawn where the Rubin children play, we can see the top of a mosque's minaret, a periscope peeking up in the Judean hills. It marks the Arab village, Um Salamuneh, closest to Efrat. It is just any village, a white spot on the map next to a road descending into the Judean wilderness. But it was there that a PLO cell was organized whose members murdered Aharon Gross, a yeshivah student from Kiryat Arba. Doesn't it frighten you to be so close to that village, we asked? Normally, Tami answered, she doesn't see it, nor can she remember its name.

Like all suburbanites, the residents of Efrat have to commute daily to Jerusalem. But unlike others, they pass Palestinian refugee camps, like Dehaishe, whose young men stone Israeli cars. When we first visited Efrat in the early 1980s, the Arab youth appeared to discriminate politically. The buses going to the most ideological settlements were much more likely to have their windows shattered. Until the Palestinian uprising began in 1987, the bus to Efrat usually escaped unscathed. Tami claimed she was not afraid to drive back and forth to Jerusalem. But, she admitted, "We've decided to invest in a little gun."

Tami and Morris were looking for more than a suburban lawn. Their house, with its deep pile carpets, its imported American toilets and chandeliers, was not just a tract house. They built it in the footsteps of the messiah.

"Is the messianic era near?" we inquired.

"We're certainly closer to it than even a hundred years ago . . . You couldn't have the messiah show up on a white horse when there were only Arabs here . . . the next step is just getting rid of the other construction on the Temple Mount . . . things are at a quickening pace. Time is just moving us closer and closer. The world is getting ready for it."

Like many settlers, Tami Rubin understands the Six-Day War as the work of God, a missed opportunity to liberate the Temple Mount.

"A mistake may have been in '67 being too overly sensitive to other religions and not keeping it [the Temple Mount] open to Jews. Now we have even a bigger problem of how to get a Temple on top of the mountain."

"You would build the Temple?"

"I wouldn't. I can't. It's not my job to build the Temple. That's part of the messianic times. You have to have a temple to worship in. You have to have."

"What do you do in a temple?

"What do you do in a temple? You worship God in a temple . . . We'll do it the same way they did it two thousand years ago. There were animal sacrifices."

"What are you going to do?" we asked. "You are going to stand in the court of the women and you'll smell the smell of burned flesh, the disgusting odor of blood drying. It will be a wretched, foul place."

"We've done it once," she assured us. "I'm sure it can be done again."

"Would you, Morris, go up there to see sacrifice where maybe two or three hundred sheep were slaughtered in a day?"

Morris didn't have a chance to answer. Tami had it figured out. "You have to eat them on Pesach . . . Morris will go into a new business of raising sheep and make a fortune. We'll worry about the details when we get to it. We've got a big backyard."

10

Defensible Borders

Like most Israelis, Jewish settlers regard Israel's pre-1967 borders as indefensible; "Auschwitz borders," Abba Eban once called them. This is not just a strategic assessment. The religious nationalists of Gush Emunim consider these frontiers to be morally indefensible.

When a people uses violence, it is an instrument, a tool by which to try pry loose resources unobtainable by other means. But violence is also an expression of commitment, a demonstration of what one holds most dear. Violence leaves bloody traces: wounds and corpses. It marks a community's values on human bodies, through blood sacrifices that only make sense in terms of the purposes for which they were offered. Violence is a language; force simultaneously a physical and a moral phenomenon. Efforts to decompose it must inevitably crumble.

Terms of Engagement

The row houses of Ofra, a Jewish suburb to the north of Jerusalem, are planted in deep red soil at the foot of Ba'al Hatzor, the highest mountain in Samaria. It should be an easy commute to Jerusalem, not unlike that separating the San Fernando Valley from Westwood; Hertford from London; or Melun from Paris. But to travel these fifteen miles along the ridge descending into the city, one has to drive through miles of Palestinian villages, smack through Ramallah and El-Bira, a major Arab metropole. Commuting to Jerusalem's Jewish suburbs has been dangerous for a long time.

Years before the *intifada*, everyone had traumatic stories. Endlessly repeated and strung end to end, these stories transformed a short drive into an ordeal. Every bend in the road could conceal a young man with a Molotov cocktail. Schoolchildren clustered at the road's edge could metamorphosize into a hostile gang. The children's stones carried their parents' politics. A Palestinian mother took her young daughter to Jerusalem's Hadassah Hospital for corrective eye surgery. Thinking the physicians didn't understand Arabic, she said to her daughter, "The doctor will make your eyes straight, so you can throw stones at the Jews." But the Jewish anesthesiologist understood; he refused to operate. On Jerusalem's suburban frontier, Jewish travelers feel relieved when they reach their destination.

A couple from Ofra were returning with their two small children from Jerusalem. Young Palestinians had hastily thrown up a barricade of burning tires, forcing them to stop. Young men and teenagers, each with a stone in his hand, began to close in on their car. Rocks shattered the windshield. The Israeli children screamed. Unable to maneuver, the husband passed a pistol to his wife. Shoot in the air, he told her. With the first shot, the barrage ceased. With the second, the young men fled. A little later, the military arrived, conducted an indiscriminant roundup of Arab men in the nearest village, lined them against a wall, ordered them to strip to their waists and then took a few back to clean the stones off the road.

The Jewish settlers contend that no Israeli government has had the political will to protect them, to impose the tough sentences that would deter Palestinian attacks. No government, not even those of the Likud, could be counted upon. "If you a throw a rock at a Jew and you crack his head open," Shifra Blass, the spokesperson for the settlement movement in the 1980s, lamented to us, you might go to jail for thirty days, you might pay a fine, which the PLO winds up paying in the end. If you go to jail for thirty days, you come out a hero."

Even though the sentences stiffened during the 1980s – three and four months for the young men who threw stones and four years for those who threw incendiary devices – the settlers complained that the Israeli military neither pursued nor prosecuted Palestinian stone throwers. Shattered windshields had to be repaired repeatedly. Delivery trucks and repair people from Jerusalem would cancel appointments. Parents feared for the safety of their children on the school buses. In 1984, a delegation of settlers met with Defense Minister Moshe Arens to protest. One of the women, Rachel Slonim, told him: "I want you to understand the awful feeling we've recently exeprienced: In the very heart of *eretz-yisrael* we feel as though we are in exile. Exile . . . is the feeling of being abused and scorned with no ability to change the situation."[1]

Israeli regulations required settlers to be armed when traveling outside their settlements. But according to settlers we spoke to before the *intifada*, the military rules regulating their use of force changed all the time. Settlers were only legally allowed to shoot in self-defense, and almost always forbidden to shoot to kill. Sometimes the settlers were told to shoot into the air and then at the suspects' feet; at other times, to apprehend the suspects and take them to the military authorities; at other times, just to report the incident to the police. Palestinians grimly joked at the time that the only way to explain the multiplication of Palestinian wounded and dead in the context of these military "orders" to shoot into the air was to assume that Palestinians were all twelve feet tall or were leaping high into the air.

Frustrated by lack of protection and humiliated by their vulnerability, the settlers exacted their own vengeance for Palestinian attacks. In the decade before the *intifada*, Jewish settlers burned Palestinian shops to the ground; fired machine guns over the heads of Palestinians; threw hand grenades at Palestinian homes near their settlements; ripped out olive trees; erected their own roadblocks; smashed and shot up hundreds of house and car windows; broke into and vandalized homes.[2] More than a quarter of the Jewish settlers polled in 1983 admitted they had participated in vigilante activity. Even then an overwhelming majority of all settlers supported those actions.[3]

Vigilantism is a logical outcome of an autonomous settler movement that is also an officially armed component of a military administration whose highest levels include people drawn from that same settler movement. When the settlements were first created, they were meant to be part of the Israeli defense network. Ofra, for example, was established in 1975 with the approval of then minister of defense Shimon Peres, who called it a "work camp for regional defense." Beginning in 1978, hundreds of settlers on active or reserve army duty were transferred to army units in the West Bank charged with protecting the settlements and controlling the Palestinian population. Many residents of Ofra, just like other Jews in the West Bank, do their active and reserve duty while living at home, sometimes administering the military governance of their Arab neighbors. Each settlement is treated as a front-line military outpost; its resident reserve soldiers carry weapons and have easy access to stockpiles of grenades, weapons, and munitions located within the settlement network.

In these circumstances, law enforcement where Jews have attacked Arabs tended to be leisurely and lax, with mild, individual punishments.[4] Jewish suspects often were unidentified and unquestioned. Criminal files were repeatedly closed with nobody booked for a crime. Those rare Israelis who were convicted received token sentences. In early 1982, to take just one example, a Jewish settler's truck was stoned by teenagers and children from the Palestinian refugee camp at Balata. The Israeli jumped out and began to fire his Uzi submachine gun at the group, killing a thirteen-year-old boy. Six years later, the Israeli was sentenced to six months of community service. The Israeli state prosecutor petitioned the Supreme Court to obtain a harsher sentence. He succeeded. The sentence was increased to three years in prison in July 1988.[5]

It was exactly the opposite in cases of Arab violence towards Jews. Military punishments were immediate and harsh: administrative detention without trial (used especially where charges cannot be proved), house arrest, long jail sentences, even deportation. Punishments were often collective: destruction of a family's residence, imposition of neighborhood and village curfews, cutoffs of electricity and water. In a polarized environment, neither Jewish nor Palestinian residents cooperated with investigations of one of their own. And the Palestinians, having no faith in the justice of the military administration and fearing revenge from Israeli settlers, refrained from reporting incidents to the Israeli authorities. Israeli settlers, anticipating what they also saw as an inadequate military response, also did not report most cases. The result was a continuous degeneration in the rule of law.

At one level, the Palestinian uprising that began in December 1987 only intensified the siege of stones. As the settlers saw it, the *intifada* meant that stones were thrown more often, in more places, at more people than ever before. The Israeli military first fired tear gas, then water cannons with colored dye by which they could mark the culprits for later arrest, and – stone for stone – machines that shot out gravel, and then bullets of metal, rubber, plastic. Three weeks into the uprising, Defense Minister Rabin announced a policy of "force, might, beatings." If neither death nor deportation could deter them, perhaps a massive deployment of pain would. It did not. Israeli soldiers broke thousands of arms and legs.

Palestinians were undeterred by curfew; by blockade; by arrest; by school closures; by deprivation of water, power, and food; by fines; and by beating. Parents were not informed where their children were being detained so that they had to go prison to prison to find them.[6] More than a thousand Palestinians, including young children and old people, were killed; tens of thousands were injured by bullets, tear gas cannisters thrown into closed spaces, and punitive beatings. Pregnant women lost their children and children their eyes. Thousands were initially detained without trial. For two decades, the Palestinians had stood in awe of the military might of the Israelis. Armed with stones and obscenities, the young generation was no longer afraid.

When the *intifada* began, Yehuda Litani carried on as usual. Litani, a longtime West Bank correspondent for *Ha-Aretz* and former Middle East editor of *The Jerusalem Post*, had been among the first Israeli reporters into Cairo, even before there was an official peace. Ordered to remain in his hotel room, he climbed out the window at night to get interviews.[7] As a longtime reporter on Palestinian politics and a former press liaison for the military administration of the West Bank, he had moved easily through the territories. He knew many Palestinians, their private lives and incidental secrets, the family relations that divide and knit together their political elite. He knew all the back roads, the dirt tracks, and who served the best lamb.

One foggy late afternoon, he told us in 1989, he realized things were different. He was driving out from Jerusalem to an interview with Reja Shehadeh, the elfin director of al-Haq, the law and human rights center in Ramallah. The clashes had been intense that day. Shehadeh, who had seen helicopters circling the main roads into town from Jerusalem, called Litani to advise him to take a back road.

Litani took a shortcut, driving along a sparsely populated back lane off the main road to Ramallah. Forced to slow by the narrowing of the road at a construction site, he spied what must have been thirty masked young men, waiting, rocks in their hands, to attack. Litani wasn't armed. There wasn't enough time or space to turn around and speed away.

Instinctively, he jumped from his car, raising his hands and yelling in Arabic, "Journalist, journalist!"

A voice called out from the building site for him to identify himself.

Hands shaking, heart pounding, he called back, "Yehuda Litani, *Jerusalem Post*."

"We know you. Let him through," the young voice called back. "Put down the stone, Abed." In unison, they lowered their arms.

Yehuda Litani saw the hatred in their faces, the desire to kill a Jew. His hands were shaking as he tried to put the key into the ignition. Three of them jumped down and ran in front of his car through the fog until he reached the main road again.

In 1989, we made our way to Jalazoun refugee camp, north of Jerusalem, crossing the remains of a hastily built stone barrier the youth had assembled to slow the almost daily entry of Israeli soldiers. The bare concrete block buildings were covered with graffiti: "Palestine is free." "General Strike, because the *intifada* has entered its 14th month." "A greeting to our martyrs who sacrificed themselves for our country – Fouad Nasser."

Massoud Safi, the Palestinian head of Jalazoun refugee camp, met us in his spare one-room office. Jalazoun provided its share of angry young men, sons who had grown up with the bitter stories of exodus, with their fathers' impotent dreams of return. This refugee camp, like others, started creating trouble many years before the *intifada*. When the Israelis invaded Lebanon, Hussein Ahmed Massoud Safi, the headman's son, was in and out of military custody. "They took him to torture him and beat him. They broke his spine," his father told us. His son was operated upon and his spinal column slowly healed. But Jalazoun would not remain quiet. In 1983, Hussein Safi was taken away again and the camp placed

Massoud Safi, head of the Jalazoun refugee camp, 1989.

under curfew. The Israeli soldiers, his father claimed, once again broke his son's spine. Hussein, twenty-three years old, began to hemorrhage. When the curfew ended, the Israelis returned him to his father, dead.

A black and white *keffiyah* framed Massoud Safi's impassive face. A kerosene heater kept the worst of the chill out of his office, but no one took their coats off. Men, women, and children floated in and out, took seats, watched for a while, interjected something, and walked out. A toothless heavy old man in a beat-up brown coat smoked his cigarette and spat on the floor. There were posters on the wall for mothers on how to put drops in their babies' eyes, treat skin infections, and purify water. A United Nations Relief and Welfare Agency (UNRWA) blackboard marked off the distribution of rations and services, a graphics of survival.

When the *intifada* began, Jalazoun rose up too. At one point, the camp was under curfew for five straight weeks. When the camp could not be pacified, the Israelis took Massoud Safi, the refugee camp leader appointed by UNRWA, to prison. It was Massoud Safi's job to distribute food rations and services to the over one thousand families of this camp. In Israeli military court, Safi was accused of distributing PLO money to the camp's residents, of organizing meetings at his house and inciting people to violent resistance. "Somebody informed on me and that was not true," Safi insisted to us. The court jailed him for nine months. Upon his release, he contended, Israeli soldiers blew up his house.

In the continuous skirmishing with the Israeli troops, hundreds of the camp's residents had been injured – bodies beaten, flesh wounded, lungs gassed. How many have died, we asked? "One young man," he replied, just one, with "his soul going out."

Amin Rajab abu Radaha died on his fourteenth birthday. The camp had again been placed under curfew after a clash. Amin looked out the window and saw his sister and brother-in-law being made to clear the road of stones. That was Israeli routine. But Amin's sister was ill, too weak, he thought, to move the heavy boulders he and his friends placed on the roads. He ran out the door to take her place, to go to help her. Before he got very far, a bullet went right through his eye. He ran a few meters more and collapsed on the ground.

Mr. Safi and other camp residents told us the Israeli military took Amin Rajab to a military center in Ramallah and from there a helicopter rushed him to Hadassah Hospital in Jerusalem. When the family caught up with him at Hadassah, he was technically dead but still connected to a life support system.[8] Camp residents alleged that the hospital asked the family whether they could have their son's organs. If the family would allow them to have the organs, they would not have to pay for the emergency care with which their son had been provided. When the family refused, it was alleged, the hospital took him off the life support system.

To Israelis involved with such matters, the Palestinian charge smacked of ancient anti-Semitic blood libel. According to a hospital official and a physician involved with organ transplantation at Hadassah Hospital, there is never any connection between organ donation and exemption from payment, irrespective of the patient's ethnicity.[9] Indeed, the hospital claimed that they had no record that Amin Rajab Abu Radha had ever been a patient.[10] In any event, Amin Rajab's body was returned to the camp and buried at night, and UNRWA, as the insurer of the camps' residents, paid the hospital bill.

Israeli repression could not quell the Palestinians. Jews traveling in the West Bank continued to be injured by stones, cut by flying glass, burned by Molotov cocktails, stabbed by knives, and occasionally shot. There were simply not enough soldiers to patrol every corner, to accompany every car, to watch the hundreds of miles of roads that wind like thick black thread through the hills. And there were just too many angry young men with too many stones.

In April 1987, Ofra Moses, a Jew, five months pregnant, was riding in a car with her husband and four children, returning to their settlement, a suburb just over the old border line, when a Molotov cocktail hit the car. Ofra Moses and her unborn child were burned to death. Another child died later. Danielle Weiss, then secretary-general of the settlement movement, led three hundred Jewish settlers on a rampage through the nearby Palestinian town of Kalkiliya. They destroyed shops, smashed car windows, burned fields, and uprooted groves of fruit trees. When soldiers rushed to the scene, the Israelis refused to obey them, throwing rocks, jeering, and cursing at them.[11] And still it continued. In October 1988, less than a week before Israel's national elections, another Jewish woman and her children, traveling through the Jordan valley up to Jerusalem for a bar mitzvah, were burned to death on a bus set aflame by a Molotov cocktail thrown by Palestinian youths. Jewish victims continued to multiply.

As the *intifada* ground on for month after month, Arab stones were answered by Jewish gunfire from settler and soldier alike. Likud Prime Minister Yitzhak Shamir had proposed already in September 1988 that rocks be reclassified as lethal weapons, to allow Jewish settlers and soldiers to open fire immediately, without the requisite "warning" shots.[12] In November 1988, Yesha, the council of Jewish settlements, resolved that their members should use live fire against stone throwers irrespective of the danger to their own lives.[13] After one incident in 1989, Rabbi Eliezer Waldman led a group of Jewish settlers on a rampage in a Palestinian village where among other things, they set fire to a mosque. "We have to shoot stone-throwers," he said. "There is nothing more absurd, immoral and dangerous than to endanger ourselves in order to safeguard the attackers' lives."[14]

In Hebron, Palestinians attacked Israeli settlers on the street without cease. Each month, there were hundreds of incidents. Rabbi Moshe Levinger was driving in Hebron with his son when a stone smashed through his windshield, injuring his son. A barrage of stones and bottles kept coming even when they reached an Israeli army roadblock. Just the week before Levinger had been hit in the head with a rock. Levinger, the Israeli prosecutor charged, then pulled out his pistol, his hand shaking, and drove back down the street firing into shop windows. Levinger maintains the Palestinians had surrounded him, threatening his life. Hassan Abdul Aziz Salah, an innocent shopkeeper, died from Levinger's bullets. "I didn't kill the Arab shopkeeper whom I am accused of killing – or I should say, rather, that I didn't have the honour of killing him."[15] Levinger, convicted of causing death through negligence, spent three and a half months in prison.[16]

With month after month of mass defiance, the shouts and shots of warning once required by Israeli law were undelivered. Shots were fired at stone throwers with the intent to punish, to injure, to kill. In 1989, the Justice Ministry gave Israeli soldiers the green light to shoot at any Palestinian who wore the mask donned to protect the activist and his family from Israeli reprisals during protests. The retaliatory and punitive violence and intimidation that were once the mark of militant settlers were becoming military policy; once-deviant behavior was becoming the norm.

The logic of the law, with individual punishment for individual crimes based on the facts of the case, was overwhelmed by the military imperative of controlling a civil rebellion. In 1985, Defense Minister Rabin had contemptuously rejected Jewish settlers' demands that villages and towns where attacks took place be punished collectively, and that Palestinians be denied the rights of due process in the courts.[17] But by 1988, punishment had become an indiscriminately used tactic of deterrence rather than a sanction for a crime. Whole towns, villages, and neighborhoods – in Jerusalem as well – were confined to their houses for days at a time, their electricity cut off, their right to market their produce denied. Curfews made each Palestinian home into a prison, large families cooped up with screaming children and dirty laundry, made to choose between getting fuel or food in the limited time available, desperate to obtain a curfew pass to make it to the doctor.

Palestinians were routinely being beaten *after* they had been taken into custody. Hands, ribs, legs, and arms were broken so they wouldn't return to the streets to throw stones. After the uprising had gone on for more than a year, the beatings sometimes became so savage that Palestinians died as a result.[18] Soldiers repeatedly violated military regulations on the use of firearms and force after a suspect had been taken into captivity, causing many Palestinian deaths and thousands of injuries. Punishments of these violations were infrequent and relatively mild, with harsher punishments meted out to soldiers who had stolen property than to those who had caused loss of life.[19]

Vigilantism had spread from ideological settlers to ordinary suburbanites just over Jerusalem's municipal line in Ma'ale Adumim. Jewish settlers who opened fire in violation of regulations, who injured or killed Palestinians, were mostly unpunished and, where apprehended, either simply had their arms confiscated or were given light sentences.[20] In 1990, a pamphlet was circulating among the settlers on how to shoot Palestinian rock throwers without getting caught. Vigilantism became so common that regular Israeli military units would claim only they stood between Palestinians and the undisciplined settlers who had no compunction about mounting a small pogrom here or there.

The degeneration of the rule of law in the territories would not respect the "Green Line" dividing the lands of the occupiers from those of the occupied.[21] At the same moment Nelson Mandela was being released from prison in South Africa, tens of thousands of West Bank Palestinians who worked on the Israeli side were still being required to carry identity cards, not unlike the hated passes used in South Africa. There is no magical divide between Israelis who administer the lives of the occupied Palestinians and those charged with law enforcement among Palestinians who are their legal equals within Israel. The same border police and soldiers who broke bones before asking questions are charged with controlling Arabs who are either citizens or residents of Israel, and of Jerusalem in particular. Israeli civilian courts judge which Palestinians in the West Bank are to be deported, which houses destroyed, which lands taken. The thousands of prisoners "administratively detained" by Israel are housed in detention centers in Israel, prisons run by the same Prison Service that would punitively warehouse any criminal.

During the *intifada*, West Bank Palestinians were often taken to the Russian Compound in Jerusalem to be interrogated.[22] Consider the case of Barakat, a thirty-two-year-old father of four accused of belonging to an "enemy organization" who was arrested on November 26, 1990, and interrogated in Jerusalem. After being handcuffed and his head covered with a smelly sack, his head was smashed against the wall until he lost consciousness. For five days, he was handcuffed without food or drink, urinating and defecating in his pants. On the fifth day, his interrogation began. According to his testimony they threatened to poison him. They poured typewriter correction fluid down his throat. They beat him until his testicles became swollen and there was blood in his urine. Barakat was released after four weeks – without charge.[23]

Because large numbers of Palestinians move daily across the old border, because Israeli Arabs are profoundly sympathetic to the political goals of the Palestinians of the West Bank and Gaza, repressive practices have begun to diffuse into Israel, and Jerusalem in particular.[24]

Stan Cohen, who documented the case of Barakat, is a criminologist who teaches at Hebrew University's law school. Cohen immigrated to Israel as an emigre from South Africa, where he had been part of the small white resistance to the Kafkaesque machine of legal repression. Israel was different. Israel never developed a theory of racial superiority. It had not forced mass migrations of Arabs after statehood as the white South Africans had. Nor did Israel ever legislate racial laws; indeed it granted Israeli Arabs citizenship.

Nonetheless, the parallels to South African apartheid pained him. In both countries, he pointed out, an apparatus of formal legalism had been built over gross injustice and political repression. In apartheid South Africa, fewer cases ever got to court, but when they did, Cohen claimed, black Africans had a better chance of a fair trial than Palestinians appearing before a military tribunal in the occupied territories.[25]

Because the administrative detention, the beatings, the blowing up of houses during the *intifada* were taking place in the occupied territories, Israeli liberals could maintain their commitment to democracy without dissonance. Out there was not really Israel. Because of this "geographic magic," Cohen said, Israeli liberals, unlike their South African counterparts, could fight for human rights without any sense that it was necessary to take a position on the "political" issue of the Palestinians' national rights.

Before the *intifada*, after two decades of sophisticated subordination and mute compliance, most Israelis had accepted the occupation as something normal: their control of another people, the absence of Palestinian political rights, the discrimination, their pervasive humiliations and intrusions into Palestinian lives unfortunate facts of life.

Faced with resistance to its rule in the territories, Israel has always been divided over the appropriate response. Before the *intifada*, cases of Israeli brutality to Palestinians usually caused controversy. For example, Yehuda Litani, the West Bank correspondent for *Ha-Aretz*, investigated the case of a sixteen-year-old Arab boy whom the military governor of Bethlehem suspected of throwing a stone that had broken his car window. The boy was the son of a former officer in the Jordanian Arab Legion, an English teacher who taught its officers and even King Hussein the language of their patron state.

An Israeli sergeant major took the boy to the Bethlehem station, where, Litani claimed, "he stood on his penis. And he said, 'You'll never have children again.' " Israeli military trucks came, forced the family to load their belongings, and then dumped them in an abandoned refugee camp in the desert near Jericho. After Litani's reportage, the outrage caused the military authorities to return the boy's family to its home. Litani had vowed to get rid of the sergeant major, "a Jew to our disgrace." The reporter went to his own former commander, to officers up and down the line, but he failed to have the sergeant removed. "It tortures me that this man still serves in the Israeli army." While the Palestinian boy, plagued by severe internal pain, was in the hospital recovering, he and Litani wrote letters back and forth. Israelis wrote to the young boy, and visited him, ordinary people from Tel Aviv and Haifa, even a general from the Israeli army. The boy's father was deeply moved. For the son, it was not enough. Shortly thereafter, he joined the PLO and was subsequently arrested and served time in Hebron prison for security offenses. "Believe me," Litani said, "I don't blame the kid. After what was done to him, I'd hate the Jews – all the Jews – really to my guts."

During the *intifada*, soldiers complained that directives from on high switched from week to week and the formal procedures were worthless in the field. This ambiguity had a function. Israel is defended by a people's army, run by an ideologically divided government, its top officers drawn from across the political spectrum. Devolution to officers in the field of the responsibility for decisions as to when to shoot, when and for how long to beat, prevented an explosive politicization of the Israeli army. Soldiers' responses in the field depended on their own views and those of their commanding officers. For some, it was too little; for others, much too much.

A number of settlers claimed to us that forces within the Israeli military had no intention of using the requisite force to crush the uprising because they wanted to keep the pressure on the Israeli public to reach a political settlement. In fact, Dan Shomron and Amram Mitzna, the army's top two generals in charge of putting down the *intifada*, opposed greater repression, arguing that a military solution was not possible. Only a political solution could quiet the territories. This enraged not only the Jewish settlers, but large segments of the Israeli public as well.

Naomi Shemer, whose song, "Jerusalem of Gold," became the anthem of the Six-Day War, blasted those Israelis who condemned their government's use of force: "At a time when the entire country is fighting for its life, its investigators, policemen and poets are driving the country to brink of insanity, and are trying to convince the people that they are mad wolves, brutal Goliaths and monsters. The *intifada* is only a prelude and an excuse to destroy Israel."[26]

The Meanings of Jewish Violence

Whether and how a community deploys its ultimate weapon, source, and marker of sanctification, its will to kill and be killed, these are keys to understanding its vision of the world. And as we might expect, in the use of force, there is a substantial difference between the vision of the social democratic Labour Zionists and that of the Gush Emunim and other religious nationalist forces whose actions and ideas so dominated post-1967 settlement in the West Bank.

To understand the Jewish settlers' violence, one must decode its meanings. It is an instrument as well as a language; the incentives for its use both material and ideal. It has its own rewards and carries its own messages. The manner and conditions under which violence is deployed also distinguish the settlement movement launched by the Gush Emunim from the early Zionist settlers.

That Jews were prepared to return the violence of their enemies was elemental. Most Israelis acknowledged the Jewish settlers' right of residence, identified with the dignity of their self-defense. But these settlements were not the same as those of the early Zionists. Before there was a state, the Zionists had had to rely largely on their own devices, extralegal and daring though they were. The Gush Emunim's settlements, in contrast, have been constructed under the watchful eye of a powerful Jewish army. Under these conditions, settler violence has been a way not simply to try to reduce Arab resistance to Jewish colonization, but to ensure more settlements will be built, for Jewish violence provokes Arab violence, which has always legitimated more settlement. Jewish settlement has long been an accepted governmental "punishment" for Palestinian violence. Under both Labour and Likud governments, Palestinian guns and explosives have left Israeli bulldozers and cement mixers in their wake. This historic cycle provided an incentive for Israeli settlers to engage in provocative and retributive acts because the vicious cycles of violence set in motion virtuous cycles of Israeli construction. The *intifada* years were initially no different. Until Labour was reelected in 1992, Likud Prime Minister Yitzhak Shamir built new Jewish settlements at an unprecedented rate. Jewish residence in the occupied territories continued to soar.

Settler violence against the Palestinians has been not only materially productive, but politically expressive. It reflects the primacy of their commitment to the land. The Jewish settlers understand their own counterviolence as a repudiation of another people's illegitimate political claim. Just as their own deployment of force indexes their commitment to the whole land, they understand the government's failure to use what they considered adequate levels of repression as reflecting the insufficiency of its territorial desire.

When the *intifada* broke, the Jewish settlers saw it as the fruit of two decades of misguided Israeli policies. The *intifada*, many claimed, was a result of government trepidation before the political pretensions of an imaginary nation. For two decades, many settlers believed, Israel had failed to deploy the necessary force to suppress the Palestinians because of the "normalized" secular nationalism upon which the state had initially been founded.

Shrifra Blass, the settlers' spokesperson, told us the government did not pursue those who harassed the settlers because it held the territories at arm's length. The reason it didn't embrace these lands as its own, she said, was that it sees itself as a sanctuary state. Those secular Zionists who understand Israel as a refuge for a persecuted people, she claimed, are morally unprepared to confront the Arab national claims their refuge has displaced. Because their state was founded as a safe haven, Israelis have a natural tendency to treat these lands as occupied, to minimize Jewish losses while waiting for a negotiated peace.

Blass thought this was an ethically dangerous posture. By not claiming Judea and Samaria, the state was knocking away the moral basis of its own claim of sovereignty over *any* land. Israel, she said in the most reasonable tone, is not a "plank for a drowning man." If the establishment of a refuge for Jews was the only justification for coming to Israel, Blass believes she would not have come and, if she had come, would not have been able to stay. "I wouldn't want to be in [the secular Zionist's] shoes . . . because I personally, coming from America, if those were my only foundations for being here, I would probably have to go someplace else where I wasn't intruding on anyone else."

Wanting the Land

For the Labour Zionists, both the force of arms and the territory it stood upon were, first and foremost, instruments of state power. In this, they were not that different from their right-wing secular opponents in Menachem Begin's Herut Party. Labour sought a power great enough to assure survival, a defensible platform on which national Jewish life might be reborn. Ultimately force would fashion the circumstances of the Jewish nation's acceptance by her Arab neighbors. A weak state was a vulnerable state, a target for invasion and intimidation. But peace has always been the Labour Zionists' ultimate goal, and land a means to the power necessary for that peace.

It was not that the Labour Zionists did not want the land they understood to be liberated in 1967. Most did: Ben-Gurion, Israel's founding prime minister; Yigal Allon, the architect of the settlement strategy, who provided the first Jewish settlers into Hebron with Uzi submachine guns; Moshe Dayan, the general who orchestrated the 1967 victory; Levi Eshkol, Israel's prime minister during that victory. The territories were strategically valuable; there was a historic claim; the lands had been acquired as the result of a war in which Israel had been attacked.

But no matter how attractive the land of the West Bank and Gaza, the Labour Zionists evaluated it in terms of its contribution to state power, to the survival of Jewish life, to the prospect of peace. Faced with apparently implacable enemies more numerous and more wealthy than they, the land was of great strategic value. But for real peace, the conquered lands were potentially negotiable. The land was a vehicle for Jewish life, not the other way round. A powerful, democratic, and Jewish state – these were their primordial values.

Despite its strategic value, many Labour Zionists saw the West Bank and Gaza as politically indigestible. Mordechai ("Motta") Gur had led his troops in bloody fighting at Mitla Pass in Israel's 1956 Sinai campaign under then colonel Ariel Sharon. And in 1967, thirty-seven-year-old Colonel Gur and his brigade of paratroopers had been on the way once again to fight the Egyptians in the Sinai. When he was rerouted to Jerusalem, it did not seem momentous. Gur led the Israeli assault on the

Jordanian-held city, capturing Mount Scopus and the Mount of Olives, then swooping down into the Old City itself. Within days, he told us, his soldiers had a "growing feeling of very deep contact with Jerusalem."

In the face of the Arabs' refusal to sue for peace, most Israelis believed their country should keep the land. But Gur did not agree, even then. With a half million Israeli Arabs, bringing more than a million Arabs of the occupied territories into Israel was unacceptable; it would leave Israel with a bare Jewish majority. "That's not a Jewish state," he exclaimed to us. The territorial choice for him was being a Jewish or a democratic nation. His solution was to cede most of the territory, except what was strategically necessary, to Jordan, as a demilitarized zone in exchange for peace and mutual recognition.

By 1977, Fatah's analysts within the PLO were arguing that Israel would be forced to choose between its Zionism and its newly acquired land. Fatah believed Israel would refuse the choice and develop a strategy of "phases," gradually confining the Palestinians to enclaves, making their lives progressively more miserable, and pushing them to emigrate. Short of that, the Israelis would use simple force. Matti Steinberg, one of Israel's top PLO watchers, first understood the difficult territorial choice after reading the writings of the PLO's own strategists.

> From them I am learning about my society, because they are a rival to my society . . . When they are analyzing developments, they are trying to push it to its logical end . . . It was the first time that I saw a contradiction between sticking to all of the land of Israel which contradicts its Zionist character. I learned it from them. Yes, I read a book from Fatah.

Such Israeli talk about Palestinian numbers strikes many Jewish settlers as hypocrisy, historical amnesia. The Jewish settlement movement, Kiryat Arba's Rabbi Waldman told us, is just following the original Zionist pattern. Harkening back to the original demand for a Jewish state in Palestine, he said, "We demanded a Jewish state in the land when there wasn't any danger of an Arab majority . . . There *was* an Arab majority! . . . Now what did these 'fanatics' at the head of the Zionist organization think?" Under any acceptable territorial scenario, whether of the left or of the right, it was said, there would always be a significant Arab minority. Annexing all the lands would just make the problem slightly more difficult. The difference was in degree, not kind. To Waldman, there was only one solution to Arab numbers: mass immigration of Jews. "There's no other choice," the rabbi said. "And where there is no other choice, it must be achieved."

One way of creating the desired outcome was to increase the number of Jews, the other to reduce the number of Arabs. When the Knesset elections were held in 1988, many settlers announced the time had come to rid Judea and Samaria of as many Palestinians as possible. "Transfer" to the east, once an ugly term redolent with fascist associations, made its way into the lexicon of the liberal state. *Counterpoint*, Gush Emunim's English-language newspaper, carried a large advertisement reminding its readers that since 1945, West Germany had resettled twenty million refugees from Poland, Czechoslovakia, and East Germany. India and Pakistan resettled fifteen million after their partition. A growing number of Israelis supported "transfer" of the Palestinians to other Arab states.[27]

To the average Israeli, Palestinians have been waiters and low-wage workers who collect garbage and clean houses. To the government, they have been a security threat to be neutralized. They have not been the remnant of a nation whom history had delivered to Israeli occupation. Meron Benvenisti, Jerusalem's former deputy mayor and the man originally charged with dealing with the city's Arabs, has long believed that Israel's unwillingness to see the Palestinians as a legitimate collectivity was a major political liability. It was easier to assimilate the Palestinians to the margins of the great Arab army intent on crushing the small Jewish state than to recognize them as a nation that might, under the appropriate circumstances, be able to make its own peace with Israel.

Most Israelis seemed incapable of recognizing the nation of Palestinians growing in their shadow. For the Israelis, Bevenisti believes, the origins of that incapacity lie in the horrible history that made Zionism both necessary and possible. Israelis easily assimilate the wars with the surrounding Arabs to their long history as powerless victims of pogroms, riots, and genocide. Because Israel could not, would not, recognize that the fulfillment of its own national aspirations was at the expense of those of another people, he believes, Zionism's original moral structures had begun to dissolve in the face of the Palestinians' violent resistance. Gush Emunim had been quick to build an explicit exclusionary scaffolding of mystical nationalism on top of the Labour Zionists' legacy.

Between Israelis and Palestinians, the denial has been mutual, both sides rejecting the other's national claim. As the Israelis converted their conflict with the Palestinians into an extension of their endless struggle with surrounding hostile Arab states or as a religious conflict with the Muslim world, the Palestinians reduced the Zionists to white colonials or infidel invaders. The PLO's program for a democratic secular state in Palestine likewise negated Jewish nationalism, making Israelis into Jews. Some PLO strategists even believed that Israel's incorporation of the territories would ultimately force it toward their own objective of a binational state. Both sides tried to manage the "other" by defining their nationhood away.

Territorial Blessings

Mordechai Gur and Yisrael Harel fought together in the battle for Jerusalem, but they do not agree on the meaning of Zion. Yisrael Harel, once the secretary-general of the settlement movement, is the editor of *Nekuda,* the movement's theoretical organ. Harel and Gur have aired their disagreements publicly. When they argued, Harel told Gur the land was given to the Jews by God. "So what's all that nonsense," Gur recalled Harel's demanding, "about Arab rights? They have twenty-one or twenty-two countries. They can go wherever they want."

Gur reduces the conflict between the two men to a fundamental disagreement about the moral meaning of being a Jew. "He thinks that what we got from the Jewish heritage is the land of Israel territorially. And I say that what we got from the Jewish heritage is the sense of equality, of decency, of understanding and it does not imply territory only."

If the choice is between Jewish land and Jewish people, Gur has no doubt which is more important. What, Gur asked Harel, if they had to choose between a million Jews from the Soviet Union willing to immigrate to Israel and keeping the territories? Wouldn't Harel prefer the people to the additional land? What about Jerusalem, Harel shot back? "And I said very explicitly," Gur told us,

> for me, Israel as a state is for the Jewish people and I have enough place . . . to receive another two million people – Jews – without Jerusalem. So if by giving back Jerusalem, it can bring two million Jews, of course I'm ready to give back Jerusalem.' . . . And let me tell you something, when we should be here five or six million, we can take Jerusalem back, because it's a territory. I mean, it's there. If you want, you take it, if you have the power. But this is not the main sense of Jerusalem, of the Jewish people, and the sense of the State of Israel. It should give a political, human, moral solution to the Jewish people. If it can be done with Jerusalem, *tres bien*, very good, but this is not a precondition to the existence of the State of Israel.

For Labour Zionists like Mordechai Gur, land is one among several means to construct a normal, democratic nation-state at peace with its neighbors. In contrast, the primary objective of those who share the world view of Gush Emunim is not peace, but territory. For real peace, the early Zionist settlers were willing to sacrifice territory, even Jerusalem. For the Gush Emunim, peace is not possible before the messianic redemption to which reclamation of the promised territory, and above all Jerusalem, is essential, even if it means war.

The foundational myth of the Israelite nation begins with the taking of lands occupied by more populous peoples. To the religious nationalist settlers, the Torah provides a precedent for dispossession. After wandering in the deserts for forty years, a new generation of Israelites had grown up under Moses's leadership. Moses hoped to create a nation that had not known slavery, a free nation centered around the laws of God. Only such a nation would be capable of possessing the lands promised to their patriarchs. In his summation of these laws to his people, Moses explained:

> When the Lord your God brings you to the land that you are about to invade and occupy and He dislodges . . . seven nations much larger than you – and the Lord your God delivers them to you and you defeat them, you must doom them to destruction: grant them no terms and give them no quarter . . . This is what you shall do to them: you shall tear down their altars, smash their high places, cut down their sacred trees, and throw their molten images into the fire . . . Should you say to yourselves, "These nations are more numerous than we; how can we dispossess them"? You need have no fear of them . . . The Lord your God will dislodge those peoples before you little by little; you will not be able to put an end to them at once, else the wild beasts would multiply to your hurt. (Deuteronomy 7:1–23)

Moses spoke to his people from the eastern side of the Jordan, on the eve of their invasion of its western bank. He described a land stretching from Iraq through Amman in the east, to the Mediterranean in the west, from Lebanon in the north to the Sinai in the south, a land covenanted to them by God. Three thousand years ago, the Jews succeeded because of their unity, their belief in one God, and the power that God bestowed upon them as a result of their obedience to his law. It was a power that could clear the ground.

Many religious settlers believe that the consequences today for Israel of not settling, and, more grotesquely, forbidding Jews from settling these covenanted territories are likely to be catastrophic. There is an essential relationship between the people and the land of Israel. Neither can be realized without the other. Moses, Rabbi Waldman reminded us, clearly laid out the curses that would befall the Israelites if they disobeyed God's law. Chief among them was that they would be driven from their land. "The Jews," the rabbi predicted, "will become desolate, meaning not fruitful nationalistically, spiritually and the land *too* will remain desolate."

There was, Waldman added, a blessing within this curse. For two thousand years, the land had failed to bear another nation. "No other people [were] ever . . . aroused nationalistically to devote themselves to developing the land . . . until the Jews came back here." When the Jews took back the land in 1967, he claimed, "80 percent of the [Arab] population was unemployed, living like dogs under the rule of [King] Hussein . . . No one revealed any devotion to the land. No one cared about it. The Arabs . . . devoted themselves to the development of their own personal property." To Waldman, the land was "empty," not in the sense of being without people, but lacking a nation devoted to it.

How, we inquired, should Israel respond to the rising tide of Palestinian nationalism in the West Bank? "There are no roots to it, the Palestinian people," Waldman quickly asserted. "Arabs yes, an Arab nation, maybe, an Egyptian nation, a Syrian nation, I don't know. Certainly not a Palestinian nation. There was no such thing."

But they understand themselves as a nation, do they not, we pressed? "The Arabs to this day, and to our sorrow," he replied, "relatively are a primitive people, the masses of Arabs, with regard to their intellectual level. It is easy to create mob rule, to drive them, just as it was in the war of liberation . . . I believe that most of the Arabs are not interested, were not interested in the first place."

Waldman could see the Palestinian nationalism rising all around him, he was no fool. "I cannot tell you," he said, addressing an imaginary Palestinian nation, "that you cannot decide now that you are a people. You didn't say it before, all the hundreds of years, Palestinian people, especially Palestinian people. I cannot tell you that you haven't the right to decide that from now on you are a people, but that doesn't give you the right to demand my land."

Whether the coerced response of a population concerned with their private progress or a belated copying of Zionist models, he believed Palestinian nationalism would eventually disappear. The Israelis only had to demonstrate their determination to stay. By not claiming these lands, he said, by suggesting that one day they may be returned, the Israeli government contributed to Arab terror, fed the fires of Palestinian nationalism. For it suggested that here, in this conquered space, there might one day be a Palestinian homeland.

"*We* are confusing the Arabs," Waldman lamented. "*We* are at fault for creating such a situation where they are given to terrorist pressure. More Arabs have been killed by Arabs in Judea and Samaria than Jews have been killed by Arabs." Given half the chance, he believed, freed of PLO coercion, the Palestinians would actually prefer Israeli governance to the inevitable bloodbath that would be unleashed if they were ever to have a government of their own. Waldman was even willing to allow the Palestinians to become Israeli citizens, provided they swore loyalty to the state. The rest could remain as a tolerated minority, a people whose only guarantees would be their quiescence and the government's good graces.

The Incitement of Peace

If the Labour Zionists understand land as a resource to be traded for peace, a small but potent component of the religious Zionists who have settled those lands view the prospect of peace, and the territorial loss it implies, as an incentive for their own provocative political violence.

In 1979, Menachem Begin signed the Camp David Accords with Egyptian President Anwar Sadat in Washington, D.C. At long last, the solid wall of Arab denial had been broken. Israel had achieved an official peace with the most populous state in the Arab world, had neutralized the military threat on its southern front. Without Egyptian support, other Arab states would not dare drive toward Tel Aviv. Sadat's visit to the Knesset profoundly moved a nation hardened by decades of its neighbors' hatred. Many cried when his plane hit the tarmac.

But not all Israelis were jubilant. Israel had sacrificed the Sinai for peace. The mountain upon which Moses had received the tablets of the law was being returned to Arab rule. The oil fields Israel had developed, which had begun to pay handsomely, were also lost. The air space in which the Israeli air force could practice was given up.

The religious nationalist settlers of Gush Emunim believed Menachem Begin had betrayed them because the Camp David Accords included provisions for Palestinian "autonomy" in the West Bank and Gaza. Surely, they believed, these accords would preclude eventual Israeli sovereignty in Judea and Samaria and might even lead to the establishment of a Palestinian state. Israel itself was repudiating God's ancient promise to the Jews. And for what?

The prospect of losing the center of the biblical Israel transformed scattered impulses to vengeance by Jewish settlers into a program for political murder; it converted vigilantism into irredentism. This superheating, this dangerous changing of state, occurred at the place where the settlement movement had been born, the city of the first Jew – Hebron.

Palestinians outraged by Begin's move as a contemptible neocolonial offering made the opening gambit. In 1980 four Arab Hebronites opened fire on a singing procession of armed yeshivah students accompanying women and children back to Hadassah House after Friday evening prayers. Their bullets and hand grenades left six Jewish students dead and sixteen wounded. These attacks departed from the pattern of Palestinian resistance: they were not executed by operatives controlled by organizations outside the territories, but by local residents acting on their own. They were personal, face-to-face attacks rather than the anonymous murder of the marketplace bombs with which Israelis were so familiar.

Hebron's mayor, Fahd Qawasmeh, belonged to the family who owned the hotel through which the Jewish settlers had first entered the city. A Palestinian pragmatist, Qawasmeh had originally supported the 1947 UN partition plan, an unusually brave position at the time. After a period in Egypt from which he returned in 1972, he had been employed by the Israeli military government as director of agricultural research and development on the West Bank.

When in 1976, under the Israelis, the Palestinians of the West Bank experienced their first free elections based on universal suffrage, Qawasmeh was elected mayor. A consummate politician, he maneuvered among the demands of the Israeli military administration, the Jordanians, and the PLO. Although Qawasmeh wanted to build a Palestinian state in the West Bank, he maintained cooperative relations with the Israeli authorities. Repeated clashes with the Jewish settlers radicalized him, the stridency of his voice growing with Jewish penetration of his city. By 1980, he was actively mobilizing to confront them. "I will not stand by silently while they go about overrunning my city," he declared. "I prefer to be deported, arrested, tried – anything but the Judaization of Arab Hebron!"[28]

After the murder of six yeshivah students in Hebron, the Israeli government deported Qawasmeh, the *qadi* (a religious judge), as well as the mayor of neighboring Halhul, Muhammad Milhelm, taking them by helicopter to Israel's northern border with Lebanon.[29] The Palestinian leadership was deemed culpable for terror and deported in the night without any charges filed, without any evidence examined, with no due process whatsoever.

But a small, clandestine group of young Israeli men from the settlement movement were already preparing for something more. It was not Palestinian violence but Israel's recognition of the legitimacy of the political claims that prompted their reply and determined its targets. Begin's treacherous peace treaty promising "autonomy" to the Palestinians had led to the formation of a settlement underground, *makteret*, the Israelis called it. Its members, who believed it was time to preempt the politicians, had already determined to orchestrate a series of violent profanations aimed at the most important symbols of Palestinian nationhood. Such provocations, they believed, would make peace and partition impossible. The politicians, even the men whom they considered their most dependable allies, had now forced them to do God's work.

This clandestine Jewish network, composed of devout young pioneers, well-trained Israeli soldiers and officers, leaders and activists at the core of the religious nationalist settlement movement, chose as their first target the Dome of the Rock, an Islamic sanctuary built in the seventh century on the same platform where Solomon constructed the first Temple. By blowing up this delicately tiled cupola built over the stone from which Muslims believe the Prophet leaped to paradise, they would clear the ground on which the Temple to their one God would ultimately be rebuilt. History was quickening. Yehuda Etzion, the leader of the underground, who had been one of the founders of Gush Emunim, believed the explosion would spark a spiritual revolution in Israel, pushing a secular state toward its destiny as a sacred kingdom.[30]

There has always been an apocalyptic stream among the Gush Emunim. Many of the underground's members believed destruction of this Islamic shrine would make war inevitable.[31] In 1948, the Arabs had fled en masse before the infant Israeli army. In 1967, they had not. As a result a million Arabs lived in the territories liberated from the Jordanians. If the Jews destroyed Palestine's most sacred Islamic shrine, they hoped the surrounding Arab states and the predominantly Muslim Palestinian population of Israel would rise in concert. At last, the conquered territories, and perhaps all Israel, could be rid of their Arab inhabitants.

Using binoculars and telescopes, they studied every movement on the stone surface of the *har ha-bayit*, the Temple Mount. Aerial photos were scrutinized. Squads trained on a model, scaling its walls with the necessary explosives. Demolitions experts made exact calculations so they could bring down the dome with a minimum of explosives; they dared not harm the Western Wall.

Because there were myriad logistical details to be worked out and rabbinical authorization was equivocal, the plot was put on hold. The murder of Jews in Hebron now set them into action. With the blessing of several rabbis, the nucleus of the same group of Gush Emunim activists who intended to blow up the Dome of the Rock met to avenge these Jewish deaths.

The Jewish underground decided to attack prominent elected Palestinian mayors, all of whom were members of the National Guidance Committee, which the Palestinians of the West Bank had formed in 1978 to resist the Camp David Accords because they stopped short of complete Palestinian sovereignty. The Jewish underground targeted five men: Ibrahim Dakkak of East Jerusalem, the Communist head of the Civil Engineers Union in the West Bank and founder of the National Guidance Committee; Bassam Shaka'a, the mayor of Nablus; Karim Khalif, the mayor of Ramallah; Ibrahim Tawil, the mayor of El Bireh; and Dr. Ahmed Hamsi Natshe, a prominent physician and nationalist deported by Peres in the 1970s who had been allowed to return to Bethlehem.

The underground attacked the Palestinian leaders simultaneously. Bassam Shaka'a had both his legs blown off by a car bomb. Karim Khalif lost a foot the same way. And Ibrahim Tawil would have suffered a similar fate had he not been warned by an Israeli army officer. The explosive charge rigged to his garage went off in the face of an Israeli Druze demolitions expert, blinding him. Ibrahim Dakkak was spared because he was out of the country. Natshe would have died if his dog had not frightened his would-be assailants away.

The Jewish settlers were jubilant when they heard the news. "Thus may all of Israel's enemies perish," declared Knesset member Haim Drukman, a rabbi and founding member of the Gush Emunim.[32] One of the settlers arrested for his part in these attacks called the Palestinian mayors "terror in municipal disguise."[33] In court, it was alleged that Rabbi Waldman, a central figure in Gush Emunim, had himself volunteered to participate in this strike.[34]

But Jewish violence did not stop Palestinian violence. On July 7, 1983, another Jewish yeshivah student, eighteen-year-old Aaron Gross, was brutally murdered in broad daylight in downtown Hebron by commandos from Islamic Jihad. As Arab Hebronites in the marketplace looked on, two Arabs grabbed him while a third stabbed him over and over again in the throat and abdomen, until his chest split open. None of the Palestinians intervened. A large Arab crowd blocked the way of settlers who desperately tried to pursue his attackers. As his friend, Uzi Sharabaf, looked on helplessly, Gross died shortly thereafter. After Israelis from the Peace Now movement held a demonstration against Jewish settlement of Hebron on the spot where Gross had been killed, Eliakim Ha-Etzni, the Jewish lawyer from Kiryat Arba, was livid. "They stood on the blood of their brother and identified with the enemy," he spat out to us. "This we will never forget."

Although Yehuda Etzion had not been able to secure rabbinical approval for the plot to blow up the Dome of the Rock, members of the Jewish underground planned their revenge against this attack with the blessing of settlement movement rabbis. Uzi Sharabaf, Miriam Levinger's son-in-law, and two others rushed into the courtyard of Hebron's Islamic College, filled with students, throwing grenades and firing Soviet assault rifles. (The Israelis had captured so many of these Russian-made guns from the PLO in Lebanon that they had been issued to Jewish settlers to defend themselves.) Three Palestinians died and over thirty were wounded.

Six months later, in December, an Israeli bus – the number 18 – was wending its way across Jerusalem. A high-explosive device had been packed with nails and placed underneath a back seat. The blast, which blew the roof off the bus, hurtled bodies through the air, caromed others off the walls, and badly burned many others. Nail fragments and glass shot out in every direction at murderous speed. It shattered ear drums. Four Jews died immediately; forty-three were injured. The PLO outside the country claimed credit.

And so six months later, in April 1984, again with the approval of some movement rabbis, Jewish terrorists attached massive explosive charges to the bottom of five buses parked in East Jerusalem. The bombs were timed to explode at 4:00 P.M. on Friday afternoon, a time when most Jews would be at home preparing for Shabbat. Hundreds of Arabs would have been killed and wounded if the Shin Bet, Israel's secret service, had not uncovered the underground and foiled the plan. In all cases, the Israeli government initially assumed and promoted the idea that the plots had been executed by clandestine Arab groups.

To reduce the legs of Palestinian mayors to stumps, to murder Palestinians in their universities and public buses, to try to blow up their most sacred sites – these acts of violence, of sacrilege, recalled for many Jews the pogroms their parents and grandparents had fled in Russia. Many in the settlement movement itself refused to believe it. The senior girls at Jerusalem's Tzviyah School, a religious nationalist high school dedicated to teaching its students the religious necessity of settling *all* of the land, certainly couldn't. Their parents knew many of the men arrested by the security forces. Surely it was a bluff. "The judges are stacked against them. The papers libel them. There is no conspiracy," one girl told us. "If such a thing existed, we're against it. I heard the rabbi of the school say that you are not allowed to kill people, especially if they are innocent, just people that were riding in a bus, just because you want *eretz-yisrael*. It's like murder." To these girls, their long hair pulled back tight, brought up with the mission of bringing the Torah to the Zionist movement, religious settlers could never do such a thing.

Other Israelis understood these events as simple acts of vengeance for the Palestinian terror that continued to plague Israel, particularly those who chose to settle in the conquered lands. Jewish buses and cars were being stoned more frequently. Yeshivah students were being murdered. These desperate Jewish acts were the logical outcome of a cycle of violence between Palestinian residents and Jewish settlers. The Jewish responses were never sufficient. Something radical was required, many Jews agreed, acts that would impose more damage on the Palestinian community than had been imposed on the Jews, that would raise the price of resistance, break the Arabs. Jewish blood was no longer cheap.

In court, Yehuda Etzion, one of those charged with assaulting the Palestinian mayors and a proponent of the plan to blow up the Dome of the Rock, offered the following:

> Planning and excuting the attack on the murder chieftains took only one month of my life, one month that started with the assassination night of six boys in Hebron . . . I insist that this operation was right . . . a pure act of self-defense.[35]

Etzion went on to say that the government, the responsible "police-man," who should have responded, not only had "stepped aside" but had developed a "friendly relationship" with the murderers.

Every day hundreds of Israelis gathered outside the jail where members of the Jewish underground were kept. Restaurant and café owners sent the prisoners cakes and cooked foods. *"Casakh* ["to break" in Arabic] is the only word the Arabs understand," one Israeli said angrily. Men nodded in agreement. In fact, a survey at the time found a majority of Israeli Jews could either justify or relate with understanding to what the Jewish underground had done.[36] After their arrest, Israel's president, Chaim Herzog, used his authority to reduce the long prison terms to which members of the underground had been sentenced.

But this was more than just a cycle of vengeance. Most religious Zionist settlers see violent Palestinian resistance to Jewish settlement as a consequence of an illegitimate nationalist claim. Palestinian violence must be countered, not just as a matter of punishing an attack on Jewish life, but as a clear repudiation of the nationalist claim that undergirds it. It is for this reason that their violent replies have not just been aimed at the perpetrators or their families, but at their most sacred symbols, their political leaders, and the Palestinian community at large.

The origins of Jewish terrorism and the groundswell of Israeli support it received were rooted as well in the changing relationship between Judaism and Zionism. The same conditions – Israel's inability to be treated like other nations, the ideological erosion of secular Zionism, the institutionalization of Judaism within the state – that gave rise to the religious nationalist settlement movement of Gush Emunim also help explain the terror in which some of its most articulate members have engaged.

When the Nightmare Arrives

And what would happen if an Israeli government were actually to cede sovereignty as part of a peace plan? The withdrawal from Yamit, a small Jewish colony in the Sinai, as part of the peace treaty with Egypt may be instructive. Wedged between Gaza and the northern Sinai, this area had been a Labour project, an Israeli stronghold against an Egyptian advance in the next war. After most of its inhabitants, predominantly not religious nationalists, were evacuated by the military, at least a thousand people from the religious nationalist settlement streamed in, maneuvering through the desert at night or wading ashore from small boats, to take the former residents' places.

In 1982, Rabbi Waldman took his yeshivah students in busloads to
Yamit. His old study partner, Moshe Levinger, told the protesters that
they, or at least their rabbis, must be willing to accept martyrdom to
prevent Yamit's surrender.[37] Some believed that, this time, there would
be divine intervention. The atmosphere was expectant, the time filled
with religious discussion and prayer. Many were relieved that Rabbi Zvi
Yehuda Kook had not lived to see this treasonous retreat. Such was the
trauma that the new rabbinical head of Merkaz ha-Rav, the Gush
Emunim yeshivah in Jerusalem, had to overrule Rabbi Levinger and
decree that suicide – individual or collective – was not permissible.

When the Israeli army arrived, the demonstrators threw buckets of
paint, toxic chemicals, and stones down on the soldiers. They had to be
dragged out from buildings, praying all the while. One by one, they were
lowered into iron cages, the buildings bulldozed as soon as each was
cleared. A dozen members of Rabbi Meir Kahane's Kach movement
barricaded themselves in a bomb shelter, demanding burial shrouds and
threatening mass suicide. Rabbi Waldman was one of the last to be
pulled out of the settlement, forcibly taken from a memorial commemorating the Israeli soldiers who fell there in the 1967 war. Shortly after,
the Israelis blew up the monument.

Within a few hours of the scheduled arrival of Egyptian troops, a
small remnant snuck back to the site and conducted a ritual of retreat.
They recited Psalm 127, "Unless the Lord watches over the city, the
watchman keeps vigil in vain." They pledged they would not forget this
"holy" city, nor would they forgive those who had betrayed them. As
they prepared to take the Torah scrolls out of the synagogue, the only
building still standing, the rabbi of the Western Wall, dressed in the
white ritual garb of Yom Kippur, recited "Avinu Malkeinu," the Jewish
New Year prayer acknowledging God's sovereignty, and rent his clothing
in mourning.

As an evacuation by choice of a small part of the "promised" land,
Yamit was a shameful precedent to these protesters. For the Gush
Emunim, Yamit was a dress rehearsal for that perfidious point in the
future when an Israeli government might dare to give up Israel's ancient
core. "We stayed almost to the end," Waldman said, "because we believed we had a slight chance of saving it, of influencing our government . . . Even if we won't succeed, the very difficult situation created
would just serve as proving to the government what could happen in
Yehudah and Shomron."

At Yamit, there were just a few true believers. The next time, Waldman was sure there would be hundreds of thousands. And next time,
Waldman believes, the government will not be able to count on the
loyalty of its soldiers to execute its orders. The commanding officers

who evacuated Yamit deeply respected those they were coming to dislodge, he argues. Many soldiers wept as their Jewish captives were evacuated. Two officers told him that they would resign rather than obey commands to evacuate Jews from Judea and Samaria. Waldman has remained friends with many of the soldiers and officers who thwarted his plans. When his daughter was married, both the general chief of staff, Moshe Levi, who was then deputy chief of staff, and the commanding officer charged with the Yamit operation gladly attended the wedding.

But how far is Rabbi Waldman willing to push? Waldman didn't hesistate. "To the limit of a civil war, but not a civil war," he said. "We wouldn't lift a hand against a Jewish soldier, certainly not arms . . . because fighting Jews against Jews, that's the worst thing. Then we don't exist . . . These are very delicate lines and you have to have control of your people, and we proved that we did."

In 1984, the rabbi was elected to the Knesset as a member of the Tehiyah Party, a party committed to the whole land. As reports began to filter back in 1985 that the Labour prime minister, Shimon Peres, was negotiating with King Hussein, the Council of Jewish Settlements in Judea, Samaria, and Gaza held an emergency meeting.

The statement they issued rocked the nation.

> The plans attributed to the prime minister, which seek to hand over rule in Judea and Samaria to a foreign body, are illegal . . . are tantamount to doing away with the State of Israel as a Zionist Jewish State whose aim is to bring Jews to the Land of Israel . . . Any government in Israel which turns over sovereignty to the enemy will be considered illegal, a government which should not be obeyed. The proposing of the division of the Land of Israel will cause the division of the people.[38]

Massive civil disobedience was endorsed. They would refuse to pay taxes or serve in the army. They would disrupt the state by any means necessary.

In the course of their struggles with the Israeli government to settle the lands, the Jewish settlers developed the distinction between actions that were legal and those that were legitimate. Zionism, a commitment to settling all *eretz-yisrael*, was Israel's constitutional foundation.[39] If the government deviated from that goal, then although its actions might be legal, they were not legitimate and must be fought. The state only had legitimacy, divine sanction, as an instrument to settle the land.

In the tussles over Jewish settlement, Gush Emunim had illegally set up tents and trailers, playing cat and mouse with the government. It had held massive demonstrations, exploiting the personal and partisan divisions that fracture the Knesset, but its members had never advocated the use of force against their own state. Rabbi Kook had insisted the Jewish state was sacred.

Now Rabbi Eliezer Waldman appeared to cross the line. Speaking on Israel Radio, he said, "I, too, warn that if any land is given up, blood will be spilled."[40] Large numbers of Gush Emunim settlers said they were willing to die rather than yield an inch of territory. A much smaller number, but enough to be deadly, were willing to kill.[41]

The *intifada* only intensified the Jewish settlers' determination to resist. Those who adhered to Kook's teachings claimed it was a heavenly message, another divine censuring of Israel's failure to embrace God's territorial gift. Without massive settlement and sufficient state repression, the Palestinians would continue to dare to reach for statehood in the land of Israel. In July 1988, six months into the uprising, Rabbi Moshe Levinger announced that it was time to make the "spiritual message" of settlement perfectly clear. By building settlements, the movement had already fulfilled the material role of the earthly messiah, son of Joseph. Now it was time to preach the message of the heavenly messiah, son of David: to prepare the people for the restoration of the Third Temple.

"The message of the Third Temple," said Levinger, who had been involved in the deliberations about blowing up the Dome of the Rock but refused to bless this operation, "will be so exalted that it will not be destroyed."[42] Normalization, peace, territorial compromise are, in his eyes, all impossible, repudiations of the redemptive promise. "Whoever wants to raise the white flag over part of the land is blemished," he continued. "The people of Israel cannot be blemished." Although Levinger's sentiments were attacked as adventurist by some settlement rabbis like Yoel Ben-Nun, they garnered considerable support within the movement.

David Grossman, the Israeli novelist, was sure that he would eventually have to fight the religious nationalists to extricate Israel from the occupied territories. "I don't like them," he told us even before the underground had been uncovered.

> I'm afraid from them. I don't like their enthusiasm of shooting, of carrying guns . . . And I cannot talk to people that involve tradition and God in the argument because in the name of God many evil things and cruel things were done all over history. And that's what they're going to do. They didn't show us yet everything that they know and they can do. They are very . . . emotional and emotions are something that's good for literature, not for life. And they are very dangerous.

The Jewish settlers played upon the average Israeli's uneasy secularism. Grossman told us he believed that unease was there from the state's very beginning, recounting an interchange beween Ben-Gurion and the esteemed *haredi* rabbi Avraham Yeshayahu Karelitz (1878–1953), who wrote under the nom de plume, Hazon Ish, "the visionary." "The two sides tested each other's power. And the Hazon Ish [asked] Ben-Gurion: 'If two carriages [are] going on the same bridge – one of them is fully loaded and the other is empty – who is to give place to the other?' " The empty one, Ben-Gurion replied.

Because the Labour Zionists conceived of themselves as the "empty carriage," Grossman said, Israel had given Judaism too much access to state power. "I'm sorry," he told us in 1983, "I'm not ready to feel like an empty carriage. I think *they're* the empty carriage [referring here to the religious nationalists]. Or maybe the carriage that is loaded with . . . everything except humanism and liberalism and real human values. They don't have it now, the people that go there to live, to fight with the Arabs, to shoot an Arab girl. He's not a Jew for me. He's not a Jew, he's a cossack. I think that I am the real Jew." If territorial compromise were ever possible, they would fight people like him. Of that, David Grossman was sure. "Nobody promised us a good end, a happy end. And I think that the end will not be happy for us."

Part III

Birth of a Nation

11

Platform for Palestine

Palestinians refer to the land as their mother. In the 1967 war, the territorial remnant from which they were to form a state was lost, their appointed lands all controlled by the Jews. But within the curse, there was a blessing, for this defeat was necessary to birth a Palestinian state.

By allying with Nasser's Egypt in 1967, the Hashemites of Jordan made a disastrous gamble. For the next quarter century, the Palestinians were caught in a triangle of Jordanian, PLO, and Israeli forces, each of which sought to turn them to their own purposes. The Jordanians hoped to retain the loyalties of their now-Israeli-occupied subjects and use their political energies to reclaim the lost lands for the Hashemite state. The PLO, formed shortly before the Six-Day War, understood these Palestinians as a subordinate component of the Palestinian nation, a pliant constituency who should support its claim to speak for all Palestinians, not only those living on the land, but the even larger diaspora throughout the Arab world. The Israelis saw them simply as Arabs, hoping they would accept circumscribed self-government under Israeli and/or Jordanian sovereignty. The Palestinians would defy them all.

Al-Quds Against Amman

Al-Nakbah, the disaster, the Palestinians call it. To the outrage of the Israelis, they sometimes translate the term for the 1948 war as "holocaust," morally equating their status as victims of Zionist expansion with the extermination of Jews by the Nazis. The Palestinians entered the war still debilitated by the civil war they had fought over territorial compromise a decade earlier. Haj Amin al-Husayni had emerged from that struggle as Palestine's leading patriot. As mufti, holder of Palestine's highest Islamic office, Husayni was the champion of an independent Palestinian nation-state, an uncompromising adversary of those Palestinians who would brook any territorial compromise with the Zionists and who largely allied with the Hashemite regime in Transjordan. As the 1948 war approached, Husayni demanded that the Arab League allow

245

the Palestinians to form their own provisional government. But under the prodding of two Hashemites kings in Jordan and Iraq, the Arab League showed little interest in an independent Palestinian state. Before the war King Abdullah had held a series of secret meetings with the Israelis in order to carve up Palestine between them.[1] Abdullah even suggested to Golda Meir that the mufti be assassinated.[2]

The mufti's forces led the Palestinians' sole domestic military organization, *al-jihad al-muqaddas*, Jerusalem Holy War, to which the Arab League granted absolutely no financial support. Abd al-Qadr, the son of Musa Kazim al-Husayni, the Jerusalem mayor deposed by the British in 1920, founded the nucleus of this guerrilla army in 1931 from young, predominantly Jerusalemite Palestinians, many of them Boy Scout commanders. After the Palestinian uprising had been crushed in 1939, the mufti sent Abd al-Qadr, his nephew, to Nazi Germany for military training. When World War II ended, Abd al-Qadr, based in Cairo, accumulated arms and trained volunteers for the coming struggle against the Jews. Among those who acquired arms for him there and was deeply influenced by him was another member of Husayni's extended family network, Muhammad Yasser Arafat, who himself claims to have been born and raised in Jerusalem, in the Arab neighborhood facing the Western Wall.[3]

The 1948 war to liberate Palestine from the Zionists was fought largely by outside Arab armies. King Abdullah of Jordan, in a move opposed by the entire Arab world, siezed Jerusalem and the West Bank, indeed all the lands the United Nations had allotted for a Palestinian state, as his own.[4] Something like 700,000 Palestinian Arabs fled what became Israeli-controlled territory into exile, leaving behind 102,000 of their brethren, who would become Israeli Arabs.[5] Hundreds of Palestinian villages were destroyed or abandoned. The cosmopolitan Arab communities built up in the Mediterranean coastal cities were decimated; Palestinian life shifted to the hill country, into what the United Nations intended as the territorial core of a new Palestinian Arab state.

After Israel and Jordan's victory in 1948, the Arab League – to prevent Jordanian annexation – allowed the Palestinian nationalists to regroup in Gaza, a small strip wedged between the Sinai and Israel, and declare an independent Palestinian state, what they called "All-Palestine Government," Jerusalem its intended capital. To convene the first Palestine National Council in September 1948, the Palestinian nationalist leader, Haj Amin al-Husayni, slipped clandestinely into Gaza with the aid of the Egyptian Free Officers and the Muslim Brotherhood.

This first Palestinian government-in-waiting issued a declaration of independence claiming all that remained of mandatory Palestine for itself. The new government rejected Amman's willingness to accept partition, its incorporation of lands meant to be part of the new Palestine, and its political claim to speak for the Palestinians.[6] After signing an armistice with Israel in 1949, the Egyptians, fearful of Israeli retaliation, and with no interest in a Palestinian state, reined in this rump Palestinian government in Gaza. Haj Amin al-Husayni was placed under house arrest in Alexandria.[7]

On the same day the mufti's provisional government was meeting in Gaza, King Abdullah convened his own meeting of Palestinians in Amman.[8] These Palestinians declared Palestine and Transjordan to be indivisible. To mark the union, Abdullah changed the country's name to the Hashemite Kingdom of Jordan. Although the new Jordan defended the Palestinians' territorial rights, it found their national rights deeply disturbing. Arabs of Palestinian origin, after all, many of them refugees from Israel, were a majority of Jordan's population. Palestinians in Jordan spoke publicly of a Palestinian entity only at great personal risk.[9]

The Jordanian regime particularly feared the Palestinian hill towns of the West Bank, centers of Palestinian nationalist resistance to Hashemite rule. The Jordanians made sure the mayors of each town reported directly to Amman; West Bank organization was strictly forbidden. Palestinians who refused to bend were imprisoned, tortured, held in desert concentration camps, and exiled. With the Mediterranean coast and its modernist Arab nationalist centers like Jaffa and Haifa in Zionist hands, Jerusalem became, more than ever, an important political center for the Palestinians. Under Jordanian rule, the Arab world continued to treat the city as Palestine's natural capital, holding conclaves of Arab states there, establishing consulates and charitable institutions, financing the refurbishment of its sacred Islamic sites.

Jerusalem's Palestinian identity threatened Transjordan's sovereign claims. After the 1948 war, the Jordanians sought to reduce the importance of the city. Many Palestinians left for Amman to be closer to power. The Jordanians expelled others they found threatening. Many members of Jerusalem's dominant families left Palestine altogether. Many Christians, who had been concentrated on Jerusalem's more fashionable western side, were forced to flee in the war. Other Christians, highly educated and anxious about the restricted opportunities the Hashemites afforded to them in general, and to Jerusalem in particular, left as well.[10]

If it hadn't been for the Hebronites, known for their merchant skills, who migrated in large numbers to Jerusalem – including the Christian quarter – Palestinians say there would have been little to stop the Jews from taking everything after 1967.[11] The wealthy Hebronites, or *Khalili*, moved into the fashionable northern quarters of East Jerusalem around the American Colony Hotel, in Sheik Jarah, and on the Mount of Olives.

Hebron villagers also gravitated to the city but often found housing only in the poor crowded sections of the city, like Silwan. In many cases, they squatted in abandoned buildings along the Green Line, just as Moroccan Jews did on the other side of the city.[12] The Hebronites now own the largest enterprises in the city and dominate the business community.

When the Hashemites took Jerusalem in 1948, they selected members of rival families from Hebron and Nablus to rule this troublesome place.[13] The Jordanians disbanded the British-created Supreme Muslim Council, which had been Husayni's fortress, subordinating control of its endowments and religious courts to Amman. The religious institutions it administered in Jerusalem were entrusted to Hebronite families. Not only were Hebronites historic enemies of the Husaynis; they had traditionally been looked down upon as uncouth country bumpkins by Jerusalem's large agrarian and commercial families.

Government offices in Jerusalem were shut down and moved to Amman. Even the administration of tourism was transferred to this dusty backwater. Jordan diverted private and public capital investment to Amman, offering tax incentives for investment on the East Bank, placing bureaucratic obstacles in the way of investment on the West Bank and especially in Jerusalem. For example, when the merchants of Jerusalem and Bethlehem lobbied to build an international airport to carry a potentially enormous Arab tourist trade, Amman stopped them cold. Abdullah had promised the Jordanian Parliament would meet regularly in Jerusalem. The promise was not kept.[14]

Anwar Nusseibeh, elected in 1950 as a deputy from Jerusalem to the Jordanian parliament in Amman, criticized the Hashemite suppression of his city. Nusseibeh had been made secretary to Haj Amin al-Husayni in that first 1948 Palestinian "government" in Gaza and was a distant member of Husayni's extended family. The Nusseibehs, like many Palestinian families, shifted their loyalties to the Hashemites because they then believed Palestinian nationalism had little chance of success. The Jordanians seemed to offer the best chance to rid themselves of Jewish rule. In 1950, Nusseibeh wrote a letter of protest against Jordanian constraints on Jerusalem's development, "in spite of the fact that Jerusalem is in the forefront of those towns affected by the catastrophe of the Palestinian holocaust."[15] Even those willing to understand Transjordan as Palestine demanded Jerusalem be made the capital of Transjordan. When the Jordanian regime resisted, Arab Jerusalemites pressured to make it Transjordan's second capital or to designate it officially as Jordan's spiritual capital.[16]

Jerusalem proved deadly to the Hashemites. On July 20, 1951, on the verge of a separate peace treaty with Israel, King Hussein's grandfather, Abdullah, was assassinated by a Palestinian nationalist – Mustafa Asha, a young tailor's apprentice from Jerusalem's Old City – as the king made his way to pray at al-Aqsa mosque in Jerusalem. Haj Amin al-Husayni's men were implicated in the attack. The monarchy's Bedouin troops stationed in Jerusalem rioted. Palestinian passersby were set upon and beaten. Hundreds were killed or wounded. In Amman, Palestinian women were taken to the central square to mourn for "their" king. Those who refused to weep were beaten until they cried from their wounds.

King Hussein had been at his grandfather's side as the Palestinian assassin shot him. Although Abdullah's father, Sharif Hussein, is buried near the Dome of the Rock, Abdullah's eldest son, Talal, refused to have his father buried in Jerusalem.[17] King Hussein, Talal's son and immediate successor, would not even pray at al-Aqsa until seven years later.[18] King Hussein hated the city, going up only to pray at al-Aqsa mosque, never, Palestinians said, staying the night.

Palestinians in Jerusalem repeatedly took to the streets to protest Jordanian moves that might lead to a separate peace with Israel. In 1955, Jordan seemed ready to enter the Baghdad Pact – an American- and British-backed anti-Soviet alliance composed of Turkey, Pakistan, Iran, and Iraq. Palestinians rose up in Jerusalem, burning Western consulates before Bedouin guns could subdue them.

The Hashemites found Palestinian nationalism profoundly threatening. For two decades of Jordanian rule, Palestinians who voiced support for an independent Palestinian polity feared for their lives and the well-being of their families.[19] Even Palestinians who rose in parliament to speak of the "two" Jordans were censured by the king. In 1961, in an effort to appease the Jerusalemites, the Hashemite regime appointed Anwar Nusseibeh governor of Jerusalem, the only Jerusalemite to hold that position under the Jordanians.[20] Palestinians in Jerusalem nonetheless mounted demonstrations and strikes to press for their national rights. And Nusseibeh supported them. When the Jordanians dismissed him in 1963, Jerusalem's Palestinians rioted.[21]

When the Palestinian riots began, Mordechai Gur, the Israeli brigade commander who would liberate Jerusalem a few years later, was positioned in Jerusalem as head of the Golani Brigade. Operational plans were developed, he told us, "to liberate the whole city as a result of the riots they had against the king."[22] King Hussein, who found the riots deeply disturbing, began to construct a royal palace on the northern edge of Jerusalem to fulfill his promise to reside part of each year in the city.

Palestinian political thinking was dominated by Arab nationalism, by the belief that the liberation of Palestine would be achieved through Arab unity.[23] But it quickly became clear that although the Arab regimes might wish Israel's military defeat, they, particularly those bordering Israel, had no interest in independent Palestinian organization. It wasn't just that Palestinian guerrilla attacks across their borders invited Israeli retaliation; the Arab regimes were threatened by the new generation of Palestinians, who believed that the Arab rulers were corrupt, overly dependent on foreign protectors, too easily bent to imperial designs.[24]

Palestinian belief in Arab nationalism was shaken by the failure of Gamel Abdel Nasser, the great Arab nationalist who so energetically trumpeted his commitment to liberate Palestine, to pursue that objective after his Free Officers' Movement had overthrown King Farouk in 1952. It later became clear that Nasser's idea was not military liberation of Palestine, but a negotiated settlement imposed on Israel through American pressure.[25] Indeed, Nasser clamped particularly harsh restrictions on all forms of Palestinian political organization and eventually, after his victory against the British and French at Suez in 1956, forced the future leaders of al-Fatah to emigrate to the Gulf.[26]

A small but growing number of Palestinians in the diaspora believed that they had to put the liberation of Palestine before Arab unity, indeed that a movement for the liberation of Palestine would be a means to mobilize the Arab masses and sweep away the politically bankrupt regimes hobbling the Arab world.[27] Only an autonomous nationalist movement could create an army willing to fight a war of liberation. This position was promulgated by al-Fatah, which grew out of a network of Palestinian student organizations led by Arafat. Al-Fatah was begun in Kuwait in 1959, largely by Cairo-educated children of middle-class Muslim Palestinian families who had fled to Kuwait both as a place to prosper and as a refuge from repression by Nasser's pan-Arab movement. Al-Fatah's first major magazine, *Our Palestine,* begun in 1959, was banned by both Egypt and Syria. Palestinians in the refugee camps in Arab countries risked torture for reading it.[28]

The Arab regimes all felt compelled to honor their commitment to liberate Palestine, but they had no interest in the formation of an independent Palestinian army operating from their territories. It took fifteen years until, finally in 1963, over the vociferous objection of the Jordanians, the Arab League called for the formation of a Palestine National Council, to be convened in Jerusalem.[29] Israel's decision to divert waters from the Sea of Galilee via aqueduct to the Negev desert in the south finally prompted Nasser to convene the first Arab Summit, in January 1964, authorizing the formation of an organization that would allow Palestinians "to play their role in the liberation of their country and their self-determination."[30]

King Hussein, who was hostile to the existence of a separate Palestinian nation-state, wanted the PLO's founding conference to be held at a

resort on the Dead Sea, not in Jerusalem. The PLO's Palestinian organizers demanded it be held inside Jerusalem's Old City. In a compromise
move, the PLO was founded at the Inter-Continental Hotel on the
Mount of Olives on the city's periphery, technically outside the municipality.[31] The PLO did not demand that the West Bank be separated from
Jordan, only that Jerusalem be made Jordan's capital.[32] Jerusalem, a
Jordanian city, was not, however, mentioned anywhere in the PLO Covenant's thirty-three articles.[33] (Even after the document was revised in
1968, Jerusalem still was not named. Only after Israel captured Jerusalem *and* the PLO had been expelled from Jordan was the PLO free to
mention Jerusalem, and only then as "the seat of the Palestine Liberation Organization.")

When the PLO finally met in May 1964, its foundational document,
the Palestinian National Covenant, had received Nasser's prior blessing.
The covenant formally denied the national rights of the Jews, who were
understood to be a religious group only; declared Zionism to be an
illegal extension of Western imperialism; and understood Palestine as
the indivisible territories of the British Mandate, to be liberated through
armed struggle. Although a majority of the population of Jordan is
Palestinian, although the Palestinians of the West Bank are related by
blood and commerce to Jordan's population, although Jordan too was
created by British fiat, nothing in the PLO covenant spoke of the national rights of the Palestinians living under Hashemite control. Nowhere was there any mention of any kind of Palestinian sovereignty.[34]
Indeed, the documents explicitly deny that the PLO had any intention of
exercising "regional" sovereignty over the West Bank and Gaza, controlled by Jordan and Egypt, respectively.

Nasser intended the PLO as an instrument for his pan-Arab policies,
as a way to prevent Palestinian guerrillas from provoking a war between
Israel and Egypt, and as a means to thwart the Jordanians, not as a
representative body concerned with Palestinian self-determination.[35]
Thus although the Arab League agreed that the Palestinians should form
a Palestine Liberation Army, the Palestinian units composing it were not
an independent fighting force, but a passel of brigades, each of which
would be stationed in, subordinated to, and expected to fight alongside
the armies of the other Arab states. Indeed, Nasser correctly reasoned
that the formation of the PLO under a leadership beholden to him
would counter the growing influence of the more radical al-Fatah. Al-
Fatah was initially devastated by the formation of the PLO, of which it
was not then a member.[36]

The politics of the PLO, which had resolved to liberate all Palestine,
had as its premise an Arab military victory. The combined might of the
Arab states' armies would defeat the Jewish colonists and their off-

spring, forcing them to return to those places whence they came, or at least establish the conditions for a democratic state in all Palestine. After the Arab states' crushing June defeat in 1967, however, the Palestinians no longer believed in these premises. Nasser's pan-Arabism had failed.

Israel's 1967 victory made an independent Palestinian nationalism and the idea of a national liberation struggle much more appealing, both to the Palestinians themselves and to Arabs everywhere who had witnessed the battlefield failures of their nations' most powerful armies.[37] Nasser, like other Arab leaders humiliated by his defeat, now changed course, aligning himself with al-Fatah. Fatah's guerrilla units soon demonstrated their ability to engage the Israelis militarily and garned massive popular Palestinian support as a result. Six months after the war, under pressure from al-Fatah and with Nasser's blessing, Ahmad al-Shuqayri, who opposed independent guerrilla actions against Israel, was forced to resign as head of the PLO. In 1968, the PLO Charter was amended: "Armed struggle is the only way to liberate Palestine and is therefore a strategy and not tactics."[38]

Nasser himself helped maneuver al-Fatah back into the PLO and helped Arafat assume its helm in 1969.[39] Al-Fatah came to power within the PLO on the strategic assumption that the PLO would have to lead the fight through guerrilla warfare supported by the Palestinian masses in Israeli-occupied territories. (Although many believed that, protected by the Arab armies, PLO fighters would liberate all Palestine, al-Fatah's leadership claimed these military operations were really intended to prevent Israel from making peace with Jordan and Egypt.)[40] After the 1967 war, many in Fatah looked to the Algerian war of liberation, which had defeated the French in 1962, as its model. "All we ask," wrote a Fatah editor, "is that you [the Arab regimes] surround Palestine with a defensive belt and watch the battle between us and the Zionists."[41] But despite hundreds of commando attacks, the Palestinians inside the territories remained largely passive. It was not difficult for the Israelis to ferret out and crush the organizational centers of Fatah, including one located in Jerusalem. Unlike in Algeria, Cuba, or Vietnam, no people's army emerged in Palestine. To Arafat's consternation, the PLO was reduced to using Jordan as its principal staging ground for assault against "the Zionist entity."

Although the Fatah leadership was willing to cooperate with Jordan and other front-line states, and even to give up armed struggle if Israel would withdraw from the territories occupied in the 1967 war, the more radical streams within the PLO and much of the rank and file within Fatah itself were not.[42] The Marxist movements – Popular Front for the Liberation of Palestine (PFLP) and Democratic Front for the Liberation of Palestine (DFLP) – both believed a social revolution led by peasants and workers was the first order of business. They looked to social revolution to sweep away the corrupt, authoritarian Arab regimes, the very states like Saudi Arabia, Jordan, and Kuwait to which Arafat turned for funds and diplomatic suport.

The PLO portrayed itself not just as the agency for the achievement of a Palestinian state, but as the vanguard of the pan-Arab movement. The language it used subordinated the particularity of the Palestinian cause to the larger Arab community's struggle to expel the Zionists, the last colonial remnant. This language allowed the PLO to keep the most radical rejectionist groups within the grand coalition on the argument that territorial compromise was a tactic, not a strategy, a stage on the road to total liberation. As a vulnerable guest of various Arab states, it adopted rhetoric that fit neatly into the ideological outlook of its hosts, and with the interests of hundreds of thousands of refugees who wanted only to return to their homes on the Mediterranean coast and on the western side of Jerusalem.

Whereas the Zionists were able to achieve unitary command in 1948, the PLO was never more than an assemblage of political militias. The radical Marxist forces within the PLO saw Jordan, their first wary host, as a colonial implant, a retrograde monarchy willing to accommodate the Zionist presence. Reclaiming the first half of Palestine from the Hashemites was thus a requisite to wresting the second half from the Zionists. These Palestinian revolutionaries intended to topple Hussein's regime with the aid of the Palestinians inside Jordan and the support of Syria, a Baath socialist Arab nationalist state allied with the Soviets.

In 1970, the Jordanians signaled their willingness to enter peace negotiations with Israel, which was based on the U.S. promise to press Israel to withdraw from most of the West Bank and to secure a role for the Hashemites in Jerusalem.[43] This threatened Israel and the PLO, both of which might lose the territories seized from the Jordanians three years earlier. Israel, to indicate its intention to keep all of Jerusalem, built massively in Jordanian Jerusalem. The more radical factions within the PLO, determined that a Jordanian–Israeli peace would not come to pass, skirmished with Jordanian troops, set up roadblocks, and commandeered private vehicles. Radical groups within the PLO twice attempted to assassinate the king and then hijacked Western airplanes, taking them to Jordan and blowing them to bits.[44]

Forces within the PLO, backed by the Syrians, believed that the time had come to bring down the Jordanian regime. Israel was launching increasingly severe reprisal raids for the PLO's *fedayeen*, or guerrilla raids from Jordanian soil. Significant segments of Jordan's military command were on the verge of revolt because of the king's failure to bring the PLO to heel.[45] In 1970, while Israel and the United States tendered

Bust of King Hussein on sale in Bethlehem, 1984.

the support necessary to keep the Syrians at bay, King Hussein crushed the PLO. During what the Palestinians call "Black September," thousands of Palestinians died in the fighting.[46] Thousands more were thrown into Jordanian prisons. Some who had fled eastward across the Jordan River from the Israeli advance in 1967 now fled back as Hussein's loyal Bedouin soldiers shot and bayonetted their way through the refugee camps.

In July 1971, Jordan drove the remains of the PLO out of the country and into Lebanon. Before killing them, the Jordanians tortured Palestinian fighters taken in battle. Many Palestinians surrendered to Israel to avoid being taken by the Jordanians; some even shot their own families and then committed suicide.[47] King Hussein would pay dearly for his stand. His wife was gunned down and killed while riding in a helicopter; two of his country's prime ministers would later be assassinated by Palestinians.

Now that the PLO had been evicted from both sides of the Jordan River, Israel hoped to create an alternative Palestinian leadership in the territories to whom civil administration could be devolved. In a parallel vision, King Hussein proclaimed his own autonomy plan for a United Arab Kingdom in which the two banks would be joined in a federal state. "Jordan is Palestine and Palestine is Jordan," declared the Jordanian Ministry of Foreign Affairs.[48]

The PLO had previously held the two banks of the Jordan to be one indissoluble entity; its expulsion from Jordan allowed them to claim the West Bank as a separate unit, an essential part of Palestine, not Jordan. The PLO now proclaimed that the Palestinians and the Jordanians consti-tuted two separate peoples, each entitled to their own entity.[49] The PLO did not claim Jordan and Jordan could not claim Palestine. By its single-minded claim to all the territories, Jordan helped push the PLO toward acceptance of a separate Palestinian state.

Israel's Labour government was internally divided as to the territory's ultimate status. Israel's most forthcoming conception was to divide the territories with Jordan, not to give them back. And certainly not Jerusa-lem. But King Hussein could not abandon Jerusalem. Hussein could not make peace with the Zionist enemy for a small piece of the Palestinian patrimony in the midst of a contest with the PLO to represent the Palestinians. Leaving Jerusalem under Zionist control would be more than dishonorable; it would be political suicide.

The first real test of PLO influence within the occupied territories was in 1972 when the Israelis decided to hold municipal elections throughout the West Bank. These municipal elections became a battleground for Israel, Jordan, and the PLO. Following Jordanian practice, only male property owners were eligible to vote. The PLO, struggling to establish a beachhead in Beirut, demanded the Palestinians boycott the elections, physically threatening those "collaborators" who dared participate and arguing that the elections were designed to normalize the occupation, to give it a patina of legitimacy.

The PLO, which saw itself as a liberating army, had spent little effort developing a political infrastructure in the West Bank. Although Palestin-ians did refuse to run for office in Jerusalem, symbol of their nationhood over which Israel claimed sovereignty, everywhere else in the occupied lands they disgregarded PLO instructions and voted in a raft of pro-Jordanian notables from landed families. The Palestinian electorate turned out in record numbers. The elected mayors and city councils were drawn from the established wealthy families who had been prominent supporters and clients of the Hashemite regime.[50] The mayors claimed that they, and not the PLO outside, should lead the transition to an independent Palestinian entity, to be federated with Jordan.[51] The PLO was desperately afraid Jordan and Egypt would make their separate peace with Israel, and that the PLO would play no part.

To many Israelis it now appeared that the PLO could be kept outside, that the Palestinians could be made to live with the Israeli occupation. Deputy Mayor Meron Benvenisti's tolerant administration of East Jeru-salem was an extension of Defense Minister Moshe Dayan's strategy of nonrepressive civilian administration on the West Bank. Dayan's idea was that life could be organized so that Palestinians never even had to see an Israeli. Palestinian political organizations were allowed to emerge, harassment and surveillance were kept to a minimum, and Israeli administrators were prepared to negotiate with whatever natural political elites came forward.

The 1973 Yom Kippur war shattered these assumptions. During the war, Palestinian passivity, which Israelis had understood as deference, evaporated. Palestinians looked back at Israelis on the street; the war had given them face value. Palestinians from East Jerusalem went to the western side to examine the houses that they believed would soon be theirs. Shots were fired at Israeli travelers coming and going into Jerusalem. The paved roads, the television aeriels, the higher incomes had accomplished nothing.

Wars involve a historically contingent array of forces. But the population often reads the battle and its outcome not as happenstance, but as a natural sign of the rightness of the purposes for which the soldiers fought. Although Israel won the contest, its enormous losses demoralized the nation. This corrosion of invincibility led many Israelis to reread history, to embrace a religious nationalist vision that would provide the will necessary to survive.

On the Palestinian side, the war, as it demonstrated Israel's vulnerability, also indicated the limits of a military Arab solution. Despite a surprise attack and the combined might of the Egyptian and Syrian armies, Israel had been able to occupy even more Arab land. The war not only pushed the PLO to the forefront of the struggle, but set it on the long road to a two-state solution. Four months after the war ended, Fatah's Central Council produced a "working paper," calling for a "national authority on any lands that can be wrested from Zionist occupation." Although this was understood as a transitional foothold, Arafat claims even then to have understood the territorial compromise the Palestinians would ultimately have to make in order to survive as a nation.[52]

Palestinians widely believed that Jordan had held back most of the Arab Legion on the East Bank in the 1967 war so that Jerusalem was not adequately defended.[53] When Jordan not only stayed out of the 1973 war but prevented Palestinian forces from passing through its territory to join the war effort, the Hashemite regime was seen to be cowardly, preoccupied with its provincial interests, unable and unwilling to play a role in Palestine's liberation.[54] In 1973, for the first time, a Palestinian, as opposed to Jordanian, flag was hoisted in a West Bank demonstration against an Israeli commando raid on PLO Beirut headquarters.[55]

After the 1973 war, the PLO was ascendant in the Arab world. In June 1974, it finally accepted the notion of an independent Palestinian "national authority," but only as a way station on the road to total liberation.[56] In October 1974, the Arab Summit Conference recognized the PLO as the sole legitimate representative of the Palestinian people. The United Nations formally recognized the Palestinian right to self-determination and granted the PLO observer status. In November 1974, when Arafat made his triumphal United Nations entry, wearing dark sunglasses and carrying a pistol on his hip, young Palestinians rioted in Jerusalem. The next year Jerusalem suffered a reign of Palestinian terror, over a hundred attacks.

Jordan fought back, pouring money into the territories, paying salaries, subsidizing hospitals and schools. In Jerusalem it tried to bolster the influence of Jordanian Islamic institutions.[57] Although the Jordanians contended they were holding the territories in trust, the Jordanian constitution claimed both sides of the Jordan River for the Hashemite kingdom. It was only after an abortive PLO attempt on Hussein's life that the monarch agreed to the Rabat resolution in 1974, conferring upon the PLO the status of sole legitimate representative of the Palestinians, with a right to establish a state anywhere in Palestine, including the territories Hussein claimed for Jordan. King Hussein could no longer negotiate alone on behalf of the Palestinians.

Although Palestinians "inside" increasingly accepted the PLO "outside" as their nationalist body, the PLO was, in fact, still weakly organized inside the territories. And as Arafat attempted to stage manage events from the outside, the Communists were the only Palestinian movement actually run from inside the territories. Centered in Jerusalem, excluded from the centers of PLO decision making, the Communists were masters of organization, with the best underground structures in the occupied territories, such as the Palestine National Front established in 1968.[58] In the Jerusalem area they created the first organizational networks combining political mobilization with the provision of social services, a model that would later be copied with such success by radical Islam.[59] Young Palestinians planted trees, helped villagers bring in the harvest, and connected outlying neighborhoods to East Jerusalem's electricity grid.

When the PLO decided in 1973 to create its own Palestinian National Front (PNF) to mobilize all Palestinian nationalists in the occupied territories, it chose to work through the Communist structures already in place. This rapprochement between al-Fatah and the Communists was, in fact, brokered by the Soviet Union and Arafat as the price to be paid for increased Soviet aid in the wake of the Egyptian expulsion of most Soviet advisers from Egypt in 1972.[60] Galvanized by the Communists using classic "popular front" tactics, young nationalists organized right across the West Bank and Gaza, bringing together all Palestinians regardless of their politics. Its organizers in the occupied territories intended it to speak for the Palestinians on the "inside" and act as a pressure group within the PLO "outside."[61] The PNF organized opposition to Israel's proposals to negotiate a return of only some of the West Bank to Jordanian sovereignty in exchange for a peace treaty, or to offer the Palestinians civilian autonomy without a state of their own.[62]

The PLO soon regretted the legitimacy it had accorded the Communist-dominated Palestinian National Front. Unlike the PLO, which still held to its vision of total liberation through armed struggle, the Communists supported partition and an independent Palestinian state.[63] Whereas the Palestinian National Front recognized the PLO as its diplomatic voice, the PNF unashamedly promoted a Palestinian state, not as a staging ground, but as the final goal to be reached through diplomacy grounded in the United Nations's original partition plan. PNF activists argued that the PLO's violence, its insistence on liberating everything from the river to the sea, only made it easier for the world to countenance Israel's growing encroachment on what little remained to the Palestinians.

Both Israel and ultimately the PLO as well did their utmost to bring down the Palestine National Front. The PLO would not tolerate an independent nationalist voice and Israel wouldn't tolerate any nationalist voice at all. Israel deported many of its members, and the PLO refused to allow the Palestine National Front to speak for itself.[64] Apprehensive that the Palestinians of the West Bank and Gaza would regroup the bickering political forces of the occupied territories into one body, Fatah instructed its activists to defect. Bashir Barghouti, a Palestinian union organizer and one of the most important Communists in the Arab world, was fired as editor of *Al-Fajr*, the PLO's paper in Jerusalem. Eventually, the PNF fell apart, many of its members deported and – except the Communists – absorbed into the upper reaches of the PLO.[65]

After the 1974 Arab summit conference at Rabat recognized the PLO as "the sole legitimate representative" of the Palestinian people, Labour leaders argued that Israel should fill the vacuum of authority left by the Jordanians. If Israel expanded the authority of the municipalities, it was argued, they might even wean the Palestinians from the PLO outside and generate locally elected officials willing to negotiate an "autonomy" in which the West Bank could be federated to either Israel or Jordan.[66]

Peres believed the PLO would boycott the next municipal elections as they had in the past. But when the Palestinian mayors came up for reelection in 1976, the PLO realized that if it could not stop this political interaction with the Israelis, it had better try to direct it and to co-opt the local nationalist leaders. Young Palestinians, mostly college and high school students, were launching wave after wave of violent demonstrations and strikes against Jewish settlements encroaching into the West Bank, against an initial Israeli court ruling that Jews had the right to pray on the Temple Mount, and against Israeli proposals for a limited form of civilian Palestinian self-rule. The youth blocked roads and stoned military vehicles. These were the first large-scale violent Palestinian confrontations with the Israelis since the occupation had begun.[67]

Israel decided to expand the electorate in the 1976 elections, loosening the property qualifications so that all taxpayers could vote. Women, too, would be allowed to vote for the first time. (Peres hoped women would be more moderate.) To the Israelis' dismay, a new generation of young, radical Palestinian nationalists who supported the PLO swept into power, particularly in the big cities: Bassam al-Shak'a (PFLP) in Nablus, Fahd al-Qawasmah (al-Fatah) in Hebron, Karim Khalaf (al-Fatah) in Ramallah, Ibrahim Tawil (al-Fatah) in El-Bireh. Only in Bethlehem did the pro-Jordanian Elias Freij, who in the late 1960s had wanted his city to become part of Israel, hold on to office.[68] Although they were still drawn from the leading families, the core of the new nationalist slates were recruited from those who had been activists in the Palestine National Front.[69]

Israel's plan for undercutting the PLO had come undone. The old landed pro-Jordanian elite had been pushed aside by young, university-educated professionals who looked to the PLO as their representative. The men who came to power as mayors and city councilmen in 1976 used their offices to confront the Israeli occupation, to resist expropriation, to build up nationalist organizations and what many understood as the infrastructure for a future Palestinian state. The municipalities became a mechanism for Palestinians in the West Bank to weld themselves into a nation, and to push the PLO to support an independent state. With Israeli consent, the Palestinian municipalities looked to the Arab states, the PLO, and the large Palestinian diaspora for funds. Israel allowed these monies to flow in, spending less and less of its own money there.[70] In 1977, the elected mayors came out en masse and in public at the Palestinian National Council meetings for the formation of a Palestinian state and PLO participation in an international peace conference.[71]

The Palestinian nationalist mayors were elected at a critical historical cusp. A year after the PLO "at home" assumed power in the cities and towns of Palestine, Likud – dedicated to settling all Judea and Samaria with Jews – began to govern Israel. Labour was willing to allow nationalist Palestinian organizations to emerge in the territories because it believed it provided the best hope for a legitimate Palestinian negotiating partner. Likud was not. The Israeli government's relation to the territories shifted from Labour's emphasis on security and a negotiated withdrawal or federation with Jordan, to a Likud determination to destroy even the Jordanian option, to hold Judea and Samaria forever.

Moreover, the Palestinian nationalists swept to power on the eve of the Egyptian peace initiative. President Anwar Sadat made peace on the premise the Israelis would ultimately cede control over the lands conquered in 1967. This was the core of United Nations resolutions 242 and 38, territorial withdrawal in exchange for peace and diplomatic recognition. When Sadat went to Jerusalem and spoke to an amazed populace, he demanded Israeli withdrawal from *all* the territories conquered by war, including East Jerusalem. The Palestinians, he stated, should be allowed to elect their own representatives to a "self-governing authority" in the occupied territories.

But there was one thing the Egyptian president did not mention – the PLO. When Sadat addressed the Knesset, he did not utter the name of the Palestine Liberation Organization even once. When the Camp David Accords were drawn up and signed in 1978, Sadat allowed President Carter to separate the restoration of Sinai to Egyptian control and diplomatic recognition of Israel from the Palestinian question. A separate accord called for Israel, Egypt, and Jordan to establish a "self-governing authority" to which the Palestinians would elect representatives. Once up and running, the Israelis would withdraw their troops to positions dictated by security considerations for a period of five years. The newly elected Palestinian body would negotiate with Israel, Egypt, and Jordan to determine the final status of the region.[72]

Egypt appeared to have betrayed the Palestinian cause. Prime Minister Menachem Begin, the man whose political life had been dedicated to an Israel on both banks of the Jordan River, had promised the Palestinians "full autonomy." But not only Israel, but Jordan, had been granted the right to determine what "autonomy" would mean. Begin's declarations on the subject made it clear it meant little more than the right to run their own schools and religious institutions, police their communities, and pave their roads – more or less the same municipal authority the Israelis had already granted. Jerusalem wasn't even mentioned.[73]

Sadat's diplomatic initiative set off an intense competition among the Palestinian factions on the West Bank. Some Palestinian leaders and elected mayors, not only pro-Jordanians but some supporters of the PLO, believed the "autonomy" talks would have a dynamic of their own leading ultimately to a Palestinian state (many Israelis agreed).[74] Most of these, however, were afraid to come out publicly for fear of the PLO, to whom the Camp David Accords had assigned no role whatsoever. Apprehensive about Jordanian and Egyptian designs, the PLO mounted hundreds of terrorist attacks, murdering many Palestinians willing to participate in the autonomy talks.[75]

But it was not just fear that prevented the Palestinians from supporting the autonomy talks. Given provisions for Israeli and Jordanian veto, many Palestinians were sure they would not get a state. Indeed, Menachem Begin announced that any elected Palestinian who demanded a state would be thrown into jail. The Israelis insisted that autonomy applied to people, not to land.[76] Israel would retain ultimate control over the land and water, and the Israeli military government would be the ultimate authority. Not only was it clear Israel did not intend to dismantle its settlements, it built new ones almost as soon as the ink on the Camp David Accords was dry.

It wasn't just Jordanian designs on the territories that frightened the PLO. From the PLO's perspective, the rising independent political organization of Palestinians in the West Bank and Gaza was equally ominous even though its leaders shared the PLO's antipathy to autonomy. In 1978, Palestinians held a huge rally in Jerusalem against the Camp David Accords, attended by most of the elected Palestinian mayors. As part of this mass mobilization, they also created the National Guidance Committee, grouping together representatives of all the major streams. Led by three elected mayors – Bassam Shak'a of Nablus, Karim Khalaf of Ramallah, and Fahd al-Qawasmah of Hebron – it mobilized local Palestinian opposition to the "autonomy" plan. These Palestinians wanted to be an "autonomous" province of neither Jordan nor Israel; they wanted their own state or nothing at all. An independent cross-partisan organization of Palestinians in Palestine could undercut the PLO's claim to be the Palestinians' sole mouthpiece. Such a prospect was particularly dangerous given its unabashed support for a two-state solution, still anathema within the PLO.

The National Guidance Committee claimed to speak for the Palestinians of the West Bank and Gaza. Akram Haniyeh, then age twenty-five, was its youngest member. Haniyeh had learned English at Cairo University and worked as a journalist in Amman. Two years later he met us in a dank East Jerusalem office where he then served as editor of the pro-PLO newspaper *Al-Sha'ab*. Haniyeh was also the chairman of the Arab Journalists Association, headquartered in Jerusalem. Although the mayors who dominated the National Guidance Committee demanded the right of Palestinians to return to their homes in Israel, justified the use of military force against Israel, and gave their tacit approval to Palestinian violence against Israeli civilians, Moshe Dayan, who served as foreign minister in Likud's first government, still saw the organization as the best prospect for a legitimate negotiating partner.[77] "When we were in the committee," Haniyeh told us, "we felt that we were free. You know, they were giving us the rope to hang ourselves. You can talk, you can write the newspaper, you can talk on the TV. They were trying to create a new leadership . . . to make a gap between the inside and the outside." Defense Minister Weizman, Haniyeh claimed, was willing to negotiate with the committee on condition they would renounce the PLO. The committee refused.

In 1980, Jewish settlers set out to maim key members of the National Guidance Committee. The same year, the Israelis placed Haniyeh, who lived in Ramallah, as well as other members of the committee, under house arrest for three years, charging him with belonging to an organization supported by Arab rejectionist states aimed at fomenting "agitation, incitement and violence."[78] This forced Haniyeh to run his paper in Jerusalem through "remote control," as he put it. In 1981, he was put in jail for fifty days, seven of them in solitary confinement.[79] When we met Haniyeh, although those Jews responsible for the violence against Haniyeh's colleagues had just been arrested, he was not reassured. The Israeli deputy military governor who had supervised his town arrest was now in jail for complicity in the bombing of Ibrahim Tawil, the mayor of Al-Bireh. "He is the man who was responsible for my security. He was giving me the order every six months and he was saying, 'For the security of the region, you are under town arrest.' " "Really, we feel afraid," he insisted. "We feel all the time that we are threatened, that they are planning to bomb all the newspapers, the same terrorists. . . I don't believe that arresting them will stop Jewish terror."

In 1981, Begin's Likud coalition swept to an even more commanding victory. Palestinians said they felt Likud's rise to power on the streets, in the form of greater harassment and humiliation. In one instance, Palestinians were reportedly rounded up and made to sing Israel's national anthem.[80] To implement Likud's vision of autonomy, a local nationalist presence, a PLO on the ground, was no longer acceptable.

The National Guidance Committee not only threatened Israel's political plans; it also disturbed the PLO and Jordan, who had once again begun a rough coordination of their maneuvers in the occupied territories. Even though representatives of Arafat's Fatah dominated the committee, the National Guidance Committee had been the brainchild of the Communists, whom Arafat mistrusted. But more importantly, this was a representative local body. The Palestinians at home wanted to make their own decisions, for which they expected PLO endorsement abroad. The National Guidance Committee insisted that it, not the PLO outside, be the one to disburse funds from the outside. Fatah expected local Palestinians to take their marching orders from the outside.

Despite considerable political and financial pressure, the National Guidance Committee countermanded Arafat's instruction; it criticized his diplomatic coordination with Jordan; it demanded the Arab states' funds go directly to their people inside the territories and not be used to engorge Fatah and Jordanian patronage further.[81] When Arafat tried to appoint Mayor Elias Freij to the National Guidance Committee, the membership beat him back.

The growing conflict between this locally elected Palestinian leadership and the Israeli government that had just negotiated the Camp David Accords ended Israel's brief effort at a democratic occupation. In 1982, Israel banned the National Guidance Committee and began to force the elected mayors from office, without any formal charges, replacing them with Israeli officials. Israel's suppression of this nationalist body did not displease Arafat at all.[82] And by deposing the nationalist mayors in cities across the West Bank, Likud only reinforced Jerusalem as the locus of Palestinian political coordination.

The Labour government's policies had both succeeded and failed. Under Israeli-supervised elections, the Palestinians had chosen leaders who repudiated the PLO's political program, who were willing to accept a territorial compromise, who accepted a small Palestinian state as a final solution. But these leaders were unwilling to renounce the PLO, unwilling to disregard the rights of their kin in the diaspora. If they had not themselves lost their homes to the Israelis, there were few who did not have refugees among their families and friends.

Israel would repeatedly expel Palestinian nationalists who supported partition and a Palestinian state. By doing so, Israel gradually increased the strength and the legitimacy of these voices within the PLO, providing credible allies to those within the PLO who understood that this would be the only way, but were unable to convince the diaspora-dominated movement to follow them. In 1980, for example, the same year the Likud government authorized the reconstruction of Hebron's Jewish Quarter, the Israelis deported one of Haniyeh's fellow members of the National Guidance Committee, Fahd Qawasmeh, the mayor of Hebron. In Palestinian circles, Qawasmeh was considered a "moderate" because he was willing to use American mediation to negotiate with Israel and to accept territorial compromise. Qawasmeh had long urged his fellow Palestinians to accept the 1947 partition plan.[83] Shortly after his deporation, Yasser Arafat appointed him to the PLO's executive committee.[84] (After Akram Haniyeh was likewise deported in November 1986, he became Arafat's adviser on the occupied territories.)[85]

In the Light of Lebanon

In March 1982, the Israeli government outlawed the National Guidance Committee and dismissed the Palestinian mayors.[86] In June, Israel invaded Lebanon. The two moves were of a piece. Prime Minister

Menachem Begin was seeking to destroy the Palestinians' political options, to suppress their legitimate leadership, and to force their quiescence to permanent Israeli possession. Israel's war in Lebanon was really a war for the West Bank. It was a war Israel and the PLO both lost.

Likud sought to close the Jordanian option by Jewish settlement, the PLO option by war. Defense Minister Ariel Sharon's invasion of Lebanon was intended to eliminate the PLO as a political threat. Despite its stockpile of Soviet arms squirreled away in bunkers beneath the refugee camps, the PLO had never really posed any military danger. Without air protection, the PLO was a fragmented set of militias, a deadly nuisance, not a menace to the state.

If the Israeli public was moving toward territorial annexation, the PLO was moving unmistakably toward a two-state solution. Right before the war, as a result of Leonid Brezhnev's initiative, the PLO finally announced its willingness to pay what it considered the ultimate price: recognition of Israel's sovereignty. Arafat was, in fact, conducting hundreds of hours of secret talks with an American emissary, John Edwin Mroz, who reported back to Secretary of State Alexander Haig. Arafat was considering recognizing Israel and renouncing terrorism in exchange for American recognition of the PLO and inclusion at the bargaining table.[87]

Israel's northern borders had not been breached by PLO attacks for almost a year before the invasion. The Begin government seized upon the attempted assassination of the Israeli ambassador in London, Shlomo Argov, to justify the deployment of Israeli troops in Lebanon. Arafat, knowing defeat was certain, argued the PLO should accept an American-mediated peace plan.[88] By driving toward Beirut, Likud intended to destroy the PLO as a state-in-waiting, to pacify the Palestinians in the territories, to fashion a space for an alternative leadership willing to countenance autonomy. The results of the war were ironic indeed.

Lebanon was a watershed for many Palestinians, particularly those in the West Bank and Gaza. This war demonstated, once and for all, that the attitude of the Arab states ranged from indifference to perfidy. As a result of the war, the PLO was denied its last territorial front with Israel, and Arafat was forced to move his headquarters from Beirut to Tunis, over a thousand miles from Israel. When Israel pushed Arafat's small army from Beirut, the PLO had to depend on the United States to secure safe exit. Israeli marksmen, it was said, actually had Arafat's visage in the cross-hairs of their high-powered rifle sights. The United States had arranged for Tunis to be the PLO's new home.[89] And it was "those good Arabs, the Greeks," who provided the ships for the evacuation, Mahdi Abdul-Hadi, the urbane director of the Palestinian Academic Society for the Study of International Affairs, recalled bitterly.

The Arab states did nothing. The great irony was that the only effective opposition to the Lebanon war was that of the Jews of Israel. Many Palestinians painted their defeat with the brave colors of courageous resistance. Hadn't other Arab states been defeated in a few days? The PLO held out against Israeli air strikes in Beirut for seventy-nine days. "At the beginning of the war when the Israelis were heading towards Beirut," Ziad abu-Zayed, the nationalist lawyer and publisher, told us,

> there was a feeling that we are finished. . . Some people, they stopped listening to the radio. . . After a few days, the people started to realize that the Israelis are not able to go inside Beirut. They started to realize that Palestinian power is still existing. . . He could stand the siege in Beirut seventy-nine days. He became in the eyes of the Palestinians a hero. And the way he came out of Beirut and he protected the honor of his fighters, it was a very good thing. People here loved it.

Ziad named his son who was born during the siege Ammar, Arafat's nom de guerre.[90]

Although some of Arafat's supporters painted his retreat from Beirut as a victory, for many Palestinians it starkly revealed the futility of "armed struggle." Shortly afterward, when the Palestinian National Council, a parliament-in-exile, met in Algiers, Issam Sartawi, a Fatah member, one of the first to push openly for mutual recognition and a negotiated territorial compromise, rose to address the gathering.[91] If the Palestinians considered the departure from Beirut a victory, Sartawi warned, then I'm afraid next year you'll be meeting in Fiji Island. Soon thereafter, Sartawi was dead, assassinated in Lisbon by those who rejected his conclusions.

"I like to be victimized by my enemy – by the Western conspiracy, by imperialist conspiracy, by the communists sending out policy," Jamil Hamad, the first editor of the PLO's *Al-Fajr* newspaper in Jerusalem, told us. "But . . . I'm against victimizing myself . . . since when was defeat a success?" As they left Beirut, the PLO fighters were allowed, in a face-saving formula, to take their personal weapons, but when the Israelis spotted a dozen jeeps on a departing ship, they demanded the ships return to port and offload them. "Is this a success? You are humiliated to the point that you are not allowed to take your jeep."

Israel was surrounded by four "front-line" Arab states: Jordan, Egypt, Syria, and Lebanon. In 1971, Jordan expelled the PLO from its realm. In 1978, Egypt signed a separate peace with Israel, making the Palestinian question secondary to Sinai, an empty stretch of desert of value for its airspace, mineral deposits, and oil. The PLO could not operate openly in Syria, which carefully controlled its border on the Golan. So the PLO's only operative continguous land base with Israel was Lebanon.

After the war in Lebanon, Yasser Arafat's forces were twice exiled from Lebanon, first by the Israelis from Beirut in 1982, and, second by the Syrians from Tripoli in 1983. The second time, some Palestinians said, Arafat was forced to disguise himself as a woman. Syria would no longer countenance Arafat's growing power in a land it considered part of its dominion. In a mirror image of Likud ideologues, President Hafez Assad has always looked at Palestine, like Lebanon, as a rightful part of "Greater Syria." In the wake of Israel's invasion, Syria used PLO weakness as an occasion to engineer a civil war within the Palestinian refugee camps in Lebanon. It was not difficult. The number of Palestinians who rejected Arafat's drift towards a two-state compromise were legion. These Palestinians, concentrated in refugee camps in the diaspora, were from cities and villages absorbed into the Jewish state; compromise would not take them home. They had given their sons to the "armed struggle" because they believed in the possibility of return to their villages, to Jaffa, to Haifa, to Ramleh, to Jerusalem, not to what Fatah had once contemptuously spurned as a "rump state."

While the world's collective memory held to the image of Sabra and Shatilla, where Israeli-backed Christian militias massacred innocents, Palestinians also found it difficult to assimilate the barbarism engineered by their supposed Arab brothers. Under the Syrians' watchful eye, the "war of the camps" continued in Lebanon for years after the Israelis withdrew.[92] Syria also tried to eliminate the PLO leadership physically, in part by sponsoring rejectionist factions who murdered PLO leaders advocating territorial compromise. The PLO sought its own vengeance, carrying out terrorist attacks right in Damascus. Before the *intifada*, Syria had as many Palestinian political prisoners languishing in its jails as Israel did.

The implication was clear: even if Syria defeated the Israelis, this would not be a victory for the Palestinians. The circle of betrayal was now complete. As the Israeli soldiers were going home, Akram Haniyeh, a former member of the National Guidance Committee, was asked by a *Time* magazine reporter which Arab government he liked best. "You know, I and my friends, we said, 'Djibouti because they didn't do anything, so they are the best.' "

The war convinced many Palestinians living in the territories that they would have to rely on themselves, that PLO military might would always be insufficient, that the Arab support necessary to make military conflict work was unlikely to be forthcoming, and that even if the Arab states did mobilize against Israel, the Palestinians would not necessarily achieve a state. Liberation need not mean independence.

The Chairman and the King

Likud intended the war to destroy the PLO as a viable political actor at a time when it was moving palpably toward a Palestinian state. After the war Likud Knesset members talked to us optimistically of a new climate in the "territories." Eliyahu Ben-Elissar, Likud's chair of the Knesset Committee on Security and Defense, told us that before Israel's incursion into Beirut, "the population . . . had the fear of being killed, being assassinated if they made any step towards the Israelis. . . The PLO is not considered anymore as strong a factor as it used to be." Palestinians, the Sorbonne-educated parliamentarian told us, were even inviting him to their homes in broad daylight. "There is a general feeling in the population of Judea and Samaria . . . of resignation to Israeli presence, as they themselves put it, forever."

Mordechai Gur, a Knesset member, in contrast, claimed that pushing the PLO out of Lebanon had done nothing to lessen Arafat's stature in the West Bank. Likud's belief that they could cut away the PLO was, he contended, an illusion born of their assumption that sheer power could solve political problems. Gur, however, did hope the stage had been set for local Palestinian leaders to lean on the PLO to change its line, to press for further cooperation between Jordan and the PLO.

When Arafat was being pushed out of Tripoli by the Syrians, Gur went to a number of "moderate," mostly pro-Hashemite Palestinians. "I said to them, 'Listen, that's your time, now when the PLO is weaker. It's your responsibility. . . Go to King Hussein, say that this is the time to negotiate." Many Palestinians spurned Gur's entreaties. Some believed they had no right. "No, sir," one told him, "my family's name will never be put in a list of Arabs who made any territorial compromise with you. . . My name will never go down in the history as somebody who gave you our territory."

With Israel's permission, a group of pro-Hashemites did go to Amman in March 1984 to press Arafat to recognition of Israel and peace negotiations, to diplomatic coordination with the Jordanians. Issam al-Anani, the tall, handsome, and always elegantly suited Jerusalem lawyer, led the delegation. There were rumors that al-Anani, who has served as the lawyer for the Jerusalem *awqaf,* the administrative board controlling Islamic properties, had been promised the post of governor of Jerusalem. Most of the Palestinians who entreated the chairman to sue for peace had no intention of raising Arafat's ire. Al-Anani told us

Arafat seemed "weak and afraid." Yet they were respectful, even deferential, all except Othman Hallak, a self-assured and cynical Palestinian of Turkish origins. Hallak has started a string of innovative businesses on the West Bank: the first pharmaceutical firm, the first feed mill, the first stone cutting factory, the largest detergent factory, a salt factory on the Dead Sea. Arafat had been dancing back and forth toward the line. Hallak was impatient and beholden to nobody. Don't do what you did last time, running away to Kuwait, Hallak claims he rebuked Arafat. "Cut this bullshit." Arafat reportedly pulled out a pen, waving it in the air. "You see this pen," he taunted, "everybody wants this pen."

Turning Point

After Lebanon Yasser Arafat now understood the Palestinians under Israeli occupation, his largest constituency, as the last front line. The demand for PLO–Jordanian coordination was not inconsistent with Arafat's own evolving orientation. The Palestinians' civil war forced the PLO to decide between its two inviolable principles: unity and independence. If the PLO chose unity, embracing even the Syrian-backed rebels, it would become an appendage of Syrian foreign expansionism. Unity, on the other hand, with the enormous influence that would give the rejectionists, would enable King Hussein to present himself as the only vehicle through which the Palestinians would ever have a hope of ridding themselves of Zionist occupation.

Arafat chose independence and continued his fateful march toward a two-state solution. Acutely vulnerable, in 1982 Arafat executed a breathless volte-face, a rapprochement with King Hussein. At the 1982 PNC meeting at Algiers, the PLO adopted a program of political coordination with Jordan, in which a joint Palestinian–Jordanian delegation would negotiate a territorial partition with Israel. Arafat made this move in the face of intense opposition from within the PLO, even from members of his own al-Fatah.[93]

What Jordan had taken by arms from the Palestinians in 1948 under the guise of pan-Arab unity, it now claimed it would return to them as an independent entity. After his troops were forced from Tripoli in 1983, Arafat was denied access to other Arab capitals. In 1984, the seventeenth meeting of the Palestinian National Council (PNC) was held in Amman. To the horror of the Palestinian left and the Israeli right, the bitterest of enemies had become allies. In their joint communiqué of February 1985, Jordan and the PLO pledged to create an Arab confederation of Palestine and Jordan to be negotiated by a joint PLO–Jordanian delegation through an international conference under UN auspices.[94] Although Arafat had obtained PLO assent for this move, it was said, by bribing Palestinian delegates and even taking some to Amman by force, this agreement became the new bedrock, the proto-type that would shape the PLO's relationship to Israel for the next decade.

The Lebanon war also pushed the Americans into a more intimate relationship with the PLO. As a result of its role in arranging the PLO's retreat from Beirut, the United States had already developed contacts. The United States's consulate in Jerusalem, seeking to broker this new relation, began to cultivate a constituency of West Bank Palestinians who would carry it forward. The American consul in Jerusalem, Wat Cluverius, having played a critical role in the Camp David Accords, was charged with the preparatory work. Through the consulate, the United States signaled to the Palestinians of the West Bank that if the PLO recognized Israel, the United States would pressure Israel. The Americans pressed the Palestinians to pressure Arafat to recognize Israel.

By its massive settlement drive and repeated refusal ever to cede sovereignty over any part of Judea and Samaria, the Likud government had destroyed a pure Jordanian option. Jordan now feared not only that there would soon be nothing about which to compromise, but that Israel would move to solve its Palestinian problem at Jordan's expense. Bringing down the Hashemite monarchy had long been an option considered by American foreign policy specialists. Hussein knew there were those within the American administration who still saw his East Bank as the logical platform upon which to create a Palestinian entity that would ultimately expand to include the most populated parts of the West Bank. King Hussein's support for Palestinian self-determination was a way to counter that threat. Besides, he knew that whatever Palestinian entity were somehow carved out of the West Bank would be dependent on his side of the Jordan River.

Arafat moved toward Jordan because he was no longer beholden to the Syrians and did not have to accommodate Syrian-sponsored rejectionism. Syria, Israel's most powerful enemy, had become Arafat's most implacable foe. Jordan was the only territorial bridge to his new constituency and a legitimate diplomatic partner for Israel and the United States. Arafat feared that a Likud-run Israel might easily seize upon war as an opportunity to expel the Palestinians in the West Bank, and perhaps to topple the Hashemite regime as well.

Ironically, by destroying the PLO's base of operations in Lebanon and establishing the conditions for Palestinian civil war, the Likud pushed the PLO to embrace the Palestinians of the West Bank and Gaza. These Palestinians stood on the only remaining part of Palestine that could become a state; their communities were intact; they alone had a real material stake in territorial compromise. By weakening the PLO outside, Israel strengthened it inside. Likud confused the PLO's military defeat in Lebanon with its own desire for political victory in the territories.

Arafat was the preeminent symbol of the Palestinian nation. But a symbol is not a leader. And the truth was that when Israel invaded Lebanon, Arafat's PLO was still weakly organized in the West Bank. After Lebanon Arafat began to remake the PLO from an umbrella for external militias into an organization that spoke on behalf of the Palestinians "inside" Palestine. Arafat finally set about organizing in the West Bank. He was itching to reassert the primacy of al-Fatah as opposed to the rejectionists and Communists who had dominated the National Guidance Committee. Fatah created new organizations and front groups in the occupied territories and spent enormous effort achieving dominance over those already there.

While Arafat condemned international terrorism, which he defined as attacks on unarmed civilians *outside* Israel, he announced that "armed struggle" inside the occupied territories would intensify.[95] The chairman appointed Khalil Wazir, known by his nom de guerre, Abu Jihad, to reconstruct a guerrilla base for operations on the Israeli side of the River Jordan. Although King Hussein would not permit armed incursions across his border with Israel, Fatah would now be able to use Amman to recruit, arm, and train West Bank Palestinians who went into Jordan for operations back inside occupied territory.

But Abu Jihad also built something that would prove more important than the infrastructure dedicated to professional violence. Al-Fatah rapidly established an extensive grass roots organization on the West Bank and Gaza, creating all kinds of community organizations, youth clubs, professional and labor associations. Fatah intended to replicate and thereby replace the network of popular organizations the Palestinian Communists had created in the late 1970s. With 70 percent of the population below age thirty, Fatah concentrated on the young people, establishing youth organizations in every town and village. Once the *intifada* started, it was this network, not the secret terror cells, that was its primary mechanism. The *shabiba*, the youth of the *intifada* who played their deadly game of cat and mouse with Israeli soldiers, were drawn predominantly from Fatah's youth organizations. In April 1988, in an attempt to stop the *intifada*, many believe the Israelis assassinated Abu Jihad in Tunis.

Likud had destroyed the PLO as a military force, as a state-in-waiting. Its central organs in Tunis were now cut off from the large Palestinian diaspora communities in Lebanon and Syria. But the PLO had been revived as a real political threat in Palestine. Inside the occupied territories, for the first time in history, the traditional notables, large landowners, and businessmen who once served and supported Jordan united politically with the nationalist supporters of the PLO, both voicing their support for a Palestinian state confederated to Jordan.[96] It appeared that, at long last, there might be not one, but two people with whom to negotiate.

The War at Home

Although the shells fell on Beirut, the Lebanon war was aimed at pacifying the Palestinian population in the West Bank. For a brief while, it seemed the blows suffered in Beirut had weakened the PLO's operational links to the West Bank and Gaza. Terrorist attacks against Israelis declined in frequency. But even during the war itself, there were signs a home-grown insurrection was in the making. The war in Lebanon *had* created a new leadership, but it was not what Ariel Sharon had had in mind. The war designed to crush, once and for all, the infrastructure of the PLO abroad created a young, radicalized generation that constituted themselves as a popular army for the PLO at home. Right after the Six-Day War, a generation of young Palestinians rebelled against their parents, who had trusted to a war of liberation led by other Arab states or the foreign policy skills of King Hussein. They had thrown in their lot with the diplomatic machinery and the guerrilla warriors of the PLO. Now after the Lebanon war, it was clear the next generation would no longer wait for their parents, for King Hussein, or even for Yasser Arafat. Right after the war we asked Palestinian high school students in Jerusalem what they thought would happen to Arafat. "Maybe he'll die; maybe they'll shoot him; maybe he'll come here," one student replied. "But whatever happens to him, he'll just be a symbol."

Before the *intifada* exploded in 1987 there was a new kind of violent resistance by Palestinians in the West Bank and Gaza. At precisely the same time the PLO was being crushed in Lebanon, the Palestinians in the occupied territories were engaging the Israelis in unprecedented attacks and demonstrations. The number of "disturbances" logged by the Israeli military in 1982–1983 increased tenfold from the levels experienced a few years earlier.[97] Jerusalemites, likewise, were increasingly being stoned, shot at, and bombed by Palestinians.[98] Soldiers doing reserve duty in the West Bank, who had put their rifles on the floor while they drank coffee in the cafés, now kept bullets always in the chamber, ready to fire. In droves, Palestinian teenagers were being taken to Israeli prisons, where, sometimes after a night standing up against a wall where Israeli soldiers would throw pebbles at them, they would confess their crimes and their families would fetch them after they had paid a fine.[99]

The Israelis returned to extensive use of curfews, shutting down of universities, house demolitions, deportation, administrative detention without trail.

It became dangerous to travel through Palestinian towns and villages on the way to the Jewish settlements that fan out from Jerusalem. Government regulations that required that groups of Israelis be accompanied by armed guards had been ignored; now suddenly, they were scrupulously followed once again. It was no longer safe to walk in the Jerusalem hills and marvel at the almond blossoms. Israeli buses and cars were being stoned, firebombed, and even shot at, not only on their way to the suburban Jewish settlements near Hebron, but in Jerusalem itself. There was a dramatic increase in face-to-face attacks with knives, rifles, and hand grenades, often against Israeli soldiers, as opposed to the anonymous terror of bombs left in marketplaces and bus stops. In the crowded *shuk*s, the marketplaces of Jerusalem, Hebron, and Bethlehem, the assailant would slash with a knife or fire a pistol and slip back into the Arab crowds. Yasser Arafat was still insisting the Palestinians would "never let the gun fall from their hands." But what was most significant about the new violence was that the assailants were local young men acting on their own, rather than operatives directed and paid from abroad.[100]

To the Israelis, the surge in Palestinian violence was unexpected. Israel had withdrawn its forces from Lebanon, freeing its elite military forces for deployment throughout the West Bank. As reserve soldiers with minimal training increasingly came under attack, Israel sent in front-line troops more accustomed to fire-fights in Beirut and Sidon. Checkpoints, surveillance, administrative detention, full-body searches instantly multiplied, conducted often by the same young men who had lost hundreds of their comrades to the ceaseless attacks in southern Lebanon. In late 1985, the Israeli air force winged its way to Tunis to bomb the PLO's headquarters in retaliation, but to no effect. The young Palestinians were not acting as Arafat's operatives: they were fighting on their own account.

Space for Palestine

Caught in the triangle of Jordanian, PLO, and Israeli political forces, the Palestinians forged themselves into an independent nationalist movement threatening to each. In opposition to Jordan, they demanded the occupied lands be the territorial base of an independent Palestinian state, not a province under Jordanian sovereignty. In opposition to the PLO, the Palestinians inside relinquished the dream of liberating all Palestine and demanded a separate Palestinian state at peace alongside

Israel, not as a stage, but as a permanent solution. In opposition to Israel, they demanded an end to occupation and Israeli recognition of their national rights.

When Israel captured the West Bank, it created a space in which the Palestinians could develop independently, free of direct Jordanian or PLO control. Israel annulled what many Palestinians considered a Hashemite usurpation. If Jordan hadn't stumbled into war in 1967, the Palestinians of the West Bank might have become, like their cousins across the river, loyal Jordanian citizens. The Israeli–Arab conflict might have remained just that, a conflict between Israel and a series of Arab states who rejected Jewish sovereignty in their midst.

By occupying the West Bank, a land it would neither annex nor cede, Israel created a natural platform for Palestine to be refashioned as a viable political project, a space where Palestinians could gradually build their own national institutions. Under Israeli rule, the Palestinians could develop a particularly Palestinian point of view. Here they did not have to pay obeisance to the ideologies and interests of the Arab countries that grudgingly absorbed them as dependent refugee communities. Here, they were less likely to be forward soldiers for the larger Arab nation, the Islamic community, or the revolutionary movement against imperialism. Zionism was culturally incapable of the kind of co-optation to which Palestinians were subject in other Arab states. Independent voices were less likely to be silenced by assassins. Just by doing its job, Israeli intelligence protected them from private militia operations so common outside.

The occupation not only cleared a logical site for Palestinian sovereignty, it created the only zone where a genuine Palestinian society could exist with national bodies for health, education, commerce, and welfare, a society composed of a population who, unlike the Palestinians of the diaspora who dominated the PLO, had a vested interest in territorial compromise.[101] The occupied territories were not just a physical zone, they were a political space in which Palestinians could form different mental maps, where they could disengage their concerns from those of the larger Arab nation, take the initiative away from the PLO outside on behalf of the Palestinians in Palestine.

12

Zion for Palestine

Israeli sovereignty over a united Jerusalem freed the city to serve once again as the national center of the Palestinians. By winning Zion, the Israelis created a privileged political space where Palestinian elites could construct a new world view, a locus where Palestinian nationalism could confront Zionism face to face. Independent, democratic Palestinian nationalism was forged in and promulgated from Jerusalem. By uniting the city, the Israelis created the conditions for Jerusalem to emerge as the capital of Palestine. Jerusalem proved to be Zionism's central contradiction.

Everything in Jerusalem is divided into Jewish and Arab – clothing, cigarettes, beer, cafés and restaurants, swimming pools, buses, blood banks, newspapers, football teams, schools, universities, houses.[1] Across the national divide, almost every relationship is marked by hierarchy, Israeli on top, Palestinian on the bottom. Arabs learn Hebrew, not the reverse. Nonetheless, this was a city where Palestinians could talk to each other, to the Zionists, and to the world. Jerusalem became a stage from which Palestinians rose to challenge not only Zionism, but Jordan and the PLO as well.

The city's political freedoms drew Palestinians who came to work, to organize, and, if they could find a way, to live there. The most important national institutions – educational councils, unions, charitable organizations, women's societies, youth movements – have been centered in Jerusalem to take advantage of this island of Israeli rule with its civil rights, adumbrated in practice, but nonetheless real. Many of their leaders are likewise Jerusalemites.[2] It was from Jerusalem that Palestinians repeatedly tried to organize the countless villages, the family and ideological factions; to overcome the local loyalties that have always hobbled them. Each time the Palestinians created a political body to coordinate their resistance – the Supreme Muslim Council in 1967, the Palestine National Front in 1973, the National Guidance Council in 1978 – to reach for influence within the PLO, they used Jerusalem as their staging ground. The united political fronts fashioned by the Jerusalem-based Communist Party helped lay the foundations for the political pluralism necessary for democracy. After the two rounds of democratic municipal elections in the West Bank and Gaza, almost every national institution in Jerusalem began to implement elections as the way to select its leadership. These democratic practices were then copied by their counterparts and branches throughout the territories.

By building Zion, the Israelis created the conditions for the Palestinians to build their center. Like the Jordanians, the Israeli government made economic development difficult on the Palestinian side of the city. The Israelis no longer allowed Jordanian banks to operate in the city; they pressed foreign companies doing business in Jordanian Jerusalem either to shut down or to consolidate their operations on the city's Jewish side. West Bank Palestinians took their produce to sell in the Old City market illicitly, paying bribes to avoid being fined or having their goods confiscated. Thousands of Arab tourists still came to Jerusalem each year, usually as pilgrims. But while Israeli high-rise hotels popped up yearly, Palestinian efforts to build and refurbish their own hotels were repeatedly frustrated.[3] A high-rise Palestinian hotel, under construction in 1967, still stands unfinished, an empty concrete carton, in the Arab downtown. To the Palestinians, it seems building permits are denied without cause and bureaucratic obstacles emerge out of thin air. Palestinian businessmen, bankers, entrepreneurs, and managers have either left or gone out of business. Even though the Palestinian population has doubled, there were fewer independent businessmen in Jerusalem in 1994 than there were in 1967. The Palestinian downtown remains tawdry, undeveloped.

Although the Israelis have tried to prevent Palestinian capital investment in Jerusalem, the metropolitan market has supported a rapidly growing Palestinian population. Even though Arab workers receive less than their Jewish counterparts, they have been able to earn much more working for an Israeli than for an Arab employer. The rapid growth of the city's economy not only drew Jews into the city, it created a complementary flow of Palestinians, who mix cement on Israeli construction sites and serve coffee in the new Israeli cafés and hotels. In Jerusalem proper, two out of every five Palestinians work for Israeli employers. Outside the city, the Arabs feel Jerusalem's economic gravity. One of three Palestinian workers in Ramallah to the north, Bethlehem and Hebron to the south, and Jericho to the east commute daily to Jerusalem to work.[4]

"Thickening" Jerusalem with Jews drew Palestinians to the metropole like a magnet. The PLO, Jordan, and the Palestinians who worked in the oil economies of the Gulf States all made their financial contribution to the Arab building spree. Tens of thousands of Jerusalem Arabs, unable to obtain sites or building permits inside the city, moved into unplanned dormitory suburbs just across the municipal line. The Israeli government has been deeply troubled that every Jew added to the city seems to add another Arab inside the city and even more around its rim. Jerusalem officials have lobbied hard for the national government to make it easier for Palestinians to build outside the city and the municipality has promoted high-technology industry, hoping it will demand highly skilled Jews, not the less skilled, lower-paid Arab workers who migrate into the city. Successive governments have sought to curtail Arab building even outside the the municipal boundaries, seeking to prevent expansion toward Jerusalem or into areas within the metropole slated for future Jewish settlement.[5] Nonetheless, after more than a quarter century of Israeli rule, Jerusalem has become the demographic center of the Palestinian population, displacing once-dominant Nablus.[6]

Jerusalem is not just the population center of Palestine; it is also its political center. Although most Palestinians have not been willing to vote in city elections and none has stood for municipal office, Israeli rule of the unified city, with its guarantees of freedom of speech and assembly, has created a privileged platform for Palestinians to build their nationalist leadership. Palestinians who live in Jerusalem are technically entitled to the same civil rights as any Israeli. The city's Palestinians have thus been able to protest, organize, complain, and litigate in a way denied to their fellows elsewhere in the West Bank and Gaza.

Outside Jerusalem, for example, military censors control what Palestinians can read. Some four thousand books have been banned since the occupation began, the head librarian at Bethlehem University informed us. Palestinian book dealers, fearing their stock will be confiscated, have learned not to carry potentially controversial books. Palestinians are not allowed to read Shakespeare's *Merchant of Venice* because of its anti-Semitic portrayal of Shylock. Many Palestinian novels are proscribed. Ghassan Kanafani's *Men in the Sun*, a collection of short stories, is forbidden, as is George Antonius's *The Arab Awakening: The Story of the Arab National Movement*, the classic text of Arab nationalism.

Against this backdrop, Jerusalem has been a fragile and imperfect island of relative freedom. Some Palestinians go to the Hebrew University to read books and journals that are unavailable or illegal just over the hill. Another example of Palestinians who make use of Jerusalem's adumbrated, but real political freedoms is Sliman Mansour, a Palestinian artist who lives just north of Jerusalem's city limits. Mansour, hirsute, shirt open well down the chest, learned to be an artist studying at Bezalel, a Jewish art college in Jerusalem, right after the Six-Day War. Mansour was just eighteen and his mother thought he was crazy. At painting exhibitions, Palestinians crowd around him. They like to talk through a painting. "Why did you put this color here?" one asks. "Why is her hand so big?"

Mansour does abstract nonrepresentational pieces for himself, but among his people, he is famous for one romantic hyperrepresentation: a heroic portrait of an exiled Palestinian peasant who carries Jerusalem in a bundle on his back. This image, first painted in 1973, has been reproduced throughout the entire Palestinian diaspora. "Especially the Palestinians outside," he told us, "they love this picture a lot. . . Although he's weak, he's beaten up, he carries his memories with him and his love with him, this . . . Jerusalem." Mansour, like other Palestinian artists, is not free to paint whatever he likes, he told us. Paintings by West Bankers are subject to censorship. Scenes of land expropriation, for example, cannot be done. Nor can Israeli shooting or beating of Palestinians. Some of his exhibits in the West Bank have been closed, his paintings and posters confiscated. His agent was once threatened with arrest for selling his work. But in Jerusalem, such repression is much more difficult. The image of the Palestinian peasant, this nationalist icon, is printed by the thousands by a Palestinian publishing house in East Jerusalem.

The Palestinian Press

It has been written that modern nations began at the breakfast table, in daily print communities, the common readers of the newspapers that assemble narratives whose appearance together on the page bespeaks a collectivity with a story worth telling.[7] Reading the news is a mundane nationalist ritual. Although Jerusalem is the Jewish capital, all the major Hebrew newspapers are published in Tel Aviv, which stands to Jerusalem like Milan to Rome. But all West Bank Palestinian newspapers are published in East Jerusalem, where Palestinians read, write, and publish newspapers, magazines, and books frequently forbidden in the West Bank. The same Palestinian journalists who commute daily to Jerusalem to write their copy can sometimes be arrested for reading it at home.

Palestinian reporting about Israel is heavily censored by the military. Palestinian writers release stories to Israeli writers so they can later reprint them in their own papers without being blue-penciled or even slapped into prison. One of the ironic consequences of strict Israeli censorship of Palestinian reporting about the Israeli occupation was that word of mouth became the conduit for dissemination of news, solidifying dense networks of trusted sources, on the one hand, and contributing to extraordinarily malevolent distortions of accidents and aberrations on the other.

Although the Palestinians have been constrained in their reportage about Israel, they have been freer in Jerusalem than in any other spot in the Middle East to criticize the Arab regimes as well as the PLO when it suits them. In Jerusalem, for instance, Palestinians buy cassettes of poetry banned throughout the Arab world. Through verse, they express their bitterness about the Arab world's lip service to the Palestinian cause. In a very popular poem by the Iraqi Muzafar al-Nawab, the Arab world watches through a keyhole as Palestine is raped.

Journalism has been the perfect political profession. One can communicate and coordinate through newspapers, not only through what is written on the page, but through the network of contacts and informants one makes in the legitimate business of collecting the news. As an editor, you have to talk to everybody. Not surprisingly the Palestinians' visible political leaders have been mostly newspaper editors, former editors, publishers, or reporters from one of Jerusalem's many Palestinian newspapers.

Although a number of Jerusalem's newspapers received financing from one or another political force, their editors and writers have proved fiercely independent and papers have been breeding grounds for a distinctive Palestinian voice. When, in 1972, al-Fatah provided the monies to found a newspaper, *Al-Fajr*, in Jerusalem, Jamil Abdul-Qadr Hamad was its first editor in chief. Hamad believed he could write truth in Jerusalem; as a result, he was pushed to the margins of his national movement.

Jamil Abdul-Qadr Hamad carries his nationalist heritage in his name. His middle name refers to Abdul-Qadr Husayni, father of Faisal Husayni. Hamad is from an affluent family who fled their home in Rafat, just down the mountain from Jerusalem. In the United Nations partition plan, Rafat lay on the Israeli side. The Israelis razed the village, which today is the site of Beit Shemesh, an Israeli suburb. The Hamad family fled to the edge of Bethlehem, where Jamil still lives with his wife and three sons in a simple but spacious house next to the main road.

Just before we arrived at the Hamad home for an interview, his wife, Raeda, had hidden her youngest son's toy pistol underneath the dishes. Her little son had been playing with it outside and, to her horror, had pointed the toy gun at an Israeli policeman. When she informed her husband what had happened, Jamil demanded they destroy the toy immediately. "I'm lucky my son isn't dead," he said.

Hamad's other son, Souheil, had almost been killed a few years earlier by an Israeli soldier. In March 1982, Souheil, then seventeen years old, was demonstrating in the courtyard at Bethlehem University against the Village Leagues, the cadre of alternative village "leaders" whom

Israel paid and armed as an alternative to the pro-PLO mayors. Israeli troops burst into the university and the students threw stones. When an Israeli soldier pulled down a forbidden Palestinian flag from the gate, Souheil rushed to raise it again. That was all he could remember. An Israeli soldier fired a tear gas cannister directly at him, cracking his head open like a hard-boiled egg. And in Jerusalem's Hadassah Hospital, an Israeli doctor painstakingly put it back together again. "God," the observant Jewish doctor told the grateful father, "decided to give you a prize."

In 1970, a decade ahead of the PLO, Jamil Hamad publicly supported a separate Palestinian state at peace alongside Israel. Both the PLO and Jordan condemned him as a traitor. Later at a meeting in the United States, a Palestinian stood up and accused Hamad of sounding like a Zionist, of defeatism, of abandoning the military struggle to liberate all of Palestine. Jamil held his tongue while the angry young man harangued him. "My family owned something like fifteen thousand dunams," Hamad finally replied.

> You want to liberate Palestine? Believe me, if Palestine is liberated, I will be one of the first people to enjoy it because I'll being going back to my land. . . I'm very poor. . . But you know, I'm not a military man. I never used a gun. But look, there is a law in Israel that he who gives a Palestinian terrorist or guerrilla fighter or liberation fighter any help, he will be jailed and his house will be demolished. Now, I am saying in front of everybody, quote me in block letters, that I, Jamil Hamad [and my family], are willing and ready to accept the risk to bring you the food and to carry the ammunition to you in any cave of the West Bank, if you come and fight the Israelis from the West Bank. . . But if you want to liberate Palestine from Fifth Avenue, my dear, I can do it better than you. . . If you want to liberate Palestine, come to Palestine. And, look, please give my address to Mr. Yasser Arafat.

As a result of Hamad's writing, the Israelis imprisoned him for violating their censorship laws. Two years later in 1974, Joe Nasser, the newspaper's publisher, was kidnapped; his body was never recovered. Some say he was taken to a cave near Hebron and murdered. But some Palestinians, especially those associated with the newspaper today, still accuse Jamil Hamad of complicity in the publisher's kidnapping, even though Hamad was himself held in prison for two months. They say that the newspaper was registered in Hamad's name and that it took a struggle to reclaim it from him.

Hamad tells a different story. Under his editorship, *Al-Fajr* attacked the pro-Jordanian notables with whom Israel believed it could do business, men from families of means like Hajj Mazuz al-Masri, the mayor of Nablus; Elias Freij, the mayor of Bethlehem; and Sheikh Muhammed

Jabari, the mayor of Hebron. To young Palestinian nationalists like Hamad, these men were corrupt figures who acted on behalf of the merchants and landowners, men too willing to subordinate Palestinian interests to Jordanian claims, too accommodating to the Israelis, and too distant from the common people, who increasingly saw the PLO as the carrier of their nationalist aspirations. As a result of his writing, the Jordanians blacklisted Hamad and accused him of being a CIA agent.

Sheikh Jabari, reelected as Hebron's mayor in 1972, was a particular target for Hamad's editorial ire. In 1948, Jabari had been president of the Palestinian congress King Abdullah convened in Jericho to ratify Jordan's annexation of the West Bank. Jabari, who had once sat in the Jordanian cabinet, was a Jordanian loyalist who used patronage and the loyalties of his extended family networks to rule Hebron. Popular democratic representation was neither in his interest nor in his makeup. Hamad claimed in print that the mayor had sold Palestinian land to the Israelis. Jabari, Hamad told us, had sold land for Kiryat Arba, the first major Israeli settlement at the edge of his town, near his own personal residence. To seal the deal ritually, Jabari invited Minister of Defense Moshe Dayan and the military governor of the West Bank to have coffee at his home. The Israeli press office called Hamad to invite him as well. But Jamil refused. "Look," he remembered telling them, "I'm not going to be involved in a ceremony of selling land to the Jews. The Jews could buy land, but why I should as an Arab give them coffee and fruits? Let them have deals in dark rooms."

Palestinian land sales to the Israelis, both past and present, are a dirty little secret of which Hamad is deeply ashamed. It is something, he proudly let us know, that does not stain his family's name. He knows that from a reputable source. Once he was part of a large group of journalists interviewing David Ben-Gurion at his kibbutz in the Negev desert. Jamil had grown up knowing that the man who forged the Jewish state lived on his family's lands.

He couldn't miss the chance. In front of everybody, Jamil said to him, "Mr. Ben-Gurion, you are enjoying your stay in the Negev at the expense of my family property." The reporters, whose eyes widened at the cockiness of this Palestinian reporter, sucked in their breath, waiting to see how the "old man" of Zionism would respond.

"Do you belong to the Hamad family?" Jamil remembered the former prime minister asked.

"Yes."

"That's true," Ben-Gurion said, "we took that land."

Jamil couldn't just leave it there. "Please tell me," he continued, "did one of my family sell you that land?"

"No, no," Ben-Gurion replied, to Hamad's great satisfaction.

Hamad contends Jabari was responsible for the disappearance of *Al-Fajr*'s publisher and for providing a pretext for his own arrest as well. The Nasser family, who controlled Bir Zeit University, were staunchly behind the young nationalist bloc then rising to challenge the Hashemites, like Jabari, whom the Israelis naturally sought to protect. In the subsequent elections, for example, when it was clear Jabari would be displaced by radical nationalists, the Israelis arranged to deport his primary opponent to Lebanon just before the election.[8]

The Israelis did their best to prevent reporters from inquiring into the publisher's disappearance. Yasser Karaki, the man charged and jailed for kidnaping Joe Nasser, served six years in jail. While in prison, he wrote to Yehuda Litani, a journalist then working for *Ha-Aretz*, that he would like the Israeli reporter to visit him in jail. Litani, he wrote, was the only person to whom he would trust his story. The minister of police refused Litani permission. Karaki, the minister told him, would lie to him. "Let me just find out," Litani remembered pleading. "Maybe he has something." But it was of no use. "It was the Labour Party," Litani complained to us, "the liberal, socialist, advanced people who want to give back the territories. . . My most bitter experience is with my people."

When Karaki was released from prison, Litani got a telephone call. "Mr. Litani, is that you?" They made an appointment. Litani arrived at the rendezvous, but Karaki never showed. Two hours before they were to meet, Karaki fled to Jordan. "He was afraid to meet me," Litani said. "He was afraid for his life. He knew a lot about it. It was Sheikh Jabari's people, them who did it."

Hamad claimed to us he had not originally known *Al-Fajr* was financed by the PLO. After he was released from prison, Hamad was approached by Paul Ajlouny, the paper's new publisher, who now lives in New York, and Karim Khalaf, the radical nationalist mayor of Ramallah. They asked him to return as editor. The PLO would pay him a handsome salary. He did not want, he explained, to be politically beholden to the PLO. "Seeing your family have nothing, no income, and you have your children, your wife, your house, your mother. And I said 'No.' " It was a costly decision. Hamad, who had edited three Arab newspapers, never worked again on the staff of a Palestinian newspaper.

As every journalist knows, it is tough working as an independent. Hamad even published op–ed pieces in *The Jerusalem Post*. Nobody escaped excoriation – not Jordan, not the PLO, not the Israelis. When Hamad wrote a blistering piece against the Village Leagues, his contact at *The Jerusalem Post* asked him to write it under a pseudonym. Jamil refused. His wife, who was a social worker with blind Palestinians, Jamil told us, paid for his refusal with her job. The Israeli military administration went to the German-funded service agency and threatened to revoke their license unless Hamad's wife was fired. She was. The Jordanians also made life difficult by refusing to renew his family's passports.

Ziad abu Zayyad is another Jerusalem journalist who pushed his profession to its political limits. He was among the first Palestinians who believed it necessary to engage Israelis in a dialogue about the prospects of a Palestinian nation-state. When we arrived at abu Zayyad's house, the table was filled with food. It was a good thing, too, because Ziad's eight children were very hungry, having fasted from sunup to sundown this Ramadan day. Ziad's wife, an English teacher born in the Gaza Strip, had stuffed zucchini, tomatoes, even carrots with rice and ground meat. There were special deserts like *hariseh* made from yogurt, honey, almonds, and semolina. A half dozen children peered curiously at us. The older took care of the younger.

Suddenly a distant staccato; conversation ceased. Ziad abu Zayyad, his face naturally shadowed with care, strained to hear. Gunshots perhaps. The night swallowed the particulate sounds; only the yelp of barking dogs and the quick song of trucks roaring down the open road from Jerusalem were heard.

The abu Zayyad family migrated to this village hundreds of years ago. It is now a small suburb of Jerusalem. As they did to his father, who was the village *mukthar*, people often go to Ziad with their problems, whether with the Israeli government or with each other. When the Israelis came, they expropriated some of the family's land for what is today Ma'aleh Adumim, a Jewish suburb at Jerusalem's eastern rim. When Ziad drives by, he tries to keep his eyes on the road. Sometimes at night, he dreams about it.

Very early on, Ziad abu Zayyad dared to formulate the conflict as between two nations whose failure to see and speak to each other was the most important obstacle to peace. Politics is a war over legitimate conversation. For forty years after statehood, for either Israelis or Palestinians to address the other by their proper name was to negate their own identity, their own territorial claims. Each nation did its utmost to make the other invisible or an essence of evil, which is the same thing. Each attempted to convert something intimate into a foreign affair. The Israelis assimilated their conflict with Palestinians to the larger Arab conflict and talked about a Jordanian option. The Palestinians assimilated Zionism to Western imperialism and hoped to bring Israel to its knees through a shift in the balance of power. A few years after Arafat became PLO chairman, he referred to the Israelis as "Arabs of the Jewish faith."[9] The Jews did not a nation make.

Given the enormous importance of the debates that occur among Palestinians in East Jerusalem, one would expect Israelis to follow them carefully. Although they are neighbors, the Israeli community of Jerusalem worked hard at making the Palestinians politically invisible. Political debates rage on the eastern side of the city, with enormous implications for Israel. But Israeli newspaper coverage of Palestinian life in East Jerusalem has been almost nonexistent. Across the airwaves, too, the Arabs who live on one side of the city almost never speak to the Jews who live on the other. When David Grossman, the Israeli novelist, worked at the *Kol Yisrael* ("Voice of Israel") radio station in central Jerusalem, he tried to interview Arabs for his program, "A Good Evening from Jerusalem." Most Arabs, he told us, didn't speak Hebrew well enough. "It's not radiophonic to translate a conversation that should be intimate," he said. But the problem was not just technical. Although there were Arabs working at *Kol Yisrael*, putting out Arabic programs, the radio station's Jewish and Arab employees didn't really speak to each other. Inside the radio station, Jewish and Arab voices kept to separate rooms, broadcast on separate programs, and spoke to separate sides of the city.

When conversation between these two nations began, it was centered in Jerusalem and Ziad abu Zayyad was one of the first to speak from the Palestinian side. In 1965, Ziad graduated law school in Damascus and began a career as a bureaucrat in Jordan's Ministry of Interior in the passport office in Jerusalem. Two years later the Israelis took Jerusalem and Ziad went to work for the the pro-Jordanian newspaper *Al-Quds*. By the end of the decade, he had switched to the pro-PLO *Al-Fajr*, first as reporter and later as managing editor.

Abu Zayyad can remember when "to say that you are going to talk to the Israelis . . . was like treason, the most awful thing that you can do." He, on the other hand, believed the Palestinians not only had to talk to the enemy but talk to them in a language they could understand: Hebrew. Ziad took the radical step of starting a Hebrew language edition of *Al-Fajr*. As he went from newstand to newstand in Jerusalem, many Israeli vendors refused to carry it. Others who did found that right-wing Israelis would steal them and tear them to pieces. One newspaper vendor agreed to carry Ziad's paper, but only inside the shop, behind the counter. The vendor had enough trouble already with *haredim* who attacked his kiosk when they spied sexually evocative magazines or ad copy. Ziad's newsboys were kicked and cursed in downtown Jerusalem when they tried to sell the paper.

But most Israelis didn't want to hear a Palestinian nationalist, even in their own language. Circulation remained very small – around twelve hundred. When *Al-Fajr*'s publisher wanted to bail out, Ziad pleaded. "For me, the Hebrew paper was very important. I did not see it as only a job where you can get money and live. For me, it was a way to talk to people . . . on the other side. . . For me, it was a bridge of conciliation." When the publisher would not back down, Ziad abu Zayyad quit *Al-Fajr* and returned to his law practice.

When high-level officials from the United States, from France, from the Netherlands would come to Jerusalem, they would often talk to abu Zayyad. And Ziad kept up the conversation with the Israelis. He worked with Meron Benvenisti and his West Bank Data Project. He spoke at *kibbutzim*, at peace conferences both in Israel and abroad. As the Palestinians became more self-confident, there were more and more, like Ziad, willing to talk. In 1986 Ziad began publishing his own Palestinian newspaper in Hebrew under the title *Gesher*, "Bridge."

Jerusalem Versus the PLO

Jerusalem was a site where Palestinians could stand up against both the PLO and Jordan. Because Israel still held to state-to-state negotiations with Jordan, it was not seriously willing to consider the creation of any kind of independent Palestinian entity. Neither was Jordan, which wanted to reabsorb the West Bank. Within the PLO, to speak of the coexistence of two states – one Palestinian Arab, one Jewish – was to reveal oneself as a quisling. At the fifth Palestinian National Council (PNC) meetings in 1969, the PLO contemptuously dismissed the idea as "a spurious Palestinian entity which would be an agent of Zionism and imperialism."[10] Rejecting it as a loathsome capitulation, a "liquidation of the Palestine problem," the PLO was unwilling even to allow the idea to be heard.[11]

Right after Jordan's bloody repression of the PLO, a delegation of Palestinians from the occupied territories approached the chairman of the PLO and announced they had decided to separate from Jordan. Arafat was livid. "The Palestinian revolution would punish any attempt to implement this decision," Arafat reportedly told them. "I hereby declare that we shall oppose the establishment of this state to the last member of the Palestinian people, for if ever such a state is established it will spell the end of the whole Palestinian cause."[12] It would not be until June 1974, after Israel briefly hovered near defeat in the Yom Kippur War, that the PLO outside would declare an independent Palestinian state as an objective, and then only as a stage on the way to total liberation.

But the Palestinian newspapers of Jerusalem, which wrote the story of and for the nation under Israeli occupation, rejected the PLO's position. The political intellectuals who edited and wrote for the city's Arab newspapers pushed for an independent Palestinian state distinct from Jordan and at peace with Israel. In 1969, the Communists, and their newspaper

Al-Talia, were the first to make the move and were roundly denounced as traitors. Then in 1970 the pro-Jordan newspaper *Al-Quds* took a similar position.[13] In 1972, Israel authorized the licensing of two pro-PLO newspapers – *Al-Fajr* and *Al-Sha'ab*, and they, too, quickly made the same move.[14] Cut off from direct PLO or Jordanian control, protected by Israeli rule, these newspapers were only printing what their readers in the occupied territories had come to understand was the only way.

The Palestinian newspapers inside not only did not support the PLO's ultimate destination, they also attacked how it intended to get there. Take December 6, 1983. Yasser Arafat and four thousand of his men waited nervously on Tripoli's docks for Greek ships to evacuate them after they had been mowed down by Palestinian rebels. That same day, a civilian Israeli Egged bus, number 18, packed with Israeli lunch hour passengers, was bombed in Jerusalem. As soon as they heard the explosion at nearby Shaare Zedek Hospital, the loudspeakers called doctors and nurses from every ward to the emergency room. A high-explosive device packed with nails had blown the roof off the bus. The blast shattered eardrums. Human bodies hurtled through the air; nail fragments and glass shot out, burrowing deep into flesh. Four Jews died immediately; forty-three were injured.

The PLO news agency, Cyprus-based WAFA, controlled by Arafat, issued a communiqué claiming credit for the explosion. The dispatch came directly from Tripoli. "Under instructions of the general command of the Palestinian revolution's forces to the guerrilla units in the occupied territories, a guerrilla unit of 'Martyr Halim' was able today to detonate explosive charges inside an Israeli military bus."[15] It was a hideous farewell card from a wounded army.

Within a few days, Jerusalem returned to normal. However, something happened that was not normal. Five Palestinians published a statement condemning the bus bombing:

> It is our belief that attacks on civilian targets are detrimental to any Palestinian–Israeli understanding. Such acts, be they in Jerusalem, in Ein Hilwe [a refugee camp in Lebanon], or in Nablus, are to be regretted. Violence against civilians, carried out by either side, is counter-productive to a just solution to the Israeli–Palestinian problem.[16]

The statement was remarkable. At this time and for years afterward, the PLO not only retained its commitment to "armed struggle," but militias allied with Arafat continued to engage in terrorist operations in which innocent Jewish civilians were murdered. For prominent Palestinians to distance themselves publicly from an attack for which the PLO claimed credit was more than noteworthy. It was courageous. Palestinians who had criticized such policies in the past sometimes paid for their position with their lives. What was even more significant was who signed the statement and where it was published. Because it was published in *Al-Fajr*, known for its support of al-Fatah, the nationalist loyalty of the signatories could not be impugned. They included two Palestinian mayors – Karim Khalaf and Mustafa Natshe – deposed by Israel for their pro-PLO activity; the editor and publisher of *Al-Fajr*; and Anwar Nusseibeh, Arafat's appointed director of the East Jerusalem Electricity Company.[17] If the PLO abroad was willing to claim credit for this massacre, the PLO at home condemned it in no uncertain terms. It was a portent of things to come.

The Shadow Mayor

Both Arafat and Hussein sought to make Jerusalem theirs. What began as a struggle between their supporters eventually became a contest between both of them and the Jerusalemites.

After 1967, the Jordanians did their utmost to maintain their leverage in the city. Jerusalem's *shari'a* or religious court was given jurisdiction for the entire West Bank. Through the Jerusalem *waqf*, Jordan funneled large amounts of monies to support Islamic schools, colleges, mosques, and welfare services throughout the West Bank.[18] As social infrastructure, job generator, and patronage machine, this complex has been the most important Hashemite-controlled institution in Jerusalem. The Jerusalem-based *waqf* also controlled a large and growing stock of real estate, much of it deeded by Palestinians fearful of Israeli expropriation.[19]

Jerusalem immediately reemerged after the 1967 war as a center of Palestinian resistance to Israeli occupation. Right after the war, Palestinians, claiming that the city was an inseparable part of the Jordanian kingdom, reestablished the Supreme Muslim Council. Although the council has never been recognized by Israeli or Jordanian law, the most important Jordanian-appointed Islamic officials sit on it and it was an important vehicle where Palestinians seeking independence sought common ground with those who wanted the Jordanians to return. In the occupation's first three years, Israel deported more than five hundred Palestinian political leaders, many of them from Jerusalem. Israel would not countenance counterclaims in its newly "united" capital, even from some of its more obstreperous Hashemites.[20]

Anwar Nusseibeh, one of the founding members of the Supreme Muslim Council, was never touched. For two decades of Israeli rule, Nusseibeh served as the shadow mayor of Jerusalem. Centuries ago, the

Anwar Nusseibeh, former foreign minister of Jordan and former head of the East Jerusalem Electric Company, 1984.

Christian churches – Catholic, Greek, Armenian, Russian – unable to agree who should be entrusted with the keys to the Church of the Holy Sepulcher, gave them over to the keeping of the Nusseibehs, a family with a distinguished Islamic lineage. In the initial years of Israeli occupation, Nusseibeh, a trusted agent of King Hussein, explored the prospects of reestablishing Jordanian rule in the occupied territories with a number of high Israeli officials. It was in this context that this refined, Cambridge-educated Palestinian negotiated personally with Teddy Kollek about a "borough plan" to obfuscate and thereby share sovereignty in Jerusalem.[21] "It was not politically acceptable at the time," Nusseibeh told us, because Jordan insisted on divided sovereignty and a return to the 1967 borders. Although Nusseibeh was then willing to countenance a separate Jordanian–Israeli peace, he believed that to accept anything less would be branded as traitorous by the entire Arab world. The talks went nowhere. (Much later Hussein would say that he could live with a solution where Israel would have sovereignty over the Jewish Quarter and the Western Wall and Jerusalem would remain an open, physicially undivided city. By then it was too late.)

Kollek's natural political allies in Arab Jerusalem were those who had served in the upper echelons of the Jordanian regime and, at least initially, supported Jordanian claims to the city. Jordan funneled monies to its clients and supporters through the officials on the Muslim Council and East Jerusalem's Chamber of Commerce. Kollek protected these Jordanian-dominated institutions and rewarded their followers. The Israeli government repeatedly deported Palestinians who threatened Jordanian influence, expelling six nationalists on the Supreme Muslim Council in 1969, for example.[22] To the Hashemites, Kollek was a subrosa ally in a troubled time. Kollek spoke quietly to Anwar Nusseibeh, the Hashemites' most respected leader, when deals had to be negotiated across the two sides of the city. Nusseibeh's brother, once Jordan's representative to the United Nations, received financial aid from the Israeli government to build middle-class apartments in the city. The mayor recognized the Palestinians distrusted Hussein, but, he wrote, "they like Arafat even less." "In an ironic fashion," Kollek wrote in 1978, "Israeli rule in East Jerusalem is almost a convenience for its Arab inhabitants."[23]

Anwar Nusseibeh walked with a limp; he had lost his left leg fighting the Israelis in Jerusalem in 1948. In 1967, the Jordanians had a machine-gun post in the backyard of his home, abutting the old armistice line. When Israeli soldiers stormed his house, a Jordanian soldier was killed there. Nusseibeh buried him and built a memorial in the yard. "The soldiers who came through the first day were extremely well behaved," he said. "The best people either die or go to fight another war."[24]

Right after the war, a number of Israelis approached Nusseibeh and others: why not negotiate independently on behalf of the Palestinians, unencumbered by either the PLO or Jordan? Nusseibeh was unwilling even to consider it. At the time, he recalled, "what was necessary for a solution was . . . an Israeli withdrawal from all of the occupied territories in exchange for a nonbelligerency agreement from Jordan. There was no need for any type of separate West Bank political body, no need for negotation."[25] Nusseibeh sought the restoration of Jordanian sovereignty.

Nusseibeh was the director of the East Jerusalem Electric Company, when we spoke in 1984, the most powerful Arab-owned enterprise in Jerusalem and the only Palestinian-owned institution linking Jerusalem to the West Bank. Although the corporation purchased most of its power from Israeli sources and was subsidized by both the Jordanians and the PLO, Nusseibeh's firm still supplied electricity to Jewish settlements and even army bases on the Jordanian side of the "Green Line."[26]

Nusseibeh had been appointed in 1979 with the support of both the Jordanians and Arafat. When the company got into administrative difficulties, he secretly turned to Mayor Kollek to provide him with a low-level Israeli technical adviser.

Nusseibeh was a natural bridge between King Hussein and Yasser Arafat. And the Higher Muslim Council, on which Nusseibeh still sat, functioned as a vehicle for PLO–Jordanian rapprochement. Nusseibeh's service to Jordan had not marked him as a quisling. "He's a gentleman. He respects himself. . . He's not like most of the people," Akram Haniyeh, a member of the militant National Guidance Committee, said. "I believe that he's a real nationalistic Palestinian although he was minister in Jordan, he was ambassador, he was everything there."

We arrived for our appointment at Nusseibeh's office promptly at 9:30 on May 22, 1984. The big clock in his office showed 8:30. We checked our watches, thinking the electricity had stopped functioning in East Jerusalem or perhaps his clock was broken. The clocks were working fine. Israel had just introduced daylight savings time. Nusseibeh's office, like all other Palestinian institutions, refused to set its clocks forward. East Jerusalem would run on Arab time. It was a foretaste of the struggle over time that would soon explode on Jerusalem's streets.

Nusseibeh had returned home to the Palestinian nationalism of his youth, and hence to the PLO. Jerusalem, he now believed, should be the site of two sovereignties. Some pro-Jordanians felt he had betrayed them; some Israelis thought so too. Anwar Nusseibeh died of natural causes on November 22, 1986. Shortly before his death, Kollek visited his friend at the hospital. As Nusseibeh's funeral cortege made its way to al-Aqsa mosque, it swelled with young Palestinians of the city.

Nusseibeh had seen the Jordanian king he once served as the necessary midwife of an otherwise illegitimate Palestinian state. Only through Hussein, Nusseibeh believed, would Arafat ever arrive in Jerusalem. Nusseibeh had been one of the Palestinians acceptable to both Arafat and Hussein as a member of a joint Palestinian–Jordanian delegation to negotiate with Israel. But by the time Nusseibeh died, the rapprochement had broken down. As Israeli soldiers armed with machine guns looked on, the Palestinians chanted, "PLO Yes! Israel No! With blood and spirit we will liberate Palestine!" The flower-covered casket carrying the Jerusalemite who had served Jordan so well slowly made its way to the cemetery. Young men mobbed the casket, yelling, "Hussein, no!" Even if many of their parents still believed Jordan was the most likely route of return to Arab rule, Jerusalem's Palestinian youth would not countenance even the suggestion. Jerusalem had become Fatah town, Arafat's most important center of political support.

Capital Crimes

Palestinian history has powerful bloodlines. Faisal Husayni is the son of Abd al-Qadr, the nationalist commander who fell in 1948 in the battle for Jerusalem. A year after Faisal was born in 1940 in Hashemite Iraq, his uncle, Haj Amin al-Husayni, the former mufti, helped engineer a pro-Nazi coup there.[27] Faisal's father led a Palestinian contingent in the fighting. The British crushed the new Iraqi regime and Abd al-Qadr spent three years in prison. After Faisal's father was released, the family made their way to Saudi Arabia. Faisal draws his memories of his father from that precious period. For the rest, after he was six years old, Faisal barely saw his father, always on the move raising money, collecting arms, mobilizing men for the coming struggle against the Zionists. "I don't know him very well," Faisal told us. "What I know about him, I hear, not what I see, what I remember." It was a legend that also spelled out an obligation.

Faisal arrived in Cairo with his father, the commander, and his uncle, the mufti, in 1946. Faisal grew up there, returning every summer to Jerusalem. Yasser Arafat, then head of the Palestinian Student League in Cairo, befriended the young son of the man he had wanted to follow into battle. Like his uncle and father, Faisal Husayni believed fervently in the pan-Arab cause. When the Syrians and the Egyptians merged to create the United Arab Republic in 1958, Faisal had been jubilant. And when it fell apart in 1961, he was devastated.

Faisal, like many other young Palestinians, began to turn to what he still refers to as a "local" loyalty to an independent Palestinian state, as opposed to a "national" position that sees the multiplicity of Arab sovereignties as a colonial residue, a Western artifice. In 1964, at the age of twenty-four, Husayni left Cairo for Jerusalem to work for the just-founded Palestine Liberation Organization. Faisal supported al-Fatah's growing guerrilla army organization, which launched its first armed operations against Israel in 1965. In Gaza, Syria, and Iraq, the PLO created the first units of a new liberation army. In 1966, Faisal Husayni left for Syria, where the Hittin Brigade was being formed, to train as a military officer. His training was still unfinished when the Six-Day War began. Husayni was sent to Lebanon in the mountains near Beirut, where he helped create the first Palestinian guerrilla training camp, an armed nucleus of what would evolve into a PLO ministate until it was destroyed by the Israelis and the Syrians years later.

The Palestinian units were not independent and Husayni chafed under Syrian tutelage. He knew he did not want to end up outside Palestine, so the young commander waded across the Jordan River, making his way back to an Israeli-occupied Jerusalem. Arafat, who was operating out of

Faisal Husayni, former director of the Arab Studies Society, 1984.

Nablus, made contact with his young friend. Al-Fatah was placing bombs in Israeli bus stations and movie theaters and Husayni agreed that Arafat's men could hide two machine guns in his home. The Israelis arrested him for illegal possession of a weapon. After a year in prison, the Israelis refused to grant him an identity card establishing his right to reside in Jerusalem. When his mother died in England, the Israelis denied his request to bring her body home for burial. After seven years of legal pressure, and seven years of peaceful employment as a radiographer, Faisal Husayni secured the precious paper establishing his Jerusalem residency. Whereupon Husayni took up the struggle once again, becoming a member of the same Jerusalem-based Islamic council and *waqf* his uncle, the mufti, once controlled.

In 1979 Husayni founded the Arab Studies Center, located at the New Orient House, a squat stone hotel owned by the family in East Jerusalem near the American Colony Hotel. Husayni's society collected anything and everything written on Palestine. Every book and article written by a

Palestinian was catalogued and shelved, every newspaper article indexed. They went house to house to persuade Palestinians to pull out old leaflets, posters, and manifestos documenting the history of their struggle. There was little available locally in Arabic on Palestinian history and politics, so Husayni underwrote studies, published new volumes, created data files on every aspect of Palestinian society from the British Mandate to the present.

Organization of memory is a powerful weapon. When the Israelis invaded Beirut in 1982, they seized the Palestinian archives and its mountain of documentary material, carting it away in boxes. Later, when the PLO negotiated a prisoner exchange with Israel, Husayni claimed the archive was treated as part of the deal. History was held hostage and then released to those who claimed it as their own. Husayni, not taking any chances, arranged to have his archive microfiched. Harvard University, among others, has part of the collection.

For the Arabs, remembering Palestine has become increasingly difficult. The Israelis bulldozed buildings that told of their prior presence, and across the country new settlements sprung up with new Hebrew names. How could the children who had never been, had never seen, remember what had been taken, what had been lost. "It's a rare thing to find a map for Palestine in Arabic," Husayni told us. His center published a "new" map of Palestine – all the lands occupied by Israel – crowded with Arabic names marking every village and town as they existed in 1934.

"Why 1934?" we asked. "Because in 1934, it is the period before the big immigration to our land, so you can find on this map all . . . the Arab villages, the 420 villages which have been destroyed after 1948. You can see it as it was in these days, a land full of villages, Arab villages, and not just a desert, not a land with no people to be a land for people with no land."

Husanyi's map, its index of place names, its catalog of empty villages, bulldozed or built over, allows the Palestinians to possess mentally what is denied them physically. "We allow our people to read and to pronounce the name of this village as it was and as it must be, not as it is now used," he said. "This index lets every one of our people know how to keep the real name in his mind."

Faisal Husayni, the PLO's highest-ranking member in Jerusalem, the hardline Fatah activist, migrated to the same political point to which Anwar Nusseibeh, the Hashemite, had migrated from the opposite direction: an independent Palestinian state at peace with Israel. Taking such a position as the son of Abd al-Qadr was not easy. "People tell me," he remembered, "that it is not right to say so . . . because you are not representative of only yourself. You are something to do with the name of your father. I can't really allow you to say so and so."

Husayni believed a Palestinian state was a precondition for peace, not its consequence. "The peace must start from an equal point. . . Don't ask me to have a solution here or there and negotiate while they are putting their boots on my neck." Prior independence was critical, too, Husayni has claimed to us over the last decade, for the Palestinian state's inevitable federation with Jordan. Landlocked between two hostile powers, an independent state could not survive. Husayni, the cartilage on his capacious nose ribbed and tubular, described it as a respiratory problem. "I need to breathe. I need lungs. And I have two lungs," referring to Jordan and Israel, "and I must choose one of these." Despite Hussein's hostility to the PLO, Husayni saw federation with the Hashemite regime as the only viable option.

The new Palestinian state, he insisted, would have to be able to protect its independence. It had to be free to gather Palestinian exiles from around the Arab world, including Jordan. It had to keep its option open that someday, somehow, there would be a union of Israel and Palestine. "[I]f I have some other atmosphere in Israel, . . . I will chase the Israeli lung." Moreover, only a Palestinian state could speak for the Palestinians living in Israel. A Jordanian state could not.

Husayni speaks in a soft, measured voice. But that does not mean he has been any less committed to armed struggle against Israel. On the contrary, he remains a soldier proud of his people's army he helped build. He considered the capacity to engage Israel's military a mark of national equality as much as anything instrumental or politically productive. He opposed random attacks against Israeli civilians. "We don't need to put a bomb in a bus," he told us in 1984.

> We have the strength, we have the respect of the whole world. I am sure that within the troops of the PLO, they have the troops [with] which they can attack some military tanks. . . To fight, it will serve. To have a military force, it will serve. To have strength, it will serve me, because I'm not so stupid to say that we want peace so we don't want battles on our side, when they have about a quarter of a million soldiers in the world. No, I'd be stupid. . . No, but what I am saying is that the targets must be in the right place, not in a bus, not in a market. It is not what we need. We are grown up.

Husayni, like many Palestinians we met over the last decade, was always waiting for the next war, the next deployment of Arab might against Israel. When we first met, Israel had largely withdrawn from Lebanon as a result of fierce guerrilla resistance, occupying only a southern buffer zone. This Israeli retreat, he admitted, nourished his hopes of an eventual Arab military victory over Israel. Husayni was waiting for the war between Iran and Iraq to end. Perhaps, then, Arabs would finally strike against the greater enemy. Without an Israeli commitment to peace, Husayni warned,

> the military option is something everyone is looking for. Especially after Lebanon, [the Palestinians] feel that somehow the Americans couldn't hold on in Lebanon and the Israelis have problems in Lebanon. So maybe Israel will say that it doesn't want [to hold on]. We are coming back now to that . . . old idea, saying let Israel occupy more territories. The more they occupy, the more they will lose. So I think it is black for us now, but in the . . . coming years, it is more black for Israel.

Husayni, like most Palestinians, still dreamed the dream of a total liberation. "The dream, believe me, I love Haifa and Jaffa. I love every piece of Palestine . . . so my dream is to be living in this home, in Palestine, to have the right to go everywhere, to live anywhere." But to be free in Palestine, he now understood, he would have to live with Israel.

> The Jewish people, most came from outside. But they are living here. . . Even if I'll have the strength that I need to conquer them and I occupied all of these places, what I am going to do with them? Am I going to throw them to the sea? Nonsense. Am I going to march on Tel Aviv to remove them? . . . Am I going to have a military sweep and stand in the roads and see if this is a Jewish car [and] . . . I search his car as they are doing to us now? It is nonsense. I can't believe that it must be. No, even if we can conquer them. So, if I want to have my dream as a reality . . . I must live with them. I can't live with them while they are under my rule or I am under their rule. We can't live one up and one down.

Husayni's dream had not changed: a Palestinian state in all Palestine. In the future, he told us, he would continue working with Palestinians and Israelis who shared his dream, "not by arms, not by revolution, but by democratic ways." He was even optimistic about the long run. "I think this dream can happen in the future. . . But I'm not going to force this dream to happen, you know . . . I'm going to try it." And if he failed, we asked? "So who in the whole world can make all of his dreams a reality?" he replied.

Faisal Husayni took an enormous leap in 1987. Together with his good friend, Sari Nusseibeh, Anwar Nusseibeh's son, a philosophy professor at Bir Zeit University, they met with Likud politician Moshe Amirav, a member of the Central Committee of Shamir's Herut Party, to search for a formula acceptable to both Israel and the PLO. Moshe Amirav, who in 1967 had been wounded as a paratrooper fighting for Jerusalem, claimed to be a government emissary. The small group drafted a joint memorandum in which Israel agreed to recognize the PLO as its interlocutor with which it would negotiate for the creation of a demilitarized Palestinian "entity" with its "administrative" capital in Arab Jerusalem.[28]

Sari Nusseibeh was severely beaten by Palestinian rejectionists, while Moshe Amirav was drummed out of his party.[29] The Palestinians didn't touch Husayni, but the Israelis did. Faisal Husayni and Sari Nusseibeh both claimed to speak with the knowledge of Yasser Arafat. Both had been in regular contact with PLO leaders on the outside with the tacit approval of the Israeli Defense Ministry.[30] Husayni was convinced Prime Minister Yitzhak Shamir stood behind Amirav's initiative.[31] Just before Husayni was scheduled to take the proposal to Arafat in August 1987, Defense Minister Yitzhak Rabin had him arrested. Husayni was put under administrative detention for nine months as a threat to state security without any formal charge, placed with thirteen other prisoners in a jail cell built for eight, where each night five prisoners had to sleep on the floor. Israeli doves took out large newspaper ads demanding that if the government were not going to charge him for a specific offense, he should be released.

Rabin's action was followed by an unprecedented meeting with West Bank Palestinian members of the Jordanian parliament, urging them yet again to take a more active role in the territories. King Hussein intended to have elections for parliament and to allocate half the seats to the West Bank. Israel still hoped it could count on Hussein to prevent PLO supporters from being seated.[32] Three months later, the *intifada* exploded and six months after that, Rabin released Husayni.

During the *intifada*, Husayni's son was arrested and beaten about the face for throwing stones. Husayni took the bold step of participating in a debate with Israelis, where he publicly endorsed a two-state solution. The Israelis threw him into prison once again and closed his Arab Studies Society for a year. When he was released in 1989, Husayni continued his political initiative.

Arafat, who had always dismissed the idea of talking to the Israelis, now changed course. In the 1988 Knesset elections, the PLO took the extraordinary step of urging Israeli Arabs to vote for those parties who would support a political solution to the conflict. The PLO decided to launch a "peace offensive" to prepare the Israeli public for the idea that they should talk with the PLO. The Tel Aviv branch of the Labour Party invited Husayni, the PLO's most important point man on the inside, to meet with them. Such meetings, Shamir contended, were "useless and unauthorized" and only served to encourage "PLO terrorism."[33]

Abu Iyad, the number two man in the PLO and head of its intelligence and covert operations, delivered the PLO's first direct message to the Israelis at a Jerusalem peace conference in 1989. The video, taped in Arabic so that it would be understood by his Arab constituents as well as the Israelis, had to be smuggled in by Israelis. Abu Iyad proclaimed that the PLO had abandoned its stage theory, that the two-state solution would be a final one, that the Palestinians were prepared to live in peace with Israel. Lova Eliav, a Labour member of Knesset and former general secretary of the Labour Party, rose to speak. "I'm proud to be here, to hear such a message from our opposite number on the other side of the bridge, on the other side of the abyss."

When Shlomo Cohen, a Jew and a civilian, was stabbed to death near Zion Gate in Jerusalem February 1989, Defense Minister Rabin blamed the PLO, denouncing the killing as a "classic attack by a terrorist organization." But Faisal Husayni, who had publicly stated that a Palestinian state would not need an army, also condemned the attack. "We regret all bloodshed," he said. "We don't differentiate between your blood and ours."

After Moshe Levinger, the Hebron rabbi, was charged with manslaughter for killing an Arab shopkeeper, Levinger led a procession to Husayni's home in East Jerusalem. Husayni went out to meet them. It was Husayni, the demonstrators yelled, who should be on trial and expelled, not Moshe Levinger. They handed him a pamphlet in which Husayni said that occupied people had the right to use force to resist. "Killer, your hands are smeared with blood," Levinger told him. "I am not the one who is standing trial for manslaughter in Hebron," Faisal retorted. Husayni, Levinger threatened, would lose his legs as Bassam Shak'a, the mayor of Nablus, and Karim Khalaf, the mayor of Ramallah, had lost theirs.[34]

In October 1989, Faisal Husayni stood in a field with a thousand Peace Now demonstrators who had intended to march into the Palestinian town of Tulkarm and have "peace talks." The Israeli army stopped them. "To the government, I say peace is made with enemies," he told the disappointed Israelis. "We have already defined our enemy and we are ready to talk peace with it. You must define your enemy, the PLO, and talk with Yasser Arafat." Husayni shared the microphone with Yael Dayan, Moshe Dayan's daughter. "Faisal Husseini's father and my father fought each other to the death," she said. "Today I am proud to stand next to him in a peace meeting. I am sure that his children and mine will live, each in his own country, in peace."[35]

13

A State of Mind

A man without a wife is like a kitchen without a knife.
A kiss without a moustache is like food without salt.
An *intifada* without troubles is likewise impossible.

– a Palestinian proverb

When the Palestinian uprising exploded on December 8, 1987, it shocked everybody. The Israelis initially didn't think it was anything unusual. Three days into the confrontation, Defense Minister Yitzhak Rabin flew off to the United States; on his return, he briefed reporters that Syria and Iran were behind it.[1] The *intifada*, or "shaking off," as the Palestinians call it, reconfigured what was politically imaginable. None of Israel's intelligence services had anticipated a civil uprising. There weren't even any contingency plans for such an event.[2] Routinely drilled for military confrontation with Syria or Iraq, Israeli soldiers had neither the training nor the materiel to do daily battle with young men and teenagers who, en masse and, unlike their parents, were willing to risk beatings, gunshot wounds, arrest, destruction of their homes, ruination of their family's businesses, deportation, and death to liberate at least some part of Palestine.

It was not just the Israelis who were stunned. The *intifada* also caught the PLO completely off guard. When it broke, top PLO United Nations officials were jetting abroad for the Christmas holidays. It took ten days for the PLO to get its first handbill into Gaza's streets.[3] The *intifada* also stunned Jordan's King Hussein. In its first months, King Hussein's supporters in Jerusalem privately complained to the Israelis that insufficient force was being used to put down a revolt that further threatened their already dwindling influence. King Hussein initially believed the Israelis wanted it to continue as a prelude to mass deportations.[4]

Weapons of the Weak

The Jordanians, the PLO, and the Israelis had each sought to subordinate the Palestinians of the West Bank to their own purposes. Pursuing divergent aims, they employed parallel tactics. None was willing to allow the Palestinians to organize politically across the occupied territories, to develop a collective voice. Each attempted to manage Palestinian politics from the outside. Each sought dependable clients and trusted agents. Each used material favors and physical coercion to architect alliances, secure positions. Nobody was willing to recognize the nation taking shape in Palestine itself.

For the first two decades of Israeli occupation the Palestinians were relatively quiescent. There were few Palestinians who had not been stopped, questioned, humiliated by Israeli soldiers; whose family members had not been arrested or beaten; who had not had to wait hours driving into Jerusalem while each car was stopped at a checkpoint while Israelis drove on by; who had not walked into Jewish Jerusalem with a nagging fear a bomb might explode, targeting them for arrest or mayhem; who had not had their luggage ripped apart piece by piece and the most private spaces of their bodies checked for explosive devices, money, or messages.[5]

Certainly, there were Palestinian terror cells here and there. But most guerrillas were trained outside, their violence imported across the borders. The mass of Palestinians did little to contest the encroaching Jewish settlements; indeed, many dug the foundations and poured the concrete upon which they were built. Palestinians worked, even as policemen, for the Israeli administration of the territories. The elected Palestinian mayors and city council members on the West Bank did little more than voice their outrage at the occupation's intrusions and dispossessions.[6]

The Israeli occupation was cheap. After the fierce repression of the first few years, it took few soldiers and very little outright force to maintain quiet in the territories. With discretionary use of their right to issue and withold permits to build, buy and sell, immigrate and plant, the Israelis were largely able to maintain control. Military regulations even allowed the Israelis to uproot unapproved fruit and olive trees. What bureaucratic sticks and carrots could not accomplish, offers of employment or threats of imprisonment or administrative detention usually did.

To many the Palestinians seemed unwilling to make the sacrifices necessary to build a nation. Before the *intifada*, not a few Palestinian activists described the Israeli occupation to us as one that, by historical standards, was civilized. And it was. All one had to do was think of the Japanese in Indonesia, the Germans in Poland, the Chinese in Tibet, or the Vietnamese in Cambodia. These others had been unprovoked conquerers. Israel had merely defended itself from conquest by Arab states who swore its destruction.

Even the Palestinians would comment on Israel's relative civility. Some of the boys who threw the stones and Molotov cocktails were sons of fathers who had already experienced both Jordanian and Israeli prisons. One father described Israeli prison to us as a "hotel" by comparison with the Jordanian cell he had occupied. Sam'an Khoury, a radical nationalist, condemned the relative barbarity of the Jordanians in no uncertain terms. "I know what happened to communists under Jordan," he told us.

> They spent years and years in these [prisons] . . . and no one would hear of the person. . . I was never in prison in Jordan, and thank God for that, because even when my parents tell me about what they used to hear about the prisons in Jordan, they would take somebody and nobody would know for ten years. . . Unless the king had [an] amnesty on his feast or his birthday or whatever, no one would go out.

From his writing table David Grossman watched the Arab workers stream into Jerusalem in the early morning. Unlike many Israelis who have learned to make Palestinians invisible, the spectacled writer saw them, these figures in blue jackets with dark, calloused hands; women carrying baskets with capers, cilantro, and sabra; men crowded into the open backs of pickup trucks; fluorescent plastic silhouettes of crescents, Mecca, and the Dome of the Rock beckoning on the front grill. They obsessed him; they carried his imagination.

"There's a way of walking in a Jerusalem street with closed eyes," the red-haired, elfin novelist told us. "You look inside. You don't see them and they do not exist. And they don't see you, I think. The Israelis did not make the Palestinians disappear as people all by themselves. They had a lot of Palestinian help." For two decades the Palestinians had been relatively passive. "How is it possible that they do nothing?" the Israeli writer asked us in 1983. When Grossman interviewed Palestinians for his first novel, *The Smile of the Lamb*, about the encounter of Hilmi, a "crazy" village Palestinian, with an Israeli officer who comes to see Hilmi's humanity, Palestinian quiescence made him feel ashamed.

> It's some kind of paradox that an Israeli should feel ashamed for them. But I know how we would react if it was the opposite situation. I don't know how they do it. They are more than a million Arabs. Statistically it should be that they would create more offenses against us. I myself – it sounds a little crazy – but I myself can think about a thousand ways in which they can damage us and make terrorist actions against us. And they do nothing.

Personal Wealth/National Poverty

Why were the Palestinians so compliant for so long? One reason is that personal prosperity took the sting out of political powerlessness. The

Israeli occupation confounded them. Conquering Arab armies had always been cruel. Israeli soldiers paid for their coffee in Arab cafés. Israeli rule brought better living standards: not only fewer babies who died before their parents could marvel at their first steps, but money for new appliances, new houses, new clothes, and new knowledge. The Israelis, who have always seen satisfied appetites as a means to prevent Palestinian protest, could proudly announce that Palestinian living standards improved dramatically under their rule. The infant mortality rate dropped. Real Palestinian incomes rose two or three times in the first two decades. In the rural villages, the improvement was even more spectacular. Palestinian villagers were eating better than ever before, better even than their Arab counterparts across the Jordan River.[7]

There was poverty, particularly in the refugee camps. And the Palestinians continued to lag behind the Israelis. But there was new-found wealth, lots of it. Many merchants, landowners, and professionals built houses whose size and ostentation dwarfed anything in Israel. Topped by enormous television antennas shaped like diminutive Eiffel Towers, gigantic family compounds – sometimes three and four stories – were built with the finest stone. Not a few new Mercedes-Benzes and BMWs were parked in the driveways. One Palestinian activist complained to us many Palestinians were more concerned about availability of Swiss chocolate in the stores than about liberation.

Going about their everyday lives as angry victims who would make do, most waited for the Arab states and the PLO to liberate them, for the nations to recognize the justice of their cause. And the Palestinians, a practical people, adapted in the same way their grandfathers survived the Turks, and then their fathers, the British and the Jordanians.

Palestinian prosperity was built on a foundation of economic dependence. Most of the money flowed in from the outside. The Arab states and the PLO sent in hundreds of millions for stipends, salaries, and services. Palestinian men migrated to the west to work on Israeli construction sites, in factories and hotel kitchens.[8] And they made their way east to the Gulf, employed in the booming oil economies starved for skilled labor. But they could not work at home.

In part, the fault lay with wealthy Palestinians who would not invest at home. Those with money sent it abroad to Jordanian and, better yet, Swiss banks. Their failure to invest so that their people might find employment at home was not completely their own fault. The Israelis made it difficult for Palestinian businesses to flourish. Palestinians with capital can all tell stories about Israeli refusal to approve one investment or another – a hotel, a cement factory, a sewage plant, a development bank.

Israel was not the only entity resistant to Palestinian economic devel-

Palestinian construction workers building Jewish homes in Ramot, 1984.

opment. Israel, Jordan, and the PLO, each for their own reasons, made productive Palestinian investment within the West Bank extraordinarily difficult. They all sought to prevent the buildup of Palestinian-owned enterprises that could make substantial capital investments and generate employment. Economic autonomy could be converted too easily to political autonomy.

As a result, Israel was able to use the West Bank as a pool of cheap labor and a captive commodity market. When combined with limited employment opportunities, the rapidly rising educational levels of the Palestinians propelled a continuous stream of emigrants across the bridges. For the Israelis, allowing investment in education without the complementary physical capital necessary to generate jobs helped alleviate the "demographic" problem. Dayan's policy of "open bridges" meant the best and the brightest Palestinians often made their way to New Jersey to be doctors, to Kuwait to be engineers, to Sydney to be grocers.

For both the Jordanians and the Israelis, stunting Palestinian economic development provided living proof an independent Palestinian state was not economically viable. It also enabled both to use their control of the bridges, and the movement of labor, money, and agricultural produce across them, as a lever to advance their own political interests. Political enemies could be easily punished and economic pressure brought to bear. Palestinian political leaders repeatedly failed to mobilize their people against employment in Israel because they did not have the resources to provide them with an alternative livelihood. "People want to eat," one activist told us. "As long as you don't give them . . . another option to work, you can't ask them not to go and work in Israel."

Jordan was the Palestinian bridge to the Arab world. Jordanian law required Palestinians leaving the West Bank to exit across the Jordan River. Jordan could confiscate their Jordanian passports and try them before military tribunals if they dared leave from Lod Airport. Palestinians put their capital in Jordanian banks and investments and were thereby tied to the health of the Jordanian regime. Just how much value the Palestinians placed on that connection was demonstrated by their vigorous rejection of a proposal in 1972 by the PLO, Egypt, and Saudi Arabia to close the bridges as a way to undercut Hussein's federation plan.[9]

Without domestic capital investment, the Palestinians were more dependent on foreign paymasters to finance their institutions. Their schools, universities, service agencies, cooperatives, municipalities, aid societies, and hospitals all got caught up in the field of outside forces – the various Palestinian factions inside and outside the PLO, the Jordanians, the Syrians, the Saudi Arabians – each of whom jockeyed for position inside the West Bank and Gaza. Because external centers were many, building a consensus among the Palestinians "inside" was accordingly more difficult.

But equally important, financial dependence on the outside reinforced Palestinian identification with political movements that made "local" nationalism less legitimate. It encouraged Palestinians to see themselves as Arabs whose homeland would be liberated by others. As a result, "local" initiatives in favor of a small, independent Palestinian state at peace with Israel were not a natural response of the population, and those who suggested them were denounced as traitors to one or another larger cause. The material lines of external dependence were reinforced by and themselves reinforced these larger, outward-looking political visions.

The Patronage Game

Billions of dollars made its way through the pockets of Palestinians in the West Bank and Gaza, much of it controlled by Jordan and the PLO, financed by the Palestinian diaspora, by Arab states, by sympathetic governments and social movements around the world.[10] Neither the

PLO nor Jordan used these monies to build a new Palestinian society. Rather they spent them to maintain political support, networks of activists and informants, to try, so they claimed, to keep the West Bank Palestinians *sumud,* "steadfast."

The monies passing through Palestinian pockets made their way through a society fragmented into family networks and intense localisms. The big families, the *hamula,* have always exterted an extraordinary gravitational pull. The Palestinian political community is still composed of families who can draw on networks of kin to protect them, who can guarantee blood debts. The most important institutions have tended to be run as private fiefdoms of one or another prominent family. For example, Bir Zeit University was registered as the personal property of the Nasser family; al-Najah University, the Masri family; and Hebron University, the Jabari family. Bethlehem University, which drew many non-Muslim professors, was the property of the Vatican.

In such a society, patronage is a binding agent. Political elites have clients as often as they have followers. Wealthy landed Palestinian families have tended to invest in conspicuous consumption to bolster their status, and in patronage payments to maintain the solidarity of their families and the loyalty of their followers.[11] A family's stature is maintained by the capacity of its most prominent members to hand out favors, which depends not simply on their wealth, but on their political power. The Israelis discovered immediately that the soft underbelly of Palestinian opposition to their rule was the eagerness of prominent Palestinians to seek favors for extended family members. Large amounts of Palestinian energy, time, and money went into penetrating state authority to secure rewards for the family network.

Although outright bribery is still relatively uncommon in Israel, the Israelis, the PLO, and the Jordanians have each played the patronage game, selectively dispersing monies to individuals, families, and whole villages who were loyal, or at least not truculent. Each sought its political clients. Political activists were beholden to the outside parties who paid them. For many Palestinian nationalists, liberation was a career. Each stream within the PLO had its paid organizers. Nobody had any interest in allowing cross-local mechanisms of organization to emerge across the West Bank and Gaza. Organizations reflect the conditions of their birth. When, in 1968, the multiple Palestinian resistance organizations banded together and seized control of the PLO, they established a mode of operation that would ultimately shackle their capacities for nation building. The leaders of these competing organizations, which were necessarily centralized military command structures, made strategic decisions among themselves. The Palestinian National Council became a hand-picked parliament of selected diaspora Palestinians with little real influence over the parameters of decision making. In the diaspora, each sought to deliver its own services, organize its own associations, using paid functionaries and bureaucratic hierarchy to assure control. Palestinian society in the diaspora was organized professionally from the center down, not popularly from the ground up.

And so, likewise, almost all organizations in the West Bank and Gaza are partisan, aligned with one faction or another. Most do not represent everybody in an area, or even all those who follow a particular profession or trade. Women's organizations, for example, include the Federation of Palestinian Women's Action Committee (DFLP), the Union of Palestinian Working Women's Committees (Communists), the Union of Palestinian Women Committee (PFLP), and the Women's Committee for Social Work (Fatah). This mode of organizing has made for ferocious party competition, reinforcing localism and weakening the Palestinian capacity to form a domestic consensus.

The distribution of largesse shifted with the balance of forces in the West Bank and Gaza, as different parties struggled to win the allegiance of Palestinians inside, to counter domestic initiatives that might move beyond their control. The Jordanians and the Israelis used patronage to undercut the PLO. For much of the period, the PLO and Jordan used it to try to erode the influence of Palestinians inside who were pushing for a Palestinian state. They all played the same game.

During the late 1970s and early 1980s, the Israelis poured monies into cooperative Palestinian villages, which they hoped to forge into a counterweight to the urban-based leadership of the PLO. To counter the independent National Guidance Committee, Arafat's Fatah and Jordan used the superfund financed by the Arab states as their own patronage porkbarrel. When the Arab states agreed to support this fund at the Baghdad summit in 1978, they had meant to arm the Palestinians with the economic means to resist annexation and emigration. Many Palestinians saw the fund as a way to create the infrastructure for their new state. These "steadfast" funds were intended to finance municipal services, teachers' salaries, economic development, housing construction, newspapers, and universities. The lion's share went to projects in Jerusalem, where they were primarily distributed through the Supreme Muslim Council, which even began to take over some municipal functions, purchasing, for example, several dozen buildings to be used as public schools.

Through the Joint Economic Committee, as it was called, millions flowed to clients of the Fatah–Jordanian bloc. Bashir Barghouti, the most important Communist leader in Jerusalem, contended that the Jordanian intelligence service actually vetted all those requesting money. Arafat and Hussein hoped to build a bloc of Palestinian constituents

who would support political directives from the outside against challeng-
ers from within, particularly left-wing Palestinian forces in the occupied
territories. Much of the money never reached its proper destination,
leeched away in patronage payments, embezzled, misappropriated.[12]
"Everybody along the line gets something," said Litani. "It starts from
the King. He took his share. Some poor clerks are now very, very rich."
Out of a hundred dinar, Litani estimated that twenty would make their
mark. Barghouti contended that many wealthy Palestinians had taken
their "steadfast" subsidies and invested the money in Amman. There
had even been a case of an administrator at al-Aqsa mosque, he recalled, who took his cut; bought Iranian rugs, which he sold to merchants in Tel Aviv; invested the money in a then-rocketing Israeli stock
market.

Much of the money went to build private homes for favored families
and clients. Need had little to do with the distribution of housing subsidies, usually around seven thousand dinar, more than twenty thousand
dollars, a substantial amount in local terms. A relative in the PLO, a
history of support for King Hussein, a friend on the committee – all
these played more importantly than individual or social need. The lion's
share of the monies went to merchants, professionals, and landed families. So abused were the funds that Palestinians bitterly pointed to the
luxurious villas to the north of Jerusalem as the "steadfast" quarter, or
"General Samud." By distributing income to individuals, particularly for
housing, the PLO and Jordan gave the Palestinians a stake in staying on
the land and a means to do so. But they also sought to make Palestinians
dependent on their external paymasters, to bolster their positions within
Palestine, not to build the general economic or political capacities of
Palestinians inside the West Bank and Gaza.

Bethlehem, for example, received around $25 million in "steadfast
funds" between 1978 and 1982, earmarked to build schools, improve the
water system, and construct sewers. The city's pro-Jordanian mayor,
Elias Freij, built an ultramodern municipal building and drove a new
brown Mercedes paid for, a number of Palestinians claimed, with *samud*
funds. But after the money had been spent, Bethlehem's schools were
still held in rented buildings; the sewage system was still hopeless; and
during the summer months, the Dehaishe refugee camp at the city's
edge often had no running water. "At least we see such money," Jamil
Hamad, the former *Al-Fajr* editor who lives in Bethlehem, told us. "We
are lucky because we are enjoying seeing the Mercedes-Benz."

Some Palestinians, a number off the record, saw the pernicious effects
of these patterns and were willing to say so. Elias Khoury, for example,
the Arab lawyer in Jerusalem known for his legal battles against expropriation, even wanted to shut down the bridges into Jordan. Because

Palestinians send their produce and their money to Jordan, he told us, "they are not thinking as they should." There is always a nagging fear that one false step will jeopardize their markets or their money. Palestinians, he claimed, think "salvation should come from outside." Many Palestinians whose lands are jeopardized by Israeli expropriation, he said, "go to Jordan, bring two or three thousand dinar back, give the lawyer five hundred dinar, keep in their pockets the balance of the sum that they brought from outside. . . [They] sit in their village, leave the lawyer and that's it. They are not fighting because they want to fight."

The Arab monies meant for Palestinian resistance, Khoury argued, should be used to serve public, not private, purposes. They should build factories and buy land, not pay out stipends and individual subsidies. "I believe the money in the Arab world can buy the whole property of Israel," he said. Hadn't Palestinians been able to buy privately held Jewish land in Jerusalem itself? "This means," he concluded, "they can buy land here,. . . they can make roads, draw planning schemes, in order to develop the area for the benefit of the locals. Those who have no dwellings, who have no houses, can build and so, by that way, we can face the Israelis."

In 1975, Khoury proposed the Palestinians in East Jerusalem form a public company to develop the unbuilt parts of the Arab city, just like the one the Israelis created in 1967 to reconstruct the Jewish Quarter in the Old City. Since the Israelis had not planned most of Jerusalem's Arab areas, the Palestinian corporation would hire architects to plan public institutions and housing that served the public interests of the local Palestinians. By submitting these plans to the municipality, Khoury said, "you put in front of the Israelis at least an obstacle if they want to expropriate." Such a move would increase the price of the unbuilt land so the Israelis would have to pay more to expropriate it. When the Israelis said the lands were being taken for public purposes, the struggle would then be between two "public purposes," rather than an Israeli public interest and an Arab private one. By the time local Palestinian elites were willing to consider his proposal, the Israelis had already encircled the Arab city with Jewish settlements. "They are interested now in the plan," he told us in 1984, "but it's too late, too late. They always miss the train; they always miss it."

The PLO, a wealthy multinational corporation, spent its resources keeping the Palestinians of the camps alive and loyal, stockpiling arms and training its militias, undertaking diplomatic initiatives and paramilitary adventures. But for four decades it did precious little to plan or build the basis of a Palestinian state in Palestine itself. Where were the plans for an educational system, for industry, for agriculture, for health care? Its energies went into cataloguing outrages, reclaiming history, and debating the constantly shifting parameters of diplomatic, political, and military strategy. What, Jamil Hamad, the irreverent former editor of *Al-Fajr*, asked a high PLO official in the 1970s, would the PLO do when it actually had a state? "I know one thing," Hamad told him,

> you will ring the Mercedes agency in Amman and say, "Prepare us five black Mercedes!" That's fine, that's easy. But I'm talking about the state. Where's your homework? What kind of education you are going to have? Now we have Jordanian books. I don't know what kind of economy you are going to have: free, socialist, capitalist? What kind of insurance system you are going to have? What kind of plates are you going to have for your cars? Are we going to use the English numbers and Arabic numbers, or only the Arabic numbers? These are the little things.

The PLO official had no reply. For two decades, little systematic work was done by Palestinians to prepare for a Palestinian state.

The Dead Language

Over the last twenty-five years, the PLO has spoken to West Bank Palestinians through violence, scrawling its political signature primarily with Jewish blood. Hundreds of Jews have been murdered by the PLO.[13] As the point of contact between Palestinians moving into Israel and Israelis moving out into the West Bank, a city where Palestinians penetrate Israeli lives, Jerusalem has been a natural target. Terror is prosaic, mundane – a bomb left in a bag in the back of a bus or in a trash can, hand grenades wired to explode in public places, knifings in the Old City, explosive charges left in refrigerators or even in pita bread. The deadly possibilities – the undetonated charges, the attempted attacks, the foiled plans, and the arms caches – pepper the papers with small items. A month doesn't go by when traffic isn't suddenly stopped, the area cleared by police, while a highly trained sapper removes an explosive device for detonation elsewhere. For twenty minutes every few weeks or so, thousands of Jewish Jerusalemites hold their breath while the deadly danger is removed from harm's way.

The prospect of Arab terrorism looms much larger in the Israeli imagination than random street crime in the American. For a Jew in Jerusalem, the chances of being a victim of Palestinian terror are tiny compared to those of dying at the hands of a maniac, drug addict, or armed robber in Los Angeles or New York.[14] Violent crimes in America are either very personal or very impersonal. A lover kills a rival or the object of love; a heroin addict murders for a twenty dollar bill to feed a habit. Palestinian violence is neither. The Palestinian with a submachine gun or hand grenades takes out whoever happens to be around. The damage is stochastic, but the violence is aimed at one's identity, one's claim to be here. The carnage cannot be neutralized. Each attack is a violation of the social body and is experienced in a deeply personal way.

By its perpetrators and its audience, the persistence of Palestinian terrorism is understood as vengeance for land taken away, for nation-hood denied, a negation by those negated. Terror is the language of those who say, "No, never" to coexistence, of men and women who will never admit the right of two nations to share this land. There are those who say the Arabs have always used violence as the language of honor. The land, they say, calls out to be freed. Lost land will always motivate people to wield a knife when the children of those who took that land are not looking. This may be so.

But Palestinian violence is also a language of weakness. The roots of Palestinian terror lie in the same factor that has now made peace possi-ble: the frailty of the Palestine Liberation Organization, both outside, as an external military threat, and inside, as a hegemonic nationalist move-ment. The PLO is and always has been an alliance of patrimonial militias incapable of mounting a serious military challenge to Israel. It depends on the political and military support of Arab states with no real interest in the establishment of Palestinian sovereignty. Al-Fatah, its central pillar, has beeen repeatedly challenged from all sides: by rejectionist groups who accuse it of treasonous accommodation to Zionism; by Is-lamic groups who reject the PLO's commitment to nationalism and civil equality of Muslims, Christians, and even Jews; by King Hussein, who has tried to make the West Bank into a Jordanian province; and most importantly by many Palestinians of the West Bank and Gaza who no longer believe in the efficacy of the PLO's "armed" or even its "politi-cal" struggle. The PLO has faced a Palestinian population in the West Bank and Gaza whom it has not been able to control and whose collec-tive voice it has feared.

Because the PLO held the Palestinians at arm's length, PLO opera-tives of the various militias who did operate in the West Bank and Gaza were sent in to engage in anonymous terror. Terrorist raids have always had more to do with assertion of the terrorist's presence and factional competition for loyalty within the refugee camps than with a reasoned military strategy to sap Israeli strength. Terror has been a political adver-tisement, a claim to, or refutation of, one's right to lead. After the PLO was declared the Palestinians' sole legitimate representative in 1974, for example, Jerusalem suffered a reign of violent attacks, over a hundred in one year. By injuring one's enemies, a group announces or affirms its existence, keeps the cause in view, salves the shame of impotence. "In fact," confessed Rashid Khalidi, "armed struggle . . . had far more impact on the Palestinians themselves than on its intended target, Israel. . . It . . . helped restore a sense of dignity to a people whose self-respect had been cruelly eroded by their expulsion by Israel and subsequent suppression by the Arab regimes."[15]

The Israelis built a society first and then an army to defend it. The PLO fatefully built itself from the beginning as a loose coalition of small militias. The unity of the organization rested on their common vow to destroy Israel, as manifested by their guerrilla activity. Violent rejection kept the PLO whole. Soldiers were paid, were honored, and had to be used. These barbarous raids were bloody signage, not military tactics. In 1948, Ben-Gurion consolidated unitary control of the several independent militias that made up the Zionist movement. He used force to do so, but not very much force was required. As this is written, Arafat has just begun to make that move, and an enormous amount of coercion will probably be required.

Without instruments of representation, the Palestinians living under Israeli occupation have had great difficulty speaking for themselves. Without means to produce new wealth and new employment, they have been beholden to the Israelis for jobs and to outside Arab paymasters who have kept their institutions afloat. They remained steadfast, living in place, no easy task, but no threat to Israeli occupation either. And so when Palestinian martyrs struck inside in the name of their freedom, they were proud. At least somebody was striking out. Most Palestinians found nothing morally objectionable in PLO guerrilla raids, nor even in civilian bus hijackings or terror bombs in which innocent Israelis died. In a 1986 poll, an overwhelming majority in the West Bank and Gaza said that not only was violent resistance justified (78 percent), but it was the most effective means by which Palestinians could make political gains.[16] By spilling Jewish blood on Palestinian soil, the guerrilla armies outside reminded the Palestinians inside that they were still there, that they had not forgotten their pledge to liberate the lands; not only that they, too, speak for Palestine, but that Palestine was there to be spoken for. Dead Jewish bodies kept Palestinian political identity alive.[17]

Palestinian violence was also a warning to Palestinians inside that there would be a price to pay for daring to speak for themselves, for promoting treacherous two-state schemes, for exploring the possibility of accommodation with Zionism. In a space controlled by Israel, terror against Jews was also designed to make Arabs afraid. The PLO repeatedly used violence to silence its political enemies. Right after the Six-Day War, a few prominent Palestinians, like Dr. Hamdi al-Taji al-

Faruqi, a physician from Ramallah, publicly proclaimed their support for an independent Palestinian state at peace with Israel. The Palestinian physician even itemized the first budget of the proposed nonaligned state and accepted the principle of compensation for Palestinians who had been refugees in 1948. Six months into the Israel occupation, a PLO operative fired a bazooka shell into his residence.[18] Hamdi al-Faruqi remained silent after that.

Aziz Shehadeh, a Christian lawyer from Ramallah, had defended the Palestinian assassin of King Abdullah. Abdullah's grandson, the young King Hussein, later jailed him for several years. Right after 1967, Shehadeh and others approached the Israelis about establishing an assembly that would negotiate with Israel to establish a state in the West Bank.[19] "The time has come for us to take the initiative in handling our own fate," Shehadeh wrote in 1968.[20] He even proposed that the Palestinian state be federated to Israel. Al-Fatah's radio station denounced Shehadeh from Cairo; the Jordanians declared him persona non grata.[21] The PLO threatened his life.[22]

Execution by the PLO remained a constant possibility for dissident Palestinians. When in 1973 the Palestinians formed the Palestine National Front, which espoused an independent Palestinian state, the PLO used threats of violence, among other tactics, to bring it down.[23] During Camp David, those Palestinians willing to participate in the autonomy talks were likewise threatened with death. In 1978 alone, there were 250 *fedayeen* attacks, killing 245 people, the majority of whom were Palestinians willing to accept a two-state solution.[24] And as we have seen, when Israel attempted to reach a new accord with Jordan after expelling the PLO from Lebanon, pro-Jordanian Palestinians who pressed Arafat to accept a Palestinian–Jordanian confederation were likewise threatened with death. For much of the last quarter century, one's life remained the price a Palestinian willing to countenance partition had to contemplate paying.

Until the *intifada*, the Israelis, similarly, were neither willing nor able to relate politically to an autonomous Palestinian nationalist movement on the West Bank and Gaza. Where the PLO relied on illicit murders by its appointed agents, Israel, as the power in place, could use jail, house arrest, and deportation. Those who called out for a Palestinian state, even those affiliated with the PLO, had to face not only physical threats from their own community, but harassment and violence from the Israelis as well. Palestinian nationalists in the National Guidance Council, for example, who demanded an independent state at peace with Israel but opposed autonomy, were terror targets of some members of the Gush Emunim, and then later deported by the Israeli government. The modalities differed, the politics did not.

Breaking the Triangle

Jordan, Israel, and the PLO all did their part to prevent the Palestinians of the West Bank and Gaza from developing a collective voice. The Palestinians' stones announced the birth of a nation – not a people dispersed around the world dreaming of return to an imaginary homeland, but a nation living daily life on territory it could call its own. The *intifada* sought to break out of the paralytic triangle, to assert the political primacy of this occupied territorial platform and its people, to force the Israelis, the Jordanians, and the PLO to make the West Bank and Gaza into a new nation-state.

The *intifada*'s roots lie in two decades of Israeli occupation that, although it did not inflict mass material suffering, systematically humiliated and repressed an entire people. The extraordinary level of popular support it elicited derives from this fact. But why in 1987, after two decades of Israel occupation? The *intifada* began, like many political upheavals, as a youth rebellion, the expression of those who came of political age during the Israeli occupation. It was the by-product of precisely those Israeli strategems intended to control the Palestinians: education at home for employment abroad and military destruction of the PLO abroad intended to weaken the Palestinians at home politically. A road accident in Gaza set the action in motion. But it was the conjunction of these two forces – rising expectations and falling political possibilities – that set a mass of young people to action.

Under Israeli rule, the Palestinians built schools and new universities and reopened the old ones closed by the Jordanians. (However, the Israelis refused to allow the Palestinians to build a major university in Jerusalem.) Because of the explosion of secondary and university education, the Palestinians have become the most educated Arab population in the Middle East, with nominal education levels approaching those of Israel.

When asked his impression of the next generation of Palestinians, Meron Benvenisti, the Israeli planner, told us there was a shock of recognition when he met them:

> They look Jewish. They adopt all the attributes that we tend to associate with Jews. They are very vital. . . The most important thing for them is to learn. They are threatened. . . The guard at the Ben-Gurion Airport was asked, "How do you know which car to stop?" he said, "I look into their eyes, and if I see Jewish eyes, I stop the car."

Israel's original intent had been to prevent Palestinians from going abroad and being recruited by the PLO. Moreover, the Israelis also reasoned it would be easier to make peace with a better educated populace. But the strategy backfired; these domestic universities became nationalist theaters of immense importance. Student body elections, one of the only legitimate forms of political activity, were closely watched by everybody. Palestinian university students provided wave after wave of political organizers despite Israel's repeated closure of the campuses during periodic upheavals.

At the same time the youth of Palestine became more educated, their employment opportunities were increasingly restricted. Only one in eight graduates found the job for which he or she was trained.[25] Palestinian parents knew their children's success was likely to result in exile, often in the oil economies of the Persian Gulf.[26] The hemorrhaging of Palestinian talent was of such great concern that Jordan and al-Fatah began a program of paying unemployed West Bank university graduates a stipend of two hundred dollars per month just to remain where they were, to stay on the land, to be "steadfast."

When the Gulf oil economy crashed in the 1980s and opportunities throughout the region dwindled, Palestinians were the first to be let go. The impact in Jordan, highly dependent on the flow of wages and subsidies from the oil-rich states, was particularly pronounced. As Jordan's economy slowed, there was a surge of popular resentment against the Palestinians, who held many of the best jobs. King Hussein, fearful of the young West Bank Palestinians, made it difficult for them to study, work, or reside in the country.

"It's for the benefit of the Palestinian people," a Palestinian teacher in Jerusalem explained to his class. "If all the young men will emigrate, nobody will stay except the old people." "No, I don't agree," challenged one of his high school students. "The reason for the restrictions are in order to avoid the establishment of an independent Palestinian state." In the eyes of this seventeen-year-old, King Hussein was trying to show the Palestinians they couldn't move without him. As usual, those whose parents were supportive of the Jordanian regime or who had friends within it were allowed to leave to study in Paris or Amman.

Credentialed Palestinians were piling up in the occupied territories without the jobs for which they believed they were qualified. With the safety valve of emigration gone, young Palestinians faced a future as migrant workers on Israeli hotels and construction sites.[27] King Hussein had caged the youth, precisely those who were the object of the PLO's organizing drive. As the downturn continued, the PLO and Jordan's ability to make patronage payments was diminishing. As standards of living began deteriorating in the territories, Israel was engaging in new forms of collective punishment, confining residents of whole neighborhoods and even cities to their homes for days and weeks at a time. Israel was also intruding deeper into Palestinian daily life through computer networks and identity cards, with permits to build, import, buy, and plant issued on the basis of political information in the computerized files.[28]

Young Palestinians were embarrassed to watch their own people build the roads and settlements honeycombing the lands they hoped one day might constitute a Palestinian state. By 1987 a generation had grown up on the West Bank that had known only Israeli rule. They found it strange, when they visited their relatives in Amman, to have to stand up at the movie theaters for the national anthem pledging loyalty to King Hussein. "You are obliged to stand," one student explained to us, "because if you don't stand, they will kick you and put you in prison." This generation had only known friends, brothers, and neighbors thrown into jail for days at a time without charge, beaten, deprived of sleep, left to stand with a bag tied over their heads, humiliated in countless ways on the possibility that they had helped build a stone barricade across the street, had talked to the wrong person, had held the outlawed Palestinian flag. They had become impatient with their parents, the PLO outside, the entire Arab world. "Arafat, he is not living under occupation," one Palestinian student, his eyes angry gemstones, told us. "*We* are living under occupation. He is not injured in the demonstrations. We are injured, yes."

This new Palestinian generation disturbed the traditional elites. Faiq Barakat, the moustached and aged pro-Hashemite head of Jerusalem's Arab Chamber of Commerce, described the change among the youth:

> Young people do not have the experience to decide what is right or wrong. . . They were kids, and maybe not even born, and don't know the king. To them the king is nothing. But the king is something and something is better than nothing. This is the result of the Communists. Young people have been selfishly educated. Go to Bir Zeit University. They have been fed by foreign ideas . . . by Communists. . . There is no respect for teachers. . . Would they respect Arafat? I doubt it. They would lean back and put their feet up on the table.

A significant component of the *intifada*'s political leadership was drawn from faculty at the Palestinian universities, while their students – who had ongoing discussions and debates with their professors on how to conduct the struggle – provided its activists. Thus was theory put into practice and practice into theory.[29]

At the same time West Bank and Gazan material conditions were eroding, the political capacity of the PLO had been seriously damaged by Israel's invasion of Lebanon and the ensuing Palestinian civil war. Palestinians in the occupied territories watched their representatives outside try to maneuver as the degrees of freedom slipped away. The war forced Arafat into Hussein's arms. The Likud government, by refusing each the possibility of a territorial partition, had pushed the two together.

The chairman and the king slowly established the conditions of their collaboration. Both knew that King Hussein had almost no Palestinian popular support, whereas that for the PLO was overwhelming. Both knew that although Israel was not willing to deal directly with the PLO outside the West Bank, it would have to deal with the PLO inside because there was nobody else with whom to talk. Folded into a joint Palestinian–Jordanian delegation, the PLO could speak through local representatives. Arafat agreed that the Jordanians would begin to appoint mayors on the West Bank in consultation with the PLO. Israel, it was understood, would not object.

Hussein and Arafat each deeply feared the other. Hussein worried that a democratic Palestinian state joined to his own Bedouin-dominated monarchy could destabilize his regime. Past experiments with democracy had brought Jordan to the brink of civil war. The Palestinians of Jordan would naturally demand the same rights as their kin across the river. Arafat feared he would deliver the West Bank to King Hussein and then be dealt out of the solution. He therefore demanded the Palestinian entity be granted sovereignty before confederation; Hussein insisted upon confederation as the starting point. Terrified of a flood of radical Palestinian refugees, many of whom had fled his own regime in the past, King Hussein also made it clear he would not accept Palestinians from Lebanon or Syria.[30] Arafat must have been vulnerable indeed, for in the final negotiations in Casablanca in 1985, it was Hussein's confederation, not Arafat's sovereign state associated to Jordan, that won out. Taher Masri, Jordan's foreign minister, claimed this confederal agreement meant the PLO no longer insisted upon an independent Palestinian state, an interpretation the PLO vociferously repudiated.

There was little indication at this time that any significant political forces in Israel were willing to negotiate with the PLO. But Arafat feared that once pried from Israeli control, the territories would become a subordinate province in the Hashemite kingdom. The PLO chairman did not intend to substitute Jordanian "autonomy" for the Israeli plan he had so contemptuously spurned. King Hussein's announcement to Jordan's Royal Military Academy in 1985 that "it will not be long before . . . the Arab flag will fly over Jerusalem" could not have reassured Arafat. What of the Palestinian flag?

When known PLO supporters crossed the bridges over the Jordan River, they often received rougher treatment inside Jordan than they had from the Israelis. Hussein seized upon his accord with Arafat to reactivate his network of supporters on the West Bank, even going so far as to appoint a new "governor" of Jerusalem. The king sent for every member of Jerusalem's Higher Muslim Council, pointedly reminding them, in the words of one of its members, "We have the relationship with the PLO, not you. You are our representative, not the PLO's." When Arafat presented his list for the joint PLO–Jordanian delegation, King Hussein rejected more candidates than did the Israelis. Arafat was not strong enough to achieve a state by himself, but was also too weak to achieve it through King Hussein.

The Israelis were more than pleased to cooperate with the king. In late 1985, Israel began to appoint figures close to the Jordanian regime to replace the elected pro-PLO mayors they had deposed and sometimes deported just a few years before. Thus they chose Zafer Masri, head of the Nablus Chamber of Commerce, to assume that town's mayorship in December 1985. Masri, who took office with the PLO's tacit approval, was the cousin of Jordan's foreign minister and one of the wealthiest Palestinian businessmen on the West Bank.

Jordanian money began pouring into the West Bank again to rebuild the lines of Hashemite influence. Jerusalem's most influential representative in the Jordanian parliament returned home looking for signatories to a memorandum of support for the king. He also had thousands of dinar to disperse to institutions likely to support the king. With the diplomatic support of the United States, Jordan announced a development plan for the occupied territories in which wealthy Palestinians would be provided capital to start or expand enterprises under the rubric of "improving the quality of life."

Jordan, as a condition of its cooperation, demanded the PLO give up its formal place at the negotiating table and accept United Nations resolutions 242 and 338 recognizing Israeli sovereignty. But neither Jordan nor the United States was willing to give assurances about Palestinian self-determination. Just as Israelis disliked these resolutions because they were interpreted to imply a return of all occupied lands, Palestinians have always found them offensive in that they refer to them only as "refugees," not as a nation. They were, the Palestinians believed, a diplomatic recipe for Jordanian restoration, for something short of sovereignty.

In October 1985, Britain's prime minister, Margaret Thatcher, engineered a meeting between her foreign secretary, Sir Geoffrey Howe, and a joint Palestinian–Jordanian delegation including two members of the PLO Executive Committee known for their moderation – Muhammad Milhelm and Bishop Elias Khoury. But Milhelm, the former mayor of Halhoul, who had been deported by Israel, refused to sign a declaration renouncing armed struggle and accepting UN resolutions 242 and 338. To Hussein's acute embarrassment, the meeting fell through.

Now, it was not just Arafat's Hashemite rivals on the West Bank who pressed the chairman to moderation – his allies did as well. This time, a delegation was formed from Jerusalem including men firmly in the PLO camp, such as Hanna Siniora, the editor of Jerusalem's *Al-Fajr* and one of Arafat's proposed delegates to the joint negotiating team. When the delegation traveled to Amman to propose to Arafat that the PLO accept the UN resolutions in exchange for international acceptance of their "right to self-determination" and a PLO role in an international peace conference, the Israeli government stopped them at the River Jordan. When the PLO Executive Committee met in Baghdad in November 1985, it again refused to endorse the UN resolutions.

By February 1986, Arafat's rapprochement with King Hussein was becoming unglued. The United States had signaled its agreement to PLO participation in peace negotiations in exchange for PLO acceptance of the UN resolutions, as well as an explicit renunciation of armed violence against Israel. Hussein had assured the Americans he could deliver Arafat, but Arafat balked. Demanding U.S. recognition of the PLO as the sole legitimate representative of the Palestinians and Palestinian rights of self-determination, Arafat left for Hungary. Hussein lashed out at the PLO for squandering the opportunity and refused further negotiation until such time "as their word becomes their bond, characterized by commitment, credibility and constancy."

Not only did Arafat fear being a junior partner to Hussein, he was also threatened by more radical factions within the PLO, like George Habash's Popular Front for the Liberation of Palestine (PFLP), which understood this diplomatic maneuver as a traitorous capitulation to Western imperialism. In early March 1986, three months after assuming office, the newly appointed mayor of Nablus, Zafer Masri, was assassinated as he walked to his office. Habash's PFLP, which claimed credit for the killing, said the death sentence was carried out for Masri's complicity in a Jordanian–Israeli plot to destroy the Palestinian cause. Yet some Palestinians claim Masri was murdered with Arafat's consent as a warning to King Hussein, who had suspended his dialogue with the PLO just a month before.[31]

Hussein saw Arafat could not control the militias within the PLO, and as the PLO rebuilt its infrastructure in Jordan, including its capacity to smuggle explosives and train assassins, the king was becoming increasingly uncomfortable. Simultaneously the Israeli Labour Party proved too weak to bring Israel to the bargaining table. Ariel Sharon and other Likud politicians were actively suggesting making Jordan into a Palestinian state. Jordan began to expel the PLO from Amman and by that summer had shut down more than twenty PLO offices.

After the breakdown of Jordanian–PLO negotiations and Arafat's departure from Amman, Hussein called upon the Palestinians of the West Bank to replace the PLO leadership, accusing them of having more interest in "ruling than in regaining the territory." Israel, as addicted to the Jordanian option as the PLO was to armed struggle, again pressed for political "devolution" to the Palestinian cities. Shimon Peres, prime minister since 1984 in a "unity" government with Likud, proposed the West Bank mayors and delegates to the Jordanian parliament, rather than the PLO, negotiate on behalf of the Palestinians. But the Palestinians were of no mind to reject the PLO, nor to return to Jordan sovereignty.[32]

At the same time the Palestinians inside offered their fealty to the PLO, they understood it would be unlikely to engineer an end to the Israeli occupation anytime soon. They watched as the Palestinian question and the PLO became ever more marginal in the Arab world. Arafat was besieged on every side: by the Israelis who bombed PLO headquarters in Tunis in 1985, by the Jordanians who had shut down Arafat operations in Amman, by the Syrians who supported the ongoing Shi'ite and Druze siege of Palestinian refugee camps in Lebanon, by Palestinian rebels in Lebanon who rejected Arafat's leadership of the PLO, by the growing strength of the Islamic movement, which repudiated the PLO's nationalism.

The PLO's position in the Arab world was so weak that the Amman summit of Arab nations held in November 1987 discussed the Iran–Iraq War without even mentioning the Palestinians. At this meeting, Egypt – at peace with Israel – was readmitted without incident to the Arab world. When King Hussein, in his opening address, equated Israeli and Iranian "expansionism," characterizing both non-Arab states as "exploiting" religion to advance their evil purposes, the message was clear: it had become easier for the Arab states to live with Israeli occupation than with a militarized Islam. King Hussein affirmed his support for negotiations with Israel based on UN resolutions 242 and 338, a position the PLO still rejected. Yasser Arafat was personally snubbed by several Arab leaders and particularly the meeting's host, King Hussein. In Jerusalem, "You could hear women cursing in the street about how poorly Arafat was treated in the summit," one Palestinian told us.

Rejectionists – both Marxist and Islamic – were rising to challenge Arafat's leadership. In late November 1987 a hang glider pilot penetrated Israel's defenses, killing six Israelis at an army base. This action, conducted by the Popular Front for the Liberation of Palestine, which had refused to rejoin the PLO under Arafat's tutelage, electrified young Palestinians. The next day Palestinian teenagers jubilantly flashed six fingers for the six Israeli victims.

Radical Islam was also threatening al-Fatah's authority. Islamic Jihad, a radical new home-grown Islamic group based in Gaza, had begun a campaign of killing Israelis. Their terrorist raids included a hand grenade attack on Israeli soldiers of the Givati Brigade who were being sworn in at the Western Wall. Israel's systematic drive to crush Islamic Jihad in Gaza finally brought the Palestinians out into the streets.

In Gaza, an Israeli truck smashed into a car filled with Arab laborers, killing four of the passengers. The rumor spread among the Palestinians that this was no accident, but retaliation for an Israeli's being stabbed to death in the market two days before. The hatred the Palestinians carried that evening in the funeral procession set the streets on fire. Young men began to throw stones, not just here or there, but everywhere. The *intifada* quickly made its way from Gaza to the West Bank, from the refugee camps to the city centers. The children had grown up with countless humiliations and their parents' helplessness. They had listened to their parents' numinous stories of what life was like before the Zionists came and their insistence that, like their parents, they must endure. But the children were ashamed. Late in 1987 they converted their shame to rage.

Violence is the angry language of the voiceless. The Israelis, the Jordanians, and the PLO all played their part in denying the Palestinians of the West Bank and Gaza a legitimate way to speak for themselves. These Palestinians waited and let others speak for them. But as that outside voice weakened, they became enraged as one Arab regime after another betrayed them. They began to question the efficacy of the PLO's heroic words and its military strategies. Parents grew impatient as their hair thinned and grayed, and still they had nothing to promise their children except a life monitored and supervised by Jews, and hard choices between living at home and making something of oneself in a world outside Palestine.

The young Palestinians refused to remain passive players who would endure the occupation's indignities while PLO diplomats abroad made "legitimate" representations on their behalf. In one well-known poem, "freedom fighters" sit in the sidewalk cafés of Paris writing military communiqués on the back of packages of expensive Marlboro cigarettes. When the PLO operated out of Beirut, stories filtered back about its leaders' lavish dinner parties, the imported whiskey, the jewels they bought their wives and girlfriends. "The age of dogs is a long time," was a common saying about the PLO among Palestinians in the diaspora.

To many of the younger generation, the PLO seemed impotent, corrupt. The first generation of Palestinians had placed their hopes in Arab nationalism; the second in the military strategy of the PLO. The third generation was unwilling to wait for Arafat, to return to live under King Hussein, or to endure the rest of their lives under the Israelis. Out of a desperate pragmatism, a majority supported an independent Palestinian state.[33]

Sticks, Stones, and Knives

With the *intifada*, the Palestinians rose up as a whole people, for the first time since 1948. After two decades, they had developed a network of institutions that could organize masses of people for resistance.[34] Tens of thousands of young men and women daily engaged Israeli troops, showering them with rocks, curses, and Molotov cocktails. The *intifada* changed the language of violence, from outside military aggression to civilian resistance from within. Ibrahim Dakkak, a central player in the National Guidance Committee, saw it this way: "The Israeli soldier, so confident in past defeats of Arab nations, is now unable to defeat a child on the street."

Given the large contraband market in Israel, it was certain that Palestinian radicals had large amounts of arms. Although Palestinians used firearms against Arab "collaborators," they did not initially use these "hot" weapons, as they call them, against the Israelis. The Israeli soldiers, in turn, maneuvered with limited fire power and a massive amount of brute force: single rifle shots, beatings, and detention were their predominant replies. It was a ritualized game in which the Palestinians voluntarily absorbed the greater share of pain so that the conflict could continue. To protect themselves, the Palestinians had only their agreement to restrict the use of weaponry, their value as fellow human beings, and their ability to convey an image of the Israelis as apparent barbarians. It was violent theater by the weak, a repertoire between the hallowed tradition of armed resistance and the alien option of nonviolence, associated predominantly with Christians.

Still Israelis had their faces lacerated by stones, their skin burned by petrol bombs, their flesh cut open by knives. Many Israeli soldiers acted with restraint, attempting to avoid engagement after being stoned, spat at, and cursed. Many hated running after Palestinian women and children who, confined for days in their homes, snuck out into the fields at night to collect a few tomatoes to replenish their barren larders. But there were also enraged soldiers who smashed windows, furniture, and bones after having spent weeks at this distasteful duty. And however restrained most Israeli soldiers were, the logic of popular defiance against state order made indiscriminate repression and growing hatred inevitable. Good soldiers became bad policemen. In the Israeli detention camps many claimed torture was becoming routine. Israeli psychiatrists and social workers confided that the endless, ugly job of subjugating a civilian population to Israeli will had driven dozens of young soldiers to suicide.

Israelis have always found expressions of Palestinian nationalism profoundly threatening. Once the *intifada* began, a large part of the confrontation was over the display of the Palestinian flag, which the Israelis contemptuously dismissed as the "PLO flag." Dozens of young Palestinians died tying its colors to the power lines. Even its colors were taboo. One Palestinian woman, an Israeli soldier told us, hung three sheets out to dry on the line, conveniently dyed green, red, and black. If the soldier left the sheets hanging, he would look stupid. If he tore them down, he would look stupid. He tore them down. Several soldiers beat a Palestinian, it was alleged, because he had a Palestinian flag tattooed on his arm. After he had been repeatedly kicked and punched, the soldiers took a sharp instrument and cut the offending image out of his arm.[35] In the late summer, Palestinians put slices of watermelon, a fruit with all the appropriate colors, in their windows.

It was contest over representation, over the writing of a nation's name on the wall. Or writing it out. In East Jerusalem, Palestinians painted the Star of David or menorah on trash dumpsters, or on the sidewalks to be walked upon. Each faction's activists spray-painted slogans on every available surface. For years, Palestinians were routinely rounded up and made to paint them out. One Palestinian man, when asked to paint out some PFLP and Islamic resistance grafitti in Arabic on his exterior wall, asked the soldier, "Why? You can't read it.[36] What difference does it make? I paint it out in white and they paint in black and I paint it out with red and they paint it in green." "Because we are in control," the Israeli soldier told him.

Before the uprising, Israelis had largely ignored the local Palestinian population. Most Knesset members, who had never been to Palestinian towns and villages, tended to see their conflict with the Palestinians as an extension of that with the surrounding Arab states. As long as violence was engineered from outside, this fiction could be maintained. But the enemy at home had now distinguished itself in no uncertain terms. Where once the Israelis viewed the Palestinians with indifference and contempt, now they feared them, and many, in a certain way, began to respect them as well.

Large segments of the Israeli public understood there was no returning to the status quo. A territorial divorce, a political settlement, was imperative. Those Israelis who rejected this vision tried to assimilate the uprising to the larger struggle with the surrounding Arab states, nothing new. Prime Minister Shamir claimed it was a war against the existence of Israel, not a struggle against occupation.[37] Defense Minister Rabin told the Knesset Foreign Affairs and Security Committee that the uprising was just a continuation of Israel's 1982 war in Lebanon. "I'm not sure any political process is going to end the violence," Foreign Minister Moshe Arens remarked in 1989, "unless we retreat into the sea. That would certainly end the violence."[38]

Graffiti in the Muslim Quarter during *intifada*, 1993.

However, that these efforts at externalization failed is indicated by the restraint with which Israelis operated on the streets of Palestine. After scores of Palestinians died in the *intifada*, essayists for the PLO's magazine, *Filastin al-Thawra*, declared, "Israel is a country with no values."[39] Yet by any historical comparison, and particularly any regional comparison, Israel's response was restrained. No villages were razed. Deportations were few. Nor were many Palestinians killed relative to the size, duration, and depth of the provocation. When the Romanian regime was challenged in 1989, for example, it killed thousands of its own people in a few weeks' time, dumping them into mass graves. In the Los

Stars of David with bullet holes painted on the walls in East Jerusalem, 1993.

Angeles "uprising" of 1992, the American police and National Guard killed dozens of looters and arsonists in a few days. Although the Israelis were too civilized to carry out the carnage required to bring the Palestinians to heel, neither were they yet courageous enough to take the political risks necessary to allow these people to govern themselves.

Economics as War

When it becomes part of conflicting national claims to territory, economics is never left to private preferences; rather it is subordinated to and becomes an instrument of power.[40] It has always been thus in Palestine. The *intifada*'s basic strategy was economic war. It tied down large numbers of the best Israeli troops in police duties, pushing up military budgets, cutting into basic training time. It began to cut off the West Bank and Gaza as markets for Israeli goods and as suppliers of low-cost labor. It dramatically reduced the flow of tourism and foreign investment. Through mass Palestinian resignations from its administration of the West Bank, it increased the cost of governing the territories by forcing the Civil Administration to employ Israelis at higher wages. And through tax resistance, it cut into the revenues the Israelis extracted from the Palestinian populace. In its first year, the *intifada* all but wiped out Israel's economic growth.

The Palestinians provided the Israeli economy with a large captive market. In January 1988, Hanna Siniora, editor of *Al-Fajr*, proposed that, wherever they could, Palestinians should stop buying Israeli products. The place to begin, he suggested, was Israeli cigarettes. Only Arab, and particularly local Palestinian, smokes, like those produced by Jerusalem Cigarettes, were appropriate. Palestinians made it more costly for Israelis to take their products into the West Bank and Gaza. After a few months of stonings, many Israeli distributors of car parts, kitchen ware, and washing machines were afraid to vend their products in what they now considered "Indian" territory. In February 1989, the Palestinians took yet another step toward disengagement, giving Palestinian shopkeepers one month to remove all Israeli products from their shops. Although Israeli products started returning to the West Bank and Gaza under false names, the boycott of Israeli producers cost the food industry tens of millions of dollars in sales.

Small Palestinian firms started to pop up, offering chocolate, biscuits, *hummus, tehina,* and yogurt.[41] In some cases, even though overall Palestinian exports to Israel dropped radically, they even penetrated the Israeli market. The Lagazel Macaroni firm in Beit Sahur, for example, sells its spaghetti in Israel. The lettering on the package is entirely in Hebrew; the seal indicates that the rabbis have approved it as kosher. Only the colors – the black, red, white, and green of the Palestinian flag – indicate its owner's nationalist sympathies. In their official complaint, Israel's angry manufacturers demanded to know whether the display of these colors violated the law. Shouldn't all packages produced by Arabs in the occupied territories be labeled in Arabic so unwary Israeli shoppers would know what they were eating?[42]

It was one thing to remove Israeli products from Palestine, another to keep Palestinian workers out of Israel. Ever since the PLO was founded, political activists had tried to prevent Palestinians from working for Israeli employers. But without jobs to offer at home, they were always unsuccessful. The *intifada* organizers nonetheless wanted to break the flow of Palestinian labor to Israeli employers. The roadblocks marking off "liberated" zones were just as much designed to keep Palestinian workers in as Israeli troops out.

Throughout the *intifada*, Palestinian workers nonetheless continued to migrate great distances to work in Israel.[43] Although the *intifada* could not control whether Palestinians worked, it could influence when they worked. Every week or so, when there were national strikes, Palestinian buses, trucks, and taxis did not move. The flow of workers to Israel would be reduced to a trickle. Construction companies in Jerusalem tried to recruit local Palestinians who could walk to work. Hotels faced similar problems. The Palestinian truck owners who haul gravel

Palestinian truckers near the Damascus Gate, East Jerusalem, 1984.

and stone to Jerusalem refused to break ranks. The few who tried had
their trucks burned.

Ironically, it was the changing geography of terror by Palestinians who
reject a two-state solution and the Israeli response that finally reduced
the movement of Palestinian workers into the Israeli economy. As the
intifada ground on, more and more Israelis were being attacked and
murdered within Israel proper, particularly within Jerusalem. "Death to
the Arabs" was scrawled everywhere in Jerusalem. Palestinians were
increasingly let go from jobs where they were in intimate contact with
Israelis. Restaurants, for example, fired their Palestinian food handlers,

replacing them with recent Russian immigrants. After Palestinian rejectionists started killing Israelis inside the "Green Line," Israel closed the occupied territories completely in the spring of 1993. Jerusalem was made off limits to almost all Palestinians from the territories. Although thousands of Palestinians were eventually allowed back into Israel to do construction, factory, and agricultural work, Israel had radically reduced the flow of Palestinian workers into its economy.

Israelis and Palestinians fought a fierce fiscal war. Although the Israelis had always been able to rely on Palestinians to work as police in the military occupation, they had never been able to recruit them to collect taxes. (The Palestinians rightly claimed their taxes went to finance their own military occupation.)[44] Once the *intifada* began, it became a badge of honor for Palestinians to refuse to pay Israeli taxes altogether. Tax resistance initially caused an enormous drop in revenue collection on the West Bank, and in Jerusalem, too.

In these revenue wars, the Israelis demanded proof of payment of taxes for every license, every permit for which Palestinians applied. The Israelis swept daily through the West Bank impounding cash, merchandise, and tangible assets like television sets, carpets, electrical appliances, and automobiles, as well as arresting those who had failed to pay. The confiscations were often arbitrary, exorbitant, and sometimes accompanied by brutality. In March 1989, Issawiya, a Palestinian village suburb of Jerusalem, suffered a five-day curfew where residents were allowed to leave their house one hour each day, as police and soldiers backed up government agents going house to house in search of withheld tax payments.[45] Israel ultimately broke the tax revolt.[46]

In Jerusalem the government suddenly stopped paying old-age pensions and child allowances to thousands of Palestinians while they checked the eligibility of each case.[47] Over a thousand people were struck from the city's national insurance rolls. The city "discovered" that Israeli civil administration had been paying the water bill of Shuafat, the one refugee camp within the city's borders, and informed the camp's residents that someone else would have to pay up.

Jerusalem's hospitals had long been a medical haven where Palestinians throughout the West Bank had sought treatment unparalleled in the Arab world. Even Jordanians presented themselves as West Bankers in order to get medical care. Israeli physicians used to accommodate this charade. After the *intifada*, Israel made it difficult for Palestinians to go to their clinics, and when they did, they made them pay full price for the services they received. Subvention of Palestinian patients virtually stopped.

Surprisingly it was the traditionally conservative Palestinian merchant class who proved able to mount the most concerted resistance.[48] As a

A main intersection in Arab East Jerusalem during a strike day, 1991.

demonstration of national solidarity, every afternoon, all Palestinian businesses – except pharmacies, physicians, newspapers, and bakeries – were shuttered everywhere. On national strike days, the shops were closed all day. Control of time, like control of space, became a battlefield. The crucial test was in Jerusalem, where the first major commercial strike went on for forty-one days straight. After breaking thousands of locks with crowbars, hacksaws, and sledgehammers, and then leaving the stores open and unguarded overnight; after imposing financial penalties and throwing shopkeepers into prison, the Israelis gave up, admitting they had lost "the shopkeepers' war."

In the main, the Palestinian shopkeepers proudly followed the rhythms of resistance.[49] Unlike during the Palestinian uprising in the 1930s, there was considerable cooperation between urban merchants and workers.[50] True, in several cases uncooperative Palestinians' shops were firebombed by their own people. Nonetheless, in the hypercharged and expectant atmosphere, it did not take many threats or much social pressure to mobilize the merchants against the full weight of the Israeli army. Fatah was not a socialist party and looked with favor on the bourgeoisie, seeing in the merchants a critical mass base for the uprising.[51] Through whatever combination of force and suasion, the Palestinian leadership demonstrated that both the merchants and the masses were with them. Consequently, after three- or four-day strikes, with people itching to get into Jerusalem to replenish vital supplies, Jerusalem's police would punitively close off the main street to traffic. If the Israelis couldn't keep business going as usual, they would make normal business as difficult as possible; the strikes, just like the physical confrontations with the Israeli soldiers, inflicted most economic damage on the Palestinians themselves.

These apparently irrational tactics were part of the ongoing struggle to control the organization and meaning of Jerusalem's time and space. In the spring of 1989, the Unified Leadership of the Intifada decided to initiate daylight savings time to mark summer in the newly declared state of Palestine. This was a full month before Israel would begin its own "summertime." In East Jerusalem, policemen would ask Palestinians for the time. If they answered according to Palestinian time, their watches were sometimes seized and smashed with billy clubs. One Palestinian from Silwan who answered, "Four o'clock" was made to stand in the street for an hour until it was 4:00 P.M. according to Israeli clocks.[52]

Leaving its constituency unable to work in Israel or to work very much at home, the *intifada* imposed an unparalleled austerity. In East Jerusalem and its surrounding Palestinian suburbs, the hard times were evident. In some refugee camps, there was real hunger, due to a shortfall of rations and constant curfews. Jerusalem restaurants frequented by Palestinians were virtually deserted. East Jerusalem's stores catering to tourists were empty. The National Hotel, once the favored haunt of King Hussein, was an empty cavern, its waiters hovering in the lobby and downstairs restaurant. Weddings, which used to go on for days, were reduced to simple marriage ceremonies, without the usual dowries and gifts of gold jewelry. Lavish celebrations would be unseemly and most could not afford them. Though merchants reduced their prices, many Palestinian families still couldn't afford to buy their children's clothing in the stores. Even middle-class mothers began to knit their children sweaters for the winter.

The Confessions of a Palestinian Nationalist

Unemployed and underemployed Palestinians needed to eat. It was only natural for Dr. Jad Isaac, a balding agronomist, to come to the aid of his countrymen. Isaac, a Palestinian Christian and a professor at the Bethlehem University, lives in Beit Sahour, a middle-class town adjacent to Bethlehem. When we visited in 1989, Isaac had just been released after six months of administrative detention in one of the sprawling prison camps Israel established for thousands of Palestinian street fighters and political activists, many of whom were imprisoned without trial. Isaac had been arrested, he told us, for being a "threat to the security of

Israel." The Israelis claimed that this man with no previous record of militant political engagement, let alone terrorism, this scholar–farmer who had links to one of the finest rural research institutes in the United States, was an organizer of the *intifada*.

Jad Isaac *had* in fact helped to sow the seeds of revolution – tomato seeds, squash seeds, okra seeds, cucumber seeds, watermelon seeds. Together with a number of local friends, he had purchased seeds and seedlings, fruit trees and fertilizer, tubing for drip irrigation, chickens and chicken coops. Many of the products were bought on the West Bank, but some were actually purchased in Israel. The idea was simple. Some people had no work at all, and others only worked in the mornings. Everybody was strapped for money and some people could no longer afford a proper meal. Small household plots could at least provide a safety net for families who had to make do with less and less.

Jad Isaac and his friends had reasoned right. In the first month they were open in 1988, thousands of Palestinians made their way to "the shed," where Isaac and a string of volunteers distributed their wares. Each week people came from farther away. Each day they came with new demands – pesticides, advice on irrigation, proposals to raise rabbits. Isaac organized a network of extension agents to help the growing number of new household farmers.

As something like 100,000 people passed through this makeshift agricultural extension center, Isaac and his staff were increasingly harassed by the Israeli military. There were one-day administrative detentions and threats of longer prison sentences. Isaac's home was put under surveillance. One afternoon, Israeli soldiers stormed into his home and arrested him in front of his terrified children. Shortly after midnight, he was released in Bethlehem to walk home alone to his worried family. The military erected a checkpost outside his home, with jeeps coming and going all night, searchlights scanning his home, telephone lines repeatedly disconnected. Over and over again, Isaac and his colleagues were summoned for questioning at military headquarters in Bethlehem. They were repeatedly made to wait for an entire day and then sent home without having been questioned. Finally, on June 5, 1989, after yet another degrading day spent at military headquarters, and reportedly at the urging of Mayor Freij of Bethlehem and Mayor Atrash of Beit Sahour, Isaac and his colleagues decided to close "the shed."

The *intifada* made survival a political issue. The more Palestinians who could eat without working for Israelis, without selling on the Israeli or Jordanian markets, without having to pass through Israeli- and Jordanian-controlled bridges, without paying taxes, without getting patronage funds from Israel or Jordan, the more difficult it would be for Israeli troops to punish the population into quiescence. Jad Isaac was not a subversive by any conventional standard. Indeed, a highly placed member of the Israeli intelligence community expressed his regret to us that such a man had to suffer half a year of imprisonment. It was, he said, a mistake made in the heat of confrontation. But he was wrong. Like it or not, Isaac is a revolutionary, if by revolutionary we understand the transformation that was taking place in the Palestinian understanding of themselves.

Isaac tends to express himself in biological metaphors. "The *intifada*," he told us, is "like a gene. It is more than rock-throwing, more than not paying taxes, more than solidarity. It is taking back the land. It's going back to the land. All our life is humiliation. Only the land will bring us back to self-respect."

Spoken like a Zionist. A. D. Gordon (1856–1922), one of the most important ideologues of the kibbutz movement, said exactly the same thing back in 1920. "It is life we want," he wrote,

> no more and no less than that, our own life feeding on our own vital sources, in the fields and under the skies of our Homeland. . . We come to our Homeland in order to be planted in our natural soil from which we have been uprooted, to strike our roots deep into the life-giving substances. . . We must study the soil and ready it for our transplantation.[53]

In his primitive experiment in populist agricultural extension, the Palestinian agronomist was seeking economic autonomy. Just as *kibbutzim* were meant to enable Jews to survive on the land without competition from cheap Arab workers who would surely underbid them in the labor markets, these household gardens were meant to provide a small margin of independence from the Israeli economy.[54] Dr. Isaac and others also opened an experimental cow farm that would show people how to feed cows their excrement. The Israelis shut it down, too. "We have a joke," he told us, his mouth turning mischievous. "The cows were arrested because they belong to a subversive organization. The cows admit this. They say P-L-mOO, P-L-mOO."

Dividing Zion

For two decades before the *intifada*, Jerusalem was relatively tranquil. Arab violence was usually executed by Palestinians who did not live in Jerusalem.[55] Though Israel expropriated large amounts of private land from local Palestinian landowners, Jews could walk without fear on the eastern side of the city. Every Shabbat, with restaurants and movie houses closed on the Jewish side, the Old City filled with Israelis looking for Palestinian needlework, *hummus*, the rich meat of pistachios and olives, painted ceramics, and, for a few, hashish from Lebanon. They were all drawn to this dirty stone warren with its unexpected passages, its unseen eyes, the wrinkled blush of apricot and sugared pastry skins gleaming against the gray stone, the mounds of Bedouin tapestries carted across the deserts, burnished brass spitoons and samovars, the ugly ferment of rotting fruit and urine, traces of ground cardamom folded into coffee brewed to a consistency of fine mud. This square fortress provided one of the few escapes for Jews with precious time and nothing to do.

In the dense crowds of the Old City's *shuk* it would have been easy for a Palestinian to shove a knife between the ribs of an Israeli soldier on leave and slip away into a dark passage leading over rooftops or through small secret vegetable gardens. But it didn't happen. Even at night, it was not unusual to see an Israeli couple moving languorously through its shuttered alleys to the other side. By Damascus Gate, Arabs and Jews ate watermelon slices and drank mint tea in the dry summer nights in open air tents. Unlike those in Hebron and Ramallah, Palestinians in Jerusalem did not pose a serious security threat to the state of Israel.[56] In the 1970s, the gun shops that once thrived here had shut their doors and closed their basement shooting galleries as the Jewish citizens of the city trusted in the efficacy of the police and the passivity, if not the goodwill, of their Arab neighbors. In the immediate aftermath of Beirut, Jerusalem and its environs were quiet. Slowly, bit by bit, it seemed the old "Green Line" was fading.

Teddy Kollek breathed a proud sigh of relief when the *intifada*'s first bloody confrontations passed his city by. Palestinian attacks came later, less frequently, and with less barbarity than elsewhere on the West Bank.[57] But the firelight of barricades burning in outlying Palestinian villages did penetrate the city.[58] Palestinian high school students faced off with stones, rock barricades, and burning tires just like their counterparts elsewhere on the West Bank. Large sections of Jerusalem became areas where Jews no longer went.

After the *intifada* began, Jerusalem became the city where Jews were most likely to be murdered by Palestinians during the uprising. Yet despite the disproportionate number of Jewish casualties in Jerusalem, of the hundreds and hundreds of Palestinians who have died at Israeli hands, almost none died in Jerusalem. Although there were shootings, beatings, strafing of buildings, intimidation, and arrests in Jerusalem, Mayor Kollek insisted that the government use police to maintain order, and they were more disciplined, less likely to beat indiscriminately, more reluctant to open fire than soldiers.[59]

The *intifada* cleaved Jerusalem back in two. The organization of Palestinian violence, by opportunity and design, redrew the old "Green Line," the barbed wired and mined strip dividing Jordanian and Israeli Jerusalem from 1948 to 1967. Jews living in the new neighborhoods beyond the old border were stoned, their cars vandalized. Hundreds of cars parked in Israeli neighborhoods abutting Palestinian areas had their windows smashed, tires slashed, and interiors torched. Many of the Palestinian political murders of Jews were carried out along the old boundary zone, known to Israelis as "the seam."[60] Property values near Palestinian areas dropped.

For most Israelis and Palestinians, movement into each other's areas was always self-conscious and slightly fearsome.[61] Because of the *intifada*, Jews stopped visiting the Old City. Tour companies no longer visited the site where King David first unified the twelve tribes of Israel because it lies in Silwan, a Palestinian neighborhood where disturbances were routine. Just as when Jerusalem was divided, Israeli students observed the Old City from a high vantage point outside because their parents did not want them to take the risk of venturing within. With the Old City and Bethlehem too dangerous for most Jews, restaurants, cafés, night clubs, and movie houses opened in Jewish Jerusalem on Friday nights for a nonobservant clientele with no place else to go. Jerusalem became once again what it was before 1967 – the end of the line.

As the *intifada* made its way into Jerusalem, Teddy Kollek was devastated. "He's one of the most intelligent Israelis," Ibrahim Dakkak said, "but he was lying to himself and to the Israelis saying that the city is unified. He knew well that it wasn't." "The city is divided," his ex–deputy mayor, Meron Benvenisti, told us. "Now Teddy Kollek and all that bullshit is swept away."

The mayor, who had just recovered from cataract surgery on both eyes, doggedly continued his daily rounds in Arab Jerusalem, often alone, without incident.[62] "I've stopped thinking," Kollek said. He briefly contemplated stepping down. But within weeks, the seventy-seven-year-old mayor proclaimed he would run one last time.

On February 28, 1989, Jerusalem held its first municipal election since the uprising began. The Palestinians of Kollek's united Jerusalem made it clear that they, too, were part of a nation under occupation, not an ethnic minority. Kollek would not remake them into de facto Israeli Arabs. Kollek's first experiment with neighborhood self-government for the Palestinians, A-Tur, was also one of the first neighborhoods closed by the Israeli army as its young people pelted Israeli cars with rocks and blocked the roads with burning tires. The *mukhtars* through whom Kollek once brokered his relationship to the Arabs had lost their prestige and power to neighborhood committees spawned by the *intifada*.

Kollek expected pragmatism to bring the city's Arabs to the polls. Certainly, he reasoned, the Palestinians understood that the right-wing alternative would be worse for them. And there were thousands of Palestinians on the municipal payroll.[63] They and their families could be counted on, surely.

The last leaflet before the election called for a "total strike, assuring the boycott of the crowds of our people in the capital of our country, the Holy Jerusalem, to the elections of Teddy Kollek." On election day, the Palestinians of Jerusalem mounted the most effective general strike ever. Salah al-Din Street, the main drag of East Jerusalem's central business district, was empty. With a strike on the Palestinian side of the city and a national holiday on the Israeli side, voting was conspicuous.

During the day, the polling places in East Jerusalem, guarded by soldiers, were virtually empty. Most Palestinians who voted came in a rush in the cover of darkness. In the event, the Arab vote was pitifully small, some 3 percent of those eligible, compared to 20 percent in 1983.[64] "Every Arab who voted is a hero and deserves a medal," Kollek said the day after the election.[65]

The city's Arabs denied Kollek the two or three seats their votes had provided him in the last election. For a brief moment, Kollek contemplated a minority government. Faced with the rising power of the non-Zionist *haredim* and the anti-Zionist Palestinians, he saw his worst nightmare coming true. In the end, Kollek decided to form a wall-to-wall Zionist coalition including a party to his left that wanted to extend greater civil rights and material equality to the Palestinians of East Jerusalem, and parties to the right that wanted to curtail them. Zion would be governed by Zionists.

The Capital of Palestine

To the outside eye, it seemed the *intifada* spread slowly to Jerusalem. The municipality's Arab workers continued to show up despite the strikes and the call for Palestinians to resign their positions on the Israeli payroll. Indeed they even asked the city to protect them – from both the Israeli Border Patrol and the Palestinian strike forces.[66] Arab employees even went to award ceremonies recognizing their service to the city as long as their names were not published nor reporters present at the ceremonies.

Jerusalem's street battles were less fierce and less frequent. By the uprising's second year, while the Israelis had locked a third of a million children out of their schools, Jerusalem's Arab schools continued to operate.[67] Hundreds of former Arab Jerusalemites who had been forced to find housing outside the municipality made arrangements for their children to study in Jerusalem.

Although the lopsided war of stone against steel may have raged more intensely elsewhere, Jerusalem was its political nerve center. The *intifada* didn't penetrate the city from the outside, it was led from Jerusalem from the outset. It was from this city that an initially uncoordinated popular rising was transformed into an organized social movement. It was in Jerusalem that Palestinian political elites created the Unified Leadership of the Intifada, the first domestic grouping of all major streams since Israel had disbanded the National Guidance Committee in 1982.[68] Unlike the National Guidance Committee, whose members were known to all, the Unified Leadership of the Intifada were invisible men and women, a rotating cast of anonymous figures who spoke for one party or institution or another.[69]

The Palestinians had always followed the lead of prominent personalities, often drawn from one of the dominant families. Years of institution building – creating associations of teachers, universities, workers, journalists, farmers, municipal officials, lawyers, students – had finally made it possible to create a new kind of leadership. "Charisma is no longer the key," Ibrahim Dakkak said. "One no longer talks about 'Mr.' and 'Mrs.', but rather of institutions working together." Dakkak felt the *intifada* had finally realized his own dream in forming the National Guidance Committee. "There is no difference between my aspirations and grievances and those of the *intifada*," he said. "The only difference is that I can put on a necktie and the *intifada* won't."

The very first organized demonstrations took place in East Jerusalem on December 19, 1987. Two days later, the first call for a general strike was made.[70] The merchants of Jerusalem began the first commercial strike, which became the model for the rest of the territories.[71] The very first political manifesto was issued from Jerusalem. The neighborhood and village committees formed to implement the leadership's directives were initially concentrated in the Jerusalem region.[72] The *intifada* leaflets were initially printed in Jerusalem, the leadership rotating its meetings across different apartments in East Jerusalem.[73]

In the uprising's first weeks, the Unified Leadership, imposed on the PLO in Tunis without prior consultation, made its decisions without even mentioning the PLO.[74] The shifting cast of leaders initially composed their demands locally, even rejecting items proposed by the PLO. They announced unequivocally that the *intifada* would continue until the establishment of a Palestinian state. A Palestinian leadership at home – identifying themselves as loyal to, yet independent of, the PLO – had decided to move, to push for an independent Palestinian state, without waiting for the PLO abroad. Like the National Guidance Committee before them, the leadership in the territories demanded that they, not the PLO abroad, be responsible for distributing funds in the occupied territories.[75] Because Israel eliminated successive ranks of local leaders, Tunis was eventually able to take political control of the *intifada*.[76] Nonetheless, the political initiative had shifted to Palestine. The Palestinians in Jerusalem composed their communiqués, then faxed them to Tunis or Baghdad, where the PLO edited them and transmitted them back.

The conversion of the *intifada* into a nationalist social movement, into a sustained civil uprising, depended upon the network of institutions – associations of merchants, social workers, teachers, workers, women, journalists, doctors, lawyers, students, nurses – that had developed over the last two decades of occupation, associations and organizations grounded in community life as much as in partisan politics. The *intifada* unleashed another organizing fever, a furious proliferation of committees – by occupation, by organization, by mosque, by town, by neighborhood, by block. This profusion of new associations, this initial chorus of nonpartisan voices, spoke in the name of Palestine.

The PLO's decision to accept a negotiated settlement meant the survival of its leadership would now depend on the strength of its political base inside Palestine, not in the refugee camps outside. But everywhere the PLO was under fire from the popular committees for the clientelistic and corrupt manner in which it distributed funds in the territories.[77] The Palestinians under Israeli occupation wanted more influence in the PLO outside; they demanded that the PLO be more democratic, less characterized by cronyism and patronage. In 1988, the domestic leadership proposed a government-in-exile in which they would have half the seats.[78] Arafat balked, but if he did not accommodate the locals, there was a danger they would go it alone. And there were important players within the PLO hierarchy, particularly given the large number of deported Palestinians, willing to support them. The American government was actively seeking to nurture a local Palestinian elite that could broker an agreement without the PLO's official involvement.

The *intifada* made it clear to Arafat that the Palestinians in the occupied territories would not allow him to operate in the same old way, that the Palestinians in Palestine demanded that the PLO represent and respect their multiple voices. In 1989, for example, Bethlehem's Mayor Elias Freij, whom many Palestinians have viewed as an accommodationist ally of King Hussein, proposed that the Palestinians announce a truce in the uprising. In exchange, the Israelis would agree to release Palestinian detainees, reopen the schools, and withdraw troops from Palestinian population centers. The Palestinians would demonstrate their discipline, would let Israelis taste the peace to which they could look forward in the event of a two-state settlement. A truce would rob the Israelis of provocation for repression.

Arafat raged against the idea, intimating that anybody who called a truce would be liable for assassination. Wafah, the Palestinian news agency, reported the chairman's rebuke of Freij. Anyone who proposed an end to the uprising, Arafat was reported to have said, "exposes himself to the bullets of his people."[79] Although Arafat's men outside claimed that he had never meant to threaten the mayor, that his comments were taken out of context, that the broadcast was in fact a fabrication,[80] West Bank Palestinians understood quite clearly what he had meant.

A number of Palestinians who disagreed with Freij complained to us about Arafat's threat. "It was the wrong time for such an idea," one Palestinian nationalist said. "But Arafat should not have threatened Freij. Any Palestinian has the right to speak about any topic he wants." Some Palestinians, "the national forces in the Jerusalem area," answered "President Arafat" with their own communiqué: We have "sacrificed hundreds of dead and thousands of injured and deformed and have tasted the worst of things . . . for the sake of forming an independent state under the leadership of the PLO." This sacrifice, they declared, gave "the local leadership the right to express what they see as suitable to put an end to the suffering of the people, without that affecting its absolute recognition of the PLO headed by President Arafat."[81]

Of course, they proclaimed, they did not agree with Freij's proposed truce or his proposal that elections be held before Israel recognized Palestinian right to self-determination and withdrew from the occupied territories. *But* they took exception to Arafat's threats against Mayor Freij. Surely Freij and his allies had only meant to advance the cause of peace and end the suffering of the Palestinian people. Wasn't Arafat committed to the same goals? "We've experienced pain in our souls," the leaflet read, because of President Arafat's "threatening with bullets and attempt to seal mouths. The President could have convinced the people to refrain from it without the use of such threats." If "democracy within the PLO" were to mean anything, not using violence against divergent opinions was its minimum guarantee. Arafat's threats, the leaflet complained, undercut the legitimacy of their own leadership. "Revolution until victory," it closed.[82]

King's Gambit

As more and more pro-Hashemites slipped into the shadows or aligned themselves with leadership of the *intifada*, King Hussein stopped paying patronage to maintain his own network of clients. And then after nine months of nationalist rising, on July, 31, 1988, Jordan's king formally renounced his claims to the West Bank. "Jordan is not Palestine," the king declared, "and the independent Palestinian state will be set up on Palestinian soil after liberation." Jordan, the king ingenuously declared, "never imagined that the continuation of legal and administrative relations between the two banks might constitute . . . an obstacle to the liberation of the occupied Palestinian land." The lower house of the Jordanian parliament in which the Palestinians of the West Bank were represented was disbanded. "We respect the wish of the PLO, the sole legitimate representative of the Palestinian people, to secede from us in an independent Palestininian state."[83]

Hussein's move was a king's gambit, an opening chess move in which one side sacrifices in order to secure room for maneuver. It was designed to put extraordinary material pressures on the West Bank Palestinians and political pressures on the PLO. Over twenty thousand Palestinians in the West Bank were receiving Jordanian salaries. Now the Jordanians would no longer pay wages or pensions, maintain schools, build housing, certify doctors and nurses, or give the high school examinations recognized throughout the Arab world. The oil slump had made the Palestinians more dependent than ever on employment and sales through the Jordanian economy. If the Jordanians closed the bridges to people and produce, and stopped issuing passports to West Bank residents as well, the Palestinians would be caged, much like their vastly poorer and stateless cousins in Gaza. Then there would only be low-wage jobs as "guest workers" in the Israeli economy, jobs that the leaders of the uprising were trying to persuade the Palestinians they should give up. At the same time that King Hussein magnanimously announced he would donate a month's salary to assist the Palestinians, Jordan radically reduced the volume of Palestinian agricultural produce allowed across the bridges, both to feed its own population and to be transshipped to other Arab markets. The PLO initially countered the king's gambit by taking their own enormous holdings out of Jordanian banks. This exacerbated Jordan's economic decline; in less than a year, the value of the Jordanian dinar plummeted to nearly half its former value.

Hussein's move generated extraordinary pressure on Arafat. Now Arafat would be solely responsible for taking the political risks necessary to regain part of Palestine. The PLO would have to act as the protogovernment for the West Bank. For the PLO to play that role, a political compromise of which it had not yet proved capable would be necessary. Arafat had been edging ever closer to a two-state solution, but if he made even more decisive steps toward compromise in the vacuum left by the Jordanians, he risked repudiation by large numbers of Palestinians in the diaspora. Hussein offered Arafat a political space, which, if he took it, would make him even more dependent on the Palestinians of the West Bank and thus more likely to have to endorse a negotiated territorial compromise.[84]

Hussein moved to show the West Bank Palestinians and the PLO that Jordan would have to be a player in any eventual negotiations. Significantly, the king kept the enormously wealthy and influential Jerusalem-based Islamic *waqf* and the Higher Muslim Council, the nerve center of his political network, in place. He still claimed their property and paid their salaries.[85] The king was betting Arafat would have to swallow his nationalist pride and cooperate with the Jordanians, both as an ally and as an intermediary to a confederal solution. Rumors circulated that, unlike the Israelis', Hussein's intelligence apparatus knew the composition of the Unified Leadership and that he had positioned assassins to eliminate them if the moment should become opportune. Hussein's strategy worked. Within two months, Arafat agreed once again to coordinate his actions with Jordan. By the beginning of 1989, Arafat was talking about raising both Palestinian and Jordanian flags in liberated Jerusalem.[86]

Hussein moved to prevent an upsurge of domestic Palestinian nationalism from engulfing his own predominantly Palestinian state. Demonstrations in Jordan in support of the *intifada* were ruthlessly suppressed. Over and over again, Hussein's troops swept through Palestinian refugee camps in Jordan, even picking them clean of stones. Hussein's grandfather, after whom he had been named, had lost custodianship of Mecca and Medina to the Saudis; his uncle had lost Syria to the French; he had lost Jerusalem to the Israelis. He stood on the last remaining portion of the dreamed Hashemite kingdom the British had promised to his grandfather during World War I. King Hussein didn't want to lose the little that remained to him.

Powerful forces within Hussein's regime advocated a "Jordanianization" of the state. The king's brother had long pressed him privately to rid himself of the Palestinian problem on the West Bank, to unburden the state of its obligation to act as an instrument of this fractious nation. Palestinians were being denounced in Jordan, in the words of one Palestinian commentator, as "foreigners" who "were enjoying the wealth of the country. . . The economy, commerce, and finance were in their hands. . . They possessed the keys to hotels and held festive gatherings with their wives or mistresses."[87] Ironically, Jews had often been similarly portrayed by their non-Jewish detractors in the countries where they lived. Jordanians who were not of Palestinian origin resented "the rapid expansion of those 'foreigners' in the banks, companies, and courts, alleging that a recommendation from one of them removes all obstacles, from contractors' deals to ministerial decisions." As a result of the king's decision, the Palestinians on his side of the river would have to decide where their loyalties lay: with the Hashemite regime in Jordan or with the new PLO state. There would no longer be an in-between.

Declaring Independence

The Palestinian children's stones both demonstrated the limits of Israeli power and restored Palestinian dignity. The shootings, the curfews, the beatings the Palestinians endured gave them both the right and the motive to demand a political solution. Their pragmatism made the Palestinians proud, even gave them a sense of superiority vis-à-vis the Israelis. The Palestinians felt that they had shed the PLO's taboos, its obsession with guarantees, its unwillingness to accept Israel. Now that they were the strong ones, they felt they could recognize the reality of Israel, in a way that the Israelis were still not able to recognize them. Against the backdrop of the *intifada*, concessions would not signify weakness. The uprising emboldened the Palestinians on the ground to push the PLO to translate their daily blood sacrifice into a two-state solution. "We do it," one *intifada* activist assured us. "It doesn't come from the outside. . . the *intifada* has forced the PLO to become moderate."

Immediately after King Hussein renounced his territorial claims and in anticipation of the upcoming PNC meetings in Algiers, Faisal Husayni brought together Palestinian political elites from almost every stream in Jerusalem to produce a Palestinian declaration of independence.[88] What was most revolutionary was the way in which this new state was to be legitimated, grounded in the very same United Nations resolution that first partitioned the area into a Jewish and an Arab state in 1947.

The Palestinians around Husayni intended to create not a government-in-exile, but a functioning government of and for the Palestinians in Palestine. They hoped to convert the *intifada* into something tangible, to achieve a diplomatic breakthrough by announcing "the birth of a Palestinian state in the homeland."[89] The Unified Leadership of the Intifada would announce the declaration in Jerusalem one week before the upcoming PNC meetings in Algiers, where it would be subsequently confirmed. Husayni was pressing Arafat to create a provisional government, headed by Arafat and Farouk Khadoumi as prime minister and foreign minister, while on the inside the Unified Leadership would appoint a legislative council made up of one hundred fifty Palestinians from the West Bank and Gaza.

But Arafat was not willing to be captive to the Palestinians in Palestine: to allow them, and not the PLO outside, to declare independence. Shamir's office dismissed the draft declaration, which had been prematurely revealed by the Israelis, as a "crazy and dangerous dream."[90] Days after Husayni had been released from months of detention, Shamir threw him back into jail for "subversive, hostile activities."[91]

The *intifada* put the Palestinian question back at center stage in the Arab world. Arafat had been inching toward public acceptance of a two-state solution, but each time rejectionists within the PLO had prevented his crossing the line. In the very first month of the *intifada*, Arafat floated a proposal for a government-in-exile claiming sovereignty over the West Bank and Gaza, which was withdrawn after it encountered intense opposition within the PLO. The Palestinian National Council meetings in Tunis in 1987 had reunified most factions, including some who had participated in the armed revolt against Fatah leadership in Lebanon. Arafat was now personally willing to negotiate with Israel without preconditions and to accept a two-state solution. Robert Friedman, a free-lance American journalist, told us that the Israeli intelligence analyst who determined Arafat was ready was under enormous pressure from his own government not to reach that conclusion, at least in public. The Labour Party did not miss Arafat's change in tone. Even before the *intifada* began, Shimon Peres informed his party the PLO appeared ready to negotiate with Israel.

However, Arafat's diplomatic maneuvering was tightly circumscribed by his need to maintain the support of those who rejected this solution, including many of the three million Palestinians in exile who still hoped one day to return to their homes. But the *intifada* finally provided Arafat with the motive and means to make his move. Six months into the *intifada*, Bassam abu-Sharif, one of Arafat's most trusted aides, released a document calling for a two-state solution based on UN resolutions 242 and 338, explicitly stating that the PLO no longer wanted to destroy Israel.[92] Rejectionists within the PLO were predictably outraged. Three months later, King Hussein cleared the field for the West Bank to become a Palestinian state. The Palestinians inside were clamoring for a declaration of statehood.

Arafat, who had always tied his willingness to accept Israel to assurances of Palestinian self-determintion, now felt he had to move unilaterally and unconditionally. He would wait only at great risk. In November 1988, the Palestine National Council met near Algiers. The initial draft of the proposed document was composed almost entirely by Palestinians from inside the occupied territories. Because of Arafat's opposition, the proposal for a Palestinian council inside the territories had to be scrapped. The different factions fought over every word. "Words, commas, semicolons and paragraphs," wrote Edward Said, "were the common talk of each recess, as if we were attending a convention of grammarians."[93]

On November 15, 1988, Chairman Arafat stood before the ecstatic gathering of delegates and declared an independent Palestinian state. "The Palestine National Council, in the name of God, and in the name of the Palestinian Arab people, hereby proclaims the establishment of the State of Palestine on our Palestinian territory with its capital Holy Jerusalem."[94] Women ululated. Intezar al-Wazir, the widow of Khalil al-Wazir, or Abu Jihad, one of Arafat's closest friends and his deputy, wept quietly in the front row.

In East Jerusalem, the streets were empty. Palestinian towns and villages were under curfew. People listened with rapt attention to radio broadcasts from neighboring Arab states. Raymonda Tawil, the Palestinian woman who had created the Palestinian Press Service, flew back from Paris. During the *intifada*, the Israelis had shut down her paper in Jerusalem, which, with its network of correspondents and informants, had been an indispensable source of information for international correspondents. Although Tawil feared being arrested for "incitement," she wanted to be in Palestine for the declaration of statehood. Because the Israelis had shut down all transportation between Palestinian towns on the West Bank, Raymonda only made it as far as Jerusalem. Israel deployed large numbers of troops to prevent Palestinians from flooding the streets with their pleasure. When the official announcement came, Raymonda Tawil stood in the lobby of the American Colony Hotel and cried. The Israeli media did not even cover the event. The Israeli writer and radio commentator David Grossman resigned over the refusal of the Israeli Broadcasting Authority to report this momentous turning point.

Dividing the land between Arab and Jew was injust, the declaration stated. Zionism had usurped their birthright. Palestine should have become a state like the others, but "yet again had unaided justice been revealed as insufficient to drive the world's history along its preferred course." The PNC still officially referred to Israel as the "Zionist entity," as a "fascist, racist, colonialist state built on the usurpation of the Palestinian land and the annihilation of the Palestinian people." Its political communiqué accompanying the declaration of independence affirmed its confidence "in victory on the road to Jerusalem, the capital of our independent Palestinian state."[95]

The document nowhere explicitly accepted Israel's right to exist, nor did it specify that the West Bank and Gaza would be the locus of the new Palestinian state, referring rather to "our Palestinian territory." And it still insisted on the Palestinian right of return to the lands lost in 1948.[96] Nonetheless, the PLO *implicitly* declared itself willing to live with the new reality. Nowhere was "armed struggle," the bread and butter of past PLO declarations, mentioned.

The declaration rooted the international legitimacy of the Palestinian state in UN resolution 181, the same 1947 resolution that had partitioned Palestine into a Jewish and an Arab state that Palestinians and the PLO had repudiated over the decades. As late as its 1984 meeting, for example, the PNC had reaffirmed the 1968 version of the National Covenant that declared "the partition of Palestine, which took place in 1947," "fundamentally invalid, however long [it] last[s]."[97] The PNC stated in 1988 that the new entity would be a "peace-loving State" that would adhere to "the principles of peaceful coexistence." The PNC now called for a peace conference under the auspices of the United Nations based on UN resolutions 242 and 338, which called for Israel to withdraw from territories captured in the 1967 war in exchange for mutual recognition of its Arab neighbors. The acceptance of these UN resolutions, which the PLO had rejected as recently as 1987, was the key to American dialogue with the PLO. However, the PLO hedged their first-time acceptance with an insistence that the conference be based, as well, on "the resolutions of the United Nations regarding the Palestinian cause." One of those resolutions (3379), of course, equates Zionism with racism. The PNC again formally supported confederation with Jordan.

Arafat walked away from the PNC meeting with overwhelming political support. The *intifada* had allowed him to move toward a two-state solution as *the* solution. In Jerusalem, Palestinians were proud that at last their chairman had moved toward the international consensus. "What more do the Israelis want?" one asked us. "Chocolate cake?"

Every year, the Palestinians have mourned the day the United Nations divided the land, making part of Palestine into a Jewish state, with strikes and demonstrations. In 1988, for the first time, the Palestinians in the West Bank and Gaza did not sadly commemorate Partition Day. Indeed, when Islamic militants, armed with rocks and Molotov cocktails, attempted to close stores to mark that black day, PLO supporters forcibly stopped them.

The majority of Palestinians interpreted the *intifada* as a victory for a political solution, for partition, for coexistence. But outside the occupied territories, even Fatah supporters still did not feel compelled to recognize Israel. After the PLO's supposed acceptance of UN Resolutions 242 and 338, al-Fatah's official newspaper, *Filastin al-Thawra*, continued to tell the faithful that it was not Israel, "the field leadership," that needed to be convinced, but the United States, "the strategic leadership." "The final decision in matters of peace and war, settlement and withdrawal . . . is nothing but an American decision and not an Israeli decision."[98] "The problem that faces us is not to convince the Jews of Israel and the Jews of the world that we are peaceful and that we don't have any thought of recovering the entire historical Palestinian land."

Israel, *al-Thawra* continued, "is . . . a state that totally follows and belongs to the U.S.A."

Although large numbers of Israelis were now willing to negotiate with the PLO, there were not enough. The unity government joining Labour and Likud was not ready to face the PLO as the legitimate Palestinian political vehicle. Ziad abu Zayyad's lifelong effort to build a conversation had come full circle. Israeli members of Knesset were now soliciting his help to convince their countrymen it was with the PLO that Israel must speak if peace were to be achieved. Abu Zayyad and other Palestinians told them that the PLO had already renounced terrorism, indicated its willingness to recognize Israel, formally accepted a two-state solution, accepted UN resolutions 242 and 338. But still, he told us, "they try to ask us what we can do for them to help them to build a front inside Israel which will support negotiating with the PLO. . . And we try to explain to them that the Palestinians have done their share."

The next year, in the wake of repeated Palestinian knife attacks in Jerusalem, the Israelis arrested Ziad and put him away for six months without trial. The Israelis charged he had helped prepare leaflets calling for revenge, distributed PLO funds, and maintained contact with the PLO abroad.[99] Held during the Gulf War, when the air-raid sirens first sounded, abu Zayyad told us he and his seven cellmates – all without gas masks – were sure they were going to die.[100] He taught his fellow Palestinian prisoners Hebrew. By the time he was released, abu Zayyad had lost a lot of weight and suffered a heart condition. "I lived like a dog and was fed like a dog," he told us.

Nothing Personal

When Arafat maneuvered the PLO toward agreement to a separate Palestinian state he abandoned the dream of liberation for which so many tens of thousands of Arabs had died. There was a heady sense of empowerment among the Palestinians of the West Bank and Gaza that they had forced the PLO's hand, that there was a connection between their daily defiance in the streets and the diplomatic pressures that the United States, Europe, the Soviet Union, and Egypt were now bringing to bear on Israel. The United States had dealt on a sub rosa basis with the PLO for a long time. Now for the first time, the United States was publicly in contact with its highest echelons.

Millions of Palestinians would have to let go of the dream of return. Palestinians in the refugee camps are organized into neighborhoods according to the towns and villages from which they fled or were dispossessed. In the Jordanian camps, a Palestinian researcher told us, the children had taken the *intifada* as a sign that they would be able to go home, to inhabit places only imagined from their parents' stories. The PLO's decision to declare a state and ground it in the United Nations resolution that divided Palestine was most momentous to those who had lost lands that they remembered reverently, but to which they would now never be able to return. After Arafat's move, Palestinian refugee camps in Lebanon polarized into armed camps where reporters who had covered the bloody beat in Beirut and El Salvador wouldn't go because their safety could not be guaranteed.

This letting go was made more palatable by the prominent role played by residents of the refugee camps in the *intifada*. Only the victims of partition could sanction its acceptance. The uprising inverted the status hierarchy among the youth. The teenagers of the refugee camps of Shuafat and Jalazoun, north of Jerusalem, and Dehaishe to the south, had the best throwing arms; they were the most audacious; it was they who took the rocks into the city centers, who clambered at night over the hills and the goat trails from village to village distributing leaflets, evading the searchlights of the Israeli patrols.

Even if the well-educated and well-heeled Palestinians of Jerusalem, Ramallah, and Bethlehem hadn't looked down their noses at the poor refugees who live in the camps and line up each day for casual labor or food rations from UNWRA, a vast social gap divided them. On the one side were families with large white-stone houses, who send their children abroad to study. On the other were the denizens of the camps, who daily commute long distances for minimum wages working in Israel's fields, kitchens, construction sites, and even military bases. In Jerusalem, Arabs charged with security violations more than likely live in a refugee camp.[101]

The refugee camps provided much of the uprising's leadership. The Palestinians hired as administrators, teachers, and health workers by UNRWA, the UN agency that runs the autonomous network of refugee camps, were particularly prominent. So were the children of the refugees who had moved up in the world through education.[102] Together with the mosques, the refugee camps provided one of the few bureaucratic structures connecting one place to another.

A few months after Arafat made his historic declaration of independence, we made our way to Jalazoun refugee camp. Massoud Safi, the camp's head, used to live in a village next to Ramleh, an Arab town near Tel Aviv. Ramleh, which the United Nations had slated as part of the Palestinian state, was a forward base for Transjordan's Arab Legion to attack Tel Aviv and the traffic up and down from Jerusalem. Because this Arab town behind advancing Israeli lines would provide irregular Arab forces to support Jordanian troops, Ben-Gurion wanted it cleared of its Arab inhabitants. As a result of Israeli shelling, heavy Palestinian civilian losses in the fighting, and a Jordanian retreat, the local residents began to flee in panic. The Israelis were able to orchestrate a mass exodus easily.

Tens of thousands of Palestinians walked with little food or water to the Jordanian lines, Safi and his family among them. In the hot dry July of 1948, the roads east were clogged with Palestinians, many of whom died of dehydration and disease before reaching safety. The Israelis were aware that this wave of refugees moving east from the demographic center of Israel would slow any westward attack by Jordanian troops.[103] After the war, the now largely Arab-free area was resettled with Jews.

Massoud Safi had paid a heavy price. His family's land had been seized in 1948 by the Israelis; his house in the refugee camp had been dyanamited into rubble; and his son had been killed in Israeli custody. Yet Safi was gladdened by Arafat's agreement to accept a state in the West Bank and Gaza. "But," he quickly added, "there remains the 1.2 million refugees who left in '48. They left their country and their villages exist till today. . . My village, which is near Ramleh . . . the United Nations recognized our right to return."

"Even though your son was killed in an Israeli prison, you would be willing to make peace with Israel?" we asked.

"Why not?" he replied.

> This is a public issue and if my son died or the son of my neighbor died, they are all my sons. . . Yasser Arafat is proposing peace. We are a people that . . . want a peace that will give us our rights, our just rights. And these are the feelings of every individual in the Palestinian people. We want to live in freedom without any guardians. We don't deny Israel, as Arafat recognizes. But at the same time, they have to recognize us as a people who have rights and they have to give us back our rights. . . Israel is founded. Nobody can deny it.

"So," we asked, "your family's land was confiscated in 1948 and you would be willing to accept, if you could have a Palestinian state, you would be willing to accept compensation for your land, your family's land?"

"Of course not. . . We don't accept compensation, but we accept people going back to their land. . . This is my own opinion . . . because I know that since '48, that no refugee would accept to give away his right to his country."

At this point, another Palestinian resident of the camp, Ahmed Hassam, his head wrapped in a red *keffiyah*, one lens of his eyeglasses cracked down the middle, interjected. "But things have changed," he half asserted, half questioned. Arafat had stated publicly that the right of return was open to negotiation. At the request of Defense Minister Yitzhak Rabin, Shmuel Goren, the Israeli coordinator of the territories, met with Faisal Husayni. Husayni told Goren that Israel had to accept the "right" to return, but how it was to be implemented was open to negotiation. Many would remain where they were. Others would want to be compensated. Less than a million, surely, he said. Israel, Husayni told them, should agree to resettle Deir Yassin, the village near Jerusalem where members of Israel's Revisionist militia had massacred the population in 1948.

Palestinians in the Jalazoun refugee camp talked about it all the time. Would they accept compensation for the lands they lost if they could have a state of their own? The debates carried on into the night. "Whoever wants wants and who doesn't doesn't. . . the point of view of the majority of people here [is] that many, many of the Palestinians are outside now and they have lands and buildings and projects outside," Hassam said. "I think they accept the condition."

But Massoud Safi didn't. "We don't know the role that international politics will take about our natural rights in our country," he said. Whatever America and Russia decided, if Massoud Safi could have a choice, he wanted to go home.

14

The Islamic Challenge

Within an hour of King Hussein's speech relinquishing the Hashemite claim of sovereignty over the West Bank, Israeli intelligence officers accompanied by police and soldiers drove from the Russian compound, its walls looped with concertina wire, to Faisal Husayni's home and ultimately to the Arab Studies Center, Husayni's research organization.[1] Husayni's staff, who were still in the office, were used to such surprise visits. The Israelis had repeatedly closed the center, claiming its real function was to coordinate PLO activities in the West Bank and Gaza.

In his secretary's unlocked desk drawer the Israelis found the Palestinian Declaration of Independence. Husayni, who had just been released from detention, was thrown back into prison, where he would remain without trial for the next half year. Husayni had planned to declare statehood in the Old City on the *haram al-sharif* the "Noble Sanctuary," with all its Islamic symbolism, and in front of the tomb of his father, Abd al-Qadir al-Husayni. There, assembled with a hundred prominent individuals to be included in the new Palestinian National Council, he would read the declaration. The Palestinian leadership in the West Bank and Gaza intended to proclaim a Palestinian state from the Temple Mount.

To the Likud government, the site of the reading must have been just as disturbing as what would have been read. Husayni, a life-long partisan of al-Fatah, wanted to locate the legitimacy of the new state in its Islamic center, on that platform where Palestinians believe the Prophet leaped to heaven. The siting of this performative gesture reflects the way in which Islam suffuses Palestinian national identity, a relation between religion and nationalism that now threatens to hobble the birthing of a Palestinian state.

Radical Islam, which has been rising everywhere in the Arab world, is the dark complement of Palestinian pragmatism. By conquering Jerusalem, Israel helped fashion the conditions for the emergence of an independent Palestinian nationalism that would accept territorial compromise, as well as the resurgence of a militant Islam that would not. By liberating Palestinian lands from Jordanian control and uniting Jerusalem under Israeli sovereignty, the Israelis created a zone in which a pragmatic Palestinian nationalist leadership could emerge. As we have seen, Jerusalem was a privileged platform for Palestinians to organize, political home to leaders who supported a small Palestinian state in which the city would be its natural capital.

But by conquering and claiming Jerusalem as its indivisible capital, by repeatedly preventing Palestinian political organization, Israeli occupation contributed to the efflorescence of militant Islam. Just as Gush Emunim understood Muslim control over the Temple Mount as a profane hole at the center of the nation, Islam considered Israeli sovereignty over Jerusalem as an abomination. Because nationalist organizations across the occupied territories were repeatedly repressed by the Israelis, Islamic institutions provided Palestinians the only legitimate cross-local form of social organization. Denied a political settlement through the PLO and effective diplomatic and military support from the Arab states, Palestinians found in the Islamic movement a means to mold history with the help of God, a way that had proved capable of humbling even the superpowers.

In combination, these two forces – an independent, pragmatic Palestinian nationalism and a militant Islam – made the *intifada* possible. But the *intifada* produced a political outcome that militant Muslims found unspeakable: partition and peace. Militant Islam not only endangers this outcome; it will seriously constrain the capacity of the Palestinian nationalist movement to fashion a sovereign state.

With the Swords of Allah

Islam, like Judaism, is a political religion, a faith meant to be conjoined with power. And like Judaism, classical Islam marks out a particular territory as its historic home. The Prophet's armies rode straight toward Jerusalem in the seventh century. For much of this century, men whose understandings of the world were refracted through Islam have taken the reconquest of Palestine as a primordial test for the political relevance of their faith in the modern world. The Prophet, after all, did not alight in Madrid.

As the Arab world fractured into nation states in the nineteenth and early twentieth centuries, its rulers, even though their reign hinged on the support of European powers, looked to Islam for legitimacy. Many Arab Muslims saw the posturing of these monarchs as so much window dressing, watching with alarm as the new middle classes took on European mores – its sexual pleasures and its godless seeking after material goods – while demeaning their own traditions. Social movements emerged in the Arab world seeking to create a true Islamic polity, to return the Arabs to the House of Islam. The most important of these was undoubtedly the Muslim Brotherhood, an Islamic movement that has decisively shaped Palestine's political culture. The Muslim Brotherhood entered Palestine through two vectors – the first, from Egypt, through Gaza; the second, under the watchful eye of the Jordanian Hashemites, from Jerusalem.

The Muslim Brotherhood was founded in Egypt in 1928 by Hasan al-Banna, a young teacher who despaired over the way young Egyptians spurned their parents' decency, scurrying after the material gadgets and the new wealth accompanying the British protectorate after World War I. Although Hasan al-Banna wanted to rid Egypt of its British-imposed monarchy, he did not want to remake Egypt in the Western image. Western colonialism, he taught, was a structure of power whose objective was not simply the extraction of wealth, but the "destruction of Islam."[2] Atheism was both the means and the end of European domination. The Brotherhood sought to refashion Arab society according to Islamic principles, creating its own network of mosques, schools, and social services.[3]

Al-Banna's Brotherhood paid more than lip service to the liberation of Palestine from Christian and Jewish invaders. Haj Amin al-Husayni, who had cast the Palestinian cause as a pan-Islamic struggle, had used Islamic pilgrimage to forge the Palestinians into a nation and conflict over the *haram* as a way to spur the populace into battle with Zionists. The Muslim Brotherhood championed the Palestinian cause, organizing demonstrations and fund-raising, closely aligning itself with Haj Amin al-Husayni's struggle to free Palestine from infidel rule. After the Second World War, the Muslim Brotherhood successfully pressed Egypt's King Farouq to grant asylum to al-Husayni, then in flight for his complicity with the Nazis.[4] The first Palestinian Muslim Brotherhood group was established in Jerusalem in 1946 with the enthusiastic support of the Palestinian nationalist leadership. Shortly thereafter, other groups were formed in two dozen other places – Jaffa, Lydda, Haifa, Nablus and Tulkaram – in Palestine west of the Jordan River. Thousands of Palestinians joined.[5] The Brotherhood sent technical advisers to Palestine to train self-defense units.

The Muslim Brotherhood understood the Palestinian struggle as an Islamic cause. "Palestine was the first line of defense of the Arab nation," al-Banna wrote in 1947, "but more, it was the heart of the Arab world, the knot of the Muslim peoples, the first of the two *qiblas* [directions of Islamic prayer]."[6] During the 1948 war, Muslim Brotherhood volunteers fought alongside the Arab armies' regular forces. Al-Banna ordered three brigades of the Egyptian Brothers, supplemented by Palestinians, to help save Palestine from the Jews. Brotherhood groups in Transjordan and Syria also sent smaller contingents of volunteers.

However, in early December 1948 the Egyptian government officially dissolved the Brotherhood after a huge weapons cache was discovered at the home of one the movement's sheikhs outside Ismailiyya. Although the Brotherhood claimed the weapons were bound for Palestine, the Egyptian government believed the Brothers intended to use them at home. Brotherhood volunteers, waiting impatiently to be deployed in Palestine, were surrounded in their camps in the Gaza Strip and ordered to surrender their weapons. There they would sit until the end of the war in January 1949. The Brotherhood, who considered it traitorous to cede any part of the historic *umma* – the community conquered by the Prophet's armies – to non-Muslims, felt King Farouq's willingness to sign an armistice with Israel and to grant Britain rights to the Suez Canal were grounds for seeking to overthrow the Egyptian monarchy. On December 28, 1948, one of its young members shot the Egyptian prime minister to death as he entered the Ministry of the Interior. Two months later, Egypt's political police retaliated and assassinated Hasan al-Banna.[7]

When the Free Officers, many of whom had connections to, or backgrounds in, the Muslim Brotherhood, finally ousted the Egyptian monarchy in 1952, their new Arab nationalist government initially looked with favor upon the Brotherhood.[8] A special section of the national cemetery was established as the Palestine Cemetery to honor their "volunteers" who died in the struggle to liberate Palestine. The Brotherhood grew so rapidly that by 1954 they were the largest political group in the Gaza Strip.

But in 1954, Nasser, like King Farouq before him, fell afoul of the Brotherhood. Nasser ordered them disbanded. Then he, too, granted Britain a presence at Suez and the right to bring its troops back to Egypt if those regimes in which the British had interests were attacked. After a Muslim Brother tried to assassinate him, Nasser banned the Brotherhood outright, jailing some of its leaders, executing others. In Gaza, the Brotherhood went into such a steep decline that on the eve of the Six-Day War its cells had almost ceased to exist.

Those Muslim Brothers living in territories controlled by Transjordan chose a different path than their comrades in Gaza. For one thing, the Hashemite monarchy drew from the Prophet's bloodline, whereas King Farouq had been of the line of Fuad Pasha, a Westernizing Turkish statesman of Albanian extraction with no kin or historic ties to the Prophet or his companions. Anxious to avoid the fate of the Gaza Brotherhood, the Jordanian Brothers, who were centered in Jerusalem, responded with alacrity to King Abdullah's offer that they would be allowed to flourish as long as they did not try to bring down his regime and refrained from armed incursions into Israel that would invite punishing retaliation.

In Transjordanian territories, the Brotherhood thus confined itself to building Islamic religious and social service organizations, not an armed militia. Although it disapproved Jordan's close relation to Britain and its failure to impose the *shari'a*, or Islamic law, by the mid-1950s the Brotherhood had become the Hashemite monarchy's ally against Palestinian nationalists, Communists, and pan-Arab Nasserists and Baathists.[9] Whereas Nasser banned the Brotherhood, the Hashemite crown allowed the Brothers to operate openly, even suppressing their political rivals. America, too, provided support for Muslim Brothers exiled to Transjordan from the Soviet-supported Egyptian regime. For all that, the Brotherhood was not a significant political threat in the West Bank prior to the Six-Day War; its message was unable to compete with Arab and Palestinian nationalism.

The Hashemites granted the Muslim Brotherhood more than freedom of operation; it gave them power over Jerusalem's sacred sites. Although the Hashemites sought to reduce Jerusalem's political importance, the city's sanctity cast an aura in the Islamic world, reinforcing the legitimacy of the Hashemites as onetime custodians of the holy places in Mecca and Medina. King Abdullah often traveled to Jerusalem to pray in al-Aqsa on Friday mornings; he extolled the city's sanctity in his public addresses; he appointed an inspector of the mosque of Umar and keeper of the holy places with the rank of cabinet minister to represent him in the city.

The Jordanians moved Palestinian nationalists out of Jerusalem's Islamic institutions, replacing them with Muslim Brothers. By giving the Muslim Brotherhood hegemony over al-Aqsa and the Dome of the Rock, the Hashemites could count on the Muslim Brotherhood to enhance the Islamic religious, as opposed to Palestinian national, significance of Jerusalem. For example, the Brotherhood, who held their annual conference in Jerusalem, instituted an all-Muslim congress in 1953 to commemorate the night of Muhammad's ascension, or *miraj*, to heaven.[10]

Jerusalem's Islamic institutions controlled more than places to pray. They controlled an enormous amount of real estate. In the five hundred years of Ottoman rule in Jerusalem, more than two-thousand Muslim endowments, or gifts of property, had attached to the *haram al-sharif* to be administered by the Jerusalem *waqf*, an Islamic trust or endowment. These properties not only generated a substantial flow of revenue, they could be used for commercial development.[11] The Jordanians appointed members of the Brotherhood, or those sympathetic to it, to positions in the *waqf*. These appointments enabled the Brotherhood to shape the flow of millions of Jordanian dinars passing through Jerusalem's *waqf*.[12]

Brothers also had considerable success in gaining and shaping appoint-

Dome of the Rock.

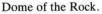

ments, both secular and religious, to the mosques, religious schools, Islamic courts, and charitable institutions of the West Bank. As vulnerable employees of the Hashemite state, the Brothers became a source of political support and information for the monarchy. Within the Islamic bureaucracy, to disagree with the Brothers could mean being transfered to a remote village school, if not being dropped entirely from the king's payroll as a prayer leader or judge.

If the Muslim Brotherood barely survived as an underground movement in Egyptian Gaza, in the West Bank the Brothers flourished, able to dominate Jerusalem's Islamic institutions; providing teachers, prayer leaders, and judges for the entire West Bank; counted on by the Hashemites as a bulwark against Palestinian nationalism.

Islam and al-Fatah

The Muslim Brotherhood wanted to liberate Zionist-held Palestine, but they had no interest in the formation of a secular democratic Palestinian state. Nonetheless it is impossible to understand the genesis of Palestinian nationalism, and that of al-Fatah in particular, without understanding their links to radical Islam.

When Yasser Arafat founded al-Fatah in 1959, he meant it to be a nucleus for a liberation army, the vanguard of a nationalist movement. Its members were required to put the interests of Palestine before those of all other transnational parties in the Arab world who likewise wanted to expel the Jews from Palestine – pan-Arab nationalists, Communists, and radical Islamic movements like the Muslim Brotherhood. A member of al-Fatah could belong to no other organization.

But these strictures should not prevent us from understanding that Arafat and those with whom he founded al-Fatah had been profoundly shaped by the Muslim Brotherhood. Although Arafat claims he himself was never formally a member, the biographical facts suggest an extraordinary intimacy with this branch of radical Islam.[13] There are reports that Arafat's father and brother, Gamal, who fought with Abd al-Qadr Husayni's forces in Jerusalem, were members of the Muslim Brotherhood. Arafat spent much of his youth in the Cairo household of Abd al-Qadr's uncle, Haj Amin al-Husayni, who, after World War II, lived in political exile there under Muslim Brotherhood sponsorship. When the Muslim Brothers formed military brigades to fight the Zionists in the 1948 war, Arafat himself joined up, leaving for Gaza with fifty other students and later joining a group of Brotherhood soldiers stationed in Jerusalem.[14]

After the war, Arafat helped train soldiers to participate in the Muslim Brotherhood–led campaign of sabotage and ambush of the British along the Suez Canal. It was there that he met Salah Khalaf, a member of the Muslim Brotherhood who would later be known as Abu Iyad, al-Fatah's security head. After the Brotherhood's attempted assassination of Nasser in 1954, the Egyptians arrested Arafat and tortured him, believing he was a member.[15] It was while he was in prison that Arafat met another member of the Muslim Brotherhood, Khalil Wazir, who would be known as Abu Jihad, with whom he later cofounded al-Fatah.

Islam pervades the language and world view of al-Fatah, the dominant party in the PLO. When Arafat speaks, he peppers his speech with Islamic language, quoting regularly from the Qur'an. His nom de guerre, Abu Ammar, "the father of Ammar," refers to Ammar ibn Yasir, one of the Prophet's companions, a great fighter from a poor family whose members were tortured for their faith in the Prophet. Significantly, this persecution led to the first emigration of Muslims from the Arabian peninsula. The Palestinian flag is modeled on the Prophet's banner kept by Jerusalem's Husayni family in the Dome of the Rock.

The word *Fatah* is a reversed acronym for *harakat al-tahrir al-watani al-filastani*, "the movement for the liberation of Palestine." But *fatah* is also a classical word from the Qur'an that means "to open" or "to conquer," referring to the Islamic conquest of infidel cities and lands.[16] Fatah modeled its freedom fighters, the *fedayeen*, "those who sacrifice themselves," after the Qassamites, followers of Sheikh Izz al-Din al-Qassam. These peasant rebels spent their days reading the Qur'an and their nights making armed raids. Qassam, who sought to forge an alliance of poor peasants on the land and their landless sons in the coastal city slums, conducted the first organized Palestinian violence against the Zionists.[17] This Islamic warrior was killed in a gun battle with the British in 1935, his martyrdom becoming a model for generations of *fedayeen*, his grave a place of patriotic pilgrimage.[18] The Muslim Brotherhood's own Gazan underground cells, formed in 1954, had likewise been called *fedayeen*.[19]

Just as Jews understand themselves through paradigms of Jewish history like the exodus from Egypt, Palestinians often see themselves through those of Islamic history. The names of Fatah's four main military battalions – Hattin, Yarmuk, Qadisiyah, and Ayn Jalut – each recall great Islamic victories over non-Muslims in Palestine, Syria, Iraq, and Iran. At Hattin in 1187, for example, Salah al-Din al-Ayyubi began the final phase of his reconquest of Jerusalem from the Crusaders. Palestinians effortlessly conjoin their struggle with these earlier Islamic struggles against infidels who made incursions into the House of Islam. Asked about these battles, one Palestinian explained that the "Palestinians have always had to fight imperialism, from the West, or from Mongols or from the Zionists."[20]

Al-Fatah's lexicon is replete with Islamic terms. "Ours is the obligation of jihad," declared Fatah's first official communiqué of January 1, 1965. Al-Fatah thus put its faith in this Islamic comandment of holy war, the liberation of Palestine being understood as the holiest of jihads, in which, al-Fatah later proclaimed, "we resolved to shed every drop of blood in our veins."[21] Fatah's soldiers who set out across the Lebanese or Jordanian borders fully expecting to die often conceived of their deeds as a reenactment of other classic Islamic narratives like Karbala, where the son and grandchildren of the Prophet were massacred by the Umayyad caliph Yazid in 630 C.E.[22]

Islamic historical imagination infuses al-Fatah's understanding of the most seminal events in the history of Palestinian resistance. In March 1968, at a Palestinian refugee camp at Karamah, Jordan, near the Allenby Bridge, Palestinian forces repulsed an Israeli tank assault. The extraordinary success of this first head-to-head confrontation with the Israeli army sent thousands of Palestinians streaming to join al-Fatah. The official Fatah statement issued in its aftermath interpreted "the Day of Karamah" as the first decisive step on the road to Jerusalem. History would continue to make Palestinian heroes, al-Fatah declared, until that day when "Bilal ascends the walls of Jerusalem in order to proclaim that the corruption has passed away." Bilal was the first *mu'adhdhim* chosen by Muhammad to call his community together for prayer. In short, Fatah's celebration of the Palestinians' new beginning recalled the foundations of the primordial Muslim polity.[23]

Al-Fatah has always sought to synthesize transnational Islam and Palestinian nationalism. This not only reflected its founders' Islamic beginnings, it was in accord with the sensibilities of an overwhelmingly Islamic Palestinian population.[24] In the squalid refugee camps of Lebanon in the 1950s, the first generation of children born in the diaspora would reverently turn to face Palestine and chant an oath that ended: "We shall never accept another homeland! Allah and history will attest: Palestine is ours, and we shall shed our blood for it."[25]

The fusion of religion and nationalism functioned not unlike that of any civil religion, grounding the authority of the nation-state in a higher divine order in the same way the United States has appropriated important themes in Christianity. Al-Fatah's ideological distinctiveness is put in relief by comparing it with the Palestinian opposition. These parties, which embraced one or another form of Marxism, were vitriolic toward religion. Significantly, Greek Orthodox Palestinians played a prominent role in these secular socialist parties. George Habash, the son of a Greek Orthodox grain merchant from Jerusalem, founded the Popular Front for the Liberation of Palestine (PFLP); Nayef Hawatmeh, a Jordanian Christian, later broke from the PFLP to form the Democratic Front for the Liberation of Palestine (DFLP). Before they were expelled from Jordan in 1971, for example, the DFLP alienated large segments of the Palestinian refugee community there by broadcasting tributes to Lenin on his one hundredth birthday from the minaret of a mosque.

Thus unlike Labour Zionism, which sought to push Judaism to the margins, the central pillar of the Palestinian nationalist movement early on developed a fusion of religion and nationalism that would not become influential among the Israelis until the 1970s. Although Fatah's grounding of national identity in Islam was a potent device for popular mobilization, it had serious limitations. For one thing, it could and did make Palestinian Christians, a disproportionate percentage of whom continued to migrate out of Palestine over the decades, very uncomfortable. And for another, it made the Palestinians particularly vulnerable to Islamic groups that could pillory al-Fatah as exploiting Islam for the profane purpose of building a modern nation-state. Over the decades, Fatah's synthesis was increasingly challenged by young men who believed that only by making Islam primary could Palestinian society be reconstructed and its territory reconquered. In the economy of divine judgment, Palestine's subjugation had an explanation – deviation from the path of Allah – and thus a ready remedy. Despite the Muslim Brotherhood's early support of the Palestinians, its form of radical Islam would prove to be the most dangerous threat facing the PLO.

The Trauma of Defeat

The Arab world was traumatized by their utter defeat in 1967, a trauma compounded by their failure in 1973, after an initially successful surprise attack on Israel, to make any territorial gains against the Zionists. These two wars shattered the Arab world's political vision. The Arab nation, even when it fought together, had not been able to defeat the Jews.

Palestine's liberation has always been the criterion against which the Arab regimes have been judged and found wanting by their opponents; this was particularly the case for radical Islam, the enemy and heir apparent to Arab nationalism. Although some secular Arabs interpreted these failures as an index of their backwardness vis-à-vis Israel, an absence of modernity marked by religion's continued influence in the affairs of Arab states, the Muslim Brotherhood reasoned differently. The Brothers argued that the Arab world's inadequacy on the battlefield derived from its failure to embrace Islam. Only Islam could instill discipline and inspire people to the necessary sacrifices. All the rest – socialism, nationalism, fascism – were Western imports. If allowed to flourish on its native soil, Islam alone would be able to conjure up the necessary forces to vanquish the infidel.[26] In Islam faith was power. Hadn't the Prophet and his followers unified the peoples of the Hijaz through Islam, extending the Prophet's community to North Africa, Palestine, Syria, and much of the Middle East? Hadn't the Ottomans, likewise, used Islam to conquer large portions of Central Europe?

Like the Gush Emunim, the Brotherhood, too, read battlefield outcomes as divine messages. Just as some Gush Emunim rabbis inter-

Haj painting indicating that a resident has made the pilgrimage to Mecca in Silwan, 1991.

preted Israel's huge losses in 1973 as punishment for its failure to incorporate God's promised lands won in 1967, the Muslim Brotherhood pointed to the Egyptians' successful crossing of the Suez Canal at the beginning of the October War as a portent of what faith could do. Hadn't Egyptian troops chanted *Allahu Akbar*, "God Is Great," as they crossed the canal? Wasn't its code word "Operation Badr," recalling the victorious battle conducted by Muhammad and his companions in 622 C.E. against their idolatrous opponents?[27] Imagine what the Arabs could do if Islam were more than a battle cry, a way of life, the true sword of state.

Bismilah al-rahim, "in the name of the Compassionate God," was how Sheikh Ikrima Said Sabri began as we sipped coffee in demitasse in his sparsely furnished house in East Jerusalem's Wadi el-Joz neighborhood in the spring of 1984. The living room walls were adorned with pictures of Mecca and Medina, where the sheikh had proudly made the *haj* – the pilgrimage celebrating Abraham's submission to God. Yes, it was true that Muhammad died five years before Jerusalem fell to his armies. But even before there were Muslims in Jerusalem, the sheik explained to us, the Prophet had destined this city to be one of the inner chambers of the House of Islam. "Jerusalem," he said with a radiant air, "is the center of the miracle of the Prophet, peace be upon him, who came here on his night journey [*al-isra' wal-miraj*]." Here he was referring to the Palestinian Muslim belief that it was from Jerusalem that the Prophet ascended heavenward. It was this miracle, not the historical conquest, that made Jerusalem a sacred Islamic trust.

The 1967 defeat had been quite unexpected, the sheikh explained, his dark tie perfectly knotted and centered against a well-starched white shirt. The Palestinians felt horrible, he said, because "the Arab leaders told us that we are strong and can destroy Israel. They lied. They lied all the time." The Arabs had been sucked into a conspiracy, he claimed, a plot hatched by the United States, France, and Great Britain, as well as the Jordanians, the Egyptians, and the Israelis. It was not really a war.

And the Arab leaders had lost because they were not really Muslims. "They are Muslims only on their identity cards. It is written there that they are Muslims. This is all. They are not Muslims more than this."

Sheikh Sabri, wearing the *imma,* the red and white turban indicating his high clerical position, spoke the language of the Muslim Brotherhood.[28] This was not some radical cleric, a rogue *imam* condemning the Arab leaders, including his own employer, King Hussein. Sabri had been the director of preaching at al-Aqsa since the 1970s, delivering its closely watched sermons on Fridays, responsible for Qur'anic education, supervising sheikhs throughout the West Bank, as well as an influential member of the *Awqaf.*

Sheikh Sabri did not venture into Jewish Jerusalem. The first time he went there, he told us, was when, filled with trepidation, he visited his brother in prison. Israel's capture of Jerusalem provided men like Sheikh Sabri, Muslim religious thinkers who would be called "fundamentalists" by Western writers after the Iranian revolution of 1979, with a potent charge to advance their claim to lead. Israel was victorous in 1967, they argued, because the Israelis conjoined their Judaism and their Zionism; they had fought so fiercely because they understood the sacrality of Jerusalem. Palestinians saw that it was the devout Jews who were the ones successfully colonizing the newly conquered lands. Palestinians, the sheikh told us, had to stop relegating Islam to a personal confession, to private ritual and personal prayer. Islam was not just for the mosque, but supplied the precepts for judgment, for rule, for war.

Sabri was nevertheless gratified by the way in which Palestinians in the occupied territories had become progressively more observant under Israeli occupation. By the 1980s, half were praying five times each day.[29] Fasting on Ramadan had become pervasive. Enormous crowds, as many as one hundred thousand according to the sheikh, were coming to al-Aqsa to pray. One out of every two books Palestinians bought contained Islamic themes. Many of these texts charged that the Palestinians had brought the Israeli occupation on themselves: powerlessness was punishment for impiety.[30]

"The Palestinians," Sheikh Sabri told us, "have tried many kinds of regimes. They understand that all of these regimes took them backwards. Now they understand that only Islam can solve their problems and move them forward. So, we can say that people who return to Islam are returning to being what they really are. It is not a new thing."

Sheikh Sabri's reasoning reflected a new mind-set that rejected the dualisms of the Enlightenment. Arab radicals and liberals had both understood religion as a reactionary force, believing that reason would construct a new polity, shucking the layers of dogma preventing the production of real Arab power.[31] False, said the radical Muslims. Look at Israel, which was both more religious and more scientific than any of the Arab states. One had to fight fire with fire.

Building an Islamic Society

The Muslim Brothers waited breathlessly after the 1967 war. Would the Israelis crack down on them? The Brothers needn't have worried. In fact, the West Bank Islamic network administered from Jerusalem soon became the primary structure for Palestinians to deliver services, to adjudicate internal conflicts, and to organize a legitimate political voice. The steady Palestinian return to Islam after the June defeat of 1967 was largely orchestrated through and capitalized upon by the Muslim Brotherhood.

After the war, the Jordanians looked more than ever to the Muslim Brotherhood as an ally against Palestinian nationalism. Sa'd Jumah, Jordanian prime minister during that war, himself called for a return to Islamic rule. Only Islam, Jumah proclaimed, could save the Arabs from what he called "barbarism and unbelief." Secular nationalism, he charged, had been imported by minorities like the Christians, who mistakenly believed Islam considered them second-rate citizens. The Jordanians, the Saudis, and the Kuwaitis poured in funds to support the growth of Islamic institutions in the West Bank and Gaza, many of which were either influenced or directly controlled by Muslim Brothers.

As a conduit of Jordanian influence in the West Bank and as a counterweight to the PLO, the Israelis protected the Muslim Brotherhood's capacity to operate. In Jerusalem, who can and cannot build is a sensitive index of favor. The city rarely stood in the way of the *Awqaf*. "We allowed them to build everything," said Yisrael Kimchi, the city's chief planner. Indeed, Aharon Sarig, Jerusalem's city manager, and Meron Benvenisti, once deputy mayor, even pressed the city to allow them to build an Islamic school, Ibrahamiyah College, run by the Muslim Brotherhood and funded by the Saudis.

Likewise in Gaza, the Israelis did not interfere significantly with the

Brotherhood, opponents as they were of Egypt's Arab nationalist regime. Beginning in 1978, the same year elected nationalist mayors formed the National Guidance Committee, Israel began to cooperate openly with Brotherhood efforts to build youth clubs and health clinics.[32]

When the Camp David Accords were signed in 1978, the Egyptian Brotherhood became vocal critics of what they understood as Sadat's capitulation to the Zionists. Sadat, in response, closed the Egyptian–Israeli border, penning the more radical and politicized wing of the Brotherhood in Gaza. He even expelled a number of Egyptian Brothers to Gaza. Jordan accordingly became the Gazan Brothers' only exit to the Arab world; naturally as they made their way across the Jordan River, they sought to influence their Jordanian counterparts.

The Brotherhood believed that they first had to build an Islamic society before they could reach for political power and eventually defeat the Zionists. A successful Islamic resistance movement would require the support of a population who walked resolutely in the path of Islam. The Brotherhood sought to form an Islamic elite, knowledgeable about the conspiracies of the past, vigilant in their exposure of traitors, persistent in teaching their people that the conflict with the Zionists was religious, not national. Violent resistance against the Jews was forbidden, not because it was not right, but because the people were not ready.[33]

Whereas the Muslim Brotherhood now eschewed armed resistance, they did not favor a politically negotiated settlement with the Israelis. Jerusalem's sanctity alone precluded a peace settlement. Sheikh Muhammad al-Jamal made this perfectly clear. From his arched office window at the corner of the platform on which the Dome of the Rock sits, you can see al-Aqsa mosque. The sheikh, a member of the Muslim Brotherhood who serves as deputy mufti of the *haram* and an influential member of the Higher Muslim Council, was explaining that when the Prophet Muhammad journeyed miraculously to Jerusalem, God sent the prophets who appeared before him "right here," gesturing to the nearby Dome of the Rock. Bearded students wearing white and brown *galabiya* listened intently as their teacher explained to us in 1991 that the Prophet's passage through Jerusalem had infused not only this city, but all the land, with sanctity. Palestinians, he asserted, had been entrusted with this patrimony for all Muslims, not just for themselves. "Many, many nations came here and fought here," he continued, "but every nation killed people here and destroyed here. Only Islam has stayed and guarded its holy places. Only Islam has had the power to push out the invaders . . . Allah knows we can do it again."

"Only Islam," he insisted, "can help this land return to its rightful custodians, to Muslims. Only Islam can achieve real peace for us. We must say 'No, no, no, my love!' " Here he was alluding to the three

Sheikh Muhammad al-Jamal, al-Aqsa mosque, 1991.

"no's" first formulated at the Khartoum summit in 1969: no to negotiations, no to recognition, and no to peace. Real peace meant Islamic victory. "All the land from the sea to the river belongs to us," he exclaimed. The *me'uzzin* would make the call for midday prayer in a few minutes; the interview was over.

The Muslim Brotherhood, like many religious Zionists, understood the Palestinians' hold on the land as a signifier of the people's faith in God. Only when the Palestinians returned to Islam would the land return to its rightful owner. The Muslim Brothers made the same kind of essential connection between possession and piety as the religious Zionists. In a Brotherhood sermon commemorating Land Day, a general strike first organized in 1976 by Israeli Palestinians to protest expropriation of Arab-owned land in the Galilee, a Brotherhood preacher argued that the Palestinians lost their land because they had severed their connections with God to serve "pathetic capitalism," "agnostic communism," and "malodorous nationalism." "What should Palestinians do?" the preacher asked. "Work the land. Do not leave it unattended, plant it with vegetables and fruit trees; . . . turn the land into heavenly gardens and orchards."[34] To remain in the land, to husband it, to refuse to sell it to non-Muslims – these, and not violent resistance, were the virtuous paths preached in the Brotherhood's sermons.

Because of the Brotherhood's hostility to secular strands of Palestinian nationalism and their disavowal of armed struggle, the Israeli civil administration allowed them to create and build communal institutions, kindergartens and schools, hospitals, social programs for the young and elderly, and stores catering to the needs of Muslim families. Sheikh Jamal, for example, had been granted the right to establish a drug rehabilitation program at the Nebi Musa mosque, the same desert complex that figured so prominently as a rallying point for Palestinian nationalists under Haj Amin al-Husayni. There on the desert floor, nubbled with the tombs of the faithful, young Muslims worked and lived, prayed and studied the Qur'an with Sheikh Jamal, cleansing the toxins from their systems, returning to Islam, waiting for the moment when the time would be right.

The Brothers steadily built their own Islamic infrastructure. In 1973, they established *al-Mujamma' al-Islami*, the Islamic Center, in Gaza, a front institution for the Gazan Brothers whose clerics they considered authoritative figures.[35] After the Camp David Accords were signed over violent PLO opposition in 1978, the Israelis registered the Islamic Center, granting it and other Islamic organizations tax-free licenses for their activities. The same year the Brotherhood established three *shari'a* colleges in Jerusalem, Hebron, and Gaza, which offered instruction in Islamic jurisprudence.[36] A year later, the Palestinians were allowed to found an Islamic University in Gaza, an institution controlled by the Brotherhood. By the early 1980s, the Brothers had captured the most important institutions for Islamic education, training young Muslims who gradually took over as clerics, judges, prayer leaders, and teachers throughout the occupied territories.[37]

As they became more influential, the Brotherhood launched its own culture wars to change permissible Palestinian behavior. Not only did it go after drug dealers and prostitutes, Brothers pronounced that women, for example, would be forbidden from public swimming in Western-style bathing suits at the beaches along the Gaza coastline. A few Spandex-clad women were even sprayed with acid. The Brothers harassed an ice cream parlor where young men and women gathered. In Jerusalem during the *intifada*, Islamicists threatened to firebomb a theater planning to show a Palestinian movie containing some nudity. The film was withdrawn. In Nablus, An-Najah University was forced to withdraw an invitation to a British band after the Brothers threatened violence if this purveyor of Western decadence were allowed to play.[38]

Among colonized peoples of the third world, women's bodies frequently carry the signs of difference, wear the marks of an oppositional identity.[39] The Brotherhood sought to promote *shari* attire, dress in accord with Islamic notions of propriety, particularly among the women of Palestine. Styled hair, rouge, lipstick were forbidden. The dark billowing gowns and scarf encasing women's heads steadily diffused throughout the schools and universities of the occupied territories. By 1984, one in three female university students in the West Bank was wearing the long-sleeved, brown or gray *hijab*, a dress covering even the ankles.[40] By supplanting the multicolored patterns delicately embroidered in pomegranate, lapis, and mustard shades, its stitched motifs indicating town and village, marking off its wearer as a Palestinian woman, the monochromatic *hijab* denoted a transnational Islamic identity.

The Brotherhood particularly disappoved of Palestinian weddings, their alcohol, the women singing a song urging the groom to relax and smoke a cigarette, the open socializing and dancing of men and women who were not married and might even be strangers to one another. Palestinian weddings were often replete with Palestinian nationalist symbolism. The Brothers sought to introduce their own "Islamic wedding" ceremony. Sometimes, their members tried to impose their own sensibilities about this rite de passage. In Nablus, for example, a wedding celebration at the Palestine Hotel was disrupted by young rock-throwing men incensed that men and women were socializing during the festivities.

As Palestinian society became steadily more Islamic, the network of mosques in the occupied territories expanded, recruiting its personnel from the new generation of clerics produced by Muslim Brotherhood–controlled institutions. Between 1967 and 1987 the number of mosques in the occupied territories doubled.[41] The mosques were not simply nodes of public piety: they became central to Palestine's political nervous system. The mosque was often the only institution able to cut across clan and partisan loyalties.

One of the reasons the mosques became so politically important, of course, was that Israel made it so difficult for Palestinians to organize any kind of cross-local, cross-partisan forms of political association. National organization would be nationalist organization. Because Israel repeatedly repressed such organizations, the ever more elaborate skein of mosques became a natural medium for cross-local organization and communication, the path of least resistance. Political activities could take place in the mosque without the same interference they would draw in other contexts. Disrupting the mosques, the Israelis well understood, would be a public-relations disaster.

Those voices arguing that Islam should be the moral bedrock of Palestinian society became progressively more influential. Among the younger generation, a growing Islamic orientation was particularly evident.[42] By the early 1980s, the Muslim Brotherhood was recruiting increasing numbers of young people in the schools and universities to its ranks. They spent their time in prayer, study circles, and commemorations of religious holidays, building reputations as upright, sober, hardworking, devout young men and women who voluntarily sat separately in cafeterias and classrooms.[43]

Muslim Brotherhood activists did not come disproportionately from the children of refugees living in concrete block houses, but from established city dwellers.[44] By the late 1970s, Brotherhood-dominated Islamic slates were regularly scoring pluralities and majorities in student body and Chamber of Commerce elections, some of the only legitimate elections the Palestinians were allowed. In one of the last comprehensive public opinion polls among Palestinians before the *intifada*, conducted by *Al-Fajr*, half of those queried wanted their state to be Islamic in some way. Only one in ten wanted a secular democracy.[45]

The Struggle Within

As their authority grew, the Islamic stream's relation with the nationalists became increasingly truculent. Whereas the Brotherhood's continued deferral of armed resistance enabled it to avoid open conflict with Israel, its repudiation of Palestinian nationalism brought it into open, and often savage, conflict with the PLO. The Brotherhood's audiocassettes and theater denigrated the PLO.[46] The PLO had abjectly failed to liberate Palestine, the Brothers charged, because it did not serve God. The imprint of godless Marxism was everywhere. The PLO's failure to embrace Islam truly had crippled its ability to liberate the land, leading it so far astray that it was even countenancing territorial compromise. The Palestinians, the Brothers urged, must "boycott all attempts to surrender to the Jews, and fight those attempts with all available means."[47]

Whom, the Brotherhood would taunt, did the PLO serve, if it did not serve God? Certainly not the Palestinians. Each Arab government, a Brotherhood tract claimed, "formed a group subservient to it ideologically, financially, and politically. Then, each regime tried to get that group into the PLO through summit conferences on the one hand, and through armed plots on the other."[48] The PLO was nothing more than a hydra-headed marionette manipulated by Egyptians, Syrians, Iraqis, Libyans. Brotherhood activists excoriated the PLO for the way in which the *samud*, or steadfastness, funds established at the 1978 Arab summit meeting in Baghdad were distributed by the Joint Jordanian–Palestinian Committee. Instead of allocating these funds to the needy or productive projects, millions of dinars, they charged, was used to buy influence among the West Bank politicians.[49]

The PLO's broadsides against the Brotherhood were equally denunciatory. Why did the Brotherhood demand Islamicization of the PLO when it did not do likewise with the Hashemite regime of Jordan? Wasn't it the case that Yusuf al-Azm, the leader of the Brotherhood in

Jordan, "stands behind the rostrum of the Jordanian Parliament to praise the king and his constitution and his royal hereditary regime"? In Egypt, hadn't the Brotherhood been allied at various times with secular parties like the Wafd Party and even the Socialist Labor Party? The Brotherhood, Fatah students at Bir Zeit charged, was nothing more than an agent of Arab regimes with deep connections to their intelligence organizations and those of the imperial powers, even to that of Israel itself.[50] The Brotherhood, they claimed, was more concerned with fighting the PLO than with fighting the real enemies of the Palestinian people. Fatah charged that when Sheikh Ahmed Yasin, a Brotherhood leader in Gaza, was arrested by the Israelis in 1984 after they linked him to a cache of weapons, he had confessed that the weapons were intended for use against the Palestinian leftists.[51]

The Brotherhood fought it out with the Palestinian nationalists on the university campuses. For example, in 1981–1982, violence between the Muslim Brotherhood and Fatah students erupted at An-Najah University in Nablus when nationalist students pushed to have four lecturers rehired after the university had terminated them. More than twenty-five persons were hurt and one faculty member, well known for his nationalist sympathies, suffered serious injuries when he was thrown out of a third floor window of a university building.

Sometimes these conflicts between the Muslim Brothers and the nationalists played on Islamic–Christian tensions within the Palestinian community. For example, in June 1983, nationalist students at Bir Zeit University were preparing to mark the first anniversary of Israel's invasion of Lebanon. Bir Zeit University, the premier Palestinian university and training ground for much of nationalist intellectual elite, was founded by a Christian family outside Ramallah, itself a major concentration of Palestinian Christians. The event ended in a brawl, with nationalists and Islamicists using fists, knives, and chains against each other. As the Brothers fled into the adjacent Christian village, they were set upon by its residents as well. According to pro-PLO students, squads of Muslim Brothers had been sent from the Islamic University in Gaza to break up the anniversary. For their part, the Muslim students claimed not only that the nationalists had prevented them from mounting their own demonstration, but that Bir Zeit University was particularly hostile to Muslim students, colluding with the nationalists out of "Phalangist hatred." Here the Muslim militants were equating Palestinian Christians with the Lebanese Christians who had massacred Palestinians in the refugee camps at Sabra and Chatilla in 1982.[52] The following fall, Muslim students drove an automobile right through the university cafeteria's wall, followed by a phalanx of Islamic militants who attacked PLO supporters with rods and knives.

In Gaza, the conflict between nationalists and Islamicists was increasingly cast in manichean terms, an all-or-nothing opposition requiring total war against the enemy within. The Brotherhood laid siege to the headquarters of the Red Crescent Society, known as a Fatah bastion, torching its library to the ground.[53] Islamicists also attacked Fatah's top man in Gaza, As'ad al-Saftawi. In November 1984, Fatah ordered the murder of Dr. Isma'il al-Khatib, an activist in the Mujamma and head of the Arabic Language Faculty at Gaza's Islamic University.[54]

For twenty years, the Brotherood built its institutions, formed its cadre, penetrated the Islamic hierarchies of the occupied territories. Although not openly claiming to be an alternative, it refused to ally with the PLO, some of its members believing it impossible because of the non-Islamic elements within it, others believing it unnecessary because the PLO would ultimately fail, both internally as the representative of an increasingly Islamic society and externally as an agent of territorial liberation. The Brotherhood would then either constitute the only viable alternative or become the hegemonic bloc within the PLO. In any event, the Brotherhood was biding its time, sure that the PLO would never achieve a state, convinced a peaceful solution would not be forthcoming, confident that the people would become ever more receptive to its message.

Certainly Arafat's most troubling move was his willingness since the 1973 war to entertain a two-state solution. Ceding a parcel of the *umma* is simply unacceptable to the Brotherhood. The only way in which the Brotherhood would be willing to go along would be as a tactical ploy, not as a strategic settlement. For this, there is ample support in the traditions of radical Islam, particularly the concept of *taqiyya*, "concealment" or "precautionary dissimulation."[55]

Sheikh Yasin, the most influential Brotherhood cleric from the Islamic Center in Gaza, for example, is a master of *taqiyya*. In April 1989, after the PLO accepted a two-state solution, Sheikh Yasin granted an interview to the Jerusalem-based newspaper *Al-Nahar* in which he seemed purposefully ambiguous. "Do you want a Palestinian state from the river [i.e., the Jordan River] to the sea?" asked the reporter. "I want a Palestinian state," the sheikh answered. The reported pushed, "What are its boundaries?" The sheikh responded by underscoring that the boundaries of Palestine are well known. And where would Israel be? "Israel," the Sheikh said, "is in Palestine . . . The Palestinian state must be founded on every inch of Palestine that we liberate, but without conceding the rest of our rights." Then did the sheikh recognize Israel's right to exist? "If I recognized Israel the problem would be finished, and we would have no rights left in Palestine." And, if Israel withdrew from the West Bank and Gaza, would the sheikh recognize it? "When it withdraws, I will say."[56]

The Brotherhood's growing strength and the popular allure of other Islamic groups pushed the PLO toward ever-greater Islamicization. Written in the heady days of Arab nationalism, the PLO's original covenant was an overwhelmingly secular text. In the decade following the 1967 war, the struggle had been drawn into the rhetoric and realpolitik of the cold war, coded in the Marxist language of anti-imperialism, class struggle, and national liberation. Not only did the PLO's leaders seek to draw hope and instruction from the successful socialist anticolonial struggles in Algeria, Cuba, and Vietnam, they relied heavily on the Soviet Union and China for arms and diplomatic support.[57] But by the mid-1980s, al-Fatah was reaching back to its Islamic roots. PLO communiqués began to carry Islamic references, every announcement beginning or ending with a Qur'anic passage. At the 1984 PNC convention in Amman, for example, a banner was hung with the Qur'anic verse from which Fatah took its name (*nasr min allah wa-fath qarib*, "succor from God and conquest soon at hand"). Sheikh Abd al-Hamid al-Sa'ih, a man with impressive Islamic credentials, was elected as the council's chairman. The PLO sheikh immediately challenged the Brotherhood's claim to have a monopoly on valid religious interpretation. And in 1985, Fatah's "Force 17," headed by Abu Tayb, which had the responsibility of guarding Chairman Arafat, set up a religious wing called the "Trusters in God's Victory" (*al-Wathikun binasr Allah*) to attack Israeli targets.[58] The Islamic trend within the PLO became so strong it helped push one of the most prominent Palestinian Christians, the Anglican bishop Elias Khoury, to resign from the PLO's executive committee in 1985.[59] At the last PNC meeting before the *intifada*, in April 1987, Arafat even opened some of the PLO's major institutions – both the PNC and the Central Council – to representatives from the Islamic streams.

Jihad for All Palestine

The success with which the Muslim Brotherhood was recruiting young, observant Muslims ultimately transformed the common understanding within the Islamic stream of what was right and possible. Because the Brotherhood refused to resist the Israelis actively, it did not enjoy much influence among the Palestinian activists, who dismissed their members as moralistic and irrelevant.[60] "Blame yourself," Faisal Husayni dismissively mimicked the Brothers to us in 1984, "because you are not on the road of God . . . It is not the Jews, not the Israelis who are making the hard work. You are making the hard work because you are not thinking of God."

Just as the young men and women who came up through the ranks of the religious Zionist movement who founded the Gush Emunim felt a sense of inadequacy because of their lack of participation in the most important Zionist settlement projects and military units in the pre-state days, so the young recruits to the Muslim Brotherhood had to endure taunts by their classmates at the schools and universities. And just as Zionists would ask contemptuously what the most anti-Zionist *haredim* were doing to secure Jewish safety in the promised land, Palestinian nationalists would ask derisively what the Muslim Brothers were doing to defend Palestinian lands against expropriation, or where their fighters were when guerrillas struck against Israeli soldiers and settlers? "They just sit and watch," Ziad abu Zayyad said contemptuously. Study and prayer, abstinence, modesty, pilgrimage, charity, the nationalists would charge, would do little to liberate Palestine.

The newly reverent generation in Palestine would not long follow what they saw as Brotherhood accommodation to the profane powers surrounding them. It was not enough to burrow through Palestinian society, creating a world within a world, cleansing souls, hardening them, preparing the ground for some distant reversal. Those young Islamic activists who grew to political maturity under Israeli occupation confronted what they saw as increasingly dangerous internal enemies as well as a world in which militant Islam was elsewhere proving itself against all odds. They also came into contact with ideas that enabled them to refashion their vision of political Islam.

Beginning in the early 1970s, increasing numbers of young Palestinians from the West Bank and Gaza went to Egyptian universities for their advanced studies. Here they came in contact with the parent organization of the Muslim Brotherhood, which had been progressively radicalized since the organization had been first reined in during the 1948 war by King Farouq and subsequently repressed by President Nasser.

Among the Egyptian Brothers, the ideas of Sayyid Qutb (1906–1966) had become very influential. If Hasan al-Banna was the Brotherhood's most powerful organizer, Sayyid Qutb was its most influential thinker. Qutb, an Arab nationalist who studied in the United States in the wake of Israel's 1948 victory, had been alarmed at the disregard with which the West held the Arab cause and the popular enthusiasm Israel engendered. By the time he returned to Egypt in 1951, he knew that the West would never look at the Islamic world as an equal. Qutb joined the Muslim Brotherhood. When Nasser cracked down on the Muslim Brotherhood in 1954, Qutb was among the thousands thrown into prison, where he would remain for the next decade.

Qutb was certain the Arab world would never regain its stature by borrowing slavishly from the West; it would always be a parvenu, a too-eager, inadequate copy. Besides, the imported secularism would destroy what was essential to Arab identity – Islam. "There is a ridiculous servility to the European fashion of divorcing religion from life," he wrote, "a separation necessitated by the nature of their religion [Christianity], but not by the nature of Islam."[61] Islam, unlike Christianity, was not concerned primarily with the human being's relation to God; Islam had always commanded the "unity of life."[62]

Qutb seized upon the Qur'anic concept of *jahiliyyah*, a term referring to the period of "ignorance" in which the people of Mecca lived prior to the revelation of God to his Prophet. Qutb argued that there was not just one *jahiliyyah*, a far-distant time endured by the Prophet's followers. No, *jahiliyyah* was a constant possibility, occurring every time a Muslim society wandered from the path of Islam.[63] Indeed, the ignorance confronting Muslims in the twentieth century was much worse than that faced by the Prophet's Meccan community, surrounded as they were by men and women who naively followed polytheistic religions. Today, Qutb wrote, Muslims must contend with those who worship no god at all.

Qutb provided the Egyptian Brotherhood with theological armature with which to engage their Arab enemies. Islam, he taught, began with the *hijrah*, Muhammad and his followers' flight from Mecca to Medina, with withdrawal and then struggle against the *jahiliyyah* of their day. The Brothers must recapitulate the Prophet's ancient practices; it was the duty of every Muslim to combat this ignorance within their own societies.[64] Qutb conjured up an Arab world flooded with Satanic ignorance. Even that which appeared to be Islamic – Islamic education, philosophy, and thought – was the product of *jahiliyyah*.[65]

Arab nationalism, too, whether shorn of religion or thinly glazed with Islam, was an expression of *jahiliyyah*.[66] Qutb excoriated the Islamic clerics in Cairo who were then proclaiming an Islamic socialism, which they held to be compatible with Nasserism. Nasser was fighting against the Brotherhood, who were then campaigning, with considerable support from Egypt's legislature, for full implementation of Islamic law. Nasser must have felt acutely threatened, for in 1966 the Egyptian president had Qutb, along with other members of the Egyptian Brotherhood, arrested for plotting the government's overthrow. Confessions were obtained through torture and Qutb and two other Brotherhood organizers were hanged for treason.

After the 1973 war, as Egypt moved toward a negotiated settlement with Israel, the Egyptian Brotherhood was throwing off small militant offshoots that condemned its failure to engage the enemies within Arab society. They were inspired not only by the tradition of Qutb, but the writings of an electrician named Muhammad Abd al-Salam Faraj (1954–1982), who went even further, arguing that the leading Islamic figures had neglected their duty of jihad.[67] Jihad was not reserved for the infidel without – Christian or Jew – but, as events were making clear, imperative against the infidel within the Islamic community as well. The putative Muslim rulers of the day, Faraj contended, were apostates who had to be destroyed.[68] One could not wait, as the Egyptian Brotherhood was doing, to build a mass popular base before overthrowing their evil rule. In the end, it would come down to force and the masses would never be ready. One of the small groups of former Egyptian Brothers who responded to Faraj's call in the late 1970s, led by Khalid al-Islambuli, a lieutenant in the Egyptian army, would assassinate President Sadat in October 1981 for making peace with the Jews. Faraj was executed with Sadat's four actual assassins on April 15, 1982.

Qutb and Faraj's ideas were eagerly consumed by young Palestinian Brothers studying in Egypt. Wasn't the passivity of the Muslim Brotherhood in the West Bank and Gaza a symptom of *jahiliyyah*? How else, they reasoned, was it possible to explain the West Bank Brothers' expedient support of King Hussein, whose not-so-secret meetings with Israelis and refusal to apply Islamic law indicated how tepid his commitment to Islam really was? The young Palestinians sought to break with the timidity of the Palestinian Muslim Brotherhood in the same way that the followers of Faraj had broken with the main organization. They, too, wanted to engage the agents of apostasy within their own society. Returning to the occupied territories, the young Muslim Brothers no longer accepted the leaders' argument that the Brothers did not participate in the armed struggle because it was led by men who were not true Muslims. More and more, they saw the Brotherhood's position as a lack of courage, as moral bankruptcy, as a failure to understand the political implications of Islam.[69]

It was in Gaza where the Muslim Brotherhood had developed a large concentration of independent institutions, had survived repeated repression by the Egyptians, had been free from the domesticating influence of Hashemite authority and employment, drawing as they did from Saudi and Kuwaiti benefactors, that a new radical Islamic Palestinian movement began. In 1980, two younger Palestinians, Dr. Fathi al-Shaqaqi and Sheikh Abdal-Aziz Odeh, formed a group in Gaza called Islamic Jihad, the Islamic Struggle. Both Shaqaqi and Odeh had grown up in Gazan refugee camps and studied in Egypt. In the West Bank, Islamic Jihad's most important leaders were two Hebronites, Sheikh As'ad Bayyd al-Tamimi and Ibrahim Sirbil, both resident in Amman. Jihad's major cells in the West Bank were around Jerusalem and Hebron.[70] Just as the national religious rabbis who had been given positions in the state-financed synagogues by the Zionists would challenge the legitimacy of the Zionist state authorizing them, so many of the Muslim Brotherhood clerics and teachers co-opted by the Hashemites would ultimately threaten their Jordanian overlords. Sheikh Tamimi, for instance, had been a preacher in al-Aqsa until he was deported by the Israelis in 1980.

The founders of Islamic Jihad, like many in their generation, had been deeply impressed by the capacity of a militant Islamic movement to topple the American-backed regime in Iran in 1978–1979.[71] The utter impotence of the most sophisticated American-supplied arms and an American-backed army and secret police against the Islamic vanguard in Iran both stunned and exhilarated the Palestinians who founded Islamic Jihad.[72]

Just at that point when increasingly large numbers of Palestinians in the occupied territories were promoting the idea of a territorial partition with the Zionists, the leader of Islamic Jihad looked to Iran for inspiration and support. Khomeini, Sheikh Tamimi asserted, had finally returned Islam to the battlefield and brought Jerusalem back into the hearts of believers everywhere. Hadn't Jerusalem been inscribed on the Iranian revolutionary flag from the very start? Khomeini had not only declared the last day of Ramadan "Jerusalem Day," he issued a *fatwa*, or legal opinion, making the elimination of the "Zionist entity" a religious duty.[73]

Khomeini believed the road to Jerusalem led through Lebanon's Bekaa Valley and Beirut's slums.[74] Shortly after coming to power in 1979, Khomeini sent the first one thousand Iranian Revolutionary Guards to Lebanon, where in 1982, they, along with a number of Lebanese Shi'ite clerics who had bolted from the Amal militia, established the Hizbullah, "The Party of God." (This name is taken from a verse in the Qur'an (5.56): "Lo! The Party of God, they are the victorious.") That Islam had routed the Americans, the French, and the Israelis from Lebanon was not lost on the men of Islamic Jihad. They looked to Khomeini to help them form what they called "the Jerusalem Army."[75]

Islamic Jihad denounced the Palestinian nationalists who understood their struggle as one against Zionists, not infidels. And they denounced the Brotherhood's quietism as "unrevolutionary" and "misguided."[76] In 1981, Islamic Jihad made its first public appearance when its partisans entered elections at the Islamic University in Gaza. In 1983, its militants drew their first blood, when one of their commando units stabbed and killed an Israeli settler in Hebron, Aharon Gross, an act that led to the Jewish underground's decision to open fire on students at the Islamic college there.

If the Brotherhood had revered the memory of Haj Amin al-Husayni, with whom they had been aligned in the pre-state struggle for Palestine, Islamic Jihad looked to other forebears who allowed them to reclaim the heritage of armed resistance. Their patron saint was Husayni's rival, Sheikh Izz al-Din al-Qassam (1882–1935), an Islamic fighter from

Latakia, Syria, who had gone to Palestine to take up arms against the Jews when he was in his fifties. Al-Qassam had been the first to call for jihad to rescue Palestine. His guerrillas had fought under the slogan "God's book in one hand, and the rifle in the other." Islamic Jihad hailed al-Qassam, killed in 1935 by the British, as the first Muslim revolutionary in modern Palestine.

The men who joined Islamic Jihad saw al-Qassam's death as an act of martyrdom to be honored and, if they were able, to be replicated as well. "We, the members of the Islamic Jihad Movement," said one member during his trial for the murder of two Israelis, "show more interest in death than we do in life. We shall either liberate our land or die bravely in the attempt." It was God's blessing, an Islamic Jihad leader explained, that allowed a *mujahid*, or fighting Muslim, to give his life while "inflicting the heaviest losses, breaking down the enemy's morale and determination." Such acts of martyrdom would inspire others to follow, increasing "the outpouring of new blood which seek jihad for the sake of God."[77]

Islamic Jihad's early leadership was drawn from disgruntled Brothers; later it was able to recruit, often through Israeli prisons, from factions of the PLO as well. Islamic Jihad, which became as much a model to emulate as a structure to belong to, eventually included many small Islamic groups throughout the occupied territories, all of which shared the principle of armed resistance.[78] Unlike the Brotherhood's mass organizational structure, Islamic Jihad on the eve of the *intifada* had a few thousand members, divided into dozens of small groups or cells, usually referred to as "families," each with its own leader or "guide."[79] There was no single head one could decapitate, no structure with lines of authority to sever.

By the mid-1980s Islamic Jihad was engaged in a full-fledged military campaign against the Israelis. In 1986 two Israeli taxi drivers were murdered in Gaza. Jihad commandos then carried out a hand grenade attack on new recruits to the elite Israeli Givati Brigade being sworn in at the Western Wall, wounding more than seventy soldiers. In May 1987 six Islamic Jihad members escaped from an Israeli prison, some of their members even making their way to Tunis.[80] This gave the group enormous prestige in the eyes of young Palestinians. A suicidal plan to blow up a truck filled with high explosives in Jerusalem was foiled by the Israeli security services in August 1987. In that same month, the officer in charge of the Israeli military police in Gaza was murdered. In October, after the Israeli Defense Forces uncovered a number of Jihad cells as well as a huge arms cache, more than fifty Jihad members were arrested. After several Jihad men, including two of the prisoners who had previously escaped, were killed in a clash with Israeli forces, Gaza's Islamic University exploded. Violence erupted again in November 1987 when Sheikh Odeh was arrested and a deportation order issued. Two thousand Palestinians assaulted the Israeli outpost at the Jebalya refugee camp.[81] As its *mujahadin* repeatedly went up against the Jews, as the Israeli troops lashed out, sweeping through the towns and refugee camps in search of their tormentors, Gaza went out into the streets, seething with rage, expecting deliverance. Islamic Jihad had prepared the ground. The uprising began at Jebalya the following month.

The New Covenant

When the *intifada* began in early December 1987 Jihad activists sought to project themselves into its leadership, sending out directives to the young people rioting in the refugee camps.[82] Israel soon managed to crush the movement, putting many of the important Islamic Jihad leaders in prison or deporting them. Crippled by Israeli repression and internal fragmentation, Islamic Jihad desperately appealed for help to Sheikh Yasin, the spiritual leader of the Muslim Brotherhood in Gaza.[83] Yasin replied curtly that the Islamic Center had no need of partners, particularly one so numerically insignificant.

Sheikh Odeh, deported by Israel in April 1988, understood that the Muslim Brotherhood had rebuffed Islamic Jihad for partisan reasons, to recapture the radical Islamic initiative for themselves.[84] Days after the *intifada* began, on December 9, 1987, six prominent leaders of the Islamic Center met with Sheikh Yasin, forming themselves into the leadership circle of a new Muslim movement that sought to move the Muslim Brotherhood back into militant resistance.[85] Unlike much of the leadership of the Muslim Brotherhood, these young Muslims did not hold positions in the Hashemite Islamic institutions and were thus not accountable as Jordanian employees. Calling themselves *Harakat al-Muqawama al-Islamiyya*, the Islamic Resistance Movement, they were soon known by their acronym, HAMAS, which means "enthusiasm" or "zeal" in Arabic. HAMAS's first leaflet, distributed in January 1988, addressed the Palestinians as "O *murabitun* on the soil of immaculate Palestine" and described the Jews as "brothers of the apes, assassins of the prophets, bloodsuckers, warmongers who have plundered the land . . . Only Islam can break the Jews and destroy their dream."[86] *Murabitun* refers to those Muslims who settled in the outlying regions during the earliest period of the Muslim conquests, here making Palestinians into defenders of Islam's exterior perimeter. Just as the Prophet had made Jerusalem the first *qibla*, or direction of prayer, so, too, they would now make it the first direction of jihad.

The Israelis did not repress HAMAS, pointedly not interfering with its strike days. Israel would not declare Hamas to be illegal until autumn 1989. HAMAS's strike forces, called Izz al-Din al-Qassam battalions, torched Israeli fields and forests, attacked Israelis and suspected Palestinian collaborators.[87] Spurning the directives of the Unified Leadership, which forbid the use of "hot" weapons, by 1989 HAMAS was engaging in fire fights with Israeli soldiers, as well as kidnapings and executions.[88] HAMAS fashioned its fighters as a spiritual elect, saved souls and selfless fighters. "[Y]outh from Fatah join HAMAS," one street activist said. "No one from HAMAS joins Fatah. We are selective; Fatah takes anyone. We are ready to die for God." Another declared, "[T]o die for God is to go to heaven. To die for Fatah is for nothing."[89]

Israeli security services had always been able to penetrate the PLO's cells and to blackmail Palestinians into collaboration. Palestinians in the territories were acutely aware of how easy it was for the Israelis to break even PLO activists, to obtain their secrets, to make them into sources of information.[90] HAMAS cells proved much less penetrable. HAMAS instructed its cadre that those who broke in detention would never know God's mercy. The tenacity and discipline of HAMAS prisoners under interrogation were in fact so much greater than those of their nationalist counterparts, that they won many other prisoners over to the Islamic stream.[91]

HAMAS gloried in the capacity of its members for martyrdom, which they read as an indicator of their superior commitment. HAMAS leaflets recalled Islamic martyrs who fought to wrest territory from the infidel, men like Ja'fr ibn Abu-Talib, who fell in battle with the Byzantines. According to tradition Abu-Talib held his battle standard until both of his hands were cut off, affixing it to his chest until he was killed. Other martrys celebrated by HAMAS included the companions of the Prophet who had been killed on the soil of Palestine, Salah al-Din al-Ayyubi, and Ahmad Abd al-Azziz, who had been the commander of the Muslim Brothers who came to fight in Palestine in 1948. "Every drop of blood" of our martyrs, a HAMAS leaflet read, "shall become a Molotov cocktail, a time bomb, and a roadside charge that will rip out the intestines of the Jews. [Only] then will their sense return."[92]

As Jordan withdrew from the occupied territories, the Islamic organization operating under its protective wing was making a bid for power. Operating through HAMAS, the Jordanian Muslim Brotherhood would be able to counter PLO hegemony in a way denied to the Hashemites. The Jordanians did what they could to bolster this fledgling organization. They channeled money through the Jerusalem *Awqaf* to HAMAS-controlled institutions and activists. In April 1989, at the request of Sheikh Yasin, the Jordanian government eased the regulations for goods and people moving from Gaza to Jordan. The Jordanian Foreign Ministry appealed to governments and international agencies to intervene on behalf of the sheikh, who was to be tried in Israeli military court in early 1990. The Jordanians even urged HAMAS to join the Unified Leadership of the Uprising as a way to have an ear and a voice inside PLO-dominated political process.[93]

HAMAS, in turn, was downright conciliatory toward the Jordanian regime, especially compared to the uncompromising criticism of all Arab regimes made by the radical Egyptian-influenced Brothers. Its leaflets and its clerics' sermons refrained from criticizing King Hussein even though his policies included acceptance of UN Security Council resolution 242, advocacy of an international conference to resolve the conflict, and Jordanian participation in the Madrid Peace Conference. HAMAS went so far as to urge King Hussein to review his decision to sever Jordanian connections to the West Bank. And the king, for his part, left that possibility open when he told his people on July 31, 1988, that he had disengaged only "in response to the request by Yasser Arafat to assume responsibility for the population of the West Bank."[94]

At one level, the decision of prominent Muslim Brothers to form an Islamic resistance movement, to resume armed struggle, can be understood as a calculated move to reach for greater influence, to rehabilitate the Muslim Brotherhood. Not only had the Jordanian withdrawal given them new opportunities: if the Brotherhood, which already had a small armed capacity in place, did not become involved, did not connect themselves to the extraordinary moral and political force of the *intifada*, they might easily be banished forever to the political periphery. Although HAMAS itself claimed it had been their people, not those of Islamic Jihad, who had really begun the *intifada*, the Muslim Brotherhood kept its public distance from HAMAS until it was clear the *intifada* would not be easily put down.

But at another level, the uprising's origins and nature themselves prompted the Brotherhood to rethink the relation between faith and history, religion and power. Emile Durkheim, the nineteenth-century progenitor of modern social theory, argued that in worshiping God, a society sacralizes its own collective powers. It is no wonder, then, that demonstrations of extraordinary collective powers so frequently suggest themselves as objects of divine action, and evoke new understandings of the role of God in history. And how much more likely this should be in religions like Judaism and Islam, whose task is not the salvation of individual souls or the provision of solace to persons in despair, but the production of moral compass and metaphysical mandate for an entire social structure.

Just as Israel's extraordinary victories in 1967 motivated large numbers of young religious Jews to read the acquisition of the promised land as divine action, requiring a new role for faith in the direction of the Jewish nation-state, so the mounting of the first apparently unstoppable popular rebellion against Israeli occupation pushed many young devout Muslims to cast this history as God's work and to understand that Islam should indeed play a central role in national liberation. After all, it had been radical Islam, not secular nationalism, that had sparked the rebellion, an explosion of popular rage that had the capacity to make history, rather than just marginally increase the cost of a military occupation.

The nature of the event embedded political calculation in a cosmic text. To many in the Brotherhood, as to the young religious Zionists, the power to move something heretofore immovable could not derive from historical contingency, from the accumulation of profane powers. "I believe," Sheikh Yasin said, "it happened as something destined by God. There is nothing called spontaneous in Islam." God had chosen his time, his place, his instrument to begin to recreate a truly Islamic state – 1987, the Aqsa mosque, HAMAS. "When all doors are sealed," Yasin said, "Allah opens a gate."[95]

In August 1988, the same month Faisal Husayni drafted the declaration of independence, HAMAS published its own "Covenant," spelling out the path of the Islamic Resistance Movement: "Allah is its Goal. The Messenger is its Leader. The Qur'an is its Constitution. Jihad is its methodology, and Death for the sake of Allah is its most coveted desire" (Article 8). This covenant, consciously designed as a countercharter to that of the PLO, now openly described HAMAS as "a branch of the Muslim Brotherhood chapter in Palestine."[96] Just as the young rabbis who founded Gush Emunim put primacy on territorial settlement above all other Jewish values and were able to seize control of religious Zionism after the Six-Day War, the young Brothers who now made jihad into the cardinal Islamic value were able to have their way within the Muslim Brotherhood.

The militant Muslims' sticks and stones of battle are addressed to different names. HAMAS understood the conflict between Israel and Palestine as a conflict between Judaism and Islam, not between Zionism and Palestinian nationalism. In an undated leaflet, HAMAS appealed to Israel: "Get your hands off our people, our cities, our camps and our villages. Our struggle with you is a contest of faith, existence and life."[97]

Palestinians, having thrown a million stones at Israel, had forced Israel to recognize them as a legitimate collectivity, a fellow nation, not a forward party for a hostile Arab nation. HAMAS sought to change the language of war from a negotiable relation between nations to an irreconcilable relation between racialized faiths. For HAMAS the enemy is not the Zionists, but Jews, who are denigrated in classic European anti-

Semitic terms. The HAMAS covenant identifies the Jews as a "vicious Nazi enemy," who are involved in a vast international conspiracy intended to accomplish only one thing – the destruction of Palestinian life and society. With their money, HAMAS charged in its covenant, the Jews ignited revolutions, including both the French and the Communist Revolutions, as well as creating secret organizations that promote the Zionist cause (e.g., the Freemasons, the Rotary and Lions Clubs). The Jews were behind the First World War, which destroyed the Islamic caliphate, and the Second World War, "where they grossed huge profits from their trade of war materials, and set down the foundations to establish their nation by forming the United Nations and Security Council . . . in order to rule the world."

HAMAS has an eschatological vision of its struggle as a war to the last Jew. Many HAMAS leaflets concluded with "*Allahu akbar* [God is great] – the hour of *Khaybar* has arrived, *Allahu akbar* – death to the conquerors.*" Khaybar* was a prosperous Jewish community near Mecca whom the Prophet Muhammad had accused of treachery. In 628 C.E., after conquering Khaybar, the Muslims massacred all its inhabitants.[98]

HAMAS understands its struggle as not just for history, but for its blessed end. The HAMAS charter prominently cites a *hadith*, or tradition, in which the Prophet says that the

> Last Hour would not come until the Muslims fight against the Jews and the Muslims would kill them, and until the Jews would hide themselves behind a stone or a tree and a stone or a tree would say: Muslim or Servant of Allah there is a Jew behind me; come and kill him; but the tree of Gharqad would not say it, for it is the tree of the Jews. (Article 7)

It is radical Islam's task not simply to liberate Palestine, but physically to rid it of its Jews. The end times depend on it; the resurrection of the dead, one HAMAS detainee explained to his interrogators, will not take place until every last Jew has been destroyed.[99]

After Saturday Comes Sunday

HAMAS wasn't just a threat to Jews, its Islamicization of the struggle made Palestine's Christian community particularly nervous. The experience of the Copts in Egypt and the Maronites in Lebanon in the face of radical Islam would give any Christian pause. Hadn't, for example, the Egyptian Islamic militant whose doctrines inspired the formation of Islamic Jihad in Gaza justified attacks on Christians? In 1981 a blind professor from the Al-Azhar faculty, Sheikh Umar Abd al-Rahman, the man who would a decade later be implicated in the bombing of New York's World Trade Center, assured young militants they would enter paradise when they killed Coptic goldsmiths during robberies committed to finance their activities.[100]

Palestinian nationalists went to considerable lengths to stress the common condition of Muslims and Christian Palestinians. Although Christians were less likely to join the rock throwing against Israeli troops, Palestinian Christians distinguished themselves by other forms of militance, such as the dogged tax resistance by Christians villagers in Beit Sahur near Jerusalem.[101] The *intifada* witnessed a marked Arabization of the Christian churches, galvanizing them into unprecedented open and united support for the nationalist claims of their parishioners, seeking to strip the Old Testament of its Zionist message, trying to develop common theological ground with each other and the Muslim clerics. After Jewish settlers in April 1990 took possession of St. John's Hospice in Jerusalem, a property owned by the Greek Orthodox Patriarchate, not only did all Christian churches and the *haram* close their doors in a day of protest, but a Palestinian flag was displayed for the first time inside the Church of the Holy Sepulcher.

"Bullets don't make a distinction between a Muslim and a Christian," read the *intifada* graffiti sprayed on a Jerusalem wall. Nonetheless, while the Unified Leadership stressed the fraternal ties between Palestinian Muslims and Christians, HAMAS not infrequently made Christian Palestinians into a collectivity worthy of contempt.[102] Palestinian Muslim women were lectured that in marrying a Christian, one risked disaster – sickness, financial loss, even death.[103] Nuns in East Jerusalem reported that since the *intifada* began, stones were being thrown into church courtyards.[104]

HAMAS used the Qur'anic term *nasara*, literally "followers of the man from Nazareth," to describe Palestinian Christians. Christians consider this term an insult, preferring to be know as *masiheyun*, "followers of the Messiah." In December 1989, HAMAS even called for a strike on Christmas Day. After a popular uproar forced it to back down, one HAMAS leader sniped, "[T]he Christians, like any minority, feel deprived; that's their privilege."[105]

In the Islamic state envisioned by HAMAS, Christian Palestinians would exist as a subordinated minority. The Covenant stated that it was only under "the shadow of Islam" that the three religions – Judaism, Christianity, and Islam – had been able to live in harmony. The followers of religions other than Islam, it stated, should stop "fighting Islam in ruling this area, because when they rule, there will only be murdering, punishing, and banishing, because they make life hard for their own people, not to mention the followers of other religions" (Article 31).

HAMAS portrayed Palestinian Christians as privileged agents of West-ernization, missionaries of the godless East and West. Sheikh Yasin publicly suggested that the Palestinian Christian community's relative affluence allowed them to enjoy "undue privilege" within Palestinian society. HAMAS sought to denigrate the factions of the PLO by the preminence of Christians within them. Why was it Christians, they asked pointedly, who led the important Communist Palestinian organizations? How could the al-Fatah-controlled PLO hope to represent Muslim inter-ests when Christians like Hanna Siniora, editor of the pro-Fatah Jerusa-lem newspaper *Al-Fajr*, controlled the mass media? HAMAS identified Christianity with the Crusading West, going so far as to attribute the PLO's misguided notion of a "secular state" to the influence of Christian missionaries.[106] As the *intifada* wore on HAMAS graffiti began to warn, "First the Jews, then the Christians."[107]

Martyr's Blood

HAMAS cast itself as Jerusalem's defender, guardian of al-Aqsa. HAMAS's favorite wall signature was a clenched fist rising out of the Dome of the Rock, usually situated within a map of Palestine.[108] For HAMAS, Palestine's sacrality flows from Jerusalem, which made Pales-tine into the "soil of *al-Isra' wal-Mi'raj*," referring to the Prophet's miraculous voyage to Jerusalem from which he ascended to paradise. The real reason God took his Prophet on the night journey to Jerusa-lem, a HAMAS leaflet argued, was to demonstrate that this city, unlike any other in the world, is the "sister of Mecca." Thus, to abandon Jerusalem to the infidel was "tantamount to the abandonment of Mecca and al-Madina."[109]

Because HAMAS understands all of Palestine as God-given *waqf* to all the Muslim generations, no one has the right to give away any part of it (Article 11). Kings, presidents, nationalist organizations have no right to cede it. International conferences cannot resolve the conflict, not only because "unbelievers" have never treated Muslims justly, but, more fundamentally, because these conferences would require partition. Sign-ing any document that would give the Jews even a single square inch of this sacred territory would be a mark of "ignominy on the brow of the Muslim Palestinian people."

If the sanctity of Palestine was not enough of a reason to oppose a peace based on partition, HAMAS's anti-Semitic vision of the Jews likewise made real peace unthinkable. Peace treaties, Hamas argued, could only be a Jewish ploy to neutralize the Palestinians, divide the Arabs, and reach for even more Islamic land. "Today," the covenant proclaimed, "it's Palestine and tomorrow it will be another country, and then another, the Zionist plan has no bounds, and after Palestine they wish to expand from the Nile River to the Euphrates. When they totally occupy it they will look towards another, and such is their plan in the 'Protocols of the Learned Elders of Zion.' "[110]

HAMAS's program was in complete contradiction to the dominant position within the PLO. As the Palestine National Council in Algiers moved toward its historic vote agreeing to partition Palestine in November 1988, HAMAS issued a a special leaflet reiterating its position of total jihad. HAMAS rejected all efforts to end jihad or to establish peace with what it called "murderers" or calls to accept "the Jewish entity on any part of our land."[111] When the PNC declared a Palestinian state, the Unified National Leadership circulated a leaflet (number 29) entitled "The Joy of the Independent Palestinian State Proclamation." HAMAS, like Israel, ignored the event.[112]

HAMAS understood the PLO as a family relative who had gone astray, mistakenly accepting the invaders' idea of a secular state as its goal. Sheikh Yasin had once derided the PLO's territorial nationalism as "idolatry."[113] HAMAS now sought to resynthesize Islam, a transnational religion, with local Palestinian nationalism, recognizing for the first time the purely Islamic legitimacy of a Palestinian nation-state. The liberation of Palestine, HAMAS insisted, must eventuate in an Islamic state, one that draws its authority from a timeless God, not from the historical will of the people. "[T]he Islamic nature of the Palestinian issue is part and parcel of our *din* [way of life] and whosoever neglects part of his *din* is surely lost." When the PLO, HAMAS declared, "adopts Islam as its system of life, we will be its soldiers and the firewood of its fire, which will burn the enemies." HAMAS offered the people of Palestine a clear choice between the PLO's non-Islamic two-state solution for a small part of Palestine or an Islamic jihad for the whole thing.

As HAMAS fought Israel, it was also fighting for hegemony among the Palestinians, to seize the streets back from the PLO, to prevent a two-state scenario in which Arafat would be king. Soon after HAMAS revealed itself as the Palestinian branch of the Muslim Brotherhood, it began to order the population to follow its own timetable for strikes, fasts, and confrontations with the enemy. HAMAS's strikes, many set to the religious calendar, were often on days the nationalists requested Palestinians not to strike. The Qassam battalions initially enforced these strikes, torching stores that refused to shut down. In early August 1988 HAMAS's strike enforcement sparked widespread violence in the Palestinians towns of the West Bank. Soon after nationalists forced open the store fronts of merchants who were following the HAMAS calls, HAMAS activists would return and demand that they shut. These violent altercations only ended when leaders of the two groups met outside the occupied territories, agreeing that the Unified Leadership would have priority in setting strike timetables, but only after the nationalists had consulted the HAMAS leadership.[114]

HAMAS grew steadily stronger in Jerusalem during the *intifada*. While the Jordanian Brotherhood initially kept HAMAS activists out of upper reaches of Jerusalem's Islamic bureacracy, HAMAS steadily penetrated its mosques by organizing study groups and collecting *zakat*, or charity, for those hit hardest by the *intifada*'s endless strikes and closures. HAMAS members routinely went to the poorest neighborhoods in Jerusalem, like Silwan and Ras al-Amud, to repair and paint houses. They fixed doors and windows; distributed blankets, heaters, and food, never great quantities, but enough to make a difference for families sometimes on the edge of starvation. They gave kerosene and food to the elderly who were unable to go the markets themselves. They gave doctors and pharmacies money to provide minimal levels of health care and medicine to whoever needed it. HAMAS provided the biers to carry the dead, as well as financing proper Muslim funerals for those too poor to afford it.[115]

Jerusalem was a central node for both the local leadership of Arafat's al-Fatah and the clerics of the Muslim Brotherhood entrenched in its Islamic bureaucracies. As self-proclaimed guardians of the stones whence the Prophet made his heavenly ascent, HAMAS naturally gravitated to it as the perfect place to engage its external enemies and internal rivals.

In April 1989, as Ramadan began, HAMAS activists from Gaza Strip went to Jerusalem and organized massive disturbances on the *haram*, hurling stones on the Jews praying below at the Western Wall. Police retaliated with tear gas and rubber bullets.[116] As a result of this conflict, the Israeli Interior Ministry only allowed Jerusalemites entrance to the *haram*, an unprecedented closure of the city. The mufti of Jerusalem, Sheikh Sa'ad al-Din al-Alami, called for Muslims throughout Palestine to pray in al-Aqsa. If the Israelis "prevent them from entering the mosque," he said, "they are to pray in the Old City of Jerusalem. If they are barred from entering the city, they are to pray on the roads leading to Jerusalem." The police and the army set up roadblocks on the highways leading into Jerusalem, so that only Muslims from Jerusalem could enter.[117] Hundreds of Muslims bent daily on the tarmac in front of the Israeli soldiers sifting out Arab Jerusalemites who were let pass.

As the *intifada* ground on without political product, HAMAS became increasingly influential, its attacks on Israeli military personnel and civilians becoming ever more frequent and ever more justified in the eyes of an exhausted and demoralized populace. In 1989, unlike in 1988, the Palestinians largely obeyed HAMAS's call to strike on Partition Day.[118]

Political events in Jordan further bolstered the position of HAMAS. At the end of 1989, inspired by the *intifada*, riots broke out in Jordan. After the Hashemite regime consented to hold its first elections since democracy had been suspended in 1956, Muslim Brotherhood candidates took thirty-two of the eighty seats in the Jordanian parliament. Among other things, the Brothers demanded that Jordan reopen the borders for guerrilla attacks on Israel.[119] King Hussein was forced to cede the Brothers new powers, five ministerial portfolios including the Ministry of Awqaf, which controlled Jerusalem's holy places. This gave the Muslim Brotherhood, and a number of young radical leaders of HAMAS in particular, enormous influence over Jerusalem's Islamic shrines.[120]

On Friday, October 5, 1990, the Islamic radicals would use their newly acquired leverage over this sacred platform to bloody effect. The sermon in al-Aqsa mosque that day included a special appeal for Muslims throughout Israel, the West Bank, and Gaza to gather on *al-haram al-sharif*, the compound enclosing the Dome of the Rock and al-Aqsa mosque, the following Monday to defend it against a small Jewish group called "The Faithful of the Temple Mount" that had announced its intention to enter the *haram* and to lay the foundation stone of the Third Temple. Not to be outdone, the Unified Leadership naturally sought to bring out its forces to demonstrate the resolve of the nationalists to defend this sacred site.

In the event, the Israeli police banned the small Jewish group from entering the Temple Mount, a ban upheld by the Israeli High Court that Sunday. Israel had few effective links to this new radical Islamic leadership for sub rosa negotiation and contact.[121] On Monday morning, as many as three thousand Palestinians gathered on the *haram*, some of them arriving before dawn. In the plaza below, in front of the Western Wall, more than twenty thousand Jews were gathered for the Sukkot morning prayers. As the Jewish service ended, the leader of the Faithful of the Temple Mount, Gershon Salomon, and about fifty followers nonetheless attempted to enter the *haram* at the Mughrabian Gate above the Western Wall plaza. When they were blocked by Israeli border and municipal police, Salomon defiantly told to the officer who ordered him to leave, "we shall continue our struggle until the Israeli flag is flying from the Dome of the Rock."[122] Salomon's group left the Old City through the Dung Gate on their way to the Shiloah Pool in Silwan carrying a banner that proclaimed "Temple Mount – the Symbol of Our People – Is in the Hands of Our Enemies."

As the Faithful of Temple Mount departed, an Israeli soldier guarding the *haram* accidentally dropped a tear gas canister, which rolled into a group of Muslim women preparing to pray. This provoked the Palestinian demonstrators to throw stones over the walls of the enclosure at the police and Salomon's group. Some of the police, who broke through the locked and barricaded Mughrabian Gate to the *haram*, where they confronted thousands of stone-throwing demonstrators, began shooting with their weapons on automatic fire. Within a matter of minutes seventeen Palestinians had been shot to death and more than one hundred and fifty had been seriously wounded.[123] It was the highest number of deaths in a single day for the nearly three-year-old *intifada*. Jerusalem had, at last, drawn large amounts of Palestinian blood.

Ambulances rushed from all over the city to ferry the wounded to the Mokassed and Augusta Victoria Hospitals in East Jerusalem, where doctors and nurses worked frantically to save the injured. The floor of the emergency room at Mokassed Hospital was flooded with blood. Hysterical relatives rushed to the hospitals looking for family members. Two Palestinian flags hung on the doors to the hospital's morgue. Palestinians stoned and set fire to buses and cars throughout Jerusalem. Hundreds were arrested in the city that day, including Faisal Husayni.

Although many Palestinians, including, for example, Sheikh Jamal, a leader of the Supreme Muslim Council, charged that the Shamir government consciously staged the confrontation, Israeli investigations concluded that the conflagration had been accidental.[124] But for Palestinians this was no random horror, but a symptom of occupation. Many also accorded the tragedy deep religious meaning. Four days later, a short allegory appeared on the front page of *Al-Sha'ab*, a Jerusalem newspaper closely identified with the PLO, describing how black birds had driven off the white doves that had nested around the Ka'aba in Mecca since the days of the Prophet Muhammad. The white doves flew off to Jordan according to the story, leaving the black birds nesting around Islam's most sacred centers.

What could this mean? Iraq was just then girding itself for the American-led onsalught. Only three days before the killings, the Israeli government began distributing gas masks in the event Saddam Hussein carried out his threats to use poison gas in rocket attacks against Israel. Thus the allegory placed the attack in the context of Allah's hoped-for intervention in the coming apocalyptic struggle between Iraq and the West. The black birds represented Allah's coming blow against the idolators – the Americans, the Israelis, the ibn-Sa'ud family who controlled Mecca and Medina and were participating in the American-led assault. Only Jerusalem remained in pious hands. The last and lowliest of Islam's three sacred sites had become the first and most important battlefield against the infidel. Perhaps the white birds in Jordan represented the Muslim Brotherhood, whose forces were on the march, who had organized the defiant defense of the *haram* against the Zionists?[125]

A cult of martyrdom enveloped the *haram*. Young people dipped their hands in the blood coagulating on the smooth stone platform, making palm prints on walls near where individuals fell or on the marble exterior of the Dome of the Rock. Spent bullet casings and tear gas canisters were collected into a case attached to one of the pillars in al-Aqsa mosque, where Palestinians approached reverently, touching it with their hands, which they then brought to their hearts. A special exhibit of the blood-soaked clothing of the dead and wounded was mounted in the foyer of the Islamic Museum on the *haram*.

The shopkeers of the Old City displayed colored pictures of the dead, often young sons, cousins, or neighbors. Majdi al-Shami, a resident of East Jerusalem, lost his sixteen-year-old son, Ayman, up there. In contrast to the convention whereby grieving guests are served bitter, black coffee, he served the mourners sweets and soft drinks. His son, he insisted, had died a martyr's death. "Ayman is a bridegroom and this was his wedding day," the father told them.[126]

Two weeks later, a Palestinian, Omar Sa'id Abu-Sirhan, only three years older than Ayman al-Shami, sought to avenge their deaths. A construction worker in Jerusalem, Abu-Sirhan suddenly dropped his trowel and took out a fifteen-inch commando knife. Screaming, "God is Great! Slaughter the Jews!" he began a deadly rampage through Bakaa, a gentrifying neighborhood inhabited by many supporters of Peace Now and the most liberal tendencies within the Labour Party. First he fatally stabbed an eighteen-year-old woman, Iris Azulaie, in uniform but unarmed. Next, he slashed a thirteen-year old, Amikam Kovner, the grandson of Abba Kovner, the revered Israeli poet who fought in the Jewish uprising in the Warsaw ghetto. Eli Eltratz, a nursery owner, died with a plant in his hands. Charlie Chelouce, a member of the antiterrorism police squad, was his final victim. As Abu-Sirhan rushed him, Chelouce first fired in the air, then at his assailant's legs, as required by military regulations, until he, too, was stabbed to death.[127] Sirhan, wounded in the leg, was finally wrestled to the ground and taken away in a police van for questioning.

Levi Kelman, a Reform rabbi, heard the news and rushed to the site, two blocks from his synagogue. A crowd had gathered around Eli Eltratz's corpse. A man with a yarmulka began to scream, "Death to the Arabs!" It would be a desecration of God's name, Kelman retorted, to incite the murder of innocents. "He's from the PLO!" the man screamed back. At this, a group fell on the rabbi, kicking him, punching him, spitting at his fallen figure.

After an Israeli policeman waded in and pulled him from the mob,

Kelman began to run to the synagogue to warn the Palestinian construction workers to go inside. As he ran, he told us, it flashed through his mind that there were Jewish children at the nursery school and that he must protect them first. Two of the Palestinians never made it to work, attacked by crowds of Israelis who beat them so badly they were hospitalized for weeks. The police, an Israeli journalist told us, intervened very hesitantly. "People," a policeman reportedly said, "needed to let off steam."

Its martyrs' blood proved that HAMAS was, indeed, as its Jerusalem graffiti claimed, "Stronger than Bullets!"[128] By defending the *haram* from the infidel, HAMAS had finally provoked Israel to engage in the same kind of uncontrolled violence in Jerusalem they had periodically practiced elsewhere in the occupied territories. Abu-Sirhan's attack was part of what Palestinians called "the war of the knives," in which more than two dozen Israelis were either stabbed or seriously wounded. These attacks, some of them uncoordinated, all increased the reputation of HAMAS on the streets.[129] HAMAS, by engaging the enemy at Palestine's most sacred center, by setting in motion a cycle of profanation, was the first force able to prompt Israel to deny Jerusalem to the Palestinians, thereby elevating HAMAS's claim to be its most valiant defender and its world view as the most adequate representation of reality. Blood offered on the center's stones was a force to reckon with.

15

Baghdad, Berlin, and Jerusalem

After more than twenty years of trumpeting its intention to destroy the "Zionist entity," in 1988 the PLO accepted a small Palestinian state sandwiched between Israel and Jordan. Tunis was reacting to the Palestinians in Jerusalem, rather the reverse. A large segment of the Israeli public was willing to talk about some kind of Palestinian government. Likud and Labour, locked together in a "unity" government, settled on the conditions under which the Palestinians would participate in "regional" elections in the West Bank and Gaza to generate a non-PLO delegation to negotiate the final status of the territories with Israel. While Likud backed away, Labour was willing to negotiate with supporters of the PLO, who, they understood, would unofficially consult Arafat. Faisal Husayni, Fatah's man in Jerusalem, was briefing Israel's Labour Party and figures across the Israeli spectrum. "I've never been in a room with so many security forces when I wasn't manacled," Husayni quipped at one meeting where a few Israeli intelligence men were present. Ziad abu Zayyad was being invited to lecture to Israeli soldiers. Because Arafat had spoken the forbidden words acknowledging Israel's right to exist, America began to talk officially to the PLO. It was the Reagan administration's last diplomatic act before passing the Oval Office to George Bush in 1989. As Israel stalled over negotiations, an about-to-be-united Europe threatened economic sanctions against Israel, which feared being shut out of its most important market.

And then, in less than a year, Arafat, most of the factions grouped within the PLO, and most importantly, the Palestinians in the territories threw their support behind Iraq as the industrial powers, Saudi Arabia, Egypt, the other Gulf States, and even Syria mobilized to reverse Saddam Hussein's seizure of Kuwait in August 1990. Across the political spectrum, PLO leaders publicly declared they would throw their operatives into action against enemy targets when and if America were to invade. In a few days the Palestinians wiped out years of diplomatic gains and political goodwill.

Scuds over Jerusalem

In the lead-up to the Gulf War, Palestinians in Jerusalem and the West Bank demonstrated daily for Saddam Hussein. His photo was plastered everywhere. Palestinians pointed to the moon, claiming they could see Saddam Hussein's face in it. During the war, there was a report of a child born with the image of Saddam imprinted on his forehead. A sheep was heard bleating Saddam Hussein's name in Arabic. The Iraqi leader was not unappreciative. "The steadfast stone-throwing people who were assigned by God to perform the duty of showing right against the wrong of the Zionists" Hussein called them in early September.[1]

Iraq has been one of Israel's most bitter foes, the only Arab country that refused at the close of the 1948 war even to make an armistice agreement with Israel. Saddam Hussein's home province had been renamed after Salah al-Din, the Kurdish warrior who retook Jerusalem from the Crusaders in the twelfth century, when the pan-Arab Baath first came to power in 1968. Hussein also wrapped himself in the mantle of Nebuchadnezzar, the Babylonian king who took Jerusalem from the Israelites in the sixth century B.C.E. And because ancient Babylonian texts claim Nebuchadnezzar's armies breached the walls of Jerusalem on the seventeenth day of the month of Tammuz, the Iraqis called their nuclear reactor, capable of producing weapons-grade plutonium, Tammuz 17. On June 7, 1981, the same day Israeli troops stormed the Old City twenty-four years earlier, sixteen Israeli jets destroyed the reactor.

After overrunning Kuwait, Hussein linked his willingness to withdraw to Israel's willingness to leave the territories occupied in the 1967 war. Progress on the Palestinian front became the Iraqi dictator's best hope of mobilizing the Arab world against the American-led assault on his acquisition of Kuwait. Saddam Hussein, whom the United States had cultivated as a moderating influence in the Middle East, left little doubt about his ultimate intentions. "With the aid of Allah," he told his people, "we will reconquer Jerusalem, all the other occupied Arab territories; and Palestine will be liberated from the Zionists, Allah is great."[2] Palestinians wanted to believe a new Nasser had emerged to the east, a man who would match the rhetoric of liberation with military action, who would use Arab oil for power and the honor it spawned, rather than for diamond brooches, Maseratis, and Christian Dior clothing as in Kuwait.[3] Palestinian parents in the occupied territories were naming their new-born sons after the Iraqi leader.

Those forces within Israel pressing for a negotiated solution with the Palestinians were immobilized. Their "pragmatic" counterparts within the PLO had undercut their ability to press their compatriots to believe a Palestinian state would not be a prelude to destruction. The hatred, the will to annihilation, would always be there, waiting for its time. A few weeks after the Iraqi invasion of Kuwait, Peace Now arranged a high-level meeting in Jerusalem to bring together Israeli peace activists and known PLO members. Only one PLO member attended. To the consternation of the assembled Israelis, who had devoted years of their lives to getting Israel and the PLO to the bargaining table, the Palestinian harangued them about the propriety of the Palestinian choice between the "American Christian Crusaders" and the Palestinian's Arab protector, Saddam Hussein.

Although the Unified Leadership of the Intifada reiterated its support for "all peoples' rights to self-determination," once the conflict had been joined, its position was unambiguous: "We stand firmly behind Iraq in its fight against the U.S."[4] According to Cairo's *Al-Ahram* newspaper, they also sent a congratulatory cable to Hussein, lauding his invasion of Kuwait as the first step to the liberation of Palestine.[5]

The Palestinians were acutely aware that Saddam's occupation had galvanized the entire world to undo it in a way their own plight never had; that no comparable opposition had faced Israel when its army had marched into Lebanon; that the United States had done next to nothing to nudge Prime Minister Yitzhak Shamir into peace negotiations. The Western world, and even its Arab allies, refused to link Iraq and the question of Palestine. America's apparent unwillingness to allow an Arab solution seemed to many Palestinians yet another indication of the West's fear of a powerful Arab world, of America's neocolonialist *macht*. Saddam Hussein presented himself as Palestine's champion; he was willing to stand up to America. Ordinary Palestinians loved it. "Banish the filth of the American army and their collaborators from Saudi Arabia, the land of the holy places," the mufti of Jerusalem told Saddam Hussein.[6]

Having served as the rhetorical coin of inter-Arab competition for so long, many Palestinians actually believed their nation's suffering was the cause of the Arab world's instability. As millions of soldiers massed in the desert, *Al-Fajr* opined: "A movement on the Palestinian question remains the most workable key to opening the door to peace, not only in the Gulf, but also in the rest of the trouble-filled Middle East. Once the Palestinian question is resolved justly, all other conflicts in the Middle East will end, stabilizing the entire region."[7]

A number of Israelis pointed out that while Germans were still celebrating in a unified Berlin, the Jews of Jerusalem were lining up for gas masks. When war came, the same question was on everybody's minds: would he or wouldn't he? Each time the air-raid sirens wailed, the Israelis had to decide whether to go into rooms sealed against poison gas, which were useless against conventional warheads, or down into hardened shelters that, with their air vents, were useless against poison gas – chemical poisons and warheads produced by the Iraqis with the aid of German corporations.

It was even harder for Israelis to explain to themselves, sitting in their sealed rooms, why they did not respond when rocket after rocket hit their homeland. The telephones rang after each air raid siren: Where did it fall? Which neighborhood? What block? Fear in the face of violent attack, doing nothing as Arabs celebrated, sang, applauded. "We're not California Beverly Hills Jews," David Hartman, a Jerusalem rabbi, said. "We're not *golus* [i.e., exile] Jews . . . We don't run." Hartman, who grew up on the basketball courts of Brooklyn, told the story of an Israeli *hasid* who was in Brownsville, Chabad's hometown, when a group of blacks attacked. While all the other Orthodox Jews fled, the lone Israeli *hasid* remained where he was. "I don't know how to run," the *hasid* reportedly replied. "I lost that unique Jewish capacity." "Because when Jews," Hartman said, "ever enter into a place, they always look where's the exit, just to know how to get out fast . . . But in Israel we don't have an exit because there's no place we want to run to. So the issue is why we don't respond . . . The whole meaning of our identity was . . . never again to lock yourself in a room waiting for the pogrom to be over."

Hartman understood Israel's restraint as an awakening, a realization that "Israel is not a shtetl with F-15's," that Israel could play its role in a larger struggle against human evil, that restraint could be a source and indicator of power. "Israel," he said, "is the freeing of the Jewish people from the trauma of Auschwitz." Nonetheless, many Israelis, who called it the war of *havlaga*, or "forbearance," were not so sanguine. "Nobody could protect us," another Jewish Jerusalemite told us. "I am still a Jew of the Holocaust."

The Gulf War was the first war fought on real-time television. As the world watched Iraqi Scud missiles land along the Mediterranean coast and it became clear Jerusalem would not be targeted, the city's hotels filled with Israelis seeking its safety. Tel Aviv's mayor condemned them as "traitors." There they were joined by relief workers, UN personnel, and several dozen Christians who arrived to be present at what they were sure would be the end days. Hussein called his deadly missiles arching into Israel "the stones," identifying their explosive powers with the chunks of granite and limestone hurled at soldiers by Palestinian teenagers. The period around the Gulf War marked the absolute high point in terms of Palestinian rock throwing and erection of barricades.[8] Because of the outpouring of Palestinian enthusiasm for Saddam and the likelihood of Palestinian obstruction in the event of military action, the Israelis clamped a total curfew on the West Bank and Gaza for the duration of the conflict. Palestinians caught outside risked getting shot.

Crops rotted and many women, under duress, delivered their babies at home.

In October 1990, Israel had informed the Palestinians that there were no gas masks for them, that the masks would have to be imported, and that they could purchase them at one hundred dollars per mask.[9] The Palestinians failed to import their own masks through sympathetic foreign consuls. It was only after Scuds started falling on Israel and the Israeli High Court, responding to a petition by a legal services unit of the Latin Patriarchate in Jerusalem, ordered them to do so, that the military distributed masks to the Palestinians. But Israel didn't have enough (only 170,000 left for a population over a million), and most Palestinians sat out the war without any protection.[10]

Nadira Kevorkian, a Palestinian in Jerusalem, was issued a gas mask. It was difficult for her and her family, she said, to have them when she knew most Palestinians did not. The Gulf War pushed Kevorkian, a Palestinian who lives in the Old City's Armenian Quarter, to existential desperation. A psychiatric social worker who works with medical crises, wife abuse, and bereavement, she had earlier worked for the Jerusalem municipality. After the *intifada* began, Palestinian clients viewed her as a collaborator; Israelis saw her as an advocate for its enemies. The *intifada* made it impossible for her to segregate politics from professional compassion. She quit and went to work for Bethlehem University.

As the Gulf War began, Kevorkian tried to use her professional skills to calm Palestinians buffeted by their desperate desire to believe Saddam would liberate them, their traumatic sense of vulnerability, and their knowledge that only the humanity of their enemy, the Israelis, could protect them. Nadira especially wanted to instruct parents how to calm their children's gigantic fears. But how to get to them? The Palestinians were confined by curfew to their homes, shut in at the very moment they most needed each other's support. The newspapers were not circulating. No radio or television channels were available to her. She called Radio Monte Carlo and Jordanian TV.

After a week of desperate immobility, together with other Palestinian mental health workers in Jerusalem, Kevorkian opened a telephone hotline. Frantic calls began to come in – women, children, people on the verge of collapse, desperate parents wanting gas masks for their children whom she could do nothing to help. (The Israelis did not originally have masks for Palestinian children in the territories under the age of fifteen, so many parents refused to take masks for themselves as well.)[11] A woman called whose husband had not yet returned from getting food during the break in the curfew; she was completely alone, ready to deliver her first baby and in total panic.

Palestinians had heard that Saddam Hussein had prayed "the prayer of the death," that he had resigned himself that in this, the mother of all wars, Israeli-occupied lands would be engulfed in a conflagration and the West Bank might be reduced to a Palestinian graveyard. Rumors circulated the Israelis were preparing mass graves for the Palestinians, which many interpreted to mean they intended a mass killing of Palestinians. (The Israelis were preparing graves for all residents in the event of chemical attacks.)

"Saddam wants to kill me," one teenage caller ranted, "the Israelis want to kill me. Both my brothers are in prison . . . The children of my brother are here. We can't protect them. We don't have any gas masks . . . I don't have school . . . I don't have a future. I have nothing. Why should I live?"

Each path Nadira Kevorkian tried, the girl closed it off. Kevorkian reminded her that in 1948, many Palestinians left their homes.

"Yes," the girl said, "my mother left her house."

"Okay, but you're not going to leave your house. You are there, so being and keeping yourself, taking care of yourself and of your house is a great power. Because then, when we'll have our state, you'll be there, and your brothers will go out of the prison and they'll find somebody is taking care of them."

At this the caller's words dissolved into sobs and Kevorkian knew the frightened girl at the other end of the line would be okay.

When the war began, anguished mothers called in, with half their children on the roof cheering for the Scud missiles streaking across the sky toward Tel Aviv, and the other half hovering inside, wailing, shaking uncontrollably. "It could tell you about our psychological state," Nadira said, "looking for a savior, looking for a future, but at the same time wanting to keep yourself. So some of the people wanted to keep themselves and stayed in the room. Others, said, 'No, we want Palestine. It's enough. We can't wait more. We've lost a lot.' "

Kevorkian could understand, even empathize with, the outpouring of popular support Hussein received. She herself had felt the fanged hatred that propelled it, the desire to inflict damage, to make the enemy suffer. During the *intifada,* she met weekly with teenagers wanted by the military, many of whom never slept at home, in Dehaishe refugee camp just south of Jerusalem. Its perimeter cased in high metal mesh to prevent stone throwing on the road, it looks from the outside like an enormous rabbit pen. As she approached their hillside meeting place at the camp's edge, an Israeli soldier lifted her in his arms, carrying her about like a baby. She pleaded with him, she said, but he continued to carry her back toward the camp entrance, laughing.

"Shout at him! Curse him!" the girls in the camp yelled.

All she could do was ask him in Hebrew, which she never spoke in the refugee camp, to please let her down.

"No, I'm enjoying it," he replied.

"I felt really bad. In front of all the people that I had to help and to give to and to be their therapist . . . In front of all the people there, he showed them, 'This is your social worker. Here is she, she's in my hand and I could play with her the way I want.' "

Nadira Kevorkian never went back to Dehaishe. "I couldn't look at the faces of the people." Later that evening, as she visited one of her professors at the Hebrew University, "I said to myself, 'In this moment, maybe I could use a knife and stab somebody.' And I am a very quiet person. I'm not a person who could use knives."

Even Nadira Kevorkian found herself thinking that perhaps Saddam Hussein was a savior, perhaps he would push the Israelis out. Nothing else seemed to be working. Kevorkian understood this fantastic hope, but when she saw Chairman Arafat on Arab television announcing that he and the Iraqi dictator would soon be in East Jerusalem, visiting the Dome of the Rock, she became apoplectic. "I got crazy. If I got a gun I could kill him. He hadn't had the limited feeling of his nation. People were suffering here so much and he['s] talking on a political [level] . . . What about the humans over here? We're not animals here." Many Palestinians, particularly parents of young children, she told us, were livid with Arafat, with the PLO outside, for failing to consider the implications of their actions for people on the "inside."

"But," she admitted, "nobody dared to open his mouth and to say something."

Arafat's Choice

There were indications Arafat knew of Iraq's plan well before the invasion of Kuwait, that Palestinians in his network who worked in Kuwaiti banks helped Iraq expropriate its neighbor's financial assets, and that the PLO provided Iraq with names and locations of key personnel within Kuwait. After the Iraqi invasion, rejectionist groups within the PLO sent their militia members to Kuwait to help the Iraqis police their new province.[12] Some Palestinians were moving in to take homes and positions left vacant by Kuwaitis who had fled for their lives.

Arafat had delegitimated the PLO as a trustworthy partner for peace in a way the Israeli right could never have accomplished. Arafat not only alienated the only two nations – the United States and Egypt – who might have mediated a solution with Israel, he outraged the PLO's most important financial backers: Saudi Arabia and Kuwait.[13] In Kuwait a large chunk of the Palestinian middle class had rebuilt their lives after 1948. Arafat himself had made his fortune there as a young man. The PLO had been born there.

By allying himself with Iraq, Arafat turned the PLO back to a military solution, believing Israel could be engaged and the status quo shattered. Ideologically, the PLO decision to support the first forcible annexation of a sovereign Arab state by another Arab regime was incredible. Consistent with classic pan-Arab Ba'ath ideology, Iraq claimed Kuwait was an artifice of British imperialism. True, but so is Palestine, which Syrian, Jordanian and Israeli forces have all coveted as their own. The PLO claimed to be a democracy, whereas Saddam Hussein was a brutal dictator who used barbarous means to solidify his personal power. The Iraqis had expelled hundreds of thousands of Kurds, another national minority, from their territory and killed thousands of others with poison gas. And they were systematically driving out Kuwait's citizenry. Local nationalist logic could not dictate the Palestinian choice.

Certainly Saddam Hussein's bellicose gestures were an intoxicant for most Palestinians. It had been almost two decades since an Arab state had seriously threatened Israel. But this does not explain the PLO's decision to support Iraq. The PLO took the path it did not because it was strong, but because it was desperately weak. It was the path of least resistance. Three factors were critical. First, pushed from one Arab state to the next, the PLO accepted Baghdad as its most important staging ground. The PLO had been denied a secure base of operations first by Egypt when it controlled Gaza, then by Jordan and Syria. Each of these states attempted to use the PLO as an instrument of its own foreign policy. After Arafat was chased from Lebanon, the PLO moved its base to Tunisia. Not only was Tunis irrelevant to the geopolitics of the region, it, too, proved an insecure haven. Baghdad, the longtime supporter and sometime home of the most radical components of the rejectionist front like Abu Nidal, had become the PLO's latest Arab patron, its last Arab station.[14]

Second, it seemed to the Palestinians they were losing their demographic weapon. Given the enormous size of the Palestinian population in the West Bank and Gaza, and high Arab birth rates, PLO strategists had long held that Israeli incorporation of the West Bank and Gaza would be the path by which Palestine would ultimately become a binational state. And then along came perestroika. The Soviet Union, desperately in need of American aid, investment, and markets, decided to let its Jews emigrate. But it was impossible for the Russian regime to legitimate this legal exodus under anything other than a logic of repatriation. If the Jews were free to go anywhere they wished, others would have to be free to do so as well. As the Soviet Union began to disintegrate, the Jewish exodus, which had begun in September 1989, received a nasty shove from an upsurge of Russian anti-Semitism. By closing their doors to new Russian Jewish émigrés, the Americans cooperated in funneling what Israeli officials then expected would be upward of two million Jews to Israel.[15] In the first year, close to two hundred thousand Russian Jews landed at Lod Airport. If the immigration continued, it now seemed possible Greater Israel would forever have a large Jewish majority, even if Israel incorporated the territories. The PLO pressed the Russians unsuccessfully to stop the outflow of Jews to Israel.

Third, the road to peace was threatening to tear the Palestinian movement into warring pieces. Arafat had taken an enormous political gamble pushing the rejectionist forces within the PLO to accept UN resolutions 242 and 338, to settle for a two-state solution as final rather than transitional. Before the PLO declared a Palestinian state, American diplomats had repeatedly assured Palestinian leaders that once the PLO formally signaled its willingness to live in peace with Israel, the Israeli electorate would respond and the United States would press Israel to negotiate. Both, in fact, initially failed to happen. Arafat had received nothing but a promise of negotiations in which the PLO would have no vote. Arafat was in no position to wait indefinitely, nor to enforce a cessation of violent attacks on Israel by member factions of the PLO.

The PLO has always been a loose coalition of militias, not a unitary state-in-waiting. Although the divergent groups went along at the Palestinian National Council meetings that declared a Palestinian state in 1988, not all of them agreed to stop their independent military operations. Even while al-Fatah initially refrained from armed attacks, units from George Habash's Popular Front for the Liberation of Palestine, from the Nayef Hawatmeh's Democratic Front for the Liberation of Palestine, and from Abul-Abbas's Palestine Liberation Front repeatedly mounted incursions from Egypt, from Jordan, from Lebanon, and from the sea, hoping to drive a wedge between the Americans and the PLO, to stop what they saw as an insidious dialogue going nowhere.

One of these independent operations stripped Arafat of the *intifada*'s most important political fruit. On May 30, 1990, Abul Abbas's sea attack on a Tel Aviv beach was intercepted by the Israeli military. Abul Abbas was the leader who had organized the hijacking of the *Achille Lauro* in 1985 in which a wheelchair-bound American Jew was murdered and dumped overboard. This time around, Iraq planned and paid for Abul Abbas's operation. Abul Abbas not only sat on the PLO Executive Committee, but he got there under Arafat's sponsorship, had an office in PLO headquarters in Tunis, and had met with Arafat days before the attack. Given the American stipulation that the U.S.–PLO dialogue was

conditional on PLO suspension of terrorism, the PLF attack was a maneuver to undercut the Cairo-mediated dialogue. The Palestinians inside
who had been negotiating with the Americans were furious. But just as
Arafat refused to condemn the attack or to support Abul Abbas's expulsion from the Executive Committee when the *Achille Lauro* was hijacked in 1985, he refused again in 1990. In June, the Americans reluctantly broke off the dialogue, instructing their British allies to maintain
contact. The American decision was a manuever, not a political end
game.

Arafat's not expelling Abul Abbas reflected his dependency on the
secular rejectionists to counter the rising challenge of militant Islam.
That spring of 1990, HAMAS felt it was strong enough to request membership in the PLO on its own terms, demanding an allocation of not less
than 40 percent of the seats on the Palestine National Council.[16] Just
how threatening HAMAS had become to the PLO was indicated by
Chairman Arafat's rejected counteroffer of 30 percent. Arafat's refusal
also reflected his dependence on his Iraqi sponsors, as well as his belief
that the Americans would not press Israel to negotiate.[17] Chairman
Arafat also feared the American plan would undercut the PLO to the
advantage of the Palestinians on the inside.

Inside the occupied territories, the Palestinians were cracking into
partisan pieces. The longer the *intifada* continued, the more its congenital defects, weaknesses born of the PLO's structure and its strategic
relation to the Palestinians under Israeli occupation, revealed themselves. The uprising was made possible through cooperation between
Palestinian factions who accept territorial compromise and those who
reject it. Israeli collective punishments whereby whole towns and villages were placed under curfew for days at a time, as well as indiscriminate roundups in which Palestinians from every stream and strata were
thrown into detention camps, played their part in building this unusual
solidarity. So did the Syrian-sponsored war against the camps, where for
years after the Israelis left Beirut, the Amal militia, with Syrian backing,
tried physically to remove the PLO from Lebanese territory. These
attacks reunited the PLO's many factions, which fought for their very
lives against the same fellow Arabs they had hailed as progressive revolutionary forces a decade before.

When the *intifada* first started, many Palestinian leaders hoped a unified, nonpartisan territorial organization would emerge. Every few
weeks the leadership announced the *intifada*'s strategy in a numbered
communiqué, whose wording was hammered out by representatives of
the different factions, then faxed or telephoned from a pay phone in
Israel to PLO headquarters in Tunis, where it was edited and communicated back. Different movements within the Unified Leadership each

had access to their own printing presses and, for the most part, printed the same version of the communiqués. When Palestinians woke in the mornings, the leaflets, possession of which constituted grounds for immediate arrest, had appeared mysteriously on the ground.

This new mechanism of Palestinian resistance, however, had its defects. The Unified Leadership remained a loose coalition of representatives from different streams; the militant Muslims largely refused to participate. The nonpartisan popular committees spawned by the *intifada* were modeled on the cross-party committees Palestinian prisoners had fashioned in the prisons in order to fight for better conditions and control collaborators.[18] These solidary popular committees gradually dissolved as leaders from the different streams within the PLO outside jockeyed for influence.[19] The leaders of each partisan militia, operating from outside the territories, were willing neither to democratize their own organizations, nor to allow nonpartisan organizations to emerge in the occupied territories, where they could not control them. The partisan centers outside were unwilling to give voice to the people inside.

Loyalties to political parties proved stronger than those to Palestine. To the bitter disappointment of insiders from other factions and even some of its loyalists inside, al-Fatah even created its own domestic "army" at the very outset of the *intifada*.[20] Fatah never took the lead in fashioning territorywide organization, even after Jordan relinquished its claim on the West Bank. To organize across the occupied territories irrespective of political party, as the Communists had years before, would create a powerful counterweight to the PLO outside. Because Arafat was unwilling to risk losing control to the inside he was reluctant to allow regional elections to form a delegation that would negotiate with the Israelis.

Although there were those who wanted to make the Unified Leadership into a central command, al-Fatah refused to relinquish its independence.[21] As a result, the Unified Leadership could only establish a framework; it did not and could not give orders or directives. The radical rejectionists centered around the Popular Front for the Liberation of Palestine, the mainline nationalists organized by Fatah, and the militant Muslims led by the Muslim Brotherhood all had their own leaflets, their own independent "strike forces," their own codes of revolutionary justice, their own conditions for a "just" settlement. Because of its balkanized, partisan structure, in which each major stream attempted to control its constituents centrally from the outside, creating organizations that functioned as parallel front groups rather than as representatives of particular social groups or localities, the PLO was proving an obstacle to nation building within Palestine itself at a most critical juncture.[22]

Moreoever, the decentralized, diffuse structure of the *intifada* gave considerable autonomy to each local popular committee organized town by town, neighborhood by neighborhood. It relied on the profusion of social service organizations, youth clubs, professional associations that each political faction had used to colonize almost every aspect of social life. Because resistance was decentralized and fragmented into thousands of small units, divided by party, by locality, by occupation and gender, the *intifada* survived wave after wave of arrest of the Unified Leadership.[23] But the very conditions making the *intifada* almost impossible for the Israelis to stop also made it impossible for the Palestinians to control the population. It was not a bureacratic command that could issue orders and ensure discipline; it was not a mechanism to aggregate popular opinion.[24] There was little coordination. Compliance depended on consent.

Israeli repression systematically sought to crack that consent. When the *intifada* began, those who had been informants for Israel, some of whom had even been issued arms, naturally feared for their lives. Palestinian activists urged suspected collaborators be warned and given a chance to repent, and thereafter they and their families be shunned, their businesses boycotted. Isolation would work as well as violence. But the Palestinians had no mechanism to establish cross-local, cross-party control. After Israel killed, wounded, and removed generation after generation of leaders and activists to its desert jails, Palestinian strategy began to shift.

Fearing for the safety of the remainder, in the spring of 1989, the *intifada*'s local leadership gave the green light for "strike forces," the *al-mulathamin*, to assassinate collaborators.[25] By the end of that year, over a hundred "collaborators" had had their throats slit, had been burned on the arms and legs, brutally beaten to death in front of their neighbors, hacked to pieces, or hung at night on power lines or on meat hooks, dumped into wheelbarrows or garbarge piles. The leadership initially claimed these executions were approved at the highest level after evidence accumulated indicating continued complicity with the Zionist enemy. But by the second year of the uprising, it was clear that small gangs of masked Palestinian youths – "strike forces" with names like "Black Panthers" and "Red Eagles" – had taken revolutionary justice into their own hands, visiting vengeance on the enemies of the people – real and imagined.

By 1993, close to a thousand Palestinians had died at the hands of their own people without any chance for the accused to defend themselves, their confessions often exacted after sustained torture.[26] Palestinian human rights organizations made no public protests.[27] Small bands of boys, electrified by their powers, were moving out of control, fearing nothing, many enamored of the ideal of martyrdom for their nation.

Teenagers wearing hoods and capes, armed with knives and hatchets, violently interrogated suspects, burned their homes and cars, ordered children out of school, and beat to death those they considered beyond redemption. In 1989, for example, a Palestinian was cut to pieces simply for selling palm branches to Jews for use during the festival of Sukkot. A fortune-teller in her midthirties in the advanced stages of pregnancy, her hands tied behind her back, was shot twice in the head in front a crowd at the center of Nablus's casbah by three hooded men for her alleged collaboration.[28] The new Palestinian enforcers, many of them with smooth hairless faces, made a mockery of the baccalaureat exams, which Jordan finally cancelled in 1991. The PLO was so disturbed it forbade them from walking hooded at night.

There were reasons for this domestic orgy of bloodletting. With tens of thousands of Palestinians in jail, the survival of the political leadership of the *intifada* was a crucial task. The Israelis, it turned out, had been able to recruit informants among activists, particularly among younger prisoners who, while being roughly interrogated, beaten, and held for indefinite amounts of time, were told they were squandering their lives for a dubious honor. The Israelis were also still able to trade precious permits for family reunification or exit visas for information about *intifada* activists. The proliferation of new informers created enormous fear among the Palestinians.

Moreover, the *intifada* had to give considerable autonomy to each local popular committee, each "strike force." When combined with localism and political fragmentation, this meant that the uprising's organizational centers did not have mechanisms to control their counterparts in the field. (Strike forces in Jerusalem proper remained much more highly disciplined than in other cities, such as Nablus or Jenin.) A disproportionate share of the killings were conducted by HAMAS, over whom the PLO-affiliated leadership had absolutely no control.

Anybody who had dealings with Israelis was suspect. For example, Aisha Husayni abu-Shweish, head nurse and deputy director of the health department in Khan Yunis, was murdered in 1991 because of a brief conversation she had had with Deputy Foreign Minister Benjamin Netanyahu when he visited el-Nasser Hospital in Gaza.[29] Political activists who stood outside the partisan structure, who were too critical of the local power bosses, were also vulnerable. These latter could be marked as traitors, have their homes firebombed, be sent death threats or killed outright because they had nobody who counted to stand up for them against political calumny and terror. And where partisan struggles overlapped with old family, personal, or class rivalries, the result could be particularly bloody.[30]

The violence recalled the French Revolution's terror, for the Palestinian revolt was also a moral renewal, an attempt to define and to purify the Palestinian "body" to make it ready for political authority. Many, particularly the Islamic militants, understood Zionism as a profaning presence; removal of the "decadent" components of an occupied culture was an essential task. HAMAS used its war against collaborators as a vehicle to enforce its moral order. HAMAS published accounts of how the Israelis lured Palestinians to become collaborators by getting them drug-addicted so that they would have to provide Israel information to feed their habit, by threatening to reveal illicit sexual liaisons among Palestinian youth, even going so far as to photograph young women in their underwear as they tried on Western dresses in shops. Parents were warned to make sure their daughters did not go around unchaperoned.[31]

The Israeli police no longer arrested criminals within the Palestinian community; their only job now was to protect Jews from Arabs, not Arabs from each other, unless the issue was "security." As a result, local popular committees saw their job as meting out revolutionary justice to thieves, pimps, and prostitutes. The nation's "enemies" were not just those who took money for information or brokered land sales to the Israelis, but also those who sold drugs to the children or their bodies to the adults. Drug dealers and prostitutes, seen as a favored conduits by which Israelis blackmailed Palestinians into becoming collaborators, were particularly subject to vigilante justice. Homosexuals, too, were subject to torture and even death. The executioners did not leave their murders unexplained, printing explanations of the "charges" in leaflets, spray-painting them on walls, writing them in letters to their victims' families.[32]

In Jerusalem, for example, HAMAS activists attacked one of East Jerusalem's best-known brothels, run by a Palestinian madame, Nina Mattar. Shortly after the Six-Day War, Mattar's daughter fell in love with an Israeli army officer, who left his wife to be with her. HAMAS shut Madame Mattar's brothel down, brutally attacking her patrons with knives, hatchets, and swords. Mattar, who fled to West Jerusalem to save her life, required more than two hundred stitches.

While hundreds of suspected collaborators – and there were Palestinian informants – were murdered, other moderate Palestinians who had pushed for federation with Jordan or an independent entity were left alone.[33] These spoke with the authority of one of the organized political streams. To kill them would unleash a partisan bloodbath.

The secret of the *intifada*'s success – its diffuse, nonhierarchical organization – helps explain Yasser Arafat's failure. The *intifada* was organized around common opposition to occupation, not a common vision of what would come after. In the event of an actual settlement, Arafat knew that he, like whatever Israeli leader was willing to pay the price of peace, faced the prospect of a civil war between those willing to accept partition and those who never would. He knew the number of Palestinian soldiers gunning for him would be legion. George Habash, leader of the PFLP, warned in October 1989 that Arafat would meet the same fate as Anwar Sadat in the event of a settlement for anything less than an independent Palestinian state. Without mechanisms of Palestinian social control, the longer Israel waited, the greater the probability the divisions inherent in the Palestinian community would explode into civil strife.

As the American-led forces massed in Saudi Arabia, the *intifada* was stretching into its third year with six hundred Palestinians killed by Israelis, tens of thousands injured and detained without trial. Israel had systematically crushed the popular committees, arrested wave after wave of the *intifada*'s leadership. Many Palestinians expected the United States to "deliver" Israel. Not only didn't the Americans generate real pressure, the Bush administration refused to support an independent Palestinian state as the ultimate outcome. Israel's Labour Party failed to form a new government. And facing a right-wing rebellion within his own Likud Party, Prime Minister Yitzhak Shamir backed off from his own plan for elections in the territories. Likud was stalling in the same manner it stalled on its agreement for Palestinian "autonomy" after the Camp David Accords, only this time there were actually Palestinians with whom to negotiate.

Lacking major political advance, the unity of the Palestinian leadership of the *intifada* was breaking apart. Rival groups within the PLO were issuing contradictory communiqués. Both the secular rejectionists and the Islamic militants were trying to change the terms of engagement with knife attacks, explosives, and firearms, seeking to polarize the situation so as to prevent a negotiated settlement in which Arafat would be central.[34]

The public leadership – centered in Jerusalem – was being attacked for its continued willingness to talk to Israelis, to Americans. Members of the Palestinian strike forces even publicly threatened leaders like Faisal Husayni with death if he betrayed their cause.[35] By the latter part of 1990, more Palestinians were dying at the hands of rival Palestinian factions – often tortured to death – than were being killed by the Israelis.[36] A few Palestinian hit-men were easier to track down than hundreds of stone throwers. For one thing the dead left grieving relatives with powerful blood loyalties. Israeli operatives armed with sniper scopes picked off the strike forces, leading to still more killings of informants.

Interfactional struggle also contributed to an increasingly violent pattern of engagement. By violently striking at the enemy, kidnaping and killing Israeli troops, the militant Islamic movement HAMAS identified themselves with the honor of armed resistance, once the PLO's central virtue. Those derided for their past passivity now sought to shame their accusers, just as Israel's national religious camp claimed to have picked up the banner of pioneering, which, they claimed, the Labour Zionists had let fall. HAMAS, which received considerable external funding from Kuwait,[37] was getting steadily stronger, not only as effective warriors, but through their ability to fill the vacuum left by the collapse of Israeli civil administration, something the other Palestinian factions could not do, in part because of their secrecy. The Islamic stream was particularly good at providing mechanisms of conflict resolution. Even Christians turned to Muslim leaders to arbitrate disputes.[38]

The leaflets of the *intifada* were becoming steadily more violent.[39] Palestinians were withdrawing from the streets from exhaustion, and, more ominously, from fear and disgust at the way in which undisciplined thugs from one party or another used terror to dictate the appropriate path to their own people. Extortion and armed robbery became increasingly common. That many Palestinian activists felt condemned to arrest and brutal interrogation irrespective of their behavior on the street also contributed to the escalation.[40] As the populace withdrew from these dangerous confrontations, Palestinian militants felt even more driven to engage Israeli troops violently to retain the face of refusal, of resistance to Israeli occupation. Popular withdrawal and militant violence fed on each other.

Iraqi troops were ransacking Kuwait City as the Palestinian National Council met on October 10, 1990, in Tunisia, this time including almost all the Palestinian nationalist factions, including those who rejected what they saw as Arafat's previous capitulations. George Habash, the PFLP leader, spoke ebulliently again of his vision of an Arab nation from the Gulf to the Mediterranean Sea.[41] Arafat moved back toward rejectionism, because in the absence of political progress, he was not powerful enough to sustain his movement to peace. By supporting Iraq, Arafat managed to reconstitute a wall-to-wall nationalist bloc.

The Palestinians confirmed every Israeli's deepest fear: that like all Arabs, they want ultimately to destroy them. For forty years, most Palestinians had suspended the present tense, imagining a golden past, believing they could endure until an Arab force sparked the cataclysm of their redemption. They tended their wounds like embers, waiting for revenge, for return, for justice.

The PLO had so long served as a righteous engine of rejection and terror that when in 1988 it finally accepted what had been offered forty years earlier – partition – it found it had helped create an Israel that refused to accept Palestinian nationhood. By refusing to respond to the PLO's acceptance of a two-state solution, to meet the *intifada* with anything other than repression and delay, the Israelis proved themselves in Palestinian eyes to be the enemies the Palestinians had always believed them to be. By its failure to respond to a dramatic shift in PLO policy, Israel contributed to the desperation that pushed the Palestinians to Saddam Hussein. Each side helped produce the enemy they knew was there in the first place.

During the Gulf War, the divide between Israelis and Palestinians widened fearfully. Judging from the way men and women from the two sides then eyed each other on the street, one might easily have concluded there would be no movement any time soon. But the communal feelings of people and the actions of state are not reducible, one to the other. The Gulf War revealed a new geopolitics that made settlement of the Palestinian–Israeli conflict possible, even necessary. Peace would be made by enemies, leaders who understood that their interests and their survival lay in realigning themselves with the new realities.

From Berlin to Baghdad

Modern states write their histories in lines. In 1989 and 1990, two borders were erased: the first across the city of Berlin, the second marking the frontier between Iraq and Kuwait. These two erasures – one successful and one failed – have brought peace and hence Jerusalem into play.

When the Berlin Wall fell, it changed the material basis of America's alignment with Israel. American military aid to Israel became monumental in the context of its efforts to contain Soviet influence around the world. In the Middle East, where oil and control over strategic waterways are at stake, where the Soviets were at various times gaining footholds in Egypt, Syria, Yemen, and Algeria, Israel had been the only reliable strategic counterweight. In a world where American military deployment was proving ineffective against determined national liberation movements in places like Vietnam, Israel had an armed force that could be depended on to fight, literally, for its life. Israel, as its American supporters always claimed, was an economical defense policy.

With the end of the cold war, battleship Israel lost part of its *raison d'être* for American strategic planners. The war against Iraq made it clear that although Israel may have been an effective ally against the machinations of the Soviet Union and its clients, it was useless against aggressive pan-Arab tyrants, still less against Islamic regimes wanting to export religious revolution. In the war against Iraq, Israel's greatest service to the U.S.-led alliance was its passivity. But reciprocally, Syria and Iraq – two rival Ba'ath regimes, and Israel's greatest enemies – lost their importance for the Soviet Union, let alone the new Russian-

dominated confederation. A heavily indebted Syria jumped behind the
coalition not only to defeat its rival, but to gain access to Saudi support,
given the end of Soviet largesse, and to gain hegemony in Lebanon,
once the Hong Kong of the Middle East.[42] Beyond defensive positioning
of troops in Saudi Arabia, Syria's primary contribution to the allied
efforts paralleled Israel's. On the one hand, Syria supported a pacifica-
tion drive to control southern Lebanon and disarm Palestinian guerrillas
who had opened a symbolic "second front" against Israel. On the other,
Syria helped restrain the terrorist networks that traditionally used its
territory as their home base.[43]

The United States and the Russians have a common interest in stabilizing the region, to protect their oil interests and to counter the rise of
militant Islam, which threatens their allies and, in the case of Russia,
members of its confederation. Even before the war began, both proved
willing to use their leverage over their respective clients to achieve
peace, to unhinge the Israeli–Arab conflict from the polarities of the
cold war. In September 1989, the Soviet Union began to allow hundreds
of thousands of Jews to leave for Israel. The Soviets also commenced an
ever-quickening pace of diplomatic contact with Israel, at the same time
brusquely informing Syria that it would no longer be able to count on the
Soviets to achieve military parity with Israel. At the 1990 Bush–
Gorbachev summit at Helsinki, Bush reversed a half century of American foreign policy by inviting the Soviet Union to join the multinational
effort in the Near East. In 1991, the Soviet Union supported a joint
Palestinian–Jordanian delegation to the Israeli–Arab peace talks. It was
no wonder the PLO in Tunis immediately welcomed the abortive Soviet
coup that briefly toppled Gorbachev.

On the American side, the United States showed a willingness to talk to
the PLO at ever higher levels, in Secretary of State Baker's reiteration to
the American–Israel Political Action Committee (AIPAC, the powerful
pro-Israel lobby in the United States) of the American policy of territory
for peace ("Israel," he said, should "lay aside once and for all the un-
realistic vision of a Greater Israel"), and in American demands that its aid
monies for Soviet Jews not be used to settle them in "occupied territory."
During the Gulf War America signaled that maintaining Israel's military
superiority to the Arabs was no longer a top American priority; it had
little compunction about providing Saudia Arabia and Egypt with increasingly sophisticated weapons. In the midst of mobilization, the Bush administration originally proposed to sell $20 billion of hardware to Saudi Ara-
bia without prior consultation with Israel.[44] "The American policy [of
assuring Israel's] qualitative edge is not being implemented anymore,"
Israeli Defense Minister Moshe Arens bluntly concluded.[45] Arabs henceforth would know the operational qualities of Israel's weapons because

they would have the same ones. During the American buildup in Saudi Arabia, for example, the Bush administration warned that the American Jewish community's anticipated opposition to a scaled-down $14 billion arms sale to Saudi Arabia would endanger American troops.[46] No wonder Israel initially argued that the "lesson" of the Gulf conflict was that the Gulf States could not defend themselves and that the only secure solution was a massive American deployment in the region.

The Gulf War had forced Israel to hold its most fundamental instincts in check. A nation founded on the premise Jews would no longer go passively to their deaths sat in sealed rooms and night after night did nothing as Iraq's missiles fell on Tel Aviv neighborhoods. President Bush personally pressed Israel not to retaliate, forcing Shamir to recall to their bases planes that were winging their way to take out Scud launchers in eastern Iraq and, some said, to bomb Baghdad.

Despite the fact Israel's most potent enemy had its war machine smashed, many Israelis felt even more vulnerable. The brute fact remained: Saddam Hussein had been able to take and hold a strategic piece of territory for a long period. Iraq withstood weeks of brutal bombing, using quantities and qualities of weaponry incomparably greater than Israel could ever amass or develop. What if that territory had been Israel's? Iraq's defeat was not complete until the American-led forces controlled the ground. In a war, Israel would have to fight alone. Every mile of strategic depth therefore had to be considered immensely valuable. Now that Jordan had shown just how vulnerable it was to Iraqi pressure, the strategic value of the West Bank seemed more important than ever before.

During the Gulf War, Israel learned once again that in a world of self-interested states, Israel is ultimately alone. In the early twentieth century, Britain supported a Jewish state because of her strategic interests vis-à-vis the Turks and then turned on the Jews when the Arabs became a more important ally against the Germans. The French (Iraq's number two arms supplier) provided military aid to Israel and then cut it off in 1967 when it decided French interests would be better served by close ties with the Arab world. The Israelis now wonder – is the United States really any different?

In 1948, the United States was the first nation to recognize Israel. Even though the ashes of death and the agony of displacement were still fresh in public memory, it is important to remember that America's decision was improbable at best. Right down to the last days of the British Mandate, it was not at all clear the United States would recognize a new Jewish state. President Truman did it over the concerted opposition of his secretary of state, George Marshall, because he believed it was the right thing to do, whereas the State Department and most of his foreign policy advisers thought it was wrong.[47] What future presidents decide is in America's interests may or may not jeopardize Israel's survival. The lesson of American recognition in 1948 is that the president of the United States has enormous discretion. Although popular and congressional support for Israel is now deep and widespread, popular sentiment has not been and will not always be the determining factor in American foreign policy.

The United States has sought to use its military victory over Iraq to obtain greater power in the Arab world. As the shah's fall in Iran proved, America's monopoly of might is worthless without moral buttress. The Arab world is acutely sensitive about the deployment of Western troops on its soil. Though the Gulf War, America helped constitute a new regional bloc made up of armed men and oil money: Egypt and Syria on the one hand, and Saudi Arabia and Kuwait on the other. America would ever more mightily arm its allies; it counts on their stability. As a result, the United States and its Arab partners needed a settlement of the Palestinian question in a way they never had before. In exchange for an American military base or positioning of materiel in Saudi Arabia after the war, the Saudis pushed the Americans hard on the Palestinian question.

The United States easily crushed Iraq's army. However, the ideas for which the Iraqis went to war emerged unscathed. Millions of Arabs still hailed Saddam Hussein as a champion of Arab honor, a man who dared strike a blow, however symbolic, against Zionism and its American patron and who survived without ever kneeling. When the Scuds struck Tel Aviv, Cairenes celebrated in the streets of Cairo. If Saddam Hussein was now the object of Arab anger and disappointment, it was much more because his armies crumbled before the allies, because he destroyed Arab unity and the Arab League, because his actions brought Western soldiers into the Arab heartland, because his defeat left a military balance significantly more in Israel's favor, than because he invaded and occupied Kuwait. Indeed, significant portions of the Arab world interpreted the American invasion as having had precisely these objectives.

In the eyes of many Arab nationalists, Iraq's conquest of Kuwait was not very different from Syria's takeover of Lebanon, both sovereign nations. The West stopped the first and confirmed the second. The first victim had oil, the second had none. The first conqueror was Arafat's patron; the second, his enemy. The differences between Iraq's occupation of Kuwait and Israel's of the West Bank and Gaza did not prevent the Arab world from making the comparison. Given its long sufferance of Israel's incorporation of the West Bank and Israel's refusal to negotiate with the Palestinians, even under conditions of its own choosing, America has not been trusted in the region as a honest broker.

After the war, Palestinians with whom we spoke compared the destructive force the United States was willing to unleash on Iraq for its refusal to end its occupation of Kuwait with the marginal reduction in monetary aid with which Israel was threatened for failing to halt settlements in the West Bank. Few believed the United States would ever press Israel.

Rajai Sbeih sure didn't. By 1991, after four years of uprising, Rajai Sbeih's Israeli patients had all dropped away. A patient in his dentist's chair looks directly at the Dome of the Rock. A sterilizing pot is bubbling on the wall in his office. Israeli soldiers are posted on his roof. This is a strategic site, a critical intersection in the Arab downtown.

Spying us waiting in the wintry hallway, Dr. Sbeih had invited us in for a coffee, which we drank while waiting for the novocaine to penetrate the gums of five patients in the outer room. On the door going into the office there is a big picture of a mouth, before and after, ragged rows of teeth straightened, capped, and whitened. In the waiting room, one man's mouth sparkles, a plateau of gold caps. Faisal Husayni, a distant cousin, is his patient.

Dr. Sbeih graciously invited us to his house in Beit Hanina for lunch. He chose a strike day; he would not be working. We should meet him at his office. Why not take a taxi to his house, we offered? "No, that would not be so good. They, the young people, might think you were Jews." "But we are Jews!" we said. "I know, I know. I meant Israelis." On the appointed day, we offered to follow him to his house just outside Jerusalem. No, he would drive us, he said. "One little mistake and they will beat me." The food was beautifully prepared, grilled meat, irreproducible casseroles. Dr. Sbeih's wife's family owned twelve houses next to the Western Wall, all razed and expropriated by the Israelis in 1967. His family hungered for peace.

Would President Bush pressure the Israelis at the negotiating table, we asked? Dr. Sbeih looked at us incredulously. "President Bush, he's afraid from the Israeli mafia," Sbeih replied. "Afraid he'll be killed." "You don't really believe that," we said. "Yes, yes. Look, somebody already tried to kill Reagan. And Kennedy, who killed Kennedy?"

The United States could not allow its use of massive force to be construed as an imperial grab for raw materials, as "a new colonialism, a new Crusade," as Michel Sabbah, the Palestinian Latin Patriarch of Jerusalem called it.[48] George Bush first sought authority for the use of force from the United Nations, not the United States Congress. In an increasingly fragmented world order, the United Nations had become the natural mechanism for the regulation of interstate conflict. America's Arab allies were watching closely to see whether the United States honored UN resolutions promising the Palestinians their national rights with as much ardor as it showed in protecting the sovereignty of Kuwait, a decidedly undemocratic, but oil-rich monarchy. After Israel refused to allow a United Nations team to investigate the killings on the *haram*, Secretary of State Baker warned David Levy, Israel's deputy foreign minister, "If Israel rejects the Security Council decision, there will be some who compare you, even though it is not justified, to Saddam Hussein and his rejection of Security Council decisions."[49]

Saddam Hussein modeled himself after Abdul Nasser, the pan-Arab Egyptian socialist who twice took his country to war, first in 1956 against the British, French, and Israelis, and again in 1967 against Israel. The parallel is as instructive as it is ominous, for Nasser's defeats gave rise to the emergence of a politicized, militant Islam. America's allies need a resolution to the Palestinian question in the superpowers' culture war with radical Islam. Before the cold war ended, each of the superpowers was defeated by militant Islam: the United States in Beirut and Iran, and the Soviets in Afghanistan. America's Arab allies are all vulnerable. Hussein's defeat may easily be converted to radical Islam's victory. In Iraq Shi'ite Islam is the logical candidate to replace the pan-Arab secular ideology. Abetted by thousands of exiles who fled to Iran, the Shia seized on Hussein's vulnerability at the close of the war and rose in the south. The United States government had unleashed the very forces that motivated its support of Iraq's military aggression against Iran in the first place. The United States, which doggedly resisted congressional pressure to stop the flow of arms and militarily useful technology to Iraq right up to the very day Iraq invaded Kuwait, stood by while the Iraqi government again mowed down its own citizens. In Jordan, militant Muslims had become the dominant bloc in the country's first democratic elections. In Algeria, the Islamic Salvation Front would have democratically swept the Socialists from power if the military had not stepped in. In Tunisia, Muslim activists have made inroads among the intelligentsia and professional classes, educated in Europe and America, dressed in Dior or Armani. In Kuwait, the Muslim Brotherhood is the most powerful group pressing for democratization against the ruling al-Sabah family.

With radical Islam, there can be no territorial settlement with Israel, no resting while the lands captured by the Prophet's armies in the seventh century are ruled by Jews, and especially no peace until Jerusalem, the city from which Muhammad ascended, is once again controlled by believers. Islam threatens the Arab states in a way the Palestinians do not. However, for the past half century, the Palestinian question has been the most important ideological battleground in Arab politics. The Arab states, and Saudi Arabia, the keeper of Islam's holiest sites, in particular, now required a Palestinian peace.

Saddam Hussein defined the terms of disengagement from Kuwait. As a result of the Gulf War, Palestine was on the international and American agenda in a way it had never been before. The Berlin Wall came crashing down on November 9, 1989, fifty-one years from the very day that Hitler's brown shirts savaged the Jewish community on Kristallnacht. At the same time Iraqi soldiers were sacking Kuwait City, Israeli passenger airlines were winging their way for the first time in history to a united Berlin. Ironically the conditions that made possible the unification of the capital of Germany, the city from which the warrant for the Holocaust went out which permitted the creation of Israel, have called into question Israel's claim to rule Jerusalem.

Part IV

Heart of Stone

16

Al-Quds and Tunis

There has always been a tension between Palestinians inside the territories and the PLO abroad, a tug-of-war between a people and an organization claiming to speak in its name. The struggle between those who have spent their lives building a national society from their Jerusalem, al-Quds, and a grizzled war-horse who has directed a nationalist movement from Tunis was becoming increasingly acute. Organizing from Jerusalem, the Palestinians under Israeli occupation forced the PLO to make peace. But after Arafat and Rabin shook hands on the White House lawn, these Palestinians understood they would still have to fight the PLO to make the Palestine for which they had given their lives.

The PLO chose its path after the failure of another war. Iraq's defeat made Israeli–Palestinian peace a requirment of American power in the region; it also weakened the PLO sufficiently to make that peace possible. Arafat's alliance with Saddam Hussein was a disastrous move. Iraq, the Palestinians' last, most powerful patron, was reduced in places to rubble. In Lebanon PLO militias were being systematically defanged by the Syrians. The possibility of "armed struggle" was closing down.

The war put Palestinians working in the Gulf in a precarious position. The postwar grafitti in Kuwait – "Amman, 1970; Beirut, 1982; Kuwait City, 1992" – foretold yet another Palestinian exodus. Palestinians who had worked for years in Kuwait and Saudi Arabia wanted to return to Palestine even though they knew there were no jobs waiting for them. PLO taxes on Palestinian wages and salaries would no longer be collected by these Arab states. Saudi Arabia and Kuwait stopped official funding of the PLO while continuing to subsidize Islamic Jihad and HAMAS, respectively. The flow of PLO funds into the territories dropped so much that the Martyrs' Committees could not pay stipends to the families of those killed and wounded by the Israelis. In Jerusalem, Gulf and PLO funding of the private schools dried up overnight, forcing them to raise their fees; as a result more than a thousand Palestinian pupils transferred into the municipal system.

Arafat's stature was in tatters. Not only had the Arab states once again sacrificed the chance to make headway on the Palestinian question to their own interests in weakening an Arab rival, their leaders now stated that neither Yasser Arafat, nor even the PLO, was essential to a diplomatic solution to the Palestinian question.[1] Knowing that the Americans, the Israelis, and many Arab states preferred a Palestinian entity tethered to Jordan, even King Hussein intimated he was prepared to go to the peace conference alone if the PLO said no. Arafat was shunned in several Arab states, including the great paymaster, Saudi Arabia. Inside the territories, as well, the extent of Palestinian derision and hostility was unprecedented. In December 1991, for the first time, we met many Palestinians – activists, public figures, ordinary people – who openly and for the record referred to Arafat as "Queen Elizabeth," "a clown," "an idiot," and "a fool."

After the Gulf War, Palestinians in the occupied territories again demanded to speak for themselves. Arafat had squandered the political capital they had accumulated through the *intifada*, paid for with their blood and their bones. The chairman had earlier resisted their demands to form a provisional government. He had repudiated Egyptian plans for peace talks because he feared local elections would provide the Israelis with a legitimate interlocutor and undercut the influence of the PLO. Now, more than ever, many Palestinians in the occupied territories were not about to let the PLO determine whether and how they would negotiate with the Israelis. A whole raft of rank and file activists, many of whom had spent years in Israeli prisons, voiced their belief that the *intifada* must be converted into a political process lest they miss a diplomatic opportunity that would not soon come again.

Stories circulated that even Abu Iyad, the number two Palestinian in Tunis in charge of the PLO's covert operations, could no longer stomach Arafat's equivocation over a negotiated settlement. Abu Iyad had been one of the first major figures within the PLO to support a two-state solution. As early as 1988, he had tried to meet with top Israeli leaders. As a result he also maintained a personal bodyguard of five men because he believed his enemies within the PLO, and perhaps even Arafat himself, might want to kill him. One month before he was in fact assassinated in 1991, allegedly by hit-men from Abu Nidal, he stated in an interview for the Jordanian media that Arafat would make a Palestinian state only when he had liquidated the entire Palestinian people.[2] The Jordanians pursuaded him not to broadcast it.

Israel's repeated arrest of *intifada* leaders had undercut the Palestinian capacity inside, bolstering the PLO abroad. But now the PLO's weakness allowed the occupied Palestinians, led from Jerusalem, to push forward once again on their own. The PLO, preoccupied with its own survival, was not paying much attention to the occupied territories.

After the war, Prime Minister Yitzhak Shamir agreed to participate in direct peace negotiations with the Arab states and a delegation of Palestinians from the West Bank and Gaza, on condition that the Palestinian representatives neither be chosen by the PLO nor be residents of Jerusalem. Although Shamir intended to offer the Palestinians another autonomy agreement, Secretary of State Baker told the Palestinians they would be building a confederation with Jordan and, as such, would have to be part of the formal Jordanian delegation. These were humiliating conditions, a return to King Hussein's 1972 proposed United Arab Kingdom, under negotiating terms worse than those they had contemptuously spurned at Camp David in 1978.

Arafat had always opposed efforts by "inside" Palestinians to meet formally with the American secretary of state on his visits to Jerusalem. In 1987, for example, when George Shultz came to Jerusalem to speak to Palestinian leaders, the "PLO at home" wanted badly to meet with him. They called Fatah in Tunis, they sent telegrams, they went abroad themselves to beg, to plead, to scream. But Arafat refused. Shultz spoke to an empty courtyard at Jerusalem's American Colony Hotel.

It was highly significant, then, that when President Bush's secretary of state, James Baker, made his first visit after the Gulf War in March 1991, the Palestinians inside demanded, and however reluctantly received, PLO endorsement for their meetings.[3] HAMAS and radical rejectionist groups threatened them with death. Faisal Husayni and his negotiating team, read an Islamic Jihad leaflet, "must know that their fate will be as the fate of the traitor King Abdallah."[4]

Faisal Husayni led the Palestinians who persuaded Arafat they had no choice but to go along with peace negotiations under Israeli–American conditions, on the "American bus," as one Palestinian strategist called it. "Okay, you don't believe in what I am doing, so what is the alternative?" was how Husayni characterized his posture to the PLO in Tunis. Palestinians like Husayni needed Arafat's protection against the radicals' charges that they were traitors. And Arafat very much needed people like Husayni not only as a base of support within the PLO, but as a means to repair his relations with the Western and the Arab world. Husayni also took comfort in knowing that his brother, Razi Abdul Khader, the number four man in the PLO military establishment, could help protect him.

When the names for the Palestinian delegation for the peace talks had been chosen, the Israelis maintained the diplomatic fiction that they were not negotiating with the PLO. More significant than the affiliation of the Palestinian delegation was how it was chosen. The Palestinians in the West Bank and Gaza initially turned to the PLO outside to form a legitimate delegation. However, it quickly became clear the PLO had neither the political will nor the capacity to form a delegation that would represent the Palestinians of the West Bank and Gaza, or to develop a practical negotiating strategy. To the chagrin of the local Palestinian leadership, Arafat pulled out all the stops to try to form a delegation that included only his loyalists. "Arafat made Tunis into the political Ka'ba [the black stone in Mecca around which Muslim pilgrims perambulate] of the Palestinians," Mahdi abdul Hadi, director of the Palestinian Academic Society for the Study of International Affairs, the Palestinian strategy think tank in Jerusalem, told us.

Husayni took the lead in the formation of a Palestinian delegation. To have influence it was necessary to have some political, professional or familial link with the "Jerusalem clique," as the Husayni-centered post-1948 generation of nationalists was called. Tensions between the outside and the inside, between younger militants, disproportionately from the refugee camps, who had spent years in prison, and older organizers, professionals from the city, who had not; between different streams and localities, made this an excruciating process. Israel and the PLO had created a situation in which there was simply no mechanism to fashion a legitimate body of representatives. Lacking territorywide organization, the Jerusalem-based leadership sometimes couldn't even judge the names debated for inclusion in the delegation. Given the strength of local loyalties, there was considerable resentment over Jerusalem's domination, particularly by nationalists in Nablus and Hebron.

To her dismay, the American consul general, Molly Williamson, was forced to broker the formation of the delegation to negotiate in Madrid in 1992. The Palestinians were initially taken aback by Williamson, not one of the State Department old-boy Arabists, but a hard-drinking, chain-smoking, fast-talking Chinese-American woman. Initially, the consul general was on the phone hourly to see whether there was still a delegation. Only when just one call was required daily, she joked to Bonnie Boxer, Teddy Kollek's press secretary, did she know the delegation would cohere.

Jerusalem's centrality proved a stumbling block. Although Jerusalemites like Husayni and Kamal Zahira, chair of the Federation of Women's Action Committees, were essential to forming the delegation, the Israelis insisted they not particiate in it. Husayni warned that no Palestinians would attend if a Jerusalemite were not included in the delegation. Arafat was equally adamant. "Do you expect me to sell or cede Jerusalem?" he thundered in August 1991. "By God, even if one put the sun to my right and moon to my left, I would not do that."[5] In the event, Husayni was allowed to go as the advisory head of the official delegation.

Five burly body guards formed a shoulder-to-shoulder barricade at the front door as we walked up the steps of Faisal Husayni's home in December 1991, on the western slope of the Mount of Olives. Why, we asked Husayni, did he support this peace process now, when he had rejected Camp David in 1978? Were the "autonomy" talks under Begin a missed opportunity? Husayni compared himself to a man offered a boat in the desert. " 'Just row there,' " he imagined being told, " 'and you will get out of the desert.' . . . And I said, 'No, I will not use it.' So suddenly, there is a flood. There is water, reaching up to me, . . . so I jumped to that boat and I will row it and I will find that yes, in this case, maybe I can . . . go out of this whole business."

In 1991 al-Fatah again did not call an official strike on Partition Day. Secular rejectionists and Islamic radicals were biding their time, sure men like Husayni would, at the end of the day, get nothing. Husayni did not feel he had much time. "If the talks will not succeed . . . after one year, you will . . . be interested in meeting someone else. Maybe he will be someone who can understand the language of the jungle more than me. Or maybe your contact, it is me."

A portrait on olive wood of Faisal's father, Abd al-Qadr, his head wrapped in a black and white *kaffiyeh*, hangs on the wall of Faisal's office. Husayni had embraced the political position of his father's and uncle's enemies, the Nashashibis, who promoted coexistence with Zionism, a position for which they were long pilloried as traitors. How would the man who died in the battle for Jerusalem in 1948 view his son's actions, we asked?

> He started from one point, the love of his people, the love of his land. And I believe . . . that what I am doing is coming onward also from this point. He didn't fight against the Jews because he hates them, but because he loved the Palestinians. And the same thing like me. So I believe that – maybe, I don't know, only God can know – but I believe that if he was now here, he would make the same thing.

Faisal Husayni continues his father's fight for the city, hoping to win where he failed. At the 1988 Palestinian National Council meeting in Algiers, where the PLO declared an independent Palestinian state with Jerusalem as its capital, sentiment for the division of Jerusalem was overwhelming. In Jerusalem itself, a majority of Palestinians also wanted to redivide the city.[6] Husayni, however, wanted Jerusalem to remain an open city, but as the capital of two states.

And if Israel refused? "I don't know what is beautiful in controlling another people who don't want to be controlled by you. Is it so beautiful to force the Israeli flag here, while you know that you can't reach here but under a heavy police guard? We can make it another way."

But if Israel refused? "In several years, there will be another war. And it will be Jerusalem."

After Madrid

When the peace conference convened in Madrid, Palestinians paraded in the streets waving olive branches, even decorating Israeli armored cars and jeeps with them.[7] The Likud government instructed state radio and television not to play peace songs during the Madrid meetings so as not to create "euphoria."[8]

Madrid was electrifying for the Palestinians who attended. They were ratified as equals by the Americans and the Russians, mobbed by the world's press, and forced to manage their own negotiating strategy, brokering the wording of statements on their own with the Americans between hotel rooms. They had been launched diplomatically and they believed there could be no return.

Arafat himself, by drawing on the Palestinians inside to support his positions within the PLO, had bolstered their claim to be Palestine's true voice. That the locus of legitimacy was sliding back toward the occupied Palestine was evident even among PLO functionaries. In late 1991, the PLO's ambassador in Britain presented himself in public as representing the people of the *intifada*. When it was pointed out to him he had not mentioned the PLO, he said that he was a member of the PLO representing the people of the *intifada*.

Arafat was profoundly jealous, feeling he had been robbed of his rightful place at the negotiating table, fearful the Palestinians who went would increasingly go their own way. Before returning to the occupied territories from Madrid, much of the delegation traveled to Tunis to meet their president. Hanan Ashrawi, the soft-spoken, articulate professor of English, a poet of lyrical rage, a woman with little history as a political activist, reportedly complained she would say something in public that would subsequently be contradicted by Arafat. "Who do you think you are?" Arafat reportedly rebuked her. "Who do you represent? Nobody! We chose you because you speak English well." Ashrawi was briefly reduced to tears.

Shortly thereafter, Arafat waltzed into the arms of his nemesis, Hafez Assad, who allowed his old enemy to begin opening PLO offices in Damascus once again. According to American intelligence and Palestinian sources in Jerusalem, Arafat asked Assad for help in fighting the "new Village Leagues," conflating Palestinians who would negotiate for anything less than statehood with the Palestinian villagers slated for material favors and physical protection in exchange for their repudiation of the PLO. Assad and Arafat both feared what the occupied Palestinians might do if the process took off. Arafat was building a cadre in refugee camps and villages of the occupied territories, including some of the very same execrated "Village League" leaders. In the event the urban Palestinian middle class betrayed him, he would turn to these forces to try to spoil the peace process.

Their entrance into the diplomatic world demonstrated just how unprepared the Palestinians were, both intellectually and institutionally, for state making. "This could take my life," one delegate half complained upon returning from Madrid. The Palestinian nation has disproportionately honored blood sacrifice, not the daily work of building a state, of planning, of investing, of working. To die for a nation, one longtime diplomat remarked, is easier for them than to live for it. The Palestinians have built a continent of words, irrigated with the blood of martyrs, that attracted money and solidarity. Inside they constructed institutions that would enable them to survive, but they had not done the intellectual or organizational work to build an infrastructure for a new nation. The Palestinians, Edward Said charged, lacked the Israeli's "discipline of detail."[9]

Now the Palestinians under occupation set out to build the core for a new state. Organizing from Jerusalem, they formed functional committees – for housing, health, elections, transportation, economic development, water, municipalities. Run by professionals, these were intended as the seeds of a national authority that would be subject to an overarching political committee established in conjunction with the PLO. Although these "higher committees" had been cleared with the PLO, the PLO had its own departmental structure and was wary at best, understanding that if these committees succeeded, these ministries-in-waiting would quickly become a legitimate governmental structure, further weakening the role of the PLO.

Tunis was besieged by telephone calls and faxes demanding membership. "Everybody now wants part of the spoils," one Palestinian remarked to us. Political leaders from Jenin, Nablus, and Tulkarm bridled at Jerusalem's centrality, at the preeminence of people who, in their eyes, had lived a relatively privileged existence during the four-year revolt and siege they had suffered. "Jerusalem is the capital," Husayni retorted, "the center for taking positions."

These planning structures initially did not go very far. Beyond the factionalism, the looking outside, the tendency to blame Israelis for every mishap, the Palestinians inside were still wary of putting their personal stature behind concrete proposals with real timetables and mechanisms. "I put more time into my thesis," a high-level American consular official in Jerusalem remarked to us, "than these guys put in their future . . . Did they think they were going to do this between writing a book or running a pharmacy?"

Looking over their shoulders to see what their factions' leaders might think, what the PLO in Tunis might do, had a crippling effect. Manuel Hassassian, a Jerusalemite Palestinian of Armenian origin whose father survived the Turkish genocide, was tapped to head the committee for elections. The Palestinians expected to elect a leadership who would govern whatever political authority they could wrest from the Israelis. There were many models to consider, Hassassian, a political scientist, told us – the Israeli, the German, the American, the Jordanian. When the spectacled cigar-smoking professor contacted the PLO in Tunis for instruction, he was told not to prepare for elections in the occupied territories; Arafat did not want them.

In other cases, the PLO simply sat on the proposals. Dr. Mustafa Bargouthi, the physician charged with overseeing the planning of a new health system, sent six hundred documents to Tunis covering every aspect of what should be done first. For months, he received no reply. Among his recommendations had been paramedic training, a proposal that would not cost much and would save many lives. All Dr. Bargouthi heard was that the PLO was negotiating with governments for new hospitals and high-tech equipment. Because the PLO would not act, very little was being done to upgrade the health system before the Palestinian Council took power. (In consequence, when Palestinians were massacred in Hebron in 1994, untrained ambulance drivers failed to give first aid and took victims to the wrong hospitals, thereby contributing to the death toll.)[10]

In Madrid, the Gulf States and the European Economic Community (EEC) signaled that they were willing to fund the occupied Palestinians directly without going through Tunis. Where once the PLO sent in $30 million per month to the occupied territories, by the end of 1992 it was only able to muster $7 million per month.[11] Direct funding would further undercut the PLO's patronage machine. But many Palestinians, bitter at their lack of representation within the PLO, saw direct external funding as a welcome corrective, validation of their independent political legitimacy. In December 1991, Husayni referred to himself as a "field command" relative to the headquarters in Tunis. Nevertheless, he was unequivocally willing to take funds outside PLO channels. "If they would like to get [these monies] from the main door, okay," he told us. "If they would like to get it from the side door, okay. If they would like to get it through the door in the kitchen, okay. The most important is that it reach the house."

After the initial hoopla in Spain, the Palestinian delegation met with their Israeli counterparts time after time, but the negotiations went nowhere. Jerusalem has always been a nonnegotiable stake for both sides. If Jerusalem had not been set aside, the Camp David agreements between Israel and Egypt would never have been signed in 1979. Disagreement between Israel and Egypt over whether or not Jerusalem's Arabs were to be included in the subsequent "autonomy" talks helped derail the process, which was finally killed by Israel's formal annexation of the city in 1980. Similarly in the post-Madrid talks both Arafat and Shamir used Jerusalem to impede progress.

Members of Likud, who had reluctantly agreed to negotiate with the Palestinians, had forced Prime Minister Shamir to proclaim that the Arabs of East Jerusalem would never have the right to participate, seeing it as a precedent for partition.[12] Unlike the governing Likud Party, Israeli Labourites were willing to allow the Jerusalem Palestinians to vote for their nation's delegation. Rabin's only qualification was that they not be allowed to run for office.[13] In June 1992, the Labour Party swept back into full control of the government for the first time since 1977. While the negotiations became somewhat more substantive, Yitzhak Rabin, in an effort to move things forward, finally allowed Faisal Husayni, a Jerusalemite, to participate officially as a member of the Palestinian delegation, a move with great symbolic significance intended to strengthen the occupied Palestinians.

The PLO delegation faced formidable opposition from within the Palestinian community. HAMAS, which had now forged an alliance with the Marxist rejectionists against the peace process, was gaining increasing popular support. In almost all the elections organized in the West Bank and Gaza after the Gulf War among physicians, jurists, engineers, and Chambers of Commerce, the HAMAS candidates garnered between 40 and 60 percent of the votes. The Palestinian delegation – unelected, unrepresentative of the range of Palestinian opinion, challenged at every turn by those who had been excluded – was unable and unwilling to make the painful concessions necessary to cut a deal. The Palestinians continued to demand the right of return, Israeli withdrawal from all lands, dismantling of Jewish settlements, guarantee of a Palestinian state, and – most explosive of all – East Jerusalem as its capital. Fearful of setting off violent internal strife among the various factions, they were incapable of generating a position that could both command legitimacy among the Palestinians and be viable for the Israelis. As a result, they neither developed a pragmatic negotiating strategy, nor were able to achieve significant independence from Arafat.[14]

Internal Palestinian incapacity and shifting geopolitics gave Arafat his chance. The immobility and vulnerability of the Palestinian delegation persuaded the Rabin government that only Arafat had a chance of delivering. But for Israel to start with an agreement with the PLO was unprecedented. The Israelis had always followed a Syria-first strategy, believing that once they made peace with their northern enemy they could force conditions on the Palestinians. It had become clear that peace with Syria was possible, but Assad's price was too high – total withdrawal from the Golan. This would be more politically explosive and strategically dangerous than an agreement with the PLO. As a result, Rabin changed course, opening the door for Arafat to walk in.[15]

Arafat, his organization bankrupt, his standing eroded, his leadership under concerted attack, knew he might lose even more if the Madrid delegation succeeded. Its members were disobeying and even publicly repudiating his direction. Constricted by Arafat's unilateral and seemingly capricious interventions, even Dr. Abd al-Shafi, the Gaza physician heading the Palestinian delegation, publicly demanded Arafat be replaced by a more democratic collective leadership.[16] In early August, three of the Palestinians' top negotiators – Faisal Husayni, Hanan Ashrawi, and Sa'eb Erakat – threatened to resign because of conflict with Arafat over the extent of their negotiating authority, his one-person rule, and his apparent acceptance of the American proposal for autonomy and an early Israeli withdrawal from Gaza and Jericho. Arafat barely convinced them to stay on, appointing them and other delegates to the PLO's Executive Committee.[17]

And there was the question of money. The PLO, once a rich conglomerate, was facing financial ruin. By June 1993, PLO payments to the occupied territories had plummeted even further, to $1.6 million per month.[18] Universities and schools couldn't pay salaries. The two most important pro-PLO Palestinian newspapers in Jerusalem – *Al-Fajr* and *Al Sha'ab* – were forced to close.[19] Without money from the PLO, the Palestinians in the territories were seeking outside funding just to keep the lights on. The oil-rich Arab states and the Europeans had begun sending money in directly, bypassing the PLO in Tunis. Over Arafat's objections, Husayni and others had gone to the Gulf States to solicit funding, with the backing of major PLO figures like Abu Mazen, one of Fatah's founders and an early promoter of dialogue with the Israeli left. The Saudis were sending millions of dollars to the Palestinians in the territories through Husayni.[20] The Palestinians under occupation were gradually cobbling together a basis for financial independence.

Events pointed to a continued erosion of Arafat's authority. The chairman had one weapon left: concessions to the Israelis. He could give away more than the occupied Palestinians, compromising on items that had always been Palestinian requisites for a deal. Operating through a Norwegian back channel to Israeli Foreign Minister Shimon Peres,

Arafat cut a deal that was inferior to the one he had called traitorous when it had been proposed by President Jimmy Carter.

In exchange for recognizing the right of "the State of Israel to exist in peace and security" and his renunciation of violence against Israel, Arafat got the Israelis to recognize the PLO as the representative of the Palestinians. Starting with the Gaza Strip and an area around the provincial desert town of Jericho, the Palestinians would elect a governing authority that would ultimately run their affairs in the West Bank and Gaza for a transitional five-year period. In addition, the world's powers would seek a vast infusion of capital investment to construct a new infrastructure, to jump start an almost moribund economy.

However, Arafat received no guarantee of a state, of dismantlement of the Jewish settlements, of control over the borders, and no assured rights of return.[21] Sovereignty and all the other items were subject to negotiation to be completed at the end of a five-year interim period. Although the ultimate settlement was to be based on UN resolutions 242 and 338 exchanging land for peace, nowhere were the territorial limits of the ultimate Palestinian entity specified. In the interim period, Palestinians were given authority over neither Jewish settlements, nor even all the lands not inhabited by Jews. Indeed, in Gaza, the Palestinian autonomy would include only about one half of all the territory, excluding much of the area's buildable land.[22] In the West Bank, the Palestinian area would be parceled into separate "cantons," squeezed between continuous zones of Jewish settlement, traversed by roads connecting those settlements to Israel, and connected to each other by twisting tubes of territory that resemble intestines more than a country. Rabin, defending the agreement in Knesset, underscored that the arrangement was perfectly compatible with the Allon plan, the proposed land-for-peace agreement with Jordan providing for three Arab enclaves surrounded by Israeli sovereignty.[23]

Even during the interim period, the ultimate structure and legislative authority of the Palestinian council were not specified in the agreement. Everything outside education, culture, health, social welfare, direct taxation, and tourism still remained to be negotiated. In the meantime, the jurisdiction of the Palestinian authority remained subject to Israeli law and military administrative orders.[24] Thus, as the Palestinian police were taking up abandoned Israeli military positions, the PLO was still insisting on a parliamentary body of one hundred eighty representatives, whereas Israel said it would allow only an administrative council of thirty.[25] In any case, whatever its size, its legislative powers would be subject to Israeli veto. While Arafat insisted on being addressed as president, the Israeli Foreign Ministry refused even to accept any piece of correspondence that included that appellation. The same month South African blacks were first enjoying political rights in a legislative body, the Palestinians were preparing for an uncertain authority that some feared would evolve into *bantustans*.

Jerusalem was the most explosive compromise of all. Although Palestinians from Jerusalem would be entitled to vote for the interim authority, they would not be allowed to run for office in it and the authority would have no jurisdiction over Jerusalem.[26] Though the Israelis agreed Jerusalem's status at the end of the interim period was negotiable, their actions suggested that they were making the city the price the Palestinians would have to pay for statehood. And Arafat, although he immediately declared Jerusalem would be the capital of the new state at the end of the transitional period, could make no guarantees that the Palestinian state would ever have any authority in Jerusalem.

It was the autonomy of Camp David with three differences: the PLO would be the interlocutor, a Palestinian state was a possible end game, and the world would commit large amounts of money. Faisal Husayni, lacking Arafat's history of armed struggle, without a mass political apparatus of his own, his authority dependent on his claim to represent the Palestinian consensus in the territories, could never have made such a deal.

On September 13, 1993, the unthinkable happened: Yitzhak Rabin and Yasser Arafat sat side by side at the White House. The agreement was signed on the same table on which Carter, Begin, and Sadat had initialed the Camp David Accords in 1979. Arafat intended to hand his pearl-handled pistol ceremoniously to President Clinton, but the idea was vetoed by the White House. At President Clinton's urging, the two men shook hands as an astounded world watched. Palestinians in Jerusalem rushed into the streets, waving forbidden Palestinian flags, one huge one unfurled atop the Damascus Gate to the Old City. In Israeli Jerusalem, the reaction was restrained, even somber.

Declaring Principles

When the Palestinian delegation learned about the Oslo accords between Arafat and the Israeli government just two days before they were signed, they were outraged, feeling that they had been used, that a deal they had previously rejected had been imposed upon them by fiat.[27] "If we have wanted the functional approach," Hanan Ashrawi complained, "we could have accepted the tasks of the civil administration, which were offered to us in '82 without negotiations, and we refused, because we weren't going to perform administrative tasks for the administration."[28] Although the newspapers were filled with pledges of loyalty to "His Excellency, the President, the leader, the symbol and the father, Arafat," Arafat's moves afterward made much of the Palestinian leadership even more uneasy, as he sought absolute personal control of both guns and money in the new entity.

The Israelis gave Arafat authority to recruit a "strong police force," some nine thousand men, who, according to his own pledge, would help "assume responsibility over all PLO elements and personnel to assure their compliance [with the accord], prevent violations, and discipline violators."[29] Just a year earlier, when Husayni, as leader of the Palestinian delegation, had proposed such an interim police force, Arafat had attacked the notion as a recipe for spilling Palestinian blood.[30] Now that the police would be under his command, Arafat's hostility to the idea evaporated.

The Palestinian police would initially be responsible for enforcing the law within Gaza and a zone around Jericho, to be extended eventually to the Palestinian population of the entire West Bank and Gaza. Israeli soldiers would pull back from populated areas to protect Jewish settlers and the borders around the Palestinian zones. Israeli and Palestinian forces would jointly patrol a number of the main roads. Palestinians suspected of cross-border attack would have to be tried by the Palestinian judiciary.[31] Israel's willingness to extend Palestinian authority to the remainder of the occupied territories would naturally hinge on how well the PLO controlled its own population.

Many local Palestinians were frightened by the new constabulary. Seven thousand of the nine thousand police, mostly veterans of the Lebanon war, were to come from the Palestine Liberation Army (PLA), the military arm of the PLO, a fighting force largely loyal to Arafat's al-Fatah.[32] The Declaration of Principles hadn't mentioned human rights even once. Rabin himself reassured Israelis Arafat would control the territories in a way Israel could not because he would not be constrained by the niceties of civil procedure and human rights watchdogs. The Palestinians would be better than the Israelis in maintaining order, Rabin explained, "because they will allow no appeals to the Supreme Court and will prevent the Association for Civil Rights from criticizing the conditions there by denying it access to the area."[33] "Once he'll be with his people, he'll be able to control his people," Mordechai Gur, the deputy minister of defense, told us. It was exactly this that made so many Palestinians uneasy. A third of the Palestinians in the West Bank and Gaza expected the new Palestinian police force to repress the political opposition.[34] (By 1995, thousands of Palestinians in Jerusalem were applying for Israeli citizenship as protection against their own regime.)

Palestinians inside were dubious about Arafat's commitment to democracy and civil rights. Arafat had never run the PLO, nor Fatah, democratically. The partisan streams composing the PLO were infused with the political culture of militias, disciplined cadres, members who received services and took orders, not citizens, armed with rights, who made demands. During the *intifada,* the PLO never condemned the wholsesale use of torture to extract confessions from thousands of Palestinians and the summary killings of suspected collaborators, most of whom were never even allowed to respond to the charges and were not, in fact, collaborators.[35]

In the diaspora, the PLO was an assemblage of armed political clans, not a deliberative community generating consent from the ground up. Palestinians in the occupied territories understood such a structure was necessary for a national liberation movement struggling to survive in the diaspora. Nonetheless many feared a wholesale transfer of Arafat's functionaries into the West Bank and Gaza could prove disastrous for the formation of a democratic nation-state.[36] When the PLO published its draft constitution for the interim period in December 1993, those suspicions were confirmed. The Palestinian authority, expected to govern during the interim period, would be appointed by Arafat and would not have an independent judiciary.[37] Such a government, one Palestinian wrote, could only regulate, not legislate.[38]

After Arafat arrived, he, in fact sought to appoint all the figures in the new administration, to make them directly and personally responsible to him.[39] Much of the Palestinian delegation from the territories was unceremoniously dumped. Arafat was promoting figures who had played little role in the *intifada*, wealthy men and rural clan leaders with little popular support for administrative positions inside Palestine.[40] He insisted on appointing Fatah-affiliated municipal officials for the Palestinian towns rather than hold elections. The core of the Palestinian police force was dominated by PLA soldiers from abroad, and recruits from the occupied territories were overwhelmingly those who accepted al-Fatah's dominance of the state.[41] By September, 1994, there were seventy-two hundred Palestinian police in Gaza, as well as five hundred intelligence operatives, more internal security people in fact, than schoolteachers. Arafat was creating a militia personally loyal to him, not a national police force accountable to the Palestinians.[42] In February 1995, Arafat created a State Security Court, a tribunal closed to outside observers, where the judges, prosecutors, and court-appointed defense attorneys were all drawn from Arafat's military forces. A Palestinian lawyer who protested was taken into custody. The secret trials, closed to outside observers, handed out summary judgments, sometimes after just a few minutes.[43] Palestinians in the occupied territories worried that Arafat would remake Palestine into Taiwan, a one-party state run by a strongman.[44]

Palestinians in the territories who supported the agreement wanted their government to be democratic and guarantee the political rights of opposition groups.[45] The PLO and its streams, although allowing for expression of divergent views, had never been democratic. It had been Israel, not the PLO, Manuel Hassassian, a Palestinian participant in negotiations, told us, that insisted that elections be held to select the council of the interim authority, which would, in turn, choose the executive. The Palestinians in the occupied territories overwhelmingly supported elections, not political appointment by the PLO, as the way to choose the Palestinian Council of the Interim Self-Government Authority.[46] And even if they were held, most Palestinians did not expect elections to be fair.[47]

Haidar Abdel-Shafi, the former head of the Palestinian delegation, claimed in early 1994 that Arafat had no intention of holding democratic elections for the interim authority.[48] Although Arafat contended his desire to delay elections was based on his fear that rejectionist forces would gain too much influence, Manuel Hassassian, the Palestinian head of the technical team charged with devising electoral procedures, flatly told us Arafat didn't want elections to the council because he didn't want to be subject to popular mandate. The sparse turnout when Arafat finally went to Gaza and Jericho in July 1994 indicated he did not enjoy overwhelming popular support. There was even a chance the old man would lose. Even within his own faction, Arafat was not about to let go. It was premature, he announced in early 1994, for Fatah to become a democratically accountable political party.[49]

Arafat's initial stance toward Palestinian political prisoners, those the Palestinians consider the crown of the resistance movement, also gave the population cause for concern. Arafat, who did not demand the release of Palestinian political prisoners in his agreement with the Israelis, apparently asked that the first Palestinian prisoners released be his partisan supporters. Israel, of course, saw this as a way to reinforce those favoring the peace accord.[50] With Israel's approval, the overwhelming number of prisoners initially allowed out were Fatah activists, a number of whom were immediately recruited into the new police force. Ziad Abu Zayyad, who had been charged with negotiating the prisoner release with the Israelis, resigned rather than accept Israel's refusal to release prisoners from rejectionist groups.[51]

A tall, lanky Palestinian with surprisingly delicate fingers, who introduced himself only as Nasr, was one of those who had just gotten out of jail. When we met at Bethlehem University's cafeteria in 1993, Nasr had served seven years for torching three Israeli buses in the West Bank with Molotov cocktails. The leadership inside the occupied territories, Nasr claimed, was "rotten and dead." Nasr described the Palestinians who had suffered in Israeli jails and detention camps as the Palestinians' real leaders entitled to take up the command posts in the future Palestinian state. He was proud of the hard-won unity supporters of different factions had achieved as they grappled with survival in Israeli jails.[52] Nasr, a supporter of al-Fatah, believed wholesale release of prisoners would help domesticate the rejectionist opposition and prevent fierce interfactional fighting. Releasing Fatah loyalists, he offered, only undercut political accord both outside and inside the prisons. Indeed he believed that was the point.

When combined with the PLO's cutbacks in funding for prisoners and their families, Arafat's approach to the prisoners created outrage among the more than ten thousand Palestinians still held in Israeli jails. "The leadership's biggest concern is to ensure their hegemony under autonomy," wrote Hassan Abdel Jawad, a former political prisoner and returned deportee. "While slashing the budgets of organizations for prisoners, martyrs and wounded," he charged, "the leadership doles out millions of US dollars monthly to ensure people's unprincipled loyalty . . . We have lost faith in this bogus leadership that uses the blood and suffering of its own people to justify its jet-set life-style and unlimited expense accounts."[53]

Many Palestinians were profoundly worried Israeli withdrawal and the arrival of the Palestinian force would be followed by internal political violence, that the cities of the West Bank and Gaza would be drawn down into the barbarity of Beirut. During the interfactional fighting that plagued the Palestinians in the later years of the *intifada*, Palestinian "strike forces" were already taking on an arbitrary strut, in one case shooting in the street a Palestinian property owner who got into an altercation with them over his refusal to lower his rents. Fatah activists in Gaza also shot at family members who were protesting an eviction order.[54]

The agreement hammered out in Februrary 1994 called for joint Israeli–Palestinian patrols on the main roads in Gaza and Jericho and for security coordination with Israel's intelligence services. Although many Palestinians hoped the rejectionist forces would be domesticated by the scramble for influence and patronage within the interim authority, there was a danger Palestinian irredentism, especially in interaction with uncontrolled violent resistance and provocation on the Israeli side, would degenerate into a full-scale civil war within Palestinian society.[55] Large numbers of Palestinians were going to the flourishing black market in Rafa to buy a gun to protect their families and properties.[56]

Arafat seemed to be presenting the Palestinians with a horrible choice: democracy or statehood. In the transitional period, the Palestinians were charged with preventing Palestinian attacks on Israeli soldiers and settlers. Such a charge, when combined with the absence of any commitment to statehoood and Israeli withdrawal, would eventually lead to massive popular oppositon. The Palestinians, PFLP leader Riad Malki contended, did not "give their lives for autonomy. Nor to be annexed to Jordan." They "died raising the Palestinian flag in order to build on their dead body a state – an independent Palestinian state."[57] To control Palestinian violence against Israeli targets and contain that opposition, Arafat would need to concentrate great repressive capacities in his own hands. The condition for Arafat's success, Riad Malki contended, was for him to make Palestine like Syria, permanently immobilizing Palestinian political opposition. "They will encircle all the Palestinian political groups, put them in prison, under administrative detention," Malki gravely warned.

One thing was certain – if the agreement did not almost eliminate Israeli casualties at Palestinian hands, the Israelis would not long let the experiment continue. Under those conditions, the Israelis were more than likely to return to the Jordanians, who had democratic institutions in place, who had redeemed themselves in Palestinian eyes by serving as the only refuge for Palestinians expelled from the Gulf. (King Hussein's restored popularity was made clear by the large number of paid advertisements published in Jerusalem's Palestinian press after his October 1992 surgical operation.)[58] A Jordanian solution would preclude Palestinian statehood. Arafat would have to control political opposition tightly in order to prevent an opening for King Hussein.

Arafat sought to muzzle the Palestinian press. In August 1994, as the conflict over Jordanian control over Jerusalem's Islamic sites intensified, Arafat banned Osman Hallak's newspaper, *Al-Nahar*, as well as another pro-Hashemite paper edited by Nasser Nashashibi, *Akbar Al-Balad*, in the autonomy areas. "A mercenary voice bearing a Palestinian name" was how Arafat derided *Al-Nahar*. Fatah youths physically threatened the newspaper's employees, allegedly on orders from PLO officials in Gaza and Jericho.[59] When a Palestinian polling organization discovered that only a tiny fraction of the Palestinians supported Arafat's action, *Al-Quds* also refused to publish its findings.[60] When *Al-Nahar* was finally allowed to roll its presses, its first editorial was uncharacteristically obsequious. Titled "A Pledge . . . and a Thank-You," it praised Arafat as "the brother, leader and symbol" of the Palestinian nation.[61] (In late September 1994 the Palestinian head of security in Jericho, Jibril Rajoub, oversaw an illegal operation in which he sent his men to East Jerusalem to kidnap the new head of Palestinian television, Samih Samara.)

Prominent Palestinians were withdrawing from the PLO in droves. In the diaspora, Edward Said had quit the PNC, saying Arafat was "mad" and would end up as nothing more than the mayor of Greater Jericho. Mahmoud Darwish, the well-known Palestinian poet, left the PLO Executive Committee. Ibrahim Abu Lughod, the PLO's representative to the United Nations, dropped from the scene to set up housekeeping in Ramallah, taking a teaching position at Bir Zeit University. Even Bassam Abu Sharif threatened to depart.

And those Palestinians who remained within the PLO could not be counted on to support the new interim authority. Many of Arafat's top personnel in the PLO, including his trusted agents, were unwilling to participate personally in the new administration. No less a figure than Abu Mazen, who negotiated the accord, declined to return to the territories, as did Abu Ala, Arafat's chief economic adviser and the managing director of the Palestine Economic Council for Development and Reconstruction (PECDAR). Most members of the PLO Executive Committee likewise refused to take up positions in the new administration, as concerned by Arafat's personalistic rule and patronage operation as by the limits of autonomy of the Palestinian authority.[62]

Inside Palestine, there were equally ominous signs of defection. When the accord implementing the autonomy was signed in Cairo, not one of the West Bank or Gazan delegates to the negotiating team showed up. Faisal Husayni pointedly remained in Jerusalem on that day. Hanan Ashrawi, the Palestinians' Abba Eban, twice refused Arafat's offer to be minister of information in the first Palestinian government, deciding rather to form an independent organization to protect Palestinian human rights in the new state. This was remarkable, for shortly before she had often been at Arafat's side as he made his diplomatic rounds, even answering national leaders' questions, responding with Arafat's full authority. It was she who initiated the "back channel" used by the PLO to strike a deal, an agreement that "flabbergasted" her when she saw it in print. She would not go along and suddenly found herself cut out from the center, marginalized by her president. She was deeply concerned about the PLO's likely mode of operation when it became a local state, concerned that, as head of information, she would end up being the Palestinians' chief political censor.[63] To stand up for human rights, she understood, would not be particularly popular with the new administration. "Somebody," she said, "has to have the guts to do it."[64]

Arafat's treatment of Ashrawi reflected what many Palestinians saw as his mode of operation, creating multiple clients with competing mandates, raising one person to prominence only to cut him or her down. Arafat has a dozen or so picture frames in his office, Osman Hallak, editor of *Al-Nahar*, a pro-Jordanian newspaper in Jerusalem, told us. The photos in them, representing people he considers most politically important, change regularly. Ziad abu Zayyad, the Palestinian lawyer, had just had his picture added to the pantheon. Abu Zayyad, who had been given responsibility for designing the security arrangements for the

new Palestinian entity, had been sent by Arafat to observe NATO maneuvers as an official PLO representative. What, the suited editor asked
us, did a lawyer know about military affairs?

The Wealth of Nations

If the political end point of the Israeli–Palestinian agreement was uncertain, the economic means that would be put at the disposal of the Palestinians were potentially considerable. The Palestinian and Israeli participants in Oslo talked money before talking politics.[65] Arafat, who had
exerted little effort in the past to build the economy of the occupied
territories, sought rapid economic growth as the key mechanism to bind
the Palestinians to the accord, to restore the finances of his organization,
and to bolster his personal authority.

The Palestinians were empowered to establish a raft of authorities –
electricity, water, communications, transportation, housing – to be financed by a Palestinian Development Bank. All of these, as well as the
even more far-reaching regional development projects that include other
Arab states – desalination, a Gazan free-trade zone and port, a petro-
chemical complex – were all legally subject to a joint committee of Israelis and Palestinians outside the authority of the Palestinian Council.[66]

Billions of dollars were expected to course through the Palestinian
development authority.[67] Its autonomy from the Palestinian Council potentially provided for a hard-headed evaluation by professionals; it was
also perfectly suited, however, for Arafat to bolster his personal power
and to use this infusion of capital to resuscitate a poverty-stricken PLO.
Arafat got Farouk Kaddoumi, head of the PLO's Political Department,
who had briefly quit the PLO because of the Oslo accords, to run it as
his deputy. Arafat demanded Kaddoumi be chosen as chairman of the
board.

This was consistent with the way Arafat has always run the PLO's
finances, making sure that the location of much of its assets remains his
personal secret. (Indeed when his plane crashed in the Libyan desert in
1992, one PLO official admitted that had Arafat died and/or his famous
"notebook" been destroyed, "nobody would have had any idea where
the money is.")[68] The PLO had once operated as the wealthiest national
liberation movement in the world, with reported annual revenues of
$675 million in 1988.[69] Much of the PLO's monies have been spent at
Arafat's personal discretion.

When Arafat chose the Board of Governors for the development
authority that would parcel out hundreds of millions of dollars to build
the new infrastructure for the new Palestinian society, to subsidize pri-

vate capital investment in critical sectors, to train the skilled Palestinian workers, to develop its fiscal administration, Palestinians inside grumbled that he chose only Fatah loyalists, many with dubious qualifications for the job, overlooking professionally qualified economists and businessmen because their political loyalties were undependable.[70] Arafat made sure that the Board of Governors was originally dominated by dependable Palestinians from the diaspora.

Arafat was so sensitive, he even demanded the authority's name be changed from PEDA, Palestine Economic Development Authority (PEDA) to the Palestine Economic Council for Development and Reconstruction (PECDAR). "Mr. Arafat," said Ibrahim Dakkak, one of six Palestinians from the inside who sat on its initial Board of Directors, "didn't like 'authority' because he preferred to keep all the authority for himself. I am on the Board of Governors and I don't know whether I'll be governing anything or not." Dakkak, the prime mover behind the National Guidance Committee, told us he would quit if the authority did not turn out to be professional. Sari Nusseibeh, who had been picked personally by Arafat to manage PECDAR from the inside as deputy director, who was even taken to Tunis to consult with his president, refused to remain in Palestine and made his way to the United States to take up an academic post.[71] That some of Palestine's best and brightest were not eager to participate in the actual delivery of the new Palestinian state for whose birth they had struggled for so long was not an encouraging sign for future Palestinian state making.

The Americans, the Europeans, and the Arab states all refused to pay their $2 billion in commitments to a development authority that could so easily be turned into a treasury of Arafat's personal political household.[72] It was an ominous sign that the PLO was seeking to tap into the flow of tax revenues that would be raised to support the administration of the Palestinian's interim authority. Many occupied Palestinians wanted to make sure the monies would not be frittered away in patronage payments, but be channeled through national institutions controlled by professionals and accountable to the Palestinians who were to be the beneficiaries of their services.[73] The World Bank, the EEC, and the Americans all insisted that standard (IMF) rules for procurement and tendering be scrupulously followed. Arafat railed that it was his sovereign right to structure the board any way he saw fit. Indeed, he demanded that PECDAR's funds be funneled through the Palestinian authority. Because of Arafat's refusal to allow PECDAR to administer the funding, only $65 million of the $750 million promised aid had been allocated as of September 1994. Arafat appeared to be using the risk that the Palestinian authority, barely able to pay its operating expenses, would fail as a way to get the Western donors to drop their demands.[74]

Arafat was pushing hard for personal control over the monies coming into Palestine. Unable to move the Americans, cold-shouldered by the Arab states, Arafat tried to persuade the Europeans to relax the conditions for receipt of foreign monies. The Israelis understood that Arafat's success in this matter was critical. "If he can't control the funds," Deputy Defense Minister Motta Gur told us in 1993, "he's finished . . . We can speak about high policy, but he will be destroyed when he doesn't have the money." Under those conditions, the occupied Palestinians would take over, displacing and domesticating the functionaries who would flow in with Arafat from Tunis and elsewhere.

Shortly after the Palestinian police took control in Gaza and Jericho, the members of PECDAR discovered that Arafat had established a parallel body in Tunis entrusted with the same authority.[75] Companies seeking contracts from the fledgling Palestinian authority were making their way to Tunisia, where Arafat made the decisions and Kaddoumi, a man with no economic expertise, signed the checks.[76] Even Abu Alaa, the man Arafat picked as minister of the economy, had no access to the monies.

Arafat was livid that one of the first American aid commitments was a $5.6 million package paid to UNRWA, rather than directly to the PLO in Tunis. When Arafat met with Secretary of State Warren Christopher in Amman in December 1993, Christopher let Arafat know that not only was the available sum less than originally thought, but the foreign community wanted accountability and was not about to create a slushfund for Fatah patronage. Arafat accused the secretary of state of being a colonialist, thundering that the Americans were trying to prevent him from building his land.

"Don't do to me," Arafat reportedly said, "what you did to Gorbachev," referring to America's failure to provide funding until Russian institutions were restructured, leading, in part, to Gorbachev's demise.[77]

A National Address in Jerusalem

Postponing discussion of Jerusalem to the final status negotiations was one of Arafat's greatest concessions. After signing the Oslo accords, Arafat gave Faisal Husayni, his newly appointed leader of Fatah for the West Bank, a portfolio everybody believed was a dead end: Jerusalem. Negotiations about the final status of Jerusalem would not begin until two years after the Oslo accords and would not be completed for five years. This would sideline the Palestinian's most important local rival and embroil him in the most divisive issue. Arafat's apparent capitulation on the Jerusalem issue was taken to be emblematic by all Palestinians opposed to the accord. After the accord was signed, the student blocs running against Fatah in the universities, for example, called themselves "Jerusalem First." Jerusalem was so fractious that the various Palestinian political parties had been unable to cooperate after Madrid on the technical committee developing scenarios and practical strategies for Jerusalem. The radical and Islamic streams would not even participate, claiming it was outrageous for the Palestinians to negotiate the city's status.

Husayni was unlikely to get much help from Tunis either. None of the Palestinian committees negotiating with the Israelis had received much technical or financial support from the PLO. Salim Tamari, negotiating on refugees, had found himself almost alone when he met with the Israelis, not even given appropriate legal advice. Arafat seemed to care only about money and soldiers. The PLO had never developed a strategy for Palestinian resistance to Israeli expansion in Jerusalem.[78] Fatah's own office in Jerusalem, which had begun to develop alternative planning scenarios for the city, had been unable to get anybody in Tunis even to read and respond to them seriously. In September 1992, Palestinians sought to reestablish the city's Arab municipality. Arafat sat on the proposal so it went nowhere. On Jerusalem, Husayni was likely to be out there by himself.

There was no public hint that the Israelis would give an inch. The furious way the Israelis were cutting into the hard red earth around Jerusalem indicated just the opposite. Almost everybody within the Palestinian community believed the Israelis would concede nothing. Husayni, they surmised, was doomed to failure, a failure for which he would be held personally responsible. Through Oslo, Arafat had knocked Husayni out of the political ring; through Jerusalem, it was frequently said, Arafat could kill him. Arafat had put Husayni in "the deep freeze," one Palestinian put it.

Husayni, it was said, had wanted to quit his post as Fatah chief for the West Bank. Arafat had quashed even public consideration of Husayni's plan to proclaim a provisional government in 1988; had kept Husayni out of the loop making real political decisions in Norway in 1993. Why should Husayni expect any better treatment now?

Husayni's friends and allies dissuaded him from quitting. With the most important rejectionist leaders spurning the accord, with large numbers of Fatah members defecting, Palestinians were themselves establishing the political conditions that would help Arafat control Palestine as a one-man, one-party state. And besides, the widely respected Palestinian nationalist began to realize, Jerusalem might prove his launching pad after all. As part of a secret side letter from Foreign Minister Shimon

Peres, Israel had assured the PLO that it would not "hamper the activity" of East Jerusalem's Palestinian institutions during the interim period.[79] Husayni understood that Jerusalem's untouchability during that period might provide him with a base from which to mobilize support and build his stature.

As a Jerusalemite, "I have sacrificed my name, my history and my family for the PLO," Husayni reportedly said. "Now I am going all the way for Jerusalem. On Jerusalem, nobody can stop me."[80]

Ever since the Madrid negotiations had begun in 1991, Husayni's base, the New Orient House, once an empty and disheveled structure, had been bustling with activity as limousines ferried diplomats to meetings on damask chairs. Enclosed with a sliding electric black steel gate, its guards were rumored to have been armed by the Israelis to defend themselves against terrorist attack by Palestinian or Israeli rejectionists. The complex enjoyed an unofficial diplomatic immunity so that Israeli police had to obtain special permission to enter.[81] Although the Palestinian delegation had been supplanted by the PLO in Tunis, the New Orient House was still a critical address for the occupied Palestinians. The Europeans, the Americans, and emissaries of a number of the Gulf States continued to arrive in Jerusalem with proposals, plans, and funding suggestions.

Husayni's Arab Studies Center, like other important Palestinian institutions, was registered as a nongovernmental organization. Yet, in reality, it was playing the role of a dual government. The major Palestinian meetings working out the nitty gritty details of institution building and even many of the negotiating strategies with the Israelis were held within it walls. Palestine could not be built from abroad. Indeed, it turned out that Arafat had done little planning for a PLO takeover in the West Bank and Gaza.[82] The New Orient House was functioning, de facto, as a critical, if indeterminate, piece of the new Palestinian state.

The all-important challenge, Husayni realized well before Arafat signed the accords, was whether the New Orient House would become a diplomatic mission in Israel or the future home of the Palestinian authority.[83] By December 1993, Husayni was discussing arrangements in Jerusalem, meeting with the Israeli ministers of housing and police. The Palestinians hoped to use the solution of municipal problems – like the city's closure to most West Bank residents, economic development, housing, and land expropriation – as a way gradually to expand their right to negotiate for new political arrangements in the city. And they would lead the struggle to prevent complete Israeli domination of the metropolitan area.

Jerusalem, given its explicit exclusion from any Palestinian authority, provided Husayni with a platform that would be independent of Arafat's control. Because Palestinians from Jerusalem would be able to vote in elections for the interim authority and because all Palestinians saw Jerusalem as their nation's capital, it was only legitimate that the political forces in the city attempt a form of national organization there. Husayni would depend on Israeli protection in his efforts to help build a democratic Palestinian state.

In late 1993, Husayni's people began to organize the Jerusalem National Council to negotiate with the Israelis at the national and municipal levels on conditions in the city, prepare for the final status negotiations, and act as a counterpart to the Palestinian interim authority in the West Bank and Gaza.[84] "The real struggle for Jerusalem began with the signing of the Declaration of Principles," Ali Ghuzlan, chairman of the Arab Lawyers Committee, a grouping of Palestinian lawyers in the West Bank, told us. "We are not going to wait for Abu Amar, or the Saudis, or wealthy Palestinians from the outside," he insisted. "We must help our leadership to take back Arab Jerusalem." Jerusalem's Palestinians, Ghuzlan said, would begin to mobilize, to bring back those who had been forced to live outside the city, to build new housing, to refuse to pay taxes. Life for Jerusalemite Palestinians had been relatively privileged during the last seven years of the *intifada*. The time of their testing had begun.

The proposed council would not only be the Palestinians' national address in Jerusalem, it would function as a strong political bloc within the interim governing council. The Jerusalem National Council also sought to be the vehicle by which the Saudis and the Gulf States, who have indicated strong interest in participating in the reconstruction of the Old City and its Islamic shrines, would funnel some of their monies to Palestine. The Gulf States had resisted giving any monies directly to Arafat, because of both his support for Saddam Hussein and his history of corruption. There were many wealthy individuals and nongovernmental institutions in the Arab and Islamic world keenly interested in restoring Jerusalem's sacred shrines, refurbishing its Arab quarter, building the Arab presence in the city. In 1994, PECDAR was working on specific projects for Jerusalem they wanted to be well executed, visible, delivering real benefits to large numbers of people, the kinds of projects that would bring honor to their Arab sponsors.

To Arafat's irritation, Husayni and the leaders of other national institutions were still shuttling to the oil-rich states with great success. Negotiating with the Saudis, Abdul-Hadi confessed, was not easy. It is often said the Palestinians are the Jews of the Arab world. Not so, said Abdul-Hadi. It is the Saudis. They are the ones, he declaimed, who are stingy and shrewd. "We hope," he added, "that we are the Jews of the Arab world, but we are too naive."

Whereas the staff at the New Orient House was almost completely composed of Fatah loyalists, the Jerusalem National Council was intended as a body that would recruit and have legitimacy across the political spectrum. Discussions were under way with opposition groups, including Riad Malki of the Popular Front for the Liberation of Palestine, who indicated to us he would consider participating if he could be sure it would not simply be an instrument in Husayni's personal rivalry with Abu-Ammar (Arafat's nom de guerre). Arafat was unlikely to get Israeli permission for Palestinian authority funding of projects in Jerusalem; this meant that with direct Gulf State funding, the Jerusalem Palestinians might make common cause with the Jerusalem *Awqaf,* using its institutions as a vehicle for the delivery of services across the West Bank and Gaza, and thereby building alliances with certain segments of the Islamic movement. There were also major Israeli businessmen looking for Palestinian counterparts to make joint investments in Jerusalem. The Jerusalem National Council might be their conduit as well.

The Jerusalem National Council hoped to distinguish itself from Arafat's emerging praetorian state in every way possible. After Oslo, Arafat's appointments were overwhelmingly composed of Fatah partisans or men tied to the Hashemites who could be counted on for support. His choices were based on loyalty, not competence. "Are quick profit and a history of servile loyalty the only criteria for service?" Edward Said sneered at Arafat's minions.[85] In contrast, the council would seek the best people the city had to offer, hoping to be a model of professionalism and to thereby build cross-party organization and legitimacy. If the Jerusalem National Council succeeded, it would be one of the first cross-partisan organizations since the National Guidance Committee in the late 1970s. Jerusalem had an unusually high percentage of Palestinians who considered themselves independent or unaffiliated with the dominant bloc (almost 35 percent in December 1993).[86]

If the Jerusalemites could get funds for projects and execute them efficiently, they might become a model for how a Palestinian state should act. Arafat had run the PLO as his personal fiefdom, using its elective bodies as ritual rubber stamps. The Jerusalem National Council would run according to democratic procedure. If Arafat's cronies failed to administer national institutions appropriately, the Council would be there to walk into the breach. And if Arafat refused to allow elections, Jerusalem would have a representative body ready to go.[87] As of July 1994, Israel was working on legislation forbidding the PLO from operating governmental institutions in Jerusalem or engaging in any kind of political organization.[88]

17

The City That Ate Palestine

Around Jerusalem, the winds of peace carry dust. As soon as Egypt, Syria, Jordan, Lebanon, and Israel agreed to the peace conference in Madrid in October 1991, Jerusalem had been put in play. Ariel Sharon, appointed minister of housing in 1990, architect of the war in Lebanon, had already chosen Jerusalem as his last and best front. Religious nationalist Jews, too, looked to Zion as the best place to assert and defend their dream, to protect redemption from the promises of an illusory peace.

Silwan, a poor Arab village hugging the steep southeastern slopes below the Old City, in the shadow of the leaded dome of al-Aqsa mosque, was one of the religious Zionists' most provocative destinations. Jews, mainly Yemenite, had lived there until the Palestinians rose against the Jews in the 1930s. After becoming part of Israeli Jerusalem in 1967, Silwan remained exclusively Arab, inhabited by many Palestinians from Deir Yassin and Hebron.

Silwan was the politically perfect point from which to assert the primacy of Jewish property rights to Jerusalem. The Jews' claim to Zion originated here. Extensive archaeological excavations had determined that Silwan, known in Hebrew as Shiloah, was the site where King David founded his city. At its base lies the Gihon spring whose waters were used in the coronation of Israelite kings. Israeli schoolchildren used to make pilgrimage to the site, candles in hand. During the *intifada,* its young Palestinian boys and girls had the same deadly face-offs with Israeli soldiers as they did everywhere else. Israelis and tourists alike stopped visiting the area.

On October 8, 1991, a small group of Jews moved forcibly into six houses in Silwan. Most of them had been affiliated in some way with Rav Kuk's Mercaz ha-Rav yeshivah, the theological center where Gush Emunim's leadership had been forged. Backed by dozens of reserve soldiers from elite army units, they woke Arab tenants before dawn and roughly expelled them. The incursion caused such a storm that the police later removed the Jews, including several members of Knesset, while the High Court examined its legality. The court allowed the Jews to remain in one house, which had belonged before 1948 to the Meyouhaus family, one of the oldest Jewish families in Jerusalem.

The politicians would not wait, however. On December 8, 1991, the fourth anniversary of the *intifada,* before the High Court even had a chance to rule, the Israeli cabinet gave its permission for Jews to move back in. Because of fear of Palestinian violence by radical rejectionists and Islamic militants to mark the anniversary and a possible Palestinian explosion in response to its decision, Jerusalem was closed to Palestinians from the West Bank. This time, police, border patrol, and army soldiers provided the protection necessary to evict the Arab tenants and secure the safety of the new Jewish residents. Yeshivah students with guns moved into one home where a Palestinian couple had lived for twenty-one years, throwing their bedding into an outhouse. The Palestinians' seven-year-old son fell on the floor, shaking in fear.

With Israeli and Palestinian delegates encamped on couches in the hallways of Washington, Silwan seemed a hastily orchestrated move to counter any notion that Jerusalem would ever be open to negotiation. But, in fact, these tactics had been in the works for a long time. Religious Zionists had been moving steadily, with as little fanfare as possible, into the Arab neighborhoods of old Jerusalem since the late 1970s. Jewish organizations, some seeking to restore Jewish control of the Temple Mount, had been slowly buying up land, leases, and buildings throughout Arab Jerusalem. The Ateret ha-Kohanim, "the Priestly Crown," a Jewish group preparing for the Third Temple service, had been purchasing Arab properties all around the Temple Mount.[1] (Ariel Sharon, in fact, moved into one of their properties.) In 1982, some of their members even tunneled under the Temple Mount in search of the room where King Solomon was believed to have hidden gold vessels used in the Temple service.

Bit by bit, the religious Zionists would make the messiah's city Jewish. Any believing Jew understands that it is to Zion that the Davidic king will return and assume the throne, and in Zion that the Temple will, at last, be rebuilt. Only Jews with faith to discern Zionism's redemptive function understand that the fact that the city's ancient core is occupied by Arabs, not Jews, blocks the way forward and that something must be done.

It was a formidable task to acquire properties and residences in the heart of Arab Jerusalem. Death is the punishment for Arabs who sell their private piece of Palestine to the Jews. Those who are not killed are ostracized. When an Arab who sold land to Ateret Kohanim later died, only his two sons were in attendance when his body was taken to al-Aqsa mosque for burial rites. Nobody would pray for this dead man. Nonetheless there were ways to maneuver. Israelis eager to acquire land in

Jerusalem traditionally used non-Jews as intermediaries. Before he was imprisoned for corruption, Rafi Levy, the Jerusalem district commissioner and head of the District Planning Committee, arranged for Greek or Armenian Orthodox to buy lands from the Palestinians, after which they would sell them to the Jews.[2] There were always Palestinians willing to deal with wealthy buyers. According to David Schafer, the American vice-consul, even during the *intifada,* Palestinians were using offers from Israelis in order to extract monies from the PLO to remain "steadfast," lest they sell to the Zionists. Palestinians with valid titles living in Australia and the United States were tracked down and richly compensated for houses to which they would never return. Other Palestinians were given one-way tickets and a packet of cash greater than they could ever attain after years of hard work. Christian families, who have neither the family networks nor the Islamic hierarchy to fall back on and who are made uncomfortable by the rising Islamic tide, have been particularly vulnerable to these material blandishments, but Muslims have sold as well.

As Israel was being pushed to the negotiations with the Palestinians, more and more religious nationalist Jews moved back to the city's ancient core, their moves becoming ever more visible and provocative. In Silwan, an organization called El Ad, an acronym for "To the City of David," had been slowly buying land since the mid-1980s. "Our past as a state began in this place," Avi Maoz, one of its members, said.[3] "This is where the kings of the House of David were anointed. It's natural that every person would want to return to the source of his existence." By 1991, El Ad boasted that it owned half Silwan's land and one out of every six of its houses. Some of the lands were in fact originally bought in the nineteenth century by the baron de Rothschild and deeded to the Jewish National Fund. Many of the so-called Arab owners were, in fact, legally only tenants. In some cases, Minister of Housing Sharon simply transferred expired leases to the Jews. In others, threatened with eviction anyway, Palestinians signed away their residual proprietary rights.[4]

Jewish entry into Silwan provoked visceral rage, invocations of terrible forces. "God's hand is here," Sheik Muhammad Jamal, a Muslim Brotherhood cleric, told us. "He will change everything." When the Jews moved in, they found HAMAS graffiti threatening the Palestinian "collaborators" who had cooperated with the Israelis with death. "They call us terrorists and treat us like fleas," an Arab teenager from Silwan exclaimed. "If they want war, then that's what we'll give them. We'll make it so the settlers will fear for their lives," another said.

Many liberal Israelis found the move into Silwan – even if it was legal – to be outrageous. Meron Benvenisti cried as he watched the Jewish settlers on television. Israel seemed to him to be slipping into apartheid, using the law to oppress another nation politically, to legiti-

Palestinian boy holding a Peace Now poster at demonstration against Jewish settlement in Silwan, 1991.

mate massive ethnic discrimination. The law was designed to make Jerusalem into Zion. For example, even though Palestinians had owned much of the Jewish Quarter, Israel's courts had refused them the right to reside there after 1967. Thousands of Palestinians who had owned homes on the western side of the city were likewise never allowed to return. Yet Jews were being allowed to reenter once-Jewish-owned houses throughout Arab quarters of the Old City. Arnon Yekutieli, a member of Jerusalem's city council, proposed to Peace Now that houses be leased on the Jewish side of the city for Arabs displaced in Silwan. Peace Now rejected the proposal as too militant, too likely to alienate the Zionist mainstream.

Thousands of Israelis and Palestinians now marched together in Silwan against the incursion, protected by lines of flak-jacketed border police. Faisal Husayni, briefly hoisted onto a wall, told the crowd, "People in Silwan can now be sure they have partners on the other side and that we can fight together to establish a Palestinian state alongside Israel." The Jews' entry into Silwan proved, he told us, that Jerusalem could not be saved for the last stages of negotiation. Too weak to force a resolution, if such radical changes on the ground continued, he warned, the Palestinians would stop the peace process. "We will find ourselves," he warned, "entrapped in the flames of a circle of blood."

Faisal Husayni at demonstration protesting Jewish move into Silwan, 1991.

Likud supporters were jubilant. This was the City of David and Jews had a legal claim to residence. That Jews could live anywhere in Jerusalem went without saying. "It is simply unthinkable that Israelis who own homes in Israel's capital should be prevented from living in them," opined *The Jerusalem Post*.[5] "Why shouldn't Jews have a right to buy homes . . . in Jerusalem?" Rabbi Waldman of Kiryat Arba asked us. "How can people be against that? What kind of distortion of human rights is that?" "Apartheid!" he replied incredulously when informed of Benvenisti's charge. Not to allow Jews to reside there would be apartheid! Can you imagine, the yeshivah head said, if American Jews were denied the right to live in a Protestant area of Los Angeles or a Catholic area in Boston? *Not* allowing Jews to live in certain areas in the land of Israel was apartheid. Didn't the Arabs have a right to buy wherever they wanted? The problem, Waldman alleged, was not with the Arabs, but with the Jews, infected with the "illness of self-hatred."

Mayor Kollek was livid when he learned – on the radio, like everybody else – about the morning move into Silwan. Kollek understood it as the culmination of Likud "harassment and intimidation of the Arab population."[6] Whatever its legality, it would radicalize the Palestinians of the city, undercut coexistence, threaten Jerusalem's ability to attract investment and Russian Jews. Sharon, as minister of housing, was funneling massive amounts of funding, some of it used illegally, to Jewish groups wanting to buy and lease in Arab sections of the city.[7] To pay for the properties in Silwan, the mayor's office asserted, Sharon reallocated funds earmarked to house new Russian immigrants. Surely, the mayor argued, it would be better to have one or two thousand new Jewish residents on lands where Arabs did not need to be displaced than thirty Jews forcibly inserted into the midst of hostile Arabs? The large police contingent needed to protect these Jews had to be taken from elsewhere in the city. It was terrible, he said, for Jerusalem's image abroad. The mayor was so angry he went personally to the site to protest and threatened to cancel the twenty-fifth anniversary celebration of Jerusalem's unification planned for 1992. "These Jewish settlers," he remarked, "dwelling morbidly on history, think that they are honoring the past, but in reality they are endangering the future." Kollek's reaction saddened Rabbi Waldman. The mayor, the rabbi told us, was confusing the "essence of the matter and the image of a matter, or how it looks through the eyes of others."

In 1993, two years after the Jews first entered Silwan, we returned to the neighborhood. It was winter and the alluvial grain of the Judean desert, stretching to the east, gleamed. Teddy Kollek's posters from the recent election, printed in Hebrew and Arabic, were still plastered on trash bins and side walls. Up and down the street, home entrances were painted with somber architectural images of the Ka'ba, indicating a resident's past pilgrimage to Mecca. Only one Palestinian flag flew in the neighborhood – over the home of an Arab working as an Israeli policeman in Jerusalem.

Aharon Horowitz, an articulate mustachioed Israeli tour guide who, with his wire-rimmed glasses, looks like a young assistant professor, lives in a small stucco house with his little children underneath a guard tower from which one can survey every approach. He says he is on good terms with his Palestinian neighbors, even though, he says, his dog ate one of their chickens. They greet each other, drink coffee at each other's homes. He even went in with some of them to tile their roofs in order to get the job done more cheaply.

There are limits, though. Although the Horowitzes are on a friendly basis with the Shabans, a Palestinian family who live just down the path, Horowitz would never let the Shaban daughter babysit for his children. "Not because of her," he explained. "I in no way have any concern that they would want to harm us. But they have cousins and they have friends and their friends have friends and we have a very strict code of security." Reciprocally when the Shaban family sons were married, the Horowitzes were not invited. The boys' mother apologized; the Horowitzes would not have felt comfortable, she explained. She gave them a video of the proceedings. "We definitely would not have felt comfortable,"

Horowitz admitted. "They were dancing with pictures of Arafat and the flag of the PLO."

Down the block, Rivka and Oren Cohen's baby was crawling on the linoleum floor of their small kitchen when we entered. The young couple moved here from Pesagot, a small Jewish enclave near Ofra. They converted part of the property Musa Abassi, a Palestinian, inherited from his father into a three-room apartment. According to Israeli press reports, this particular Abassi compound was inherited by five brothers, four of whom had moved on to Jordan. Under Israeli laws regarding absentee property, the four brothers thereby lost all claims. Arguing that Musa, the only brother left, had no right to the whole compound, the court approved the transfer of the four absentee brothers' shares to the new Jewish residents. Musa Abassi lives in two rooms surrounded by hostile Jews. Every legal decision, Rivka proudly pointed out to us, had been in the settlers' favor. "We don't do anything against the laws of the country," Rivka emphasized. "This is our country." Unlike her Arab neighbors, many of whom have built illegally, she claimed they bought and built according to the book.

The Abassis, who number in the thousands, are the dominant Palestinian family in Silwan. Its young men and women figure prominently among the staff and bodyguards of Faisal Hussayni's apparatus at the New Orient House. Aharon Horowitz had had dealings with an Abassi many years before. An Abassi, he told us, was once in charge of the entrance to Warren's shaft, an underground tunnel connecting into an ancient aqueduct through which King David is believed to have conquered the city of Jebus, as it was then named. Horowitz was always asking permission to lead Israeli soldiers through the tunnel and Mr. Abassi was always saying no. "You know," Horowitz remembered telling Abassi, "this is the spot that supposedly King David captured Jerusalem three thousand years ago and these are his descendants, soldiers of the Israeli army, and they'd like to see it." Abassi, never very accommodating, was ultimately fired, Horowitz remembered. "Things in that family started going bad a while ago."

Ali Ghuzlan's office is on the third floor of an unlit decrepit building on al-Asfahani St., a small dark side road strewn with trash in the Arab downtown. Ghuzlan had an intense interest in the Israeli court's annulment of the Abassi brothers' property rights. A specialist in land cases, he was not only the representative of the Abassi family; his own mother is an Abassi. According to Ghuzlan, the balding chairman of the Arab Lawyers Committee, this particular compound had originally been inherited by all twelve children of his maternal grandfather. All told, said Ghuzlan, who smoked one gold-banded cigarette after another, there are twenty-seven living heirs. Although many did move to Jordan, and thus forfeited their rights under Israeli law, there are many more still living in Jerusalem with a valid claim.[8] In 1989, he told us, the property had, unbeknown to its Palestinian owners, been reregistered as absentee property. It was, he claimed, all part of Sharon's plan to create a continuous band of Jewish habitation from the Old City's Jewish Quarter into the Arab villages clustered around it to the south. The goateed lawyer expected the Central Court in Jerusalem to overturn the Jewish occupancy. Besides, he insisted, Silwan was not really the City of David, as Israeli archaeologists claimed. In his own countergeography, the real location of David's first capital was around Mount Zion, with its contemporary sites marking David's burial place, his palace, and a synagogue.

A Jewish presence in Silwan has been normalized. There are eleven families spread throughout the neighborhood, living in compounds surrounded by barbed wire and protected by private guards paid for by the state. One of the guards, a young university student who took the job for the money, tells us it is quiet in the neighborhood – just a couple of rocks. You see, Rivka quietly pointed out, before this had been a violent place, a haven for drug pushers, a free zone for HAMAS activists, a place even Israeli soldiers were wary of entering.[9] Now it is all quiet. Do they feel safe, we inquired? Oren replied that only an army presence would make them feel truly safe. Now, he added, it is that way in the whole country.

Teddy Kollek wanted Jews and Arabs to live separately, Rivka said, "but we changed his plans." Rivka Cohen was grinning.

The City That Ate Palestine

Although it was a particularly noticeable move in the battle for Jerusalem, Silwan was part of a larger logic. Since 1967, the thrust of the settlement movement had been outward from Jerusalem. As geopolitical forces realigned and Israel was being nudged into peace negotiations, the religious and right-wing Zionists turned back to the center, to the Arab heart of Jerusalem, to Zion.

On March 3, 1991, when President Bush referred to East Jerusalem as "occupied territory," he signaled what everybody always knew, that Jerusalem would be up for grabs in the diplomatic and financial press with which the United States would cajole and strong arm the Arabs and the Jews to peace.[10] Sharon's sponsorship of the move into Silwan was not an isolated feint, but part of a overall plan to fill in as much of the Jerusalem region as possible with Jews.

Ariel Sharon and Teddy Kollek: the first holds to a vision of Greater Israel and the second rejects it. But, on Jerusalem, there was no substantial division between the former right-wing minister of housing and the city's liberal former mayor. Although barely on speaking terms, they had differences on Zion that were only matters of style. In response to Secretary of State Baker's demand in October 1990 that American monies not be used to finance housing construction in East Jerusalem, Sharon announced he planned to build seventeen thousand new apartments in Jerusalem, almost all of them in the portions annexed in 1967. In that same month, after the 1990 explosion of Palestinian violence in the city in the wake of Israel's massacre of Palestinians on the Temple Mount that prompted a United States–supported UN resolution referring to Jerusalem as "occupied," Kollek stated, "The solution is to bring as many immigrants to the city as possible and make it an overwhelmingly Jewish city, so that they will get it out of their heads that Jerusalem will not be Israel's capital."[11]

Indeed, Sharon's settlement policies as minister of housing were closer to those of the Labour government than to Likud's.[12] Unlike his Likud predecessors, such as David Levy, Sharon poured money into the municipality and metropolitan region of Jerusalem. Though Kollek publicly opposed Sharon's idea of a "Greater Jerusalem" that included massive Jewish settlement outside the municipality, the mayor had already been a willing partner to the expropriation of Palestinian lands in East Jerusalem and the construction of a ring of new Jewish neighborhoods surrounding the Arab population core in East Jerusalem. Sharon was only consolidating the work of previous Labour governments. Even Sharon's settlement plan of 1981, when he headed Likud's Inter-Ministerial Settlement Committee, was, more or less, his own version of the Allon plan, Labour's proposal for a territorial settlement with Jordan.

As housing minister, Sharon so massively expanded Ma'aleh Adumim, a settlement just over Jerusalem's eastern border, that it became the first Israeli city on the West Bank. Sharon was closing, widening, and tightening the Jewish circle around Jerusalem that Mayor Kollek had begun long ago. The Palestinians were not only being encircled inside the city, they were being encircled on the outside as well. Palestinians outside the city would then have to pass through Jewish areas to make it into Jerusalem's Arab center. Sharon was a savvy strategist. The Israeli consensus on Jerusalem is rock solid. Through Jerusalem, Israel could consume the center of Palestine.

When Sharon had taken the Ministry of Housing, he demanded that the Israel Lands Authority, the body with the power to acquire lands for the state, be transferred to his ministry. After 1990, he used that power to buy and bully space for Jewish expansion everywhere in and around Jerusalem. Silwan was part and parcel of Sharon's plan to fragment the remaining Palestinian field. By 1991, Sharon had identified twenty-six new sites all over Jerusalem, many of them in densely populated Arab areas, for new Jewish construction. One of them was Karem ha-Mufti, a large olive orchard adjoining Haj Amin al-Husayni's old home. For Ateret ha-Kohanim, which intended to build residences there for their yeshivah students, it was a delicious choice. Although these initiatives enraged then-mayor Kollek, Sharon's "constructive" reaction to American peace plans was nothing new. Ramat Eshkol and French Hill had likewise been built by Labour governments in response to Secretary of State Rogers's peace plans two decades earlier. (George Bush, who was then ambassador to the United Nations, supported the Security Council in 1971 in condemning Israel's construction at the time.)[13]

As a result of its rapid expansion, the city had run out of lands on which to build the Jewish city without further expropriation. Israeli planners understood that to maintain the demographic balance between Arabs and Jews in the city, they needed to provide more jobs and there just wasn't any land left to build new factories and offices. A commitment to the low-lying premodern skyline prevented building upward. Although urban rationality might have pointed to dispersal into other areas, there was a cross-party consensus that more Jewish residents were necessary to strengthen Israel's claim to the city. But which way? Despite the fact that most of the "land reserves," unpopulated area taken by the state for future Jewish development, were concentrated to the east of the city, beyond the "Green Line," Kollek's liberal planners wanted to push the city westward, back into Israel, to prevent absorption into the network of Likud settlements around the city. Some left-leaning Israeli planners saw the creation of a new economic region joining Jerusalem and Tel Aviv with a high-speed rail link not only as good economic policy, but as a way to help achieve that objective.[14] Though most Labour Zionists wanted the city to expand in a westerly direction, Sharon wouldn't yield, demanding that Jerusalem expand to the east.

On June 23, 1992, the Israeli electorate threw Likud out of power. For fifteen years, men drawn from the tradition of Revisionist Zionism had been able to orchestrate the settlement of Judea and Samaria as they saw fit. Labour moved swiftly to repair relations with the United States, to initiate substantive negotiations with the Palestinians. There was a difference, the newly elected prime minister said, between "political" and "security" settlements.[15] Rabin's government would support the latter; the former would be slowly choked off. Government subsidies of up to twenty-eight thousand dollars per apartment that had gone to Jewish settlements under Likud would henceforth be denied to the "political" settlements.[16] While Rabin allowed Jewish construction already under way to continue, he stopped new construction in most areas heavily populated with Palestinians. Israelis who were building homes in these zones complained they were denied electrical and water hookups, and so unable to move in. Suddenly, banks refused them loans for remodeling and construction. The government even helped a number of Palestinians dispossessed by Sharon's Housing Ministry in Jerusalem to regain tenancy in their houses. It sought to bring charges against some Israeli civil servants who had participated in Sharon's campaign to replace Arab tenants with Jews; it demanded that the Jewish organizations that had received financing for these ventures refund the money to the state. Rabin banned mobile homes, used to settle Jews quickly in the territories.

But there was one place that the pace of construction and government funding was untouched–metropolitan Jerusalem. By 1993, there were 130,000 Jews living in the West Bank. But within East Jerusalem, there were another 160,000, more Jews, in fact, than Arabs. During the first year of Rabin's tenure as prime minister, another 13,000 housing units for Jews were readied in East Jerusalem.[17] Although the newly elected Labour government finally approved westerly expansion for Jerusalem, the Rabin government was forging ahead with a $90 million tunnel connecting Efrat and Gush Etzion, a bloc of Jewish suburban settlement to the south, directly to Jerusalem, passing right under Arab Bethlehem.

Jewish Jerusalem has spread far to the east, cutting the north–south ribbon of Palestinian population in two. Rabin moved to consolidate that Jewish wall. After the Oslo accords, his government made plans to expand Maaleh Adumim, kissing the city's eastern perimeter, into a continuous bloc of Jewish settlement, Gush Adumim, linking up with Jewish suburbs being constructed inside East Jerusalem, encircling Palestinian areas built up near Jerusalem's eastern borders, establishing an almost continuous Jewish corridor through which the main road up from the Jordan valley would run, and pushing eastward all the way down to the Jericho region to be ceded to the Palestinians.[18] Plans were also on the books to build a tunnel to Maaleh Adumim. (Twenty-eight thousand of the thirty-one thousand government-built apartments in the 1995–1998 program are in the Jerusalem region.)[19]

"Experience has proved that in order to defend Jerusalem, one must have a strip of defense surrounding it in the north, south, east and west," Mordechai Gur, deputy minister of defense, said in 1994.[20] Unlike those in outlying settlements where housing prices dropped by as much as half, prices for Jewish homes in commuting distance of Jerusalem did not drop after the peace treaty. Indeed, some settlements close-in got more expensive.[21] The Israeli government has made it clear that the Palestinians will have to sacrifice big chunks of the metropole in order to get statehood. And Israeli housing prices indicate that the Jews believe it.

The King Is Dead: Long Live the King

In the immediate aftermath of Israel's peace agreement with the PLO, Jerusalemites went to the polls in the 1993 municipal elections. Prime Minister Rabin told the Israeli public that their vote would be a plebiscite on his diplomacy. This was a dangerous maneuver, nowhere more so than in Jerusalem. Through his negotiations with the Palestinians, Rabin had himself put Jerusalem into play. He had allowed a Palestinian from Jerusalem to lead the Palestinian delegation. He had allowed Palestinians from Jerusalem to vote and even run for election to the Palestinian legislative council that would run Palestinian affairs in the West Bank and Gaza in the interim period. And Jerusalem was explicitly included among the issues to be negotiated during the final status talks scheduled to be concluded by December 13, 1999.

In the midst of the breakthrough with the PLO, Prime Minister Rabin sought to convince the eighty-three-old and ailing Kollek to run again, even though Kollek had already announced he would retire because of poor health. Maintaining the peace of Jerusalem in the face of an emerging Palestinian state would require the mayor's unique gifts. Liberal Zionist rule of the city would be critical if Israel were going to deliver changes in the city that would have any chance of satisfying even minimal Palestinian aspirations.

Likud's candidates for mayor had typically been marginal figures with little national visibility, token challenges to an apparently unbeatable Kollek. The Likud campaign budgets for Jerusalem were meager compared to those allocated for cities like Tel Aviv. But in 1993, Likud's candidate was Ehud Olmert, a former Knesset member who had once served as Shamir's minister of justice.

Kollek did not see anybody on the horizon who could beat Olmert. And he remembered the words of an eighty-nine-year-old violinist who had told him never to stop working. "It will sign your death warrant," she reportedly told him. Kollek gamely threw his hat back into the ring. Facing a formidable opponent with substantial resources, Kollek raised campaign funds in the United States. In October 1993, Frank Sinatra and his wife hosted a fund-raiser in an exclusive Los Angeles restaurant in an effort to raise $850,000. Sinatra invited his friends, including Barbra Streisand, Gregory Peck, Roseanne Arnold, and Don Rickles, and picked up the $16,000 bill for the dinner. The "whole world has to have an interest in Israel and Jeusalem," Sinatra said, "and Teddy has been a good friend for many years."[22]

During the campaign, Olmert pounded on Kollek's apparent weakness vis-à-vis Palestinian political rights in Jerusalem. Olmert's campaign-ers warned of a secret "covenant between Teddy, Arafat and Faisal Husayni."[23] Olmert promised he would launch a massive building campaign to erase the relatively undeveloped "seam" still dividing the Arab and the Jewish city, a partition reinforced by the construction of a big north–south road built by Moshe Amirav, the dove who had served as head of transportation in Kollek's last government. Omert stressed he would expand Jerusalem to the east, not the west. Agudat Yisrael's Meir Porush likewise stated, "The Oslo agreements revealed plans that had been hidden to us. This makes us think . . . that maybe there are hidden plans about Jerusalem, too . . . The people feel that Olmert will stop any plans to divide Jerusalem."[24]

Labour understood Kollek would need substantial Palestinian turnout to retain municipal power. They thus approached Meron Benvenisti, who had administered East Jerusalem immediately after the Six-Day War, to run on the ticket. Benvenisti, who had come to understand Israeli policies as leading to a genteel apartheid, surprisingly agreed. Benvenisti ran because he believed reconciliation might now, indeed, be possible. He demanded the portfolio for the Arab city and assurances from the Labour government that he could use the resources and power of his office to push for major improvements in housing, infrastructure, and economic development on the Palestinian side of the city. When news of the Oslo accords broke, it bolstered his sense that a major psychological threshold had been crossed: Israel had recognized the Palestinian nation and the PLO as its legitimate enemy, not just as an incarnation of evil to be suppressed or expelled. And the Palestinians, to Benvenisti's amazement, had done something of which he had never imagined them capable: acknowledged their defeat. Every item in the Declaration of Principles, he told us in 1993, contained language that expressed Israeli supremacy. It was, he said, "a *diktat*." If he were a Palestinian, he said, he could never have signed.

Benvenisti pulled out all the stops to encourage the Palestinians to vote. He wrung a statement out of Faisal Husayni that the PLO would not punish Palestinians who wanted to vote, given the importance of defeating the right. But other Palestinians, like Mahdi Abdul-Hadi, called Arafat, demanding he order a total Palestinian boycott. In the end, Tunis's response was equivocal. As far as most Palestinians were concerned, there was not much difference between Israelis on the Jerusalem question. Benvenisti discovered, he told us, just how much the Palestinians of the city hated Teddy Kollek.

Meir Porush, the rotund Agudat Yisrael city leader, mounted his own campaign for mayor. But the night before the election Porush recommended to Agudah's rabbinical court that he withdraw his candidacy and that the *haredim* be instructed to vote for the Likud candidate. With only twelve hours to go before the polls opened, Agudat's Council of Torah Sages gave its approval and Kollek's fate was sealed.²⁵ Porush's candidacy had been a feint, leading Kollek's supporters to believe his secular and religious opponents would divide their votes, at worst leading him to a run-off with Olmert. Given the huge distrust of Agudat Yisrael's self-serving domination of the municipality in years past, the *haredi* turnout was astonishing. Nearly 85 percent of eligible *haredim* cast their ballots for Olmert. The *haredim* also disliked the secular mayor and his cosmopolitan plans for the city. It was the first time in the history of the city, Benvenisti told us, that the *haredim* had actually voted for a known "pork-eater, a shrimp-eater, a secularist."

Although the PLO provided a flickering green light, the level of Palestinian participation was very low (3 percent). "Their own political processes are more important to them than what the white man has to offer," Bonnie Boxer, Kollek's spokesperson, told us after the election. As a result of low Arab and secular turnout (25 percent), combined with very high *haredi* turnout (85 percent), Kollek's One Jerusalem Party's share of the council's seats was almost cut in half, from its already reduced position, to just six mandates.²⁶ As the last votes were being tabulated, Kollek, without congratulating Olmert, conceded the contest. "I thought that the policy we always followed in the past, and that we still follow, was the right one," he told his exhausted campaign workers. "Now the policy is not correct. I feel sorry for Jerusalem and its residents, who will have to bear the future policy."²⁷

The religious parties – United Torah, Shas, and the National Religious Party – all told, won thirteen seats, more than the two liberal parties – One Jerusalem and Meretz – combined. The United Torah Party won seven seats, more than any other party. Omert formed a municipal government with both *haredi* blocs, the Ashkenazi United Torah Party and the Sephardi SHAS Party.²⁸ The Ashkenazi *haredi* party were given three deputy mayors and five portfolios, putting them on an institutional par with Likud itself. Porush was expected to get some 40 percent of the city's education budget to allocate as he desired. The Ashkenzi and Sephardi *haredim* were both granted their own independent education departments with their own substantial budgets, as well as a separate department for the national religious stream. Olmert sexually segregated the buses for Mea She'arim.

Ornan Yakutieli, elected to the city council in 1989 on the Meretz (a left–Zionist party) slate, felt a sense of doom. "If they take our kids and try to give them a *haredi* brainwash," he said, "I will not send my two 7-year-old kids to school."²⁹ The *haredim* were pushing to close twenty more roads, including Bar-Ilan Avenue, a major thoroughfare. The *haredim* were also given control over municipal building and planning in the city and would now be able to move into any secular Israeli neighborhood. For example, they purchased a small hotel in Beit ha-Karem, a completely secular, even bohemian, Israeli enclave, and converted it into a yeshivah. Such moves, Israel Kimchi, Kollek's longtime chief planner, told us, would never have been permitted under previous administrations, even if everything were legal. It was expected that although existing establishments would be allowed to remain in operation, the *haredim* would not allow permits for new establishments intending to remain open on Shabbat.[30] Slowly, but surely, many secular residents say, the city will close down.

After Kollek's defeat, Benvenisti was blamed by both sides. Benvenisti, who reviews restaurants for the local paper, had been asked by Kollek not to write articles reviewing nonkosher establishments during the campaign. Meir Porush wrote a public apology to Kollek, claiming Benvenisti's presence on the list had forced his hand. And Labour, in its turn, grumbled that the presence of Benvenisti, who has supported Palestinian national rights in Jerusalem, had alienated the centrist voters of the city, who found any hint of Palestinian sovereignty unthinkable. Shortly after his election to the city council, Benvenisti told us he intended to step down. Why should I sit with thirty morons? he groused. He was even playing with the idea of leaving Jerusalem for the Galilee, working at a kibbutz, teaching the Crusades and Palestinian geography. Benevenisti quit the council in 1994.

Kollek's quarter-century reign was over. It was questionable whether One Jerusalem would outlive the man who had founded it. Within weeks, Labour activists were maneuvering to fold it back into their party. Kollek's rule had been aberrant, his charisma conquering the political proclivities of his constituents. Despite the high culture, the orchestrated pilgrimage of the avant garde to the walls and stages of the city, Jerusalem had never ceased to be a bastion of the old *yishuv,* its streets increasingly dominated by black hats and skullcaps covering the heads of the sons of the *haredim* unable to keep up with the growing affluence of the rest of Israeli society, and the exuberant and now increasingly angry children of the religious Zionist *yeshivot* who watched in horror as their government edged toward a traitorous dispossession of their divine birthright. Under unquestioned Israeli sovereignty, Kollek's pluralism had been a viable project. But with sovereignty now at stake and Jerusalem in play, a huge portion of the electorate voted for a man who made it clear that Jerusalem was home to only one nation.

Right after his election, Olmert showed just how averse he was even to contact with Palestinian nationalists. Invited by an Israeli Arab television program to discuss the future of Jerusalem, Olmert walked out of the studio when he discovered Faisal Husayni was going share the stage. The new mayor later demanded Husayni's Orient House pay $300,000 in municipal taxes, levies from which Husayni claims the building, as a diplomatic institution, is exempt.[31] Mayor Olmert not only led massive demonstrations against the way in which Orient House was functioning, de facto, as a Palestinian government, but threw his institutional weight behind the right's efforts to mass Jews, a half million they hoped, who would seek to block Arafat from praying at al-Aqsa mosque.[32]

An Unsettling Agreement

If the peace settlement made the Jews of Jerusalem uneasy, it terrified the Jewish suburbs. When Rabin's hand reluctantly reached out to Arafat's on the White House lawn, it sent a shock wave through the settlement movement. Thundered Yitzhak Shamir, former Likud prime minister,

> After six wars and a permanent struggle against the Arab terror-
> ist organizations whose objective was and remains to this day the
> elimination of what they call "the Zionist entity," today, elements
> are in control who are celebrating what they call the end of the
> occupation. This word means that our presence in Judea, Samaria,
> Gaza . . . and Yerusahalayim for twenty-six years was illegal and
> unjust. Mr. Chairman, Ladies and Gentlemen, I have to reject this
> concept with all my heart and strength. In 1967 we liberated . . .
> those areas, . . . never to be separated from them again. Yeru-
> shalayim was united never to be divided again, to be the capital of
> Israel forever and ever.[33]

Shamir, his hair pearl white, was exhorting American Jews to give money to keep the settlements going as the government shut down its support. Private American Jewish donations would be critical to keep the settlement movement alive, and Likud politicians were fund-raising across the United States on their behalf. (The Rabin government had not banned private funding of settlement, which, in fact, continued in all settlements, allowing the Jewish population to continue growing.) The settlement movement was also looking to the former Soviet Union, Bangladesh, India, even Burma, for Jews who might join them if the conditions were right.[34]

Speaking to a Conservative synagogue full of Los Angeles Jews shortly after the agreement was signed, Shamir explained to his audience,

> It is clear that in terms of the Rabin policies, these settle-
> ments . . . will not be able to exist for any length of time, mainly
> because of the lack of any possibility to expand and develop, with-
> out any reserve of land and water, . . . in a territory that will be
> handed over to strangers who will pursue the permanent growth of
> Arab terror in order to get rid of them.

The government, he said, would wait for the settlers to tire; it would gradually convince "the nation that there is no sense in endangering our soldiers because of some messianic idea of fanatics."

Back in Israel, when the parties of the right failed to bring large numbers of people into the streets against the Oslo deal, there was a sense of profound disappointment among the religious Zionist settlers. Even though Syria had yet to be very forthcoming, the grafitti and protest signage in every other window indicated widespread opposition to withdrawal from the Golan Heights, where so many Israelis had died in previous wars. But there were few signs and little talk on the street about Judea and Samaria, let alone Gaza, a squalid headache where so many Israelis felt they had wasted months of their lives doing guard duty. Clearly, the settlers had failed to educate the Israeli people about the essential import of the land. In building the land, many settlers now said, they had lost touch with the people. The Jews of Judea and Samaria had their world turned upside down. Men and women who had understood themselves as heroes were now being denigrated as obstacles to peace, vigilantes, and "cry babies" in Rabin's felicitous phrasing. Speaking to the settlers, we found a strong sense of depression, abandonment, and rage.

The settlers were unprepared to move back into the posture of an extraparliamentary movement. Initially, settlement leaders were unable even to mobilize their residents; they had ceased to be a social movement, their pioneering elan institutionalized into bureaucratic directives, incentives, and a network of municipalities and housing agencies. Efforts to revive Gush Emunim failed. With Likud immobilized and bickering, unable to posit an alternative vision for the new circumstances, with Israelis seeking separation from the Palestinians, not reconciliation, the settlement movement leaders understood they would have to premise their political strategy, just as the Palestinian rejectionists had, on what they believed was the high probability of failure. Failure meant peace would not produce security, that Jews would continue to die – maybe even more Jews. The prospect of losing patrimony did not provoke a revulsive outpouring of Israelis into the streets. Dead and maimed Jews, politically gratuitous deaths, would, however, galvanize the Israelis.

As the rock throwing continued, as Jewish settlers were targeted for murder by Palestinian opponents to the accord, soldiers serving in the territories were increasingly vilified and Israelis began to move into the streets. In December 1993, as the Rabin government negotiated the implementation of the Oslo principles, there were demonstrations almost every night, drawing thousands into the main intersections. Bonfires flared into the Jerusalem night near the monumental stolidity of the

Great Synagogue, the seat of the Chief Rabbinate, where the fusion of Judaism and Zionism takes concrete form. Masses of religious nationalists, dominated by young yeshivah students and families, young children in tow, heard speaker after speaker denounce the prime minister as a traitor, backed by a huge portrait of Rabin, swathed in a red-checked *kaffiyah*. "Rabin + Arafat = Murderers," read one placard. "Don't let the murderers multiply," read another poster, this one with Rabin handing Arafat a gun. "Today, it is Jericho and Gaza," roared Hanan Porat, a founder of Gush Emunim and member of Knesset. "Tomorrow it will be Gush Etzion, Elon Moreh, Tel Aviv and finally Jerusalem. Then there will be no Jews in the land of Israel." "The government will be brought down," he shouted. Yeshivah students danced around bonfires, burning Palestinian flags, as well as images of Rabin, Arafat, and even Kollek.

After a few moments of silence, the crowd in Jerusalem recited the psalm for the soul of the dead. Just a few days before this demonstration, a Russian refusenik and kindergarten teacher, Mordechai Lapid, as well as his nineteen-year-old son, Shalom, had been murdered near Kiryat Arba by HAMAS guerrillas as the Lapids waited for a bus into Jerusalem. The Lapids' funeral procession had been stoned with rocks and cinder blocks thrown from Palestinian rooftops as it passed through Hebron. That the government had sent no official representative to the funeral was not just shocking to the settlers: it was obscene.

The lesson the settlers had drawn from Yamit, where the Jewish settlers forcibly opposed Israeli withdrawal from the Sinai, was the importance of being with the Israeli people and of not waiting until the moment of evacuation. Through civil disobedience and massive protest years before any Jews might be moved from their homes in the land, they hoped to shift government policy as protesters against the war in Lebanon had. Where the people had once made it impossible for the government to remain in Lebanon, they hoped they could make it politically impossible not to remain in Judea and Samaria. "The house is burning," said Ehud Sprinzak, Israel's best analyst of the settlement movement. "It is no longer theoretical issues. Legal civil disobedience is something that all of them are talking about. They've got to show *mesirut ha-nefesh* [extreme devotion] for *eretz-yisrael*."

Yisrael Harel, longtime editor of *Nekudah*, the settlers' political organ, had no faith Rabin would protect the Jews living in the territories. Why should he? When Rabin had been defense minister, Harel spoke with him regularly. "He practically failed to shut down the *intifada*," Harel pointedly replied, "which is what brought all this. I don't expect him to act differently, more decisively, then he did a few years ago." When we met a few months after the agreement was signed, Palestinians had stoned Harel's car for three days from exactly the same position. He had called the military and identified the spot, but no soldiers had been deployed there. He claimed HAMAS, PFLP, even renegade militants from Fatah were shooting and stabbing Jews in the territories. It was, he said, absurd how the Israeli government was vilifying Jews trying to protect themselves and simultaneously releasing Palestinians charged with attacking Jews for the new Palestinian police force, whereupon they posed, armed, for the world's press. The Labour government was seeking to annul the political laws of gravity by declaration. The insanity would not continue for long, particularly as the Jewish body count mounted. The government would fall, he was sure.

Although Rabin repeatedly swore no settlement would be uprooted during the five-year transition period, he said nothing about what would happen at the end. And even in the interim his aides indicated that evacuation of isolated settlements was being considered.[35] Anxiety mounted that Rabin was using the settlements as a bargaining chip and whole communities would eventually be evacuated or left to their own devices under Palestinian sovereignty. Israeli supporters of partition worried that unless the government soon laid out a viable future for the Jews living in Judea and Samaria the situation would push people, fearful of losing a whole way of life without any sense of the alternatives, into massive civil disobedience, even create the conditions for irridentists to resist evacuation and extension of Palestinian authority violently.

The Rabin–Arafat pact was also a profound theological blow to the religious nationalists who believe the settlement of the land is a divinely sanctioned pathway to redemption. If, God forbid, Jews should be evacuated with the consent of the Israeli public, it could only mean that the people were not ready for redemption. Now voices were heard that perhaps redemption would not come in their days, that perhaps the secular Labour elites were creating a Palestinian state that would become a hostile beachhead in the next war, a war that would enable Israel finally to clear the land of its Arab inhabitants. Only then would Israel understand it must embrace the lands, free from Arabs. Only then would Israel be on the road.

Jerusalem was now at risk. Yisrael Harel, one of settlers' key strategists, had no doubt. "If the agreement works in Judea, Samaria and Gaza, Jerusalem will follow," he said. "At the end, if this agreement will be implemented successfully in the territories, Jerusalem will not stop it. If the Arabs will be clever, they will get Jerusalem, too."

It had been precisely this fear that prompted Aharon Horowitz to move into the City of David in 1992. A student of Rabbi Zvi Yehuda Kook, Horowitz believes that Israel, and hence the world, is on the verge of redemption. How would he react, we asked, if Palestinians were given sovereignty in *eretz-yisrael,* in any part of Jerusalem, particularly over the *haram al-sharif?* He replied that a government that could give away land, or "national treasures" as he called it, was steeped in secular democracy, where the aggregation of individual people's pleasures was more important than collective identity, than the sacred purpose of a people.

When Horowitz, an Israeli tour guide, spoke of Jerusalem, his change in tone marked the danger. "It would," he said, "probably throw us into an abyss of lack of identity because you see Jerusalem is at the very core of Jewish identity. It always has been. And now that you have it in your hands and you're letting it go it means you are making yourself out to be somebody else. [It] would be a . . . regression into oblivion for the Jewish people." It would begin, he said,

> a dismal spell of emptiness. Emptiness is really what there would be left for a people who really has no business here. We're mostly Europeans, the Ashkenazic Jews, who have occupied a land which is really very Oriental, very Middle Eastern. . . . If we're not a continuation of Abraham, Isaac and Jacob and the tribes, then we don't belong here. We lose our reason for existence. We lose our reason to defend ourselves . . . if we let go of Jerusalem.

What would he do in such an eventuality?

> In my mind, the value of the land of Israel is very great . . . but there's one value that is considered more vital and that's the unity of the people. And should it come to a situation, which I think would be tragic and I think it would be spiritual suicide, maybe not only spiritual, but definitely the identity of the state would be in peril, but I could never lift a gun against another soldier, against an action that was taken by the wish of the people.

"Peace till the last Jew," Israel Medad called the peace accord. To Medad, a wiry, politically seasoned settlement leader who has participated in the parliamentary struggle to extend Jewish ritual rights on the Temple Mount, it appeared that while Jews in the settlements were being wounded and dying daily, the government was doing nothing. Government ministers weren't even going to funerals, he said bitterly. "They don't give a damn for us anymore."

Medad knew the time for the big battle over the land had finally arrived. "Finally there is history meeting history. Does the Arab win or the Jew win? People just don't get excited about water," he told us. Arafat announced one of his first acts on arriving in Palestine would be to walk up from Jericho, with maybe as many as a quarter million other Palestinians, to pray at al-Aqsa mosque. Medad was already preparing to mass as many Jews as possible to stop him. He was organizing parlor meetings throughout the outer suburbs of Jerusalem. The Jewish settlement movement is the front line, he told them. "Hey, guys," he says, pointing out their living room windows, "autonomy is right over there. "If we fail you are going to find yourself in a very difficult situation."

A remarkable shift in political culture has been taking place as a result of the accord, a reaching out between the *haredim* and the religious Zionist settlement movement, once wary enemies mutually contemptuous of each other's understandings of the national significance of Judaism. Though they do not agree on the redemptive significance of Jewish settlement, many in both non-Zionist and Zionist Torah-observant communities instinctively feel threatened by the peace accord with the Palestinians.

It was striking that the very first protests against the accords were led neither by Likud, torn by internal factional bickering, nor by the Jewish settlers, who had become a comfortable community of suburbanites. Rather they were led by activists from Chabad, a Hasidic constituent of Agudat Yisrael. With their Brooklyn-bound *rebbe* partially paralyzed and dying, Israel's Chabad *hasidim* appeared to transfer their ardor from the dying person of Menachem Mendel Schneersohn to the land of Israel, from a threatened messiah to an endangered land.

A red-haired Chabad woman, carrying a picture of the *rebbe,* was standing outside the American consulate to protest the accords. She had just returned from Brooklyn, where she had gone to pray and to see the *rebbe.* She had gone there, she told us in a heavy French accent, to see whether Schneersohn might indeed be the messiah. When she first saw him, he looked like an ordinary old man who might be dying. But Friday, during *minhah* afternoon prayers, the light shone on the rebbe's face in such a way that he appeared to her as a forty-year-old man. She realized, she said, that all his wisdom was contained in his bushy, white luminous beard. Scheersohn was the king messiah, the Davidic redeemer.

Why, we asked, had Chabad not been involved in Israeli politics until recently? The messiah, she replied, could only come to Israel when the people of Israel were ready. God created everything. The land of Israel had been created expressly for the Jews. It could not be given up by anybody, even if he were the prime minister of Israel. The conflict over the accords, she told us as though it were a confession, was part of a grand plan for Israel to do repentance, because it would lead the people to turn to God in refuge from the strife. Arafat knows, she insisted, that the messiah is coming and is trying to prevent it. That is why, she said, he was willing to make peace.

But it was not just the Chabad *hasidim* who were galvanized against the accord. "The leftists in the government have proven that they are not Zionists at all, but Canaanites," charged Agudat Yisrael Knesset member Menachem Porush at Agudat Yisrael's party convention in January 1994. Large numbers of *haredim* from many different communities were coming out to demonstrate against the agreement; thousands attended a massive protest at the Western Wall in early 1994, the largest of its kind.

That Agudat Yisrael, the non-Zionist party representing the descendants of the old *yishuv,* would criticize the government for being insufficiently Zionist was astounding. The *haredi* impulse against the accord derived from an urge not to hold on to Jewish land, but to protect Jewish life. For the same reason many would never even go to the territories during the *intifada,* even to their relatives' gravesites on Mt. Zion, because that would put Jewish life in danger, many have been profoundly troubled by the agreement with Arafat. *Pikkuach nefesh,* the precedence of saving of Jewish life over even adherence to critical commandments such as Shabbat observance, is a central *haredi* value enshrined in the Talmud. Thus a Gerer *haredi* yeshivah in the West Bank town of Immanuel was the first institution to relocate back inside Israel voluntarily in 1994 because of security concerns in the wake of the agreement.[36] Just as the Jewish settlement movement has been unable to get the *haredim* even to consider living in areas that might be dangerous, the failure of the accord to stop Palestinian attacks on Jews and the fear that pullbacks of Israeli troops will endanger even more Jewish lives have mobilized thousands of *haredim* against the agreement. Just as the *intifada* and the prospect of partition it engendered pushed the Muslim Brotherhood to recognize the Islamic legitimacy of Palestinian nationalism, so the same forces seem to be pushing significant segments of the *haredi* community to rethink the religious significance of the Zionist state.

From the other side, there has been a renewed appreciation by the Jewish settlement movement of the antistatist orientation of the *haredim.* The religious Jews of the settlement movement now understood the *haredi* sense of themselves as a denigrated observant community at odds with a Jewish state that appears to have forgotten what it is that makes it Jewish in the first place. Jewish settlers complained to us that Israeli police were instructed to take off their badges, each imprinted with an identification number, before confronting the settlers. This, the settlers charged, enabled the police to take hefty whacks without fear of being charged. A number of settlers pointed out that Yitzhak Rabin himself had shot the "sacred cannon," executing Ben-Gurion's order in 1948 to sink the *Altalena,* bearing arms for the Revisionist armies of the Irgun. Would he hesitate this time, they wondered, before using violence against Jews who opposed his perfidious partition? History seemed to be repeating itself.

Danny Felsenstein, when he was younger, had jumped onto a London stage to disrupt the Bolshoi Ballet to protest repression of Soviet Jewry.

He has the lean body of a long-distance runner. Felsenstein, an expert on high-technology development, makes the long commute from his home in Karnei Shomron up to Jerusalem to teach geography at the Hebrew University. Calling the Declaration of Principles "a bag of rats," he is proud his was the first settlement to fire the Arabs who cleaned the streets in the wake of the *intifada,* replacing them with Russians.

The peace accord is one of the most painful experiences Felsenstein has had since migrating here. "I write this to you in a month in which we have been blessed with guesting Madonna, Michael Jackson and the U.S. professional wrestling troupe," he wrote to us right after the agreement was signed.

> The willingness to give up land, the callousness and cynicism against those who love the land and the brutality being waged against those opposing the government is simply a reflection of a wider "Madonna culture." Those viewed as interfering with this process have to be delegitimized (cry babies, not real Israelis, "wasn't worth wasting a Scud on them" and other Rabin gems over the last few weeks) . . . Thus genuine love of *eretz-yisrael,* its scenery, historical memories . . . is interpreted as "political" by those who have lost that feeling . . . Whoever is therefore perceived as spoiling the Israeli dream of tickets to Madonna, holidays in Turkey and general cheap materialism is a threat. Settlers have now joined that category, previously reserved only for *haredim.* The government media orchestrated euphoria over the peace package is sold on the basis of hyped-up predictions of further material well-being, less *miluim* [reserve army duty], more Madonna . . . People like myself are being faced with a choice that we don't want to make: *eretz yisrael* versus *medinat yisrael* [land of Israel versus state of Israel].

As the moment of implementation of the accords approached, some ten thousand Palestinian police drawn primarily from the Palestine Liberation Army were due to enter Jericho and Gaza as Israeli troops withdrew. The prospect horrified many Israelis. The settlers vowed not to obey them. The idea of issuing Khalishnikov rifles, captured from the PLO during the Lebanon war, to thousands of former terrorists boggled many Israelis' minds. As Palestinian guerrillas, both self-appointed and operating under instruction from a variety of rejectionist groups, attacked Jews in the territories with automatic rifles, axes, and knives, settlers blocked the road into Jerusalem and stoned Palestinian cars. The settlers formed a new internal volunteer militia, called Hashomer, named after the very first pre-state units of self-defense, which eventually evolved into the Haganah, the core of the new state's army. The attorney general's office was so frightened it immediately denounced Yesha, the organization representing all Jewish settlements in the occupied territories, as a "subversive organization," backing off when it realized that there was nothing illegal about the militia, under the command of high-level reserve army officers directing Jewish settlers concerned to protect themselves against a highly visible increase in Palestinian terrorism.

Although the overwhelming majority of Jewish settlers were law-abiding citizens who expected the continuation of Palestinian violence toward Jews to undermine Israeli support for the agreement, a small number of Jewish settlers did not intend to allow the political process to evolve to its natural conclusion. Given Arafat's inability to control the Palestinian violent rejection, there was ample occasion for revenge, for bloodletting that could escalate into intercommunal war. And though Gush Emunim may have been transformed into a religious settler bourgeoisie, there were still small but dedicated and well-organized groups able and willing to set the bloody concatenation in motion.

There was also some theological support for Jewish violence against Palestinians. In 1991, the rabbis in the Jewish settlement organized themselves into the Council of Yesha Rabbis in order to provide religious leadership to the settlers who felt besieged by the burgeoning peace process and the territorial partition it implied. It was this group, not the lay leadership, that brought the settlers into the streets after each Palestinian terrorist attack. This rabbinical council has taken upon itself to set the halakhic boundaries for the religious settlers. Opposed to the death of innocent Arabs, it nevertheless made judgments that legitimized violent Jewish retaliation. Such explosions cannot be condoned in advance, they argued, but if an individual, acting in the name of God, in a divinely inspired way, opens fire on a car full of Palestinians after an attack, the rabbis have been willing to give him retroactive legitimacy.

A number of Jews have already engaged in provocative and retaliatory violence. According to Ehud Sprinzak, the Committee for Safety on the Roads, originally formed in 1985 by Rabbi Meir Kahane's Kach Party to protect Jewish transport when the Israeli army was not present, has been an important vehicle for this kind of activity. During the *intifada,* the committee expanded to include over one thousand registered volunteers drawn from throughout the settlement movement. Now, using scanners to identify army positions, small groups of eight or twelve men were moving into Palestinian neighborhoods, smashing windows, torching cars and storefronts, bludgeoning those who resisted with their rifle butts. (They avoid live fire to prevent later ballistic identification.) In ten minutes, they cut a wide swath of destruction. According to Sprinzak, everybody knows who is involved, but there is never any proof.

Yisrael Harel, a Yesha leader, sees groups such as these as greater political threats to the Jews' ability to hold on to the land of Israel than murderers from HAMAS. "In order to survive and continue our vision, we need the support of the majority," he explained.

> They are practical people. But most of them have a natural feeling. They are Jewish. They want the safety of the country . . . They feel very much troubled when a Jew is killed. If we convince them that though members of our community are killed here and there, there is a hope for better days, then they will continue to support us. But once Arabs will kill Jews, Jews will retaliate and kill Arabs and there's going to be Lebanon, they will say: "This is our limit. If so, if you cannot be safe, if you have to go out on a small war, then we don't support you anymore." Some will say: "It is not that we don't support you. We are very troubled and worried about you. There is no use for your struggle. Come back."

The Israeli military, which had for so long given carte blanche for settler self-defense, confessed they were unable to control settler violence. (In the sixteen months after the accord was signed in September 1993 in Washington, D.C., Palestinians killed 101 Israelis, while Israeli civilians killed 48 Palestinians. Israeli troops killed 116 Palestinians.)[37] Both the police and the Shin Bet, Israel's intelligence apparatus, for the first time began to concentrate some analytic ability on the settlers. Settlers angrily reported being approached as informants, their homes and offices being bugged. Rabin, for his part, deployed large numbers of Israeli troops in the territories to be ready for violent confrontations of Jewish settlers, Palestinian radicals, and probably the Palestinian police force as well. Israel's chief of police, Rafi Peled, remarked in late January 1994 that if Jewish settlers continued to engage in civil disobedience, Israel should consider the construction of temporary detention centers. "While the government is releasing Arab terrorists," the Yesha council replied, "It is arresting good Jews who do not endanger the public."[38]

In January 1994 former chief rabbi Shlomo Goren issued a halakhic ruling that soldiers should refuse to obey government orders to dismantle Jewish settlements, prompting Israel's attorney general to see whether this constituted seditious behavior. By that spring, more rabbis, including another former chief rabbi, Avraham Shapira, the head of Mercaz ha-Rav, the yeshivah established by Rav Kook, had issued a similar judgment. "You must refuse it as you would refuse an order to eat pork," the rabbi declared.[39] A rabbi in Ma'aleh Adumim went so far as to compare his government to that of the Nazis.[40] Even former prime minister Shamir said that removing Jews from "the homeland" would be equivalent to killing one's parents.[41]

In the settlers' eyes the Israeli state was being stripped of its sacred purpose. Many would no longer give it their blessing. In 1993, for the first time since 1948, they stopped saying the traditional Israeli Sabbath blessing – "O God, radiate Your light and truth upon Israel's leaders, ministers and advisers." Many Israelis now believed peace would entail civil war.[42] If keeping all the lands, with their enormous Palestinian population, might undercut democracy, it began to appear that giving them back might lead to the same result.

On Friday, February 25, 1994, a Jewish doctor offered a blood sacrifice at the feet of his first ancestor's grave, the tomb of Abraham in Hebron.[43] Dr. Baruch Goldstein, Kiryat Arba's chief physician, clothed in his army reserve uniform, walked into the Muslim prayer area of the al-Ibrahimi mosque, the room containing the tombs of Isaac and Rebecca; shoved clip after clip into his Galil assault rifle; and mowed down the tightly packed Muslims prostrate on the carpeted stone floor. Goldstein, a follower of Rabbi Meir Kahane, who had been murdered in 1990, was able to get off over a hundred rounds, killing dozens of Palestinians, before his gun jammed and he was overpowered, knocked unconscious with a fire extinguisher, and beaten to death by the crowd.

Goldstein's killing of Muslims while they prayed in Ibrahim's mosque, cutting them down during Ramadan the month-long fasting period comparable to the Jews' Yom Kippur, could not have been better calculated to trigger calls for jihad, to push the Islamic militants into furious violence, to conjure and strengthen the enemy with whom Israel could not make peace. Ever since the horrible handshake at the Rose Garden, it was clear to all the settlers that catastrophe was closing in. Goldstein's outrageous cruelty was calculated to continue the conflict, to prevent partition, to foment a situation in which Israelis would be compelled to use their powers to subdue and even expel the Palestinians. It was, Goldstein surely believed, a kindness.

The attack immediately reverberated in Jerusalem, where 100,000 Muslims were attending Friday Ramadan services at al-Aqsa mosque. During Ramadan, East Jerusalem's streets are awash with people going to pray and visit their friends and family. There are mounds of date and nut pastries, stacks of *kenaffih,* vendors' stacks of licorice-root drink, delicacies to break the daily fast. Friday prayers ended this time with violent attacks on the Israeli police post on the *haram* as well as showers of stones thrown at Jews worshiping below at the Western Wall. For hours, young men, some carrying the green flag of HAMAS, fought pitched battles with the Israeli riot police on the *haram.* The Israelis refrained from using live fire, fearing a repeat of the bloodshed. For most of the day, East Jerusalem was controlled by bands of young Palestinian men who directed cars and ambulances ferrying the wounded to Makassed Hospital. Jerusalem was shut entirely to Palestinians from the West Bank.

The Palestinians suspended the negotiations, demanding protection from the Jewish settlers and an international armed presence in the territories, insisting that the status of the Jewish settlements be discussed immediately, not at the end of the transitional period. The United States publicly urged Israel to consider steps – including the PLO proposal to allow United Nations observers or even PLO police to be deployed in Hebron – to assure Palestinians' security.[44]

Many Palestinians around the world pointed to Goldstein as representing Zionism's true face. But the Palestinians, too, had created the conditions under which such acts became thinkable, for a large percentage of Israeli Jews to believe that as long as they stood anywhere in the land they would continue to die at Palestinian hands simply because they were here. It was not just HAMAS and PFLP members who were still trying to kill Jews. Fatah members themselves had been involved in twenty-one attempted murders of Israelis since the signing of the accords.[45] Thirty Israelis had been murdered by Palestinians since the Oslo accords were signed, yet the PLO had refused to condemn the the murders, had offered no visible expressions of remorse, had given no indication that those who perpetrated such deeds would be accountable to Palestinian justice, no suggestion that it would use its considerable force to crush those who executed such barbarity.

Goldstein's actions eroded support for Arafat and his peace accord. Once again the West Bank Palestinians reasserted their moral claim to dictate the terms of negotiation with Israel. Indeed there were even reports the United National Leadership of the Intifada, the secret body that once directed the *intifada,* had reconstituted itself.[46] The Palestinians understood the massacre as horrible proof that they could not co-exist with the Jewish settlements, that the Israeli army was incapable of protecting them, and that full withdrawal and sovereignty were essential preconditions of peace. In sum, many understood Arafat's agreement in Oslo as a terrible capitulation.

Indeed, in the massacre's aftermath, the Israeli army put the Palestinian residents of Hebron under a blanket curfew for weeks, while Israeli settlers were allowed to move about freely. A million Palestinians were under various forms of curfews and confined to the West Bank and Gaza. Israeli soldiers killed dozens of Palestinians in subsequent clashes. Everywhere in the territories, Arafat was being denounced as a traitor. The Palestinian flag, associated with the PLO, became almost unpresentable in certain areas. Fatah Hawks, the irregular militia once aligned with Arafat, marched together with HAMAS activists in towns across the West Bank and Gaza. Fatah leaders inside the occupied territories were realigning with HAMAS against Arafat's tutelage outside.[47]

Arafat was so weak, when HAMAS subsequently orchestrated a campaign of terror, using explosives, sometimes carried by suicide bombers, inside Israel itself, that all he could manage to say, even after Rabin's public display of contrition, was, "These actions are unfortunately directed only against innocent people." Faisal Husayni went no further. When asked by an Israeli television reporter whether he condemned a bomb blast in the Hadera bus station that killed five Israelis and injured thirty-one, his reply was: "Why should I? Did you come to ask me how I felt about Fatma Ralida?" (Ralida, a pregnant nineteen-year-old, was killed while cleaning her carpet by a stray bullet fired by a Jewish settler who had opened fire on Palestinians stoning his car.)[48] That one was done by an individual under attack and the other by a Palestinian political party did not register. Dr. Goldstein's profanation had pushed the discourse of carnage to a higher level; the PLO's moral incapacities threatened to send it further.

On the Israeli side, Goldstein's actions dealt a serious blow to the nobility of the settlement movement. Yisrael Harel's nightmare had come true sooner than he had imagined. "Of the 111 bullets that Dr. Goldstein shot into the Arabs, some of them exited them and came back to hit us. That's what this madman did," Harel said.[49] The government moved to disarm and administratively detain the most militant Jewish settlers associated with Kach. Kach and its offshoots were declared illegal "terrorist" organizations.[50] The greatest change, however, was that a majority of the government's ministers openly supported the removal of Jewish settlements in the midst of Arab population centers like Hebron. Against the backdrop of Goldstein's barbarity, the military vulnerability of the few hundred Jews living there, their capacity for provocation, had finally left them open to public attack. The Israeli government, by the first such discussion of evacuation of Jews, had crossed a political "red line."[51] Almost half of the Israeli public supported the removal of Jews from inside Palestinian Hebron.[52] And so in April 1994, the Israeli government had almost decided forcibly to evacuate a few isolated Jewish residences in the midst of the Arab city. The Jewish settlement council was aghast:

> It is inconceivable that a Jewish government could make Hebron *"Judenrein."* Hebron is the birthplace of Judaism and the Jewish People, with an unbroken chain of Jewish life until the Arab massacre of 1929. The Rabin government has no mandate for an "ethnic cleansing" of Hebron, or to carry out its policies of capitulation.[53]

Only the settlement movement's announcement that it would bring ordinary life in Israel to a halt, block the roads with its supporters' bodies, shut down the prisons, encircle the Knesset, averted it. A Jewish physician had put the territorial limits of Israel's body politic on the public agenda.

18

Heart of Stone

It began with knives and a swelling pool of blood. On the verge of an apparent peace Israelis were being stabbed to death by Palestinians who enfold seedlings in the earth of Israel, scrub pots in its kitchens, and spread mortar in its new suburbs. On March 31, 1993, Israel closed the arteries linking Palestinians of the West Bank and Gaza to its sovereign body – a closing out, not in.[1] The closure of Israel to almost all Palestinians from outside became a permanent feature of the landscape. Hundreds of thousands of Palestinians who used to work or shop in Jerusalem were forbidden to cross into Zion from the West Bank.[2] Although a few thousand had their jobs taken by new Russian immigrants desperate for employment, about fifty thousand Arabs – mostly construction and agricultural workers – were eventually given permission to go in and out of Israel each day, a fragile privilege that could be revoked at any moment.[3]

It is December 1993 and the hopoe birds, feathered in funereal shades, scavenge in twos and threes in the Jerusalem hills. Rabin and Arafat are bickering over the implementation of the Declaration of Principles, and still Jerusalem is forbidden to most Palestinians, closed to all but the very old and the very young. A couple of Palestinian flags hang limply over the major hotels in the Arab downtown. A furniture store sells a big office chair, its leather carefully ruled into red, green, black, and white. The boisterous waving, the explosive display, of long-forbidden Palestinian colors is over.

At blockades on all West Bank roads entering the city, Israeli soldiers slowly inspect and question each Palestinian car seeking al-Quds. Palestinians with blue license plates indicating residence on the West Bank must stop for questioning, show their orange computerized identity cards, open their trunks, and allow the soldiers to reach under the seats. Men from the West Bank who have waited for two or three days to get permission to enter Israel from military offices show their papers. Even the yellow Israeli-plated cars driven by Arab Jerusalemites may be stopped. At each crossing of the line, even Jerusalemites debate how much to slow, whether to presume free passage. Nothing is certain. The city's Israeli residents have been visibly relieved since Jerusalem has been sealed. The impulse to look over one's shoulder, to watch each Arab on the street, has diminished.

In Arab Jerusalem, Palestinian women still descend from buses, balancing enormous burlap or plastic bags of produce atop their heads. They sit, big skirted, on the sidewalks and esplanade near the grey pastry walls of Damascus Gate, guarding small hillocks of *za'ata* and cilantro as trucks, one metal hand bolted to their grillwork to guard against evil, muscle down the street. There are huge stacks of *The Jerusalem Post,* now a mouthpiece for the Israeli right, at the newstand. The city's Palestinians read it in great numbers; they want to know what their enemies on the city's western side have in mind. They are sure it is the worst, the "Judaization of Jerusalem," they call it.

After the Oslo peace accords, after six years of uprising, the Palestinians are exhausted, resigned. They understand the agreement is a capitulation. Some seem relieved to have bent their necks to a singular American power. Their eagerness to reassert the daily round is everywhere apparent. The city's merchants were seriously hurt by the endless strikes, the boycotts, the closures. For the first time, there are wedding gowns, white and gossamer, in shop windows. Once-boycotted Israeli beer is for sale again in Palestinian restaurants. Children have returned to school, their collars and jumpers carefully pressed.

Those who come to Jerusalem to buy, to pray, and to ask permission for one thing or another produce an apparent bustle. They pick out the warmest *ka'ek,* round sesame breads, from corner vendors. They hand Jordanian currency to moneychangers standing on the sidewalks who shuck bills from enormous rolls of Israeli shekels back out to them. There are tourists again in the Arab hotels, Italian Catholics on pre-Christmas pilgrimage. But Arab Jerusalem is a shadow of its former self. Choked off from its clientele outside, made into an uncertain, potentially forbidden destination, an Arab island enclosed by Israeli settlement, the streets are sparsely populated. Soldiers rigorously check each vendor for permission to be there. On Fridays, women, their faces encased in white cloth like cookies wrapped in tissue, fill the sidewalks.

After six years of afternoon strikes, local Palestinians have gotten used to doing their business in the mornings. In the afternoons, the streets are ceded to stray cats, overdue bills, and gossip, as those commercial forces of which the city is capable have already spent themselves in the morning. On Salah al-Din Street, the Arab downtown, only two storefronts adorned with red Christmas decorations and plastic Santa Clauses remain open by late afternoon. Even the Old City's fabled alleyways, the caravansary, the cotton merchants' gallery, are shuttered and gloomy after midday. Men strain to steer carts, heavy with goods, to restock the stores for the morning. A few yeshivah students, rifles on their backs, walk defiantly through the stone maze, seen but unacknowledged by the Arabs whom they pass. By dinner's end, nothing moves in Arab Jerusalem, not even cars. The public space is voided, evacuated by force and the habits of resistance.

We are returning from Ramallah's jammed and viscous streets, its lots striated with garbage, buildings scrawled with factional graffiti, inching past a dusty yard swathed in grape and ruby carpets for sale, back on the long road to Jerusalem. Passengers in a long Mercedes, its body tightly partitioned into four rows for its Arab riders, we are descending the mountain spine to Jerusalem. The power poles festooned with Palestinian flags welcome the first political deportees the Israelis have allowed to return as part of their agreement with the PLO. We are in the taxi because it is unsafe to take an Israeli rental car into Palestinian areas. Even in Jerusalem. Palestinian children stone the cars, easily identifiable by license plates, by the rental company decals on the window. Just a few days before, we barely scrambled out of reach of a barrage of children's stones. The agencies hand out city maps with the car keys. All of East Jerusalem is marked "VULNERABLE AREA!"

Now, down the road in front of us is the Jerusalem roadblock. Israeli soldiers, their hands resting on semiautomatic muzzles, peer at each car, scrutinize the papers, run computer checks on the security record of each Palestinian without a Jerusalem identity card. The line is liable to lengthen at any moment. There are so many questions that can be asked, so many places to look. Israelis jump the slow queue, slipping by in a separate lane.

Unexpectedly, our car, packed with eight passengers – village women in embroidered dresses with bright dental work, a hairdresser, a travel agent who works part-time as a theater director – turns off the main road. Pavement becomes rutted dirt and then our laden vehicle is thundering along a muddy track, the cab bottom scraping the ground. Where are we headed? For an instant, we each imagine the driver knows they have two Jews in the car. We are passing through a small Bedouin encampment, goat skins and tin jerried into human habitation, children's faces caked with mud and dry mucus. They will leave us in a deserted spot. Just a few days ago, a Jew was stabbed to death while shopping for less expensive produce in Bethlehem. It is understood. Nobody will say anything.

But nobody in the cab has remarked upon our circuitous route. Conversations continue as though the detour is routine. None of the passengers points, questions the driver, looks around. And then, there, farther up the hill, we see yet another Arab taxi slithering through the mud.

This is a regular route! We pass the lapis blue dome of the new mosque under construction in Beit Hanina. We have regained the solidity of pavement, driving along a suburban Arab street in East Jerusalem.

The security blockade is neither. We knew Palestinians from outside Jerusalem, who, when closed out of Jerusalem, walked across goat tracks in the hills to get in, risking fines and imprisonment. The Jewish heart of Israel is not protected by borders, hermetic with guarded passages and earthworks. It is rather a walkable and, now we find, a drivable frontier.

Palestinians who intend to slash with a knife or plant explosives can easily enter the city. Indeed, they are already here. The leaders of HAMAS have declared that the time has come to kill the Jews, that one approaches God by bathing in their blood. HAMAS graffiti are daubed and spray-painted everywhere. Blood drips from scalloped blades, images painted on rough stucco and cement walls in the Arab suburbs, knives plunging deep into roughly painted maps of Israel. Palestinian youth burn Torah scrolls at the Mount of Olives cemetery. The knives live here.[4]

The blockades are real even though their security rationale is made up. Jerusalem has no cage that can keep it secure as Israel's united capital. Protected only by the horrible prospect of communal war, the city waits for more outrage and profanation. The blockade is Israel's statement that it is legitimate to cut off Arab Jerusalem from Palestine. Severing normal traffic between the Palestinian city and its hinterland under the guise of security, Israel appears to deny, perhaps even seeks to undo, the city's commercial centrality within an emergent Palestine. A Hebronite wanting to get to Ramallah cannot drive directly through Jerusalem, but must take the dangerous "Valley of Fire" road, constructed by the Jordanians in 1953, circumventing the city at the edge of steep dry ravines to the east, a tortuous 100- (as opposed to a straight 40-) kilometer trip.[5] The closure is a military marking of a boundary line, an armed statement of what will be inside Israel and what will be, in some still unstated way, outside. The blockade asserts, makes visible, a line for all the world to see. It is part of a geopolitical conversation.

Although it was countered by a congressional vote declaring that Jerusalem should remain the undivided capital of Israel, President Bush's post–cold war statement of March 3, 1990, "We do not believe there should be new settlements in the West Bank or in East Jerusalem," stunned the Jewish community. The president promptly "clarified" his stand in a private letter to Teddy Kollek in which he stated that Jerusalem should never again be divided.[6] Nonetheless the Americans made it clear Jerusalem was negotiable. This was reconfirmed after the October

Popular Front for the Liberation of Palestine graffito, Ras al-Amud, Jerusalem, 1993.

1990 clash on the *haram al-sharif* in which Israeli troops killed eighteen Palestinians. The United States supported a United Nations resolution referring to East Jerusalem as "occupied territory." In that same month, before the Gulf War began, Secretary of State Baker tied $400 million in American loan guarantees for Soviet immigrants to Israeli assurances that the new citizens would not be settled anywhere in occupied territories, including East Jerusalem. Even after the war, during which Israel absorbed Iraq's repeated missile attacks on its cities without responding, President Bush again faced down Congress and a mobilized Israeli lobby in order to make $10 billion in loan guarantees conditional on Israel's behavior in the peace process.

President Bush had not been beholden to a Jewish vote; President Clinton decidedly was. Nonetheless, a year after Clinton was elected, the American administration shocked the Israelis by tacking a token $6.5 million for Israeli construction in Jerusalem to the $437 million penalty from the annual loan guarantee deducted for settlement activities in occupied territories.[7] And then in March 1994, President Clinton instructed America's delegate to support a United Nations resolution condemning Dr. Baruch Goldstein's mass murder of Palestinians in Hebron that included language referring to Jerusalem as occupied territory, even though eight-two senators demanded he veto it.[8] The Americans were going to press. Peace would make Jerusalem into a battle royale.

The Invisible and the Indivisible

Two peoples demand one city be the capital of their independent states. The prospects for peace between Israelis and Palestinians will hinge on the way they manage their contradictory claims.[9] Though most Palestinians want to divide the city, Palestinian leaders have spoken out against redivision, promoting the idea that a physically united city can function as two nations' capitals.[10]

But for most Israelis, the very idea of Palestinian sovereignty in Jerusalem is outside the envelope of permissible thought. "Anyone who would give up sovereignty," Aharon Sarig, the former city manager, told us in 1989, "would be considered a collaborator. Jerusalem is a unified city under Israeli sovereignty and no one will dare to consider a different solution . . . We have no power to think even." His boss, Teddy Kollek, adamantly rejected the idea that Jerusalem might be the capital of two states. "I think," he said in his 1989 preelection news conference, "it is a concept that has no historical justification. Jerusalem was never a capital of an Arab state . . . In 1948, they could have made their capital in this part of Jerusalem, but they didn't . . . This is a holy city. They have not made Mecca a capital; it's in Riyyad. Why should it be made in Jerusalem?" Beside, two sovereignties in one city would mean two sets of laws, criminals escaping from one side to the other. If Israel were going to give the West Bank back to the Palestinians, the Palestinians could put their capital someplace else. Why not Ramallah, he queried? "This will remain one city," he concluded, "the capital of Israel."

Behind the public no, Kollek was involved with a private initiative to think out the varieties of yes. In March 1989, his Jerusalem Committee, composed of international experts, met; among the options formally considered was a plan to divide Jerusalem. The jurisdictional structure of the new Jerusalem would look something like the olives produced by the gnarled trees that dot the city's hills. The capital of Palestine would be composed of a crescent running from Ramallah in the north to Bethlehem in the south; that of Israel would be the contemporary Jewish Jerusalem. The Old City, the "pit" of the olive, would have a unique constitutional status allowing both sides some measure of sovereignty. Haim Cohen, former chief justice of the Israeli Supreme Court, had even drafted a constitution for the new structure. The proposal, however, remained an impotent abstraction.

Even after the Oslo peace accords between Israel and the PLO, nobody in the Israeli government was officially even planning for the negotiations mandated for Jerusalem. Nobody in the government had been officially charged with coordinating the Israeli position. "Everybody is basically afraid," said Yisrael Kimchi, head of Jerusalem planning at the Jerusalem Institute for Israel Studies, whose organization has been authorized and financed to explore alternative planning scenarios for the region. Kimchi himself would talk in only the vaguest generalities. Even though he had forty people working on Jerusalem, the politicians in the Israeli government seemed decidedly unwilling to engage the planners' ideas openly. Part of the problem, too, Kimchi told us, was that nobody on the Palestinian side had come forward with clear authority, professional expertise, and concrete proposals. The public posture on the Palestinian side was also evasive. "You cannot touch the question of Jerusalem at this stage," Manuel Hassassian, a Jerusalemite Palestinian close to the post-Oslo negotiations with the Israelis, told us.

But ever since Madrid, in a number of small gatherings and in secret committees, prominent Israelis and Palestinians have been exploring alternative visions for Jerusalem, making proposals, testing the waters. And beyond that there have been serious negotiations and discussions at high levels among Israelis, Palestinians, and several foreign bodies about a framework for the future status of the city. Despite repeated vociferous denials, Jerusalem was already being tackled. Through interviews with Israelis and Palestinians working on the Jerusalem question, we were able to determine the kinds of solutions under consideration by some of the most influential planners and negotiators who have the ear of their nation's elites.

Israel's approach is to disaggregate the problem of Jerusalem. At the most bread and butter level of social services, health, housing, and education, Israel believes it can cede authority to the Palestinians in Jerusalem, allowing them to govern themselves and to be subject to the same institutions as their brothers and sisters elsewhere in the West Bank and Gaza. After all, the Israelis have for the last quarter century allowed the Palestinians to follow the Jordanian curriculum in the schools and take the Jordanian baccalaureate. Similarly, the Palestinians' Housing Council is located in Jerusalem, as is the Council for Higher Education, which has authority over Palestinian housing and university education everywhere in the occupied territories.[11] Even Teddy Kollek is reportedly now willing to support a separate Palestinian municipality in the context of a peace agreement if Jerusalem remains under Israeli sovereignty.[12]

Moreover, the Jews and Arabs of Jerusalem are still, more or less, demographically segregated from each other. This is so, even though more Jews than Palestinians live in East Jerusalem. All efforts to create mixed areas or even to locate Israeli housing areas in the midst of Arab zones, as in Neve Yakov, have failed. Designing a patchwork of separate Israeli and Palestinian municipal or neighborhood units is thus still a possibility. There is also experience with neighborhood government in several Palestinian areas, sponsored by Kollek, which could function as the basis for local Palestinian delivery of services.

The second problem involves land-use planning, infrastructure, and the control of capital investment necessary for economic development. The natural way to deal with these issues is to look beyond the current boundaries. There can be no return either to the pre-1967 Jordanian city boundaries for Arab Jerusalem or to the new post-1967 boundaries of the Israeli city. One must handle these issues at a metropolitan level, precisely what both Israelis and Palestinians are thinking right now.

In 1991, the Likud Ministries of Housing, and Interior and the Kollek-dominated Municipality of Jerusalem put out a contract to plan the metropolitan area. The planners drew the boundaries of a new metropolitan unit that would include Arab Ramallah to the north and Bethlehem to the south. This made perfect sense from a technical point of view. After all, the metropole has become an integrated ecological and economic entity, and yet nobody was planning the development of the region, some of it inside Israel, most of it outside. But Palestinians were in no way the subject of the operation, only its objects. The exercise was driven by a desire to bolster the Jewish center, not to achieve balanced growth, equitable distribution, or shared sovereignty. Past expropriations were treated as topographical facts. It was an ethnic marking of the earth in which the Israelis were the only legitimate public. Although its Israeli planners claimed it was a technical exercise that left political options wide open, Meron Benvenisti dismissed it as "a battle plan disguised as a planning process."

Two years later, in 1993, top planners on both sides of the city were poring over the same metropolitan "Jerusalem" maps. From his small, poorly equipped office in East Jerusalem, Dr. Abdallah Abdallah, director of the Palestine Geographic Center, who is developing the geographic data system for the new state of Palestine, showed us a metropolitan map that looked strikingly like that we had seen two years before at the Jerusalem Institute for Israel Studies. It quickly became clear that metropolitan Jerusalem is not only a sociological fact and a planning reality: it has become the medium through which both sides hope to solve thorny political conflicts.

Jerusalem is, like any metropole, a physically integrated unit. The Israelis intend both to supply and to control the region's infrastructure. Just as the East Jerusalem Electric Company used to supply power to much of the population in its old service area, whether Arab or Jewish, now the Israeli Electric Authority in Tel Aviv provides power to pretty much the entire area, whether Arab or Jewish. It would be too costly to bring power all the way from Jordan, which doesn't have the capacity to deliver it anyway. Given the rudimentary nature of Palestinian resources, the Palestinians of the area will likely have no choice but to integrate into the Israeli system. Likewise Palestinian towns in the metropolitan area, like Bethlehem and Ramallah, are already making plans to link up to the Israeli sewage system.

The Israeli road network knits Arabs and Jews within the region as well. Under the autonomy arrangements, a critical issue is how Jericho is to be connected to Gaza, Hebron to Ramallah. The main lines of Palestinian communication will undoubtedly lay out future claims to sovereignty. It is thus notable that the Israelis have insisted the Jericho–Gaza road skirt far to the south of Jerusalem. With the road connecting the northern and southern portions of Palestine, there is less room to maneuver. The Israelis had begun building a road passing through the deep *wadis* between Ma'aleh Adumim, the Jewish suburban city a few miles to the east, and Jerusalem proper, as a conduit for Palestinians along the north–south axis. Because this road would lay out the eastern perimeter of Israeli sovereignty and reinforce Jerusalem's centrality in the eventual Palestinian entity, construction was stopped as some Israeli officials sought to reroute it on the far eastern slopes of the Judean mountains. "In our eyes, Ma'aleh Adumim is part of Jerusalem," said Mordechai Gur.[13] Israeli planners like Meron Benvenisti suggested to us it would be both topographically impossible and politically explosive to push the road eastward, given the amount of private Palestinian land that would have to be expropriated to find the right of way. Yet at the end of December 1993, Housing Minister Binyamin Ben-Eliezer had given the go-ahead to build the eastern loop right along the borders of the new autonomy area.

All this suggests the Israelis are unlikely to cede control over capital investment, whether public or private, to Palestinians within the metropolitan area. In that people follow jobs, which follow capital investment, the Israelis are likely to seek a monopoly on the flows of capital and granting of permissions to build Jerusalem. While arrangements were made for the Jordanians and the Egyptians to open new Arab banks in the West Bank and Gaza, no permissions were given for Jerusalem. In 1993, when the World Bank proposed a list of projects they were interested in funding, they intentionally avoided new investments in Jerusalem. However, included among the items was continued funding for al-Mukaddasi Hospital and Auguste Victoria Hospital – two Jerusalem institutions to which they have long contributed. Although it backed off, Israel initially objected vociferously even to their inclusion.

The Palestinians were pushing to develop Jerusalem economically. PECDAR, the Palestinian development council, began deliberations over the granting of funds to Palestinian investment projects in Jerusalem. PECDAR's emergency program included training, infrastructural development, and credits to develop Jerusalem as a center for Arab tourism, including the restoration of a variety of sacred sites. The Palestinians hoped to locate PECDAR's central offices in Jerusalem, but Israel forced them to locate them just outside the municipal boundaries, in Dahiyat al-Barid. And Arafat, to get around Israel's refusal to allow international funds slated for the Palestinian authority to be spent on Jerusalem projects, had to drop the development projects in East Jerusalem.[14]

The Palestinians are nonetheless jockeying for investment capital in East Jerusalem. Wealthy Palestinians have not been very willing to make investments in Jerusalem because they are wary of the economic uncertainty involved and because they are subject to the same taxes in Jerusalem as the Jews whereas Palestinian incomes are much lower than those of the Israelis. Palestinians who made their fortunes in the diaspora came to Jerusalem after the accords were signed to discuss investment possibilities. Israeli business concerns also started pairing up with Palestinian businesses for projects in the territories. No less a figure than Jaweed Al-Gussain, the PLO minister of finance, a very successful developer, reportedly joined with Koor Industries to finance a number of major projects.[15] The Palestinian businessmen, however, have reportedly been so daunted by the conditions Israel has imposed in Jerusalem that they have so far demurred.

The Palestinians have shown considerable interest in making Atarot Airport, within the northern panhandle of Jerusalem, once the Kalandia Jordanian airfield, into a Palestinian facility. Not only would air access to Jerusalem be vital to Palestinian plans for Arab tourism, they see it as the kind of penetration that would bolster later claims for sovereignty. At the minimum, they hope to secure Israel's agreement that Palestinians will be able to use it during the interim period. Muslims from around the world, Palestinian planners claimed to us, would stream into Jerusalem as pilgrims and tourists if they could go directly to Jerusalem and land on Palestinian rather than Israeli land. Maybe two to three million visitors more per year, said Dr. Abdallah Abdallah, head of the Palestine Geographic Center. Not so, said Yisrael Kimchi, top planner at the Jerusalem Institute of Israel Studies. "The Arabs are not tourists," Kimchi said. The contest over the site broke into public view in January 1994, when Aeroflot, Russia's airline, under pressure from the Arab League, suddenly suspended its newly inaugurated direct flights from Moscow to Jerusalem loaded with Russian Jews.[16]

The third part of the problem is control over non-Jewish sacred sites. The Israelis have been scrupulous about protecting the status quo in the holy places as they found it in 1967. It now appears the Israelis are considering ceding sovereignty over different religious sites to Muslims and Christians on a spot basis within the Old City. For the Palestinians, the *haram al-sharif*, the platform containing the Dome of the Rock and al-Aqsa mosque, has figured as a nationalist symbol and shrine ever since they first faced off against the Zionists early in this century. But the site is also religiously central to Muslims all over the world. No one holds it more dear than King Hussein and his Hashemite family, who once claimed the title of sharif, custodians of Medina and Mecca, until they were ousted by the ibn Sa'ud family in 1919.

Until the Israelis took it in 1967, the Hashemites had only one sacred spot left to administer, al-Quds. Right after the Six-Day War, Moshe Dayan proposed that Jordan be given extraterritorial control over the *haram*, connected to the West Bank by an underground tunnel.[17] It was striking that when King Hussein abdicated all claims to the West Bank in 1988 and summarily stopped paying Jordanian civil servant salaries there, he maintained the Jerusalem *waqf*, its network of mosques, and the *shari'a* courts. In 1990, before the Gulf War, pro-Jordanians proposed that areas to the east of the current municipality be formed into a new capital for a Jordanian–Palestinian federation, with the *haram* serving as a Palestinian capital on which Jordanian and Palestinian flags would both fly.[18]

In the wake of the Gulf War, the ibn Sa'ud family, sensing Hussein's desperate straits, made a play for the *haram* as well, offering to finance its renovation and to gild the Dome of the Rock, which was badly in need of repair. The Saudis, whose puritanical Wahhabi Islamic movement seized Mecca and Medina from King Hussein's grandfather, Abdullah, in 1919, were hoping to complete their sweep of the holy sites from their old Hashemite rivals. The Saudis paid for Egyptian engineers and architects to travel to Jerusalem under the auspices of UNESCO to offer their services.

The Saudis even were willing to realign themselves with Arafat in order to deny the walled city of Jerusalem to Hashemite spawn. Arafat, who believed he could regain access to Saudi largesse after his disastrous alliance with Saddam Hussein, initially supported the Saudi move. The Saudis pressed Arafat to demand control over the *haram*, for whose renovation and upkeep, they would, in turn, foot the bill. But the Saudis drove a hard bargain, demanding that Arafat be more conciliatory to Israeli peace conditions, that the PLO be democratically restructured, and that the Saudis be allowed to pay monies Arafat requested in return directly to the West Bank Palestinians. The Fatah-dominated Higher Muslim Council and President Arafat refused, "allowing" King Hussein to pick up the bill for reconstruction, which he financed by selling one of his luxury apartments in Europe. In 1994, Hussein was paying a Northern Irish company that specializes in the restoration of church domes to restore the Dome of the Rock, using the wooden joints dictated by ninth-century architectural plans and eighty-two layers of microthin gold. Barred from the *haram,* the Saudis then began angling to finance the reconstruction of the Muslim Quarter of the Old City.[19]

King Hussein had regained considerable support among the Palestinians of the diaspora. After the Gulf War, when the Palestinians had been expelled from Kuwait and other Gulf States, Jordan was the only state to welcome them. The money they brought in with them helped revitalize Hussein's moribund economy. King Hussein pressed the idea that Jerusalem's Islamic shrines be put in the care of an Islamic trust in which he would be dominant. It was therefore significant that when he made his pilgrimage to Mecca and Medina in February 1994 nobody from the Saudi monarchy was there to meet him. An unconfirmed report even suggested the Saudis were paying tribal leaders from southern Jordan to spark a civil war with the Palestinians.[20]

By late 1993, work had resumed on King Hussein's unfinished palace north of Jerusalem, an area reserved for him ever since he had lost the city in 1967. When Hussein spoke at the opening of the Jordanian parliament in 1993, he referred to Jerusalem as a city sacred to Muslims throughout the world without even mentioning its status as the capital of Palestine. The king also fired Hassan Tabub as director of the Jerusalem *waqf* and refused to recognize his election as president of the Supreme Muslim Council because Tabub, a Hebronite, was too close to Arafat's al-Fatah. In March 1993, the king appointed Sheik Suleiman al-Jabari, a loyal ally, to the position of mufti in Jerusalem.

During Friday prayers at al-Aqsa, there is a traditional prayer for the legitimate ruler. However, when Muslims kneel on their prayer rugs on the *haram,* this prayer is not said. The city's proper sovereign is too contested. Most Palestinians find the idea of King Hussein's being restored as *sharif* of Jerusalem distasteful in the extreme.[21] No one more so that Yaser Arafat. Speaking to South African Muslims, Arafat interpreted a secret letter he had received from Shimon Peres in October promising that Israel would not "hamper" the activity of "Palestinian institutions" in East Jerusalem to mean that Israel would ultimately grant Palestinians authority for the city's Christian and Muslim holy places.[22] In January 1994, Arafat again seized on the contest between the Hashemites and the Saudis to regain entry to Saudi Arabia, securing his first audience with King Fahd and Prince Salman, the governor of Riyad, who chairs the committee channeling Palestinian taxes to the PLO. Arafat not only apologized for his stance in the Gulf War, he pointedly urged King Fahd to take responsibility for the al-Aqsa mosque.[23] Using the sacred sites of al-Quds as his lure, Arafat sought to offer the PLO as the Saudi road into Jerusalem, to counterbalance his two enemies and thereby use Saudi largesse to capture the loyalties of the Jerusalem *waqf*. (Significantly, Arafat demanded and received from the Israelis a guaranteed safe passage from Jericho to Nebi Mussa, where Palestinian Muslims believe Moses is buried. Arafat would likely revive pilgrimage to the site, begun during the mufti's time, as a nationalist rite by which to mobilize his emergent nation.)

The logic behind Arafat's maneuvers became clear when, on July 25, 1994, King Hussein and Yitzhak Rabin initialed a peace treaty on the White House lawn promising "to bring an end to bloodshed and sorrow." Israel forswore forcible Palestinian transfer to the Hashemite kingdom. To Palestinian astonishment, Israel agreed to respect Jordan's "historic role" in administering Islamic sites in Jerusalem and to give that role "high priority" in its future negotiations with the Palestinians scheduled to begin in 1996.[24] The king had personally insisted that Israel confirm his standing in Jerusalem as a requirement for signing the peace treaty.[25] Jordan had moved in part to preempt the Saudis' cutting their own deal with the PLO.[26]

Arafat, when he entered what he termed the "first free land" in Palestine on July 1, 1994, promised to "achieve a Palestinian state, with Jerusalem as its capital." "We are here in Gaza," he told the crowd of Palestinians who had packed into Gaza City, "on the way to the *haram* . . . There, we will pray together, as we promised the fallen, that we will pray there on their souls."[27] Arafat had not pressed to visit Jerusalem, fearing it would only feed the Israeli right, weakening support for the Labour-led negotiations.[28]

So when later the same month, four days before Rabin and Hussein signed their declaration, the Israelis formally invited King Hussein to pray there, Arafat raged: "They have no right to issue any invitations. It is my duty and my responsibility to invite my brothers and friends to come visit the holy Christian and Muslim sites, which are under Palestinian jurisdiction." Arafat, who had stiffed the Jordanians by making a separate deal with Israel, was now himself being squeezed.

Rabin boasted that he had written the portion of the Jordanian peace treaty recognizing Jordanian privileges over Jerusalem's Islamic sites.[29] From an Israeli point of view, the idea of putting the *haram* under some kind of wider Islamic authority of which King Hussein would be head makes perfect political sense, denationalizing Jerusalem's most sacred Islamic shine.[30] Not a few Arab leaders have privately approached the Israelis and expressed their grave concern about Palestinian control of Islam's third most sacred site. Arafat is neither trusted nor deemed worthy as its guarantor. In 1993, Rabin traveled to the Islamic conference in Jakarta to discuss future arrangements in Jerusalem. By ceding sovereignty over the platform of the *haram* and giving authority to an Islamic council, the Israelis would be able to win legitimacy in the larger

Islamic world, perhaps securing widespread Islamic recognition of their state and maybe even their control over the rest of Jerusalem. When the Israelis allowed King Hussein to fly his jet over Israeli airspace on his way home from Britain, Rabin pointedly told him, "Your Majesty . . . I hope that in your flight over Jerusalem you will see the tremendous development of this holy city."[31] King Hussein, for his part, did not take umbrage at Israel's cleaving off religious real estate from the issues of sovereignty and settlement. "Religious and political sovereignty over the holy city were two separate issues," the king told Jordanian journalists. "As regards the Muslim shrines there, we believe the whole Muslim nation should have jurisdiction over them."[32] There was virtually no protest from the Arab world, even from Saudi Arabia.[33]

There is evidence that the Israelis intend to grant some kind of collective Christian sovereignty over Jerusalem's sacred Christian sites as well. With a peace agreement in the air, Jerusalem's churches have suddenly returned to geopolitical jockeying not witnessed since the nineteenth century. The Russians, for instance, have resumed their position as patron and protector of the Greek Orthodox Church. The Armenian flag now flies over the Armenian Quarter, to the great irritation of Palestinian nationalists. Previous Israeli Labour governments have been willing to cede sovereignty in the Christian quarter to some larger Christian authority if they felt it would serve Israel's political interests. Unlike in the *haram,* few Israeli leaders believe there was much at stake for non-Jews to exercise sovereignty over the place where Pontius Pilate had executed Jesus as a political criminal, placing a sign, "King of the Jews," on his crucifix.

In January 1994, the Vatican finally concluded a pact according diplomatic recognition to the state of Israel. The desire to protect its Arab parishioners and theological discomfort with Jewish sovereignty, particularly on the site of the Lord's crucifixion, had both played a part in the Vatican's past hesitation to grant recognition. But recently the Holy See had become increasingly concerned about the deteriorating position of the Christian population in the Holy Land and in Jerusalem in particular, as well as about the way in which the rise of militant Islam has made life increasingly uncomfortable, and even dangerous, for Christians throughout the Arab world. Moreover, the Latin Church, as the Roman Catholics are called, has always been bitter about its restricted access to Christianity's most sacrosanct sites, with Israel enforcing the same allocation of sacred Christian space among the numerous churches inherited from the Turks and the British.

It was highly significant, therefore, that before the Palestinians could negotiate any new conditions in Jerusalem or Bethlehem, the Vatican suddenly struck a deal with Israel and Jordan as well. Most notably, the

Vatican did not support Jerusalem as the capital of a Palestinian state.[34] Although the Vatican had taken the remarkable step of appointing a Palestinian, Michel Sabah, as the Jerusalem Patriarch in 1987, the experience of the Christian Copts in Egypt, gunned down and knifed by Islamic militants while the nationalist regime looked on more or less helplessly, shocked the Holy See. The Vatican reluctantly concluded Palestinian nationalist control of Jerusalem and Bethlehem would be a vehicle through which militant Islam, already quite strong in the Islamic hierarchy in Jerusalem, would gain even greater influence among the population. Moreover, because Palestinians Christians are predominantly Greek Orthodox, to allow Palestinian control over the Church of the Holy Sepulcher, for example, would not be beneficial to the Latin Church, as well as disconcerting to the many other Christian churches, which have no representation in the Palestinian community, let alone the Arab world.[35]

In its accord with Israel, the Vatican did not recognize Israeli sovereignty in Jerusalem, notably locating its diplomatic mission in the village of Jaffe, an Arab town adjacent to the municipality of Tel Aviv. However, neither did the Vatican push for a Palestinian capital in the Old City, coming out strongly for internationalization of that part of Jerusalem. Ifrah Zilberman, an Israeli researcher at the Truman Institute who participated in a Vatican seminar on Jerusalem just before the agreement was signed, told us that the agreement included a secret annex guaranteeing the Vatican equal membership in a council of Christianities that would eventually be formed to govern Jerusalem's sacred Christian sites, as well as the right to establish new tax-exempt Catholic institutions in the city at some unspecified point in the future.[36] Even if the Vatican couldn't immediately get more access to the sacred spaces of the Church of the Holy Sepulcher and the Church of the Nativity, it was making sure it would be in a position to expand its institutional position in the sacred cities containing them and to politic for new arrangements once the Israelis left the field.[37] On July 12, 1994, Foreign Minister Peres finally made a public announcement that Israel was considering giving control over Islamic and Christian sacred sites to a council composed of representatives of Jordan, Morocco, Saudi Arabia, the Vatican, and the Palestinians.[38]

The fourth and most explosive issue in the city is Palestinian sovereignty, and whether Jerusalem will serve as its real or symbolic locus. "Jerusalem is like a part of our body. We cannot negotiate it away," a Palestinian student told us. Where should the Palestinian national government be built, we asked Dr. Abdallah Abdallah, the civil engineer who directs the Palestine Geographic Center? "I prefer it will be built very near to the Old City," he replied, "because they will represent . . . the sovereignty of the Palestinians over the area."

Though most Palestinians want to divide the city into two sovereignties, they are willing to consider joint governance. Most Israelis, on the other hand, are not willing to divide the city or to consider losing sovereignty over a united city. But even here on this explosive issue there are forces within the Israeli Labour government willing to make concessions. For example, in a post-accord Cairo meeting attended by important figures in the PLO and the Labour government such as Eli Dayan, Yossi Katz, Professor Yehoshafat Harkabi, Yael Dayan, and Shmuel Toledano, the principle of territorial unity and political division was accepted, even by Eli Dayan, Knesset head of the Labour Party, who said, according to one participant, that he would deny his support of this principle if he were quoted puiblicly. The major sticking point between the Palestinians and the Israelis in these discussions has been the status of the new Jewish neighborhoods in East Jerusalem. The Palestinians have demanded that they be under Palestinian sovereignty and that their Jewish residents be relocated in Israeli Jerusalem, whereas the Israelis have insisted that zones of sovereignty be determined demographically, not geographically.

So how to accommodate Palestinian sovereignty within a unified Jerusalem? The framework that was espoused by highly placed Israelis and Palestinians in more or less the same terms was the creation of a new Jerusalem, whose enlarged boundaries would allow each side to have its sites and its sovereignties within it. Metropolitan Jerusalem, originally a political program to prevent partition, might become the mechanism to allow it.

Jerusalem was not supposed to be discussed formally by Palestinians and Israelis until December 1995. Nevertheless, when the Palestine Geographic Center was created in 1992 to generate data to plan the new Palestinian state, Dr. Abdallah, its director, told us that one of its first orders of business had been to develop planning maps for the Jerusalem region. Metropolitan Jerusalem, he told us, was important "for political reasons." By 1993, Yisrael Kimchi, associate director of the Jerusalem Institute for Israel Studies, told us they had developed the concept and planning maps for a federal metropolitan district with a two-tiered government, whose upper tier would be subject to greater central government control than other Israeli cities, not unlike Washington, D.C., or Paris. Israel would remain the sovereign government in metropolitan Jerusalem, but Palestinians would be able to share in its governance as a devolution of authority by the state of Israel.

The idea of a metropolitan district first originated immediately after the 1967 war in the context of the Labour government's secret pursuit of a separate peace with Jordan. Mayor Kollek was then willing to explore how the governance of Jerusalem might be shared. In 1968, the Labour

government asked Meron Benvenisti to be part of a group, along with
Moshe Dayan, to devise a seemingly impossible plan – to assure Israeli
sovereignty over a united Jerusalem, and yet at the same time to satisfy
Jordanian interests. Benvenisti proposed a new metropolitan district,
Greater Jerusalem, including both the new Israeli municipality of Jerusalem as well as the large, unincorporated Arab area that was a natural
part of the metropolis. The metropolitan district would be under dual
sovereignty and jointly administered by Israel and Jordan. The entire
metropole would then be subdivided into nationally homogenous, constituent "boroughs," each delegated its own powers (education, welfare,
and planning). Benvenisti saw the proposal, still known as the "Borough
Plan," as a way to "blur" the problem of sovereignty by assigning national functions to local governments.

In the current proposal for a metropolitan district, infrastructure,
police, and fire fighting could be jointly governed by an umbrella body
directly subject to control by the two national governments, but operating under Israeli sovereignty. This metropolitan unit would allow a
disaggregation of the demographic units composing the city into separate governmental units, whether municipalities or boroughs, which
would then be granted functional sovereignty according to their demographic composition. Jerusalem's planners have been quite successful in
sustaining an ecology on the ground, in terms of actual human flows,
that would allow a rough territorial partition between a Jewish and an
Arab bloc. Exploiting the centrifugal forces of any postautomobile city,
Jerusalem's top planners have managed to keep major new economic
and administrative activities out of the old city center, which has remained a historic, but relatively undynamic and functionally unimpor-
tant area. Palestinian development has been concentrated to the north
and south of the city, while the Israeli center of gravity has moved
steadily westward. In 1991, for example, Israeli planners quashed a
proposal to unify Arab and Jewish bus transportation at a central station
just outside Damascus Gate. In 1993, they deflected proposals for commercial development, again near Damascus Gate, making the area into
an open-air pedestrian zone instead. Except for the new municipality
building, the city's core has remained administratively undeveloped.

Some within the Labour Party establishment also see a metropolitan
district as a way to allow the Palestinians to establish their national
capital "in Jerusalem," by creating new spaces in which it would be
possible to locate the institutions and symbols of Palestinian sovereignty.
There were indications that in exchange for Israeli sovereignty over the
metropolitan area, the Palestinians were to be granted the right to have
their capital within Jerusalem. Israel would exercise sovereignty over

Jerusalem, in which Palestine would be allowed to locate its sovereignty. In a secret forum of planners from the Ministry of Housing, Kollek's municipality, and the Israel Lands Administration that began meeting in spring 1993, Ranan Weitz, the architect of the Labour government settlement policies, promoted the idea that perhaps the Palestinians could, after all, have their capital "in Jerusalem." He even proposed a site for the Palestinian parliament in the northeast quadrant of the metropole, not far from where the Palestinians are now building their own television station within an old Israeli army base. Here, the Palestinians would be able to build a new city, called al-Quds, of 300,000 residents.[39] Just as the Israelis were forced to build their Knesset far to the west of the Old City, the Palestinians could likewise be granted such a site. Those Palestinian negotiators with whom we spoke did not expect to succeed in securing a location within the Old City or even the modern Arab downtown for their capital. A Palestinian capital in Greater Jerusalem was the best they expected.

Such a metropolitan unit, Labour planners imagine, would allow them to develop an area over which Israel could claim overall sovereignty while allowing the Palestinians to assert suzerainty, in the words of both Israeli planners and Palestinian negotiators, over their own municipalities and even to locate the institutions of national sovereignty within them. This idea had already been discussed with top PLO negotiators by late 1993.

Separating sovereignty and suzerainty was initially discussed and agreed upon in April 1987 in discussions between King Hussein and Israeli Foreign Minister Peres, placing Jewish neighborhoods in East Jerusalem under Jordanian suzerainty, while still under Israeli sovereignty. Cecilia Albin, an Oxford University scholar who had carefully tracked the history of proposals for Jerusalem, told us that "a right-wing high-level Likud advisor to Shamir once suggested to me confidentially – following a successful transitional period Israelis could come to see that allowing for Palestinian 'pockets' of sovereignty over Arab areas of East Jerusalem is compatible with, and indeed necessary for, a (physically) united city."[40] By a conceptual sleight of hand, the suzerain, an ancient Persian concept for relations between independent and dependent states, the Israelis could maintain their preeminent claim over the metropole, while allowing the Palestinians control over pieces within it.[41] According to the Israeli version, Israel would appoint the mayor, the Palestinians the vice-mayor, with the Old City governed by representatives of the three religions. Alternatively, if conditions were propitious, it could also evolve to joint governance of the metropolitan unit. Within a properly structured metropolitan district, the Arab and Jewish populations are more or less equally balanced. No wonder the Likud introduced a bill in Knesset in January 1994 trying to extend Israeli sovereignty over the entire metropolitan area.

Just as Emperor Franz Josef sought to take Vienna out of the hands of Karl Lueger's populist anti-Semitic party, a metropolitan government would enable the national Labour government to neutralize the Likud-run municipality's efforts to sabotage the peace accords by provocative acts, particularly Mayor Olmert's drive to build Jewish employment and residence along the "seam" still marking the old no-man's-land between Arab and Israeli Jerusalem, as well as in Palestinian neighborhoods down the hill from Mt. Scopus and elsewhere.[42] Unlike Kollek's administration, which actively promoted the idea of neighborhood self-government, a Likud-run municipality would be less likely to cede powers to Palestinian areas. A metropolitan district would take that discretion out of the hands of city officials.

The metropolitan unit would also allow the government to bring the overwhelming majority of Jews living over the "Green Line," including 30 to 40 percent of the Jews elsewhere in the West Bank, within Israel. When combined with the 30 percent who have indicated their willingness to move in exchange for compensation, this would cut away a huge chunk of the Jewish population nervously watching to see whether, when, and under what conditions they may have to be evacuated from the Palestinian entity.[43]

The metropolitan district would also solve an increasingly nettlesome issue for the Zionist state, namely that within Jerusalem proper, the *haredim* will soon predominate. Their children fill the delivery rooms. They are the ones who migrate and remain here. Because a Jew is a Jew and Israel is determined to maintain a Jewish majority in the city, the *haredim* will not and cannot be denied housing. Unless large numbers of immigrants displace them – seemingly unlikely given the tendency of overwhelmingly secular Russian immigrants to settle elsewhere in the country – these non-Zionists are likely to be Jerusalem's power brokers in the not too distant future.[44] Experts prophesy they will compose 40 percent of the population by 2010.[45]

Over the last decade, increasing numbers of secular or traditional Jerusalemites have told us that young, less observant Jews in Jerusalem, unlike their parents, intend to migrate away from the city after their army service.[46] Why stay in a city that will be more and more unreceptive to their cultural needs and has not produced lots of new jobs in those sectors for which they are prepared? The election of Ehud Olmert of Likud, a cosmopolitan secularist, predicted Ari Shachar, Safdie professor of geography at Hebrew University, was a transitional phenomenon. The city's future was in the hands of the *haredim;* the next mayor would be one of their own, one of Jerusalem's best students bravely predicted.[47] That occurrence would be the sign for even more secular Israelis that it was time to take their leave. A city ruled by non-Zionists, even if they are Jewish, is not a scenario any Israeli government can take lightly.

Broken Heart, Bloody Stage?

In a few days in 1967 Israel captured Jerusalem, its ancient capital. But in the years since, it would be more appropriate to say that Zion captured Zionism. Bringing the ancient ritual and sovereign center into modern Israel strengthened those who give precedence to religion over nationalism, Torah over state. Sovereignty over Jerusalem has always been the key messianic index, the sign that God might once again honor his promise to his chosen people. The *haredim,* Jews who have understood Zionism as a false messiah, were forced to react in a way that the mere fact of Jewish sovereignty on a coastal strip far from the ancient hill country never required. The *haredim,* who had always pushed to make the state enforce religious law, strove now to make the Jews of Zion live publicly by that law. As the *haredim* have become steadily more populous in the center and more powerful at both the municipal and national levels, they have threatened Jerusalem's status as a cosmopolitan capital of a modern state. Though the secular populace have fought back, the *haredim* will, bit by bit, become the dominant community in Jerusalem.

Israeli sovereignty in Jerusalem not only set in motion a new wave of religious nationalism but transformed the way in which religious Zionists thought about the law and the land. Before Israel controlled Zion, the religious Zionists shared the general strategic orientation of the Labour Party, which treated territory as secondary to the Israeli people and their ability to live in peace. With the Arab world so dogged in its determination to eliminate the state, they never had to decide between territory or peace. Territory was held because it was strategic to do so. It was not a matter of principle. Taking Jerusalem changed that orientation forever. What had been beyond reach was, incredibly, now in their hands. Galvanized by young men trained by rabbis who had developed a new messianic theology of the state, Jerusalem's conquest pushed the religious nationalist movement to interpret their mandate in a radically new way. Holding and building the historic lands became the central religious obligation and suburbanization of Jerusalem the prime mechanism for knitting the newly conquered heartland of *eretz-yisrael* to the sovereign territories of Israel.

If secular nationalists are under siege within Zion, religious nationalists are in danger outside it. Jewish settlements, particularly those more distant and dangerously located in the midst of Palestinians, are acutely vulnerable. It will be difficult for their leaders to challenge evacuation if Israel's military establishment determines that dismantlement is the most efficient response to continued Palestinian violence and, as is likely, settlers are targeted by Palestinian rejectionist groups that the Palestinian authority must either repress or co-opt. This prospect was understood long before the Hebron massacre, when Palestinian street fighters and guerrillas made the settlers their primary targets. The massacre and the popular wave of Palestinian vengeance it provoked proved just how politically fruitful that dance of death could be. Meeting with the pope after the Hebron massacre, Prime Minister Rabin declared that to allow Jews to remain in Hebron was "dumb from a security point of view."[48]

The settlements also include a large constituency that can be compensated, as much as a third of those Jews living in the West Bank and Gaza, according to one estimate.[49] Knesset members began to make initiatives to compensate Jews living in Judea, Samaria, and Gaza. By February 1994, a hotline established by Knesset members for Jews considering relocation was receiving hundreds of calls.[50] Many interpreted the ground breaking a few months after the agreement was signed for Modi'in, a new city between Jerusalem and Tel Aviv planned for a quarter million Jews, as part of a plan to evacuate and relocate settlers. Perfectly sited in commuting distance to both Tel Aviv and Jerusalem, the city would provide a viable alternative venue for the suburban commuters who overwhelmingly populate the settlements today.[51] If Israel does accept a new metropolitan area in which another third of the Jewish settler population could continue to live under Israeli sovereignty, a remnant of the most ideologically committed settler movement who remained would be forced to accommodate themselves to the new realities.

Now that an Israeli regime that will cede or compromise sovereignty over the West Bank and Gaza has taken power, the ideological core of the settlement movement will increasingly return to the center – to Jerusalem – as its best battleground. The militants of the settlement movement will challenge the Palestinians in that place where they are most likely to bring the Israeli public along with them. Here an orchestrated strategy of group conflict is more likely to pay off politically than in Hebron or Nablus. If the settlers cannot live in peace in their suburbs, then the Palestinians of Jerusalem will not be allowed to live normally in Jerusalem. Palestinians will be increasingly subject to their attacks and harassment.

With the municipality in the hands of right-wing opponents of peace, as the headquarters of the settlement movement, with its large number of religious nationalist *yeshivot* who can fill the streets on command, and with the city's enormous *haredi* community being steadily drawn into the antipartition camp, it is reasonable to expect that large segments of the Israeli city will participate in massive civil disorder in the event Israeli control of Jerusalem is compromised in any way. Although the settlement movement may not be able to mobilize the Israelis to defend Kiryat Arba or Ophrah, they can count on mass support to prevent Palestinians from touching Jerusalem. If, as is likely, Jerusalem is increasingly chosen as a target for terrorism by those Palestinians opposed to the peace plan, the prospects for massive manifestations of disobedient rage are very great.

When Arafat came to Gaza for the first time, 100,000 Israelis massed at the Western Wall in protest, more than came to hear Arafat's first public address in Gaza City. Demonstrators threw themselves onto the streets into the city, pouring concrete and nails on the main road up from the new Jericho autonomy zone. Mayor Olmert, who provided support for the demonstrations, said, "We are not fighting against the Government. We are fighting to protect the unity of Jerusalem."[52]

For the Palestinians, Israel's conquest of al-Quds, the ultimate humiliation, provided them the site from which to fashion a nation. By liberating Jerusalem, the Israelis freed the city to serve again as the symbolic and organizational center for the Palestinians as well. Unlike the Israelis, the Palestinians have had the misfortune of being surrounded by people with whom they can readily identify, peoples who take their struggle as their own. To develop their local nationalist movement, the Palestinians have had to disengage and defend their destiny from pan-Arab and Islamic movements that have attempted to assimilate their conflict against colonization to their own aims. The diaspora PLO, caught in the force field of ideological conflict and murderous rivalry among the Arab states, has had to adapt constantly to the foreign policies of its host countries in Amman, Beirut, Tunis, Damascus, and, most recently, Baghdad.

Like the Jordanians before them, Israelis played their part in economically stunting Palestinian Jerusalem, but because the Israelis defined Jerusalem – all of it – as part of Israel, they felt compelled to provide the Palestinians with political rights – no matter how compromised – that were denied to their confreres living in occupied territory. As a result Jerusalem reemerged once again as the political center of the Palestinian nation. Its Palestinian political elites were better able to give voice to the unique perspective of the Palestinians under Israeli occupation and to devote their energies to organizing the population of all the territories conquered by Israel. Every time the Palestinians tried to organize across the occupied territories, they did so from Jerusalem. Jerusalem became the base from which the Palestinians inside pushed the PLO outside to recognize Israel and to accept, after forty years of steadfast and violent refusal, the original United Nations partition plan.

But just as making Zion central left a religious imprint on Zionism, so al-Quds has made its mark on the ways in which Palestinians understand their struggle with the Jews. As long as Jerusalem was controlled by the Hashemites, a ruling family with impeccable Islamic credentials, the quest to return to all of Palestine, to purge the Arab homeland of an alien intruder, dominated the Palestinian struggle. The conflict was understood in the language of Arab nationalism. Once the sacred center fell to the Zionists, liberating the holy city from the infidel increasingly became a rallying cry; the contest between colonist and native increasingly was understood as a war between infidel and believer.

The PLO's political weakness, the failure of its armed struggle, its inability to achieve a state, its crescive withdrawal from one principle after another, have been shadowed by the strengthening of militant Islam. As we have seen, HAMAS has gained progressively greater influence over the network of mosques and religious schools controlled from the central *waqf* of Jerusalem.[53] HAMAS clerics regularly attack the PLO from the pulpit. During the Gulf War, the walls of East Jerusalem were covered with Islamic graffiti.

After the Gulf War, in December 1991, with the Palestinian delegation ensconced in the hallways in Washington, D.C., when we met with Sheik Muhammad Jamal, the Jerusalem head of the *shari'a* courts and key player in the Muslim Brotherhood claimed he was a friend of Faisal Husayni. Jamal repeatedly refused to condemn or distance himself in any way from HAMAS, which repudiated both the nationalist leadership and the peace process. Not just this platform, the *haram al-sharif,* he told us, was holy, but *all* the land, from the river to the sea. The goals of the PLO and HAMAS remained the same, he insisted; only the means to attain them differed.

It was thus striking that in a bid to regain legitimacy in the Arab world after his disastrous support of Saddam Hussein, but before he signed the peace agreement, Arafat pressed the need to liberate Jerusalem by jihad at the Islamic conference in Dakar, Senegal. By abandoning the PLO, his Arab brothers were turning their backs on their sacred obligation to free al-Quds, he declared. And then again, even after signing the peace accord, speaking in South Africa, where Nelson Mandela was being sworn in as president, Arafat not only called again for jihad to liberate Jerusalem, but compared his agreement to the Prophet Muhammad's treaty of Hudaybiyah, a truce by which the tribe of Quraysh exiled Muhammad to Medina with limited rights to visit Mecca. The truce, enormously unpopular among the Prophet's followers at the time, broke down two years later and the Prophet's forces vanquished the Quraysh. "The prophet Muhammad accepted [Hudaybiyah], and we now accept the peace agreement, but in order to continue on the way to Jerusalem," Arafat told the listeners in the mosque in Johannesburg.[54]

If the nationalist camp falters on the road to statehood, it is only a matter of time before the Islamic militants gain the upper hand. While PLO fighters police their own, HAMAS's Qassamite brigades' continued violent attacks against Israelis allow them to claim that they alone now carry the mantle of the *fedayeen*. Even after it was evident that the agreement had massive Palestinian support, Arafat did not consider the PLO strong enough to repress the Islamic opposition. In the spring of 1994, Arafat used his historic ties to the Egyptian Brotherhood to make a truce with HAMAS. HAMAS was being pressured by the Jordanian-dominated Muslim Brotherhood, as well as its financial backers in Saudi Arabia, Kuwait, and the United Arab Emirates. HAMAS, it appeared, now offered to be a loyal opposition within the new Palestinian jurisdiction, and an armed one without.[55] Musa Abu Marzouk, HAMAS political head, declared that HAMAS would only cease its attacks on Israelis if Israel withdrew from all the occupied territories.[56] Given that Israeli soldiers and settlers were going to remain, HAMAS and the PLO would thus divide the labor, the former providing the latter with the inducement for Israeli withdrawal. "We are with you, Ahmad Yassin, and we will not rest or be quiet until you stand with us here," Arafat proclaimed in Gaza on his first visit to Palestine, referring to the still imprisoned leader of HAMAS.[57] Arafat offered HAMAS six seats in the authority, began trying to secure the release of HAMAS prisoners from Israeli jails, and instructed his police force not to shoot at their guerrillas.[58]

At the same moment right-wing and religious forces have captured power on the Israeli side of the city, militant Islam has become increasingly influential on its Palestinian side. When combined with the strategic position of Islamic militants or those sympathetic to their goals within the Jerusalem-centered Muslim institutions, there is a sufficient base for provocation and engagement in the event that Jerusalem is excluded from the eventual Palestinian entity. Islamic influence has grown to such an extent that when other Palestinian towns held elections for the Chamber of Commerce, Palestinians in Jerusalem delayed them in 1993, fearing Fatah would be defeated by the Islamic bloc. After Israel promised to give priority to King Hussein's ritual rights in Jerusalem, Sheik Jamil Hamimi, a former aide to HAMAS leader Yasin and HAMAS's most prominent leader in Jerusalem, approached Faisal Husayni about coordinating their struggle for Jerusalem.[59] Just like the religious nationalists on the Israeli side, the militant Muslims find Jerusalem the best place to engage the enemy, to stage profanations, to press the boundaries of permissible confrontation.

The logic of both Israeli and Palestinian national unity points to Jerusalem as a likely battlefield. The overwhelming majority of Israeli religious nationalists and revisionists, on the one side, and Islamic militants and Palestinian secular rejectionists, on the other, want to avoid violent conflict with their countrymen. For Jewish religious nationalists, there is a powerful theological tradition that makes the Jewish state and its army sacred. To do anything that weakens its force would be anathema to most Jewish settlers. The long and short arm of historical memory is also a deterrent for both peoples. The Israeli memory of the violent civil war accompanying Jerusalem's fall to the Romans in the first century C.E. and the Palestinian memory of the debilitating civil war that destroyed any nationalist capacity in the 1930s are both alive as cautionary tales.

Jerusalem is the best battleground for those Israelis and Palestinians opposed to a partitioned peace. On Jerusalem, there is an almost congenital consensus on nonnegotiability in both nations. Elsewhere in the West Bank and Gaza, Palestinian and Israeli troops will be jointly responsible for controlling Palestinian violence. But in Jerusalem, there will be no Palestinian police. If the Labour government follows a strategy of separation – closing Israel to most Palestinians from the territories – in response to continued Palestinian terrorism, Jerusalem will become an even more critical conduit and staging ground for Palestinian violence. And in Jerusalem, those Palestinians who reject the peace plan can engage the enemy without fear of confronting their own. Indeed, such attacks will likely contribute to Arafat's claim to the city. It will be politically suicidal for Arafat to repudiate them as long as Jerusalem is excluded from Palestine. And they will bolster his argument that only if the Palestinians have a sovereign stake in the city will the Jews be able to live safely in Zion.

And the Palestinians in the city will have plenty to provoke them. Backed by the municipal government, Jews will seek to penetrate more Palestinian neighborhoods. One of Mayor Olmert's first acts was to approve the movement of the Beit Orot yeshivah into an Arab neighborhood on the Mount of Olives that Kollek had zoned for a Palestinian girls' school.[60] Most ominously, one can expect not only efforts by religious nationalist Israelis to assert their ritual rights on the *har ha-bayit,* or Temple Mount, but violent attacks on the Dome of the Rock and al-Aqsa mosque as well. The more peace beckons, the more likely this stone platform will become a target for those who value territory more highly than the possibility of living at peace upon it. Right after her husband was assassinated in 1990, Kibby Kahane, Meir's widow and a librarian at Hebrew University, helped found the Temple Mount Religious Seminary, dedicated to rebuilding the Temple. In November 1993 the seminary's leader, Rabbi Avraham Toledano, was arrested for seeking to smuggle materials for making of bombs and weapons components into Israel. Five of Toledano's followers were also arrested, including Andy Green, who had been jailed with Kahane for planning to blow up the Dome of the Rock.[61] At least one rabbi, Ehud Sprinzak, who chronicles the Israeli right, informed us at the close of 1993, was actively preparing for an armed attack on the *haram*.

From their side, the Palestinians of the city will not only seek to assert their national rights in Jerusalem, they will try to build housing for their children and to provide residences for those forced to move outside the municipal boundaries by Israeli restrictions on their building rights. HAMAS, for whom Jerusalem is the second most important redoubt after Hebron, is likely to try again to engage the Israelis and Arafat from the *haram,* which, they will allege, he has bartered away for a mess of pottage. The struggle among Fatah, the Hashemites, and HAMAS for primacy on the Prophet's platform will lead to a competition over who can best protect it from the Israelis who police its sacred ground.

The options for Jerusalem are stark and painful. The Palestinians demand an independent state with Jerusalem as its capital. The Israelis, although they might accept a Palestinian state, will not accept Jerusalem as a Palestinian capital. If the benefits and pressures are great enough, Israel will make Jerusalem the price the Palestinians have to pay in order to get sovereignty elsewhere. However, without some at least symbolic claim to Jerusalem, it is unlikely the PLO will ever be able to agree to a secure and legitimate territorial partition with Israel. Without Jerusalem, both Arafat and the local "moderate" Palestinian leadership will simply lose control.

In Jerusalem, as we have seen, the hard structures of the city are built upon foundations that are more enduring, more materially effective, than stone or concrete. The city is built upon a set of symbols that threaten to tear it apart. As Israelis and Palestinians move toward peace, Jerusalem is being prepared as a battlefield for war.

Notes

Introduction

1 A considerable amount of theorizing went into this study. We have, however, written this book so that the theoretical constructs we deploy and the problematics we engage are invisible to the untutored eye. Most of our readers will care about Jerusalem, not about social theories and methodology in the fields of urban ethnography, sacred centers, nation building, and social movements. Our theoretical commitments are embodied in the account, in the method, in the explanation, in the very language we use to describe the worlds of Jerusalem. Our theoretical and methodological position will be made explicit in another book, *At the Center,* which is in progress.

2 We use the more secular notation C.E., referring to the common era, rather than B.C. and A.D. with their Christian connotations.

3 Saul Friedlander and Adam Seligman, "The Israeli Memory of the Shoah: On Symbols, Rituals and Ideological Polarization," in Roger Friedland and Deirdre Boden, eds., *NowHere: Space, Time and Modernity* (Berkeley: University of California Press, 1994), pp. 356–371.

4 The first four leaders following the Prophet – Abu Bakr, Umar ibn al-Khattab, Uthman ibn Affan, and Ali ibn Abi Talib – were all immediate companions of the Prophet and are called *rashidum*, or "rightly guided" caliphs.

Chapter 1. A Fearful Fusion

1 David Fromkin, *A Peace to End All Peace: The Fall of the Ottoman Empire and the Creation of the Modern Middle East* (New York: Avon, 1989), pp. 293–295.

2 David Vital, *Zionism: The Formative Years* (Oxford: Oxford University Press, 1982), esp. pp. 146–162.

3 Pp. 107–108 in an editorial published in the *New York Daily Tribune* on April 18, 1854, "Declaration of War: On the History of the Eastern Question," in *Karl Marx and Frederick Engels: Collected Works* (New York: International Publishers, 1980), vol. 13, pp. 100–108.

4 S. Zalman Abramov, *Perpetual Dilemma: Jewish Religion in the Jewish State* (Rutherford, N.J.: Fairleigh Dickinson University Press, 1976), p. 46.

5 Ehud Luz, *Parallels Meet: Religion and Nationalism in the Early Zionist Movement, 1882–1904,* trans. by Lenn J. Scramm (Philadelphia: The Jewish Publication Society, 1988).

6 "The Proclamation of the State of Israel," in Itamar Rabinovich and Jehuda Reinharz, eds., *Israel and the Middle East: Documents and Readings on Society, Politics and Foreign Relations, 1948–Present* (New York: Oxford University Press, 1984), p. 14.

7 Marek Halter, *The Jester and the Kings: A Political Autobiography*, trans. by Lowell Bair (Boston: Arcade Publishing, 1989), pp. 35–36.

8 This term *khalifa* was originally understood as a viceroy or deputy of God (Qur'an, Sura 38.257). Patricia Crone and Martin Hinds, *God's Caliph: Religious Authority in the First Centuries of Islam* (Cambridge: Cambridge University Press, 1986).

9 In 1774, the Russians forced the Ottomans to recognize the independence of the Crimean Tartars, prior to their annexation by Russia. In exchange for ceding political sovereignty, the sultan was allowed to claim he was "the supreme religious head of Islam," and hence still the religious head of the Tartars. The first Ottoman constitution a century later still made the claim that the sultan occupied this role. This remained official Ottoman doctrine until 1924 when the Turkish republic abolished the caliphate. The sultan's claim was pressed as a way to bolster support for the Ottoman regime. It was in this context that the Hejaz railway was built to take pilgrims to Mecca and Medina. See Bernard Lewis, *Islam and the West* (New York: Oxford University Press, 1993), pp. 20–22, *The Political Language of Islam*, pp. 49–50, and Albert Hourani, *A History of the Arab Peoples* (Cambridge: Harvard University Press, 1991), pp. 346–347. On the Hejaz railway, see Jacob M. Landau, *The Hejaz Railway and the Muslim Pilgrimage: A Case of Ottoman Political Propaganda* (Detroit: Wayne State University Press, 1971).

10 Hourani, *A History of the Arab Peoples*, pp. 207–230, and Lewis, *Islam and the West*, pp. 15–29, 72–84, and "Ottoman Observers of Ottoman Decline," in *Islam in History: Ideas, People, and Events in the Middle East*, New and Revised Edition (Chicago: Open Court, 1993), pp. 209–222.

11 Fromkin, *A Peace to End All Peace*, pp. 219–227.

12 Ibid., p. 324.

13 Janet Wallach and John Wallach, *Arafat: In The Eyes of the Beholder* (New York, Lyle Stuart, 1990), pp. 25–27. As the Wallachs point out, Arafat claims Jerusalem as his birthplace whereas his birth certificate indicates Cairo.

14 Baruch Kimmerling and Joel S. Migdal, *Palestinians: The Making of a People* (New York: The Free Press, 1993), p. 47, on Palestine. Martin Gilbert, *Jerusalem History Atlas* (New York: Macmillan, 1977), pp. 59, 61.

15 Meron Medzini, "The International Relations of Jerusalem," *The Center Magazine*, 18.1 (January/February, 1985), pp. 41–50, and Silvio Ferrari, "The Vatican, Israel and the Jerusalem Question (1943–1984)," *Middle East Journal*, 39.2 (1985), pp. 316–331. Cecilia Albin argues that there may have been an explicit deal with the Vatican exchanging support for partition in exchange for internationalization. "Strategies and Options in the Jerusalem Conflict," in Ifrah Zilberman, ed., *Palestinian Society and Politics in Jerusalem: Twenty-Five Years of Israeli Rule* (Privately circulated manuscript, 1992).

16 See Steven L. Spiegel, *The Other Arab–Israeli Conflict: Making America's Middle East Policy, from Truman to Reagan* (Chicago: University of Chicago Press, 1985), esp. pp. 16–49; as well as Clark Clifford and Richard Holbrooke, "Annals of Government (The Truman Years – Part I)," *New Yorker*, March 25, 1991, pp. 40–59.

17 Hourani, *A History of the Arab Peoples*, pp. 257–258.

18 Avishai Margalit, "The General's Main Chance," *New York Review of Books*, June 11, 1992, pp. 17–22.

19 Tom Segev, *1949: The First Israelis* (New York: Free Press, 1986), p. 14.

20 Saul B. Cohen, *Jerusalem: Bridging the Four Walls: A Geopolitical Perspective* (New York: Herzl Press, 1977), p. 43. Meron Benvenisti, *Jerusalem: Study of a Polarized Community* (Jerusalem: The West Bank Data Base Project, 1983), p. 70.

21 Even the sympathetic Palestinian biographer Philip Mattar believes it most likely that the mufti either "ordered or acquiesced in the assassination." See his *The Mufti of Jerusalem: Al-Hajj Amin Al-Husayni and the Palestinian National Movement* (New York: Columbia University Press, 1988), p. 137.

22 See Meron Benvenisti, *Jerusalem: The Torn City* (Jerusalem: Isratypeset, 1976), pp. 17–29. For population data, see Ziva Wainshal and Dafna Pelli, *Jerusalem: Statistical Data* (Jerusalem: Jerusalem Municipality, 1983).

23 Moshe Dayan later told Rabin that this operation, plus a daylight armed convoy attack on Jordanian soldiers the previous year, pushed Nasser into aggressive action. Ben-Gurion made the same inference. See Avishai Margalit, "The General's Main Chance," *New York Review of Books*, June 11, 1992, pp. 17–22, p. 19.

24 See Moskin, *Among Lions, The Battle for Jerusalem, June 5–7, 1967* (New York: Ballantine Books, 1982), p. 63.

25 Moshe Amirav claimed that Teddy Kollek opposed immediate opening of the borders, fearing that it was too soon and there would be a disaster. He was overruled.

26 Michael Romann and Alex Weingrod, *Living Together Separately: Arabs and Jews in Contemporary Jerusalem* (Princeton, N.J.: Princeton University Press, 1991), p. 65.

27 In addition to our interviews with Tawil, we have also made use of her autobiography, *My Home, My Prison* (New York: Holt, Rinehart and Winston, 1979).

28 Tawil was arrested during a period when Palestinian merchants were closing their shops in protest against the imposition of a new value added tax of 8 percent. Tawil claimed that the tax was simply a device Israel was using to force greater Palestinian emigration. Tawil, who was put under house arrest at about the same time as Bassam Shakaa, the mayor of Nablus, was released shortly after the tax protest ended. William Farrell, "Tax Protest a Gauge of West Bank's Deeper Tensions," *New York Times*, August 23, 1976, p. A4.

29 Uzi Narkis, *The Liberation of Jerusalem: The Battle of 1967* (London: Vallentine, Mitchell, 1983), pp. 252–256. Abraham Rabinovich, *The Battle for Jerusalem, June 5–7, 1967: 20th Anniversary Edition* (Philadelphia: The Jewish Publication Society, 1987), p. 370.

30 Avraham Shapira, ed., *The Seventh Day: Soldiers Talk About the Six-Day War* (London: Andre Deutsch, 1970). Adapted from the original Hebrew edition, *Soldiers Talk* (Tel Aviv: General Kibbutz Movement, 1970).

31 Shapira, *The Seventh Day*, pp. 139–140.

32 Benvenisti, *Jerusalem, The Torn City*, p. 84.

33 Hanna Siniora, "A Palestinian Perspective," in Stephen J. Roth, *The Impact of the Six-Day War: A Twenty-Year Assessment* (New York: St. Martin's Press, 1987), p. 95.

34 Hisham Sharabi, "Liberation or Settlement: The Dialectics of Palestinian Struggle," *Journal of Palestine Studies*, 2.2 (Winter, 1973), pp. 38–48.

35 Under British rule, Palestinian leaders used the term *democratic* to refer to

the determination of the regime by the Arab majority. Neither the 1964 nor the 1968 revision of the Palestinian covenant contains an explicit commitment to democracy. In 1971, the Palestine National Council (PNC) committed itself to a democratic state and the idea that all Israeli Jews would be allowed to remain provided they relinquish their national claims. See Y. Harkabi, *The Palestinian Covenant and Its Meaning* (London: Vallentine, Mitchell, 1979), pp. 51–53.

36 Friedman, "The State of Israel as a Theological Dilemma" in Baruch Kimmerling, ed., *The Israeli State and Society: Boundaries and Frontiers* (Albany: State University of New York Press 1989), p. 204.

37 Gideon Aran, "A Mystic–Messianic Interpretation of Modern Israeli History: The Six Day War as a Key Event in the Development of the Original Religious Culture of Gush Emunim," in *Studies in Contemporary Jewry*, edited by Jonathan Frankel (Jerusalem and Oxford: Institute of Contemporary Jewry of the Hebrew University and Oxford University Press, 1988), vol. 4, pp. 263–275, esp. p. 265.

38 Fouad Ajami, *The Arab Predicament: Arab Political Thought and Practice Since 1967* (Cambridge: Cambridge University Press, 1981), pp. 60–63, suggests that pan-Arabism itself began to draw again on the military traditions of jihad.

Chapter 2. Zion Against Zionism

1 Cited in Amos Elon, *Jerusalem: City of Mirrors* (Boston: Little, Brown, 1989), p. 239.

2 After 1948, Jerusalem's Armenians continued their classic function as land brokers in Jerusalem, negotiating clandestinely between Zionists who were forced to secure long-term leases on properties on the Jewish side of the city and Arabs on the Jordanian side who managed to maintain their ownership of those properties. This point derives from a number of necessarily anonymous sources who were in a position to know.

3 Originally named Itamar by his father, he changed his name in deference to Jerusalem custom of naming the first son Ben-Zion, "son of Zion." At age twenty-one, his son retook his intended name, but changed his last name to Ben-Avi, not only because it means "son of my father," but because in Hebrew *Avi* is an acronym for his father's full name, Eliezer Ben-Yehuda.

4 Itamar Ben-Avi, *Memoirs*, translated in Levi Soshuk and Azriel Eisenberg, eds., *Momentous Century* (New York: Cornwall Books, 1984), p. 54.

5 Half of all Jews in Palestine lived in Jerusalem. Yehoshua Ben-Arieh, *Jerusalem in the 19th Century: The Old City* (Jerusalem and New York: Yad Izhak Ben-Zvi Institute and St. Martin's Press, 1984), based on British figures.

6 H. H. Ben-Sasson, "The Middle Ages," in *A History of the Jewish People*, ed. by H. H. Ben-Sasson (Cambridge: Harvard University Press, 1976), pp. 632–633.

7 Halper, *Between Redemption and Revival: The Jewish Yishuv of Jerusalem in the Nineteenth Century* (Boulder, Colo.: Westview Press, 1992), pp. 52–61.

8 Ben-Arieh, *Jerusalem in the 19th Century*, p. 357.

9 Halper, *Between Redemption and Revival*, pp. 143–144.

10 Ben-Arieh, *Jerusalem in the 19th Century*, p. 388.

11 Yoel Rappel, *Yearning for the Holy Land: Hasidic Tales of Israel*, translated by Shmuel Himmelstein (New York: Adama Books, 1986), p. 142.

12 In the mid-1850s, Ben-Arieh reports, only 4 percent of the Jewish population

worked. *Jerusalem*, p. 324. Halper, however, argues that most families could not live on *hallukah* in the later part of the nineteenth century and had to supplement them with various forms of work. Halper, *Between Redemption and Revival*, pp. 88–89, 126–127, 152. This is at variance with S. Zalman Abramov's estimate that at the beginning of the twentieth century, some 80 percent of Jerusalem's Jews did no productive labor. *Perpetual Dilemma: Jewish Religion in the Jewish State*, p. 27.

When queried about the discrepancy, Halper replied (personal communication, November 17, 1993): "My reading of the material indicates that *haluka* represented only a portion – larger or smaller – of Ashkenazis' income. . . It might cover an important expense – rent, for example, or a supply of wheat – but could not begin to cover actual living needs of most people." Halper argues that "in the vast majority of cases," *hallukah* was supplemented by wage labor. As early as 1823, he notes, even the centrist leadership, or Perushis, those who tried to reduce the conflict with the Jerusalem Sephardim, had given tacit approval for its people to work. Halper contends that high estimates such as Abramov's reflect Zionist antipathy to the community as "parasitical" and "unproductive." "Ideologically speaking," Halper writes, "the crucial point was not whether or not one found employment to 'supplement' *haluka*, but rather that one not see employment as the main thing, overshadowing spiritualism, yeshiva study, etc., and certainly not as a value in itself."

13 They also sought to convert Eastern Christians. Ben-Arieh, *Jerusalem in the 19th Century*, pp. 333–348.

14 They also wanted to reduce their dependence on Arab merchants, who often held a monopoly position.

15 There were exceptions, particularly among the *hasidim* and some of the children of the Ashkenazi founders.

16 Rappel, *Yearning for the Holy Land*, p. 159.

17 Abramov, *Perpetual Dilemma*, pp. 39–40. The windmill was constructed using sixty thousand dollars left by Judah Touro, a Sephardi magnate from New Orleans, to aid poor Jews in Jerusalem. Halper, *Between Redemption and Revival*, p. 98.

18 See Abramov, *Perpetual Dilemma*, p. 34.

19 Halper, *Between Redemption and Revival*, pp. 179–181.

20 Quoted in Ben-Arieh, *Jerusalem in the 19th Century*, p. 393.

21 Halper, *Between Redemption and Revival*, p. 178.

22 Ibid., p. 200. A few months later, when one of the mourners placed a wreath of flowers on his dead daughter's body, the Ashkenazim declared it a non-Jewish custom and said they would not bury her. Only when Ben-Yehuda grabbed a shovel and threatened to bury her himself did they relent.

23 Halper, *Between Redemption and Revival*, p. 224.

24 The term *haredim* appears in Isaiah 66:5, where the prophets says, "Hear the word of the Lord, you that tremble [*haharedim*] at his word."

25 Ibid., p. 63.

26 Ibid., p. 66.

27 Menachem Friedman, "The State of Israel as a Theological Dilemma" in *The Israeli State and Society: Boundaries and Frontiers*, ed. by Baruch Kimmerling (Albany: State University of New York Press, 1989) pp. 173–174.

28 M. Amit, *Rebellion: Chapters in the History of the Jewish Haredi Community in the Land of Israel* (Bene Berak: Ra'am, 1983), p. 19 [Hebrew]; Abramov, *Perpetual Dilemma*, pp. 119–120; Menachem Friedman, *Society and Reli-*

gion: The Non-Zionist Orthodox in Eretz-Yisrael: 1918–1936 (Jerusalem: Yad Izhak Ben-Zvi Publications, 1977), pp. 247–250 [Hebrew].

29 Menachem Friedman, *Society and Religion,* pp. 315–333.
30 Cited in Friedman, "The State of Israel as a Theological Dilemma," p. 175.
31 Ibid., p. 178.
32 Ibid., p. 239.
33 Talmud of the Land of Israel, Hagigah 1:7.
34 Haim Shapiro, "Naturei Karta Rabbis Bring Kosher Food," *The Jerusalem Post*, February 10, 1988, p. 10.
35 Amram Blau, Neture-Karta's founder, was arrested 153 times.
36 Both Rafi Davara, spokesman for the municipality of Jerusalem, and Aharon Sarig, deputy general of Jerusalem, estimated that as of 1981, of the twenty thousand people who lived in Mea She'arim proper, about seven thousand belong to the Edah Haredit and about three hundred openly support the Neture-Karta. In a June 13, 1992, letter to the *New York Times*, Chaim Katzenel, the head of Neture-Karta, estimated about seven thousand people belonged to his group. This number is approximately the same in the analyses of Yosef Shilhav, "Communal Conflict in Jerusalem: The Spread of Ultra-Orthodox Neighborhoods," in N. Kliot and W. Waterman, eds., *Pluralism and Political Geography: People, Territory and State* (London: Croom Helm, 1983), pp. 100–113, and Yosef Shilhav, *Growth and Segregation: The Ultra-Orthodox Community of Jerusalem*, 2nd Edition (Jerusalem: Jerusalem Institute for Israel Studies, 1989).
37 Babylonian Talmud, Ketubot 111a. There have been a number of alternative interpretations of this passage.
38 Chris Hedges, "Rabbi on the Messiah's Team, and Now Arafat's," *New York Times*, August 20, 1994, p. 2. Hirsch's posture evokes strong emotions. In 1991, somebody threw a bottle of acid in his face, forcing the removal of one of his eyes. *The Jerusalem Post*, January 12, 1992, p. 4.

Chapter 3. Black Zion

1 "Songs of Continuity," in Chana Bloch and Stephen Mitchell, trans. and ed. *Selected Poetry of Yehuda Amichai* (New York: Harper & Row, 1986), p. 115.
2 Our interpretation of the Lurianic Kabbalah relies on Gershom Scholem, *Major Trends in Jewish Mysticism* (New York: Schocken Books, 1961), pp. 244–286, *The Messianic Idea in Judaism and Other Essays in Jewish Spirituality* (New York: Schocken,1971), *Sabbatai Sevi: The Mystical Messiah,* trans. by R. J. Zwi Werblowsky, (Princeton, N.J.: Princeton University Press, 1973), and *Kabbalah* (New York: New York Times Press, 1974).
3 Raphael Mahler, *Hasidism and the Jewish Enlightenment* (Philadelphia: Jewish Publication Society of America, 1985), pp. 177–181.
4 The term *hasid* originated during the second century B.C.E. Maccabean revolt to designate those who resisted assimilation to Greek culture.
5 On Hasidic prayer, see Louis Jacobs, *Hasidic Prayer* (New York: Schocken, 1978), pp. 32, 46–50, 55–103.
6 Gershom Scholem, "The Neutralization of the Messianic Element in Early Hasidism," *The Messianic Idea in Judaism and Other Essays on Jewish Spirituality* (New York: Schocken, 1971), pp. 176–202.
7 Aryeh Rubinstein, *Hasidism* (New York: Leon Amiel, 1975), p. 22.

8 Samuel H. Dresner, *The Zaddik: The Doctrine of the Zaddik According to the Writings of Rabbi Yaakov Yosef of Polnoy* (New York: Schocken, 1974), pp. 125–128.

9 Joseph Weiss, "The Saddik: Altering the Divine Will," pp. 183–193, in Joseph Weiss, *Studies in East European Jewish Mysticism* (Oxford: Oxford University Press, 1985).

10 Jerome R. Mintz, *Legends of the Hasidim* (Bloomington: Indiana University Press, 1978), p. 360.

11 Joseph Dan, *Gershom Scholem and the Mystical Dimension of Jewish History* (New York: New York University Press, 1987), p. 321.

12 Jeff Halper, "Mosaic in Black: An Outsider's Guide to the Haredi Community," *Jerusalem Post Magazine*, September 21, 1984, pp. 8–9.

13 Robert Rosenberg, "Cops and Rebbes," *The Jerusalem Post*, July 8, 1983, p. 3.

14 Haim Shapiro, "Feud in Rebbe's Family Shakes Kiryat Viznitz," *The Jerusalem Post*, June 2, 1985, p. 2.

15 Arthur Green, *Tormented Master: A Life of Rabbi Nahman of Bratslav* (New York: Schocken, 1981), pp. 63–93.

16 Cited in Friedman, "The State of Israel as a Theological Dilemma," p. 201. On the demonization of the Zionists see Aviezer Ravitzky, "Forcing the End: Zionism and the State of Israel as Antimessianic Undertakings," *Jews and Messianism in the Modern Era: Metaphor and Meaning* in Jonathan Frankel, ed., *Studies in Contemporary Jewry*, vol. 7 (New York: Oxford University Press, 1991), pp. 48–50, and Tzvi Rabinowicz, *Hasidism and the State of Israel* (Rutherford, N.J.: Fairleigh Dickenson University Press, 1982), pp. 222–242.

17 Rabinowicz, *Hasidism and the State of Israel*, pp. 103–104.

18 On the individualization and internalization of redemption see particularly, Rivka Schatz Uffenheimer, "History and National Redemption," in *Hasidism as Mysticism: Quietistic Elements in Eighteenth Century Hasidic Thought*, trans. by Jonathan Chipman (Princeton, N.J., and Jerusalem: Princeton University Press and the Magnes Press of the Hebrew University, 1993), pp. 326–339.

19 Mordecai L. Wilensky, "Hasidic–Mitnaggedic Polemics in the Jewish Communities of Eastern Europe: The Hostile Phase" in Gershon David Hundert, ed., *Essential Papers on Hasidism: Origins to the Present* (New York: New York University Press, 1991), pp. 244–271.

20 The title *Gaon* is the Hebrew cognate of the Greek title *Exilarch*, who represented the Jewish community to the outside world, first to the Byzantine Christians, later to the Muslims.

21 This appellation was originally given to them by the Hasidim. The Gaon's followers called themselves *perushim*, or those who separate.

22 Aryeh Rubinstein, *Hasidism* (New York: Leon Amiel, 1975), pp. 62–71.

23 Halper, *Between Redemption and Revival*, p. 40.

24 Roger Friedland and Richard Hecht, "The Two Banks of Jerusalem," *Tikkun*, 4.3 (1989) pp. 35–40.

25 Asher Wallfish, "A Super-Star Surrenders the Limelight," *The Jerusalem Post International Edition*, August 6, 1988, p. 13.

26 Samuel Heilman, *Defenders of the Faith: Inside Ultra-Orthodox Jewry* (New York: Schocken, 1992), pp. 43–44, and Daniel J. Elazar, *The Other Jews: The Sephardim Today* (New York: Basic, 1989), pp. 65–67.

27 Jane Satlow Gerber, *Jewish Society in Fez: Studies in Communal and Economic Life*, Ph.D. dissertation, Columbia University, 1972.

28 On the co-incidence of housing-class segregation and ethnic discrimination as a precipitant of urban social movements among the North African Jews, see Shlomo Hasson, *Urban Social Movements in Jerusalem: The Protest of the Second Generation* (Albany: State University of New York Press, 1993).

29 Issachar Ben-Ami, *Saint Veneration Among the Jews of Morocco* (Jerusalem: Magnes Press of the Hebrew University, 1984) [Hebrew].

30 Hasson, *Urban Social Movements in Jerusalem*, 1993, p. 38.

31 In the July 1984 Knesset election SHAS won 4 seats, Agudat Yisrael 2, and the National Religious Party 5. In 1988 and 1992, they won 6 of the 18 seats captured by all religious parties in the 120-seat Knesset.

32 Mark Featherman, "Lubavitch Hail Rebbe's Birthday," *Forward*, April 17, 1992.

33 In 1992 the *rebbe* suffered a debilitating stroke that confined him, unable to speak, to a wheelchair. In late 1993, he sank into a deep coma; he died on June 12, 1994, sending his community searching for the meaning of his death.

Chapter 4. Sabbath Wars

1 Yehuda Lev, "Birthing a State," *Jewish Journal,* May 15–21, 1992.

2 Mishnah *Shabbat* 7:2.

3 In the event of danger to human life, travel by car, like other forms of prohibited activity, is permissible. Indeed, Judaism has allowed Jews to disobey any commandment, including the observance of Shabbat or *kashrut*, in order to save human life.

4 Only the Oriental Jews living in areas like Musrara and Nachla'ot had similar levels of population density in 1967. U. O. Schmelz, "The Population of Reunited Jerusalem, 1967–1985," *American Jewish Yearbook, 1987* (Philadelphia: Jewish Publication Society, 1989), and *Modern Jerusalem's Demographic Evolution*, Jewish Population Studies, No. 20 (Jerusalem: Institute of Contemporary Jewry of the Hebrew University of Jerusalem and the Jerusalem Institute for Israel Studies, 1987).

5 Saul B. Cohen, *Jerusalem – Bridging the Four Walls: A Geopolitical Perspective* (New York: Herzl Press, 1977), esp. pp. 145–171.

6 Other city planners claimed the siting of the road was based on topography alone. Israeli Kimchi, Jerusalem's chief planner, contested Benvenisti's claim. "Who asked him?" Kimchi said. Benvenisti, he said, was just a member of the city council at the time. The road, Kimchi said, was planned as a simple connection between Ramot and the main body of the city. "That's all," he said. And if it were to be a boundary, why did Benvenisti choose a road that was bound to be controversial, rather than an orchard of olives? "It's unreasonable," he concluded. Aharon Sarig, deputy general of Jerusalem, on the other hand, conceded that Benvenisti argued for a compact, Jewish city, which the municipal government opposed.

7 Abraham Rabinovich, "The Stony Way to Ramot," *The Jerusalem Post*, January 16, 1979, p. 6.

8 *The Jerusalem Post*, December 28, 1978, p. 3.

9 Ibid., January 7, 1979, p. 2.

10 Ibid., January 26, 1979, p. 3.

11 Ibid., February 21, 1979, p. 3.
12 Ibid., December 9, 1979, p. 2.
13 Ibid., February 8, 1980, p. 3.
14 Ibid., March 15, 1981, p. 2.
15 Ibid., March 29, 1981, p. 4.
16 Schmelz, "Population of Reunited Jerusalem," pp. 39–109.
17 In 1979, the *haredim* cancelled a planned sports stadium that would have generated an enormous weekly flow of fans each Shabbat. They also opposed, unsuccessfully, a national highway, on the planning boards since 1968, running north–south through Jerusalem. When Route 1 opened in October 1991, several thousand *haredim* rioted against the road. As mounted policemen waded into the crowds, they threw stones at them, shouting, "Nazis! Nazis!" *The Jerusalem Post International Edition*, October 21, 1991, p. 2.
18 This has happened in Mekor Baruch, Rehavia, Shmuel Hanavi, Ramot Eshkol, and French Hill. Bayit Ve-Gan is a noncontiguous *haredi* suburb.
19 Heilman, *Defenders of the Faith*, pp. 324–325.
20 Ibid., p. 326.
21 "The Religious Laws of the Groom on the Marriage Night," mimeograph, n.d. [Hebrew].
22 Joshua Trachtenberg, *Jewish Magic and Superstition: A Study in Folk Religion* (Philadelphia: Jewish Publication Society of America, 1961), p. 185.
23 Raphael Patai, "Exorcism and Xenoglossia Among the Safed Kabbalists," *On Jewish Folklore* (Detroit: Wayne State University Press, 1983), pp. 314–333.
24 Heilman, *Defenders of the Faith*, p. 320.
25 Rachel Biale, *Women and Jewish Law: An Exploration of Women's Issues in Halakhic Sources* (New York: Schocken, 1984), esp. pp. 165–174.
26 *Happiness in Married Life* (Jerusalem: Central Committee for Taharath Hamishpachah [Family Purity] in Israel, n.d.).
27 Trachtenberg, *Jewish Magic and Superstition*, p. 186–187.
28 Biale, *Women and Jewish Law*, esp. pp. 10–43.
29 Heilman, *Defenders of the Faith*, p. 319.
30 Ibid., p. 318.

Chapter 5. To Control the Center

1 Abraham Rabinovich, "For Heaven's Sake," *The Jerusalem Post*, November 4, 1983, p. 3.
2 *The Jerusalem Post*, October 18, 1983, p. 2.
3 This, according to Truman Madsen, president of the Brigham Young University Jerusalem Center for Near Eastern Studies, December 1991. See *Doctrine and Covenants* 45:51–53; 133:13. The Mormons are known for their positive attitude toward the Jews. In the *Book of Mormon*, it is written: "Yea, and ye need not any longer hiss, nor spurn, nor make game of the Jews, nor any of the remnant of the house of Israel; for behold, the Lord remembereth his covenant unto that which he hath sworn" (3 Nephi 29:9).
4 See Naomi Shepherd, *The Mayor and the Citadel: Teddy Kollek and Jerusalem* (London: Weidenfeld and Nicolson, 1987), esp. pp. 96–99.
5 It is twelve hundred meters, or almost a mile, away.
6 "I'm Having a Good Time in Tel-Aviv," *Kol Ha'ir*, August 26, 1983, p. 8;

Thomas L. Friedman, "Orthodoxy of Jerusalem Drives Away Young," *New York Times*, July 21, 1987, p. A2.

7 Yosef Goell, "Fighting Back," *The Jerusalem Post*, October 21, 1983, p. 9.

8 Dan Fisher, "Secular Jews Retaliate in Jerusalem 'Sabbath Wars,' " *Los Angeles Times*, August 26, 1987, p. A7.

9 The map was developed by Arnon Yekutieli, a Meretz Party member of the city council.

10 An informal poll conducted by Anat Hoffman asking Ratz–Shinui voters why they had chosen the party indicated that anti-*haredi* sentiment was the paramount factor. Personal communication to the authors, November 1993.

11 "The *Haredim* Are Satisfied with Election Results," *Kol Ha-Ir*, March 3, 1989, p. 13.

12 Naomi Gutkin-Golan, "The Heikhal Cinema Issue: A Sympton of Religious–Non-Religious Relations in the 1980's," in Charles S. Liebman, ed., *Conflict and Accommodation Between Jews in Israel: Religious and Secular* (Jerusalem: Keter Publishing House, 1990), describes the role of the press and the *haredi* use of photographs of the conflict over cinema opening in a Tel Aviv suburb.

13 Micha Odenheimer, "A Society in Flux," *The Jerusalem Post Magazine*, January 6, 1989, pp. 7, 8.

14 Peter Hirschberg, "Defender of the Dead," *Jerusalem Report*, 1993, pp. 12–13.

15 Yisrael Kimchi, Jerusalem's chief planner, claimed, for example, that the *haredim* had approved the location of Jerusalem's soccer stadium. It was *after* they had been brought into the Likud coalition in 1977 that they made it into an issue. "They were looking," he told us, "for any excuse, anything, to make pressure on the government."

16 Peter Hirschberg, "Votes for Sale," *Jerusalem Report*, November 28, 1991, pp. 14–15.

17 Thomas L. Friedman, "Fight for the Religious Future Builds in Israel," *New York Times*, June 29, 1987, p. A5.

18 Table XIII/9, "Classes and Pupils in Primary Schools, by Type of School and Grade, 1987/88," in Shimon Bigelman, ed., *Statistical Yearbook of Jerusalem, 1987* (Jerusalem: Jerusalem Institute of Israel Studies, 1989), pp. 240–241. Eric Silver, "The Rise of the Ultra-Orthodox," *Jerusalem Report*, December 2, 1993, p. 11.

19 E. P. Thompson, "Time, Work-Discipline, and Industrial Capitalism," *Past and Present*, 38 (1967), pp. 56–97.

Chapter 6. A Few Footsteps for the Messiah

1 See, for example, Dan Kurzman, "The Shadow of Ben-Gurion," *New York Times,* September 19, 1993, p. 17.

2 It was also clear to some of the first anti-Zionist Arab nationalists. Muhammad Y. Muslih, *The Origins of Palestinian Nationalism* (New York: Columbia University Press, 1988), pp. 76–78.

3 Leon Poliakov, *The History of Anti-Semitism* (London: Oxford University Press, 1985), vol. 4.

4 See Erik Cohen, *The City in Zionist Ideology*, Vol. 1 of Jerusalem Urban Studies (Jerusalem: Institute of Urban and Regional Studies and the Eliezer Kaplan School of Economics and Social Sciences of the Hebrew University of Jerusalem, 1970).

5 This turning was associated with the institutionalization of the Holocaust in Israeli national ritual and educational programs. Amos Elon, "The Politics of Memory," *New York Review of Books*, October 7, 1993, pp. 3–5.

6 They based their argument on Babylonian Talmud Ketubot 111a. On the "three oaths," see Amos Funkenstein, "Theological Interpretations of the Holocaust: A Balance," in François Furet, ed., *Unanswered Questions: Nazi Germany and the Genocide of the Jews* (New York: Schocken, 1989), esp. pp. 276–280, and Ravitzky, "Forcing the End: Zionism and the State of Israel as Antimessianic Undertakings," esp. pp. 44–50.

7 Despite Kook's importance, no definitive biography has been completed. J. B. Agus, *High Priest of Rebirth* (New York: Bloch, 1972), which was originally published in 1946, is the best source available.

8 Here we differ from those who argue that Maimonidean tradition opposed messianic thinking or called for Jews not to become active nationalists because Maimonides warned against the disastrous failed revolts against Roman rule in the first and second centuries C.E. See, for example, Ian S. Lustick, *For the Land and the Lord: Jewish Fundamentalism in Israel* (New York: Council on International Relations, 1988), and Gideon Aran, "From Religious Zionism to Zionist Religion: The Roots of Gush Emunim," in Peter Y. Medding, ed., *Studies in Contemporary Jewry* (Bloomington: Indiana University Press, 1986), vol. 2, pp. 116–143, p. 456.

9 *The Code of Maimonides*, 14:5.11, translated by A. M. Hershman (New Haven, Conn.: Yale University Press, 1949), pp. 239–240. See also Amos Funkenstein, "Political Theory and Realistic Messianism," in *Miscellanea Mediaevelia*, Band 11: *Die Machte des Guten und Bosen* (Berlin and New York: Walter de Gruyter, 1977), pp. 81–103.

10 Mishnah *Sotah* 9:15.

11 Abraham Isaac Kook, *The Lights of the Holy*, ed. by David Cohen (Jerusalem: Mossad Ha-Rav Kook, 1985), p. 323 [Hebrew].

12 *Hazon Ha-Geulah, Vision of the Redemption* (Jerusalem: Agudah Lehotzoat Sifre Harayah Kook, 1941), pp. 140–141 [Hebrew].

13 S. Zalman Abramov, *Perpetual Dilemma: Jewish Religion in the Jewish State* (Cranbury, N.J.: Associated University Presses, 1976), p. 101.

14 Zvi Yehuda ha-Cohen Kook, *The Paths of Israel: A Collection of Speeches* (Jerusalem: Menorah, 1969), pp. 17–19 [Hebrew]. See also Richard L. Hoch, "The Politics of Redemption: Rabbi Tzvi Yehudah Ha-Kohen Kook and the Origins of Gush Emunim," Ph.D. dissertation, Department of Religious Studies, University of California, Santa Barbara, 1994.

15 Aran, "From Religious Zionism to Zionist Religion," p. 240; Yohai Baruch Rudik, *Land of Redemption: Ideological Roots of Religious Zionism, Gush Emunim, the Jewish Underground, and Their Relations with the Secular World in the State of Israel* (Jerusalem: Institute for the Study of the Teachings of Rabbi A. I. Kook, of Blessed Memory, 1989).

16 Lustick, *For the Land and the Lord*, p. 106.

17 Richard L. Hoch, *The Politics of Redemption*, pp. 296–334.

18 The group who called themselves Gahelet, or "embers," who would become leaders of the Gush Emunim. Rabbi Moshe Levinger, Rabbi Eliezer Waldman, Rabbi Hanan Porat, and Benny Katzover all studied with him. See Aran, "From Religious Zionism to Zionist Religion," pp. 116–143, and Hoch, *Politics of Redemption*, pp. 233–236.

19 Hoch, *Politics of Redemption*, p. 24.

20 Ehud Sprinzak, *The Ascendance of Israel's Radical Right* (New York: Oxford University Press, 1991), p. 44.
21 Hoch, *Politics of Redemption*, p. 25.
22 His proclamation, called *Lo Taguru*, was, Danny Rubinstein argues, the inspiration for the founding of Gush Emunim. *On The Lord's Side: Gush Emunim* (Tel Aviv: Hakibbutz Hameuchad, 1982), p. 30 [Hebrew].
23 Sprinzak, *Ascendance of Israel's Radical Right*, pp. 46–50.
24 See Walter Laqueur, *A History of Zionism* (New York: Schocken, 1976), pp. 338–383.
25 Shabtai Teveth, *Ben-Gurion and the Palestinian Arabs: From Peace to War* (Oxford: Oxford University Press, 1985), and Avi Shlaim, *Collusion Across the Jordan: King Abdullah, the Zionist Movement, and the Partition of Palestine* (New York: Columbia University Press, 1988).
26 Laqueur, *History of Zionism,* p. 353.
27 Marie Syrkin, "The Revisionist in Power," in *The State of the Jews* (Washington, D.C.: New Republic, 1980), pp. 155–162.
28 Howard M. Sachar, *A History of Israel: From the Rise of Zionism to Our Time* (New York: Knopf, 1976), p. 187.
29 The point is the political distinctiveness of the urban and rural areas, not the geographical distinctiveness of the fighting forces. Given the number of Jews living in them, the cities, in fact, may have provided a majority of the Haganah's fighting forces.
30 See Kurzman, *Ben-Gurion*, p. 293. See Mark Segal, "Arms and the *Altalena*," *The Jerusalem Post*, August 22, 1980, p. 11, where he summarizes Shlomo Nakdimon's book, *Altalena*, and interviews Claire Vaydat, the French connection for Irgun.

Chapter 7. Staking the Claim in Judea and Samaria

1 *Ha-aretz,* September 11, 1967, p. 27.
2 Hoch, *The Politics of Redemption*, pp. 140–141. See also, Danny Rubenstein, *On the Lord's Side: Gush Emunim* (Tel Aviv: Ha-Kibbutz Ha-Meuchad, 1982), p. 30.
3 Sprinzak, *The Ascendance of the Israeli Radical Right*, p. 40.
4 David H. K. Amiran, "Jerusalem's Urban Development," *Middle East Review*, 23.3–4 (Spring/Summer 1981), esp. pp. 59–60, and Saul B. Cohen, "Jerusalem's Unity and West Bank Autonomy: Paired Principles," in Alice L. Eckardt, ed., *Jerusalem: City of the Ages* (Lanham, Md., and New York: University Press of America and the American Academic Association for Peace in the Middle East, 1987), pp. 344–353.
5 Teddy Kollek with Amos Kollek, *For Jerusalem*, p. 225.
6 Hirsh Goodman, "The War That Led to Peace," *Jerusalem Report*, October 7, 1993, pp. 12–14, p. 13.
7 See David Newman, "The Role of Gush Emunim and the Yishuv Kehillati in the West Bank, 1974–1980," Ph.D. dissertation, University of Durham, England, 1981, and W. W. Harris, *Taking Root: Israeli Settlement in the West Bank, Golan, Gaza and Sinai, 1967–1980* (New York: John Wiley, 1980).
8 *The Jerusalem Post*, August 9, 1976, p. 3.
9 Ibid., p. 27.

10 Geoffrey Aronson, *Creating Facts: Israel, Palestinians and the West Bank*, p. 36.

11 Gideon Aran, "Jewish Zionist Fundamentalism: The Bloc of the Faithful in Israel (Gush Emunim)," in Martin E. Marty and R. Scott Appleby, eds., *Fundamentalisms Observed* (Chicago: University of Chicago Press, 1991), pp. 268–271, suggests that Elon Moreh and Sebastia provided the Elon Moreh group with unparalleled moral authority to map out Gush Emunim's ideological, political, and operative front.

12 Sprinzak, *Ascendance of Israel's Radical Right*, p. 145.

13 Sharon meant this as a contingency plan in the event of war with Syria. Uzi Benziman, *Sharon: An Israeli Caesar* (New York: Adama, 1985), pp. 97–98.

14 Sprinzak, *Ascendance of Israel's Radical Right*, p. 127.

15 "A Framework for Peace in the Middle East Agreed at Camp David, 17 September, 1978," in Yehuda Lukacs, ed., *Documents on the Israeli–Palestinian Conflict, 1967–1983* (London: Cambridge University Press, 1984), pp. 63–67.

16 In 1981, it won three Knesset seats; in 1984, five; in 1988, three; and in 1992, it failed to pass the threshold necessary to gain any seats at all.

17 Sprinzak, *Ascendance of the Israeli Right*, pp. 131–132.

18 Meron Benvenisti, *1986 Report: Demographic, Economic, Legal, Social and Political Developments in the West Bank* (Jerusalem: The Jerusalem Post, 1986), pp. 56–57.

19 A. Gerson, *Israel, the West Bank and International Law* (London: Frank Cass, 1978).

20 On the "greenbelt" around Jerusalem see Shaul Ephraim Cohen, *The Politics of Planting: Israeli–Palestinian Competition for Control of Land in the Jerusalem Periphery*, Geography Research Paper No. 23 (Chicago: University of Chicago Press, 1993), esp. pp. 109–131.

21 Interview, Arnon Yekutieli, December 17, 1991.

22 Benvenisti, *Conflicts and Contradictions* (New York: Villard Books, 1986), p. 154; Benvenisti and Shlomo Khayat, *The West Bank and Gaza Atlas* (Jerusalem: The Jerusalem Post, 1988), pp. 59–63.

23 Howard M. Sachar, *A History of Israel, From the Aftermath of The Yom Kippur War* (New York: Oxford University Press, 1987), vol. II, p. 97.

24 Saul Raskin, *Artzenu ve-Amenu: The Land of Palestine* (New York: Saul Raskin, 1947) [Hebrew-Yiddish].

25 A. Abbu Ayyash, "Israeli Regional Planning Policy in the Occupied Territories," *Journal of Palestine Studies*, 5.3–4 (1976), pp. 83–103, and Newman, "The Role of Gush Emunim and the Yishuv Kehillati in the West Bank, 1974–1980."

26 When Likud stepped down in 1984, there were thirty-eight thousand settlers. Meron Benvenisti, *The West Bank Data Project* (Washington, D.C.; American Enterprise Institute, 1984), p. 61; *1986 Report, Demographic, Economic, Legal, Social and Political Developments in the West Bank* (Jerusalem: West Bank Data Project and the Jerusalem Post, 1986); and Benvenisti and Khayat, *West Bank and Gaza Atlas*, pp. 32–33. See also Ibrahim Matar, "Israeli Settlements in the West Bank and Gaza Strip," *Journal of Palestine Studies*, 11.1 (Autumn 1981), pp. 93–110.

27 "From Messiah-Son-of-Joseph to Messiah-Son-of-David," translated interview from *Nekudah*, July 22, 1988, in *New Outlook*, September/October 1988, pp. 15–17.

28 Daniel Williams, "Israel's Ambitious Plans for West Bank Settlement Revealed," *Los Angeles Times*, January 9, 1991, p. A9 and "Israel to Fund New West Bank, Gaza Housing," January 3, 1991, p. A8.

29 Arieh Ya'ari, *Is Annexation Irreversible?* (Tel-Aviv: International Center for Peace in the Middle East, June, 1985), pp. 1–7, and Ian Lustick, *State-Building Failure in British Ireland and French Algeria* (Berkeley, Calif.: Institute of International Studies, 1985).

Chapter 8. Building the Capital

1 Teddy Kollek, with Amos Kollek, *For Jerusalem*, pp. 31 and 121–124.

2 Yossi Klein Halevi, "The Man Who Put Teeth into Moderation," *Jerusalem Report*, December 6, 1990, p. 13.

3 Teddy Kollek, "Sharing United Jerusalem." *Foreign Affairs* (Winter 1988/1989), p. 167.

4 Naomi Shepherd, *The Mayor and the Citadel: Teddy Kollek and Jerusalem* (London: Weidenfeld and Nicolson, 1987), pp. 32–33.

5 See Abraham Rabinovich, *Jerusalem on Earth: People, Passions and Politics in the Holy City* (New York: Free Press, 1988), p. 18, and Shepherd, *Mayor and the Citadel*, p. 26.

6 Tom Sawicki, *The Jerusalem Handbook* (Jerusalem: Jerusalem Institute for Israel Studies and the Anti-Defamation League of B'nai B'rith, 1987), p. 64.

7 Gershom Gorenberg, "Jerusalem and the Uprising," *Present Tense*, Vol. 17, No. 1 (November/December 1989), pp. 45–47.

8 Usama Halabi, "The Jerusalem Arab Municipality" (Jerusalem: PASSIA, 1993) [Arabic].

9 Ashkenasi, "Israeli Policies and Palestinian Fragmentation: Political and Social Impact in Israel and Jerusalem," Policy Studies 24 (Jerusalem: Leonard Davis Institute for International Relations, 1988), pp. 38–39. See also his book, *Palestinian Identities and Preferences: Israel's Jerusalem Arabs* (New York: Praeger, 1992).

10 See Yehuda Z. Blum, "The Juridical Status of Jerusalem," in J. M. Oesterreicher and Anne Sinai, eds., *Jerusalem* (New York: American Academic Association for Peace in the Middle East and John Day Company, 1974), pp. 108–125.

11 In 1994, there were 162,000 Jews living in East Jerusalem, compared to about 140,000 Jews in other occupied territories. *Report of Israeli Settlement in the Occupied Territories*, 5.1 (January 1995), p. 4.

12 Newman, *The Role of Gush Emunim and the Yishuv Kehillati in the West Bank 1974–1980*, pp. 129–133, and Shepherd, *Mayor and the Citadel*, p. 62.

13 As Ibrahim Mattar points out, a number of Palestinian villages' lands were included, while their population centers, such as Beit Hanina and Beit Iksa, Izma, Anata, Bethany, and Abu Dis, were excluded. "From Palestinian to Israeli: Jerusalem 1948–1982," *Journal of Palestine Studies*, 12.4 (Summer 1983), pp. 57–63. The new 1967 boundaries tripled the size of the city and included seventy thousand Arab residents, half of whom had never been residents of Jordanian Jerusalem. Gershon Baskin and Robin Twite, eds., *The Future of Jerusalem* (Jerusalem: Israel/Palestine Center for Research and Information), p. 36. In 1967, Yitzhak Rabin then advised Prime Minister Levi Eshkol and Defense Minister Moshe Dayan to include a much

greater land area in Jerusalem, but they objected because of the number of Arabs who would necessarily be included in Israel's enlarged capital. "Rabin Builds on the Vision of a Permanent Jewish City," *A Report on Israeli Settlement in the Occupied Territories*, Feburary 1994, p. 8. In contrast, Moshe Amirav argues, on the basis of his own interviews with the principals involved in mapmaking at the time, that nobody actually knew how many Arabs there were in the annexed area at the time. Interview, December 19, 1991.

14 Table III/3, "Population in Jerusalem, Tel-Aviv and Haifa," p. 51, and Table III/1, "Population in Israel and Jerusalem, by Population Group," p. 50, in *Statistical Yearbook of Jerusalem* (Jerusalem: Jerusalem Institute of Israel Studies, 1989). By 1991, the population had jumped to over 540,000 people and was continuing to grow rapidly. *Statistical Yearbook of Jerusalem* (Jerusalem: Jerusalem Institute of Israel Studies, 1993).

15 Table III/1, "Population in Israel and Jerusalem, by Population Group," in *Jerusalem Statistical Year Book* (Jerusalem: Jerusalem Institute of Israel Studies, 1989), p. 50.

16 Bill Hutman, "At Least 10,000 Palestinians Live in Jerusalem Illegally," *The Jerusalem Post: International Edition*, May 9, 1992, p. 5.

17 Shepherd, *Mayor and the Citadel,* p. 133.

18 Nathan Krystall, "Who Has the Right to Live There?" *News from Within*, 10.7 (July 1994), pp. 9–13. See also his *Urgent Issues of Palestinian Residency in Jerusalem* (Jerusalem: Alternative Information Center, 1993).

19 In 1991, for instance, the city's total population was 544,200 people, of whom 392,800 were Jews and 151,300 non-Jews. *Statistical Yearbook for Jerusalem, 1991* (Jerusalem: Jerusalem Institute for Israel Studies and the Municipality of Jerusalem, 1993).

20 According to Yisrael Kimchi, Jerusalem chief planner under Kollek, Jerusalem contained – before the most recent expansion in the 1990s – 108 square kilometers. In 1967, Jerusalem was expanded by about 70 square kilometers. Of that, about 25 square kilometers was expropriated. (And of that 25 square kilometers, Kimchi estimated, about 5 square kilometers was Jewish-owned before the 1948 war.) Thus as of 1991, Palestinians owned about 42 percent of the land area and Jews about 48 percent. Interview, Yisrael Kimchi, December 18, 1991.

21 A master plan for the entire city, 3000B, that would allow Israel to confiscate up to 40 percent of Arab areas for public infrastructure – schools, roads, recreational areas – was still under consideration. It would also make possible major Palestinian commercial and industrial development for the first time. Interview, Elinoar Barzaki, December 18, 1991.

22 According to the Palestine Human Rights Information center, as of 1994, of the seventy-three thousand dunam in East Jerusalem, twenty-nine thousand has been or will soon be expropriated, thirty-five thousand dunam was still unplanned, and ten thousand dunam remained on which Palestinians could still potentially build. "Homelessness in Jerusalem," *News from Within*, 10.7 (July 1994) pp. 15–17.

23 PHRIC argued in 1994 that Israel had provided subsidized housing for 70,000 Jewish families in East Jerusalem, while providing such housing for only 555 Palestinian families. See "Statistics on Israeli House Demolition and Planning Policy in East Jerusalem," *News from Within*, 10.7 (July 1994) p. 17. Moshe Amirav, former city council member, claimed in 1990 that

Israel had built seventy thousand apartments for Jews since 1967, and only five thousand for Arabs. "Toward Coexisting in the Capital," *The Jerusalem Post*, October 18, 1990, p. 3.

24 Geoffrey Aronson, "Israel Builds Greater Jerusalem at the Site of the Eternal City," *Settlement Report*, February 1994.

25 Ashkenasi, "Israeli Policies and Palestinian Fragmentation," p. 41.

26 Shaul Cohen, "The Political Geography of Jerusalem: Demographic–Territorial Aspects of the Israeli–Palestinian Conflict" (Jerusalem: Truman Institute, 1992), unpublished paper.

Chapter 9. Suburbs of the Messiah

1 Sprinzak, *The Ascendance of Israel's Radical Right,* pp. 48–49.

2 Moshe Kohn, *Who's Afraid of Gush Emunim?* (Jerusalem: Jerusalem Post Press, 1978), p. 13.

3 Sprinzak, *Ascendance of Israel's Radical Right*, p. 140.

4 Robert I. Friedman, *Zealots for Zion: Inside Israel's West Bank Settlement Movement* (New York: Random House, 1992), pp. 210–211.

5 Benvenisti and Khayat, *West Bank and Gaza Atlas*, p. 10. In 1994, in response to our inquiry, the Israeli government's Office of Information stated that the percentage had not changed.

6 As of 1991, Abraham Ashkenasi estimated that the differential in terms of the cost of a four-room apartment was roughly about $200,000 in central Jerusalem, $100,000 in Pisgat Ze'ev on the inner suburbs, and $65,000 in Maaleh Adumim, a suburb just outside the municipal boundaries.

7 Sprinzak, *Ascendance of Israel's Radical Right*.

8 See Matthew Nesvisky, "Those So-Called Settlements," *Moment*, January/February 1987, pp. 15–19.

9 Ian S. Lustick, *For the Land and the Lord: Jewish Fundamentalism in Israel* (New York: Council on Foreign Relations, 1988), pp. 159–160.

10 Joel Greenberg, "Suburbia in the West Bank," *The Jerusalem Post*, July 9, 1988, p. 5.

11 Robert I. Friedman, "The Brooklyn Avengers," *New York Review of Books*, June 23, 1994, p. 45.

Chapter 10. Defensible Borders

1 Haggai Segal, *Dear Brothers: The West Bank Jewish Underground* (Woodmere, New York: Beit-Shamai, 1988), pp. 162–163.

2 "Settler Vigilante Danger in Areas," *The Jerusalem Post*, March 19, 1988, p. 6. For a catalog of Israeli settler involvement during the *intifada*, see *Punishing a Nation: Human Rights Violations During the Palestinian Uprising, December 1987–December 1988* (Ramallah: Al-Haq, 1989).

3 David Weisburd with Vered Vinitzky, "Vigilantism as Rational Social Control: The Case of Gush Emunim Settlers," in M. Aronoff, ed., *Cross Currents in Israeli Culture and Politics*, *Political Anthropology* (New Brunswick, N.J.: Transaction, 1984), vol. 4, pp. 80–81. On the necessity of independent settler response to Palestinian attacks, see David Weisburd, *Jewish Settler*

Violence: Deviance as Social Reaction (University Park: Pennsylvania State University Press, 1989), pp. 64–85.

4 See, for example, the Israeli-commissioned Karp Report, headed by Yehudit Karp and written by a panel of Israeli jurists appointed by the Israeli attorney general in 1981.

5 "Sentence Increased on Settler Who Shot Palestinian Boy," *The Jerusalem Post*, July 9, 1988, p. 2.

6 F. Robert Hunter, *Palestinian Uprising: A War by Other Means* (Berkeley: University of California Press, 1991), p. 103.

7 It was illegal for Israelis to meet the PLO, but Litani made sure his reporters were at the press conference where Arafat would speak.

8 According to the Database Project on Palestinian Human Rights, Radaha was shot in the head on May 25, 1988, and died two days later. We made repeated efforts to contact the Israeli consulate and embassy in Los Angeles and Washington, D.C., to inquire about this case and received no reply.

9 Letter from Yossi Shoval, director, External Relations Division, April 19, 1994, and Dr. Ran Tur-Kaspa, May 9, 1994.

10 Letter from Zvi Dagan, director, Patient Services Administration, Hadassah Medical Organization, June 20, 1994.

11 Sprinzak, *The Ascendance of Israel's Radical Right*, pp. 159–160.

12 "Shamir Seeks to Ease Rules on Firing at Rock-Throwers," *Los Angeles Times*, September 1, 1988, p. A5.

13 *The Jerusalem Post*, November 13, 1988, p. 4.

14 Joshua Brilliant, "New Militancy Among Settlers," *The Jerusalem Post*, May 19, 1989, p. 3.

15 *The Jerusalem Post: International Edition*, June 3, 1989, p. 7 and Susan Hattis Rolef, "Not All Settlers Are Fanatics," *The Jerusalem Post*, June 6, 1989, p. 2.

16 The original charge was manslaughter. Excerpt from clarifications by Israel to U.S. Undersecretary of State Richard Schifter Concerning the State Department 1990 Human Rights Report, December 13, 1990.

17 Hirsh Goodman, " 'New Lebanon' on West Bank?" *Bulletin*, October 10, 1985, reprinted from *The Jerusalem Post*.

18 The first Palestinian to die as a result of beatings, according to Israeli sources, was Iyad Aql, on Feburary 8, 1988. See Michael Sela, "Soldiers to Be Tried for Beating," *The Jerusalem Post*, April 2, 1989, p. 3. For another case, involving four members of the elite Givati Brigade, see Daniel Williams, "Israeli Army Chief Testifies in Arab's Death, Cites Troops' Vague Orders," *Los Angeles Times*, March 2, 1989, p. A9.

19 Joel Greenberg, "An Erosion of Norms," *The Jerusalem Post: International Edition*, March 10, 1989, p. 3.

20 See, for example, *Al-Fajr*, October 21, 1991, pp. 1, 15.

21 See, for example, Stanley Cohen, "The Myth of 'the Rule of Law,' " *The Jerusalem Post*, January 23, 1989, p. 7. See also David Kretzmer, *The Legal Status of Arabs in Israel* (Boulder, Colo.: Westview Press, 1990).

22 During the first three years of the *intifada*, twenty-five thousand people were arrested annually, eight thousand of whom were subjected to formal interrogation, two thousand of whom were subjected to "intensive methods." In 1988 and 1989, five Palestinians died as a result of the methods of interrogation. See Stanley Cohen, "Talking About Torture in Israel," *Tikkun*, Vol. 6, No. 6, pp. 23–30, 89; Stanley Cohen and Daphna Golan, *The Interrogation*

of Palestinians During the Intifada: Ill-Treatment, 'Moderate Physical Pressure' or Torture* (Jerusalem: B'tselem, 1991). Cohen and Golan show that during the *intifada* force was used when the charges were allegations of assault, stone throwing, belonging to an illegal organization, or participating in a demonstration. "Many interrogations," they note, "are not even aimed at extracting a confession to secure a conviction. Their purpose is general information gathering, random deterrence, intimidation or harm for its own sake."

According to a survey of five hundred ex-prisoners conducted by Dr. Eyad Saraj of the Gaza Community Mental Health Program, 96 percent reported beating, 69 percent suffocation, and 66 percent pressure on their testicles. "Torture: Anomaly or Policy?" *April 17* (August 1993), p. 24.

23 Cohen and Golan, "Interrogation of Palestinians," pp. 84–86.

24 See Abraham Ashkenasi, *Palestinian Identity and Preferences: Israel's Jerusalem Arabs* (New York: Praeger, 1992).

25 Cohen argued that this was true in terms of rights to counsel, due process, and independence of the judiciary.

26 Giora Shamis and Louis Rapoport, "Army Upheaval," *Jewish Journal*, June 9–15, 1989, p. 11.

27 See Ephraim Yuchtman-Yaar, "Democracy in Israel: The Test of Israel's Arab Minority," Department of Sociology and Anthropology, Tel Aviv University, unpublished, January 1988.

28 Rafik Halaby, *The West Bank Story: An Israeli Arab's View of Both Sides of a Tangled Conflict* (New York: Harcourt Brace Jovanovich, 1981), p. 154; Moshe Ma'oz, *Palestinian Leadership on the West Bank: The Changing Role of the Mayors Under Jordan and Israel* (London: Frank Cass, 1984), pp. 156–159, 165–170, and 182–183.

29 After his deportation, Qawasmeh was elected to the PLO Executive Committee. In 1984, rejectionists from Black September murdered him in Amman for his willingness to endorse a territorial compromise with Israel. After shooting him in front of his home, they denounced him as a "Jordanian cop" who had "plotted against the revolution for the benefit of Arafat and King Hussein." John Rice, Associated Press, December 29, 1984.

30 Sprinzak, *Ascendance of Israel's Radical Right,* pp. 96, 256–257.

31 See, for example, the testimony of Daniel Ben-Simon, an underground member, reported in *Davar*, February 27, 1994, cited in "Is a Civil War Between the Israeli Jews Forthcoming?" *Shahak Report*, No. 136 (April 6, 1994), p. 6.

32 Sprinzak, *Ascendance of Israel's Radical Right*, p. 97.

33 Segal, *Dear Brothers*, pp. 95–109.

34 According to the court testimony of Menachem Livni, a leader of the terrorist underground and, with Etzion, mastermind of the plot to blow up the Dome of the Rock, Waldman and Levinger participated in a meeting after the 1980 Palestinian terrorist attack in which the six yeshivah students were murdered in Hebron. At this time it was decided to attack Palestinian political figures. Upon the basis of this testimony, Waldman was arrrested and interrogated. But under Israeli law, the testimony of an accomplice is insufficient evidence upon which to prosecute.

35 Sprinzak, *Ascendance of Israel's Radical Right*, p. 93.

36 See Lustick, *For the Land and the Lord*, p. 190.

37 Here and later, our account of Yamit relies on Segal, *Dear Brothers*, pp. 143–157. See also the special issue of the *Journal of Applied Behavioral*

Science, ed. Erik Cohen, "The Price of Peace: The Removal of the Israeli Settlements in Sinai," vol. 23.1 (1987), and Gideon Aran, *Eretz-Israel Between Politics and Religion: The Movement to Stop the Withdrawal from Sinai*, Jerusalem Institute for Israel Studies, no. 18 (Jerusalem: Jerusalem Institute for Israel Studies, 1985).

38 *Hadashot*, November 5, 1985, p. 4.

39 Sprinzak, *Ascendance of Israel's Radical Right*, p. 67.

40 *The Jerusalem Post: International Edition*, November 16, 1985. Eliakim Ha-Etzni, too, argued that Jews had the right to overthrow the government if it relinquished parts of *eretz-yisrael*. See Lustick, *For the Land and the Lord*, p. 114.

41 Lustick, *For the Land and the Lord*, pp. 159 and 216. Thirty percent of the residents of Kiryat Arba, for example, said they would take up arms rather than evacuate.

42 "From Messiah-Son-of-Joseph to Messiah-Son-of-David," translated interview from *Nekudah*, July 22, 1988, pp. 21–23, in *New Outlook*, September/October 1988, pp. 15–17.

Chapter 11. Platform for Palestine

1 Avi Shlaim, *The Politics of Partition: King Abdullah, the Zionists and Palestine 1921–1951* (New York: Columbia University Press, 1990), esp. pp. 114–134.

2 Philip Mattar, *The Mufti of Jerusalem: Al-Hajj Amin Al-Husayni and the Palestinian National Movement* (New York: Columbia University Press, 1988), pp. 118–119.

3 Alan Hart, *Arafat: Terrorist or Peacemaker?* (London: Sidgwick and Jackson, 1985), p. 75.

4 Mattar, *Mufti of Jerusalem*, p. 117. See also Mary C. Wilson, *King Abdullah, Britain and the Making of Jordan* (Cambridge: Cambridge University Press, 1987), pp. 179–180.

5 Benny Morris, *The Birth of the Palestinian Refugee Problem, 1947–1949* (Cambridge: Cambridge University Press, 1987), pp. 297–298.

6 See Avi Shlaim's abridged version of *Politics of Partition, Collusion Across the Jordan: King Abdullah, the Zionist Movement and the Partition of Palestine* (New York: Columbia University Presss, 1990), pp. 296–303, and Laurie A. Brand, *Palestinians in the Arab World: Institution Building and the Search for State* (New York: Columbia University Press, 1988), pp. 23–25.

7 Helena Cobban, *The Palestine Liberation Organisation: People, Power and Politics* (Cambridge: Cambridge University Press, 1984), p. 180; Zvi Elpeleg, "Why Was 'Independent Palestine' Never Created in 1948?" *Jerusalem Quarterly*, 50 (Spring 1989), p. 20. The Arab League dissolved it in 1952; see Wilson, *King Abdullah*, p. 181.

8 Wilson, *King Abdullah*, pp. 180–182.

9 Shaul Mishal, "Jordanian and Israeli Policy on the West Bank," in Anne Sinai and Allen Pollack, eds., *The Hashemite Kingdom of Jordan and the West Bank* (New York: American Academic Association for Peace in the Middle East, 1977), pp. 210–221. See also Brand, *Palestinians in the Arab World*.

10 See Stavro Danilov, "Dilemmas of Jerusalem's Christians," *Middle East Re-*

view, 13.3–4 (1981), p. 43. Daphne Tsimhoni, "Demographic Trends of the Christian Population in Jerusalem and the West Bank, 1948–1978," *Middle East Journal*, 37 (1983), p. 57.

11 Bernard Sabella, *The Christian Community in Jerusalem and the West Bank and Employment Prospects in the Next Five to Ten Years: A Report Submitted to the Order of the Holy Sepulchre of the Hold Land* (Bethlehem: Privately circulated manuscript, 1987); Ifrach Zilberman, "The Hebronite Migration and the Development of Suburbs in the Metropolitan Area of Jerusalem," in Aharon Layish, ed., *The Arabs in Jerusalem: From the Late Ottoman Period to the Beginning of the 1990's – Religious, Social and Cultural Distinctiveness* (Jerusalem: Magnes Press of the Hebrew University, 1992), pp. 43–63 [Hebrew].

12 See Michael Romann and Alex Weingrod's discussion of the Abu Tor in *Living Together Separately: Arabs and Jews in Contemporary Jerusalem* (Princeton, N.J.: Princeton University Press, 1991), pp. 63–81.

13 Benvenisti, *Jerusalem: The Torn City*, p. 48. Five of the six governors of Jerusalem were from Nablus during the city's Hashemite period. The *shari'a* was dominated, on the other hand, by Hebronites, who were known for their loyalty to the crown. Meron Benvenisti, *Jerusalem: Study of a Polarized Community*, p. 32.

14 Benvenisti, *Jerusalem: The Torn City*, pp. 25–27.

15 Ibid., p. 23.

16 The petition was only published in full in a Lebanese newspaper. See Naim Sofer, "The Political Status of Jerusalem in the Hashemite Kingdom of Jordan, 1948–1967," *Middle Eastern Studies*, 12 (1976), pp. 86–87.

17 Talal, who had suffered a nervous breakdown shortly before, was crowned king in 1952. Shortly afterward, the Jordanian parliament found him mentally incapable, whereupon he abdicated in favor of his eldest son, Hussein, the current king. Wilson, *King Abdullah*, pp. 207–209, 214–215.

18 Except for a quick trip shortly after his coronation in 1953 to inspect repairs. Sofer, "Political Status of Jerusalem," in p. 270.

19 Shaul Mishal, "Jordanian and Israeli Policy on the West Bank," in Anne Sinai and Allen Pollack, eds., *The Hashemite Kingdom of Jordan and the West Bank* (New York: American Academic Association for Peace in the Middle East, 1977), pp. 210–221. See also Brand, *Palestinians in the Arab World*, 1988.

20 Benvenisti, *Jerusalem: The Torn City*, p. 48.

21 Sofer, "Political Status of Jerusalem," in pp. 83–85.

22 The proposal in 1962, he told us in 1993, was for the Golani Brigade to take the south and the paratroopers the north.

23 Cobban, *The Palestine Liberational Organisation*, pp. 24–25; Hart, *Arafat*, p. 97.

24 Cobban, *Palestine Liberation Organisation*, pp. 21–22.

25 Hart, *Arafat*, pp. 161–162.

26 All the Arab governments bordering Israel placed "ruthless restrictions on Palestinian political activity right up until 1967," notes Cobban, *Palestine Liberation Organisation*, pp. 22–23. See also Hart, *Arafat*, pp. 81–82.

27 Cobban, *Palestine Liberation Organisation*, p. 33.

28 Hart, *Arafat*, pp. 128–130.

29 Brand, *Palestinians in the Arab World*, pp. 55–58.

30 Hart, *Arafat*, pp. 162–163.

31 Mishal, "Jordanian and Israeli Policy on the West Bank," in Sinai and Pollack, eds., *Hashemite Kingdom of Jordan and the West Bank*, p. 213.

32 Benvenisti, *Jerusalem: The Torn City*, p. 29.

33 Yehoshafat Harkabi, *The Palestinian Covenant and Its Meaning* (Totowa, N.J.: Vallentine, Mitchell, 1979).

34 Alain Gresh, *The PLO: The Struggle Within – Towards an Independent Palestinian State,* trans. by A. M. Berret (London: Zed Books, 1988), pp. 9, 22.

35 Ibid., p. 21, and Hart, *Arafat*, pp. 160–166.

36 Hart, *Arafat*, pp. 168, 172.

37 Rashid Khalidi, "The Palestinian People: Twenty-Two Years After 1967," in Zachary Lockman and Joel Beinin, eds., *Intifada: The Palestinian Uprising Against Israeli Occupation* (Washington, D.C.: Middle East Research and Information Project, 1989), p. 118.

38 Shaul Mishal, *The PLO Under Arafat: Between Gun and Olive Branch* (New Haven, Conn.: Yale University Press, 1986), pp. 7–8.

39 Hart, *Arafat*, p. 274.

40 Ibid., pp. 172–173, 238–246, 282–283.

41 Gresh, *PLO: The Struggle Within*, p. 23.

42 This eagerness to topple the Hashemite regime was shared by a majority of al-Fatah's own membership. Hart, *Arafat*, p. 303.

43 Henry Kissinger, *The White House Years* (Boston: Little, Brown, 1979), pp. 345, 600.

44 See ibid., p. 598.

45 Hirst, *Gun and the Olive Branch*, p. 307. See also Kissinger, *White House Years*, p. 603.

46 See William B. Quandt, "Politcal and Military Dimensions of Contemporary Palestinian Nationalism," in *The Politics of Palestinian Nationalism* (Berkeley: University of California Press, 1973), p. 128.

47 Hart, *Arafat*, pp. 326–327.

48 Quoted in Gresh, *PLO: The Struggle Within*, p. 83.

49 Ibid., p. 113.

50 Mishal, *PLO Under Arafat*, pp. 114–118.

51 Moshe Ma'oz, *Palestinian Leadership on the West Bank: The Changing Role of the Arab Mayors Under Jordan and Israel* (London: Frank Cass, 1984), p. 120.

52 Hart, *Arafat*, pp. 378–384.

53 Clinton Bailey, "Changing Attitudes Toward Jordan in the West Bank," *Middle East Journal* (Spring 1978), pp. 155–166.

54 See Cobban, *Palestine Liberation Organisation*, p. 56.

55 Gresh, *PLO: The Struggle Within*, p. 89.

56 Ziad Abu-Amr, *Emerging Trends in Palestinian Strategic Political Thinking and Practice* (Jerusalem: Palestinian Academic Society for the Study of International Affairs, 1992), pp. 7–8.

57 Ibrahim Dakkak, "Back to Square One: A Study in the Re-Emergence of the Palestinian Identity in the West Bank, 1967–1980," in Alexander Scholch, ed., *Palestinians over the Green Line: Studies on the Relations Between Palestinians on Both Sides of the 1949 Armistice Line Since 1967* (London: Ithaca Press, 1983), p. 72, and Ma'oz, *Palestinian Leadership*, p. 121.

58 The Communists had created Committees for National Guidance and a National Front in 1968. The front was composed of representatives of banned political organizations, as well as professional associations. Initially concen-

trated in Nablus, the front was repressed in 1969 by Israel and went underground. See Ma'oz, *Palestinian Leadership*, pp. 88, 112–113.

59 Hillel Frisch, "Between Diffusion and Territorial Consolidation in Rebellion: Striking at the Hard Core of the Intifada," *Terrorism and Political Violence*, 3.4 (Winter 1991), pp. 39–62.

60 Cobban, *Palestine Liberation Organisation*, p. 223.

61 Emile Sahliyeh, *In Search of Leadership: West Bank Politics Since 1967* (Washington, D.C.: Brookings Institution, 1988), pp. 42–86.

62 Ibid., pp. 54–57.

63 In 1973, the Palestinian Communists briefly turned to the formation of an armed underground and were crushed by the Israelis. Since then, they have been committed to a path of nonviolent resistance and recognition of Israel within the 1967 borders. Ze'ev Schiff and Ehud Ya'ari, *Intifada: The Palestinian Uprising – Israel's Third Front* (New York: Simon and Schuster, 1990), pp. 199–200. The Palestine Communist Party broke away as an independent party from the Jordanian Communist Party in 1982. See Dakkak, "Back to Square One," p. 75, and Abraham Sela, "The PLO, the West Bank and the Gaza Strip," *Jerusalem Quarterly*, 8 (Summer 1978), pp. 66–77.

64 Sahliyeh, *In Search of Leadership*, pp. 58–63.

65 Ma'oz, *Palestinian Leadership*, p. 118.

66 See Ann Mosely Lesch, *The Political Perceptions of the Palestinians on the West Bank and the Gaza Strip*, Special Study 3 (Washington, D.C.: Middle East Institute, 1980), pp. 65–66, and Sahliyeh, *In Search of Leadership*, p. 55.

67 Ma'oz, *Palestinian Leadership*, pp. 117–118, 124–126.

68 Ibid., p. 119.

69 Ibid., p. 136; Mishal, *PLO Under Arafat*, pp. 110–111.

70 Ma'oz, *Palestinian Leadership*, pp. 139–143.

71 Sahliyeh, *In Search of Leadership*, p. 68.

72 Mark Tessler, "The Camp David Accords and the Palestinian Problem," in *Israel, Egypt, and the Palestinians*, ed. Ann Mosely Lesch and Mark Tessler (Bloomington: Indiana University Press, 1989), pp. 3–22.

73 Begin and Sadat discussed Jerusalem on the last day of their negotiations. Sadat's proposal was to divide sovereignty in Jerusalem but maintain the city as a single municipality with a rotating mayor. Although President Carter had originally referred to East Jerusalem as "occupied territory," the Americans ultimately proposed that the two parties simply agree to negotiate the city's ultimate status as part of the negotiations on the final status of the territories. Begin threatened to walk out of the negotiations if this language were included and the Camp David Accords thus did not mention Jerusalem by name. William Quandt, *Camp David: Peacemaking and Politics* (Washington, D.C.: Brookings Institutions, 1986).

74 Mishal, *PLO Under Arafat*, pp. 120–121.

75 Sachar, *A History of Israel: From the Aftermath of the Yom Kippur War*, p. 87. Ma'oz, *Palestinian Leadership*, p. 181.

76 Sachar, *A History of Israel: From the Aftermath of the Yom Kippur War*, pp. 88–92.

77 Ma'oz, *Palestinian Leadership*, pp. 180–183; Aronson, *Creating Facts*, p. 64.

78 Ma'oz, *Palestinian Leadership*, p. 196.

79 Aronson, *Creating Facts*, p. 259.

80 Ibid., pp. 282–285.

81 Mishal, *PLO Under Arafat*, pp. 134–139, and Sahliyeh, *In Search of Leadership*, pp. 73–77.

82 A number of Palestinians told us this. See Neil Partrick, "Democracy Under Limited Autonomy," *News from Within*, 10.9 (September 1994), pp. 21–24, for a description of the PLO's efforts to undercut the elected mayors associated with the National Guidance Commitee, such as favoring Jordan's opening independent passport offices in the territories so that Palestinians would not be dependent on the mayor's offices, through which passports were normally issued.

83 Gresh, *PLO: The Struggle Within*, p. 44.

84 On December 29, 1984, Qawasmah was assassinated by those who found his politics odious. Arafat blamed the Syrians, whom he denounced as "Arab Zionists" at the funeral.

85 Suha Tawil, "Akram Haniyeh: The Deported Editor of *Al-Shaab* Newspaper," *Return* (October 1988), pp. 16, 31; Joel Greenberg, "Arab Editor Deported," *The Jerusalem Post*, January 1, 1987, p. 3.

86 Bernard Sabella, "Manipulating the Municipalities," *Return* (February 1989), pp. 15–20.

87 Robert I. Friedman, "The PLO in Exile: Waiting for Allah," *Village Voice*, October 23, 1984, pp. 19–23. See also, Hart, *Arafat*, pp. 448–453.

88 Friedman, "PLO in Exile," p. 21.

89 Mary Anne Weaver, "The Chairman and His Wife," *New Yorker*, May 16, 1994, p. 81.

90 John Wallach and Janet Wallach, *The New Palestinians: The Emerging Generation of Leaders* (Rocklin, Calif.: Prima, 1992), p. 136.

91 See the interview with Sartawi, "Dr. Sartawi Speaks His Mind," *New Outlook* (March 1982), pp. 15–16, and Simha Flapan, "Dr. Sartawi – and the Dilemma of Israeli–Palestinian Dialogue," *New Outlook* (March 1982), pp. 17–22.

92 There were at least three cycles of conflict in the "War of the Camps," involving first the Palestinians against the Shi'ite Amal and Druze militias from 1985 to 1987, then the Palestinians against the Syrians from 1987 through 1988, and then finally conflict between Arafat loyalists and the Fatah rebels of Abu Musa with Syrian support from 1988 through 1991. On the Palestinian losses, see Rex Brynen, "PLO Policy in Lebanon: Legacies and Lessons," *Journal of Palestine Studies*, 18.2 (Winter 1989), pp. 48–70, and "Palestinian–Lebanese Relations: A Political Analysis," in Deirdre Collings, ed., *Peace for Lebanon? From War to Reconstruction* (Boulder, Colo.: Lynne Rienner Publishers, 1994).

93 Over half the PLO members in Jordan refused to meet with him when he went to Amman. Joel Greenberg, "Palestinians Back Terror and PLO," *The Jerusalem Post: International Edition*, September 20, 1986, p. 2.

94 Ehud Ya'ari claims that the accord was never signed. "Back to the Future," *Jerusalem Report*, April 9, 1992, p. 28.

95 Gerald F. Seib, "Arafat Asserts He Is Opposed to Terrorism," *Wall Street Journal*, October 21, 1985.

96 Arafat's supporters, ironically, now pressed the Israelis to hold elections yet again, believing they would win. But Israel refused, knowing full well that the PLO, and al-Fatah in particular, would emerge victorious.

97 Aryeh Shalev, *The Intifada: Causes and Effects* (Tel-Aviv and Boulder, Colo.: Jaffee Center for Strategic Studies and Westview Press, 1991), p. 207.

98 See Table XVIII/3, *Statistical Yearbook of Jerusalem, 1984* (Jerusalem: Municipality of Jerusalem and Jerusalem Institute for Israel Studies, 1986), p. 341, and Table XVI/3, *Statistical Yearbook of Jerusalem, 1987* (Jerusalem: Municipality of Jerusalem and Jerusalem Institute for Israel Studies, 1989), p. 275.

99 Edward Norden, "Stars over Jalazoun," *Present Tense* (September/October 1989), pp. 54–56.

100 *Los Angeles Herald Examiner*, November 11, 1985, p. A8; Ze'ev Schiff and Ehud Ya'ari, *Intifada: The Palestinian Uprising*, p. 58.

101 Jamil Hilal, "PLO Institutions: The Challenge Ahead," *Journal of Palestine Studies*, 23.1 (Winter 1993), pp. 46–60.

Chapter 12. Zion for Palestine

1 Romann and Weingrod, *Living Together Separately.*

2 *Palestinians in Profile: A Guide to Leading Palestinians in the Occupied Territories* (Jerusalem: Panorama, 1993).

3 See Romann and Weingrod, *Living Together Separately*, p. 119.

4 Don Peretz, *The West Bank: History, Politics, Society and Economy* (Boulder, Colo.: Westview Press, 1986), p. 93.

5 Shaul Cohen, "The Political Geography of Jerusalem" (Jerusalem: The Truman Institute, 1992), unpublished paper.

6 Benvenisti and Khayat, *West Bank and Gaza Atlas*, pp. 28–29.

7 Benedict Anderson, *Imagined Communities*, pp. 23–46.

8 Ma'oz, *Palestinian Leadership on the West Bank*, p. 135.

9 Gresh, *PLO: The Struggle Within*, p. 44.

10 Accepting the right of Jews to remain in Palestine was a major change in PLO thinking. Ibid., pp. 101–103.

11 Ibid., p. 66.

12 Ibid., p. 105.

13 Ibid., pp. 73–80.

14 Sahliyeh, *In Search of Leadership*, pp. 42–43.

15 *The Jerusalem Post*, December 7, 1983, p. 2.

16 David Richardson, "West Bank Leaders Condemn Terror Attack," *The Jerusalem Post*, December 8, 1983, p. 2.

17 Mel Layner, United Press International, December 8, 1983.

18 The Jerusalem *waqf*, or endowment department, is run by the Council for Endowments and Islamic Affairs. Yitzhak Reiter, "Islamic Religious Organization in Jerusalem," in Ifrah Zilberman, ed., *Palestinian Society and Politics in Jerusalem: Twenty-Five Years of Israeli Rule* (Jersualem: Truman Institute, 1992), unpublished manuscript.

19 Yitzhak Reiter, *Islamic Awqaf in Jerusalem, 1948–1990* (Jerusalem: Jerusalem Institute for Israel Studies, 1991), p. 3. Aharon Layish, "The Muslim *Waqf* in Jerusalem Since 1967: Beneficiaries and Management," in Abaron Layish, ed., *The Arabs in Jerusalem: From the Late Ottoman Period to the Beginning of the 1990's – Religious, Social and Cultural Distinctiveness* (Jerusalem: The Israel Oriental Society, Jerusalem Institute for Israel Studies and Magnes Press of the Hebrew Univerrsity, 1992), pp. 95–114.

20 Sahliyeh, *In Search of Leadership*, pp. 24–33; Ma'oz, *Palestinian Leadership*; Mishal, *PLO Under Arafat.*

21 The first borough plans were developed in the 1930s and 1940s as communal

conflict in Jerusalem became increasingly intractable. Cecilia Albin, "Strategies and Options in the Jerusalem Conflict," in Zilberman, ed., *Palestinian Society and Politics*.

22 Dakkak, "Back to Square One: A Study in the Re-Emergence of the Palestinian Identity in the West Bank, 1967–1980," pp. 71–73.

23 Teddy Kollek, with Amos Kollek, *For Jerusalem*, p. 241.

24 Moskin, *Among Lions: The Battle for Jerusalem, June 5–7, 1967*, p. 232.

25 Martin Malin, "The West Bank: Israel's Policies and Palestinian Political Behavior, 1967–1976," unpublished paper (Hebrew University of Jerusalem, 1983).

26 Michael T. Dumper, "Jerusalem's Infrastructure: Is Annexation Irreversible?" *Journal of Palestine Studies*, 22.3 (Spring), 1993, pp. 78–95. See also Naomi Shepherd, *The Mayor and the Citadel: Teddy Kollek and Jerusalem*, pp. 130–132.

27 Elpeleg, "Why Was 'Independent Palestine' Never Created in 1948?" *Jerusalem Quarterly*, pp. 3–22. Beyond our interviews with Husayni, we have also consulted John and Janet Wallach, *Still Small Voices* (San Diego: Harcourt Brace Jovanovich, 1989), pp. 77–97, and Shukri Abed, "Profile of a Leader: Faisal Hussaini," *Return*, August 1988, pp. 10–11, as well as assorted clippings and articles from *The Jerusalem Post* and *Jerusalem Report*.

28 Schiff and Ya'ari, *Intifada*, pp. 274–278. During the three-year transitional phase, the self-governing authority would have its own flag, national anthem, independent broadcasting service, identity cards, and travel documents. This was very much the kind of agreement that the Labour government would strike six years later.

29 Although Schiff and Ya'ari argue that Amirav negotiated well beyond the scope of what Shamir would tolerate, Amirav himself claimed to us that Shamir "knew about all the meetings," that he reported to Shamir, and that it was his going public that made Shamir back away. The crunch, Amirav claimed, occurred when Shamir learned from Israeli intelligence services that the Romanian president would discuss proposals that Amirav and Husayni had formulated. "Moshe, that's it," Shamir reportedly told him on the phone.

30 Yehuda Litani, "Palestinian Leaders from Areas Meet PLO in Tunis or Cairo – with Knowledge of Defence Ministry," *The Jerusalem Post*, September 27, 1989, p. 2.

31 Abed, "Profile of a Leader: Faisal Husseini," pp. 10–11.

32 Dvorah Getzler, "Rabin Signal to Jordan: No PLO," *The Jerusalem Post: International Edition*, August 8, 1987, p. 6.

33 Dan Petreanu and Menachem Shalev, "Shamir Lambasts 'Useless' Meetings with Husseini," *The Jerusalem Post*, February 17, 1989, p. 1.

34 Daoud Kuttab, "Deaths and Deportations," *Middle East International*, No. 358 (September 8, 1989), pp. 5–6.

35 Joel Greenberg, "IDF Prevents Peace Now from Entering Tulkarm," *The Jerusalem Post*, October 8, 1989, p. 3.

Chapter 13. A State of Mind

1 Schiff and Ya'ari, *Intifada*, pp. 23, 25.

2 Yehuda Litani, "For the Sake of Friendship," *The Jerusalem Post*, July 7, 1989, p. 9; Schiff and Ya'ari, *Intifada*, pp. 33–40, 117–118.

3 Schiff and Ya'ari, *Intifada*, p. 47.
4 Ibid., pp. 267–268.
5 *Journal of Palestine Studies*, 16.2 (Winter 1987), p. 202.
6 Thomas Parker, "Les maires de la Cisjordanie et de Gaza: Leur politique et leurs doleances," *Politique Etrangere*, 3 (1978), pp. 331–345.
7 Benvenisti, *West Bank Data Project: A Survey of Israel's Policies*, p. 13.
8 This is also the case in Jerusalem. Romann and Weingrod, *Living Together Separately*, p. 117.
9 Asher Susser, "Jordanian Influence in the West Bank," *Jerusalem Quarterly*, 8 (Summer 1978), pp. 53–65.
10 Schiff and Ya'ari, *Intifada*, p. 203.
11 Pamela Ann Smith, *Palestine and the Palestinians, 1876–1983* (New York: St. Martin's Press, 1984), p. 24.
12 This statement is based on interviews during the last decade with Palestinians, men and women who came from many political streams within the PLO as well as a number of people identified with the Hashemites. These kinds of statements were always made off the record and we do not attribute them. By 1994, charges of PLO corruption were being made publicly by many Palestinians aligned with the PLO.
13 Between 1967 and 1984, 343 people died in 332 separate violent Palestinian attacks in Israel.
14 Based on data for murder and nonnegligent manslaughter figures, *Crime in the United States* (Washington, D.C.: Federal Bureau of Investigation, 1985).
15 Khalidi, "The Palestinian People: Twenty-Two Years After 1967," in Lockman and Beinin, *Intifada*, p. 119.
16 *Journal of Palestine Studies*, 16.2 (Winter 1987), pp. 196–207, contains the poll and the results.
17 Cobban, *Palestinian Liberation Organisation*, p. 257.
18 Mishal, *PLO Under Arafat*, pp. 31–32.
19 Gresh, *PLO: The Struggle Within*, pp. 68–69. See also Dan Bavly, "A Palestinian Who Wanted to Make Peace," *The Jerusalem Post*, November 28, 1986, p. 7.
20 Aziz Shehada, "The Voice of the Forgotten Palestinian," *New Middle East*, December 1968, pp. 14–15. And the next year, Muhammad Ali al-Jabari, a Hebronite Muslim, put forward the same idea.
21 Jamil Hamad, "Palestinian Future: New Directions," *New Middle East* (August 1971), pp. 16–19, and Malin, "The West Bank: Israel's Policies and Palestinian Political Behavior."
22 Clinton Bailey, "Changing Attitudes Toward Jordan in the West Bank," *Middle East Journal* (Spring 1978), p. 159.
23 Sahliyeh, *In Search of Leadership*, p. 58.
24 Howard Sachar, *History of History*, vol. II, p. 87.
25 Ashkenasi, *Palestinian Identities and Preferences*, p. 86, provided an estimate in 1992 of twelve thousand unemployed Palestinians with university degrees. Schiff and Ya'ari, *Intifada*, p. 91.
26 Of the 800,000 Palestinians working in the Gulf, 165,000 were from the West Bank and Gaza as of 1990. Samir Barghouthi, "Palestinian Economy Is Also Suffering from Gulf Crisis," *Al-Fajr*, October 8, 1990, pp. 5, 15.
27 This was true in Jerusalem as well. See, Ashkenasi, "Israeli Policies and Palestinian Fragmentation: Political and Social Impacts in Israel and Jerusalem," pp. 21–31.

28 Meron Benvenisti, *1987 Report: Demographic, Economic, Legal, Social and Political Developments in the West Bank* (Jerusalem: West Bank Data Base Project, 1987), pp. 34–35.

29 Schiff and Ya'ari, *Intifada*, pp. 213.

30 For the same reason, Hussein opposed an international solution to the Lebanese civil war in 1989, fearing an enforced cantonization would inevitably lead to expulsion of the Palestinians. See Lamis Andoni, "Jordanian Alarm Bells," *Middle East International*, September 8, 1989, pp. 5–6.

31 Sahliyeh, *In Search of Leadership*, p. 174.

32 "The *Al-Fajr* Public Opinion Survey," *Journal of Palestine Studies* 16.2 (Winter 1987), pp. 196–207.

33 See also the *Al-Fajr* poll conducted in September 1986, discussed by Daoud Kuttab, in *Journal of Palestine Studies*, 16.2 (Winter 1987), pp. 149–153. Among the Israelis, the only option then capable of generating even a modicum of support was Labour's proposed Jordanian confederation. Michael Inbar and Ephraim Yuchtman-Yaar, "The People's Image of Conflict Resolution: A Comparative Survey of Israelis and Palestinians," Department of Sociology, Tel Aviv University, 1987, unpublished paper.

34 Joost Hiltermann, *Behind the Intifada: Labor and Women's Movements in the Occupied Territories* (Princeton, N.J.: Princeton University Press, 1991).

35 Knesset member Shulamit Aloni charged this according to *The Jerusalem Post*, August 2, 1989, p. 3.

36 See Paul Steinberg and A. M. Oliver, *The Graffiti of the Intifada: A Brief Survey* (Jerusalem: Palestinian Academic Society for the Study of International Affairs, 1990), and Ziad Abu-Amr, *Islamic Fundamentalism in the West Bank and Gaza* (Bloomington: Indiana University Press, 1994), p. 78.

37 Edy Kaufman, "Israeli Perceptions of the Palestinians' 'Limited Violence' in the Intifada," July 1991, unpublished paper.

38 *The Jerusalem Post*, February 5, 1989, p. 4.

39 Jahal Ahmad, "Israel Has to Accept the Palestinian Reality," *Filastin al-Thawra*, September 25, 1988, pp. 4–5.

40 See Gershon Shafir, *Land, Labor and the Origins of the Israeli–Palestinian Conflict, 1882–1914* (New York: Cambridge University Press, 1989). On the conflict over limited land in generating collectivist Jewish institutions, see Baruch Kimmerling, *Zionism and Territory: The Socio-Territorial Dimensions of Zionist Politics* (Berkeley, Calif.: Institute of International Studies, 1983).

41 Salim Tamari reports that because of their monopoly on the Palestinian market, Palestinian manufacturers were able to do very well despite the enormous drop in the Palestinian standard of living. This caused considerable resentment among Palestinian merchants. "Revolt of the Petite Bourgeoisie: Urban Merchants and the Palestinian Uprising," in Michael C. Hudson, ed., *The Palestinians: New Directions* (Georgetown, Md.: Center for Contemporary Arab Studies, 1990), p. 39.

42 Judy Maltz, "PLO Colours on Spaghetti Packaging," *The Jerusalem Post*, October 26, 1989, p. 3.

43 In 1993, about 130,000 Palestinians from the territories worked in Israel; their wages accounted for about one third of its GNP. "Economic Impact of Israeli Military Closure," *News from Within* (June 1993), pp. 7–9.

44 See Benvenisti, *West Bank Data Project*, p. 10.

45 Andy Court, "Issawiya Curfew Lifted After Five Days," *The Jerusalem Post*, March 14, 1989, p. 5.

46 Tamari argues that because of Israeli retaliation and the Palestinian granting of exemptions to Palestinian manufacturers, allowing them to pay their taxes so that they could continue to provide employment for Palestinians, tax resistance ultimately failed. This was due both to the economic losses suffered and to the emergence of a conflict between merchants and manufacturers. "Revolt of the Petite Bourgeosie," pp. 37–39.

47 Andy Court and Ben Lynfield, "Histadrut Plans High Court Appeal Against NII for Suspending East Jerusalemites' Payments," *The Jerusalem Post*, March 15, 1989, p. 5.

48 Tamari, "Revolt of the Petite Bourgeoisie," pp. 26–27.

49 Ibid. However, city officials told us some merchants pleaded with the Israelis to "force" them to open.

50 Kenneth W. Stein, *The Intifadah and the 1936–1939 Uprising: A Comparison of the Palestinian Arab Communities* (Atlanta: Carter Center of Emory University, 1989).

51 Tamari, "Revolt of the Petite Bourgeoisie," p. 34.

52 Yehuda Litani and Joel Greenberg, "Complaints over Smashed Watches Set According to 'Palestinian Time,' " *Jerusalem Post*, April 25, 1989, p. 1.

53 A. D. Gordon, "Our Tasks Ahead," in Arthur Hertzberg, ed., *The Zionist Idea: A Historical Analysis and Reader* (New York: Atheneum, 1986), p. 381.

54 Likewise in 1990, when Palestinian industrialists sought to create a Chamber of Industry under the United Nations Development Program, Israel stopped them. Barghouthi, "Palestinian Economy," *Al-Fajr*, October 8, 1990, pp. 5, 15. In fact, so many Palestinians planted new crops that they flooded the market, causing prices to plummet so that many people lost their initial investment.

55 Robert Rosenberg, a reporter for *The Jerusalem Post*, told us in 1983 that of the 150 successful and attempted bombings in Jerusalem between 1977 and 1982, in only 4 were the suspects from Jerusalem.

56 This inference is based on discussions with numerous Israeli officials over the years. Using empirical data to bolster such a conclusion is fraught with difficulty. Ashkenasi, *Palestinian Identities and Preferences,* p. 84, points out that in 1984 the ratio of security cases tried in Jerusalem to those in the West Bank was one to ten. Given that the ratio of population of the two areas is one to seven, this suggests a significant underrepresentation of Jerusalemite Arabs. However, Ashkenasi believes that this is partly the result of the Arab Jerusalemites' living under the Israeli civil legal system and not the "ambitious, arbitrary and often provocative military system" of the occupied territories. However, at the same time, all incidents are likely to be reported in Jerusalem when compared to other occupied territories, where detection and reportage are both less likely. See Aryeh Shalev, *The Intifada: Causes and Effects* (Boulder, Colo. and Jerusalem: Westview Press and The Jerusalem Post, 1991), p. 195.

57 Ashkenasi, *Palestinian Identities and Preferences,* p. 84. However, in the *intifada's* first full year, 1988, there were, for example, 92 arsons reported in Jerusalem compared to 315 in the West Bank, a ratio of 0.29, more than twice Jerusalem's proportion of the Arab population. We cannnot estimate the extent to which this proportion is biased upward by the greater likelihood of reporting in Jerusalem. Thus, for example, examining the number of Palestinians arrested, the proportion of Jerusalemites arrested in the first

year was about 10 percent, an underrepresentation. See Shalev, *Intifada: Causes and Effects*, pp. 74, 208–209, 219.

58 The very first confrontations, which began on December 19, 1987, were, in fact, organized by outsiders. Schiff and Ya'ari, *Intifada*, pp. 106–113. A majority of the *intifada* "activists" in Jerusalem came from outside the Palestinian-defined city of Jerusalem, from other villages in the West Bank like Ram, al-Azariya, or Abu Dis. See Ashkenasi, *Palestinian Identities and Preferences*, p. 84.

59 Schiff and Ya'ari, *Intifada*, p. 112. In addition, in response to Palestinian incidents, Israeli police, who were not allowed to use plastic bullets as elsewhere in the West Bank and Gaza, were likely to be rapidly and strongly reinforced. Shalev, *Intifada: Causes and Effects*, p. 78.

60 Nadav Shraga'i, "Jerusalem a Border Town Again," *Ha-aretz*, July 9, 1993, reprinted in *Middle East International*, 455 (July 23, 1993), p. 22.

61 Romann and Weingrod, *Living Together Separately*, 1991, pp. 53–55.

62 Abraham Rabinovich, "Teddy Holds the Fort," *The Jerusalem Post: International Edition*, March 11, 1989, pp. 9–10. His adviser for East Jerusalem affairs, Amir Cheshin, suffered a serious heart attack.

63 Romann and Weingrod, *Living Together Separately*, pp. 107–108.

64 And the real count was probably even less. Kollek's opponents found large numbers of fraudulent Arab votes. Yizhar Be'er, "Controversy Arises over Election on Beit Safafa," *Kol Ha-ir*, March 17, 1989, p. 11 [Hebrew], and Andy Court, "Likud Wants Probe of Reported Election Fraud in J'lem," *The Jerusalem Post*, March 20, 1989, p. 2.

65 Municipality of Jerusalem, press release, March 1, 1989.

66 Interview, December 12, 1991, Bonnie Boxer, spokesperson, Mayor Teddy Kollek's office.

67 *New Israel Fund Report*, 8.3 (Fall 1989).

68 The command initially grew out of an existent committee in the city to coordinate demonstrations and strikes and to mediate political conflicts among al-Fatah, DFLP, PFLP, and the Communists. Schiff and Ya'ari, *Intifada*, p. 195.

69 Schiff and Ya'ari argue that they purposefully kept their identities secret, even after being apprehended or exiled, both to conceal their ordinary and undistinguished backgrounds, as well as to avoid repression by the PLO outside. *Intifada*, pp. 190–191.

70 Penny Johnson and Lee O'Brien with Joost Hiltermann, "The West Bank Rises Up," in Lockman and Beinin, eds., *Intifada*, p. 30.

71 Tamari, "Revolt of the Petite Bourgeoisie," p. 34.

72 Joe Stork, "The Significance of Stones: Notes from the Seventh Month," in Lockman and Beinin, eds., *Intifada*, p. 73.

73 Schiff and Ya'ari, *Intifada*, pp. 194–195, 209.

74 On the formation of the leadership as a fait accompli, see ibid., p. 195.

75 Ibid., p. 217.

76 Ziad Abu-Amr, "The Politics of the Intifada," in Hudson, *Palestinians: New Directions*, p. 17. It was Arafat who demanded that their handbills bear the PLO's signature, initially proposing it be understood as an "arm" of the PLO. When its members were deported, Arafat refused to give them any kind of public standing. Eventually, leaflets were read and then composed in Tunis. Schiff and Ya'ari, *Intifada*, pp. 191–192, 216–217.

77 Interview, Salim Tamari, January 3, 1989. Tamari argued that the critiques

came just as much from within the dominant partisan streams, including Fatah, as they did from opposition forces that had been disadvantaged by this structure.

78 Adam Garfinkle, "Getting It Right? US Mideast Policy in the Bush Administration," *Jerusalem Quarterly*, 52 (Fall 1989), p. 64.

79 Joel Greenberg, "Freij Not in Hiding – Working as Usual," *The Jerusalem Post*, January 6, 1989, p. 2.

80 "Statement Issued by Arafat's Office, 20 January, 1989," *Return* (Feburary 1989), p. 14.

81 There were a large number of forged leaflets. That this, however, was given to us by a prominent Palestinian nationalist, Dr. Jad Isaac, suggests it was not.

82 The Unified Leadership issued its own condemnation of Freij's call for a truce. Although it also said that those who wanted to stop the *intifada* should be silenced, it made no mention of killing them. Abu-Amr, "Politics of the Intifada," p. 14.

83 The king claimed that Jordan had supported an independent Palestinian state ever since 1972. Directorate of Publications, Jordan, "Jordan's Recent Position on Jordanian Palestinian Relations," August 1, 1988, John Kifner, "King Warns Palestinians Residing in Jordan to Maintain Stability," *New York Times*, August 1, 1988, pp. A2, A9, and "Speech by King Hussein of Jordan Renouncing Claim to the West Bank and Gaza, July 31, 1988," *American Arab Affairs*, 25 (Summer 1988), pp. 194–198.

84 The notion of Hussein's withdrawal as a lure that pushed Arafat to the West Bankers is developed in Garfinkle, "Getting It Right?" pp. 57–58.

85 Yitzhak Reiter, *Islamic Awqaf in Jerusalem* (Jerusalem: Jerusalem Institute for Israel Studies, 1991), pp. 3–4.

86 Garfinkle, "Getting It Right?" p. 64.

87 Mahdi F. Abdul-Hadi, "The Jordanian Disengagement: Causes and Effects" (East Jerusalem: Palestinian Academic Society for the Study of International Affairs, 1988), p. 4.

88 The draft bore striking similarities to a strategy proposal made by an American Jewish academic, Jerome Segal, which was published in Jerusalem's largest Arabic paper, *Al-Quds*, in April 1988.

89 See Schiff and Ya'ari, *Intifada*, pp. 278–280, for an account of Husayni's political plan.

90 The entire text of the draft, "The Palestine Independence Document Prepared by Faisal Husseini of the Jerusalem Arab Studies Society," is reprinted in Peretz, *Intifada*, appendix 4, pp. 204–207. Yehuda Litani, Elaine Ruth Fletcher, and Joel Greenberg, "PLO Statehood Plan Is Dismissed a 'Crazy Dream," *The Jerusalem Post: International Edition*, August 13, 1988, p. 9.

91 Dan Fisher, "Israel's Arrest of Arab Tied to Plan for West Bank State," *Los Angeles Times*, August 7, 1988, pp. A1, A13.

92 Bassam Abu Sharif, "Prospects of a Palestinian–Israeli Settlement, Algiers, June 7, 1988," in Don Peretz, *Intifada: The Palestinian Uprising* (Boulder, Colo.: Westview Press, 1990), appendix 5, pp. 208–210.

93 Edward W. Said, "Intifada and Independence," in Lockman and Beinin, eds., *Intifada: The Palestinian Uprising Against Israeli Occupation*, p. 16.

94 From the official English translation, "The Palestinian Declaration of Independence," *Return* (December 1988), pp. 32–34.

95 "Palestine National Council, 'Political Communiqué,' Algiers, 15 November

1988," in Peretz, *Intifada: The Palestinian Uprising*, appendix 7, pp. 215–219, and "Political Statement – Adopted by the Palestine National Council at the Conclusion of Its Meeting Held in Algiers November 11–15, 1988," *Return* (December 1988), pp. 35–38.

96 Phil Baum and Raphael Danziger, "A Regenerated PLO? The Palestine National Council's 1988 Resolutions and Their Repercussions," *Middle East Review* (Fall 1989), pp. 17–25.

97 Baum and Danziger, "Regenerated PLO?" p. 20.

98 Ahmad Abdul Rahman, "The Settlement Is with America and Not with Israel," *Filastin al-Thawra*, July 5, 1989, p. 13.

99 Daniel Williams, "Israel Jails Two Palestinian Nationalist Leaders," *Los Angeles Times*, November 14, 1990, pp. A1, A14.

100 Wallach and Wallach, *New Palestinians*, pp. 134–135.

101 Shimon Bigelman, ed., *Statistical Yearbook of Jerusalem, 1987* (Jerusalem: Jerusalem Institute for Israel Studies, 1989), pp. 274–275.

102 Don Peretz, "Intifadeh: The Palestinian Uprising," *Foreign Affairs*, 66.5 (1987), pp. 964–980.

103 Benny Morris, *The Birth of the Palestinian Refugee Problem, 1947–1949* (Cambridge: Cambridge University Press, 1987), esp. pp. 203–212.

Chapter 14. The Islamic Challenge

1 Schiff and Ya'ari, *Intifada,* pp. 273–279. See also Dan Fisher, "Israel's Arrest of Arab Tied to Plan for West Bank State," *Los Angeles Times,* August 7, 1988, pp. 9–10.

2 Richard P. Mitchell, *The Society of the Muslim Brothers* (London: Oxford University Press, 1969), p. 5.

3 John Voll, "Fundamentalism in the Sunni Arab World: Egypt and the Sudan," in Martin E. Marty and R. Scott Appleby, eds., *Fundamentalisms Observed: The Fundamentalism Project* (Chicago: University of Chicago Press, 1991), vol. 1, pp. 362–363.

4 Mattar, *The Mufti of Jerusalem: Al-Hajj Amin al-Husayni and the Palestinian National Movement*, pp. 108–110.

5 Raphael Israeli, *Muslim Fundamentalism in Israel* (London: Brassey's, 1993), p. 16.

6 Mitchell, *The Society of Muslim Brothers*, p. 267.

7 Ibid., pp. 66–73.

8 Hart, *Arafat*, p. 84.

9 Mohammed K. Shadid, "The Muslim Brotherhood Movement in the West Bank and Gaza," *Third World Quarterly*, 10.2 (1988), p. 662.

10 Sofer, "The Political Status of Jerusalem in the Hashemite Kingdom of Jordan," p. 261.

11 Yitzhak Reiter, *Islamic Awqaf in Jerusalem, 1948–1990* (Jerusalem: Jerusalem Institute for Israel Studies, 1991), pp. 13–14.

12 For example, six million dinars came in from Jordan in 1992. Reiter, "Islamic Religious Organization in Jerusalem," p. 12. Hasan Tabbub, elected as the president of the Supreme Muslim Council in 1993, told us that the council's budget had always required massive infusion of funds from Jordan. He estimated that the income from endowments and entrance fees amounted to no more than 20 percent of their budget.

13 See Hart, *Arafat*, pp. 86, 104.

14 Janet Wallach and John Wallach, *Arafat: In the Eyes of the Beholder* (New York: Lyle Stuart, 1990), pp. 74–75.

15 Hart, *Arafat*, pp. 104–105.

16 Khalil Wazir claimed that they chose the name *Fatah* with no thought of the Islamic past. Hart, *Arafat*, p. 127.

17 David Hirst, *The Gun and the Olive Branch: The Roots of Violence in the Middle East* (London: Faber and Faber), 1984, pp. 75–78; Migdal and Kimmerling, *Palestinians*, pp. 61–63.

18 See, for example, Fadwa Tuqan, *A Mountainous Journey: A Poet's Autobiography*, trans. by O. Kenny (Saint Paul: Graywolf Press, 1990), p. 82.

19 Israeli, *Muslim Fundamentalism in Israel*, p. 18.

20 Nels Johnson, quoting a Palestinian informant, *Islam and the Politics of Meaning in Palestinian Nationalism* (London: Kegan Paul International, 1982), p. 81.

21 Ibid., p. 82. *Jihad*, loosely translated as "holy war"; *mujahid*, one who struggles or a fighter in a holy war; and *shahid*, martyr or one who has died on the path of God, all function as synonyms for Fatah's central nationalist terminology of *thawrah*, "revolution," and *fida'i*, one who sacrifices for the national cause. Many Palestinians equate jihad and *thawrah*, or "revolution," and even Christian Palestinians use jihad as a nonreligious term for the "struggle" to regain Palestine.

22 Ibid., p. 78.

23 Ibid., pp. 91–92.

24 Matti Steinberg, "The PLO and Palestinian Islamic Fundamentalism," *Jerusalem Quarterly*, 52 (Fall 1989), p. 39.

25 Cited in A. L. Tibawi, "Visions of the Return: The Palestine Arab Refugees in Arabic Poetry and Art," *Middle East Journal*, 17 (1963), p. 523.

26 Fouad Ajami, *The Arab Predicament: Arab Political Thought and Practice Since 1967* (Cambridge and New York: Cambridge University Press, 1981), pp. 50–51. Shadid, "Muslim Brotherhood Movement in the West Bank and Gaza," pp. 668–669.

27 Abu-Amr, *Islamic Fundamentalism in the West Bank and Gaza*, p. 11.

28 Sabri did not explicitly state that he belonged to the Muslim Brotherhood. However, three sources indicated to us that he either belonged or was sympathetic to its world view: Osman Hallak, editor of *Al-Nahar*, December 15, 1991; Ifrah Zilberman, researcher, Truman Institute, December 17, 1991; Clinton Bailey, professor of anthropology, Tel Aviv University, December 15, 1991.

29 The difference in religiosity between West Bank and Gazan Muslims, though it may be statistically significant, is not great in terms of magnitude. Shadid, "Muslim Brotherhood Movement in the West Bank and Gaza," pp. 663–664.

30 Ibid., p. 672.

31 Ajami, *Arab Predicament*, p. 70.

32 Mishal, "Paper War," p. 72.

33 Emile Sahliyeh, *In Search of Leadership: West Bank Politics Since 1967* (Washington, D.C.: Brookings Institution, 1988), p. 145.

34 Shadid, "Muslim Brotherhood Movement in the West Bank and Gaza," p. 673.

35 Abu-Amr, *Islamic Fundamentalism in the West Bank and Gaza*, p. 16.

36 Sahliyeh, *In Search of Leadership*, p. 145.

37 Abu-Amr, *Islamic Fundamentalism in the West Bank and Gaza*, p. 17, suggests that as of the early 1990s, Al-Mujamma'a al-Islami directly controlled about 40 percent of the mosques in Gaza.

38 Shadid, "Muslim Brotherhood Movement in the West Bank and Gaza," pp. 673–674.

39 Michael Taussig, *Mimesis and Alterity: A Particular History of the Senses* (New York: Routledge, 1993), p. 185.

40 Shadid, "Muslim Brotherhood Movement in the West Bank and Gaza," p. 671.

41 Abu-Amr, *Islamic Fundamentalism in the West Bank and Gaza*, pp. 15–16. In the same period, total Arab population grew by much less, about a quarter.

42 Shadid, "Muslim Brotherhood Movement in the West Bank and Gaza," pp. 663–664.

43 Lisa Taraki, "The Islamic Resistance Movement in the Palestinian Uprising," in Lockman and Beinin, eds., *Intifada: The Palestinian Uprising Against Israeli Occupation*, pp. 171–177.

44 Jean-François Legrain, "Palestinian Islamisms: Patriotism as a Condition of Their Expansion," in Martin E. Marty and R. Scott Appleby, eds., *Accounting for Fundamentalism: The Dynamic Character of Movements* (Chicago: University of Chicago, 1994), pp. 413–427.

45 Matti Steinberg, "PLO and Palestinian Islamic Fundamentalism," p. 43.

46 Shadid, "Muslim Brotherhood Movement in the West Bank and Gaza," pp. 670–671.

47 Abu-Amr, *Islamic Fundamentalism in the West Bank and Gaza*, pp. 28–29.

48 From "The PLO: From One Ordeal to Another," cited in Abu-Amr, *Islamic Fundamentalism in the West Bank and Gaza*, p. 29.

49 Sahliyeh, *In Search of Leadership,* p. 157.

50 Abu-Amr, *Islamic Fundamentalism in the West Bank and Gaza*, p. 34.

51 Sahliyeh, *In Search of Leadership*, p. 156. Abu-Amr, *Islamic Fundamentalism in the West Bank and Gaza*, p. 35.

52 Abu-Amr, *Islamic Fundamentalism in the West Bank and Gaza*, pp. 43–45.

53 Ibid., p. 45.

54 Steinberg, "PLO and Palestinian Islamic Fundamentalism," p. 45. Abu-Amr does not specify culpability, only saying that the Brotherhood held al-Fatah responsible. See his *Islamic Fundamentalism in the West Bank and Gaza*, p. 46.

55 Abdulaziz A. Sachedina, "Activist Shi'ism in Iran, Iraq, and Lebanon," in Martin E. Marty and R. Scott Appleby, eds., *Fundamentalisms Observed* (Chicago: University of Chicago Press, 1991), esp. pp. 433–437.

56 Abu-Amr cited this interview as an example of *taqiyya. Islamic Fundamentalism in the West Bank and Gaza*, p. 32.

57 Cobban, *Palestine Liberation Organisation*, pp. 221–228.

58 Steinberg, "PLO and Palestinian Islamic Fundamentalism," *Jewish Quarterly*, 52 (Fall 1989), pp. 42–46.

59 Charles P. Wallace, "Anglican Cleric, Leaving PLO Leadership, Denounces Abbas as 'Absolute Traitor,' " *Los Angeles Times*, November 7, 1985, p. A18.

60 Legrain, "Palestinian Islamisms," p. 415. See also Legrain's "A Defining Moment: Palestinian Islamic Fundmentalism," in James Piscatori, ed., *Islamic Fundamentalisms and the Gulf Crisis* (Chicago: American Academy of Arts and Sciences, 1991), pp. 70–87.

61 Quoted in Voll, "Fundamentalism in the Sunni Arab World," p. 369.

62 Mitchell, *Society of the Muslim Brothers*, p. 244.

63 Here Qutb repeated the interpretation of this term from the Muslim thinker Maulana Abul-Ala Mawdudi of pre-state Pakistan. Yvonne Y. Haddad, "Sayyid Qutb: Idealogue of Islamic Revival," in John L. Esposito, ed., *Voices of Resurgent Islam* (New York: Oxford University Press, 1983), p. 85.

64 Voll, "Fundamentalism in the Sunni Arab World," p. 372.

65 Haddad, "Sayyid Qutb: Idealogue of Islamic Revival," p. 85.

66 Kepel, *Muslim Extremism in Egypt: The Prophet and the Pharaoh*, p. 45.

67 Faraj's treatise, called *The Neglected Duty*, is translated by Johannes J. G. Jansen, *The Neglected Duty: The Creed of Sadat's Assassins and Islamic Resurgence in the Middle East* (New York: Macmillan, 1986), pp. 159–234, p. 160.

68 Kepel, *Muslim Extremism in Egypt*, p. 193. See also Hamied N. Ansari, "The Islamic Militants in Egyptian Politics," *International Journal of Middle East Studies*, 16 (1984), pp. 123–144.

69 Abu-Amr, *Islamic Fundamentalism in the West Bank and Gaza*, pp. 92–93.

70 Legrain, "Palestinian Islamisms," pp. 416–417.

71 For example, Abu-Amr, *Islamic Fundamentalism in the West Bank and Gaza*, pp. 93–94, notes that in 1979, Shaqaqi published a book, *Khomeini: The Islamic Solution and Alternative*, which attempted to apply the lessons learned in the Iranian revolution to the Palestinian situation.

72 Elie Rekhess, "The Iranian Impact on the Islamic Jihad Movement in the Gaza Strip," in David Menashri, ed., *The Iranian Revolution and the Muslim World* (Boulder, Colo.: Westview Press, 1990), p. 193.

73 Peter Chelkowski, "Khomeini's Iran as Seen Through Bank Notes," in David Menashri, ed., *Iranian Revolution and the Muslim World*, pp. 85–101; Rekhess, "The Iranian Impact on the Islamic Jihad Movement in the Gaza Strip," p. 195.

74 For a discussion of Hizbullah's pan-Islamic discourse, see Martin Kramer, "Redeeming Jerusalem: The Pan-Islamic Premise of Hizballah," in Menashri, *Iranian Revolution and the Muslim World,* pp. 105–130.

75 Rekhess, "Iranian Impact on the Islamic Jihad Movement in the Gaza Strip," p. 194.

76 Ibid., p. 193.

77 Abu-Amr, *Islamic Fundamentalism in the West Bank and Gaza*, pp. 95 and 102.

78 Ibid., pp. 94–95.

79 Rekhess, "Iranian Impact on the Islamic Jihad Movement in the Gaza Strip," p. 191.

80 "Palestinian Prisoners Successfully Made Their Way out of Gaza Prison to Tunis," *Al-Awdah*, July 13, 1987, p. 1.

81 Schiff and Ya'ari, *Intifada*, p. 26.

82 Don Peretz, *Intifada: The Palestinian Uprising* (Boulder, Colo.: Westview Press, 1990), p. 104. Schiff and Ya'ari, *Intifada*, pp. 228–229, doubt the role of the Islamic Jihad in the initial stages of the *intifada*.

83 Legrain, "Palestinian Islamisms," pp. 418–419.

84 Schiff and Ya'ari, *Intifada*, pp. 228–229.

85 Abu-Amr, *Islamic Fundamentalism in the West Bank and Gaza*, p. 63.

86 It was also in this leaflet that the term *intifada* was first used to describe the events that had begun the month before. Clinton Bailey, "Hamas: The Fundamentalist Challenge to the PLO," *Policy Focus*, The Washington Institute

for Near East Policy, Research Memorandum, 19 (April 1992), p. 3. Bailey indicates that previous disorders in the occupied territories in 1974–75, 1976, 1977, and 1981 had also been described as *intifada*. The full text of this leaflet is reprinted in Mishal and Aharoni, *Speaking Stones*, p. 201.

87 Legrain, "Palestinian Islamisms," p. 420, and Abu-Amr, *Islamic Fundamentalism in the West Bank and Gaza*, p. 67.

88 HAMAS's first direct military confrontation with Israeli soldiers took place in late May 1989 in the village of Beit Aula, north of Hebron, when a group of Palestinians pursued by an army patrol opened fire with rifles and grenades. Dan Williams, "Arabs, for First Time, Use Guns; 4 Killed: Soldier Among Dead; Another 5 Palestinians Slain in Gaza Strip," *Los Angeles Times*, May 20, 1989, p. A11, and Daniel Williams "Leaders of Uprising Call for Revenge on Israelis: Latest Leaflet Urges Attacks on Soldiers, Settlers 'to Make the Enemy Pay,' " *Los Angeles Times,* May 21, 1989, pp. A6, 14.

89 Daniel Williams, "Islamic Fundamentalists Gain Strength in West Bank, Gaza at Expense of PLO," *Los Angeles Times*, June 3, 1990, pp. A9–A10.

90 Schiff and Ya'ari, *Intifada*, pp. 63–64.

91 Ibid., pp. 230–233.

92 Mishal and Aharoni, *Speaking Stones*, p. 202.

93 Bailey, "Hamas: The Fundamentalist Challenge to the PLO," pp. 16–17.

94 Ibid., pp. 16–17.

95 Cited in Abu-Amr, *Islamic Fundamentalism in the West Bank and Gaza*, pp. 66, 68.

96 Article 2. HAMAS used the very same Arabic word, *mithaq*, used by the PLO for its national covenant. All citations from the covenant are taken from Muhammad Maqdsi, trans., "Charter of the Islamic Resistance Movement (HAMAS) of Palestine," *Journal of Palestine Studies*, 22.4 (Summer 1993), pp. 122–134.

97 Shaul Mishal, "Paper War," p. 79.

98 Mishal and Aharoni, *Speaking Stones*, p. 32.

99 Schiff and Ya'ari, *Intifada*, p. 227.

100 Kepel, *Muslim Extremism in Egypt*, pp. 206–209.

101 Daphne Tsimhoni, "Between the Hammer and the Anvil: The Christians in Jerusalem and the West Bank During the Intifada," unpublished paper, 1993.

102 Mishal, "Paper War," p. 79.

103 Diane Baxter, "Women's Islamic Groups in Jerusalem: A Study in Identity Alienation and Agency," in Ifrah Zilberman, ed. *Palestinian Society and Politics in Jerusalem: Twenty-Five Years of Israeli Rule*, unpublished manuscript, 1992.

104 Tsimhoni, "Between the Hammer and the Anvil," 1993. By 1994, Christians were being subjected to increasingly public Islamic attack. See Bill Hutman, "Concern over Increasing Moslem Attacks on Christians in Old City," *The Jerusalem Post: International Edition*, July 30, 1994, p. 2.

105 Bailey, "Hamas: The Fundamentalist Challenge to the PLO," p. 12.

106 See Article 15 and Article 27.

107 Robert I. Friedman, *Zealots for Zion: Inside Israel's West Bank Settlement Movement* (New York: Random House, 1992), p. 108. In Bethlehem, the common saying was "After Saturday comes Sunday." Tsimhoni, "Between the Hammer and the Anvil," 1993.

108 Steinberg and Oliver, *Graffiti of the Intifada*, pp. 27, 37

109 Mishal and Aharoni, *Speaking Stones*, p. 217.
110 Article 32.
111 Ziad Abu-Amr, "The Politics of the Intifada," in Michael C. Hudson, ed., *The Palestinians: New Directions* (Washington, D.C.: Center for Contemporary Arab Studies Georgetown University, 1990), p. 9.
112 Bailey, "Hamas: The Fundamentalist Challenge to the PLO," p. 8.
113 Graham Usher, "The Rise of Political Islam in the Occupied Territories," *Middle East International*, June 25, 1993, p. 19.
114 Legrain, "Palestinian Islamisms," pp. 420–421.
115 Ifrah Zilberman, interview, April 10, 1992.
116 Daniel Williams, "Muslims, Israel Police Clash at Islamic Holy Site," *Los Angeles Times*, April 8, 1989, pp. A7–8.
117 Sabra Chartrand, "For the First Time, Israel Restricts Palestinians' Freedom of Worship," *New York Times*, April 15, 1989, p. A2. Dan Izenberg, "Moslems Urged to Flock to al-Aksa," *Jerusalem Post*, April 21, 1989, p. 1.
118 Mishal, "Paper War," p. 81.
119 Lamis Adoni, "King Hussein Leads Jordan in a New Era," *Middle East International*, November 17, 1989, pp. 3–4.
120 Ifrah Zilberman, "Jordan's Temple Mount Role," *The Jerusalem Post: International Edition*, November 17, 1990, p. 12.
121 Meron Benvenisti, *Fatal Embrace* (Jerusalem: Maxwell-Macmillan-Keter, 1992), pp. 15–40
122 Daniel Williams, "Israelis Slay 19 Arabs in Clash in Jerusalem," *Los Angeles Times,* October 9, 1990, pp. A1, 9, 10.
123 The number of Gazans killed and wounded in the incident suggests that HAMAS was an organizer of the defense of the *haram al-sharif*. Of the 17 killed, 2 were from Gaza. Of the nearly 150 wounded, 27 were residents of Gaza. That so many Gazans, by chance, would be on the *haram* that day is unlikely. *News from Within*, 6.10 (November 5, 1990), p. 10.
124 For a detailed discussion of the event see our "Divisions at the Center: The Organization of Political Violence at Jerusalem's Temple Mount/al-Haram al-Sharif – 1929 and 1990," in Paul R. Brass, ed., *Riots and Pogroms* (New York: Macmillan, forthcoming).
125 Benvenisti, *Fatal Embrace*, pp. 15–40.
126 Shyman Bhatia, "Massacred on the Mount," *Sunday Observer*, October 14, 1990, p. 23.
127 Daniel Williams, "Palestinian Stabs 3 Jews to Death in Jerusalem," *Los Angeles Times*, October 22, 1990, pp. A1, 13; "Israel Seals Off West Bank, Gaza After New Violence," *Los Angeles Times*, October 24, 1990, pp. A4, 19; Louis Rappoport, "Violent Days," *Jewish Journal*, October 26–November 1, 1990, p. 23.
128 Steinberg and Oliver, *Graffiti of the Intifada*, p. 55.
129 Legrain, "Palestinian Islamisms," p. 423.

Chapter 15. Baghdad, Berlin, and Jerusalem

1 Ofra Bengio, *Saddam Speaks on the Gulf Crisis: A Collection of Documents* (Tel Aviv: Moshe Dayan Center, Shiloah Institute, and Tel Aviv University, 1992), p. 143.
2 Magdi Allam, "Vinceremo perche Allah e con noi," *La Repubblica*, Septem-

ber 6, 1990, p. 3. See also Ennio Caretto, "Se sara guerra, durera anni," *La Repubblica*, September 21, 1990, p. 9.

3 See, for example, Ahmad Awad, "Support for Saddam Is Support for Change," *Al-Fajr*, October 1, 1990, p. 16.

4 Matthew Seriphs, "Palestinian Support for Saddam Increases," *The Jerusalem Post: International Edition*, August 25, 1990, p. 2.

5 *Al-Ahram*, August 5, 1990.

6 Ziad Abu Amr, "The Gulf Crisis: A Palestinian Perspective," *Al-Fajr*, January 7, 1991, pp. 8–9.

7 "Taking Wrong Road," *Al-Fajr*, January 7, 1991, p. 4.

8 Israeli Defense Forces, Information Branch, "General Disturbances in Judea, Samaria and Gaza District, 1988–1992." See also Shlomo Gazit, ed., *The Middle East Military Balance, 1992–1993* (Jerusalem and Boulder, Colo.: The Jerusalem Post and Westview Press, 1993), p. 122.

9 Hisham Abadallah, "Israelis to Get Gas Masks, Palestinians Maybe," *Al-Fajr*, October 8, 1990, p. 3.

10 Mousa Qous, "Palestinians Say a Fraction of Population Received Gas Masks," *Al-Fajr*, January 28, 1991, p. 2.

11 Ibid. The Palestinians also claimed the adult kits that were distributed were incomplete in that they did not include atrophine injections or powder for use on burns.

12 Laurie Mylroie, "Blood Brothers," *The Jerusalem Post: International Edition*, November 3, 1990, p. 9.

13 Between 1980 and 1990, Kuwait, Saudi Arabia, and the United Arab Emirates probably contributed more than $10 billion to the PLO. Legrain, "A Defining Moment," p. 79.

14 Alain Gresh, "M. Saddam Hussein, l'homme a abattre," *Monde Diplomatique*, September 1990, p. 16.

15 Bill Hutman, "Russian Aliya Far Exceeds Expectations," *The Jerusalem Post: International Edition*, September 29, 1990, p. 3.

16 Bailey, "Hamas: The Fundamentalist Challenge to the PLO," p. 11.

17 Mylroie, "Blood Brothers."

18 Schiff and Ya'ari, *Intifada*, p. 214.

19 Jamil Hilal, "PLO Institutions: The Challenge Ahead," *Journal of Palestine Studies*, 23 (Autumn 1993), p. 54. See also Hunter, who also points out that the banning of popular committees contributed to factionalization because only the factions had a structure for clandestine activity. *Palestinian Uprising*, pp. 77–78, 213.

20 Hillel Frisch, "Between Diffusion and Territorial Consolidation in Rebellion: Striking at the Hard Core of the Intifada," *Terrorism and Political Violence*, 3.4 (Winter 1991), pp. 39–62.

21 Schiff and Ya'ari, *Intifada*, pp. 196–198.

22 See Jamil Hilal, head of the PLO's Information Department in Tunis, who wrote "PLO Institutions: The Challenge Ahead," *Journal of Palestine Studies*, 23.1 (Autumn 1993), pp. 46–60.

23 Schiff and Ya'ari, *Intifada*. Ian Black and Benny Morris argue that about half of all the "terrorist cells" uncovered by Israel in the first year of the *intifada* were "local" and independent of the PLO. *Israel's Secret Wars: A History of Israel's Intelligence Services* (New York: Grove Wiedenfeld, 1991), p. 481.

24 Nasir Arruri, "A New Climate of Opportunity for Palestine," *Middle East International*, December 2, 1988, pp. 16–19.

25 Daniel Williams, "Intifada's 'Shock Troops' Masked," *Los Angeles Times*, October 29, 1989, p. A12.

26 Joel Greenberg, "The Intifada: Both Sides Digging In," *The Jerusalem Post*, October 20, 1989, pp. 1 and 14. Jon Immanuel, "B'tselem: Palestinians Have Killed up to 950 Fellow Arabs," *The Jerusalem Post: International Edition*, January 22, 1994, p. 4; Clyde Haberman, "Israeli Rights Group Critical of Arab Slayings of Arabs," *New York Times*, January 10, 1994, p. A7; Michael Parks, "PLO's Role in Collaborator's Executions Hit," *Los Angeles Times*, January 10, 1994, p. A9.

27 Lamia Lahud, "Murdered for Disgracing the Honor of the Nation," *Yerushalayyim*, May 22, 1992, p. 8.

28 Ibid.

29 Ibid.

30 Ronny Shaked, "Masked Youths Raped Me Three Times in Front of My Husband and Children," *Yediot Ahranot*, April 10, 1992, p. 10.

31 Schiff and Ya'ari, *Intifada*, p. 231.

32 Kenneth Kaplan, "Intifada Hit Squads Send Letters to Families to Justify Killings of Collaborators," *The Jerusalem Post*, October 22, 1989, p. 3.

33 According to the Israeli Defense Ministry, of the 1,751 attacks on Arabs by other Arabs that took place in the first twenty-one months of the *intifada*, 970 were against suspected "collaborators." Of these 970, 572 were against Palestinians associated with Israel. Kenneth Kaplan, "Big Increase in Attacks on Collaborators," *The Jerusalem Post*, September 3, 1989, p. 2.

34 The number of Palestinian shootings reported by the IDF steadily increased from 42 in 1988, to 112 in 1989, 169 in 1990, 299 in 1991, and 512 in 1992. Gazit, ed., *The Middle East Military Balance, 1992–1993*, p. 122.

35 Frisch, "Between Diffusion and Territorial Consolidation in Rebellion."

36 The number of Palestinians killed by other Palestinians (compared to the number killed by Israeli soldiers, in parentheses) was 21 in 1988 (279), 138 in 1989 (248), 184 in 1990 (119), 194 in 1991 (82), and 223 in 1992 (101). "Arabs Killed in Judea, Samaria and the Gaza District, 1988–1992" (Jerusalem: Israeli Defense Forces, Information Branch, 1993).

37 Legrain, "A Defining Moment: Palestinian Islamic Fundamentalism," p. 79.

38 Dr. Ziad Abu Amr, "Emerging Trends in Palestinian Strategic Political Thinking and Practice" (Jersualem: PASSIA, 1992), pp. 23, 45, and *Islamic Fundamentalism in the West Bank and Gaza*, pp. 69–70.

39 Mishal, "Paper War," pp. 71–94.

40 Abu Amr, "Emerging Trends," pp. 20–21. Abu Amr also argues that the turn to violence and the use of firearms was due to the fact that they felt condemned to arrest and brutal interrogation anyway.

41 Alberto Stabile, "Faro riesplodere il terrorismo," *La Repubblica*, September 19, 1990. Syria closed the offices of the DFLP and PFLP in Damascus in response to their decisions.

42 Syria was $20 billion in debt, $15 billion of it to the Soviet Union. Bernardo Valli, "E Israele aspetta dietro lo scudo Usa," *La Repubblica*, August 26, 1990, pp. 1, 7.

43 Michael Wines, "International Teamwork May Have Foiled Terror," *New York Times*, March 4, 1991, pp. A3, 14.

44 George P. Shultz, "Middle East: Diplomacy for the New Facts of Life," *International Herald Tribune*, March 8, 1990, p. 4.

45 "Arens: 'We Can Deter Iraq,' " *The Jerusalem Post: International Edition*, September 29, 1990, p. 1.

46 James David Besser, "Inside Washington," *Jewish Journal*, November 29, 1990, p. 17.
47 Clark Clifford, "Annals of Government: Serving the Government (The Truman Years – I)," *New Yorker*, March 25, 1991, pp. 40–59.
48 Domenico Del Rio, "Il patriarca di Gerusalemme 'Via gli americani dal Golfo,' " *La Repubblica*, September 27, 1990, p. 19.
49 David Landau, "Shamir Takes the Offensive on U.N. Vote," *Jewish Journal*, October 19–25, 1990, p. 2.

Chapter 16. Al-Quds and Tunis

1 Edward Cody, "Arafat's Role as 'Iraq Lawyer' Wins No Friends," *International Herald Tribune*, September 26, 1990, p. 9; Youssef Ibrahim, "The Debate on Saudi's Future," *International Herald Tribune*, August 27, 1990, p. 6.
2 Kimmerling and Migdal allege that he was "probably" assassinated by Iraqi agents. *Palestinians*, p. 213.
3 Khaled Abu Aker, "Palestinians Leave Meeting with Baker Optimistic," *Al-Fajr*, March 18, 1991.
4 *Jerusalem Report*, August 15, 1991, p. 6.
5 Ibid.
6 Abraham Ashkenasi, *Palestinian Identities and Preferences: Israel's and Jerusalem's Arabs*, pp. 124–167.
7 Imad Musa and Khaled Abu Aker, "Palestinians Take to the Streets to Celebrate Opening of Madrid Conference as Delegation Presents Peace Message," *Al-Fajr*, November 4, 1991.
8 *The Other Front*, No. 146, October 31, 1991.
9 Edward Said, "Rally and Resist for Palestinian Independence," *Nation*, February 14, 1994, pp. 190–193.
10 Mark Fineman, "For PLO, a Long Climb Out of Chaos," *Los Angeles Times*, May 3, 1994, p. H3.
11 Mary C. Cook, "Arafat–Rabin Agreement Comes at Depths of PLO Financial Crisis," *Washington Report on Middle East Affairs* (November/December 1993), pp. 48, 82.
12 Ruth Ginsberg, "Milo Says Israel Should Have Backed PLO Take-Over of Jordan in 1970," *The Jerusalem Post*, November 2, 1989.
13 *New York Times*, June 11, 1993.
14 At one point, Rabin dismissed Husayni as a "mailbox" for the transmission of orders from Tunis. Avi Shlaim, "The Oslo Accord," *Journal of Palestine Studies*, 23.3 (Spring 1994), p. 29.
15 Interview with Moshe Ma'oz, December, 1993; Shlaim argues that the move was designed to reduce Syria's bargaining power. See Shlaim "Oslo Accord," pp. 28, 30.
16 Haydar 'Abd al-Shafi's open letter to the "Palestinian Masses," published in *Al-Quds*, July 10, 1993, is reported in *Journal of Palestine Studies*, 23.1 (Autumn 1993), p. 169. See also G. H. Jansen, "Victims of Despair," *Middle East International*, July 23, 1993, pp. 5–6 and "Haider Abed al-Shafi on the Peace Talks," *News from Within*, August 5, 1993, p. 9.
17 Daoud Kuttab, "Confusion in the Territories," *Middle East International*, August 28, 1993, pp. 3–4; "PLO Rejects Resignations of 3 Negotiators,"

New York Times, August 13, 1993. See also *Journal of Palestine Studies*, 23.1 (Autumn 1993), p. 174.

18 Reported in *Al-Hayat*, June 7, 1993, cited in *Journal of Palestine Studies*, 23.1 (1993), p. 165. There are those who question just how "poor" Arafat really was, given that the PLO had amassed a stock of assets worth $12 billion before the Gulf War. According to the PLO, it was forced to cut its annual budget after the 1990 war from $320 million per year to $140 million. The crucial question is to what extent Arafat was forced to sell off his assets in order to maintain operating expenses at this level. See Steve Rodan, "Peeking into the 'Poor' PLO's Piggy Bank," *The Jerusalem Post: International Edition*, July 9, 1994, p. 12.

19 Rodan, ibid., argues that Arafat pulled the plug on *Al-Fajr* because of its criticism of PLO spending policies.

20 Jonathan Broder, "Playing Chess with Israel," *Jerusalem Report*, May 20, 1993, pp. 26–27; "U.S. Asks Saudis to Fund Palestinians in Territories," *Forward*, April 30, 1993, pp. 1, 3.

21 Negotiations on the final status were to be begin no later than December 13, 1995. For texts of the letters of recognition, signed on September 9, 1993, and the Israel–PLO Declaration of Principles, signed on September 13, 1993, see *Journal of Palestine Studies*, 23.1 (Autumn 1993), pp. 114–121.

22 Tania Reinhart, "The Era of Yellow Territories," *Ha-Aretz*, May 27, 1994, as reprinted in *Other Front*, May 31, 1994, p. 275.

23 *International Herald Tribune*, September 11–12, 1993, cited in Burham Dajani, "The September 1993 Israeli–PLO Documents: A Textual Analysis," *Journal of Palestine Studies*, 23.3 (Spring 1994), p. 21.

24 Ibid., p. 15.

25 Leslie Susser, "Where Do We Go from Here?" *Jerusalem Report*, June 2, 1994, p. 13, and Dr. Mahdi Abdul-Hadi, "The Transitional Phase," *PASSIA Annual Report 1993* (Jerusalem: PASSIA, 1994), pp. 69–74.

26 Ussama Halabi, "Jerusalem and the Declaration of Principles," *News from Within*, 10.7 (July 1994), pp. 2–4.

27 Kuttab, "Confusion in the Territories."

28 Claudia Dreifus, "A Separate Peace: Hanan Ashrawi," *New York Times Magazine,* June 26, 1994, p. 24.

29 Dajani, "The September 1993 Israeli–PLO Documents," p. 7.

30 Jon Immanuel, "Doubt Surrounds Palestinian Leadership," *The Jerusalem Post: International Edition*, October 3, 1992.

31 Dore Gold, "Security After Gaza–Jericho," *The Jerusalem Post: International Edition*, May 21, 1994, p. 8b; Steve Rodan, "After the Ball," *The Jerusalem Post: International Edition*, May 14, 1994, p. 9.

32 Jon Immanuel and David Makovsky, "Palestinian Police Begin Arriving," *The Jerusalem Post: International Edition*, May 14, 1994, pp. 1, 4. On the point that the pro-Arafat sympathies of the police were part of the agreement, see Shlaim, "Oslo Accord," p. 33.

33 *Yediot Ahronot*, September 7, 1993.

34 Poll, December 12, 1993, *Palestinian Elections and the Declaration of Principles* (Nablus: Center for Palestine Research and Studies, 1993).

35 Jon Immanuel, "B'tselem: Palestinians Have Killed up to 950 Fellow Arabs," *The Jerusalem Post: International Edition*, January 22, 1994; Clyde Haberman, "Israeli Rights Group Critical of Arab Slayings of Arabs," *New York Times*, January 10, 1994; Michael Parks, "PLO's Role in Collaborators' Executions Hit," *Los Angeles Times*, January 10, 1994.

36 See, for example, Ziad Abu-Amr, "The View from Palestine: In The Wake of the Agreement," *Journal of Palestine Studies*, 23.2 (Winter 1994), pp. 75–83.

37 See also Neil Partrick, "Democracy Under Limited Autonomy," *News from Within*, 10.9 (September 1994), p. 23.

38 Hassan Abdel Jawad, "A First Reading of the Palestinian Constitution," *News from Within*, 10.6 (June 1994), pp. 8–10.

39 Ehud Ya'ari, "Can Arafat Govern?" *Jerusalem Report*, January 13, 1994, pp. 10–12.

40 "An Interview with Salim Tamari," *Middle East Report* (January/February 1994), pp. 17–19; Ya'ari, "Can Arafat Govern?"

41 Ya'ari, "Can Arafat Govern?" See also Ehud Ya'ari, "Palestinian Preparation for Arafat's Move to Gaza/Jericho," *Peacewatch*, No. 22 (June 17, 1994). Graham Usher, "Proliferating Police Forces," *Middle East International*, September 23, 1994, pp. 4–5.

42 Ya'ari, "Can Arafat Govern?" p. 11.

43 Joel Greenberg, "Palestinians Hold Quick, Secret Trials," *New York Times*, May 3, 1995, p. A4, and "Arafat Critic Is Detained in Gaza," *New York Times*, February 16, 1995.

44 Ziad Abu-Amr, "The View from Palestine," p. 80.

45 Poll, November 11, 1993, *Palestine Elections: Results of Public Opinion Poll #2 (November, 1993)* (Nablus: Center for Palestine Research and Studies, November 1993), and Bill Hutman, "Most Palestinians Support Cairo Accords," *The Jerusalem Post: International Edition*, July 30, 1994, p. 3.

46 *Palestinian Elections and the Declaration of Principles* (Nablus: Center for Palestine Research and Studies, 1993).

47 *Palestinian Elections: Public Opinion Poll, 5–10 October, 1993* (Nablus: Center for Palestine Research and Studies, 1993).

48 Reported in *Ma'ariv*, January 13, 1994. See also Abu Alaa, "The Challenges of Palestinian Economic Development," *Peacewatch*, No. 24 (June 29, 1994).

49 Daoud Kuttab, "Concern over Democracy," *Middle East International*, February 4, 1994, p. 9.

50 Interview, Mordechai Gur, December 1993.

51 "Ziad Abu Zayyad Suspends His Participation in the Negotiations," *April 17*, No. 4/5 (December 1993), pp. 9–11.

52 Schiff and Ya'ari, *Intifada*, p. 214.

53 Hassan Abdel Jawad, "Prisoners Pay the Price," *April 17*, No. 4/5 (December 1993), pp. 17–19.

54 Clyde Haberman, "Doctor, an Old Ally, Confronts Arafat," *New York Times*, January 23, 1994.

55 For example, after the "Jerusalem First" bloc opposed to the Oslo accords won the student election at Bir Zeit University in November 1993, Fatah activists ransacked the Student Council offices, breaking the furniture and knocking out the windows. *Palestine Report*, November 1993, p. 4. See also Abu-Amr, "View from Palestine," esp. p. 79.

56 "Palestine – Birth Pains," *Economist*, April 2, 1994, pp. 19–21.

57 Wallach and Wallach, *New Palestinians*, p. 227.

58 Dr. Ziad Abu Amr, *Emerging Trends in Palestinian Strategic Political Thinking and Practice* (Jerusalem: PASSIA, 1992), p. 43.

59 Lamis Andoni, "PLO Gets Danger Signals," *Middle East International*, August 5, 1994, p. 6; Khalid Amayreh, "Left in the Lurch," *Middle East Interna-*

tional, August 5, 1994, p. 7; Lia Collins, "Two Papers Banned in Autonomous Areas," *The Jerusalem Post: International Edition*, August 6, 1994, p. 4. Jon Immanuel, "Arafat Demands Immediate Negotiations on Jerusalem," *The Jerusalem Post: International Edition*, August 13, 1994, p. 2.

60 Jon Immanuel, "Ban on Papers Opposed," *The Jerusalem Post: International Edition*, September 3, 1994, p. 24.

61 Parks, "A Full-Court Press." Bill Hutman, "Jericho Security Chief's Capital Operations Cause Furor," *The Jerusalem Post: International Edition*, October 1, 1994, p. 5.

62 Lamis Andoni, "Arafat's Troubles Deepen," *Middle East International*, May 13, 1994, p. 8. See also Ya'ari, "Palestine Liberation Disorganization," 1994, p. 15.

63 Lamis Andoni, "Confusion and Paralysis," *Middle East International*, June 24, 1994, p. 5.

64 Dreifus, "A Separate Peace," p. 24. Ashrawi launched the Palestinian Independent Commission for Citizens Rights in East Jerusalem in June 1994.

65 Shlaim, "Oslo Accord," p. 30.

66 Dajani, "The September 1993 Israeli–PLO Documents," pp. 11–13; Isabel Kershner, "Where's the Dough?" *Jerusalem Report*, June 16, 1994, p. 2.

67 The World Bank had pledges of $2.1 billion for five years as of October 1, 1993. See "The World Bank and International Aid to Palestine," *Journal of Palestine Studies*, 23.2 (Winter 1994), pp. 64–74.

68 Mary Anne Weaver, "The Chairman and His Wife," *New Yorker*, May 16, 1994, pp. 72–85.

69 This paragraph relies on Neil C. Livingstone and David Halevy, *Inside the PLO* (New York: Quill, 1990), pp. 162–198.

70 "Palestinian figures, memorandum to Yasir Arafat, December, 1993," *Journal of Palestine Studies*, 23.3 (Spring 1994), pp. 154–155. Daoud Kuttab, a film producer charged with establishing a Palestinian broadcasting authority, likewise complained about the predominance of politics, rather than professional expertise, in Arafat's appointments. Fineman, "For PLO, a Long Climb Out of Chaos," p. H3.

71 Without much support from the prison activists, Nusseibeh feared for his life, not only from HAMAS, which had already targeted him for assassination, but from local Fatah activists jealous of his role as well. Arafat was pressing Nusseibeh to return from Washington.

72 See Frank Collins, "World Bank Awaits Donor Countries' Approval of PLO Commission," *Washington Report on Middle East Affairs* (January 1994), and "Temporary Commission May Speed World Bank Palestinian Funding," *Washington Report on Middle East Affairs* (February/March 1994). Indeed, in June 1994, the PLO was demanding that the funds to finance economic development projects be merged with those financing the personnel of the new Palestinian authority. Abu Alaa, "The Challenges of Palestinian Economic Development," *Peacewatch*, No. 24, June 29, 1994, p. 2.

73 For example, 120 Palestinian activists sent a petition to Arafat in December 1993 demanding democratic reform of the PLO. The signatories were members of parties that supported the agreement including members of the Palestine People's Party (the Communists), a branch of the DFLP, and members of Fatah itself.

74 Michael Parks, "Fight to Control Purse Imperils Palestinian Plans," *Los Angeles Times*, September 25, 1994, pp. 1, A8–9.

75 Ya'ari, "Palestine Liberation Disorganization," p. 15.

76 Kim Murphy, "Frustrations Mount as PLO Leadership Begins Paying the Price for Autonomy," *Los Angeles Times*, June 12, 1994, pp. A9–10.

77 This remark was reported to us by a high American consular official, as well as two Palestinian leaders.

78 Edward Said, "Rally and Resist," *Nation*, Feburary 14, 1994.

79 William Safire, "If I Forget Thee, O Jerusalem," *New York Times*, June 13, 1994.

80 Interview, Mahdi Abdul-Hadi, December 1993.

81 *Ha-Aretz*, February 21, 1994, p. A9.

82 For two years before the Oslo accord was first implemented, Husayni had some three hundred technical experts working on three dozen areas developing specific plans for a Palestinian state. See, for example, John Kifner, "In a Palestinian Center, a State Is Taking Shape," *New York Times*, September 7, 1993; on the absence of PLO planning, see Ya'ari, "Palestine Liberation Disorganization," p. 15.

83 Arafat himself saw it as a critical part of his emerging government. The right to operate the Orient House as part of the self-rule institutional complex was the last remaining point in the Israeli–Palestinian negotiations in Norway. See David Makovsky, "Rabin Was More Involved in Oslo Than People Realize," *The Jerusalem Post: International Edition*, July 23, 1994, p. 8b.

84 See "Towards a Jerusalem National Council," in *PASSIA Annual Report 1993* (Jerusalem: PASSIA, 1994), pp. 41–46.

85 Said, "Rally and Resist."

86 Poll conducted December 12, 1993. Special tabulations provided by Dr. Nader Sa'id, *Palestinian Elections and the Declaration of Principles,* pp. 1–2.

87 Arafat was threatened by Husayni's maneuvers, trying to bypass him as much as possible. In May 1994, the two men clashed in Tunis. Husayni charged Arafat with trying to convert him into a symbolic figure. "I am too big to accept this," he said. Andoni, "Arafat's Troubles Deepen," p. 8.

88 "Ministry of Justice Proposes Law to Limit PLO Political Activities in Jerusalem," *Other Front*, No. 282 (July 20, 1994), pp. 1–2.

Chapter 17. The City That Ate Palestine

1 Robert I. Friedman, *Zealots for Zion: Inside Israel's West Bank Settlement Movement* (New York: Random House, 1992), pp. 96–122.

2 See, for example, *Al-Fajr*, August 16, 1993. See also Naomi Shepherd, *The Mayor and the Citadel: Teddy Kollek and Jerusalem* (London: Weidenfeld and Nicolson, 1987), pp. 160–162; Friedman, *Zealots*, pp. 108–110.

3 Clyde Haberman, "Battle on Jerusalem's Future Has Roots 3,000 Years in Past," *New York Times*, January 6, 1992, pp. A1 and 14.

4 Palestinian land sales to Israelis continued even after the Palestinian agreement with the Israelis in September 1993. "Arafat: Sell Jerusalem Land to PLO, but Not to Israelis," *The Jerusalem Post: International Edition*, July 23, 1994, p. 3.

5 "The City of David Dispute," *The Jerusalem Post,* December 9, 1991, p. 4.

6 Beyond our interviews with Kollek's press secretary, Bonnie Boxer, see also Teddy Kollek, "An Ill Wind Is Blowing," *Jewish Journal*, January 23, 1991.

7 Michal Yudelman, "Irregularities in Property Deals," *The Jerusalem Post: International Edition,* March 20, 1993, p. 3.

8 Ghuzlan's account varies from that reported in Isabel Kershner, "The Second Conquest of the City of David," *Jerusalem Report,* January 30, 1992, pp. 4–8. Kershner describes how the El Ad group used the "Absentee's Property Law" of 1950 and the Israel Land Authority to acquire the properties. *Absentee* was originally defined as any Palestinian who left and became a national of or even visited "Lebanon, Egypt, Syria, Saudi Arabia, Trans-Jordan, Iraq or the Yemen." The law transferred absentee property to state custody to be held in trust. It was amended after the Six-Day War so that East Jerusalem residents living in the city before June 28, 1967, would not be considered absentees. However, Palestinians living in the West Bank who own property in Jerusalem are still considered absentee owners. Even if the custodian makes a mistake "in good faith" in the determination of absentee status, properties acquired under the law need not revert to their former owners.

9 See also Ashkenasi, *Palestinian Identities and Preferences,* p. 121.

10 He had voiced the same opinion privately to Mayor Kollek in 1990. "Don't quarrel with Bush!" *The Jerusalem Post: International Edition,* September 28, 1991, p. 2.

11 *The Jerusalem Post,* October 22, 1990.

12 Sharon's "twelve star" plan to build large Jewish settlements concentrated new development along the old "Green Line," not deep into the Palestinian heartland.

13 Donald Neff, "Jerusalem in U.S. Policy," *Journal of Palestine Studies,* 23.1 (1993), p. 35.

14 Yisrael Kimchi, a member of that committee, argued that this was not the source of the initiative. Rather the concern was maintaining Jewish demographic strength in Jerusalem, given the expansion in *haredi*-free, lower-cost housing and employment opportunities between Jerusalem and the coastal area.

15 "Rabin Considers 100 of the 142 Settlements to Be 'Political,' " *Jerusalem Report,* July 30, 1992, p. 5.

16 "Rabin Slashes Grants to Settlers," *Forward,* August 28, 1992; *Current Insights,* No. 4 (Summer 1993).

17 Between July 1992 and March 1993. *Report on Israeli Settlement in the Occupied Territories,* 3.6 (November 1993), p. 3. The Labour government's program for 1995–1998 includes fifteen thousand apartments in East Jerusalem and thirteen thousand in the larger metropolitan area. *Report on Israeli Settlement in the Occupied Territories,* 5.2 (March 1995).

18 *Report on Israeli Settlement in the Occupied Territories,* 4.1 (January 1994). See also Bill Hutman, "Ben-Eliezer Speeding Up J'lem Plans," *The Jerusalem Post: International Edition,* January 1, 1994, p. 3.

19 *Report on Israeli Settlement in the Occupied Territories* (March 1995).

20 Clyde Haberman, "Israelis Are Rushing to Build a Greater Jerusalem," *New York Times,* February 19, 1994, p. 3.

21 "Settler Population Grew by 10 Percent in 1993," *Report on Israeli Settlement in the Occupied Territories,* 4.3 (May 1994), p. 3; "House Prices Soar by up to 40 Percent at some W. Bank Settlements," *Jerusalem Report,* February 9, 1995, p. 2.

22 Steve Leibowitz, "Ballot Box," *In Jerusalem,* October 1, 1993, p. 1, and Tom

Tugend, "Teddy Kollek: Campaigning in L.A.," *Jewish Journal,* October 1–7, 1993, p. 2.

23 Liat Collins, "Olmert Camp Lauds 'Revolution,' " *The Jerusalem Post,* November 3, 1993, p. 3.

24 Abraham Rabinovich, "Porush's Daring Gamble Pays Off," *The Jerusalem Post,* November 3, 1993, p. 2.

25 Ibid.

26 Bill Hutman, "Low Arab Turnout at Polls Deals Lethal Blow to Kollek," *The Jerusalem Post,* November 3, 1993, p. 1.

27 Clyde Haberman, "Kollek Defeated, 3–2 as Mayor in Jerusalem, a Blow to Laborites," *New York Times,* November 3, 1993, p. A7.

28 The United Torah Party was a coalition of Agudat Yisrael and Degel Ha-Torah.

29 Carey Goldberg, "No Dividing Jerusalem, New Mayor Vows," *Los Angeles Times,* November 4, 1993, p. 12.

30 Bill Hutman, "How Jewish Will the Jewish Capital Get?" *The Jerusalem Post,* December 10, 1993, p. 10.

31 Khaled Abu Toameh, "Mansion of Controversy," *Jerusalem Report,* April 21, 1994, pp. 26–27.

32 "Ehud Olmert: 'I'll Bring 500,000 People to Keep Arafat from Temple Mt.,' " *Jerusalem Report,* May 5, 1994, p. 5.

33 Israel Bonds fund-raising speech at Congregation Magen David, Los Angeles, November 30, 1993.

34 Mary Curtis, "Lost Tribe Applicants Stir Debate on Israel Citizenship," *Los Angeles Times,* August 29, 1994, pp. A1, 6, 7.

35 Steve Rodan, "After the Ball," *The Jerusalem Post: International Edition,* May 14, 1994, p. 9.

36 Yossi Klein Halevi, "Troubled in Paradise," *Jerusalem Report,* February 24, 1994, pp. 18–19.

37 Eric Silver, "The Pulse of the Nation," *Jerusalem Report,* February 9, 1995, pp. 16–17.

38 *Yesha News Service,* February 1, 1994.

39 Published in the *Journal of the Rabbis of Judea, Samaria and Gaza. The Jerusalem Report,* January 13, 1994, p. 9; Hillel Halkin, "When Rabin Ran into the Rambam," *Forward,* April 8, 1994, pp. 1, 3. Clyde Haberman, "Defy Orders on Settlers, Rabbis Tell Troops," *New York Times,* April 19, 1994, p. A6.B.

40 *The Jerusalem Post,* April 23, 1994, p. 3.

41 Haberman, "Defy Orders on Settlers," p. A6.B.

42 Shahak, "Is a Civil War Between the Israeli Jews Forthcoming?", p. 9.

43 Our account of the attack is based on CNN television news coverage, as well as Joel Greenberg, "Sounds of Chanting and Gunfire Echo in a Town Awash in Blood," *New York Times,* February 26, 1994; Clyde Haberman, "40 Slain in West Bank Mosque as Israeli Militant Opens Fire: Clinton Moves to Rescue Talks," *New York Times,* February 26, 1994; Chris Hedges and Joel Greenberg, "A Seething Hate, a Gun, and 40 Muslims Died," *New York Times,* February 28, 1994; Clyde Haberman, "Israel Orders Tough Measures Against Militant Settlers," *New York Times,* February 28, 1994; "The Hebron Attack: Countering the Lies," *Yesha News Service,* February 28, 1994; "After Hebron," and "No Protection," *Economist,* March 5, 1994.

44 Steven Greenhouse, "U.S. Urges Israel to Give the P.L.O. a Role in Hebron," *New York Times,* March 16, 1994, pp. 1, 7.

45 *Al-Hamishmar,* March 10, 1994, reported in *Yesha News Service,* March 13, 1994.
46 Graham Usher, "A Rubicon Has Been Crossed," *Middle East International,* March 18, 1994, pp. 4–5.
47 Tikva Honig-Parnass, "Palestinian and Israeli Reactions to the Massacre," *News from Within,* 10.4 (April 1994), pp. 2–5.
48 Hillel Halkin, "Israelis Brace for New Terror After Second Bombing," *Forward,* April 15, 1994, p. 3; Clyde Haberman, "5 Killed in Israel as Second Bomber Blows Up a Bus," *New York Times,* April 14, 1994, pp. 1, 4; Bill Hutman, "Pregnant Palestinian Killed by Shilo Man," *The Jerusalem Post: International Edition,* April 23, 1994, p. 2.
49 Clyde Haberman, "Rabin in Tough, Maybe," *New York Times,* March 2, 1994.
50 Any organization that wanted to establish a "theocracy" or violently expel the Arabs was now banned. Clyde Haberman, "Israel Votes Ban on Jewish Groups Linked to Kahane," *New York Times,* March 14, 1994, p. A5; Michael Parks, "Israel Outlaws 2 Extremist Groups," *Los Angeles Times,* March 14, 1994, p. A12.
51 Clyde Haberman, "Israeli Ministers Debate Evictions of Jews in Hebron," *New York Times,* March 7, 1994, pp. 1–2; Ina Friedman, "Pressure on the Peace Process," *Jewish Journal,* March 4, 1994, p. 7.
52 Haim Baram, "Has Hebron Sounded Oslo's Death-Knell?" *Middle East International,* March 4, 1994, p. 3.
53 Statement by Yesha Council and Mateh HaMeshutaf.

Chapter 18. Heart of Stone

1 The first major closure of the West Bank and Gaza in which Palestinians from outside – excluding, of course, those resident in East Jerusalem – were forbidden from entering Israel proper was for six weeks during the Gulf War.
2 Yifat Susskind, "The Disintegration of Palestinian Society," *News from Within,* September 5, 1993, pp. 30–31.
3 Tivka Honig-Parnass, "Military Blockade: One Step Closer to Bantustan," and Dr. Adel Samara, "Closure and Its Economic Ramifications," both in *News from Within,* 9.5 (May 1, 1993), pp. 2–7; Eric Silver, "Living Without Them," *Jerusalem Report,* April 22, 1993, p. 21.
4 Indeed since the closure Palestinian terrorism declined in the rest of Israel, but increased in Jerusalem. Nadav Shraga'i, "Jerusalem a Border Town Again." *Ha'Aretz,* July 9, 1993, reprinted in *Middle East International,* July 23, 1993, p. 22.
5 Mary C. Cook, "Israel–Occupied Territories Closure Marks First Anniversary," *Washington Report on Middle East Affairs* (June 1994), pp. 13, 90.
6 Photocopy of personal letter to Mayor Teddy Kollek from George Bush, March 13, 1990; personal letter to Mel Levin from James A. Baker III, March 16, 1990; personal letter to Rudy Boschwitz from George Bush, March 20, 1990; personal letter to Shalom Comay, president, American Jewish Committee, April 18, 1990.
7 "U.S. Loan Guarantees Cut by $437 Million: 1993–1994 Penalty Shocks Rabin Government," *Report on Israeli Settlement in the Occupied Territories,* 3.6 (November 1993), pp. 1, 6.

8 Paul Lewis, "Massacre in Hebron Mosque Condemned by U.N. Council," *New York Times*, March 19, 1994, p. A1 and 14.

9 The best review of proposals is Cecilia Albin, "Negotiating the Future of Jerusalem" (privately circulated manuscript). See also her essay, "Negotiating Indivisible Goods: The Case of Jerusalem," *Jerusalem Journal of International Relations*, 13.1 (1991), pp. 45–76.

10 Orit Galili, "Feisal Husseini, After Conferring with Labor Doves, I Am Very Optimistic," *Ha'Aretz*, July 31, 1989, p. A9.

11 The official offices of the Council of Higher Education are actually located just outside Jerusalem in El-Bireh, but the Council has always held its meetings in Jerusalem proper.

12 See Albin, "Negotiating the Future of Jerusalem."

13 Haberman, "Israelis Are Rushing to Build a Greater Jerusalem," *New York Times*, February 19, 1994, p. 3.

14 Alan Makovsky, "The Israel–PLO Accord at One Year: Taking Stock," *Peacewatch*, August 9, 1994; Shada Islam, "Another Oslo Agreement," *Middle East International*, September 23, 1994, p. 6.

15 Mary C. Cook, "Palestinian Investors Eye West Bank Opportunities Cautiously," *Washington Report on Middle East Affairs* (February/March 1994).

16 *Yediot Aharonot*, January 14, 1994.

17 Leslie Susser, "The City That Defies Solutions," *Jerusalem Report*, December 6, 1990, pp. 17–18.

18 The new Arab municipality would be under Palestinian sovereignty, but Jordanian suzerainty. Albin, "Negotiating the Future of Jerusalem," p. 7.

19 "Saudi Arabia Funds Restorations of Islamic Holy Sites in Jerusalem," *Saudi Arabia: The Monthly Newsletter of the Royal Embassy of Saudi Arabia, Washington, D.C.*, 11.6 (June 1994), p. 4.

20 Reported by A. Jaber on *Palestine Net* in March 1994.

21 Jon Immanuel, "Ban on Papers Opposed," *The Jerusalem Post: International Edition*, September 3, 1994, p. 4.

22 Safire, "If I Forget Thee, O Jerusalem," *New York Times*, June 13, 1994, p. A21. David Makovsky, "Peres Letter in October '93 Encouraged Palestinian Institutions in Jerusalem," *The Jerusalem Post: International Edition*, June 18, 1994, pp. 1, 4.

23 Najm Jarrah, "The PLO and Saudi Arabia," *Middle East International*, February 4, 1994, pp. 4–5. Ehud Ya'ari, "O Jerusalem!" *Jerusalem Report*, July 14, 1994, p. 31.

24 "Text of Washington Declaration Signed by Jordan and Israel," and Youssef M. Ibrahim, "Confirmation of Jordan as Guardian of Shrines," *New York Times*, July 26, 1994.

25 Ya'ari, "O Jerusalem!" p. 31.

26 Dr. Jawad Al-Anani, "Jordan and the Peace Process," *Peacewatch*, No. 22, July 29, 1994, p. 3. George Hawatmeh, "Jordan's Dramatic Peace Gestures," *Middle East International*, 22 (July 1994), p. 3.

27 "Arafat's Return: Unity Is 'The Shield of Our People,' " *New York Times*, July 2, 1994, p. 2.

28 Isabel Kershner and Tom Sawicki, "The Battle for Jerusalem," *Jerusalem Report*, July 28, 1994, pp. 11–16.

29 Hillel Kullter and David Makovsky, "Rabin and King Hussein: State of War Over," *The Jerusalem Post: International Edition*, August 6, 1994, pp. 1, 2, 9.

30 Michael Parks, "PLO Assails Jordan over Jerusalem," *Los Angeles Times,* July 27, 1994, p. A3.
31 Mary Curtis, "Israel, Jordan Move Closer to Peace Treaty," *Los Angeles Times,* August 4, 1994, pp. A1, 4.
32 George Hawatmeh, "Why the King Signed," *Middle East International,* August 5, 1994, p. 4.
33 Najm Jarrah, "Muted Arab Reaction," *Middle East International,* August 5, 1994, p. 8.
34 Ussama Halabi, "Jerusalem and the Declaration of Principles," *News from Within,* 10.7 (July 1994), p. 3.
35 The Greek Orthodox were notably absent from these discussions about the future of Jerusalem. Haim Shapiro, "Greek Orthodox Not Consulted over Jerusalem," *The Jerusalem Post: International Edition,* July 30, 1994, p. 3.
36 See also Haim Shapiro, "Israel, Vatican Sign Agreement Paving Way to Diplomatic Ties," *The Jerusalem Post,* January 8, 1994, pp. 1, 4.
37 In the "Fundamental Agreement Between the Holy See and the State of Israel," the Holy See "affirms the Catholic Church's continuing commitment to respect the . . . 'Status Quo.' " As reported by Israel Internet, December 30, 1993.
38 *Jerusalem Report,* August 11, 1994, pp. 8–9.
39 *Yerushalayim,* October 6, 1993; Isabel Kershner and Tom Sawicki, "The Battle for Jerusalem," *Jerusalem Report,* July 28, 1994, pp. 11–16.
40 Albin, "Negotiating the Future of Jerusalem," and personal correspondence, September 6, 1994.
41 "Jerusalem – Capital of Israel, Al Quds – Capital of Palestine," *Other Front,* 243 (October 20, 1993). This may be the basis of press reports that Israel was preparing to "hand over to the Palestinians all the Arab neighborhoods of Jerusalem." See, for example, Hillel Halkin, " 'Secret Plan May Sunder Jerusalem,' " *Forward,* January 14, 1994.
42 See, for instance, Leslie Susser, "Keeping Tabs on Olmert," *Jerusalem Report,* December 2, 1993, pp. 15–16.
43 Emily Bazelton, "Many Settlers Ready to Leave," *Forward,* February 18, 1994, p. 8.
44 Herb Keinon, "Newest Citizens Are Secular," *The Jerusalem Post: International Edition,* November 3, 1990, p. 17.
45 "By 2010, 40% of Capital's Jews Will Be Ultra-Orthodox," *Jerusalem Report,* April 21, 1994, p. 5.
46 Between 1967 and 1993, about 100,000 mostly secular Jews have emigrated from Jerusalem. Eric Silver, "The Rise of the Ultra-Orthodox," *Jerusalem Report,* December 2, 1993, p. 11.
47 See also Eric Silver, "Who's the Boss?" *Jerusalem Report,* December 2, 1993, pp. 10–13.
48 Clyde Haberman, "Israel Considers Relocating Settlers Within Hebron," *New York Times,* March 19, 1994.
49 Peter Hirschberg, " 'Replace This and I'll Leave,' " *Jerusalem Report,* January 27, 1994, pp. 16–17.
50 *Yediot Ahranot,* February 27, 1994, p. 13.
51 Abigail Wisse, "Settlers See Plot in Plans for New City," *Forward,* December 24, 1993, p. 9.
52 "Jerusalem Anti-Arafat Rally Draws Well over 100,000," *The Jerusalem*

Post: International Edition, July 9, 1994, p. 4; Joel Greenberg, "Protests Jam Israel Roads over Arafat," *New York Times,* July 1, 1994, p. A6.

53 Ifrah Zilberman, "Jordan's Temple Mount Role," *The Jerusalem Post: International Edition,* November 17, 1990, p. 14.

54 Alan Makovsky, "Assessing Arafat's Johannesburg Speech," *Peacewatch,* No. 20 (May 27, 1994).

55 Lamis Andoni, "Arafat's Tactics," *Middle East International,* April 29, 1994, p. 4; Judith Wrubel, "Hamas 'Peace Overtures' – a Closer Look," *Peacewatch,* No. 19 (May 11, 1994). Mariam Shahin, "The PLO and Hamas," *Middle East International,* January 8, 1993, pp. 7–8; Ziad Abu-Amr, "The View from Palestine: In the Wake of the Agreement," *Journal of Palestine Studies,* 23.2 (1994), p. 79.

56 "Palestinian Preparations for Arafat's Move to Gaza/Jericho: Preliminary Observations," *Peacewatch,* No. 22 (June 17, 1994). See also Bassam Jarrar, "The Islamist Movement and the Palestinian Authority," *Middle East Report* (July/August 1994), pp. 28–29.

57 Robert Satloff, "The Themes of Arafat's Return to Gaza/Jericho," *Peacewatch,* No. 25 (July 6, 1994).

58 Daoud Kuttab, "The New Arafat?" *Middle East International,* July 9, 1994; "Gaza Police Chief: We Won't Shoot at Hamas," *The Jerusalem Post: International Edition,* August 27, 1994, p. 1.

59 Graham Usher, "Arafat Fears Hussein's Shadow," *Middle East International,* August 5, 1994, pp. 7–8; Bill Hutman, "Hamas Offers to Join PLO on Jerusalem," *The Jerusalem Post: International Edition,* August 6, 1994, p. 3; Khalid Amayreh, "Left in the Lurch," *Middle East International,* August 5, 1994, p. 7.

60 "Olmert 'Freezing Out Kollek' with New Fund-Raising Effort," *Jerusalem Report,* February 24, 1994, p. 4.

61 Friedman, "Brooklyn Avengers," p. 42.

Index